creating MOTION GRAPHICS

with after effects

Trish & Chris Meyer

DEDICATION

to the memory of **Vera McGrath**,
who always said I could do anything I put my mind to – Trish

and to the memory of **Leroy Meyer**,
who taught me to be curious about how all things worked – Chris

Published by CMP Books
600 Harrison, San Francisco, CA 94107

An imprint of CMP Media Inc.
Publishers of DV Magazine

Distributed to the book trade in the U.S. and Canada by
Publishers Group West, 1700 Fourth Street, Berkeley, CA 94710

Library of Congress Card Number: 0 0 - 1 0 2 6 7 3

ISBN 0-87930-606-8

Printed in the United States of America

00 01 02 03 04   5 4 3 2

Table of Contents

 PART 1 Getting Started, Animation

TechTips

The CD-ROM contains PDF files of additional chapters, appendices, and tweaky tips. They include:

TechTip 01: Alpha Channel Types
The difference between Straight and Premultiplied alpha channel types.

TechTip 02: ElectricImage Issues
Getting the most out of the Z-depth information from this popular 3D package from Play.

TechTip 03: Luminescent Premultiply
Using this transfer mode to handle a variation on premultiplied alpha channels, often created by 3D programs and color keyers.

TechTip 04: Luminance and IRE Issues
How to manage the different hardware and software luminance range definitions in video.

TechTip 05: Truth in Aspect Ratios
Pedantically correct aspect ratios for nonsquare pixels in a variety of formats.

TechTip 06: Cineon Issues
Technical bulletins on the Cineon format; plus an article on using the Cineon Converter originally published in *DV* magazine by Jonathan Banta.

TechTip 07: Advanced Rendering
How to use Collect Files for archiving and distributed rendering, including tips on using the Production Bundle's Render Engine.

TechTip 08: Video Issues
Details on safe areas, safe colors, and testing field order — including fixing field issues.

TechTip 09: The Definitive Rendering Pipeline
The steps After Effects executes when it's rendering a composition.

TechTip 10: Interpretation Rules
Creating simple scripts to set Interpret Footage parameters automatically for specific footage items.

TechTip 11: Photoshop Layer Effects
How After Effects recreates certain Photoshop layer effects.

TechTip 12: Slimming Straight Alphas
Tricks to reduce the disk space required to save straight alpha files.

The Road Home

Visual Magic

How Far We've Come

Harry Marks is rightfully acknowledged by many as the father of modern broadcast motion graphics. From a typography background in England, he eventually moved to Los Angeles in the mid-1960s, where he worked for both ABC and CBS as Vice President and Creative Director for On-Air Promotions. He also served as an independent consultant to NBC for six years. Harry initiated the move from animation stands to computer-generated graphics, and in doing so forever influenced what we see on television. He is an Apple Master, and was the first recipient of the Broadcast Designers Association Lifetime Achievement Award. Harry remains active to this day learning new tools and teaching them to others. He's also an incredibly nice guy. We're proud to have him write our foreword.

Foreword by Harry Marks

Motion graphics can involve any of a number of different tasks, from creating eye-popping special effects, to building reality-twisting commercials, to saving someone's job by subtly repairing a shot that would otherwise be unusable. My favorite is creating compelling images from scratch that help promote or sell a show or concept. Performing this visual magic used to be far more tedious and difficult than it is today.

War Stories

It seems not that long ago that in my position as Vice President of On-Air Advertising for ABC-TV, I was struggling to inject some semblance of graphic design into our promos. It was 1966, and even though I was given the leeway to experiment graphically, the tools available then were, by comparison to today's technology, crude and slow. Everything we tried had to go through a laborious process of hand setting type, shooting everything graphic on an animation stand, and combining the results in an optical printer. The process took days and invariably resulted in a product that was not exactly as visualized. We either settled for what we saw, or began the whole process over again. Needless to say, our resulting promotion spots for the network were not exactly graphics-intensive.

Even after teaming up with such visual effects pioneers as Douglas Trumbull and Bob Abel, and in spite of the gradual introduction of the computer into the process, our production of innovative graphics was painfully slow – and unrepeatable, thanks to unreliable computers and the variables of the film lab. But we worked with what we had, and designed and produced work that was quite startling on the screen. This helped enhance the upstart network's image as an innovator.

In 1977 ABC moved from a perennial No. 3 in a three-way ratings race to No. 1. I'm convinced that our promotional style was in a large way responsible for the success of the network; by this time, graphics had become a major element of promotion. People were becoming aware of motion graphics, and a new industry was born.

Enter Desktop Video

By 1985, the desktop computer was a required device in every graphic designer's toolbox. Some of us went a bit further and started to produce images for broadcast on our little computers. Images that had previously required the use of exotic and expensive broadcast tools were now being routinely produced on the desktop.

In my case, this was out of dire need. Those were the times of seemingly unlimited budgets, but limited facilities. Sometimes we had air time to fill and no way to produce the material to fill it with. Necessity being the mother of invention, we used our Macintoshes just to get on the air.

Software that allowed us to go further began to appear. Video capture cards made it possible for us to capture full-screen, "broadcast quality" video, albeit frame by frame, and audio tools enabled us to perform what would have been hitherto complex sound editing with ease. Before we realized it, a revolution was under way. On a limited basis, we could, on our desktops, produce video that would withstand the rigors of a broadcast engineer's scrutiny, without ever going to an expensive facility.

The downside was that the process was sometimes treacherous and always slow. But we new desktop video enthusiasts were undaunted, and we continued, with the help of faster desktop machines, to push the envelope. While nothing could compare with the speed and quality of exotic dedicated systems housed in rooms full of creature comforts at ever more deluxe facilities, budgets were being scrutinized, and the new tools were looking interesting to producers working on a shoestring.

Enter After Effects

What happened next was remarkable. In Rhode Island, a small group of intensely creative people going by the name of CoSA, The Company of Science and Art, created a product for manipulating video with plans to do what nothing else could. The product, which became After Effects, had a lot of unique properties, as well as a

ABC Fall Campaign, 1989*
ABC Sunday Night Movie*

Two NBC Fall Campaigns:
Let's All Be There, 1984*
Come Home to NBC, 1985*

Two Scenes from NBC
Monday Night at the Movies, 1989*

* with Dale Herigstad

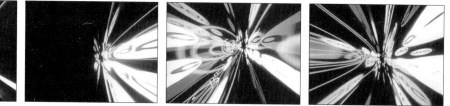

Early slit scan tests for
ABC Movie of the Week, 1969
with Douglas Trumbull

Experiments in streak photography
Kung Fu ABC, 1974
with Robert Abel

ABC Promo title –
one of a series, 1974
with Robert Abel

baffling interface. On the positive side, it was completely resolution independent, meaning that it didn't matter what the resolution or size or shape of the material it worked with was. And if you had the horsepower in your machine, it would output in any resolution you asked for.

The significance of this was that the television screen was no longer the boundary. After Effects could produce images for theatrical motion pictures – the big screen. In addition, the software could manipulate images with what I can only describe as exquisite precision. There'd never been anything like it before, and it still stands as the software of choice for the motion graphics industry. It's a common mantra in the business – if you're good with After Effects, you'll always work. And always being able to work is a good thing.

After Effects has evolved dramatically since "The Daves" – Herbstman and Simons – led their little band of computer scientists into the demanding waters of Hollywood production. Aldus Corporation and then Adobe Systems Inc. purchased it, the interface has been dramatically improved, and it "talks" very well to other industry standard software like Adobe Photoshop and Adobe Illustrator – both essential tools for the motion graphics designer. I can't imagine a production that somewhere and in some way doesn't use After Effects.

In the hands of an inexperienced artist, After Effects can be nothing short of dangerous, but in the hands of a master, it's brilliant, and all of its visual trickery is invisible to the eye. Trish and Chris Meyer are such masters; to me they are a walking, talking manual. Wherever they teach, classes are sold out. Whenever they write an article in a trade magazine, the piece gets promptly torn out of the magazine and filed like a great recipe. This is how vast their knowledge of the subject is and how invaluable their words are. I'm proud and happy to know Trish and Chris – after all, it's good to be able to call a walking manual. I'm personally very pleased that they've finally agreed to put all of their knowledge and experience on this subject in a book, and I'm sure that if motion graphics turns out to be your chosen path, you'll be the beneficiary of this remarkable couple's gifts.

Harry Marks

Los Angeles, January 2000

http://www.apple.com/applemasters/hmarks/

Welcome to Our World

We would not be what we are today if it was not for After Effects. We literally owe our careers to this program; we know this is true for many of you as well.

As you read in Harry Marks' foreword, not that long ago professional video production could be accomplished only on expensive, dedicated pieces of hardware. Only large facilities could afford such equipment; artists were hired to operate this gear; clients had to pay a lot of money to get both.

Then came After Effects – originally code-named Egg – from the tiny Company of Science and Art (CoSA) in Providence, Rhode Island. After Effects' graphics routines calculated images with precision equaling or exceeding the very best hardware available, so quality was not an issue. After Effects also ran on computers virtually anyone could afford. It gave you the tools to create almost any image you could imagine, tempered only by the amount of time or computing horsepower you had. With After Effects, the artists could afford the equipment themselves, and clients could hire these artists directly.

By Trish and Chris Meyer

The result has been a profusion of small artist-driven studios creating really cool graphics for television, film, multimedia, and the Web – many of whom use After Effects as one of their primary tools. We run one of those studios ourselves.

We have enjoyed working on a wide variety of creative (and technical!) challenges, including film and television opening titles such as *Now and Then* and *The Talented Mr. Ripley;* graphics for trade shows and press events such as Comdex for Xerox, CES for Clarion and Sun JavaOne; and special venue presentations for NBC's AstroVision sign in Times Square and the four-block-long Fremont Street Experience in Las Vegas. And we continue to do this work today.

But we weren't born knowing how to design graphics for video and film; using desktop computers was a new frontier in the industry when we started. We learned because virtually everyone involved in the early days was willing to share what he or she knew with each other, so we could all participate in this revolution that has come to be known as *desktop motion graphics*. Most of this activity was based

Keep Up to Date

Check our Web site for more information on other available training materials, including *VideoSyncrasies*, as well as information about scheduled classes and workshops.

We promise to add an "errata" page for *Creating Motion Graphics*, in case we discover errors after the book has been printed, third-party vendors have changed their contact information, and so on. The page to bookmark:

www.cybmotion.com/training

on the American Film Institute's Advanced Technology Program, where you would see a new technique demonstrated, then go home and literally pull out of your mailbox an industry magazine that predicted you wouldn't be able to see the same thing for several years.

Remembering those beginnings, we continue to share what we've learned with others who enter this field – as well as fellow old pros. We have taught at the American Film Institute and run a professional user group of fellow artists known as Motion Graphics Los Angeles (MGLA). We write numerous articles, including the monthly *Motion Graphics* column for *DV* magazine and speak at various trade shows and conferences. (We used to joke that our *DV* column *was* our book, appearing one chapter per month. However, the column has broadened to cover a wider variety of subjects including hardware and design, while this book goes into far greater depth than any individual column ever could.)

We've also created a training tape – *VideoSyncrasies* – that covers most of the technical gotchas that creep up when the computer world collides with video. And now, we present you with this book. We hope it will help you master this amazing program that is so central to much motion graphics production today – so you can then focus on being an artist, creating cool images for the rest of us to watch.

Trish and Chris Meyer
CyberMotion
March 2000

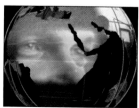

THANK YOUS

It is customary to thank all of those who have helped us get this far. But that would take a book in itself, and then we would still undoubtedly forget someone important. Needless to say, everyone we have come in contact with during our careers has shaped the path we've taken, and we thank you all. But we want to at least recognize those who contributed directly to the creation of this book:

▶ Everyone who was ever part of the After Effects team, as it wound its way from CoSA to Aldus to Adobe – thank you for creating this wonderful tool. In particular, thank you to team members Dan Wilk, David Simons, James Acquavella, Lazarus Long, and Barbara Vrana who answered our numerous questions during production, and Erica Schisler and Steve Kilisky for encouraging us along the way.

▶ Steve Tiborcz for his excellent technical edit – he sacrificed many an evening and weekend rigorously checking every concept and project to make sure the information presented here is correct.

▶ Harry Marks for his back-to-the-future *Foreword*, and David Simons who delved into the history of CoSA to write the *Afterword*.

▶ All of those who contributed tips, tricks, techniques, and tutorials. They are identified throughout the book where their wisdom is shared, with a special nod to Richard Lainhart, JJ Gifford, and Trevor Gilchrist, who graciously wrote guest tutorials for the CD, and Brenda Sexton who donated a project she designed for her *CoolMoves* CD. Thanks also to everyone who participates in the email lists and Web forums we frequent – the ongoing sharing of knowledge in these venues is simply amazing.

▶ The numerous companies, studios, and artists who created the source material used throughout this book. Specific contributors are thanked in the **Credits** section on page 466 and in the chapters where their footage is used.

▶ The companies who contributed free effects for you to use: Adobe, Atomic Power, Boris FX, Cycore, DigiEffects, ICE, and Puffin Designs.

▶ Ronny Schiff, David Biedny, and John Sledd, who gave generously of their experience and helped us wend our way through the legal issues involved.

▶ Everyone who was a member of the old AFI Advanced Technology Program, including in particular Harry Mott, who first brought us into the fold, and Harry Marks, who literally changed the look of what you see on television.

▶ Lynda Weinman, one of our earliest role models for a video artist using desktop tools, who gave Trish her first real After Effects gig (a nine-screen Circlevision using CoSA 1.0 on screamin' Quadra 950s…).

▶ All of our clients who patiently waited for us to get back to work(!) while we finished this project, as well as Lachlan Westfall of Quiet Earth Design plus Peter Lehrack, who covered for us when the jobs couldn't wait.

▶ Our editors at *DV* magazine, Dominic Milano and Jim Feeley.

▶ Kendall Eckman and Tina James, who test-drove the Bonus Tutorials included on the CD.

▶ Mandy Erickson, our copy editor, who made us seem like we actually knew how to write plain English. And Ken DellaPenta, our proofreader, who checked what took us months to write in mere days.

▶ And of course, our publishers – Matt Kelsey, Dorothy Cox and Gary Montalvo of Miller Freeman Books – who humored our outrageous demands for this large a book with this many color pages that took this long to write. Thank you for understanding our goal was to make the absolute best product we could, so we would all be proud.

Production Credits: The book and cover were designed by Trish Meyer; the icons were designed by Trevor Gilchrist. The chapter page layouts were performed by Paul Hillson and Trish Meyer; front/back matter by Trish Meyer. Peter Lehrack did the page layouts for the TechTips and Bonus Tutorials.

How to Use This Book

This book is not a rewrite of the After Effects 4.1 manual and online Help files. After all, you already own them; why pay to read them again?

This book is the culmination of more than seven years' experience using After Effects to create graphics in the real world for a wide variety of projects, teaching it at the Hollywood branch of the American Film Institute, and speaking at numerous conferences. This book will not cover every single function and keyboard command inside After Effects. However, it *will* cover – at great depth – how After Effects works, and how we use it to solve real-world design and production challenges. The goal is to help you understand the program and use it efficiently and creatively for your own tasks. As another artist shared with us, "Give me a fish, and you've fed me for one day. Teach me how to fish, and you've fed me for the rest of my life." We want to teach you how to fish.

We've restricted this book as much as we can to After Effects 4.1 as shipped by Adobe, noting sections specific to the Production Bundle version of the program as they occur. However, there are also numerous wonderful third-party extensions available for After Effects; we'll mention our favorites where appropriate in asides to the main text. (Check out the ad in the back of this book to get a free CD from ToolFarm of demos of virtually all the available third-party effects.)

We also assume you already have, or are familiar with, **Adobe Photoshop** (version 5 or later) and **Adobe Illustrator** (version 8 or later): these are essential companion programs to After Effects, and they should be in your arsenal if they're not already.

Which Part Comes First?

Throughout this book, we've tried to make sure an emphasis on design is not lost while learning the concepts – it's the "why" behind doing something. Before teaching a technique, we continually asked ourselves "Would *we* do that?" If not, we won't waste your time showing *you* how to do it. On the other hand, many of the examples have additional layers and objects added to them that are otherwise unnecessary to teach a concept, because we *would* do that – our bottom line is creating interesting imagery.

For those of you who are new to After Effects, the chapters have been arranged in a primarily linear fashion, grouped by general subject. If you already have some experience using After Effects, you can jump to later chapters, or into specific topics. As the chapters progress, so will our assumptions about your knowledge base. Later in the book, the information will get more specialized (there are chapters dedicated to color keying, motion tracking, or working with film); these can obviously be skipped and referred to later as needed.

Bonus Tutorials

After you have mastered the concepts covered in the individual chapters, there are a number of Bonus Tutorials on the CD that include concepts from a variety of chapters, showing you how it all comes together. Each tutorial has a corresponding Acrobat PDF file for you to read and a finished movie if applicable. A summary of tutorials is on page 454 so you can preview which tutorials are of interest; we have tried to grade them in a range between "easy" and "strenuous" – choose accordingly. Some tutorials are step-by-step; some show a finished project and describe the major tricks to look for. If they don't make sense, they will cross-reference which chapters in the book should be reviewed to understand their concepts. (If you don't have Acrobat Reader, it's included in the book's CD>_Installers folder; the latest reader can also be downloaded from www.adobe.com.)

Iconography

The content inside each chapter is also usually presented in a linear fashion. However, you will find numerous asides throughout. In addition to sidebars, which focus on specific ideas or techniques, you will also see:

Tips: These contain additional tricks and shortcuts, or info on a third-party effect we recommend.

Factoids: These are tweaky bits of specific information that might help demystify some subjects.

Gotchas: These are important rocks you might trip over or holes you might fall into.

Connects: Mini-indexes at the end of each chapter point out additional chapters that contain information related with what you just learned.

Production Bundle: After Effects comes in two versions, Standard and Production Bundle. The latter includes powerful features such as motion stabilization and tracking, plug-ins for keying and distortion, and additional keyframe assistants. Whenever a chapter *requires* the Production Bundle, you will see this icon beside the chapter title. If the icon appears beside a subhead instead, this means that the chapter is applicable

For Instructors Only

Much of this book is modeled on the After Effects beginning and advanced classes Trish has taught for many years at The American Film Institute in Hollywood. If you're an instructor, we hope that you will use this book to teach After Effects, adapting it to your specific needs.

Recognizing the budgets and time constraints of most instructional situations, we've built 95% of the example projects using 320×240 comps and similar low resolution sources. This requires less memory all around, and results in faster demonstrations and previewing.

We'd love for you to use our book to help you teach After Effects to the masses, and hope the examples and sources supplied will encourage your students to create great motion graphics as they learn key concepts.

If all the students own a copy of the book, they can review the material covered after class – without wasting valuable class time writing reams of notes. Students can open the Chapter Example project from the CD, make changes to it, and save the edited project to their own folders on the hard disk or removable media. At the next class, if they load the CD *before* opening their modified projects, the sources should relink properly.

If your school has the available disk space, students may copy contents from the CD to their computer (see also sidebar, *Faster Retrieval and Relinking,* on the next page). However, each student must still own a copy of the book if you are using the sources, projects and tutorials on multiple machines. If a school, company or instructor distributes copies of the sources, or the tutorial projects and PDFs, to any person who has not purchased the book, that constitutes copyright infringement. Also, it goes without saying that copying pages of the book, or any PDFs included on the CD, is also a copyright no-no. That includes modifying tutorials and paraphrasing step-by-step instructions without proper attribution.

If you're an instructor you no doubt appreciate how much time and effort it takes to prepare examples and class materials that both teach and inspire. Thank you for protecting our copyright, and those of the many vendors and studios who contributed sources.

(For more information on copyrights for sources, please read the End User License Agreements that are included in the **Credits and Info** folder on your CD.)

for the most part to the Standard version, with the exception of a few examples or ideas that use Production Bundle features. (In these cases, you will also find that some plug-in references are removed when you open the Chapter Example Project file; only comps tagged in the project's Comment field as "PB Only" should be affected.)

Assumptions We've Made

As we mentioned, for the most part this book does not repeat information that is easily found and clearly presented in the manual and online Help (which contains useful information not in the manual, by the way). If you can't find it here, refer back to those documents. We felt it more important to use these pages to explain concepts, gotchas, design tips, and working practices that couldn't be gleaned from the documentation provided. That said, the first several chapters do provide a good overview of how to get into using After Effects, if you're the type who just can't bring yourself to read the manual (you know who you are).

Adobe After Effects is currently available for the MacOS and Windows operating systems. Since the Macintosh version has been available longer, it is the platform we personally use. Rather than clutter up the copy with multiple keyboard commands, all of the key commands are given for MacOS. We've provided an accompanying table with the appropriate keyboard conversions. We know some will take great offense at this, but we give Windows

MacOS	->	Windows
Command	=	Control
Option	=	Alt
Control	=	right mouse button

users credit for being smart enough to translate as they go. Plus, you'll no doubt memorize the most often-used shortcuts with a little practice.

Before You Start...Load That CD!

We hope at this point that you're ready to tear into the book proper. Before you start, however, check out the enclosed CD. *If you never load it, you're missing out on at least half of what this book has to offer.* It contains a companion After Effects project for virtually every chapter in this book and will really reinforce each concept as you read it.

Hand in hand with the Chapter Projects is a folder full of source material (complete with a Portfolio catalog which includes creator contact information). This Sources folder contains content used by these projects, some of the TechTips, and the twenty-two Bonus Tutorials also contained on the CD.

The CD also contains numerous Effects Favorites we've created for you, updated Motion Math scripts, templates for film and video work, 12 free fully-functional plug-in effects from a variety of manufacturers, and even a tryout version of After Effects 4.1! The CD Roadmap on the next page explains what is where and how best to use the CD.

Retrieving and Relinking

If you have free hard disk space, copy the entire CD to your hard disk (you can throw away bits you don't need later). By copying the whole shebang, you'll maintain the "links" that each After Effects project has to the master Sources folder. Copying just a small project folder will not speed up your workflow if the larger sources (especially the movies) are still being retrieved from the CD.

If files become "unlinked" for some reason, they will appear in *italics* in the Project window. Simply *double-click the first missing item*, which opens the Open dialog, and navigate to it on the CD or your drive. Select this item and After Effects should now search all folders for the other missing items. Provided their relationship has not changed (movies are still in the Movies folder, and so on), this should be successful.

CD ROADMAP

The enclosed CD contains many useful resources for you to explore while reading this book. Here's what is in each folder:

▶ Catalog of Sources.fdb

This is an Extensis Portfolio catalog of all the footage items in the SOURCES folder on the CD. In addition to being a great visual reference, it contains contact information for all of the content contributors. If you do not already have Portfolio, run Portfolio Browser (PortBrws.exe for Windows users) in the Installers folder.

▶ CD Tutorial Projects

Contains twenty-two bonus tutorials in PDF form for you to practice after you've mastered some of the chapters in this book. Most come with an After Effects project plus a QuickTime movie of the final result; some contain additional source material as well. Inside this folder is a Portfolio catalog of the final tutorial movies. See also page 454 for additional information; a summary of each tutorial starts on page 455.

▶ Chapter Example Projects

Virtually every chapter has a corresponding After Effects example project. This way, you can actually see each concept discussed in action, and try it for yourself. Some have additional source material specific to that chapter which are used in addition to the shared Sources folder on this CD.

▶ Credits and Info

Info on the numerous stock footage houses, studios, and individual artists who contributed content for this book, should you want to work with them directly. Also contains the End User License Agreements that you agree to when using their content provided on the CD.

▶ Free Plug-ins

Adobe, Atomic Power, Boris FX, Cycore, DigiEffects, ICE, and Puffin Designs have contributed a dozen free, fully-functional plug-in effects for you to add to your collection. Install them; they will be used throughout this book. You'll also find information on other effect packages, and where to find more free effects.

▶ Goodies

A pot pourri of additional tools such as Effects Favorites, updated Motion Math scripts, and a subfolder full of Templates of guides and safe areas for various film and video frame sizes.

▶ SOURCES

Over 400 megabytes of movies, music, mattes, objects, stills, sequences, and text elements that are used by the various projects and tutorials throughout this book. Each file has a two-letter prefix that identifies its creator; a key is provided in the Credits and Info folder as well as on page 466. Make sure you read their respective End User License Agreements in the Credits and Info folder – many of the sources may also be used in your own projects.

▶ TechTips

An additional dozen mini-chapters in PDF format on tweaky subjects such as alpha channel types, video-specific issues, working with 3D programs, and the Kodak Cineon file format.

▶ _Installers

Contains a try-out version of After Effects 4.1, in addition to the Extensis Portfolio Browser to view the Catalog of Sources and the Catalog of Tutorials on this CD.

How After Effects Thinks

After Effects is a very logical, predictable program – if you know how it works.

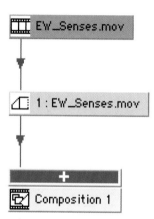

The flow of images through After Effects. Footage items (such as the red-colored file EW_Senses.mov) become layers (the green bar with the name of the source footage it came from) inside compositions (the blue item at the bottom of the flow).

Ever use a piece of software that seems to have a mind of its own? Things just happen, for reasons that aren't exactly clear? After Effects can be that way – if you don't know how it works. However, when you step back and learn the overall structure of how images flow through it, After Effects becomes very logical to use. You then can move on to solving artistic challenges, rather than randomly searching through menu items, or trying to remember ritualistic procedures that you swear worked the last time you tried them… In this chapter, we will give a conceptual overview of After Effects' internal flow. Subsequent chapters will build on this basic structure, as we go into more and more detail on how you can combine and animate your source elements.

Gimme Structure

Here is the thumbnail overview of how images flow through After Effects:

• *Footage* is your original source material which you capture, create, or otherwise prepare before bringing into After Effects. It can include movies (self-contained movie files or sequences of consecutive still image files), stills (pixel- and vector-based), layered still images, and audio.

• You combine your footage inside entities known as *compositions*. When you drag a footage item into a composition ("comp" for short), it becomes a *layer* inside that comp. A single footage item can be a layer in any number of compositions, or it can be used for several layers inside a single composition – you don't need to create or bring in multiple copies of the same source. Inside a composition, you can also create layers, which are simple blocks of color, known as *solids*.

• You can have essentially an unlimited number of compositions inside a single After Effects file. Any composition can turn around and serve as a source for a layer for a new comp, allowing grouping and other organizational tricks. When we're talking about layers, we will quite often refer to the material that made them as sources, rather than explicitly footage or other comps.

• After Effects gives you a number of ways to manipulate the appearance of each layer. In order, you can Mask off portions of the layer to hide or reveal them; Transform them with various geometric manipulations such as Position, Scale, Rotation, and Opacity; you can also apply *effects* – plug-ins that changes the appearance and behavior of a layer – to each layer in a composition. After Effects comes with a wide range of effects, even more are included in the Production Bundle version; and additional effects are available from third parties.

- You can render any composition to create a final movie. You can also render a still of a particular point in time inside a composition. If you have a chain of compositions – one serving as a layer for another – you often will render the last composition in this chain.

- All of this is contained inside a single After Effects file known as a *project*. Projects do not contain the sources; they point to the sources wherever they exist on your hard drives or network. The job of a project is to keep track of the structure of how you want to combine and treat your sources.

- To save your work, you save the project file, not individual compositions. Saving the project (File> Save) saves the links to the imported footage items, the compositions, keyframes, effects references, and so on. (You can safely close the Composition and Time Layout windows, without "saving" first.) Project files may incorporate the bulk of the time and effort spent on a job – lucky for you they're easy to back up frequently due to their small size. To protect against a corrupt project file (an unusual occurrence with After Effects, but it happens), perform a Save As with a new version number at least daily.

To review: Footage items are your raw source material. They can be used as layers in a composition, where you combine multiple elements together and animate them to create your final image. Entire comps can be used as layers in other compositions, further increasing the power. Each layer can be manipulated using Masks, Effects, and Transformations. The structure of all this is remembered in a file known as a project.

This structure is significantly different from that of a typical video editing or paint program. Perhaps the most powerful aspect of After Effects is the fact that you can build these sub-projects known as compositions, then use these comps as elements in other comps. An example is building a complex picture-in-picture window that might include a moving image, a frame created in Photoshop, and a text overlay – then treating all that as one element to scale and position over a second video scene.

Now let's dive underneath this surface to see how these files actually flow through After Effects.

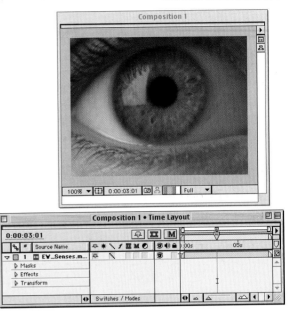

A composition contains two windows: the Comp window, which is the "stage" on which you arrange the objects that make up your layers, and the Time Layout window, where you order and animate them. Eye courtesy Eyewire/Senses.

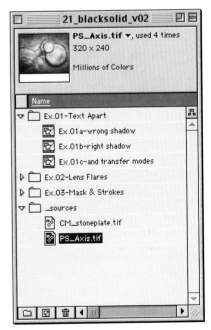

A simple project, with compositions organized inside folders, and a couple of source footage items shared by multiple comps.

RGB Value Display

To read the color value of any pixel, make sure the Info window is open (Window> Show Info, or Command+2) and move the cursor over an open Composition, Source, or Layer window. Its RGB and Alpha value will be displayed in this window.

Object Oriented

Some people refer to After Effects as being "object oriented" – in other words, it strives to treat all types of layers equally, whether they are movies, stills, solids, or entire compositions. This means you can learn one set of rules and apply them to virtually all of your images, rather than having to remember different rules for different types of media. The one exception is the difference between audio and visual files: they have their own effects and their own parameters to manipulate.

Peeling Back the Layers

After Effects works in RGB (Red, Green, and Blue) color space, where every pixel is the combination of the three color channels. After Effects uses 8 bits of resolution per pixel per channel, so each channel is actually a grayscale image with 256 possible values. The "value" of each color component can range from 0 to 255, with 0 being no contribution by that primary color to this pixel, and 255 being 100 percent contribution. These three values add their color weightings to give you the final "color" of a pixel. If all three values are 0, the result is black; if their values are all 255, the result is white; any other mixture yields a color of some description. If a source image is in another color space, such as grayscale, it is automatically converted to 24-bit RGB for handling inside After Effects.

After Effects also carries a fourth channel of information for every image, known as the "alpha" channel. It also has 8-bit resolution, which when combined with the 24-bit RGB color channels result in a 32-bit image. The alpha channel decides the transparency of every pixel built by the RGB color channels. A value of 0 (black in the alpha) means the pixel underneath is totally transparent, 255 (white in the alpha) means totally opaque. Values between these numbers are partially transparent: if you were to put this image on top of another, you would see part of the image behind these pixels.

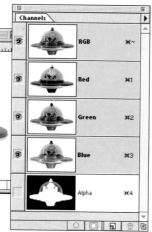

As viewed in Photoshop, this image consists of four channels: Red, Green, Blue, and Alpha, each of which is an 8-bit grayscale channel. When imported in After Effects, the combination of RGB channels creates the color for each pixel, while the corresponding alpha channel determines the pixel's opacity. Spaceman from Classic PIO/Nostalgic Memorabilia.

The concept of the alpha channel is crucial to everything After Effects does. Every source, layer, and comp has one. If an original source file does not have an alpha, After Effects automatically gives it an all-white (all-opaque) one that can then be manipulated later. You control the transparency of each layer in a comp by scaling the values in its alpha channel. You can carve out sections of an image with *masks*. An alpha channel for one layer can be borrowed from another layer; in this case, it's called a *matte*.

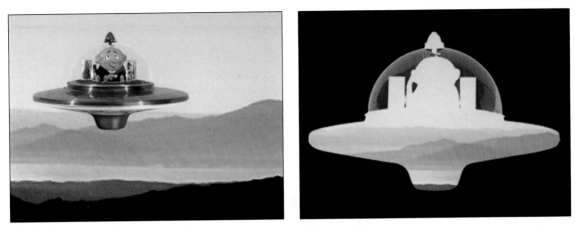

There are also effects that can create or modify the alpha channel – by keying out the blue screen behind an actor to make those areas transparent, for example. We will discuss all of these techniques in later chapters.

The concept to remember at this point is that everything has transparency, which, combined with transfer modes, allows you to blend images together in interesting ways.

The Spaceman's alpha channel is used in After Effects for compositing against a background (left); the alpha channel can also be used as a matte for the background layer (right).

Time Machine

Another important characteristic of After Effects, which sets it apart from paint and drawing applications, is the concept of time. You can use it to create still images, but things are far more interesting when they're animated. Movies and sequences themselves are series of still images that change over time, and After Effects can animate the properties of, and effects applied to, any comp's layer over time.

The way movies and sequences change over time is based on their frame rate. A single still image in a movie is referred to as a frame. The interval of time between calling up new stills in the sequence is its rate, usually expressed in *frames per second* (fps): the number of frames that are supposed to appear in each second. For example, film commonly projects 24 new frames a second; NTSC video changes frames 29.97 times a second. If it is easier for you to grasp, consider that the duration of time each frame is displayed before the next one comes along. In the case of film, that's 1/24th of a second. After Effects also gives you a number of ways to fudge this frame rate, which we'll discuss later.

You can combine sources of different frame rates inside After Effects. It keeps track of each one individually, incrementing to the next image when each one's time is up. Compositions also have their own frame rates, which is how it decides which images to display – i.e., when you move forward one frame on the comp's timeline, how much later in time are you? The comp's frame rate is typically set to equal the rate you intend to render at later, and it is the default rate used for rendering. However, when you actually render the comp, the frame rate set in the Render Settings overrides the comp's frame rate.

Audio Sample Rates

Sound files have their own "frame rates" known as sample rates – how many audio samples pass by in a second. Again, After Effects can mix together sources of different rates, with the render settings deciding the rate of the final movie you create.

Memory Requirements

After Effects renders one layer at a time in a composition. Therefore, the amount of RAM it needs is greatly impacted by the dimensions of the largest layer in a composition. After Effects leaves the contents of your sources unaltered on your drives, but it needs to load a copy of either the still image or the current frame of a movie into RAM to work on it. It doesn't matter if you are rendering a small movie for the Web or a film resolution title – if both are using a large photo as its source, both will require enough memory to load that photo into RAM. Masks, certain effects (such as those that point to other layers), and nested compositions will also increase your RAM requirements. Prior to version 4.0, we would consider 100 megabytes to be the smallest amount of RAM we would recommend for video work and still feel safe (64 is dancing on ice); film resolution work can take two to three times more.

Version 4.0 and later have added a RAM Preview function that eats up additional RAM – but for a good cause. Rather than having to render a movie and then play it to see how your animation is coming along, you can now render to RAM while still inside the program, and play back your test from there. The price: you need to have enough RAM available to buffer up this preview. As a result, on the Mac, we now rarely run After Effects with less than 250 megabytes of RAM assigned. We discuss RAM Preview, along with optimizing previews, at the end of Chapter 4.

Rendering Pipeline

Now it's time to dig a little deeper into After Effects' internal flow. We know that sources become layers in comps, which can become layers in other comps, and then get rendered. But beyond that, different operations take place on those layers – in a certain order – inside a comp. This used to be known as the *rendering pipeline*, but has since been rechristened as the *render order*. It is a concept that initially strikes fear in the non-technical, but it's one of the secrets to understanding what After Effects is really doing to your sources on their way to the final render. This is the sequence of what happens:

- A source comes into a project with its own properties, such as its frame rate.
- How some of these properties, such as alpha channel type, are interpreted can be modified by the Interpret Footage dialog (covered in more detail in the next chapter). These interpretations apply to every use of the source in any and all comps.
- Layers in a comp are calculated bottom (back) to top (front). Layers placed on top paste over the layers underneath, depending on their own transparency, and any other trickery such as transfer modes.
- Each layer has a Mask (additional cutout to its alpha channel). This is cut before any other operations take place on a layer.
- Up to thirty-one effects may be applied to each layer. They can be ordered in the Effects Controls window and are calculated from top to bottom.
- Next come the transformations: Anchor Point, Position, Scale, Rotation, and Opacity. These transform the layer after the mask has been cut and any effects applied.

Rendering Reminder
Twirl down a layer's properties in the Time Layout window. The order that properties are stacked – Masks, Effects (in order), and Transform – is how they are rendered.

Rendering Pipeline • Time Layout

Rendering Pipe...						
0:00:00:00					00:15f	01:
⌕ #	Source Name				:00f	
▽ ☐ 1	🖺 CP_Spaceman.tif					
	▷ Masks					
	▽ Effects					
	▷ Hue/Saturation	Reset				
	▷ Drop Shadow	Reset				
	▽ Transform					
	⌂ Anchor Point	150.0, 100.0				
	⌂ Position	150.0, 100.0				
	⌂ Scale	100%				
	⌂ Rotation	0.0°				
	⌂ Opacity	100%				
	Switches / Modes					

Layers are altered, in order, through Masks, then Effects, then Transform. Once all the layers in a composition are calculated, the result can be passed on as a new layer in a new composition – meaning the group can then get its own Masks, Effects, and Transform.

• The layer ordered immediately above the layer being calculated can act as an additional alpha channel modifier for the current layer, and is called a *track matte*. If a track matte is being applied, its effect on a layer's alpha channel is calculated after Masks, Effects, and Transform.

• Layers are calculated from the bottom up, and a composite takes place after each layer is rendered. For instance, in a comp with three layers, the background (Layer 3) is rendered first. Then Layer 2 is rendered and composited with Layer 3 and a new 32-bit image is created. Then Layer 1 is rendered and composited on top of the *result* of Layers 2 and 3.

• Calculating all the layers in a comp results in a temporarily saved image with alpha. It is either output at this point, or passed onto another comp which may use it as a layer: here this process repeats.

Note that these steps occur only when an image needs to be displayed or rendered. The original source material is never permanently changed. All a project does is remember the processing steps you want to perform on your sources. This means every parameter is always "live": you can go back and change your mind later, without worrying about backups or image degradation.

"Masks, Effects, Transform" will become a mantra that you will learn to memorize. Understanding the order in which After Effects is manipulating your layers is important, as it explains all sorts of mysteries, such as why the direction of the drop shadow is rotating with the layer instead of acting like the light is always in the same place. (Because Drop Shadow is an effect, and Rotation is a transformation, and transformations – such as the rotation – get rendered after effects.)

Knowing what After Effects is doing empowers you to thwart it, if need be. Part 4 of this book is dedicated to understanding the rendering order and building comp hierarchies that work.

Onward

Now you have a handle on how After Effects thinks. So we can move onto gaining a greater understanding of each of the above steps. Hold onto your hats…

Connect

Importing Footage items is covered in Chapter 2.

Creating Compositions, and their various parameters, is introduced in Chapter 3.

Various Transformations are covered in Chapters 4, 5, and 6.

Managing and manipulating Layers is discussed in Chapters 8 and 9.

Ways of manipulating the frame rate of a source are discussed in Chapter 10.

Masking is covered in Chapter 13; Track Mattes in Chapter 14.

The power of nesting Compositions inside other Compositions is covered in Chapters 16 & 17.

Applying and using Effects is discussed in Chapters 19–24.

Alternate ways of creating and managing transparency are revealed in Chapter 25.

Audio in general is covered in Chapter 30.

Rendering options are explored in Chapters 43–44 and TechTip 07 on the CD.

Alpha channels are discussed in greater detail in TechTip 01 on the CD.

Customs and Immigration

Getting files in, interpreting their information, and changing your mind later.

Now that we have a handle on how After Effects operates, we'll examine each stage in greater detail. In this chapter, we will cover importing files, plus the Project and Footage windows. Then we'll move on to more specific issues for movies, stills, sequences, and audio, as well as Adobe Photoshop and Illustrator. We will also reveal additional options and tricks in later chapters as they come up. If you're new to After Effects, follow the *To Do* prompts. These will encourage you to practice importing various sources from the accompanying CD. More advanced After Effects users might wish to simply scour the copy for tips, or explore the final project file.

New Project

You can create a new project by using File>New>New Project, or Command+Option+N. If no project is currently open, Command+N will also create a new project.

Example Project

If you're a beginner, we encourage you to create this chapter's project from scratch by following the *To Do* prompts. The result is included on the CD as 02-Example Project.aep.

The Project File

The way you handle different image sources, regardless of their file type, is similar. This includes importing them, navigating the Project window where they are sorted and managed, and setting the type of alpha channel each file has.

When you first boot After Effects, a new Project file will open by default. You can access the various Import options via File>Import>Footage File… or >Footage Files…. Double-clicking in the blank Project window,

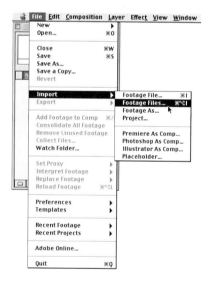

You can import a single file, or multiple files at a time. Still image file formats that contain layers of component images (such as Photoshop and Illustrator files) can be imported either merged or as layers. You can also import whole projects created in After Effects, Premiere, and others that are enabled with their own special plug-ins, such as Media 100. Finally, you can set the size and duration of a dummy file known as a Placeholder, and replace it later when you have the actual file.

or the keyboard shortcut Command+I, will get you to the most used Import Footage File dialog used for importing movies, sequences, stills, and audio. You will need to use the other options under File>Import menu for more complex tasks such as importing a multilayered Photoshop file and keeping its layers separate.

If you are using After Effects 4.1 and MacOS 8.5 or later, there is an alternate Import Footage dialog available that allows you to either import one item, or Shift+click to select and import multiple items. Go to File> Preferences>Import and enable Enhanced Open & Save Dialogs. The Shift key acts as a toggle for temporarily switching to the Open/ Save dialog style that's the opposite of the one set in Preferences. You will also need to use the older dialog when you want to import any file types QuickTime needs to translate, such as .avi and CD audio tracks.

> *To Do:* With a New Project open, select File>Import Footage File... (Command+I). Navigate to the CD>Sources>Movies folder. From this folder, select the first movie, AB_CloudChamber_Fill.mov and click Import. The movie will now appear in the Project window.

If you select a single source in the Project window, thumbnail information about the file will appear at the top of the Project window. Here you can see the file's name, how often it is used, frame size, duration, frame rate, color depth, and additional information such as the QuickTime codec it was compressed with.

If the source is an audio file or a movie file that contains audio, the sample rate, resolution, and number of channels will also be displayed along the bottom, as well as a squiggle underneath the thumbnail that represents a generic audio waveform.

Remember that the act of importing a source does not *copy* the file into your project – all that gets stored in the project is a pointer to the source on your hard disk.

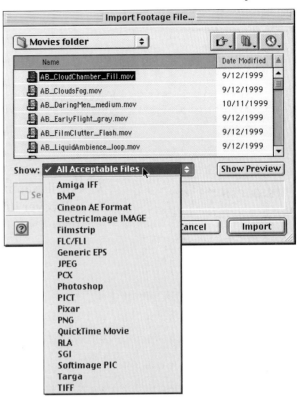

The Import dialog is shown here using the Enhanced Navigation Services option on the Mac. It can recognize a wide range of file formats. QuickTime can read an even wider range of formats, including AVI and MP3 audio; After Effects can import any file format QuickTime can read. However, it does not read non-image or non-audio tracks of a QuickTime file, such as text; it also cannot access multiple streams of the same type.

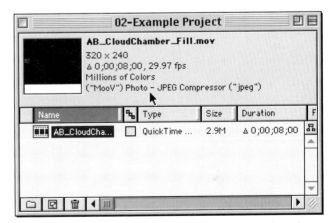

The top of the Project window displays useful information about the currently selected source. Option+click on a name in the Project window to additionally display the file type code and codec code, as shown.

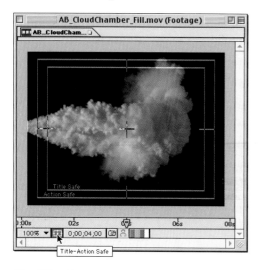

After Effects' Footage window is the best way to view your sources before adding them to comps. If you pause the cursor over the icons along the bottom, you will get a hint as to what that feature does (such as display the alpha channel by itself, or turn on Title-Action Safe). These Tool Tips can be turned on or off in the File>Preferences>General dialog. Movie courtesy Artbeats Cloud Chamber CD.

When an alpha is unlabeled, After Effects defaults to asking you what type of alpha channel. If you don't know, click Guess – most of the time its guess is as good as anyone's...

Viewing Sources in the Footage Window

If you simply double-click an imported movie, the generic Quick-Time viewer will open. (Note that movies on the CD are often saved with light JPEG compression to maintain quality – they are not optimized for realtime playback.) Holding down the Option key before double-clicking will open it in After Effects' own viewer, which adds the ability to view individual color channels and the alpha channel, zoom the view resolution, display an action-safe overlay, and otherwise use After Effects' time navigation features. A similar window is used for stills and sequences.

> *To Do:* Option+double-click on the imported movie to open it in After Effects' viewer. Hit the spacebar to Play. The movie will play better the second time around, after it's been cached. The Tool Tips will help you in exploring the switches.

Importing Footage with Alpha

As mentioned in Chapter 1, After Effects bases its life around the alpha channel of an image. If it does not detect any alpha channel, it will automatically create one that is 100% opaque (i.e., it will show the entire image). If After Effects actually created the file, it will have saved a tag with it indicating the alpha type (Straight or Premultiplied), and will use that; it also knows that some files always have a certain type (for example, Illustrator files have Straight alphas).

If After Effects detects an alpha without a tag saying what type of alpha it is, After Effects then refers to the setting in File>Preferences>Import to decide if it should ask you what type of alpha it is, assume an alpha type, or guess. If you selected the option to have it always ask you, After Effects will present you with four choices: Guess, Ignore, Treat as Straight, and Treat as Premultiplied (the last choice includes a color swatch).

Import As

Ever have a file that you know is in the correct format, but After Effects refuses to see it when you go to import it? Chances are, it lost its identity – either its File Type resource (Mac) or format extensions (Windows). You can force After Effects to see it by using the File>Import>Footage As command, and setting the Show popup to the file format you think it is. If you're wrong, you'll merely get an error dialog. There are numerous utilities that can change or repair these file type designations for you, but this may be a quick fix.

To Do: Select File>Import Footage File… (Command+I) and select the CM_bikewheel.tif still image from the Objects folder. This image has an alpha channel. When the Interpret Footage dialog opens, click Guess, and the file will be interpreted correctly as Straight Alpha.

Ignore means replace the alpha with a solid white (opaque) one. Straight and Premultiplied are two different types of alpha channels, with Straight often being preferred. These types are discussed in TechTip 01 on the CD. Guess means you want After Effects to take its own best shot at deciding the alpha type. It does a pretty good job, with a known weakness of wrongly guessing that alphas which are Premultiplied with White (the correct setting for most still image object libraries shot against a white background) are Straight.

Project Window Organization

When you import your sources, they appear in the Project window. If you open the Project window wider, you see not only the source names, but also media types, durations, and the file patch (where they are located on your drives). You can rearrange these information fields by dragging their headings to the left or right over each other. Most headings also have a handle on their right edge – this allows you to resize the field, in case you want to see more or less text for it.

After Effects sorts the contents of the Project window based on which of the information fields, or *panel* (file type, name, and so on) you last selected and highlighted. When you create new compositions, they are also added to the Project window; we'll get to them in the next chapter. Throughout After Effects, you can also Hide or Show various panels using a context-sensitive popup menu. Control+click in the header area of the Project window to bring up the menu.

> **To Do:** Control+click in the header area of the Project window and select Panels>Comment. The Comments field will default to the right side of the window. Open the Project window wide and drag the Comments panel to the left. Clicking in a source's Comment field will allow you to type in notes; hit Return to accept your typing. You'll see we've added comments throughout our Example and Tutorial Projects.
> To Hide a panel, Control+click and select Hide Panel from the popup. You might want to Hide the colored Labels panel to reduce clutter.

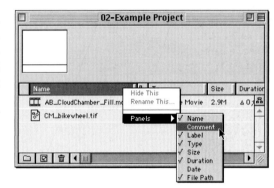

Opening the Project window wider reveals additional information about the footage files. Individual panels can be widened and rearranged by dragging them left and right. The window defaults to sorting by Name, so that panel is shown highlighted.

Control+click in the header area to Hide and Show individual panels. If you Show the Comment panel, it will open to the far right; drag it to the left where it's easier to see and use.

The Comment field allows you to type notes about items in the Project window.

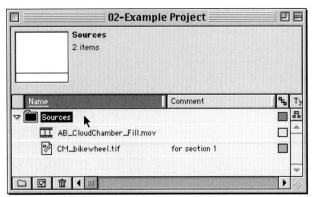

The imported footage items after being dragged into a new folder named Sources.

You probably sort your source materials on your hard drives by using directories and folders, and you can do the same inside After Effects. New Folders can be created from File>New>New Folder. Drag any sources you want into this new folder. To reveal what is inside, either double-click on the folder, or twirl down the arrow to its left. To hide the contents of the folder, click on the arrow again to twirl it up. We strongly suggest using folders to help organize your sources (movies, audio, backgrounds, titles, and so on).

To Do: Select File>New>New Folder (Command+Option+Shift+N) to create an Untitled folder. Immediately hit Return, type in the name Sources, and hit Return again to accept the new name. Marquee all your imported footage items to select them, and drag the sources to the new folder. Double-click the folder to reveal its contents.

Drag and Drop a Folder

You can also import sources by simply dragging them from the desktop into the Project window. You can even drag them directly into a folder you've created in After Effects. However, if you have already sorted your sources by folders on your hard drive, you can import these folders and their contents directly into a project using a similar drag-and-drop technique. This is probably one of the most useful, underdocumented features in After Effects, and once you get the technique nailed, you'll save time on every project:

Step 1: Make sure both the Project window and the folder you wish to import from the desktop are both visible before you begin (you may have to move windows around).

Step 2: Select the CD>Sources>Objects folder on the desktop and Option+drag the folder to the Project window.

Step 3: Drop the folder into the Project window, then let go of the Option key. A new folder will be created inside the After Effects project. It will automatically guess any unlabeled alpha channel, but will stop for instructions if it encounters a file with layers. Embedded folders will keep the same hierarchy as in the directory.

Alpha and Folders

When you drag and drop a folder of sources, After Effects will always guess any unlabeled alpha channel rather than presenting you with a dialog, regardless of how the Interpret Alpha in File>Preferences> Import has been set.

Sluggish Thumbnails

The display of thumbnails in the Project window is useful, but it slows you down because it has to retrieve the image or render the comp to display the thumbnail. If you've had too much caffeine, set the "Disable thumbnails in project window" option (File>Preferences>Display).

If you're having trouble with this drag-and-drop technique, you might be dropping the folder and releasing the Option key at exactly the same time. If After Effects does not have a chance to acknowledge that the Option key was held down, the folder will be interpreted as a sequence of frames – great if that was your intention (we'll discuss sequences in more detail below).

After Effects is aware of the contents of an external folder only at the time you import it. If you later add or delete items in this directory folder, they are not added to or deleted from your After Effects project. If you move already-imported files out of the folders they were originally in when you imported them, After Effects will attempt to track them and relink the items, but will not resort them in the project.

When working on the Mac, we've occasionally found that the simple Option+drag technique above fails to work. To ensure success, modify the steps slightly: In Step 1, make sure After Effects is the foreground application, not the Finder. In Step 2, select the folder on the desktop and hold down the mouse. (If you let up the mouse, the Finder will come to the foreground.) Now add the Option key, and drag the folder to the Project window. (Don't just Option+click on the folder directly, or the Finder will come forward and hide After Effects.) Release the mouse, then release the Option key. This exact series of steps never fails to work.

Reloading and Missing Sources

If you need to replace a source (perhaps you updated it on disk), select it, and use File>Reload Footage (Command+Option+L). If its name or location on the disk has changed, you might need to use File>Replace Footage instead (Command+H). After Effects will automatically update this source in any composition that used it.

If After Effects cannot find a source file when you open a Project, missing footage will be displayed in *italics* in the Project window. Double-clicking on a missing item will bring up the standard file import dialog, where you can relink or replace the missing footage. All other missing items will also be found automatically, provided that their relationship to the first item remained the same. Note that if you save the project with footage tagged as "missing," then reopen it later, After Effects may lose the ability to automatically go searching for missing items. In that case, use the File>Replace Source feature to relink sources manually.

Import Specifics

Now that we've covered the basic issues of bringing sources into After Effects, let's focus on more specific issues with each media type:

Movie Issues

A movie is actually a series of still images known as frames. The most common format for movies is QuickTime files. QuickTime is just a container for media; After Effects can import and use any format of movies, stills, and audio that can be contained inside a QuickTime file.

Uncompressed image data takes up a lot of disk space. Therefore, most QuickTime movie files have been data compressed in some way. Even so-called "lossless" files have some specific data format or packing. The compression or packing method is usually referred to as a movie's codec (which stands for compressor/decompressor). QuickTime supports several different codecs natively; many video cards and nonlinear editing systems also employ their own proprietary codecs, even though their data is stored inside a QuickTime file container. To use a movie that has a non-native codec, you need to add the codec to the operating

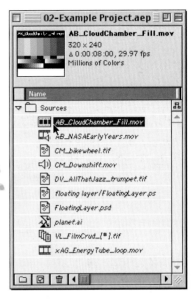

If After Effects is unable to link to footage when you open a project, the "missing" items will appear as color bars, and their names will be in italics. Double-click the first item and relink to it on your drive. If you're lucky – and the other items are in the same relative positions to the first item as when the project was last saved – all other footage will be relinked automatically.

After Effects Viewer

Option+double-click a movie to open it in the After Effects' viewer, which displays the footage after the settings in the Interpret Footage dialog have been taken into account.

The Interpret Footage dialog: Conform any 30 fps animation or stock footage to 29.97 fps if working with NTSC video. Also, interlaced footage should be separated Upper Field First or Lower Field First, as dictated by the video card that captured it.

system (see the sidebar *In Search of the Lost Codec*). Alternatively, you can ask that the movies be translated and supplied to you using a codec you have or one that is native to QuickTime.

There are several other parameters that can be associated with movie files. A series of settings accessed through the File>Interpet Footage> Main dialog sits between these sources and any composition that uses them. These settings govern how movies are treated. Many of these parameters are a bit on the techie side; since we assume you want to get busy creating rather than tweaking, we've deferred a detailed discussion of them until Chapter 36 and later. However, here is an overview of some of the parameters, just so you know that they exist and why they're important:

• **Conform to Frame Rate:** Movies have frame rates – the speed at which the individual stills that make them up are displayed – associated with them. Most of the time, they will be tagged with the correct rate. However, sometimes they are tagged wrong. For instance, when outputting to NTSC video at 29.97 fps, it's important that sources are also tagged at 29.97 fps, not 30. The Interpret Footage dialog lets you conform the frame rate of 30 fps sources to 29.97 fps.

• **Separate Fields:** Through a process called interlacing, most video actually packs two fields of images from different points in time into single frames. After Effects has the capability to separate fields, effectively doubling their frame rate in the process (see Chapter 37). As of version

Re-Interpret Footage

If you later find out that the alpha type or any other Interpret Footage parameters were set incorrectly, you do not need to re-import the file. After Effects allows you to go back and change the alpha channel type as well as other parameters in the Interpret Footage dialog. This window contains several other settings, such as frame rate and field separation, that have a great impact on how After Effects treats your sources.

As of version 4.1, After Effects added a simple scripting feature called Interpretation Rules that allows you to choose specific parameter settings for certain files, such as alpha type for files of a specific format (for example, set alpha interpretation to "straight" for all ElectricImage files). Interpretation Rules and the Interpret Footage dialog are covered in more detail in Chapter 36. In these earlier chapters, we'll focus on more fundamental concepts.

To re-interpret the alpha channel type if After Effects' guess was wrong, select the footage item in the Project window, then select File>Interpret Footage>Main.

4.1, After Effects automatically separates fields on some movies, and you can set up scripts to perform other automatic footage interpretations using the Interpretation Rules.

• **Remove Pulldown:** When film is transferred to video, a process called *3:2 pulldown* is used to spread 24 film frames over "30" (actually, 29.97) video frames per second. Often, you'll want to get back to the original film frames for manipulation in After Effects. This Remove 3:2 Pulldown process is again regulated by the Interpret Footage dialog; we cover it in detail in Chapter 38.

• **Pixel Aspect Ratio:** Not all video and film is ultimately projected the same way your computer monitor displays images. Quite often, the individual pixels are actually displayed wider or taller than the perfect squares a computer usually tries to mimic. Combining images with different pixel aspect ratio definitions can get confusing; again, After Effects can interpret the most common ratios and internally manage their differences to make compositing easier. Chapters 39 through 41 deal with working in D1 NTSC, D1 PAL, and Widescreen aspect ratios respectively.

• **Looping:** There is one Interpret Footage item we'll discuss here. Many stock footage backgrounds or 3D renders used in our examples have been created so that they can loop seamlessly, allowing a short clip to be repeated for as long as you need it. When you import a movie into After Effects, it defaults to playing the movie once, but you can set it to repeat up to 9,999 times in the File> Interpret Footage>Main dialog. If a source on our CD includes "_loop" in its file name, it is capable of looping seamlessly.

> *TO DO:* Select File>Import Footage File... and navigate to the Mattes_ Maps_Spices folder. Select the xAG_EnergyTube_loop. mov and Import. This is a 256-grayscale movie, with a duration of 6 seconds. With the movie selected, go to File>Interpret Footage>Main (Command+F) and enter 5 in the Looping box. Click OK and the movie will now appear to be 30 seconds long.

Sequences Issues

An alternative to movies is importing a series of still image files as a continuous sequence. While you're using the File menu's Import dialog, if you select a valid still image, a checkbox will become active with the file type (PICT or TIFF, for example) and the word "Sequence" will appear. Check it, click Open, and After Effects will now try to match up the rest of the files in the same folder to see if it can build a sequence. If there are missing numbers in the sequence, After Effects will import what it finds, but it will give you a warning dialog with the number of missing files.

The conditions by which After Effects considers a collection of stills to potentially be a sequence changed from version 3.1 to version 4.0, and changed again in version 4.1, so both new and longtime After Effects users should go over these conditions.

Assume Frame Rate

Changing the frame rate of a source in Interpret Footage is a handy way to "time-stretch" footage without affecting any keyframes applied to it in a composition.

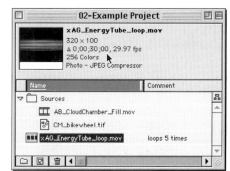

You can loop a movie or sequence in the Interpret Footage dialog. This 6-second movie is set to loop five times and now appears as 30 seconds long. It's best to loop movies that were designed to loop seamlessly or consist of random frames.

Random Sequences

Sequences can be a series of stills created at random for a nervous "grunge" effect, or a series of soft abstract backgrounds. Set the frame rate in Interpret Footage, and turn on Frame Blending (Chapter 11) to crossfade between them.

In Search of the Lost Codec

You open a movie in After Effects or QuickTime Player (previously known as MoviePlayer), and instead of the desired image, you get a white screen and an error message. You select it in After Effects' Project window, and all it says is "Compressor." This means you don't have its codec installed. Don't panic; you can often find out what the missing codec is. Inside After Effects, Option+click on a name in the Project window to display both the file type and codec codes.

If the codec code is too obscure, open the movie in Apple's QuickTime Player. Select Get Info under the Movie menu item, set the left popup to Video Track, and the right popup to Format. Next to Data Format, it will tell you the codec used, even if you don't have it installed.

```
┌─────────────────────────────────────────────┐
│ ▢ ▤▤ TOC title E-lowres-V100 Info ▤▤ ▤     │
├─────────────────────────────────────────────┤
│  ┌──────────────┐ ▲   ┌──────────────┐ ▲   │
│  │ Video Track ◆│ ▼   │ Format      ◆│ ▼   │
│  └──────────────┘      └──────────────┘     │
│                            ▶                  │
│        Width: 640                             │
│       Height: 480                             │
│       Colors: Millions                        │
│  Data Format: HDR Media 100® NTSC             │
│                                               │
└─────────────────────────────────────────────┘
```

To tell what codec a movie uses, open it in Apple's QuickTime Player, Get Info, and set the popups as shown here. Other useful information (such as copyright) can be viewed and set through these Info options.

On the Windows side, opening an AVI movie with a missing codec in the Windows Media Player will prompt it to automatically attempt to download the missing codec from a Microsoft repository. If it was unsuccessful, you will get a message telling you at the bottom of the Media Player window. File>Properties in the Media Player will also give you more information about the movie (more so than context-clicking on the movie itself and selecting Properties>Details).

Some video cards and nonlinear editing systems insist that you have their hardware installed to be able to render a movie to their codec. However, nearly all have a "software only" codec that will allow you to read their movies without hardware. Ask the person who gave you the mystery movie if he or she has a copy of the codec handy. If not, most hardware vendors have it buried somewhere on their Web sites, usually in the Support or Downloads section. Install the codec, reboot, and now you should be able to at least read the movie. If the software-only codec is read/write, it will also appear as a QuickTime codec option when you render.

Swiss Codecs

When there is concern over sending out or receiving a movie with a codec that either we or our clients do not have, a neutral codec supported natively by QuickTime is usually the best choice. For maximum quality, we like the Animation codec, set to Millions of Colors for RGB movies or Millions of Colors+ for those with alpha channels. We set the Quality slider to 100 for lossless output; the Animation codec uses lossless run-length encoding, akin to a PICT file. We also turn off any keyframing in the QuickTime dialog. Keyframing, which stores a whole reference frame at desired intervals and then just the data that changed between the intervals, may not update reliably in an editing application as you jump around in time. We've also seen quality issues with keyframing, so we have learned to avoid it.

If the resulting Animation movies are too large, we'll use the Photo JPEG codec, again with quality set in the range 95 to 99. It should be perceptually lossless. The downside is that you lose alpha channel capabilities and will have to output the Alpha channel as a separate movie (see Chapter 43).

(Thanks to Paul Whitelock for the Windows Media Player suggestions.)

All of the stills must be in the same folder, and it's best if they are the same size and format. In version 4.0, they must also all have the same name, followed by a number (with the same number of digits per file). On the Mac, you can use a period to separate the number from the name, but this can confuse file type tagging on Windows (where a period usually precedes the file type); an underscore is more common now.

In version 3.1, After Effects allowed any random collection of like-sized images to be a sequence – it simply imported them in alphabetical order. In version 4.1, After Effects again tries to make a sequence out of a collection of files in a folder, as long as the first file in the sequence does not have a number in it. Otherwise, the program will look for similarly named files to form a sequence – handy for those who have multiple numbered sequences in the same folder.

If you drag and drop a folder of images into the Project window and do not hold down the Option key while doing so, After Effects will attempt to make a sequence out of stills in that folder. If the sequence is not considered valid, you'll get an error message that it can't generate a sequence.

Occasionally, the MacOS will create an invisible "icon" file inside a folder that can prevent drag-and-drop importation of a sequence of files from that folder. The workaround on the Mac is to use the normal import procedure (File>Import); on Windows, move the files to a new folder and try again.

When you import a sequence of stills, After Effects automatically assigns it the frame rate set in the File>Preferences>Import dialog. We suggest you set this Preference to 29.97 fps for NTSC video sequences. You can change the preference before importing the sequence, or change the frame rate later in the source's File>Interpret Footage>Main dialog.

To Do: Practice importing a sequence and changing its frame rate. Select File>Import Footage File… and navigate to the Sequences folder. Open the VL_FilmCrud sequence folder, select the first file, and check the "TIFF sequence" checkbox at the bottom of the dialog. Click OK.
The sequence is a short (01:00) grungy animation.
Let's slow it down by changing its frame rate: select the source in the Project window, and select File>Interpret Footage>Main. Change the Assume This Frame Rate to 10 fps – each frame will now play for three frames in a 30 fps animation. Click OK. The sequence will appear as 03:00 in duration at 10 fps. You can also loop the sequence to extend the duration further.

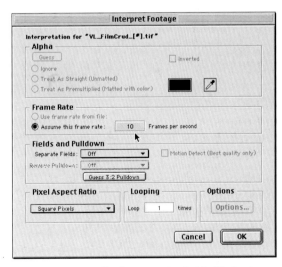

When you select a still image to import, you get an extra checkbox option to interpret it – and others like it, named and numbered sequentially, in the same folder – as a sequence. This example shows the Mac's Enhanced Open/Save dialog. Note that the file extension is optional on Mac, but it is recommended when creating sequences for PC.

The frame rate for the VL_FilmCrud sequence can be changed in the Interpret Footage dialog. At 10 fps, the sequence will be 03:00 in duration. It can also be looped to extend its length. Sequence courtesy VideoLoops CD.

.ps versus .psd

Many people use the extension .ps to indicate a Photoshop format file. However, After Effects may confuse this with a Postscript format file so use the .psd extension instead.

.PIC versus .PCT

Don't use the extension .PIC to indicate a PICT format file as After Effects 4.1 may confuse this with a Softimage format file. Use .PCT for PICT files instead. On a Mac, the extension can also be omitted.

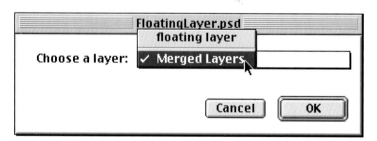

Import>Footage File for a Photoshop file with a floating layer(s) will prompt you to choose a single layer or merge the layers. Importing a single layer will create an image that's (auto) cropped to just fit the pixels on that layer. Merging layers will result in a file that's the same size as the Photoshop file, and the alpha channels for all layers will be merged.

Importing Stills from Photoshop

After Effects works internally at 32-bit resolution, assigning 8-bit red, green, blue, and alpha channels to every source. If the native color space of an image is less, such as grayscale, or uses an 8-bit color lookup table, After Effects will convert it to full RGB color when it displays it. If there is no alpha channel present, After Effects will automatically create a full white (opaque, or full-visibility) alpha channel for it.

To Do: Import a TIFF image saved from Photoshop. Navigate to the Sources>Stills folder, select DV_AllThatJazz_trumpet.tif, and import. This image is RGB only, no alpha channel. It was created on a background layer in Photoshop.

When you create an Adobe Photoshop file, you can either create it as a single image, or as a layered file. A single image would normally consist of one "background" layer. When a file *appears* to be a single image in Photoshop, it could in fact be a background layer (flattened) or a "floating" layer. If you create type in Photoshop, it's likely to be on a floating layer with transparency.

Flattened layers can be saved in a variety of file formats. Floating layers must be saved using the Photoshop file format – all other options are grayed out. If a file is saved with floating layers, After Effects can import one of the component Photoshop layers at a time, or merge (flatten) all the layers down to a single still image on import.

To Do: Import a Photoshop file with a floating text layer. Navigate to the Sources>Text folder, select the image FloatingLayer.psd and import. You'll be prompted to Choose a layer – select Floating Layer and click OK. Double-click the image in the Footage window. Notice the file size is 200×125, the same size as the layer, so the layer boundary is right up against the type. Next, import the same file again, but this time, at the Choose a layer prompt, select Merged Layers. Double-click to display the image. This time the type sits inside a 320×240 image, the same size the file was created in Photoshop.

When a Photoshop file has layers that you wish to retain as individual layers in After Effects, save it as a Photoshop format file. To use this layer information in After Effects, use the File>Import>Photoshop as Comp option. This will import all the layers as separate sources, and After Effects will automatically create a comp that rebuilds the layer stack. If you imported the layers one by one, each layer would come in (auto) cropped to just fit the pixels on each individual layer. Chapter 29 covers issues that arise when working with layered Photoshop files.

Illustrator Issues

After Effects will automatically rasterize vector-based Illustrator files into bitmaps as needed, with very clean edges. Areas that would be considered the "paper" in Illustrator will be converted to an alpha channel in After Effects.

To Do: Import an Illustrator file. From the Sources>Text folder, select the Planet.ai file, and import. Double-click the image to open it in the Footage window. The image is not visible, as the type was created as black type, and the Footage window's background is also black. Click on the white (alpha channel) swatch at the bottom of the window. This displays the alpha channel only, and the type will be visible. Click again to turn off the swatch when you're done.

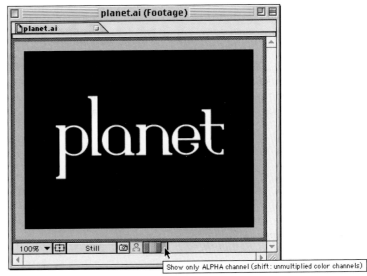

When you open an Illustrator file that consists of black text, it's a bit hard to see against the black background in the Footage window. Click on the alpha channel swatch to view the outlines of the text. Anywhere that's "paper" in Illustrator is automatically transparent in After Effects.

Prior to version 4.0, After Effects imported an entire Illustrator file as one vector art image. However, many artists create their Illustrator artwork in layers. You can now select an individual layer by name, and import just that. Even more useful, After Effects can now import layered Illustrator 7.0 or later files as a composition, with each Illustrator layer appearing as a separate layer. Use the File>Import>Illustrator as Comp command, rather than the normal Import command, if you wish to retain the layer data.

We cover working with Illustrator files in detail in Chapters 27 and 28. If you choose to do color gradients in Illustrator, and notice that color blends look bad, refer to the Interpret Footage options in Chapter 36 for fixing this problem.

Premiere and Media 100 Issues

After Effects v4.0 and later has the ability to import a project from video editing applications. The ability to import Adobe Premiere 5.0 or later projects is built in (File>Import>Premiere as Comp); Media 100 v6.0 has an extension to take advantage of this feature, too.

Before you get all excited, the features of this import routine are rather limited – you won't get any of your transitions, filter applications, or essentially anything beyond your video edits. Plain solids are inserted into the After Effects composition that is created as placeholders where the transitions take place, as well as where titles and color mattes were.

"Hot Key" to Edit Source

The Edit>Edit Original feature allows you to hot-key from After Effects to Photoshop, Illustrator and other applications to edit a file. More on this in Chapter 8.

However, keep in mind that After Effects is not a very good video editor. For example, it has to render its timeline (a composition) to disk or RAM to play it in realtime, unlike many nonlinear editors (NLEs) that can play back directly from their timelines. Therefore, it is not a bad idea to do offline cuts-only edits for timing in a NLE application like Premiere or Media 100, then bring that into After Effects as a head start on building your project.

Save Different, Save Often

After Effects is very stable. This doesn't mean your hard drives or power are (you do back up every night and have uninterruptable power supplies, don't you?). Save your projects often, and Save As under a new version number every time you make a major change.

Audio Issues

After Effects also supports audio. In many cases, audio is embedded in a movie file along with the image, but QuickTime movies can contain just audio. In fact, After Effects supports any audio file format QuickTime supports as it essentially reads it by using QuickTime's own "import" routines to internally turn it into a movie. Later versions of QuickTime support more file types (for example, QuickTime 4.0 has better support for MP3), so this is one reason to keep up to date.

Unfortunately, After Effects does not give you many options to reinterpret how audio files are used – for example, you cannot conform the sample rate, unlike being able to conform a movie file's frame rate. Also, to hear audio in the Footage window, you must use the QuickTime player – the After Effects viewer does not preview audio.

To Do: From the Sources>Audio folder, import the audio-only movie, CM_Downshift.mov. Double-click the audio to play it using the QuickTime player. Next, from the Movies folder, import the AB_NASAEarlyYears.mov. This movie of President Kennedy includes both video and audio. To hear the audio, you must play it by using QuickTime's viewer.

3D Channels Issues

There are several 3D programs that have special file types, which can save information beyond simple color and alpha channel. After Effects refers to these as Footage with 3D Channels. One of the most common is .RLA, originated by Alias/Wavefront and extended by Discreet/Kinetix. The most basic .RLA file also carries *Z buffer* information, which is how far away each pixel was from the camera. More advanced channels include object or texture groups. All of these are embedded in the same file, so nothing different is required during import.

Play's ElectricImage has the ability to render a separate file that contains just Z buffer information. Normally you render using the extension .EI, then prepare a separate Z buffer render saved with the extension .EIZ. Make sure the two renders are in the same folder. When importing into After Effects, select just the .EI file, and it will automatically find and use the .EIZ file. We have included details for using ElectricImage Z buffer files in TechTip 02 on the CD-ROM.

3D Channels footage

3D_stairs.rla			
640 x 480			
Z-depth, Material Effects, Object ID, UV-coordinates, Normal Vector, Z coverage			

Name	Comment	Type	Size	Du
3D_stairs.rla	3D Gear	RLA	5.5M	
CM_metropolis.ei	CyberMotion	ElectricImage IMAGE	661K	

Some 3D renders have additional channels of information that After Effects can now use to perform more advanced compositing tricks. Stairs image rendered in 3D Studio MAX by 3D Gear.

Opening Old Projects

Most new versions of After Effects introduce a number of new features, which requires an updated Project format. You usually cannot open a project created in a newer version of After Effects (such as 4.1) in an older version (such as 4.0). When opening an old project in a new version, After Effects creates a new project, usually with appropriate version translations. Save this under a new name.

One known exception is converting version 3.x projects to newer versions. The fonts used by plug-ins such as Path Text, Basic Text, and Numbers might not get converted. Reset the font in the Options dialog of the plug-in. Note that with Numbers, sometimes your placement will shift as well.

In general, when a new version ships, consider "mothballing" the old version (freeze it at a certain point in time, and don't update any of the third-party plug-ins). When you archive a project, make a note of what version and fonts were used to create it. If you need to make changes in the future and the latest version exhibits problems, you can always open the old project with the mothballed version and everything should render exactly the same.

You can use a similar procedure for Softimage PIC files: name the normal render with the extension .PIC, the Z buffer renders with the extensions .ZPIC, keep them in the same folder, and import just the .PIC file – After Effects will automatically find the Z buffer file.

Importing Projects

Finally, you can import entire After Effects Projects into your current Project (File>Import>Project). The entire project, with all of its sources, comps, and settings, will appear in a folder in your current project. This works particularly well if you've set up a template for a specific effect as a standalone project: when you want to use that technique or template again, import the whole project.

Sometimes you will find yourself going back and importing prior versions of a project you are working on, just to remind yourself what you were doing previously. This might mean you end up with multiple references to the same sources inside your project – which is unnecessary, since After Effects can re-use a source limitless times. To clean up organizational messes like this, use the File>Consolidate All Footage command. It will search for identical sources, link all references to one copy of the source, and delete the duplicates. This command is undoable, but it's a good working habit to remember to save before doing anything this drastic, regardless.

To Do: Save the project you're working on. Now practice importing another project into your project: Select File>Import>Project... Navigate to the Chapter Example Projects folder on the CD, open it, and open the 02-Example Project folder. Select the 02-ExampleProject.aep (which is our finished version of the same project you've created in this chapter), and click Open. The project will appear in its own folder, named as per the Project file, with the folder structure intact.

Connect

Frame Blending is explained in Chapter 11.

Effects are covered in Part 5 (Chapters 19 through 25).

Working with Illustrator files is discussed in more detail in Chapters 27 and 28; Photoshop files in Chapter 29.

All things audio are discussed in Chapter 30.

The all-important Interpret Footage dialog, and the Interpretation Rules scripting option, are uncovered in Chapter 36.

Interlacing, 3:2 pulldown, non-square pixels, and other video issues are covered in Chapters 37 through 41.

Chapter 42 is dedicated to film issues, including handling the Cineon file format.

Rendering the RGB and Alpha channels separately is covered in Chapter 43.

Alpha channels and their types are explained in more detail in TechTip 01 on the CD.

③ Creating a Composition

Procedures and shortcuts for setting up a blank canvas.

This chapter will show you how to create a composition and navigate in both space and time. You'll add sources to the comp, then position, scale, and rotate them. These basic concepts, techniques, and shortcuts will prepare you for creating animation in the next chapter. If you're a more experienced user, you might still want to skim this chapter and see if there are any navigation shortcuts or tips you've been missing out on.

The New Composition

The previous chapter concentrated on importing footage into the Project window. Now we'll move on to creating a composition and adding sources to it. Open the accompanying **03-Example Project.aep** on the CD (in the Chapter Example Projects folder). We've already imported various footage items, but feel free to import your own sources.

The area where you do all of your work inside After Effects is called a *composition* (often called a "comp" for short). This is where you layer your source material, position and size them on your virtual canvas, and navigate through time. There are several ways to create a new composition: mousing through the menus to Composition>New Composition, using the Command+N shortcut, or clicking on the New Composition button at the bottom of the Project window.

Whichever method you choose, when you select New Composition, you'll be presented with a dialog to set up the basic working parameters of your blank canvas. Many people overlook the parameter at the very top: the Composition Name. After Effects defaults to naming new compositions Comp 1, Comp 2, Comp 3, etc.; if you don't rename them, your project will soon become a string of comps you can't tell apart. We strongly suggest you give each comp a more meaningful name as soon as you create it. As you gain experience, try to develop a working practice where you number the compositions based on their position in the multicomp hierarchies you will eventually build (we'll get to all that in later chapters).

The next step is to set the visible area of your composition. You can type in pixel dimensions manually or use a number of presets in the popup menu to the right of these parameters. The overall aspect ratio of the comp is calculated underneath; you can lock in the current

When you create a new composition (Command+N), After Effects presents you with this dialog to set up its basic parameters. Once you create the comp, you can change any of these settings by selecting Composition>Composition Settings (Command+K).

Example Project

Explore the 03-Example Project.aep file as you read this chapter; references to [Ex.##] refer to specific compositions within the project file.

aspect ratio if you choose. If you do so, typing in one dimension will automatically update the other accordingly.

We're going to make most of our comps in this book at 320×240 pixels, square pixel aspect ratio, so they'll respond fast and fit comfortably on-screen on virtually any computer. (Real video and film size comps will be larger and have different pixel aspect ratios; we'll be covering those in more detail in Chapters 39 through 42.) We'll also be using the NTSC video frame rate of 29.97, although other frame rates are popular, such as 25 for PAL video and 24 for film.

When you're working on real projects, it pays to decide what your final image size will be and to set up your comps based on this. It can be a pain to go back and change things after you have already arranged and animated your sources; simply re-scaling them to fit can lower the quality of your final image. You can still work fast even at larger image sizes by temporarily changing the resolution of your comp; we'll discuss that later in this chapter. In the meantime, remember that you don't create comps at 320×240 if your final output needs to be 640×480 or higher – the small size is only for our examples and tutorials.

If you must change the comp's size later, the Anchor selector in the Composition Settings window decides which area of the comp it will hold steady – it will expand or shrink the surrounding areas, keeping track of layer positions as it does so. When you're making a new composition, the Anchor selector will be grayed out. For the remainder of the settings, set the Pixel Aspect Ratio to Square, Frame Rate to 29.97 fps, Resolution to Full, and the Duration to 10:00. Click on OK (or hit Return) and the comp will be created. You can change all of the parameters you've set – including comp size and duration – later by selecting Composition>Composition Settings (Command+K).

You'll now see two windows: the Composition window (the *stage* or *canvas*) and the Time Layout window. The Comp window is where you see the image you're creating at the current point in time. The Time Layout window is your *sequencer*,

After Effects provides a number of preset composition Frame Sizes for some of the most common media formats. Using a preset automatically sets the Pixel Aspect Ratio popup to match the Frame Size, which reduces the chance that you'll forget to set it manually.

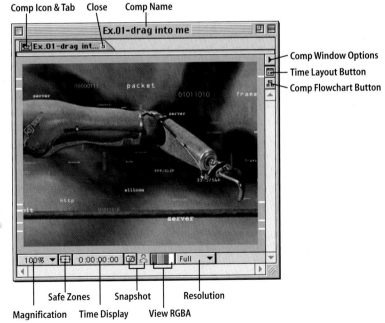

Comp Icon & Tab   Close   Comp Name

Comp Window Options
Time Layout Button
Comp Flowchart Button

Safe Zones   Snapshot   Resolution
Magnification   Time Display   View RGBA

The Comp window where you will be arranging and animating your source material. Artificial arm image courtesy Classic PIO/Medical; movie courtesy Artbeats/Microbes.

Time Display

Comp Tab

Comp Name

Time Marker

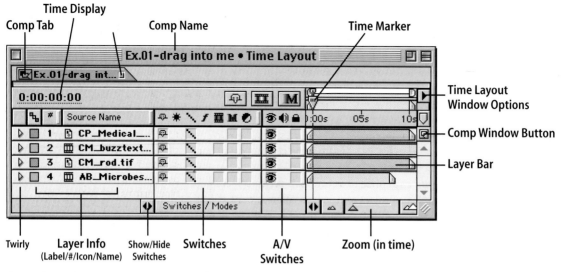

Time Layout Window Options

Comp Window Button

Layer Bar

Twirly

Layer Info
(Label/#/Icon/Name)

Show/Hide Switches

Switches

A/V Switches

Zoom (in time)

Companion to the Comp window is the Time Layout window, where you navigate and arrange your sources in time. The two are a pair that you usually want to keep open at the same time – if you accidentally close one, the buttons on the right side will open the partner window again. We will be referring to details of these two windows throughout this and later chapters.

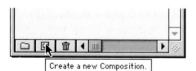

Footage = New Comp

Drag a footage file in the Project window onto the New Comp icon at the bottom of the window to create a new composition with the same size, duration, and frame rate as the source.

where you control the time at which the sources begin and end, and how they animate over time. The current time is displayed in both the Comp and Time Layout windows, and is also indicated by the blue time marker in the Time Layout window.

The Comp and Time Layout windows include a myriad of buttons and switches. We'll discuss the ones we need to master to get started below; we'll dive into the tweakier ones in later chapters, particularly Chapter 8. You can customize the look of the Time Layout window by resizing the settings column headers that have embossed vertical bars on their right edges, and by dragging the settings column headers around vertically – for example, we prefer the Keyframe Navigator to be at the right, just before the timeline. Context-clicking on the tops of these columns (Control+ click on the Mac, right-click on Windows) allows you to customize what panels you do or do not want to see. If you're just learning, leave them as they are for now; you might accidentally hide something you need.

Once a comp has been created, After Effects adds it to the list in the Project window. As we mentioned in Chapter 2, you can drag comps into folders for better organization. (You might want to create a new folder in the Project window – File>New>New Folder – to organize the practice comps you create while trying out the concepts in this chapter.) If you need to re-open a comp after it has been closed, double-click on it in the Project window, or select it and hit the Enter key on the numerical keypad.

Adding Layers

Once you've made a new composition, practice dragging some sources into your composition. (Tip: For now, leave the current time at 00:00 so that when you add layers, they will start at the beginning of the comp.) There are several ways to add footage to a comp. One is to drag it straight from the Project window to the Comp window, placing it roughly where you want it on the composition's stage; it will also try to "snap" to the corners or center. Another is to drag it from the Project window either to the open Time Layout window or onto the composition's icon in the Project window; this will add and center it in the composition. Selecting a source in the Project window and hitting Command+/ (slash) will also add and center it in the current comp.

Once you add a source to a composition, it becomes known as a *layer*. The "eyeball" switch determines the overall visibility of the layer. You can use sources in as many comps as you want, and as many times as you want in the same comp. Comps can have an unlimited number of layers.

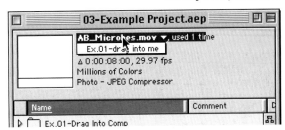

You can add multiple sources at once to a composition. To select multiple sources, Shift+click in the Project window to select a contiguous list of sources, drag a marquee around them, or Command+click to select sources that are not continuous with each other in the list. Then drag or use Command+/ as before. Layers are added in alphabetical order, top to bottom, not in the order selected.

Layers stack with the top-most item in the Time Layout window being the forward-most layer in the Comp window. You can re-order this stacking by simply dragging layers up or down the list in the Time Layout window. You can also move them using the keyboard shortcuts:

Move up (forward)	**Command+] (right bracket)**
Move down (backward)	**Command+[(left bracket)**
Bring to front	**Command+Shift+] (right bracket)**
Send to back	**Command+Shift+[(left bracket)**

Layers default to mapping one pixel of source to one pixel in the comp, giving a scaling of 100% of the source size. Note that if a source is much larger than the composition, you may need to open the Comp window to see the pasteboard, and/or reduce the magnification (zoom level) of the comp to see the entire range of the image.

Or you can scale your layers. Which brings us to discussing the various properties a layer may have in a composition.

The Transform Interactive Tour

The whole point of After Effects is to be able to animate the layers that make up a composition. Make a new composition (see above) and add one source to it. Open the Comp window a bit more in size, so you have some extra pasteboard around your display stage to work with.

To view the main properties that After Effects can animate, twirl down the arrow to the left of the layer name in the Time Layout window. This reveals the main property categories: **Masks**, **Effects**, **Transform** (and if the source layer has it, **Audio**).

We'll just concentrate on the Transform properties for now. Twirl down the arrow to the left of the word Transform, and you'll see a list

After you have dragged a layer into a comp, select the layer in the Project window. To the right of its name is a popup arrow, and a note of how many times that footage has been used. Click on the name of the footage to see a list of these comps. Release the mouse while selecting a comp, and that comp will open or come forward.

No DPI or PPI

Any dots per inch, pixels per inch, or similar scaling of a source image has no relevance in After Effects, because there are no inches in video – just pixels. The same full-screen image can be displayed on anything from a 13-inch monitor to a 25-foot projection screen. We will be concerned only with the number of pixels – not their dpi or ppi – in our source layers and comps.

A high resolution image (one with lots of pixels, regardless of the ppi setting) may appear many times larger than the size of the comp, with most of the image on the pasteboard. This allows you to pan around a large image without having to scale the layer past 100% – this *motion control* technique is covered in Chapter 6.

Time Layout window (partial):

```
                    My second comp • Time Layout
 My second comp
 0:00:00:00
    # Source Name
 ▽ □ 1  CM_spherecream1.tif
    ▷ Masks
    ▷ Effects
    ▽ Transform
        Anchor Point        100.0, 100.0
        Position            168.0, 115.0
        Scale               100%
        Rotation            0.0°
        Opacity             100%
                    Switches / Modes
```

Twirl down the arrow to the left of the layer name to reveal the main layer properties: Mask, Effects, and Transform. Transform is shown twirled down, revealing the animation properties: Anchor Point, Position, Scale, Rotation, and Opacity. Notice that when you reposition the layer, the Position I-beam will be highlighted.

Realtime Drag

Hold down the Option key as you position, scale and rotate in the Comp window for an interactive update instead of just the bounding box.

Tools

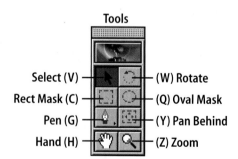

Select (V) —— —— (W) Rotate
Rect Mask (C) —— —— (Q) Oval Mask
Pen (G) —— —— (Y) Pan Behind
Hand (H) —— —— (Z) Zoom

The arrow tool (V to select) is the one you will use most often. It can be used to position and scale layers. Note that the Pan Behind (aka Anchor Point) tool may look like a "mover" tool in other programs – don't be fooled (more in Chapter 6). The Rectangle and Oval tools create Masks (more in Chapter 13) and are normally grayed out.

of these, which include the main animation properties: Position, Scale, and Rotation.

Let's practice manipulating the Transform properties interactively by pulling handles and using the arrow and rotation tools. The following chapters will cover animating these properties and using more keyboard shortcuts. If you're a beginner, start with just one layer in a comp so it's easy to see exactly what's going on. If the Tool palette isn't open, select Window> Show Tools (or use the shortcut, Command+1).

- **Anchor Point:** The Anchor Point is the point around which After Effects scales and rotates a layer. It defaults to the middle of a layer, as indicated by the "X" symbol. You can change and even animate the Anchor Point over time; we'll cover that in Chapter 6. Let's leave it alone for now.
- **Position:** Make sure the Selection (arrow) tool is selected in the Tool palette. Now click anywhere on the layer in the Comp window and hold the mouse down to move it around. A bounding box will appear and follow your dragging; the image will redraw when you mouse up. Don't drag by the handles at the corners; this scales the image rather than moving it. Notice that dragging anywhere else on the layer will work – don't waste time zeroing in on the anchor point icon in the center. Hold down the Option key while you drag to get a realtime update of what the layer looks like in its new position. Add the Shift key after you start dragging (or Option+dragging) to constrain the motion to the vertical or horizontal axis.

As you change Position, notice the values updating in the Time Layout window for the X (left-right) and Y (up-down) axes, as well as the bottom of the Info window (Window>Show Info, or Command+2) if you have it open. After Effects considers the upper-left corner of a comp to be position 0,0 with X being the horizontal axis and Y being the vertical axis.

These coordinates are based on how far the anchor point (mentioned above, defaulting to a layer's center) is moved away from the upper left. Notice that you can drag layers completely onto the pasteboard – this is handy for animating a layer that starts off-screen.

- **Scale:** With the selection tool again, this time grab one of the corner handles of your layer – as you drag the mouse, you'll scale the layer in the X and Y axes. Drag a handle on the side of the layer to scale on the X axis only, or the top or bottom to scale along the Y axis only. Notice that this time the Scale property is changing in the Time Layout window, as well as being updated in the Info palette while you drag. The bounding box isn't very informative, so again, press the Option key to get a realtime update as you drag. Add the Shift key *after* you start dragging (or Option+dragging) to maintain the aspect ratio of the layer as you scale. If you make a mess, double-click the Selection tool to reset Scale to 100%.

As you drag a layer, the Info Palette gives realtime feedback, displaying the new coordinates and how many pixels the layer has moved from its previous position. In this case, the layer has been moved 55 pixels to the left, to a new Position of X 105, Y 120. (Note that the X and Y in the upper right indicate the position of the mouse when you started dragging the layer, and are not relevant when setting Position.)

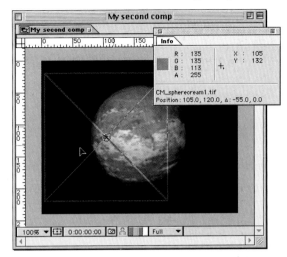

- **Rotation:** Select the Rotation tool (W) from the toolbox and drag one of the corner handles to rotate the layer. The Rotation value changes in the Time Layout window and updates in the Info window while dragging. Again, press the Option key to get a real-time update as you rotate the layer, and add the Shift key *after* you start dragging (or Option+dragging) to constrain the rotation to 45° increments. If you make a mess, double-click the Rotation tool to reset Rotation to 0°. Return to the Selection tool (V) when you're done.

- **Opacity:** Opacity sets the transparency or visibility of a layer. After Effects uses the term *opacity*, rather than *transparency*, so 0% Opacity is 100% transparent. This time click on the Opacity value in the Time Layout window. A dialog box appears; here you can enter a precise value. Enter 50% and hit OK. The image will appear darker, as it is composited against the black background, which is now showing through some. Add a second layer to the comp and drag it to the bottom of the stack. This should confirm that the layer is semitransparent.

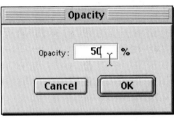

If you click on the value for Opacity in the Time Layout window, you can enter a precise value in the Opacity dialog. (The same applies to any value that appears "underlined" in After Effects.)

Although you have been changing the properties for a layer, you have not created an animation – you've just been changing its otherwise static transform properties. To animate, you need to do two things: set keyframes for parameters and have these parameters change over time. We'll get into keyframing these properties in the next few chapters. For now, let's continue with our tour of the Comp and Time Layout windows.

Keeping Tabs on Comps

If you open or create more than one composition (go ahead and create yet another new composition with a different name), you will notice that they go into the same Comp and Time Layout windows. Multiple tabs start to accumulate along the tops of these windows with the names of the comps in them. Clicking on the tabs brings that comp forward as a pair (if you bring Comp 1 forward, then the Time Layout window for Comp 1 will also come forward). Dragging a tab outside their windows creates a new window, which allows you to see two Comp windows side by side for comparison

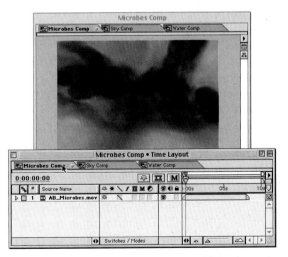

Selecting a tab in the Time Layout window will bring forward the partner Composition window, and vice versa. Footage courtesy Artbeats/Microbes.

Locking Windows

You can "lock" a tabbed window by double-clicking in the region just underneath the tab(s). Opening another comp will then create a second window. Double-click a second time unlocks the window.

and ease of editing. When you open or create a new composition, it opens into the forward-most Comp or Time Layout window. To open it in a window set of your choice, make sure you bring that window forward before opening the comp.

Closing a tab in one window (Command+W, or clicking on the tiny "close" box near the tab's right edge) closes the partner window as well. You can drag the tabs back and forth horizontally to sort them in the same window; when you have a lot of tabs, a scrolling bar will appear underneath the tabs. The name of the current composition is always in the window title along the top.

There are a few ways to modify this behavior, if you so choose. If you want to close, say, only the Time Layout window of a comp but keep its Comp window around for visual reference, Option+click on the close box in the tab of the window you wish to close. (De-selecting the Window>Closing in Groups option will also disable this feature, with Option+clicking now closing the windows as a pair.)

However, when you're editing, make sure that the two forward windows belong to the same composition, or you'll get very confused! If one window is missing its partner (or you accidentally close an entire window), click on the Open Time Layout button to the right of the Comp window, or the Open Comp Window button to the right of the Time Layout window, to open the partner window.

The introduction of tabbed windows was one of the biggest visual changes in version 4.0. However, you can set After Effects back to its pre-4.0 behavior (no tabs) by de-selecting Tabbed Windows in File> Preferences>General. (Note: Some figures in this book were created with tabs deselected to save space on the page – we don't normally work this way!)

Navigating in Space

It is important to know that you're not stuck viewing the Comp window at 100% – you can zoom in to get a detailed view, or zoom out to see more of the pasteboard area around your composition's visible stage.

There are many ways to zoom around the Comp window; we're going to focus on the ones we use the most. (The Quick Reference Card that comes with After Effects contains every shortcut, if you're curious.) The easiest keys to zoom with are the period and comma keys, which zoom in and out respectively. These keep the Comp window the same size and just zoom the visible area.

If you want to zoom in or out around a specific area, use the Zoom tool in the Tool palette. It can be selected by clicking on it, or by hitting Z on the keyboard. The cursor becomes a magnifying glass; click

Magnification can be set in the Comp window popup, with various shortcuts, or the Zoom tool. When a layer is larger than the comp size, zoom out to see the layer boundaries (indicated by the white outlines on the pasteboard). If you zoom in so far that the image area is larger than the window, you can use the Hand tool (H) to pan around.

in the Comp window to zoom in centered where you click. Hold down Option before clicking to toggle to the Zoom out tool. If you zoom in so that the canvas ends up larger than the window, use the Hand tool (H on the keyboard) to move the image inside the visible area of the window. Note that magnifying does not rescale any of the actual layers in the comp; it just changes the magnification of your view of them. Don't forget to revert to the Arrow tool (V) to return to normal operation when you're done zooming and panning.

If you're a Photoshop user, there are a couple of commands that you'll have to unlearn. The spacebar in Photoshop pans around an image (sort of a temporary Hand panning tool), but in After Effects, the spacebar starts playback. Also, the shortcut to switch to the zoom tool (Command+spacebar) doesn't work; use Z instead. On the plus side, there are a couple of Photoshop shortcuts that translate well:

Zoom in and resize window   Command += (equal, on main keyboard)

Zoom out and resize window   Command +– (hyphen, on main keyboard)

Partnering Up

Make sure the two windows you're viewing belong to the same comp. Select Windows> Closing in Groups to reduce the confusion of mismatched windows.

Resolution

Separate from a composition's magnification or zoom factor is its Resolution. This setting tells After Effects how many pixels to render when calculating images to show in the Comp window. The current setting is indicated by the right-most popup along the bottom of the Comp window; it can be set using this popup, from the menu via View> Resolution, in the Composition Settings dialog (Command+K), or by using the following shortcuts:

Full resolution   Command+J

Half resolution   Command+Shift+J

Quarter resolution   Command+Shift+Option+J

Full resolution means After Effects calculates every pixel in a composition. Half calculates only every other horizontal pixel, and every other line, resulting in only every fourth pixel being created – meaning calculations proceed up to four times as fast. If the zoom level is at 100%, the missing pixels are filled in with duplicates, resulting in a more pixelated look. That's why it's common to set the zoom level to 50% when the resolution is at Half, so that you're displaying 1:1 (one comp pixel per one screen pixel). The other resolutions follow the same scheme – for example, Quarter calculates every fourth pixel and every fourth line, resulting in calculations proceeding up to 16 times as fast.

Reducing the resolution is a great way to work more quickly with larger file sizes. It's common to set the resolution down to Half resolution (and

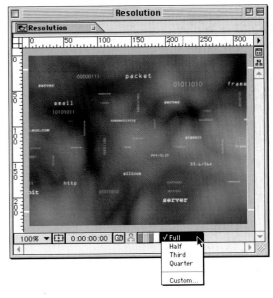

Resolution determines how many pixels should be processed. You can set it to Full, Half, Third or Quarter from the menu in the Comp window – or select Custom to set a different number of pixels and lines to be skipped.

50% Zoom) when working with full resolution video, and Quarter resolution (and 25% Zoom) when working at film resolution. Screen updates and previews occur much faster, and most effects properly scale to look more or less the same at reduced resolution (although you should go back to Full resolution occasionally as a confidence check). Resolution and magnification do not need to be set the same, but it usually makes the most sense to keep them in sync; you will also get the best RAM Preview performance if they match (more on this Chapter 4).

When you change Resolution, you can change Magnification automatically to match, with the "Auto-zoom when resolution changes" preference (File>Preferences>Display). It sounds great, but we find the auto-zoom preference to be somewhat irritating. Set to taste.

Quality

Different from both Resolution and Magnification is Quality. Whereas the first two are parameters that affect an entire composition, Quality is set on a layer-by-layer basis in the Time Layout window. In the Switches/ Modes panel (the one with all the icons along the top), Quality is the column with the backward-leaning slash.

If the icon for the layers below looks the same, they are set to the default Draft mode, where they will render using the faster "nearest neighbor" method. This means they will look pretty crunchy whenever you scale, rotate, or otherwise cause a change to the image that requires resampling pixels. However, setting layers to Draft Quality will speed up your workflow.

Clicking on the Quality icon for a layer toggles it between Draft and Best. In Best, the layer is calculated with the highest precision whenever any of its parameters that require resampling pixels are changed. Of course, this takes longer to process. It's therefore common to work in Draft quality whenever possible, and to render using Best.

A holdover from earlier versions of After Effects, when computers were much slower than they are now, is the Wireframe quality option. It reduces a layer to just its outline and an X going through the middle – really fast to draw, but not very informative visually. It you really need it, you can set a selected layer to this mode using the shortcut, or Layer> Quality>Wireframe.

To set multiple layers to Best or Draft quality, click on the first switch and drag down the layer stack. The keyboard shortcuts for Quality are:

Best Quality	Command+U
Draft Quality	Command+Shift+U
Wireframe Quality	Command+Shift+Option+U

Magnification, Resolution, and Quality may seem confusing if you're a beginning user, but you will come to appreciate the flexibility they give you to work more efficiently. The idea is to optimize your workflow by having After Effects think less while you're editing and previewing. When

Overworked, Underdisplayed

If your comp is set to 50% zoom but Full Resolution, After Effects is processing more pixels than the monitor can display. Work faster by changing the Resolution to Half.

Draft vs Best • Time

Click on the Quality switch to toggle between Draft (broken line) and Best (solid line). When you render a movie, the Render Settings can override these settings and force all layers to render in Best quality.

Undo

You can undo nearly any action in After Effects by hitting Command+Z. You can also redo your undo with Command+Shift+Z. If you're not sure what you're about to un- or redo, check under the Edit menu; it should give you a brief description next to the Undo and Redo menu items. The number of undos can be set in File>Preferences>General, with a limit of 99; more undos require more RAM, and the default of 20 is usually sufficient. By the way, changes to Composition Settings is one of the few things you can't undo.

The End, Really

If you drag the time marker to the "end" of a composition, the Comp stage appears gray. Instead, use the End key to jump to the last visible frame.

it comes time to render, the Render Settings will override these switches so you can easily render at Full Resolution/Best Quality for all layers without having to set switches manually.

Navigating in Time

When you're animating layers, the concept of the *current time* is very important, as most events happen at the frame currently being displayed in the Comp window. Learning how to navigate in time quickly and efficiently involves learning a few shortcuts.

Graphically, you can grab and move the blue time marker, which will change the current frame you are viewing in the Comp window as soon as you mouse up. However, you don't need to drag the time marker – simply click in the ruler in the Time Layout window to jump to a new time. Also, holding down the Option key while you drag the time marker will update the Comp window as fast as your computer can process (sort of like a jog/shuttle control). This is especially handy when one of your source layers is video, or the layers are otherwise animating over time.

Numerically, you can click on the current time display in either the Comp or Time Layout windows, which will bring up a dialog box to enter a new time. Command+G is a shortcut to open this dialog. (The time units used in these displays are set by a preference that we'll discuss at the end of this chapter.)

There is a Time Controls palette (Command+3), but we never use it for navigating in time, only for Previews. The following keyboard shortcuts replace those navigation controls nicely (an extended keyboard is recommended):

Max Comp Size

Comps were previously limited in size to 4000×4000 pixels; as of version 4.1, the limit has increased to 30,000×30,000. Just stock up on RAM first…

Go to beginning	**Home (or Command+Option+left arrow)**
Go to end	**End (or Command+Option+right arrow)**
Forward one frame	**Page Down (or Command+right arrow)**
Forward ten frames	**Shift+Page Down (or Command+Shift+right arrow)**
Backward one frame	**Page Up (or Command+left arrow)**
Backward ten frames	**Shift+Page Up (or Command+Shift+left arrow)**

Fit to Screen

To fit a Comp window to a second monitor, drag the Comp window to that monitor and hit Command+Shift+\. This sizes the Comp window to the current screen and hides all menus. Repeat the shortcut to undo.

After Effects' concept of time is such that each frame starts at the frame increments in the Time Layout window, and expires just before the next frame increment. If you use the End keyboard shortcut above to jump to the "end" of a composition, the time needle locates to a position just short of all the way right. The time indicator will also seem to be one frame short of the total duration of the comp – for example, 09:29 is the last frame in a 10:00 second long, 30 fps comp. It stops here because this is the beginning of the last visible frame; go any further, and you would be beyond the last frame.

This concept carries throughout the program, and will explain some other on-screen displays that might otherwise seem weird (such as locating to the Out Point of a layer also does not go to its right-most extreme). So when you drag the time marker all the way to the right, you get a solid gray image in the Comp window, indicating you are now at time 10:00, one frame past the end of the composition. This is useful when creating comps that seamlessly loop, but for now, use the End key to jump to the last visible frame.

Zooming in Time

You can zoom around in time, in addition to zooming in space. The Time Layout window allows you to decide what portion of time it is displaying. This will become a lot more important as we start animating in future chapters, when you need to zoom in to look at the detail of a set of rapid-fire keyframes, or zoom out and get an overview of how a project flows.

Centering Time

Zooming the Time Layout view does not center around the current time marker. To recenter the displayed area of time around the time marker, hit D on the keyboard after zooming.

The overview in the Time Layout window not only shows you where you are in a composition, but also allows you to change what portion of the comp you are looking at, and to move the time marker if it is otherwise out of view. Slide the center white area to move the zoom area in time.

There are a couple of graphical ways to zoom around this window. One is the set of "mountains" at the bottom of this Time Layout window. As you drag the triangle between them, the degree of zoom updates in realtime, attempting to center the visible portion of time around the current time represented by the blue Time Marker.

Another is to use the "overview" portion of the Time Layout window, above the layer bars and time ruler. The white area of this overview bar is what you can currently see; the dark gray areas are the regions of time before and after the visible area. Dragging on the half circles that default to the left and right edges sets the beginning and end times of the visible portion of this window; once they are dragged in from these ends, you can drag on the white portion to slide the visible area. Option+dragging this white area updates the layer stack and keyframes underneath in real-time – a handy way to zoom around in time.

Of course, there are keyboard shortcuts to zooming in time:

Zoom in time	=	(equal on main keyboard)
Zoom out time	–	(hyphen on main keyboard)
Zoom to/from frame view	;	(semicolon)

The Work Area

Beyond zooming in time to see a particular portion of the timeline in more detail, you can also define a "work area" time range in a comp. You'll see how this will come in handy when we discuss previewing and rendering. Previewing your work in a comp uses the currently set work area as the section to preview; you may also render just the defined work area of a composition.

The work area is defined by a gray bar in the Time Layout window that resides between the timeline and the overview. It has handles at its ends to adjust its length. It can now also be repositioned by grabbing the middle area and sliding it left and right, which maintains the same duration.

Move Layers to 00:00

When you add new sources to a composition, they start at the current time. If you intend for them to start at the beginning, select the layer(s) and hit Home (go to time 00:00). Then hit [(left square bracket) to set the In Point for any selected layers to the current time.

Ex.01–drag into me • Time Layout	
Ex.01–drag int...	
0:00:00:00	:00s 02s 04s 06s 08s 10s
# Source Name	
▷ ☐ 1 ▦ CM_buzztext...	
▷ ☐ 2 ▦ CM_rod.tif	
▷ ☐ 3 ▦ AB_Microbes...	
Switches / Modes	

Even more useful are the keyboard shortcuts to automatically move either the beginning or end points to the current time:

Set work area beginning to current time	B
Set work area end to current time	N
Set work area to length of selected layers	Command+Option+B
Go to beginning of work area	Shift+Home
Go to end of work area	Shift+End

The work area is indicated by a gray bar between the timeline and overview in the Time Layout window. Its ends can be dragged to resize it; you can also grab the center area (where the mouse cursor is positioned here) and slide it in time. The keyboard shortcuts B and N set its beginning and end to the current time, respectively.

When it comes to moving the work area triangles, note that After Effects will not allow you to drag one end point past the other; for example, if the current time is past the end of the work area, hitting B will bring the beginning up to one frame before the end, but no further. You'll have to either drag the work area itself, or (in this particular case) set the end (N) and then the beginning (B), which will at least move the work area end handles to the current time.

Retrieve Time Layout Window

Command+\ resizes the currently selected window between a tidy height and its current size. It also brings a window that's partially out of the screen back onto the screen.

Frame Rate = Time Grid

Frame rate is an important concept: It defines how often new image frames are read from a source, and how many times per second new frames are calculated during a render. The comp's frame rate does not alter the frame rate of any of your sources; it sets the time intervals at which sources are sampled and where animation keyframes can be placed. Each composition can have its own frame rate (Composition> Composition Settings). However, when you render the comp, the frame rate in Render Settings will override the comp's frame rate. (Later, when we explore building a hierarchy of nested comps, it's important to realize that the entire chain of comps will be "sampled" according to the frame rate set in Render Settings.)

For example, if your source material is 24 frames per second, setting the frame rate of a comp it is in to 29.97 fps does not speed it up, nor create new frames where there were none before. To see this, open the comp

Displaying Time

After Effects has three different ways of displaying time: the SMPTE (Society of Motion Picture and Television Engineers) format, the number of frames since the beginning, and the film measurement style of feet and frames. Normally, you set which one you want to be in use under File>Preferences>Time.

![Preferences dialog showing Time display settings with Display Style options: Timecode Base 30 fps, NTSC Non-Drop Frame, Frames, Feet + Frames 35mm, Start numbering frames at: 0]

The Time preferences allow you to select the display style, timebase, and frame offset of the counting method throughout the project.

Cool Tip: *You can also Command+click on the time displays in the Comp and Time Layout windows to rotate through these three styles.*

SMPTE timecode is represented as hours:minutes:seconds:frames. The number of frames in a second can be set to any number in a composition; for the sake of display, only the most common "timebases" (such as 30, for NTSC video) are available in the time display popup. It is generally a good idea to use the same timebase as you plan to set as the frame rate of your composition.

There is no timebase of 29.97, as fractional frames cannot be easily displayed inside the SMPTE timecode format – 30 is used instead. This brings up a pair of options for counting methods: "drop frame" and "non-drop."

The Drop Frame timecode attempts to resolve the difference between 29.97 and 30 by skipping certain frame numbers in the timeline. It is confusing, and almost never used for programs under a half hour in length. Unfortunately, After Effects defaults to this method. Unless you know precisely why you want drop frame counting (explained further in Chapter 39), set this preference to non-drop immediately.

The most common time format you will probably be using in After Effects is SMPTE timecode. All compositions start from time 00:00:00:00 with (unfortunately) no optional offset. In drop frame, the timecode numbers are separated by semicolons; when you switch to drop frame counting, you'll see

[**Ex.02**] in this chapter's example project. Step through the comp using the Page Up and Down keys. You will see some frames of the source repeated, because the time steps in your comp are smaller than the steps at which new frames appear in the source. Change the comp's frame rate to 24 fps (Command+K to open the Composition Settings): Now one frame in the comp equals one frame in the source.

It is usually a good idea to set the composition's frame rate to the same rate you intend to render at, so as you step through the timeline, you'll see the points in time that will be rendered. (An exception is when editing interlaced footage on a field-by-field basis, when you set the comp to double the frame rate. This is covered later, in Chapters 13 and 37.)

It is generally not a good idea to change a comp's frame rate after you have started adding layers, as the layer start and end points, as well as any animation keyframes you set, will remain at the points in time you set them at under the old frame rate. If you need to render at a different frame rate, change it in the Render Settings.

What Time You Got?

Changes made to settings in Preferences>Time are not applied per project. When you open a project that is designed to work with a certain counting method or timebase, make sure you check the Time preference is appropriate.

---

colons instead. After Effects allows you to type in a SMPTE number without the colons; it will fill them in automatically. You also don't need to type in any leading zeroes. As an example, typing a number such as 110 will take you to 0:00:01:10 in the composition.

If you type in any two-digit number that is greater than the number of frames in a second, the program will calculate how many seconds and frames it works out to – for example, typing in 70 with a timebase of 30 frames per second results in the time 2 seconds and 10 frames. Finally, you can type in a positive time offset, such as +15, and After Effects will add this time to the current time and advance 15 frames. To subtract (or back up) 15 frames, you must enter + –15 (typing simply –15 will jump to 15 frames before the beginning).

Most non-video animators, and many working with film, prefer the frames counting method. It simply refers to which frame you are on from the start of the composition. You can set a frame offset in the preferences, but unfortunately, not per comp. It is usually used to adjust between those who count "0" as the first frame and those who count "1" as first.

Many traditional film editors prefer a "feet+frames" counting method, which was initially used to literally measure the physical length of film involved for a shot. Neither options are directly related to film's

You can skip the colons and leading zeroes when you're typing in SMPTE time code numbers. For example, 110 equals 00:00:01:10.

typical frame rate of 24 per second: 35mm film has 16 frames per foot; 16mm film has 40 frames per foot. You get used to it. The first frame in each foot is counted as 0; the frame start number parameter also offsets this count.

Warning: *After Effects remembers the settings in Preferences>Time on an application level, not per project. You will need to reset them when you're opening a project that is designed to work with a different counting method or timebase. This is particularly important if you're switching between video and film projects on the same machine.*

The "safe area" borders shown overlaying the Composition window. Place all critical elements and type within the Title Safe area.

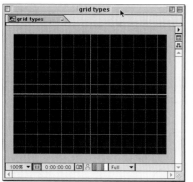

How the various Grids are displayed can be defined in File>Preferences> Grids & Guides (above). These are overlaid on the Comp window (left); the gray lines are the Proportional Grid, the green lines the regular Grid.

Visual Aids

There are a few more useful features and preference that we'll cover before moving onto animation, which affect the way compositions look and behave:

Rules, Grids, and Guides

After Effects has several ways of adding overlays to the Comp window that can come in handy when positioning layers: Safe Areas, Proportional Grids, User Grids, Rulers, and Guides.

Safe areas exist because a significant portion of a composition you are creating for video or film playback will not be visible once it is projected. Video images are "overscanned" in that they extend beyond the edges of the picture tube's bezel to conceal irregularities in aging or maladjusted sets. Even motion pictures have their edges cropped to neaten up projection. In normal video, the *action safe* area is considered to be inset 5% from the outer edges all the way around an image (10% in all); it's a good idea to assume the viewer won't see imagery in the action safe zone.

Older picture tubes in particular distort an image more around the edges. Therefore, we have a *title safe* area, which is inset an additional 5% from action safe (chopping off a total of 20% of the image in each dimension). It is considered unwise to put any text or other detailed critical information outside this title safe area, lest it be unreadable to the viewer.

There are a couple ways to toggle the safe areas overlay on and off: clicking on its button in the Comp window, or hitting the apostrophe key. This overlay can be toggled on and off on a comp-by-comp basis. (You can change the default settings for the safe areas in File>Preferences>Display in the Safe Margins area of the dialog.)

In addition to safe areas, After Effects has two options to overlay a grid of evenly spaced lines onto the Composition window. Grids are handy when you need help visualizing the comp in halves or thirds, or you need help delineating a specific number of pixels of spacing.

Newer versions of the program added the Grid common to other Adobe programs, in which the user can define the grid color, how it is drawn, pixel spacings between the bars of the grid, and displayed subdivisions of the grid. You can toggle them on and off on a project-wide basis, and invoke them with the menu command View>Show Grid. You can also turn on and off the ability for layers to have an affinity to snap to these grids (making regular pixel alignments easier) with View>Snap to Grid.

All of these grids and guides have convenient keyboard equivalents:

Toggle Safe Areas: ′ (apostrophe) (per comp)

Toggle Grids: Command+′ (apostrophe) (project-wide)

Toggle Snap to Grids: Command+Shift+′(apostrophe) (project-wide)

Toggle Proportional Grids: Option+′ (apostrophe) (per comp)

Finally, there are also rulers and user-definable guides, also accessible under the View menu, that will be familiar to users of other Adobe applications. The rulers reinforce the X and Y coordinates, in pixels, of a composition. If you have the rulers turned on (select View>Show Rulers), you may also create and view guides. To make a new guide, mouse down in the ruler margins, drag the mouse into the Comp window area, and release where you want the guide. The Info palette will tell you the precise position you are dragging the guides to. You can Lock Guides to protect them from being moved accidentally. Drag them back to the rulers to delete them.

Guides are handy aids for lining up multiple layers in the Comp window, either visually, or by turning on the Snap to Guides feature. Check out [**Ex.03**] where we've created some guides and simple Solids for you to experiment with; try out the different Lock and Snap options for the guides. You can view guides with the rulers turned off, but you can't create or delete guides without rulers. Again, rulers and guides also have keyboard shortcuts:

Toggle Rulers: Command+R

Toggle Guides: Command+; (semicolon)

Snap to Guides: Command+Shift+; (semicolon)

Lock Guides: Command+Shift+Option+; (semicolon)

Saving Comps

When you save a project (File>Save…), all comps are saved automatically. You don't need to save individual comps before closing their windows.

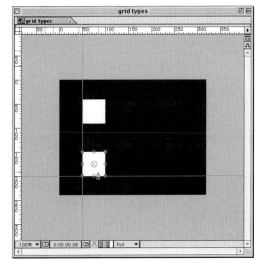

Rulers appear around the edges of the Comp window, even showing negative position coordinates. Guides have user-definable color and appearance; a handy feature is enabling Snap to Guides to help position objects.

The Channel Swatches

As we mentioned in Chapter 1, After Effects thinks in terms of Red, Green, Blue, and Alpha channels throughout. This includes inside a composition and the Comp window. Normally, you see all these channels at once, with the alpha already calculated into the equation. At the bottom of the Comp window is a series of four buttons where you can view these channels individually. The buttons latch on and off; Shift+clicking on them displays them in their color (i.e., degrees of red) rather than as grayscale values.

Black is Black – Not!

It's important to differentiate between a black Background Color setting, and black that resides in RGB colorspace. Open the **[Ex.05]** comp, where we have created a black "Solid" layer. It's not visible against the black background, but if you select the layer you'll see its bounding box. Now click on the Alpha Channel swatch (the white switch) at the bottom of the Comp window. The black solid exists as pixels in the RGB channels – the black background does not.

Change the background color to blue, and note that the color has no effect on the comp's alpha channel. If you render as an RGB-only movie, the background color will be used as the background for the movie, so set the color accordingly.

However, if you render an RGB+Alpha movie, the background will render as black regardless in the RGB channels; where the background color was visible will result in "transparency" in the Alpha. In later chapters, where you'll nest one comp inside another, you'll also notice that the background color becomes transparent when a comp is nested.

What if you really want a composition's background to consist of black pixels in RGB space? The answer is to create a black solid layer and send it to the bottom of your layer stack.

Creating a Solid

To create a solid-color layer, select Layer>New Solid (Command+Y). The Solid Settings dialog includes a handy button to automatically size it to fill the comp, or you can enter any values in pixels or as a percentage of Comp. Set the color using the eyedropper or by clicking on the swatch. As with comps, it is a good idea to name solids as you create them. Solids are really useful; we'll be using them more in later chapters.

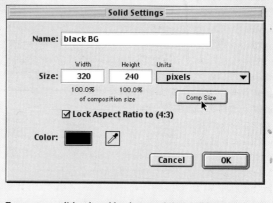

To create a solid-colored background that will be visible when you nest the comp or render with an alpha channel, select New Solid (Command+Y), click on the Comp Size button, and select your color.

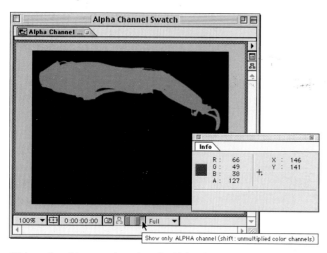

Click on the white swatch to view the Alpha Channel – don't forget to toggle it off again or everything will appear as grayscale.

Of greater use is the Alpha Channel button (the white one), where you can view the alpha channel in isolation. Shift+clicking on this one shows the color channels without the alpha matted on semi-transparent edges. This is a way to see the "bleed" or "overspray" of the color channels beyond the alpha's edge (this is covered in more detail in TechTip 01 on the CD).

With one layer visible in a comp, change its Opacity to 50%. The image might appear darker, but what's really changed is the value of its alpha channel. Click on the Alpha Channel button in the Comp window and notice that the alpha channel appears as 50% gray (if you drag your mouse cursor over it, the Info Palette will display a value of 127 or 128 out of a possible 0–255 range).

The Background Color

The background color is a temporary back plate to make viewing the contents of a comp easier [**Ex.04**]. You'll often need to change the background color from the default black particularly when masking dark layers or using black text. You can change this color on a comp-by-comp basis via Composition>Background Color (or *Command*+Shift+B). Once you change the color, new compositions you create will use this new color.

Some other programs, such as Photo-shop and many 3D programs, depict transparent areas as a checkerboard pattern. If you prefer this, you can set it by selecting the Checkerboard Background option in the Comp Window Options menu (not to be confused with the normal Composition Settings) in the upper-right corner of the Comp window. You can also toggle the checkerboard background on and off by Option+clicking in the rectangle area immediately to the right of the resolution menu at the bottom of the Comp window. Note that viewing the checkerboard pattern will slow down window redraw.

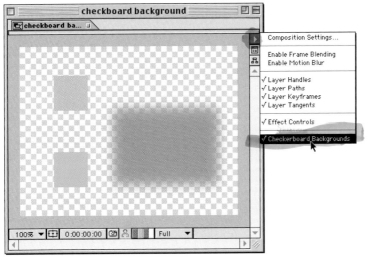

You can change the background color easily (Composition>Background Color) by eyedropping another color. Click on the color swatch to bring up the color wheel. Artificial arm image courtesy Classic PIO/Medical.

The Comp window's background color can be replaced with a checkerboard pattern in the Comp Window Options menu.

Cool Tip: You can also toggle the checkerboard on and off by Option+clicking in the rectangle area immediately to the right of the resolution popup at the bottom of the Comp window.

Connect

Animating the Transform parameters is covered in Chapters 4, 5 and 6.

More details of the Layer and Comp windows will be discussed as we delve further into layer options in Chapter 8.

Nesting comps is covered in Chapters 16.

Working at video and film resolutions and frame rates are demonstrated in Chapters 39 through 42; interlaced video footage is discussed in Chapter 37.

Alpha channels and their types are covered in more detail in TechTip 01 on the CD.

Additional video issues, such as Safe Areas, are discussed in TechTip 08 on the CD.

A Matter of Time and Space

Mastering the use of Position leads you on an essential journey through spatial and temporal keyframes, motion paths, and interpolation types.

Ex.0

Ex.01–stopwat...

0:00:00:00

	#	Source Name				
▽ ☐	1	🗋 Spaceman.TIF				
		▷ Masks				
		▷ Effects				
		▽ Transform				
		⊘ Anchor Point	150.0, 100.0			
		▷ ⊘ Position	0.0, 120.0			
		⊘ Scale	100%			
		⊘ Rotation	0.0°			
		⊘ Opacity	100%			
			◀▶ Switches / Mod			

The stopwatch is turned on for Position, which creates the first keyframe. Unless the stopwatch is on for a property, changing the value changes it throughout the animation.

Example Project

Explore the 04-Example Project.aep file as you read this chapter; references to [Ex.##] refer to specific compositions within the project file.

One of the most important components of motion graphics is controlling how an object moves over time, so this chapter explores Position keyframes in depth. The techniques covered, however, are not limited to this one property. Rules and tips for creating keyframes are generic to all parameters throughout the program. Creating a motion path using Position keyframes is similar to creating an Anchor or Effect Point path, as well as manipulating Mask shapes. And understanding how velocity curves are manipulated for Position keyframes will get you most of the way to understanding velocity curves for all other parameters. You could call this a "keystone" chapter.

Keyframes 101

The traditional animation industry devised *keyframes* as a way for master animators (the ones paid the big bucks) to draw the important movements of a character, while the lowly apprentice draws the frames between them. In our computer kingdom, we dictate the keyframes, and the computer calculates the points inbetween by *interpolating* values (computers are good with numbers, after all; plus it gives us more time to spend those big bucks).

After Effects uses a "stopwatch" icon alongside the name of a property in the Time Layout window to show whether or not that property is set to animate [**Ex.01**]. The stopwatch is off by default, which means that if you change the value of the property, that change takes place for all frames in the animation. This Constant setting (indicated by an "I-beam" in the property track) is useful when you don't need a property to animate, as you can make a global change at any point in time.

To turn on the stopwatch for a property, you simply click on it. This creates the first keyframe. Since this property is now set to animate, if you make any change to this property later in time, it will automatically create a new keyframe.

Some programs force you to explicitly "make keyframe" – not so with After Effects. What this means is that once you turn on the stopwatch, pay attention as you edit to avoid unplanned keyframes. For instance, if you select layers by clicking on them in the Comp window, try not to be heavy-handed – if you so much as move the layer by a pixel, you may create a new, unwanted Position keyframe. Selecting layers in the Time Layout window can be a safer bet if you're a novice.

An important concept is that editing happens at the current time. The position of the blue time marker indicates the active frame. If a property is set to animate (stopwatch is on), changing the value of this property at this point in time either (a) edits a keyframe if one exists on this frame, or (b) creates a new keyframe.

Some animation programs default to setting a keyframe for every property on the first frame. Resist the urge to re-create this working environment in After Effects by turning on the stopwatch for every property when you begin animating. If you do, you'll either be forced to return to the beginning of the layer to make a global change, or you'll introduce unwanted animation by accidentally adding keyframes later in time.

If this is your first day on the job, here are a few other simple rules to help you avoid a classic "doh" experience:

• Unless you turn on the stopwatch, the property will never animate.

• Turn on the stopwatch for the property you wish to animate (making the size smaller changes Scale, not Position).

• There is no animation unless you create at least two keyframes at different points in time.

• These two keyframes must have different values.

• Turning off the stopwatch deletes all the keyframes for that property. Turning back on the stopwatch won't bring them back. That's what Undo is for.

Finally, if you're feeling overwhelmed managing lots of keyframes and their associated interpolation and velocity curves, you might be making your life unnecessarily complex by creating too many keyframes. Take a

Smooth as Glass

After Effects resolves to 16 bits of subpixel resolution, so each pixel is divided into 65,536 parts width and height. With that kind of resolution, there are more than *4 billion* subpixels. Technically speaking, that's known as "a lot."

Replace Layer

Once you've animated a layer, you can replace its source with another footage item while maintaining all keyframes and other attributes. Simply select the layer, then select the new footage item from the project window, and Option+drag-and-drop to the Comp or Time Layout window. (More tips for managing layers are in Chapter 8.)

Ex.01-stopwatch on • Time Layout

Ex.01-stopwat...

0:00:02:00

	#	Source Name									:00s	02s	04s
	1	Spaceman.TIF											
		Position		160.0, 120.0		◀	▶		◇			◇	

Switches / Modes

With the Position stopwatch on, and the time parked between two keyframes, changing the value of Position (either by dragging the layer in Comp window or entering a numerical value) will automatically add a keyframe at the current time.

moment to study some TV or movie titles. You might be surprised to find that most titles consist of only one or two animated properties, and just two keyframes per property. A title moves left to right (two Position keyframes). A title grows larger (two Scale keyframes). A title fades in (two Opacity keyframes). We bet you won't find many titles buzzing around the frame doing figure eights (you know who you are)…

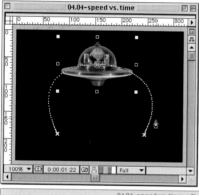

As you drag a layer in the composition, the Info palette updates the current position as well as its offset from the previous position.

The motion path in the Comp window determines the direction the layer travels, while the spacing of the keyframes and the velocity graph in the Time Layout window set the speed. The keyframe types used in both windows are independent of each other. Spaceman from the Classic PIO CD Nostalgic Memorabilia.

Getting into Position

The Position property determines a layer's value on the X (left-right, or horizontal) and Y (up-down, or vertical) axes in the comp, computed from the top-left-hand corner. To be precise, the value represents the position of the Layer's Anchor Point (the "X" which defaults to the center of the layer) in relationship to the composition. If the Info palette is open, as you move a layer in the composition, you'll see the Position value update in real time.

When a layer is set to Draft Quality, After Effects computes all Position values on whole pixels. When set to Best Quality, movement is calculated using subpixel positioning (covered later in this chapter), resulting in smoother animation.

When you animate Position you create a motion path in the Comp window. This path can be manipulated using Bezier handles, which create different "flavors" of keyframes. After Effects calls this *spatial* interpolation, or how the layer interpolates between keyframes in space. Only properties that have values which contain X and Y axes have a spatial component – namely, Position, Anchor Point, and Effect Point. (We'll look at these two other properties in later chapters.)

Once you've created a motion path, you control the speed of the object as it travels along this path using curves in the Time Layout window. This is referred to as *temporal* interpolation, or how the layer interpolates between keyframes over time.

Obviously, we're talking about two different concepts here – *space* and *time*. The keyframe flavor you chose for your motion path is independent of the keyframe types available for the velocity curve. We'll see later that space and time can even be disconnected from each other for the ultimate in independence.

Position Keyframes in Space

After Effects identifies its keyframe types by important-sounding names, such as Linear, Auto Bezier, Continuous Bezier, and Bezier. After all, without names, the manual writer would be forced to identify Bezier as the "keyframe with handles sticking out in different directions" (or KWHSOIDD for short). Don't get too hung up on the keyframe names – it's more important to know what the bezier handles are doing, and how to edit them so that you can quickly change the keyframe behavior without a lot of aimless fiddling. Creating motion paths is easy – making them do exactly what you want them to do takes a little practice.

In order to run through the different keyframes and show you how to manipulate them, we've set up a simple example file [**Ex.02*starter**] for you to open. If you're a beginner, you may want to re-create this composition so you know how we got there:

Step 1: Create a new composition at 320×240, 29.97 fps, with a duration of 5:00.

Step 2: Drag in an object to animate and place it in the bottom left-hand corner. Scale the layer quite small so that it doesn't get in the way.

Step 3: To animate Position, turn on its stopwatch. Rather than twirl all the properties down to find Position, with the layer selected, hit P to solo the Position property in the Time Layout window. Turn on the stopwatch to the left of the word Position to set the first keyframe at 00:00.

Step 4: Move in time to 01:00, and drag the layer to the top of the Comp window. The second keyframe is created automatically, along with a motion path made up of dots. Each dot indicates the position of the layer on each frame from 00:00 to 01:00.

Step 5: Move to 02:00 and drag the layer to the bottom right-hand corner to create the third keyframe. Notice that the motion path is now rounded at the second keyframe. (The Time Layout window has three diamond-shaped keyframe icons, which we won't worry about for now.)

Step 6: In the Comp window, select the keyframes individually by clicking on their X icon, and notice the associated handles that look not unlike the dots for the motion path itself. The first keyframe has just one handle, while the middle keyframe, when selected, shows a handle on each side. These are *Auto Bezier* keyframes, the default keyframe in the Comp window. Since the middle keyframe has both incoming and outgoing characteristics, we'll concentrate on its behavior for now. Resist the urge to touch these default handles, or you'll convert them to another keyframe type (undo if that's the case).

Step 7: Return to time 00:00 and play your animation by hitting the Spacebar. We'll explore other previewing options later in this chapter.

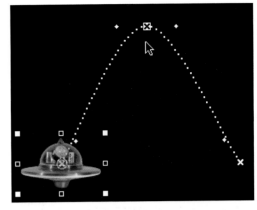

The Auto Bezier keyframe is the default spatial keyframe and displays as two dots each side of the keyframe icon. These dots form an imaginary line, the angle of which is determined by the position of the keyframes before and after.

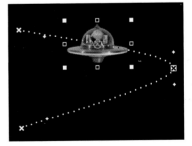

Trouble Getting a Handle?

If you're having trouble finding the default Auto Bezier handles amid the motion path dots, hold down the Command key and drag out handles from the keyframe. Some dots are just not worth looking for…

The Spatial Keyframes Grand Tour

Auto Bezier Keyframe

As the example above shows, the default keyframe type in space is Auto Bezier. The role of Auto Bezier is to create a smooth angle into and out of a keyframe, with no hard angles or sudden changes in direction. Select the middle keyframe and imagine a line connecting the two handles on each side of the keyframe. Now imagine another line connecting the first and third keyframes. Unless your imagination is playing tricks on you, these two lines should be parallel to each other.

To see what's automatic about Auto Bezier, move the three keyframes around in the Comp window by selecting their X icons and dragging them to new positions, again avoiding dragging the keyframe handles. Notice that no matter where you drag the keyframes, the two imaginary lines remain parallel.

The orientation of the Auto Bezier handles for the middle keyframe now appear vertically and parallel to the imaginary line created by the first and last keyframe.

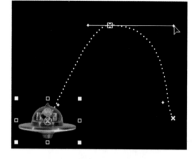

Dragging one of the Auto Bezier dots converts the keyframe to Continuous Bezier, which maintains a straight line through the keyframe.

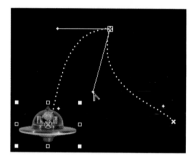

Dragging a Continuous Bezier handle with the Command key pressed breaks the direction handles and gives you independent control over the incoming and outgoing handles. This technique is a toggle.

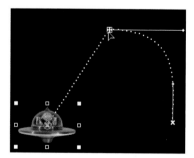

You can drag just one Bezier handle to a keyframe to retract it. The incoming handle is now Linear, while the outgoing handle remains Bezier.

Continuous Bezier Keyframe

More often than not, you'll end up manually editing the default Auto Bezier handles so that you can control the size and shape of the curve. You do this by selecting one of the default handles and dragging, which turns the imaginary line connecting the handles into real direction handles.

This keyframe type is called Continuous Bezier. You'll notice that as you edit a handle on one side, the opposite handle moves also (similar to a see-saw action). The two direction handles are lengthened or shortened independently of each other, but the handles maintain a continuous straight line through the keyframe.

Bezier Keyframe

For the ultimate control, you can break the incoming and outgoing handles and create a hard angle at the keyframe – this is the Bezier keyframe type, upon which all other interpolation methods are based.

If you use Bezier handles in other programs, you know there's always a secret key you need to hold down to break the handles; to make matters worse each program seems to be different. After Effects 4.1 uses the Command key. When you move the cursor over a handle with the Command key down, the regular arrow toggles temporarily to the "convert control point" tool (the upside-down V symbol). If you Command+click on one of the handles, you'll convert it to a Bezier keyframe. Now you can use the arrow tool to drag each handle independently of the other.

You'll soon realize though, that the most efficient way to convert to Bezier is to Command+click-and-drag in one fluid movement. It takes a little practice, as there's a tendency in the beginning to Command+click and then Command+click-and-drag. Remember that each time you Command+click on a handle, you toggle the keyframe type between Bezier and Continuous Bezier.

Once you've broken the handles, practice reverting back to Continuous Bezier by repeating the procedure. Command+click-and-drag on a handle, and watch how the opposing direction handle jumps to form a continuous line again. Note that if you just Command+click on a broken handle, nothing appears to change, and the handles will form a continuous line only when you move one of them later.

Linear Keyframe

Up to now we've dealt with curves and handles, but there are many occasions when you need absolute straight lines and hard angles in your motion path. You do this by "retracting" the handles into the center of the keyframe. You can retract just the incoming handle by dragging it to the keyframe and use the outgoing handle to create a curve – or vice versa. To retract both handles, simply Command+click right on the keyframe X icon. The handles will disappear, and the result is a Linear keyframe type with a corner point. To pop out the handles again, Command+click on the keyframe – the Auto Bezier handles reappear, and you're back where you started. Note that retracting handles and reverting back to Auto Bezier in this manner works across multiple keyframes – select more than one keyframe and Command+click on any one of them.

If you need to switch from a Linear keyframe directly to Continuous Bezier, you can also Command+click-and-drag out from the keyframe in one move. Examples of each spatial keyframe type is included in [**Ex.02-complete**].

The Five-Second Spatial Test

Now that you've been on the long tour of spatial keyframes and have arrived back where you started with Auto Bezier, try changing from one keyframe type to the next until you have the technique down without guesswork. Remember that you'll use these steps throughout the program when you're editing all motion paths and even mask shapes. So do not pass Go, do not collect $200, until you can do the following in five seconds or less:

A start with the default middle keyframe (Auto Bezier);
B drag handles to edit curve manually (Continuous Bezier);
C break handles for more control (Bezier);
D reconnect handles (revert to Continuous Bezier);
E retract handles (Linear);
F pop out handles (Auto Bezier).

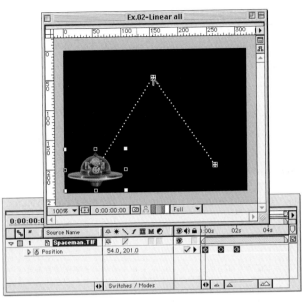

To convert all keyframes to Linear in one go, click on the word Position in the Time Layout window to select all Position keyframes. Then Command+click on one of the keyframe icons in the Comp window. To convert back to the Auto Bezier default, Command+click a second time.

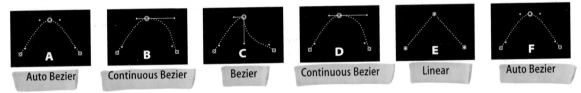

| Auto Bezier | Continuous Bezier | Bezier | Continuous Bezier | Linear | Auto Bezier |

Navigation Tips

Once you've created a few Position keyframes, you'll notice that the Keyframe Navigator area in the Time Layout window became active. The navigator consists of a left and right arrow and a checkbox in the center. When the checkbox is selected (checked), this indicates that the time marker is positioned exactly at a keyframe. When the checkbox is empty, it means that you're parked between keyframes.

In AE3.x, the navigator controls were placed in an area directly to the left of the Time Layout window's sequencer area, close to the keyframes. In 4.x, the navigator was moved to the far left and grouped with the A/V Features column (Visibility, Audio, and Lock), so navigating between keyframes involved more mousing around. The first thing we did after installing 4.x was to move the A/V Features column from the far left to the far right, beside the sequencer area. (We did this by selecting the

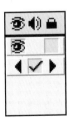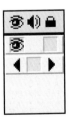

The state of the Keyframe Navigator indicates whether the time marker is positioned exactly on a keyframe left (checked) or between keyframes right (unchecked). The left and right arrows are a handy way to navigate among keyframes.

```
╔════════════════════════════════════════════════════════════════════════╗
║         keyframes one frame apart • Time Layout                          ║
╠════════════════════════════════════════════════════════════════════════╣
║  keyframes one... ▢                                                      ║
║  0:00:01:29              [⊡] [Ⅲ] [M]           20f   02:00f  10f   20f  ║
║  ▤ # │ Source Name │ ⊹ ✳ ↘ ƒ ⊞ M ● │ ◉ ◀) ⌂ │                          ║
║  ▽ ▢  1  🅑 CP_Spaceman.tif  ⊹   ╱           ◉                          ║
║     ▷ ⏱ Position    257.4, 190.1   ◀ ✓ ▶              ◇◇                 ║
║                          Switches / Modes                                ║
╚════════════════════════════════════════════════════════════════════════╝
```

A common beginner mistake is to navigate to keyframes by dragging the blue time marker. If you miss by a frame, and then edit the layer, you'll have two keyframes one frame apart – and a likely glitch in your animation. So get in the habit of navigating by clicking the arrows in the keyframe navigator area.

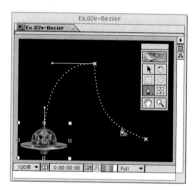

Add and edit keyframes along a motion path directly with the Pen tool – just click on a dot to add a keyframe.

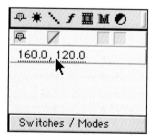

Anywhere you see a value that's underlined, clicking on it will open a dialog box.

column header and simply dragging it to the new position.) After Effects will remember this preference for all future compositions.

To edit a keyframe value, it's usually necessary to move the time marker to that point in time, and the navigator is a great way to do this. It might seem more natural to drag the blue time marker to a keyframe to make it the active frame. The problem with this method is that it's all too easy to drag the time marker to a frame close to the keyframe, but not *exactly* on top of it. When you move the layer, instead of editing the intended Position keyframe, you create a *new* keyframe just one frame to the left or right. This error will show up in your animation as a *glitch*, or motion artifact. The two keyframes tend to overlap when the Time Layout is zoomed out, so if this happens to you, zoom in until you can see the two keyframes clearly. Now delete the unwanted keyframe. You can avoid this problem entirely if you navigate to keyframes using the navigator arrows, not the time marker.

Using the Pen Tool

You might be inclined to reach for the pen tool when you're editing motion paths, but as you've seen, you can create any keyframe type with just the selection tool, adding the Command key when you need it. We find the pen tool gets used mostly when creating mask shapes (see Chapter 13). However, you can use the pen tool (shortcut: G) for editing the motion path if you find it more intuitive:

• To add a keyframe anywhere along the motion path, select the pen tool and move over the motion path. The pen changes to a pen+ icon, and clicking on a dot will create a Continuous Bezier keyframe on the frame represented by that dot.

• When you move over an existing keyframe, the pen changes to the convert control point tool, and clicking the keyframe will retract the handles.

• When the pen tool is active, hold down the Command key to temporarily change back to the arrow to move a keyframe.

Positioning by Numbers

Up to now we've created Position keyframes interactively by moving the layer around in the Comp window to set new keyframes or to edit existing ones. Throughout After Effects, however, you also have the choice to enter precise values for a keyframe by entering them into a dialog box.

To enter a precise value for Position, click on the current value in the Time Layout window (or use the shortcut Command+Shift+P). You can type a value on the X and Y axes in pixels, or select from a number of options in the Units popup. The most useful options are Pixels and % of Composition (we doubt if you'll use Centimeters and Inches too often).

Watch out for this gotcha: The numerical value shown in the Time Layout window is the value *at the current time.* A common mistake is to select a keyframe at another point in time, then click on this value to type a new number into the dialog box. This does not edit the keyframe you selected – it edits the value at the current time. If you want to edit a specific keyframe, double-click the keyframe icon to open the dialog box. Or simply navigate to the keyframe you want to edit so that it now lies at the current time.

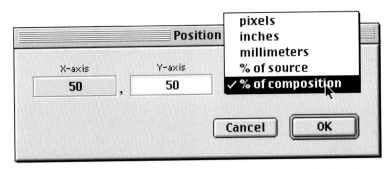

Click on the value of Position in the Time Layout window to open the Position dialog where you can enter values using various criteria. For instance, to center a layer in the comp, set the Units menu to % of Composition, and the X and Y values to 50%.

Gotcha! Selecting a keyframe, then clicking on the Position value does not edit that keyframe – it adds a new one at the current time. (In this case, double-click the keyframe to open the Position dialog box if the keyframe is not at the current time.)

Where Does Speed Come From?

The speed of a layer as it moves along its motion path is determined by the number of pixels it has to travel (the distance) and the amount of time it is allotted for that journey (the spacing of the keyframes in time). No amount of fiddling with velocity curves is going to make a slow-poke animation suddenly fast and exciting or calm down a frenzied animation.

In After Effects, you set the path of a journey from A to B in the Comp window, and you set the duration by spacing these two keyframes in the Time Layout window. The default Linear interpolation in time results in an average and constant speed for the trip, which ideally is close to the desired speed. If you slow down the takeoff (outgoing from keyframe A)

using a speed curve, After Effects will speed up the rest of the journey – otherwise you'd arrive late at keyframe B. Similarly, speeding up your takeoff will slow down the remainder of the trip – or you'd arrive too early. If you slow down both the takeoff and landing, you'll travel much faster than the average speed in the middle. So adjusting speed curves is always a balancing act.

Before you adjust the curves, preview the animation using Linear keyframes. If your animation is going too fast on average at this point, you may have to deal with the big picture by giving keyframes more time to play out. If the animation seems sluggish, bring the keyframes closer together in time so they have less time to play. Then start tweaking the curves for smooth takeoff and landings.

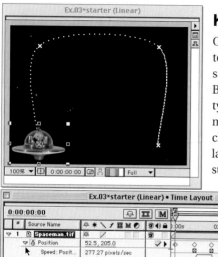

Keyframes in Time

Once you've mastered creating Position keyframes in space, it's time to control how they change over time in the Time Layout window. We saw how the default keyframe type in the Comp window was Auto Bezier, which produces an automatic curve. The default keyframe type in time is actually Linear (the familiar "diamond" icon), which maintains a constant speed between keyframes. This robotic rate of change can be useful at times, but to many an eye, linear motion lacks sophistication and hints at inexperience. The cure is to add subtle timing changes to your animation using speed curves. So grab a really hot cup of tea and wrap your head around velocity curves, once and for all.

For this exercise, move a small object around the comp from one corner to another using four keyframes, or use our example [**Ex.03*starter**]. Space the keyframes starting at 00:00 and ending at 04:00. Don't worry about perfecting the motion path, but do introduce variety in the speed by placing the keyframes at irregular intervals in time. The speed between each segment is represented by the spacing between the motion path dots – dots that are closer together indicate a slower speed than dots that are spaced further apart. Play the comp, and note the changes in speed between keyframes.

Our spaceman is animated moving around the comp; each segment results in a different speed. Twirl down the arrow to the left of the word Position to reveal the speed graph.

Twirling down the arrow to the left of the Position stopwatch reveals the time graph area. You should have a graph similar to our example with segments at different heights, indicating a variety of speeds. Before we move on, pat yourself on the back for not shrieking and twirling back up the graph (we all did that the first time, trust us).

Understanding the Graph

Before creating curves, it's useful to understand how the graph works. The speed of a layer is measured in pixels per second, and the middle number of the graph always shows the speed at the current point in time. Move the current time marker between your various keyframes and take a reading – lines that are higher indicate a faster speed than lines that are close to the bottom. Watch out for the graph display directly under the keyframes – the graph appears to ramp up and down, but this is misleading. If you zoom in in time, you'll see that the speed changes abruptly at the keyframe.

Although the speed graph appears to ramp up and down around the keyframes, this is a display anomaly. When you zoom in in time, the graph draws correctly. Step through the keyframes frame by frame (Page Up/Down shortcuts) and notice how the current speed value changes abruptly at each keyframe.

The top and bottom numbers indicate the range of the graph, and the middle number indicates the speed of the layer at this particular frame. The bottom number for Position is always 0, or completely stopped. Since you can't get much slower than stopped, the graph for Position doesn't allow for negative numbers. After the last keyframe, the line drops to 0 pixels per second, and the right side of this keyframe icon is grayed out to indicate that no interpolation is taking place.

The top number indicates the fastest speed achieved by your layer, which is taken from the fastest portion of the motion path. For instance, if the layer travels at some point at 400 pixels per second, the top number will read 400 and the curve will hit this peak at least once. All other portions of the motion path are drawn *relative to this peak*, so a speed of 200 pixels per second will appear halfway up the graph (200 relative to 400).

While this makes perfect sense, the ever changing dynamics of the graph can be confusing, since editing the fastest segment can make the other segments jump up and down. For instance, if you edit the motion path segment that was previously 400 pixels a second so that it now zips along at 600 pixels a second, the graph range will readjust to reflect the

Stopwatch Shortcut

Option+P is the shortcut to turn on the stopwatch for Position and set the first keyframe without having to twirl down the property. To check your Position keyframes, type P, or the über shortcut, U, which twirls down all properties that have been animated.

Ex.03*starter • Time Layout

0:00:00:12

#	Source Name			:00s	02s	04s
▽ ☐ 1	🗋 **Spaceman.TIF**		◉			
▽ ⓣ Position	39.7, 125.1	◀ ▶				
Speed: Position	584.05 pixels/sec					
	202.17 pixels/sec					
	0.00 pixels/sec					

Switches / Modes

---

new peak of 600. The line representing 200 pixels a second will then move down to the one-third mark (200 relative to 600). But remember that the speed of 200 pixels a second has not been changed – only its relationship with the graph's range.

To see this strange behavior in action, in [**Ex.03*starter*Graph**], place the time marker at 00:10, between keyframes (KF) #1 and #2, and read off the current speed value from the middle number. Now drag KF #3 to around time 03:20 so that it's much closer to #4 and so that segment becomes the tallest (moving the fastest). This will redefine the range of the graph. Notice that the line segment between KF #1 and 2 moves up and down the graph, yet the speed of the layer does not change. Only the speed on either side of the keyframe being moved (KF #3) is actually being changed.

Moving Keyframe #3 closer to #4 moves the fastest portion of the graph to this segment and reconfigures the graph's range. Although the first line segment moves up and down as the graph's range changed, don't be misled– the speed between Keyframe #1 and #2 has not changed.

Graph Height

Place your cursor on the bottom of the time layout graph and it will change to the "cell resizer" icon (left). Drag down to make the graph taller. You can also change the default height of all graphs under File>Preferences>Display.

Ex.03*starter • Time Layout

0:00:00:00

#	Source Name			:00s	01s	02s	03s	04s	0
▽ 1	🗋 **Spaceman.TIF**		◉						
▽ ⓣ Position	52.5, 205.0	✔ ▶							
Speed: Position	277.27 pixels/sec								
	202.17 pixels/sec								
	0.00 pixels/sec								

Switches / Modes

Motion Paths Meet Masks

Position motion paths can be pasted to a Mask shape, or vice versa, as well as copied and pasted to an Effects Point to animate the position of, say, a Lens Flare center. See Chapter 13 (Masking) and Chapter 19 (Animating Effects) for more info.

Cycling through Temporal Keyframes

Position keyframes in time have incoming and outgoing ease handles which are used to adjust the speed curve. After Effects also refers to these controls as *ease in* (incoming to a keyframe) and *ease out* (outgoing from a keyframe). Just as with motion paths, you use the arrow tool in conjunction with the Command key to cycle through all the keyframe options. These keyframe options are similar to those of the motion path: Linear, Auto Bezier, Continuous Bezier, and Bezier. There's also a Hold keyframe type which we'll look at later.

For now, ignore the tiny checkbox below the keyframe icon (see *Roving in Time* later in this chapter) – if you uncheck it by mistake, undo or select the checkbox again. And remember that you need to select a keyframe to see both handles. Let's start our tour with the same four Linear keyframes we manipulated earlier [**Ex.03*starter*Linear**]:

◇ Linear Keyframe

The default keyframe in time is Linear, the familiar diamond icon. Linear interpolation creates a constant speed between keyframes #1 and #2. When the KF #2 is reached, the speed instantly changes to the rate set by the segment between KF #2 and #3. When the last keyframe is reached, the layer stops suddenly, and the overall effect is quite mechanical. With Linear interpolation, the Bezier handles, although visible on either side of the keyframe, are aligned with the speed lines and are basically inactive.

Linear keyframes display handles that align perfectly with the line segment, so they have no effect. The handles are "broken," and the lines are at different heights, indicating that the incoming and outgoing speeds are different.

Since the incoming speed is different from the outgoing speed, the handles are "broken," which has a different meaning in a time graph. In the comp window, broken handles mean that a path enters and exits a spatial keyframe at different *angles* – broken handles in the time graph indicate different incoming and outgoing *speeds*.

◯ Auto Bezier Keyframe

When you preview your Linear animation, the speed change at each keyframe creates a little bump in the motion. Often, all you really want to do is smooth out this ugly bump. You can do this easily by changing the Linear keyframe to Auto Bezier by Command+clicking directly on the Linear keyframe (you don't even need to have the graph twirled down). The diamond will change to a circle, indicating Auto Bezier. Change the two middle keyframes to Auto Bezier and Preview the smoother motion. We think of Auto Bezier as an automatic gear change.

The Bezier handles in the time graph have now been converted to two handle dots, one on each side. The distance of the handle dots from the

Bezier Rules

All interpolation methods in After Effects are based on the Bezier interpolation type, with constraints placed on the handles to render them automatic, continuous, or retracted.

keyframe is called the influence amount, which is measured from 0% (at the keyframe) to 100% (at the midpoint between two keyframes). Each incoming and outgoing handle has a possible *influence* range of 0 to 100%, but Auto Bezier sets the influence automatically

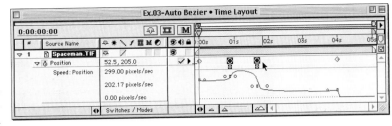

at 16.67%, or one-sixth the distance from the keyframe to the middle of the line segment. What this means is that the layer ramps from one speed to another over a set number of frames in and around a keyframe, based on a percentage of the time between keyframes.

Continuous Bezier Keyframe

Although Auto Bezier will smooth out the worst of the bump, you may want to adjust the influence handles manually to increase the amount of time taken to adjust from one speed to another as you roll through a keyframe. You do this by dragging the Auto Bezier handle dots, which add direction lines to the handles. The Info palette updates the velocity and influence values as you edit.

Since both handles maintain a continuous line between them, a keyframe's incoming speed is identical to its outgoing speed. Dragging the handles left to right adjusts the amount of influence – notice you can't drag past the halfway point (or 100% influence). Dragging the handles higher in the graph increases the speed through the keyframe, while dragging them lower decreases the speed. You can even drag the handles above the top of the graph – when you let go, the graph range will readjust itself to the new peak in speed. Dragging to the bottom of the graph will make the layer stop at the keyframe before taking off again.

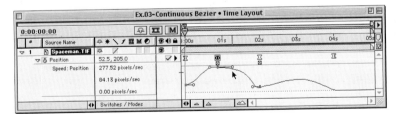

Experiment with various settings and don't forget to preview often so that you can see the effects – the shape of the graph should be a fairly good indication of how speed is changing. The motion path dots are a further clue to the speed of the layer (wider dots being faster – remember).

The single handle outgoing from the first keyframe can also be edited. You might want to ease out of the first keyframe starting at 0 pixels a second for a smooth takeoff. Drag the handle down to the bottom line and create a smooth ramp-up curve. The handle incoming to the last keyframe can also be edited in a similar fashion to create a smooth ramp-down to zero.

Command+click on Linear keyframes to convert them to Auto Bezier and smooth out speed bumps. The handles will appear as dots on both sides of a keyframe, and the incoming and outgoing speeds will match.

Made a Mess?

If you want to return to Linear keyframes, Command+click right on the keyframe icon until it cycles back to the familiar diamond icon. This also works with multiple keyframes selected.

Dragging the Auto Bezier handles converts the keyframe to Continuous Bezier. The direction lines allows you to change the length of the influence handles (drag left and right). The line is continuous, ensuring that the incoming and outgoing speed through the keyframe is consistent. You can adjust the speed at the keyframe by dragging the handles up and down.

Bezier Keyframe

Yes, the Bezier and Continuous Bezier icons look exactly the same, in case you were wondering. The Bezier interpolation allows for an incoming speed that's different from the outgoing speed, and you get there by breaking the Continuous Bezier handles. Hold down the Command key and drag one of the handles to break them. You can now drag the incoming handle to the bottom of the graph for a total ease in, and drag the outgoing handle up high to set a speedy outgoing motion or vice versa. Create a few different scenarios and preview your results. To return to Continuous Bezier, repeat the Command+drag routine and the handles will snap together again.

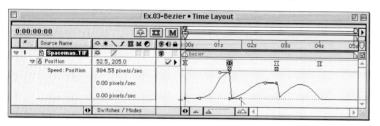

Break the Continuous Bezier handles by dragging a handle with the Command key pressed. The incoming and outgoing speeds will now be different. Repeat the Command+click-and-drag technique to toggle back to continuous direction lines.

Remember that all interpolation methods are based on Bezier, the most flexible of the bunch. By adding constraints to how the handles operate, you end up with Linear, Auto Bezier, and Continuous Bezier keyframes.

The Ten-Second Temporal Test

To return to the default Linear keyframes, click on the word Position to select all keyframes, and Command+click directly on one of the keyframes. All the keyframes will switch back to Linear, where you started. Deselect the keyframes (shortcut: F2).

To reinforce the steps learned, try changing one of the middle keyframes from one interpolation to the next without guesswork. You'll use these steps throughout the program when you're editing other velocity curves, so see if you can do the following in ten seconds or less:

Handles with Influence

The distance of the handles from the keyframe is called its influence. Think of this as the deceleration time when slowing down, or the acceleration time when speeding up. If in doubt, you can't go wrong with influence in the 20 to 40% range.

- start with default middle "diamond" keyframe (Linear);
- smooth out the speed bump with the "circle" keyframe (Auto Bezier);
- drag handles and edit curve manually (Continuous Bezier);
- break handles for more control (Bezier);
- snap handles to continuous again (revert to Continuous Bezier);
- return to Linear.

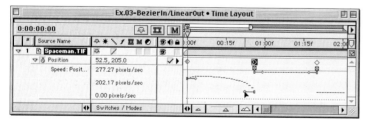

Starting with a Linear keyframe, drag the incoming handle to convert that side to Bezier. The outgoing side remains Linear.

Linear to Bezier Directly

For our final exercise, we'll start again with a Linear keyframe. Notice that if you manipulate just one of the handles of a Linear keyframe, that side of the keyframe converts to Bezier interpolation, while the other side remains Linear. If you also edit the handle on the other side, you'll have the equivalent of a Bezier keyframe. If you want to change from Linear to Bezier (with broken handles) directly, this is the way to go. The only advantage of converting from Linear to Bezier via Auto Bezier (the circle) is that (a) smoothing the bump may be all you need and you can do this without even twirling down the graph, and (b) the handles will be continuous if you then decide to edit the influence handles.

Things to Avoid with Graphs

There are no hard and fast rules for how curves should be manipulated, but there are a couple of problems that are easy to avoid. Re-create these problems in your project and preview the results, or check out the examples in the [**Ex.04**] folder:

• Influence handles are too long [**Ex.04a**]: If you drag opposing handles to their maximum 100% and drag them to the bottom, you'll create a spike in the graph. Spikes indicate that a layer is traveling very fast for just a frame or two, which is also indicated by a gap in the motion path dots.

• Layer slows to a crawl [**Ex.04b**]: Similarly, if the handles are so long that they meet higher up the graph, they'll create a large dip in the center of graph, where the layer is traveling at 0 pixels per second (it comes to a complete stop).

• Influence handles are too short [**Ex.04c**]: If a handle is very close to the keyframe, it basically has no effect. Just because you drag the handle down to the zero line doesn't add an ease in. If the influence amount is 0%, the layer has *no time* to slow down, so it will appear to stop suddenly. Drag the handle away from the keyframe and watch the curve emerge.

Velocity by Numbers

As in other areas of the program, you can edit the speed graph interactively by dragging handles, or you can enter precise values in a dialog box. Select a keyframe and open the Keyframe Velocity dialog from the Layer menu (Command+Shift+K). If the keyframe has continuous handles, the Continuous checkbox will be selected, and the incoming and outgoing speeds will be identical.

This dialog can also be accessed by *context*-clicking on a keyframe (Control+click on the Mac, right-click on Windows), or by Option+ double-clicking on the keyframe. Or if the graph is twirled down, you can double-click on the keyframe *nubbin* (the point between the ease handles). Incidentally, you may have assumed that you could use this keyframe nubbin to move the handles up and down, but for some reason it doesn't do anything for Speed or Velocity graphs, just Value graphs (such as those used for properties like Scale and Rotation).

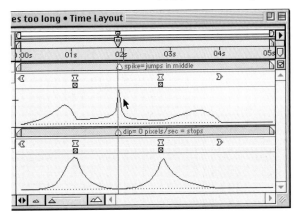

Example of a spike created by handles that are too long (top graph) – the layer travels very fast for just a frame or two. Another problem created by long handles is a dip in the center where the layer literally stops when it reaches 0 pixels a second.

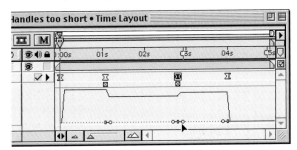

When influence handles are too short (0%), they have no time to work on accelerating or decelerating the layer. In this example, the Bezier handles are so short that the motion approximates linear keyframes.

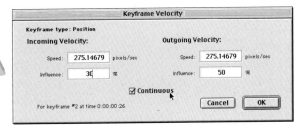

The Keyframe Velocity dialog offers statistics for incoming and outgoing speeds and influence amounts.

Roving Keyframes

Until you've become frustrated while trying to create a consistent speed across multiple keyframes, or a simple velocity curve for a complicated motion path, it's hard to appreciate Roving Keyframes. But when you need this feature, believe us, you need this feature.

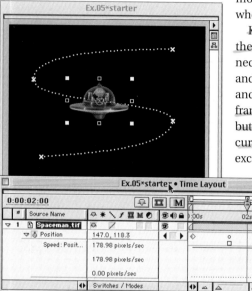

Keyframes that *rove in time* are basically disconnected from the timeline (the spatial component is active, but their connection to time is not). Only keyframes that have *both* spatial and temporal qualities can rove in time: Position, Anchor Point, and Effect Point. When you convert a keyframe to a roving keyframe, their existing X and Y positions in the comp are honored, but the time at which this event occurs is determined by the speed curve of the keyframes before and after. Multiple keyframes, except the first and last keyframes, can be set to rove in time.

To see roving in action, start with a motion path with at least four Position keyframes creating an S-curve, as we did in [**Ex.05*starter**]. Imagine how you would create a consistent speed for this animation by moving keyframes around… The real solution is to uncheck the tiny boxes underneath the two middle keyframes in the graph. The keyframe icons will change from Linear to small circles to indicate they are roving in time, and will likely jump to a new position in the time line. The graph will flatten to one flat line, indicating that one speed applies to the entire motion path. Drag the last keyframe later in time and notice how all the roving keyframes move accordion-style.

When the roving checkboxes are unchecked for the middle two keyframes, the speed graph becomes a flat line, indicating a consistent speed across the entire motion path.

With keyframes set to rove, it's easy to create a simple speed curve for multiple keyframes.

Now change the ease handles for the first and last keyframe and see how easy it is to create a simple speed curve over multiple keyframes [**Ex.05-complete**]. Roving keyframes are incredibly useful when you're creating a complicated motion path where you need a consistent or simple speed change for multiple keyframes.

Roving 'Round the Bend

In this example, we've created an S-curved motion path **[Ex.06*starter]** and set the middle two keyframes to rove in time. This should create a consistent speed along the path. But if you preview the comp, we think you'll agree that the object appears to go faster around the tighter bends. Without going into the reasons for this (we'll avoid hard-core math as much as possible), when an object changes direction, it creates an illusion that it also picks up speed. We need to counteract this behavior by reducing the speed around the bends:

Step 1: Select the two middle roving keyframes and check one of their checkboxes – the selected keyframes will switch back to Linear keyframes.

Step 2: With the keyframes still selected, Command+click on one of the keyframes. Both middle keyframes

will change to Auto Bezier and the ease handles will be continuous. Deselect (shortcut: F2).

Step 3: Select each of the middle keyframes separately, and pull down the ease handles so that the speed is slower at each of the bends. Preview until the motion *feels* consistent. You might be surprised to end up with a speed curve like ours.

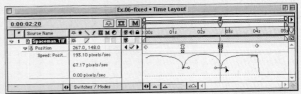

Because speed appears to pick up when objects change direction, you may have to reduce the speed at corners in order to appear to be maintaining a consistent speed.

Hold Interpolation

Before you head off where no animator's gone before, there's one more interpolation method that unfortunately gets overlooked by many users. It's possible that the Hold keyframe remains undiscovered because no matter how much you fiddle with keyframe handles, you never stumble across the Hold keyframe. (And stumbling across features is how most of us learn…) But if you don't know how to make keyframes "hold," you're creating extra work for yourself, and possibly encountering motion glitches with imperfect workarounds (see the sidebar, *Hold It Right There*).

The Hold interpolation's job is to *not* interpolate. When a Position keyframe is set to Hold, the layer maintains that Position value until it reaches the next keyframe, and the speed drops to 0 pixels per second. Hold keyframes are great for creating more rhythmic animations, and they can be used on any property or effect parameter, not just Position.

To create a Hold keyframe, select any keyframe and invoke Toggle Hold Keyframe (shortcut: Command+Option+H) from the Layer menu **[Ex.07*starter]**. A Hold keyframe takes over the entire segment of time until the next keyframe is reached, when the layer immediately jumps to the new position or value. The incoming ease handle for the next keyframe is inactive, and that keyframe is grayed out on the left side to indicate this. However, the next keyframe could use any keyframe type

With all four keyframes converted from Linear to Hold, our spaceman moves from corner to corner without interpolating between them.

Accordian Keyframes

New in 4.1: To expand or contract a group of keyframes in the Time Layout window, Option+ drag the first or last keyframe, and all selected keyframes will move accordion-style.

for its outgoing interpolation, since After Effects can freely mix and match interpolation methods.

You can also toggle a keyframe to Hold without going to the menu by Command+Option+clicking on it in the Time Layout window. Or you can use the context-sensitive menu: Context-click on the keyframe and select Toggle Hold Keyframe from the popup. Either method works with multiple keyframes selected.

Remember that this feature is a toggle – you can revert back by repeating the Toggle Hold Keyframe on a selected keyframe, or by Command+clicking on the keyframe icon until the icon reverts to a diamond, indicating Linear.

Continuing from Hold

If you need a property to hold on a value and continue from there, the Hold keyframe and the one following should both have the same value [**Ex.08**]. It might also be appropriate to apply an ease out of the second keyframe. Remember that if you change the value of the first Hold keyframe, you'll need to update the following keyframe also. Here are a couple of tips for achieving this:

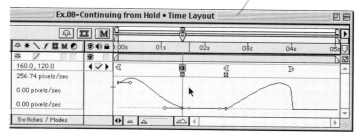

• Select both keyframes, and double-click one of them to get a dialog box where you can type in a new value. This value will apply to both keyframes, but will not change their individual interpolation types.

To hold on a value and continue from that point, make sure the Hold keyframe (shown selected) is followed by a keyframe with exactly the same value. You can ease into a Hold keyframe, and ease out of the following keyframe – the Hold keyframe has control only of its own outgoing curve.

• For Position keyframes, select both keyframes and park the time marker on one of the keyframes. Use the arrow keys to nudge the layer in the Composition window.

• For other properties, such as Scale and Rotation, you can select both keyframes and use the keyboard shortcuts to nudge both values – see Chapter 5 for more info. Provided both keyframes stay selected after your edit, both values will have been changed.

Things to Do with Keyframes

When you're in the throes of creativity, it's not always possible to place keyframes in exactly the perfect spot every time. After Effects provides many options and shortcuts for selecting, deleting, moving, copying, and pasting keyframes:

• To add a new keyframe at the current time using the current value, select (make the check mark visible) the keyframe navigator checkbox for that property.

To create a keyframe at the current frame using the current value, select the checkbox in the keyframe navigator.

• To delete a keyframe, select it and hit the Delete key. Delete all keyframes for a property by turning off the stopwatch.

• Select multiple keyframes by Shift+selecting them, or drag a marquee around multiple keyframes. You can even marquee across multiple properties and multiple layers, which is handy when you're moving many keyframes while maintaining their relationship to each other.

Hold It Right There!

The Second Field Glitch Problem

Users who haven't discovered Hold keyframes have devised all sorts of workarounds to make a property's value hold in place. The most common one involves creating a duplicate keyframe one frame before the next keyframe value [**Ex.09**].

Let's say you want a layer to hold at Position A for one second from 00:00 to 2:00, then jump to Position B when 02:00 is reached, without interpolating between the two points. You create two Linear keyframes, at 00:00 and 02:00. Then, to make the layer hold steady, you duplicate keyframe A at 01:29, one frame before keyframe B is due to occur. When you preview your animation, everything looks fine, and no interpolation occurs.

When you render the animation with field rendering turned on (discussed in Chapter 37 and beyond), you notice a glitch in the motion right around 02:00. Unfortunately, there is a position between frame 01:29 and 2:00. It's called the second field. If you examine the movie field by field, you would see that on frame 1:29, the layer is at Position A for the first field, but has jumped to an interpolated position *between* A and B for the second field.

Don't duplicate a keyframe in order to make it "hold" – you'll introduce a glitch when you field render.

There is no reason to ever use this ugly workaround – this is what the Hold keyframe lives and breathes for. Not only does this workaround create a glitch if you field render, but if you edit the value of keyframe A at time 00:00, you have to remember to update the duplicate keyframe at 01:29.

Now that you know all about Holds, you can simply use Toggle Hold Keyframe on the first keyframe at 00:00. The Position will hold steady until the next keyframe occurs at 2:00.

The Loop-de-Loop Problem

If in the course of creating a motion path you create two default Position keyframes (let's call them C and D), with exactly the same Position values, After Effects will automatically retract the outgoing Bezier handle from C and the incoming handle for the duplicate keyframe, D. With these handles on the motion path retracted, you'll have the functional equivalent of a Hold keyframe for C. (It's not exactly a Hold keyframe, but the layer will remain rock steady.)

But have you ever created two Position keyframes with exactly the same values, assuming the layer would hold steady – yet the layer ends up wandering around in a loop instead? This problem occurs because the handles on the motion path at keyframe C were manipulated before keyframe D was created. In this situation, After Effects will honor the position of the handles and create a small loop in the motion path [**Ex.10**]. (You can see the loop in the motion path more clearly by zooming in and moving the handles.) To fix this problem, select keyframe C and change it to a Hold keyframe. The loop will disappear as the outgoing handle for C and the incoming handle for D are retracted. This won't affect the motion path you've created; it will just remove the unwanted loop in the middle.

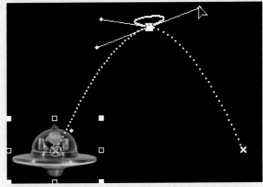

If you manipulate handles and then create two Position keyframes with the same value, those handles sticking out will create a loop in the motion path. Convert the first keyframe to a Hold keyframe to fix the problem.

Copying Layers

If a layer has been edited, one of its properties or a keyframe will be highlighted. If you then Copy, the program will copy the *property value*, not the layer. So when you Paste the layer, nothing happens. To copy the layer, deselect all (F2) first, then select the layer and Copy.

- If you don't animate a property, the I-beam (instead of a keyframe icon) represents the property's values for the duration of the comp. While not being a keyframe per se, it does contain a value that can be selected, copied, and pasted just like a keyframe. To include it in a marquee selection, park the time marker inside the area to be marqueed.
- Select all keyframes for a property by clicking on the name of the property (click on the word Position to select all Position keyframes). Shift+click multiple properties to select more tracks.
- To move keyframes in time, simply drag them along the Time Layout window. To make the selected keyframe stick to the time marker, hold down the Shift key after you start dragging.
- To nudge keyframes in time by one frame, use the Option+left-arrow and Option+right-arrow shortcuts.

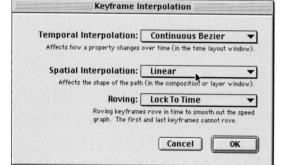

The Keyframe Interpolation dialog is useful for changing interpolation for multiple keyframes in both space and time – just select from the popups for Temporal, Spatial, and Roving.

Keyframe Interpolation Dialog

A handy shortcut for changing multiple keyframes at once is the Keyframe Interpolation dialog (Command+Option+K). For instance, you can retract the handles on a motion path so that all Spatial keyframes convert to Linear, while at the same time setting the Temporal keyframes to Continuous Bezier.

You can also use this dialog for checking the status of a selected keyframe. However, if a menu says simply Current Settings, this means that you have multiple keyframes selected of different interpolation types. If that's the case, you can set them all to the same interpolation type by selecting it from the menu.

Copying and Pasting Keyframes

You can copy keyframes in the time honored fashion (Command+C, or Edit>Copy). You can paste these keyframes later in time on the same layer or paste them to another layer anywhere inside the program. Keyframes do not reference the time from which they were copied; rather, they

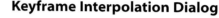

paste in at the current time. So when you paste, pay attention – the first keyframe in the copied sequence will be pasted at the time marker, and any subsequent keyframes will paste in later maintaining the same relationship.

When keyframes are pasted, the first keyframe is placed at the current time. Subsequent keyframes follow, maintaining the same relationship as when they were copied.

Position keyframes remember their spatial and temporal interpolation settings, so velocity curves are pasted along with the values of the X and Y axes. (Unfortunately, there is no way to copy just the velocity curves without the values.)

Keyframes are copied and stored as a set of numbers, but when they're pasted they default to using the same property as the source. So if you copy Position keyframes from one layer, then select another layer and paste, the keyframes will be pasted by default to the Position track. But keyframes can also be pasted from one property to any other, provided it makes sense to the program. You set the destination property by clicking on its name in the Time Layout window. For instance, to paste Position keyframes, which have two values (for the X and Y axes), you need to select another property with two channels, such as Anchor Point. Click on the word Anchor Point in the Time Layout window to set the destination track, and Paste. (To achieve more complicated copy and paste operations, you'll need to turn to Motion Math, Chapter 35.)

This smart paste feature can sometimes be too smart when you want to copy and paste keyframes between layers. For instance, if you copy Position keyframes from one layer, then adjust the Opacity on the destination layer before pasting, the Opacity property will be the active track. The program will then attempt to paste Position keyframes into Opacity and, as these properties are not compatible, return an error message. Worse yet, it may paste into an unintended, albeit compatible, property. (If you successfully pasted but the keyframes are not appearing on the intended track, check whether they pasted into the wrong property.) All in all, it's a good practice to copy keyframes, select another layer and paste *immediately* so that the keyframes paste to the same property by default.

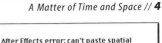

If you attempt to paste keyframes to a layer but instead trigger an error message, don't panic. In this example, the Opacity I-beam was highlighted, and the program attempted to paste Position keyframes to Opacity (which is not allowed). Click on the word Position to activate that track, and try your paste again.

Moving and Nudging Motion Paths

You can move individual keyframes in the Comp window by selecting the keyframe's X icon and dragging to a new location – you don't need to first navigate in time to where the keyframe occurs. The Info palette gives a running update of the new position as you drag the X icon. If you select multiple keyframes, you can drag one keyframe icon and have all of them follow – so you can drag the entire motion path to a new position easily.

You can nudge a layer by using the up/down/ left/right arrow keys to move a layer by one screen pixel at a time, or ten screen pixels with Shift pressed. What's not so obvious is how to use the nudge tools to move the entire motion path in small increments. The key is to make sure the time marker is parked on one of the selected keyframes when you nudge. If it isn't, hitting any arrow key will add a new keyframe at that point in time.

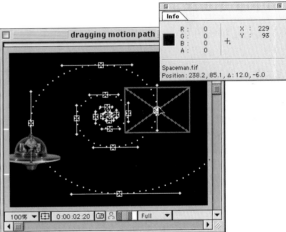

To move an entire motion path, select all the keyframes by clicking on the word Position in the Time Layout window. Drag any of the keyframe icons in the Comp window to move the path.

To nudge a path using the arrow keys, make sure the current time marker is parked on one of the keyframes you're moving.

Option+drag a layer to move with real-time preview, then add the Shift key to constrain the movement to the horizontal or vertical axis.

Sticky Shift

Press the Shift key when you're dragging the time marker and it will "stick" to keyframes, in and out points, markers, and so on.

Constraining and Snapping

When you're dragging layers to create Position keyframes, there are some handy keyboard shortcuts for constraining movement and snapping to the edge of a comp. Invoking the different states requires some subtle timing decisions:

• Use the Shift key to constrain a layer to vertical or horizontal movement only. Since Shift+clicking a layer deselects it, you must introduce the Shift key after you start moving the layer.

• Add the Option key when you're moving a layer to see a realtime preview of the new position.

• New in version 4.1, you can make the layer both constrain *and* show a realtime preview: Option+drag the layer first, *then* add the Shift key.

• Similar but different: to make a layer snap to the edges of a comp, or the comp's center, start dragging the layer first, *then* add Shift, then add Option.

Subpixel Positioning

As we mentioned earlier, when a layer is set to Draft Quality, movement is calculated using whole pixels only. While this lets you set up keyframes and preview them more quickly, you might find the results a little bumpy. Subpixel positioning allows for a layer to be positioned using less than one pixel for smoother motion.

To see the numerical results of this precision, park the time marker between two interpolating keyframes and click on the value for Position. The dialog will show values for the X and Y axes: numbers to the left of the decimal point are the integer numbers used by Draft mode, while the fractional numbers indicating subpixels are used in Best Quality.

Position

X−axis	Y−axis	Units:
70.991535	53.417627	pixels ▼

Cancel OK

When Position is interpolating between keyframes, check out the current value – the subpixel numbers to the right of the decimal point are used when the layer is set to Best Quality.

If you're previewing velocity changes with a critical eye, you might want to set the layer to Best Quality. Subpixel positioning is also used when a layer is scaled and rotated (see Chapter 5). However, all that extra precision (and antialiasing) take time, so in general we use Draft Quality for editing, and Best Quality when rendering.

Mutant Icons

Each temporal keyframe has an icon indicating the interpolation being used. But what's with these strange mutants? If you slice them down the vertical center, you'll see that they're combinations of diamonds, Bezier, and squares (you'll never see half a circle, though). If one side is grayed out, it means that no interpolation is taking place.

The regular set of icons include, left to right: Linear, Auto Bezier, Continuous Bezier/Bezier, and Hold.

Combinations of incoming and outgoing icons can create a strange mix. See if you can ID these mutants…

Resample: The Good, the Bad and the Avoidable

A second benefit of Best Quality and subpixel positioning is that layers are antialiased (or resampled) when they are transformed, as well as when distorted with an effect that pushes pixels around. However, this resampling adds additional softness and can be unwanted when you're doing nothing more than placing, say, a non-moving image or title created in Illustrator or Photoshop in your comp.

To avoid this unwanted resampling for stills, we need to understand why and when it kicks in. As it happens, After Effects resamples a layer whenever it uses subpixel positioning, and that means *whenever the difference between the Anchor Point value and Position value is not a whole number.* (After Effects defaults to using the center of a layer as the Anchor Point, and it takes the position of this Anchor Point in relationship to the comp for the value of Position.) Check out the following examples in this chapter's project:

- **[Ex.11a]** Your layer is even-sized, 300 pixels wide by 300 high, which places the Anchor Point at (150, 150). You drag this image into an even-sized 640×480 comp and Position it in the center (320, 240). The difference between (150, 150) and (320, 240) is a whole number, so the layer does not get resampled. Change the layer from Draft to Best Quality, and you'll see that there is no change.
- **[Ex.11b]** Your layer is odd-sized, 301 pixels wide by 301 high, which places the Anchor Point at (150.5, 150.5). You drag this image into an even-sized 640×480 comp and Position it in the center (320, 240). The difference between (150.5, 150.5) and (320, 240) is not a whole number, so the layer

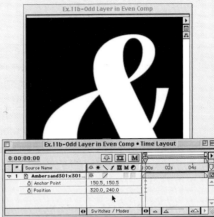

In **[Ex.11b]**, the Anchor Point defaults to a half pixel for this odd-sized layer. The difference between the Anchor Point and the Position is now a half pixel, so the layer is softened by resampling.

will be resampled. Change the layer from Draft to Best, and you'll see the image soften.

- **[Ex.11c]** Your layer is even-sized, 300 pixels wide by 300 high, which places the Anchor Point at (150, 150). You drag this image into an odd-sized 601×480 comp and position it in the center (300.5, 240). The difference between (150, 150) and (300.5, 240) is not a whole number on the X axis, so the layer will be resampled.

As you can see, you can avoid resampling for non-moving images by creating all sources with even sizes in Photoshop or Illustrator, and create comps with even sizes also. A single Photoshop image is relatively easy to create with even sizes; after creating or scanning an image, open Canvas Size in Photoshop and check that the width and height are even numbered – trim by one pixel if that's not the case.

The size of an Illustrator file is determined by its bounding box, which you can create manually (see Chapter 28) instead of relying on the size as determined by the objects. But if you create a bounding box manually using even values, After Effects will usually add a pixel to the width and height, thus making the image odd-sized. It is possible to carefully create an even-sized file by following a list of rules, but it's simply easier to create an odd-sized bounding box which imports into After Effects as an even-sized file. Usually. (Go figure.) We've supplied a variety of Illustrator Templates in the CD>Goodies folder that are guaranteed to be even-sized.

When you drag footage to a comp, take note of the magnification level. At 100%, the Position value will default to a whole pixel. But at 200% zoom or higher, it's possible to place a layer on a subpixel, which will negate your efforts to avoid resampling. Instead, drag images to the Time Layout window, which automatically centers them in the comp regardless of zoom level. If you then drag layers at 100% or 50% zoom or less, the Position will remain on a whole pixel.

If all else fails, you can always avoid unnecessary resampling by changing the Position of the layer by a half pixel up or down, left or right, until the image pops into sharpness. The easiest way to do this is to set the layer to Best, and Magnification to 200%. Use the arrow keys to nudge the layer one screen pixel at a time (at 200% zoom, one screen pixel will be a half pixel to Position).

Position

X-axis		Y-axis		Units :
260	,	248*1.25		pixels ▼

Cancel   OK

Arithmetic expressions (add, subtract, multiply, divide) can be used inside dialog boxes – handy when you can't find the calculator.

Math Tricks

All numerical dialog boxes in After Effects can perform simple math tricks using the arithmetic expressions + – * and /. For instance, to move a layer to the right by 64 pixels, type +64 after the current X axis value in the Position dialog. Subtract amounts by using minus values (100–64), multiply with an asterisk (10*64), and divide with the slashkey (100/20). The exception is the Go To Time dialog: entering –15 frames will jump to 15 frames before the beginning of the comp. The rule for Go To Time is that to advance 15 frames, type +15; to rewind 15 frames, type +–15 frames.

Easy Easing

Three Keyframe Assistants are available for automatically easing into and out of a keyframe. The assistants set the speed to 0% and the influence to 33.33%. See Chapter 7 for details.

Preferences for Position

Before we wrap up all that's specific to Position keyframes, there are a few preferences (found under the File>Preferences) that are worth familiarizing yourself with:

• General Preferences>Default Spatial Interpolation to Linear: In older versions of After Effects, Linear keyframes were the default for spatial keyframes, so this switch allowed users to stick with the old default instead of using the new Auto Bezier default. Switching back to Linear can be useful, though, particularly if you're animating a lot of small layers that move only in a straight line, where handles are getting in the way. If you find yourself constantly retracting Auto Bezier handles, turn on this preference temporarily and all new spatial keyframes will be created as Linear.

• Display Preferences>Motion Path: These preferences are useful for tweaking motion paths that are displayed only partially or are too busy to be editable. The default is to show keyframes for just a few seconds around the time marker. However, if the motion path is simple but extends over a long duration, the motion path will be cut off – and you'll have to

Preferences

| Display ▼ |

Motion Path
◉ All keyframes
○ No more than: [5] keyframes
○ No more than:
  [0:00:05:00] is 0:00:05:00
                   Base 30
○ No motion path

Safe Margins
Action-safe margin:
[10] %
Title-safe margin:
[20] %

OK
Cancel
Previous
Next

☐ Disable thumbnails in project window
☐ Auto-zoom when resolution changes
☑ Synchronize time of all related items
☐ Show rendering in progress in Info palette
  Default height of time layout graphs: [4] cells
                                          1 cell = 14 pixels

The Motion Path area of Display Preferences controls how much of the motion path or the number of keyframes are visible at any point in time. Set it to All Keyframes to avoid motion paths being cut off.

move in time in order to see and edit the path. In this case, change the preference to All Keyframes. We prefer the All Keyframes option overall.

On another project, though, you might have hundreds of keyframes on a motion path that crosses over itself, which makes it difficult to distinguish and select individual keyframes easily. In this case, use constraints for the number of keyframes, or the time period, to limit the visibility of keyframes to an area immediately around the current time.

Preview Possibilities

After Effects provides various previewing options, all of which are useful at some time or another. For instance, you might use the faster previewing options when the animation is taking shape, and the more time-intensive RAM preview when finalizing the effects and finishing the design. Most of these previews use the work area (explained in Chapter 3) as the preview area.

The Time Controls palette can be used to navigate in time, though we much prefer the keyboard short-cuts (Chapter 3). The defaults have Audio playback and Looping on, and you'll probably want to keep these on permanently. Your preview choices include:

• **The Shuttle Preview** (Option+drag): When you move the time marker along the timeline, the frame is rendered to the Comp window only when you mouse up. But if you press Option as you drag along the timeline, you'll get a rough and ready preview as fast as your machine allows. Add the Command key to also scrub the audio track. This is great for getting a quick overview of a long animation before you launch a more time-intensive preview. The jog and shuttle controls in the Time Controls palette do roughly the same thing, though the latter is rather like playing a video game when you're tipsy…

• **Wireframe Preview** (Option+0 on numeric keypad): Previously this was the only realtime preview option available in After Effects. It only draws a wireframe outline of a layer's mask or alpha channel (so you can't use it for testing effects), it doesn't honor opacity, and animated nested comps are drawn as rectangles. In its favor, the Wireframe preview starts almost immediately, and since it plays long sequences without heavy RAM requirements,

it's still useful for testing animation moves. It works on selected layers only, so you can even preview and loop a portion of the audio track this way. If no layers

Wireframe preview (Option+0) needs little RAM, plays back immediately, and is useful for testing motion before committing to a full RAM preview.

are selected, all layers will preview, so it's common to Deselect All (F2) before doing a Wireframe preview.

• **Standard Preview** (Spacebar): This preview displays all frames in the Composition's work area as quickly as possible using the current settings. To start and stop the standard preview, hit the Play button in the Time Controls Palette or the Spacebar. This preview tends to play back less efficiently than RAM Preview, but it does display with guides, grids, and title safe overlays.

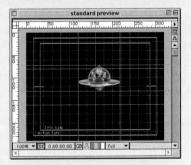

Standard preview (spacebar) is capable of playing back with grid, guides, and action/title safe areas displayed, though at the expense of playback performance.

Continued on next page/

/continued from previous page

- **RAM Preview** (0 on the numeric keypad): The most important new feature introduced by After Effects 4 is the RAM Preview. In earlier versions, proofing your animation necessitated a trip to the Render Queue to create test renders, and before long your hard drive was littered with test movies. With the addition of RAM previewing, you can test your design without having to go near the Render Queue. To launch a RAM Preview, set the work area appropriately, and hit either the 0 key on the keypad, or the RAM Preview button in the Time Controls palette. Shift+0 will preview every second frame. When complete, the preview plays at the composition's frame rate or as fast as your system will allow.

The RAM Preview Balancing Act

Getting the best of RAM Preview requires balancing your patience, quality needs, and RAM availability to get good feedback of a decent duration in a reasonable time frame. You'll quickly build up a feeling for how much time and patience you have versus the capability of your system. We find the Half Resolution/ 50% Magnification settings a good compromise for getting good feedback and image quality, along with fairly speedy previews. There are a number of issues to keep in mind during this juggling act, particularly the difference between the time taken to compile a preview, and the RAM needed to play it back:

- On the Mac, After Effects can use only RAM that's allocated to the program, and it doesn't play well with Virtual Memory. If the RAM preview stops after only a few frames, or you're otherwise getting Out of Memory errors, allocate more RAM to After Effects, or consider installing additional RAM. After Effects won't necessarily run faster with more RAM (unlike, say, Photoshop), but you will be able to preview more frames.

- Holding down the Shift key when you click on the RAM Preview button (Shift+0 shortcut) will preview every second frame. This is useful when you don't need to see every frame, as it cuts the render time in half. Another way of looking at it is that you can preview twice the duration with the same amount of RAM.

- Once a frame is rendered, the amount of RAM consumed is determined by the composition's Resolution setting. This amount is calculated based on an uncompressed frame. For instance, a 640×480 (Full Resolution) frame would take approximately 900K (kilobytes) when rendered, whereas a 320×240 (Half Resolution) frame would take only 225K. Setting the resolution to Half will allow you to render four times as many frames with the same amount of RAM.

- All layers and their effects are rendered at the current Quality settings. Layers set to Best Quality will take longer to render than those set to Draft. But once they are compiled, the amount of RAM they consume is identical. You can save render time by turning off layers that you don't need to see, setting layers to Draft Quality, and turning off any effects that are not critical for your test.

- Once the preview is compiled, the Time Controls palette will report how many of the requested frames it can hold in RAM, and the playback speed. If you're basing critical animation decisions on how the preview looks, check that playback is in realtime. Note that audio will always play realtime, so it may stop before the video if the video's frame rate is less than realtime.

- The playback frame rate is largely determined by the performance of your display card and how much data you're sending to it. Another factor that helps performance is for the screen depth to be at Millions of Colors on the Mac, and True Color on Windows. Make sure that system windows, such as the Control Strip, aren't overlapping the comp's window. And most important, match Resolution to Zoom (see *Testing 1000 Blits*, below).

- Once you've viewed the preview and continued editing, invoking RAM preview again should take less time as After Effects will do its best to cache frames from source movies or nested compositions. If it feels like it's starting over from scratch each time, keep adjusting the work area to focus on just the frames you've tweaked, and avoid rerendering frames you've signed off on.

Playing from RAM: 150 of 150
fps: 14.5/29.97 (NOT realtime)

The rightmost button in Time Controls (or 0 on keypad) starts a RAM preview display. The palette will display a "NOT realtime" warning in red if playback is less than the comp's frame rate. If you're making critical timing decisions, make sure audio is in sync and playback is realtime.

Saving RAM Preview as a Movie

Command+click on the RAM Preview button in the Time Controls palette to save the preview as a movie. You'll be prompted to name the movie and select a destination. Click Save. The Render Queue will come forward and the progress bar will immediately activate.

But how does it know what settings to use for saving to disk? The RAM Preview uses the Current Settings Template as the default for Render Settings, for obvious reasons (it's done already). The size of the resulting movie will be determined by the resolution of the comp – the magnification setting has no bearing on the movie's size. So if you previewed a 640×480 comp at Half Resolution, the preview movie will be 320×240.

The movie by default saves as QuickTime Animation, RGB Channels only (no alpha), which is a fine choice for smaller movies as it saves quickly. But the Output Module can be set to whatever codec works for you, and you might want to choose your video card's codec if applicable. Under File>Template >Output Module, the Default template for RAM Preview is, surprise, a template called RAM Preview. You can change the default to another Output Module, or edit the existing RAM Preview module. (See Chapter 43 for more on editing templates.)

If you need to render the RAM Preview with an alpha channel, make sure the selected Output Module is set to render RGB+Alpha in the Channels popup and that the codec supports alpha. QuickTime Animation supports RGB+Alpha, but many compressors do not. Since the images created for RAM Preview contain a premultiplied alpha, the output module cannot be set to save as a Straight Alpha. Also, the Background Color for the comp should be set to black if the output module is set to render alpha.

Finally, the idea is not to spend hours rendering your final rendered movie to RAM – particularly since the result is so volatile, and running out of RAM is a distinct possibility. Other drawbacks include the inability to render with fields, and the fact that alpha channels are always premultiplied.

Testing 1000 Blits

Yes, it would make a great name for a rock band, but it's actually an undocumented way to test the RAM preview capability of your display card using certain settings. To set the test in motion, with a Comp forward, hold down Command+Option+Shift and click on the RAM Preview button in the Time Controls palette. The program "blits" the display card up to a count of 1000, and the result of the test is shown in the Info palette as a frames per second result. This is an indication of the maximum frame rate attainable by your hardware configuration using the current settings of Resolution and Magnification.

Info				
R :	0		X :	302
G :	0		Y :	224
B :	0	+.		
A :	0			

testing 1000 blits
206.8966 fps

Try a few tests using various settings and write down the results. If you have more than one monitor, repeat the test for each monitor. The results can be quite surprising. For instance, testing a 640×480 comp at Full Resolution/100% Magnification gave much better results than Half Res/100% or Full Res/50%. The best performance results when the resolution (the number of pixels created) matched the number of pixels on the monitor (the magnification). We achieved the best performance with Half Res/50% zoom level.

A Trio of Transformations

Applying our newfound animation knowledge to additional transformation parameters.

We introduced you to the Scale, Rotation, and Opacity properties in Chapter 3, but now it's time to go into more detail and to learn to animate them. We will assume you've read Chapter 4 – *A Matter of Time and Space* – as it explains in depth the various keyframe interpolation types and how the velocity curves work. We promised that once you got these basics down, that knowledge could be transferred to almost all other properties, and that's what we'll do here. So rather than repeat ourselves, we'll focus on how Scale, Rotation, and Opacity differ from animating Position. By the end of this chapter, you'll be ready to animate multiple objects against a background.

The Scale numeric parameter defaults to keeping the original aspect ratio of the source; you need to uncheck the Preserve box if you want to scale a layer non-uniformly. The Units popup allows you to work in a system other than Percentage of Source, which is used to display Scale values in the Time Layout and Info windows.

Example Project

Explore the 05-Example Project.aep file as you read this chapter; references to [Ex.##] refer to specific compositions within the project file.

S is for Scale

First, let's reacquaint ourselves with manipulating the Scale property of a layer – and learn a couple of quick shortcuts and tips while we're at it. Open [**Ex.01.1**], select the CM_spherecopper layer in the Time Layout window, and type S – this is the shortcut to twirling down just the Scale parameter for a selected layer.

You can alter the Scale of a layer by clicking the numeric value on the same line as the word Scale. Enter a value for Width and Height. If the Preserve Frame Aspect Ratio is checked, you need to enter only one value; if you want to distort the image, uncheck this box and type in different numbers. Typing the same number for Width and Height automatically rechecks this option the next time you open the dialog box. The Units popup allows you to scale in Pixels, % of Source, and % of Composition (and other measurement units that have no real meaning in video), although all units are presented as a percentage of source in the Time Layout window when you close the dialog.

As we saw in Chapter 3, you can edit Scale interactively by dragging its handles in the Comp window. Press the Option key to get a realtime update as you drag, and add the Shift key after you start dragging (or Option+dragging) to maintain the aspect ratio of the layer as you scale.

If you make a mess, double-click the selection (arrow) tool in the toolbox to reset the layer to 100%.

You can also edit this property interactively by Option+clicking on the word Scale in the Time Layout window. This pops up the "magic slider" (well, it's magic if you didn't know it was there…). Drag the slider up and down to adjust the scale.

Selected layers can also be resized from the keyboard by holding down the Option key and hitting + or – on the numeric keypad. This increases or decreases Scale by 1% per click. Also, holding the Shift key results in 10% increments. The keyboard shortcuts also work for multiple keyframes, provided the time marker is parked on one of the selected keyframes.

Selecting a layer and typing S twirls down just the Scale property. Then Option+clicking next to the word Scale brings up a "magic slider" to interactively adjust its value.

What if the handles aren't visible? Open [**Ex.01.2**]. In this case, the layer CP_Radio is so much larger than the comp size that the handles are out on the pasteboard somewhere. You can obviously zoom down the Comp window to see more of the pasteboard, or use another little keyboard shortcut: Hold down the Command key and drag the image in the Comp window to scale it interactively without grabbing a handle. Again, add the Option key while dragging to view the actual image, and add Shift to constrain the aspect ratio. Also remember that you can look at the Info floating palette (Command+2) to see an update of the precise numeric values as you drag.

Animating Scale

Now that we know several different ways to manipulate Scale, it's time to animate it. Close any lingering windows and open [**Ex.02*starter**].

Step 1: Select the CP_Spaceman layer, and type S to twirl down the Scale parameter in the Time Layout window.

Step 2: Make sure the time marker is at the beginning of the comp, and click on the stopwatch icon for Scale. This enables animation and sets the first Scale keyframe at the current time. The current size – 100% – is used for this keyframe. Double-clicking on the keyframe icon opens its own Scale dialog, giving you another way to change this parameter.

Step 3: Leaving the time marker at the start of the comp, change the scale of the layer however you choose (bearing in mind that values over 100% will blow up pixels and decrease quality). Notice the value changes in the Time Layout window.

Step 4: Move the time marker further along the Time Layout window's timeline. Notice that the Scale parameter remains the same until you set a second keyframe and create an animation.

Step 5: Rescale the spaceman to a size different from the first keyframe. Notice that a new keyframe is created in the Time Layout window. Whenever Scale's stopwatch is on, changing the Scale results in a keyframe being created at that point in time, or updated if there was already a keyframe at that point in time, just as with Position keyframes.

If you can't see the Scale handles of a layer, Command+dragging the layer allows you to resize it without grabbing the handles. Image from Classic PIO/Classic Radios.

Blowing Up Pixels

Try to avoid scaling a layer above 100%. This creates new pixels that weren't originally available, resulting in softening or aliasing artifacts.

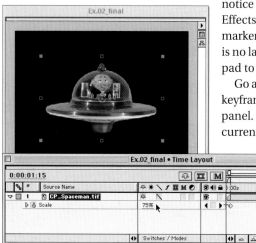

Ex.02_final

Ex.02_final • Time Layout

As you scrub (Option+drag) the time marker along this window, notice that the spaceman changes size between keyframes, as After Effects automatically interpolates the Scale values. Drag the time marker after the last keyframe, and its size no longer changes; there is no later keyframe to interpolate to. Hit zero on the numeric keypad to preview your animation (covered at the end of Chapter 4).

Go ahead and set more than two Scale keyframes. Jump between keyframes using the keyframe navigator arrows in the A/V Features panel. Note that clicking on one of these check marks removes the current keyframe; clicking in an empty box when parked between keyframes creates a new one with the current value. Selecting a keyframe and hitting Delete also removes it. Clicking on the stopwatch erases all keyframes – oops. Undo (Command+Z) to get them back. These techniques apply to all parameter keyframes.

When the time marker is between two keyframes, the Scale parameter automatically interpolates between the values of the nearest keyframe – in this case, 100% and 50%. Notice the image looks a bit crunchy in Draft Quality – turn on Best Quality to see the layer antialiased. Spaceman from Classic PIO/ Nostalgic Memorabilia.

The Value Graph

Unlike Position, Scale and Rotation have both a Value graph and a Velocity graph. Let's look closely at Scale [Ex.03]; you'll see later that the Rotation graphs are similar:

The **Value : Scale** graph (the top one) allows you to edit the value of Scale keyframes by moving the points up or down. The Value graph is a visual guide to whether the Scale value is increasing (the line ascends) or decreasing (the line descends). The default range for the Value graph is 0% to 100%, but if you scale above or below these values, the range will automatically realign itself to the new maximum and minimum values. If you scale below 0%, the image will flip either horizontally (width) or vertically (height).

To change the value of a Scale keyframe using the graph, drag the keyframe "nubbin" (the dot on the graph underneath the keyframe) up or down, and add the Option key to see the layer update in the Comp window. The Info palette displays the current Scale value as you drag.

If you're used to changing the velocity graph for Position, remember that adjusting the Value graph for Scale changes the *actual value*, not the rate of change between keyframes.

However, you'll notice that as you edit the Value graph, the Velocity graph also changes. In fact, both graphs are inherently linked together – you can't adjust one without affecting the other in some way.

Ex.03-adjust the nubbin • Time Layout

Twirl down Scale, and you will see both Value and Velocity graphs. The first shows how a parameter is changing; the second, how fast it is changing. You can click and drag the "nubbin" at the keyframe locations in the Value graph to directly edit the Scale amount; add the Option key to also update the Comp window as you drag.

The Velocity Graph

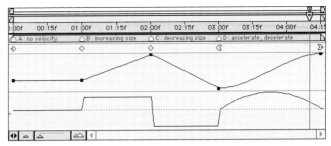

The second graph, **Velocity : Scale**, depicts and adjusts the rate of change between keyframe values. This graph is a little more complicated than the corresponding velocity for Position because Scale can be either increasing or decreasing. That's why there's a centerline in this graph – it represents zero change. The further away the graph is from this centerline, the faster the parameter is changing. To "read" the different shapes this graph might take, look at the corresponding figure and [**Ex.04.1**]:

A: If the velocity graph sits along the centerline, this indicates that the layer's Scale value is constant at that point in time – not that the size is 0 percent, but that there's no change in size over time.

B: If the velocity graph sits above the centerline, the layer is increasing in size. If the line is flat, the rate of change is linear (the layer is interpolating between linear keyframes).

C: If the velocity graph sits below the centerline, the layer is decreasing in size. Again, if the line is flat, the rate of change is linear.

D: If the velocity graph ramps up or down toward the centerline, the keyframe's interpolation has been changed from the default linear interpolation. The closer the curve is to the centerline, the slower the rate of change in Scale.

Remember that there is a numeric readout of how velocity is changing to the left of the graphs, so read that for confirmation. The middle number explains how fast the Scale parameter is changing per second for this frame, forward from the current time.

Although it's not initially intuitive, you can learn to "read" the Velocity : Scale line to understand what a value is doing: the centerline means no change; above means getting bigger; below means getting smaller; and the further away from the centerline, the faster it's changing.

Changing Keyframe Interpolation

In Chapter 4, we covered in great detail the various keyframe interpolation types and how to change from one to the other. You should therefore be familiar with Linear, Auto Bezier, Continuous Bezier, Bezier, and Hold keyframe types. The good news is that you can apply that knowledge to every other animated property inside After Effects, from Scale and Rotation, to animating effects. (This is a nice way of saying that we're not going to repeat the same information in every chapter…)

Scale has only Temporal keyframes (keyframes in time). Experiment in [**Ex.05**] with changing the default Linear (diamond) keyframes in the Time Layout window. Start with Auto Bezier (Command+click on the diamond and it will change to a circle). This will pop out the handles on both graphs and force the incoming and outgoing handles to be continuous. Now you can adjust the handles on the Velocity graph by dragging the hollow handles up and down (clicking on the actual nubbin does nothing). This is the Continuous Bezier keyframe type. The Command key will split the handles and reconnect them, just as with the curves in the Position graph.

Mirror Reflections

You can scale a layer by a negative amount: either type in a negative number, or drag the handles "through" zero until it flips around. This mirrors the layer, as if you were looking at its back side. To flip a layer horizontally, click on its Scale parameter, uncheck the Preserve Aspect Ratio option, and make the Width a negative number, such as –100%. To flip vertically, do the same to the Height.

Note that when one of these parameters is negative, resizing with the keyboard shortcut acts a little strange, since it in essence now adds to one size and subtracts from the other. Consider flipping layers in a precomp (see Chapters 16 and 17), or if you have Boris AE set of plug-ins, use its Boris Fast Flipper effect.

Seeing Double

Scale is one of those parameters that has two parts: X and Y dimensions. What if you chose different values for these, resulting in the scale in the X dimension animating at a different rate than in the Y dimension? You'd get two sets of lines in the Value and Velocity graphs. An example of this is in **[Ex.04.2]**. On the other hand, if you didn't intend to split these two dimensions and keep the image's aspect ratio constant, then seeing double in these graphs means you accidentally distorted your image. You might want to turn on Preserve Frame Aspect Ratio in the Scale dialog box to fix this. Remember to use the Shift key when dragging a layer's handles if you want to keep the aspect ratio constant.

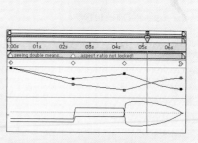

If the X and Y dimensions of Scale (or similar parameters) are animating differently, you'll see two lines for the Value and Velocity graphs.

Exponential Scale

If you animate Scale from a small to a large value, the zoom may appear to slow down over time. Check out the Exponential Scale Keyframe Assistant in Chapter 7.

The Gray Areas: Overshooting

When you're adjusting the handles for the Value graph, be aware that if you create a graph shape that extends higher than the relative position of the keyframe's nubbin, the layer will be temporarily larger than the value of the next keyframe. Preview **[Ex.06]** to get a feel for this action.

Another clue that overshooting is occurring is that a gray line appears along the centerline in the Velocity graph. This indicates that the layer is scaling, for that period of time, *in the opposite direction than the keyframes would indicate.* For instance, if you animate a layer from 50% to 80%, you would expect the layer to be always increasing in size between the two keyframes. However, it's quite easy to drag either the Value graph or the Velocity graph handles in sucha way that the layer scales *past* 80% and then *decreases* in size for a period of time as it approaches the second keyframe.

If the Value graph is bent so that its line extends beyond the next keyframe's resting place, the result is an overshoot in Scale as it approaches that keyframe. This is also indicated by a gray line along the center-line in the velocity graph. Press Shift as you adjust either graph to avoid this behavior.

This overshooting behavior may be exactly what you want for a cartoony animation style – or it could be a mistake. If you want to avoid this overshooting behavior, hold down the Shift key as you adjust the handles on either the Value or Velocity graph. This tip works for all graphs that have a centerline.

R is for Rotation

The Rotation parameter has its own set of keyboard short-cuts and alternate methods of manipulation that are worth learning. Close any compositions that might be cluttering up your window and open [**Ex.07**]. Select the CM_bikewheel layer, and type R on the keyboard – this is the shortcut for revealing just the Rotation parameter.

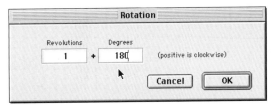

You can enter Rotation as just degrees, or number of rotations plus degrees.

You can edit Rotation numerically by clicking on its parameter value, which opens its own dialog. The right-most box is for entering degrees; one full revolution is 360°. The left-most box is a shortcut for entering whole rotations. You can enter more than 360° for more than one revolution, enter values in both boxes, and enter negative values as well.

As we saw in Chapter 3, you can interactively rotate a layer in the Comp window with the Rotation tool (shortcut: W for Wotate – seriously, that's what they told us). Again, hold down Option for realtime updates as you drag; add Shift to constrain to 45° increments. If you make a mess, double-click the Rotation tool to revert to 0°.

Option+clicking on the word Rotation also brings up the "magic slider" for interactively rotating a layer; the limit is plus and minus one full rotation. Plus and minus on the numeric keypad increments or decrements rotation in 1° increments; adding the Shift key rotates it in 10° increments.

If the wheel looks a bit crunchy at some rotational values, again, this is an artifact of a layer being in Draft quality with its corresponding nearest neighbor sampling. Set the quality switch in the Time Layout window to Best for smoother drawing, with a corresponding small penalty in calculation time.

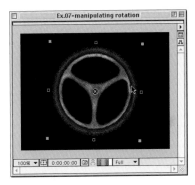

If rotated layers look a bit sliced or disjointed, they are probably in Draft quality. Set to Best to turn on antialiasing.

Animating Rotation

Time for a little practice animating rotation, using [**Ex.08*starter**]:

Step 1: Select the CM_bikewheel layer, and type R to twirl down the Rotation parameter in the Time Layout window.

Step 2: Make sure the time marker is at the beginning of the comp, and click on the stopwatch icon to the left of the word Rotation. This enables animation and sets the first Rotation keyframe at the current time. We'll use the current rotation amount – 0 – for this keyframe. Alter the initial rotation value if you wish. As with Scale, double-clicking on the keyframe is another way to access the Rotation parameter's dialog box.

Step 3: Move the time marker to a new place along the Time Layout window's timeline. Notice that the Rotation parameter stays the same; again, this is because it takes more than one keyframe to create an animation.

Step 4: Rotate the wheel, either interactively or numerically. Note that a new keyframe is created in the Time Layout window. Option+drag the time marker or preview the comp to see the effects of your rotation animation. Use the keyframe navigator arrows to jump between keyframes and edit the values. You can also delete a keyframe by unchecking the checkbox when you're parked on a keyframe.

Stretch to Fit

Command+Option+F will force a layer to scale and position itself to fit the size of the comp exactly – though this may distort the image. It will also reset any Rotation value applied.

Rotation Rules

After you've rotated the layer a few times in a still image program such as Illustrator or Photoshop, it's often difficult to reset the orientation back to the starting position. This is because once rotation is processed, the image assumes a rotation value of 0 again.

After Effects, however, always remembers the initial orientation. When you rotate a layer, the value displayed is always in relation to the original starting value of 0°. When animating rotation, therefore, we recommend you create the first keyframe at 0° if possible, as it'll provide a point of reference when setting additional keyframes.

If the value of any particular Rotation keyframe is its rotational position, it stands to reason that the value does not indicate how the layer will animate. For instance, a value of 90° does not necessarily mean the layer will rotate clockwise 90°. That would be true only if the previous keyframe was 0°.

In [**Ex.09*starter**], our CM_bikewheel layer rotates from 0° to 180° clockwise over one second. If you now wish the layer to animate counterclockwise by 180°, the third keyframe should be set to 0° (not minus 180° as you might think). The layer will interpolate between the absolute values of keyframes; thus 180° back to 0° is counterclockwise 180°. So whether or not a layer is rotating clockwise or counterclockwise can really be gauged only by checking the values of keyframes before and after, or by consulting the Value : Rotation graph.

Rotation Value and Velocity Graphs

Everything you learned about Value and Velocity graphs and interpolating between keyframes for Scale applies to Rotation, except it's easier – there is only one dimension to Rotation, so you don't have any split graphs to deal with. You can edit Rotation by dragging the keyframe nubbins up and down; Command+clicking on keyframes toggle them between Linear (no acceleration or deceleration) and Auto-Bezier (smooth speed changes), and adjusting handles gives you Continuous Bezier and Bezier controls. By now, you should be getting good at changing interpolation types and "reading" these graphs [**Ex.10.1**]:

A: Flat Value : Angle lines means no change in rotation.

B: Upward-sloping Value lines means increasing angle; the distance of the Velocity : Angle line above its centerline indicates clockwise speed. A flat Velocity line means constant speed.

C: Downward-sloping Value lines means decreasing angle; the distance between the Velocity line and its centerline indicates counterclockwise speed. In this case, the fact that it is not ruler-straight means the speed is changing over time between the keyframes. A nice taper to the centerline means it decelerates nicely to 0 rotational speed.

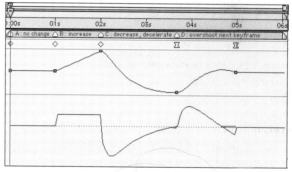

Can you "read" the Value and Velocity graphs now to predict what the layer is generally going to do, even before you preview it?

D: A Value handle coming out of a keyframe at anything other than a flat angle means we are undershooting or overshooting our approach to a keyframe. A second clue is the Velocity handle being off the centerline. If there is a gray line along this centerline, it means you are overshooting your next keyframe along this period of time; preview the comp to get a feel for that. Holding down the Shift Key as you adjust the handles on the Value graph will constrain it from overshooting the next keyframe. Note that you can accomplish the same trick (or sin, depending on what your intentions were) as you leave a keyframe, making an object appear to "rear back" before taking off. If you are having trouble accomplishing the exact animation, try using multiple keyframes – there is no rule that says every move can consist of only two keyframes, although the fewer the keyframes, the easier the move will be to manage.

Comp [**Ex.10.2**] is a variation of the example above, showing overshoot at the start; practice manipulating the keyframes using the handles in these graphs. (Remember that you have to click on a keyframe to see the handles.) Preview often to get an idea of the results, resetting the work area as needed.

If you are more comfortable manipulating numbers than graphs, you can open the Keyframe Velocity window by Option+double-clicking on a keyframe, context-clicking on a keyframe and selecting Keyframe Velocity, or selecting a keyframe and typing Command+Shift+K.

To numerically manipulate interpolation through a keyframe, select it and open its Keyframe Velocity window. Unchecking the Continuous button allows different incoming and outgoing speeds through a keyframe; the same can be accomplished by Command+ clicking on the influence handles.

Auto-Orient Rotation

After Effects has two ways of handling rotation for a layer. In addition to the Rotation transformation property, it can automatically orient the rotation of a layer to point along a motion path it is following. To enable this for a selected layer, either context-click on it or go to the Layer menu and select Transform>Auto-Orient Rotation (Command+Option+O).

To try this for yourself, open [**Ex.11-AutoOrient*starter**], select the spaceman layer, and turn this option on. Note how the spaceship suddenly snaps to be tangential to the motion path. Preview to see how it follows the path around the bends, with no Rotation keyframes set.

The important thing is that Auto-Orient is separate from the normal Rotation value. You can offset Rotation to better point a layer along its path, or even animate it. You cannot animate Auto-Orient; however, if you need to switch it on or off during a composition, split the layer into two pieces and turn it on for one (more on divide-and-conquer concepts like this in future chapters).

The problem with Auto-Orient Rotation is that there's usually a slight hitch at the beginning and end of the motion path, as seen when you preview [**Ex.11-Auto-Orient*starter**] after you turn this option on. Zoom into the Comp window and select the first keyframe's icon (move the current time marker to later in time if the CP_Spaceman image is in the way). If you carefully examine the motion path, you'll see that the spatial keyframes are all of the default Auto Bezier type, whose handles are represented by tiny dots. The handle for the first keyframe does not align with the motion path, so the layer orients itself at a slightly different angle for a few frames, resulting in a twisting motion.

To fix this, drag the handle dot and the direction line will appear, which is an indication that its interpolation has changed to Continuous Bezier. Now align the direction line with the

Auto-Orient Flip

If a layer flips upside down when Auto-Orient is enabled, change Rotation to 180° to turn it right side up. Other angles give other alignments.

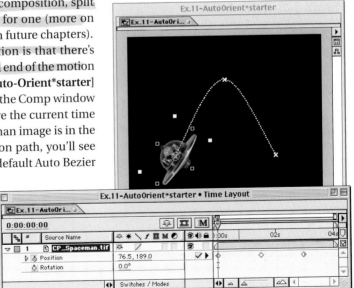

When Auto-Orient Rotation is turned on (Command+Option+O), the layer automatically aligns itself to be tangential to its motion path, with no Rotation keyframes necessary.

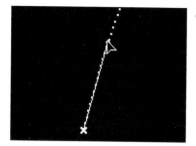

To avoid rotation twists at the ends of animations, zoom in and grab the dot that represents the Auto Bezier handles. Drag the handle to convert to Continuous Bezier and make sure the Position handles are tangential to their path.

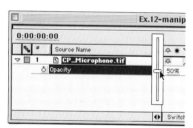

Option+clicking to the right of the word Opacity brings up a slider to interactively edit its value – the only interactive tool you have for Opacity.

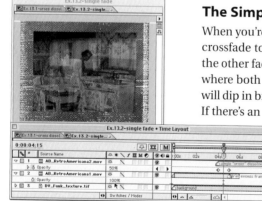

When both layers are the same size and centered over one another, you can just fade one of the layers. Retro Americana footage from Artbeats; background from Digital Vision/Data:Funk.

motion path. Repeat for the handle at the last keyframe. Preview again and the motion should be smooth at both ends (check out the [**Ex.11-Auto-Orient_fixed**] comp to compare with our version).

T is for Opacity

Actually, T is for Transparency, but the O was being used already to jump to the Out Point. After Effects uses the term *opacity*, rather than *transparency*, so 0% Opacity is 100% transparent. To practice editing Opacity, open [**Ex.12**], select the layer, and type T to solo Opacity. Click on the current value and enter a value between 0 and 100 in the Opacity dialog box.

Probably the best way to edit Opacity is to use the handy slider we mentioned earlier: Hold down the Option key and click on the word Opacity in the Time Layout window. A popup appears on the right side, just to the left of the Opacity value. Drag the cursor directly over the slider, and drag up and down to set transparency. The Info palette gives real-time feedback of the exact value. Since you have to move the cursor directly over the slider to change it, practice Option+clicking on the right side of the highlighted area – right where the slider pops up. This cuts out some mousing around.

When you edit Opacity, the layer's alpha channel is being changed, making the layer more or less transparent. For instance, toggle on the Alpha swatch along the bottom of the Comp window as you play with the Opacity slider in [**Ex.12**] to see what is going on.

You've probably guessed already that turning on the stopwatch for Opacity and setting two keyframes with values of 0% to 100% will fade up a layer. Try it now if you need the practice. Notice that the reverse will fade off a layer. When keyframes have been set, you can also twirl down Opacity and edit the velocity curve with all the tools we've already mentioned, although this is usually optional when you're animating Opacity.

The Simple Cross Dissolve

When you're crossfading from one layer to another, don't take the word crossfade too literally. If you crossfade by fading one layer down while the other fades up [**Ex.13.1-crossfade**], you'll notice a dip in the middle where both layers are at 50%. If the background is black, the crossfade will dip in brightness as some of the black background becomes visible. If there's an image in the background, it will be partially visible.

If both layers are the same size, you need to fade up only the top layer from 0 to 100%, as in [**Ex.13.2-single fade**]. Once the top layer is fully opaque, trim out the bottom layer (even though the bottom layer is obscured, you'll waste time retrieving frames from disk). This does not always work; problems occur when the layers are not the same size, are animating, or have their own alpha channels and partial transparencies. Also, the layer behind might still be partially visible, and pop off, as in [**Ex.13.3-problems**]. In this case, go ahead and crossfade both layers (or try the Blend effect, Chapter 23).

Advanced Opacity

Opaque Logic

You might expect that when you stack two layers on top of each other, each with opacity 50%, that the result would be 100% opaque. But that's not how opacity works – it multiplies, rather than adds. This may not seem intuitive, but consider putting on two pairs of 50% opaque sunglasses: You can still see through them; it's just darker.

Think of opacity as filling up a glass, with a full glass being 100% opaque. The first 50% opaque layer would fill the glass half full. You now have 50% of opacity left to work with. The next 50% layer fills half the remaining opacity, resulting in a glass now three-quarters full (75% opaque). This works with any combination of values. For example, if the first layer was 60% opaque, you would have 40% left at the top to work with; if the layer on top was 75% opaque, it would use up 75% of the remaining 40%, resulting in 90% opacity where the two overlap. (The math: $0.60 + [0.75 \times 0.40] = 0.90$.) The only way to go fully opaque is to have a layer somewhere in the stack that is 100% opaque, or to stack so many layers (put on so many pairs of sunglasses) that no one will notice the tiny amount of transparency that might be left.

This little fact about opacity can cause problems, such as when two feathered layers have edges that are supposed to overlap perfectly, or when one layer is fading out while another is fading up on top. Luminance dips caused by these partial, scaled transparencies will result. Fortunately, After Effects has cures for these two particular cases – the Alpha Add transfer mode and the Blend effect, respectively – we'll discuss both of these in future chapters.

Not Fade Away

This bit of trivia also affects less esoteric issues, such as fades. When you fade down multiple layers individually from 100% to 0% Opacity, you will end up with a "staggered" fade-out **[Ex.14-FadeOut*problem]**. As the top layer fades out, it becomes transparent, revealing the layer below. In our example, in the middle of the fade-out at time 02:00, the cloud

When previously opaque layers are faded individually, you start to see through the front objects during the fade (left) – perhaps not what you intended. The solution is to fade the layers as a group (right), either using Adjustment Layers or nested compositions (both covered in more detail later in this book). White Puffy Clouds background from Artbeats; clock from Classic PIO/Classic Sampler.

background layer shows through the clock layer in the foreground.

Ideally, both layers should be fading out as one unit. Therefore, the solution is to apply the Opacity keyframes to the layers as a group, after they've been composited together. (The following solutions are based on techniques "not yet in evidence" in the previous chapters, so if you're a beginner they may not make sense just yet.)

The easiest way to fade out a group of layers all in one comp **[Ex.14-FadeOut_fixed]** is to apply an Adjustment Layer (Layer>New Adjustment Layer) and apply the Transform effect (Perspective submenu). By setting keyframes for the Opacity parameter in the effect instead of the regular Opacity keyframes, the fade-out affects all layers below after they've been composited as a group.

Another solution is to use a nested comp to solve the problem (nesting is covered in Chapter 16). Using two compositions in a chain, no fades are applied in the first comp **[Ex.15-Opacity-1]**. This comp is nested in a second comp **[Ex.15-Opacity-2]**, and Opacity keyframes fade out the nested comp layer as a group. These regular Opacity keyframes will now apply to the group of layers after they've been composited together. This might be a better option if you need to also apply other animation and effects to the group.

Gotchas to Avoid

• **Creating a keyframe at the beginning of a layer for no reason:** If you want a title to scale down at the end of the animation, place two Scale keyframes (100% and 0%) at the end of the layer [**Ex.17.1-Gotcha#1**]. The layer will start out using the value of the first keyframe (100%). When it passes the first keyframe it will then interpolate down to 0%. (Contrary to what we've read elsewhere, there's no need for a keyframe of 100% at the start of the layer to make this simple animation work.)

• **Turning on a stopwatch for a constant value:** Turn on the stopwatch only for properties you plan to animate so you can edit its value at any point in time without introducing unwanted animation.

• **Creating keyframes at the same time on all animated properties:** If you have three Position keyframes, there's no equal opportunity rule that you also must have three Scale and three Rotation keyframes, all synched to the same points in time. Create keyframes only where needed: The fewer keyframes you have to manage, the easier the animation will be to edit.

• **If a layer's Position, Scale, and Rotation are all animating,** it's best to apply the same amount of ease in and out to keyframes that align in time. If you ease in and out of Position but not Scale and Rotation, for instance, the animation may appear to "slide" into position. Preview the Before layer (#1) in [**Ex.17.2-Gotcha#2**] to see the problem. Now turn on the After layer (#2) instead and preview again – you should be able to see the improvement.

• **Creating extra keyframes to adjust speed:** To rotate or scale a layer at different speeds, try adjusting velocity curves with the minimum number of keyframes, adding keyframes only if necessary.

Handy Transform Keyboard Shortcuts

Solo Property in Time Layout window:

Anchor Point	A
Position	P
Scale	S
Rotation	R
Opacity	T
to add and subtract	Shift
Turn on property stopwatch	Option+respective solo key
If stopwatch on, add/delete keyframe	Option+respective solo key
Set value in dialog box	Command+Shift+P, S, or R
Scale layer without using handles	Command+drag on image
Constrain Scale to aspect ratio	Drag to Scale, add Shift
Constrain Rotation to 45° increments	Rotate with tool, add Shift
Double-click Selection tool	Reset Scale to 100%
Double-click Rotation tool	Reset Rotation to 0 degrees
Auto-Orient Rotation on/off	Command+Option+O
Show all properties that animate	U (selected layers)
Select all keyframes for property	Click property name

Render Hit or Miss

If a layer's Opacity is at 0% or its visibility is off, the layer takes up no RAM and no rendering time (unless it's being accessed by a second layer).

Multiple Solos

To solo multiple properties, type the shortcut for the first one (S for Scale), then Shift+type the shortcuts to add and subtract properties (i.e., Shift+R to add Rotation).

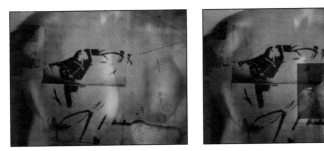 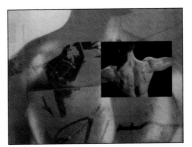

All Together Now

To sum up what we've covered to date, we've created a couple of compositions that animate all four properties (Position, Scale, Rotation, and Opacity), using a variety of keyframe interpolation types. Both examples use more than one layer. When additional layers are added to a comp, they default to the top (foreground). You can rearrange the stacking order by simply dragging the layers up and down in the Time Layout window (more on managing multiple layers in Chapter 8).

- **[Ex.16-AllTogether#1]:** Three layers animate using some Linear keyframes and others that ease in and out. (The Easy Ease Keyframe Assistants come in handy when you have multiple keyframes to effect – more on those in Chapter 7.)

- **[Ex.16-AllTogether#2]:** In this example, the background (Hand) layer animates Rotation and Scale using Hold keyframes at the beginning, then the last movement interpolates. The foreground (Eye) layer starts at 01:20, and blinks on and off (thanks to Hold keyframes set for Opacity) before scaling down and fading off.

Creating motion graphics begins with motion, and manipulating keyframes and velocity curves is a large part of the job. After you've checked out these examples, check out the step-by-step beginner tutorials on the CD. Most of all, experiment and have fun until you feel comfortable with the animation techniques covered in Chapters 4 and 5. Create a new comp and design your own animation. Remember: It's only software; you can't break anything.

All Together #1: Three layers blending with opacity and some slight rotation. Background still images from Digital Vision's The Body and Naked & Scared CDs; inset video footage from EyeWire/Fitness.

Connect

The Anchor Point (discussed in Chapter 6) is critical to Scale and Rotation, since both center their actions around this point. Animating it is also great for motion-control moves.

Useful Keyframe Assistants such as Easy Ease and Exponential Scale are explained in Chapter 7.

More tips on managing layers, including hot-keying to another program, are covered in Chapter 8.

Trimming layers is covered in Chapter 9.

Motion Blur, which makes many animation moves look more realistic, is the subject of Chapter 11.

Chapter 16 discusses nesting compositions, and using Transform to animate groups of layers.

Animating effects are covered in Chapter 19; Adjustment Layers are in Chapter 20.

All Together #2: Two layers rotating, exploiting Hold keyframes to make one of them "blink." Both images from Digital Vision/The Body.

The Anchor Point

To transform a layer, it's best to know what you're transforming it around.

Central – quite literally – to changing the position, scale, and rotation of an image is its anchor point. This is the pivot around which these activities take place. Judicious placement and animation of the anchor point can help you avoid a lot of headaches. Once we have a good grasp on the anchor point, we will show you how to use it to simulate motion control moves.

Anchors Away

Open comp [**Ex.01**] in the examples project for this chapter, or create a new composition (Command+N) and make a new Solid (Command+Y) that's the same size as the comp (click on the Comp Size button in the Solid's dialog). Select the solid layer, and notice the anchor point in the center of the layer. With the layer selected, type A to solo Anchor Point, and Shift+P to add Position so only these two properties are displayed in the Time Layout window.

Both Anchor Point and Position appear to have the same values on the X and Y axes, so how do these numbers differ? Move the layer in the comp window and notice that only the value of Position has changed. The value of Position is *the position of the layer's anchor point relative to the comp* (the Position's X and Y axes are in comp space).

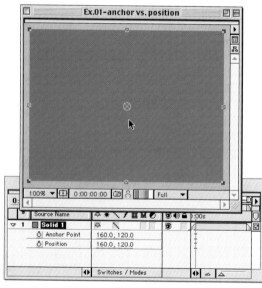

The Anchor Point X and Y values are in relative to the layer itself, and default to the center. The value of Position is relative to the Composition.

Example Project

Explore the 06-Example Project.aep file as you read this chapter; references to [Ex.##] refer to specific compositions within the project file.

Double-click the layer to open the Layer window, where you can trim layers, create masks, and edit the motion path for Anchor Point and Effects Point. We'll concentrate on moving the anchor point for now.

The anchor point (a circle with an X in the middle) is visible in the center of the layer; notice that you can't drag this anchor point around with the default settings. Check the Layer Window Options menu in the upper right corner of this window. Masks is checked by default; check Anchor Point Path instead. Grab the anchor point with the mouse and move it around. Note that only the value of the Anchor Point parameter changes in the Time Layout window. The Anchor Point value is *the position of the anchor point relative to the layer itself* (the anchor point's X and Y axes are in layer space).

Holding down the Option key while dragging with the selection tool in either window will give you a realtime update as you edit. Also, the arrow keys nudge either Position or Anchor Point by one screen pixel, depending on whether the Comp or Layer window is active, respectively. Adding the Shift key will nudge by ten screen pixels.

When you move the anchor point in the Layer window, the image will appear to move in the exact opposite direction in the Comp window. Obviously, this is not very intuitive! But the Position property has no sense of the layer; it only keeps track of where the anchor point is in the comp. Considering that the anchor point's position in the Comp window has not changed, but the position of the anchor point relative to the layer has, it makes sense that the layer is "offset" in the Comp window. Fortunately, it's easy to reposition the layer in the comp so that your layout appears unchanged. (For multiple Position keyframes, Chapter 4 includes tips for dragging or nudging an entire motion path.)

Don't forget why you're moving the anchor point in the first place: When you move the anchor point, then scale and rotate the layer, the image will anchor itself around this new position. With some images it'll be obvious that scale and rotation should happen around a certain point – the center of a wheel or gear, for instance. Because of the offset behavior mentioned above, it's best to decide on the position of the anchor point as soon as you drag the layer into the comp – before the layer's Position property has been animated over time.

Moving Anchor and Position Together

As you've discovered, in order to change the center of rotation and scale without changing your layout, you have to move the anchor point and then reposition the layer in the Comp window. But can't we do this in one step? This is where the Pan Behind tool comes in handy: It can edit two properties at the same time.

The Pan Behind tool (shortcut: Y) is the sixth tool in the toolbox. By clicking directly on the anchor point in the Comp or Layer window, you can move the anchor point while maintaining the layer's visual position in the comp. It achieves this feat by changing the value for both Anchor Point and Position at the same time. Try it in [**Ex.01**] while watching how these parameters update in the Time Layout window. Obviously, this is of little use if Position is already animating, unless you want to make a mess

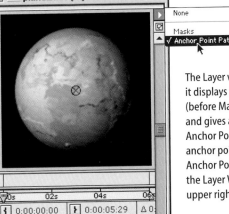

The Layer window serves many purposes: it displays a layer in its original state (before Masks, Effects, and Transform) and gives access to properties such as Anchor Point and Masks. To move the anchor point in the Layer window, Anchor Point Path must be selected in the Layer Window Options menu in the upper right corner.

Pan Behind What?

What we call the Anchor Point tool is known as the Pan Behind tool because its original purpose was to pan an image behind a window created by its mask, while keeping the mask's position stationary in a comp.

The Pan Behind tool (which we also call the Anchor Point tool) is the sixth icon in the Tool palette. It can be selected by hitting Y on the keyboard. Return to the selection tool when you're done.

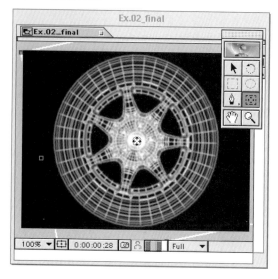

Ex.02_final

In **[Ex.02*starter]**, you'll need to recenter the anchor point to remove the wobble when the wheel rotates. You can either edit the anchor point in the Layer window, or Option+drag it with the Pan Behind tool directly in the Comp window, as shown here.

of your motion path. But if you set the anchor point in the Comp window before creating Position keyframes, it sure beats fussing about in the Layer window.

In version 4.1, you can now also use the Pan Behind tool while pressing the Option key and dragging the anchor point in the Comp window. This has the same effect as dragging the anchor point in the Layer window with the selection tool – when you mouse up, the layer's position will offset in the comp as only the value for Anchor Point is changed, not Position. But at least it allows you to move the anchor point without having to open the layer window.

A warning: Beginners sometimes mistake the Pan Behind tool for an innocent "move" tool – with disastrous results. If you have already created a mask, then you "move" the layer, the mask could be dragged completely off the layer – at which point the layer disappears. Don't panic. Undo if possible, and return to using the selection tool. If you catch the problem later on, open the Layer window, and select Masks from the menu. You'll no doubt find the mask on the pasteboard; reposition the mask shape to fix the problem.

With this in mind, as soon as you're finished using the Pan Behind tool, don't forget to immediately revert back to the arrow tool (V) before you start moving layers around. You've been warned.

Arcs, Orbits, and Transitions

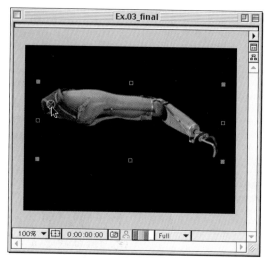

To animate the arm rising and falling using simple rotation, its anchor point (where the cursor is pointing) should be placed at the shoulder joint. Now it will rotate around its natural pivot point. Artificial arm courtesy Classic PIO/Classic Medical Equipment.

This chapter's example project file demonstrates several applications of manipulating the anchor point of a layer. For example, comp [Ex.02*starter] shows a simple 3D wireframe of a tire and wheel. The source layer has been centered in the comp, but the tire is not centered in the source layer. If you preview the animation (0 on the keypad for RAM preview), you'll see how the tire wobbles. To fix this, open the Layer window, make sure Anchor Point Path is selected from the pop-out menu, and reposition the anchor point to the center of the wheel. Zoom in the Layer window for position on a sub-pixel. Preview the animation again, and tweak until the wobble is cured, as in [Ex.02_final].

Comp [Ex.03*starter] is a trickier example, as it uses an artificial arm. The anchor point is centered in the original footage item. If you preview the comp, the arm pivots about this center, rather than moving from the imaginary shoulder joint. This time, try using the anchor point tool (Y) to reposition the anchor point at the left end where you imagine the joint should be, and preview again. Return to the selection tool (V) when you're done. If you're stumped look at our version in [Ex.03_final].

Stretch Transitions

You can create transitions in which a layer stretches from one corner or side to the other by moving its anchor point to the point where the stretch is supposed to start, then animating Scale. For instance, if you set the anchor point on the left side of a layer, and animate Scale from 0% width and 100% height, to 100% width and height, your layer will stretch open horizontally to full screen.

Composition [**Ex.04a**] shows a variety of these transitions. Study their Scale keyframes and anchor point, then try the techniques with your own sources – even text lends itself well to this effect. Comp [**Ex.04b**] takes this a touch further, coordinating keyframes so one layer appears to "push" another off as they scale. Notice that Hold keyframes are used for Anchor Point and Position so that a layer can push in from the right side, then be pushed out to the left side later.

Coordinating Anchor Point, Position and Scale keyframes allows one layer to "push" off another layer.

Orbits and Arcs

One of the simplest and most useful things you can do by offsetting an anchor point is to have one object rotate around another, as demonstrated in [**Ex.05a*orbit_final**]. RAM Preview the final result – notice that the orbit is even seamless. Let's re-create this effect from scratch:

Step 1: Open [**Ex.05a*orbit_starter**]. Drag the movie CM_ planet_loop.mov (Sources>Movies folder) to the Time Layout window so that it's centered in the Comp window. Do the same for the CM_sputnik.tif (Sources>Objects folder). It's important that both layers share the same Position value. Scale the sputnik to 20% and make sure it's the top layer.

Step 2: Double-click the sputnik layer to open the Layer window, and select Anchor Point Path from the pop-out menu. Hit the comma key shortcut a couple of times to zoom from 100% to 25%, where you'll have lots of pasteboard to work with. Move the Layer window aside so you can see the Comp window at the same time.

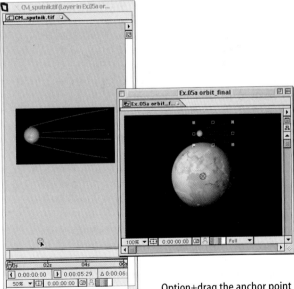

Option+drag the anchor point in the Layer window (left) until the sputnik is positioned at an appropriate orbit position in the Comp window (right).

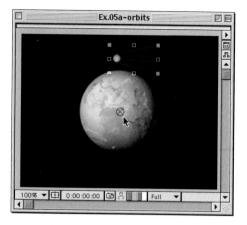

To make one object orbit another, offset its Anchor Point so that it lines up with the center of the object it is orbiting.

Step 3: With Option pressed, drag the anchor point in the Layer window until the sputnik is positioned at about 12 o'clock in the Comp window. When you're happy with the position, close the Layer window.

Step 4: At time 00:00, turn on the stopwatch for Rotation, which will set the first keyframe at 0°. For the second keyframe, drag the time marker off the end of the comp, to 06:00, one frame after the end. Click on the value for Rotation and enter a value of –1 Revolutions + 0 Degrees, and click OK. RAM preview your animation. The sputnik will revolve counterclockwise around the planet, using its new anchor point, which just so happens to be the center of the planet. It seamlessly loops because the value of the keyframe one frame after the end is a whole revolution from the starting keyframe.

You don't have to orbit in a perfect circle; sometimes you might want to have an object move through your frame in an arc. Visualize what the center of rotation would be to match the desired arc, and offset the layer's anchor point by that amount. Now, just animate its rotation. Composition [Ex.05b] shows a simple example of this. Beats making a motion path…

Separating Stacked Anchor Points

If you create two Anchor Point keyframes right on top of each other, you can't drag the anchor point to a third position to set another keyframe; you'll just end up moving the first keyframe. You'll usually encounter this situation only if you animate the anchor point, hold it in position, then continue from there. Holding in position necessitates that you have two keyframes with the same value – hence, two keyframes on top of each other in the Layer window.

One solution is to move to the point in time where you want your new keyframe, then use the "nudge" arrows in the Layer window to move the anchor point until it's free of the problem area. Now you can drag it anywhere you like. Comp [Ex.08] is set up with this problem for you to practice on. (Try moving the anchor point in the Layer window at 02:00 and notice how an earlier keyframe moves instead.)

Motion Control Moves

The ultimate use for the anchor point is for creating motion control moves, popular for panning around photographs documentary-style. Perhaps the most well-known example of this is the documentary *The Civil War: A Film by Ken Burns*. Here, numerous photographs of the American Civil War era were placed on stands, then a camera under motion control zoomed in, out, and panned around them. By introducing movement to otherwise still photography, you'll hopefully engage the audience and help tell your story. This technique is used today on a variety of source material, with either manual or motion control cameras.

This technique is easy to replicate, with greater control and higher quality, inside After Effects. It's important to start with an image that's much larger than the comp size so you can avoid scaling past 100% at your tightest zoom, which will blow up the pixels and render a softer, lower quality image. You could then just animate Position keyframes, but problems will creep in as soon as you try to simulate a zoom by animating the Scale as well. Since layers scale around their anchor point, your image may start to creep sideways unless your anchor happens to be centered in the Comp window. An example of this mistake is shown in example comp [Ex.06_final-bad]. The larger the image is in comparison to the comp size, the more exaggerated the problem becomes. Zoom down (comma shortcut) and you'll see that the anchor point starts off out on the pasteboard, so scaling occurs around this point, not the center of the Comp window.

How do you keep the anchor point centered? Easy: Center the Position, and animate the Anchor Point instead. The anchor point now becomes the crosshairs your virtual camera is aimed at as you pan around an image. Comp [**Ex.06_final-good**] shows the same move and zoom, but with animating the anchor point instead; notice that the zoom no longer makes the focal point of the image creep off screen. Position is placed dead center and does not animate.

Smooth Operator

If you need the practice, re-create a similar motion control move from scratch. Use the same image, or one of your own:

Our desire is to fake a camera move on a still so that we start tight on a tree (top left) and end up with a wide shot, pulled back and panned slightly left (top right). If we use Position to animate the pan and leave the Anchor Point centered, our pull-back will drift (bottom left). However, if we animate the anchor point to be where the "camera" is pointing, our pull-back remains framed correctly around the tree (bottom right).

Step 1: Open comp [**Ex.06*starter**]. Add the CM_BigMorongo.tif image (Sources>Stills folder) by using the Command+/ shortcut. This adds and centers the image in the Comp window. Zoom down the Comp window (Command+hyphen key on keyboard) to 50%, and position the window to one side. Consider this window your viewfinder.

Step 2: Double-click the layer to open the Layer window and resize if it's too large (Command+hyphen shortcut works here also). Make sure you can see both the Layer and Comp windows at the same time, though you'll be editing mostly in the Layer window.

Step 3: Select Anchor Point Path from the menu. Hold down the Option key while moving the anchor point, and the Comp window will update in realtime. Notice that wherever you drag the anchor point, that spot will be what's centered in the Comp window, provided the position of the layer is the exact center of the comp.

Step 4: Type A, then Shift+S, to twirl down Anchor Point and Scale. Set keyframes for these properties to taste, and ease in and out of keyframes for smoother motion. Twirl down the Anchor Point velocity graph to edit the velocity curves – the graph behaves just like Position. It might look more realistic if the rate of change is not exactly the same for both properties – real camera operators aren't that smooth!

You're not limited to panning around just photographs. You can use this technique on moving sources (remember that you want the source to be larger than the comp you are panning in, such as film or a large 3D render), or even another comp. Note that if you have more than two keyframes set for Anchor Point, the middle keyframe(s) can Rove in Time, just like Position (Chapter 4).

Connect

Stretching and squashing layers look even better with Motion Blur; see Chapter 11.

Masking, which is also accessed through the Layer window, is covered in Chapter 13.

Issues with NTSC and PAL frame sizes and pixel aspect ratios are covered in Chapters 39 through 41.

Dots, Pixels, and Inches

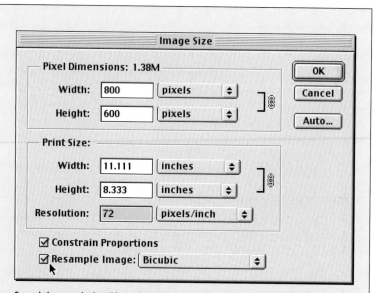

So you've decided to use After Effects as a faux motion control camera to pan around on a scan of a photo. How large should be the photo be? Good question, particularly because scanning for animation has different considerations than scanning for print. For example, there are no dpi or ppi in video and film.

Scanning for Video

When you use a scan, or indeed any image, in an After Effects project, how big will it appear? What dpi should you make it? The general consensus is that video is "72 dpi" and therefore you should set the resolution to 72. But since After Effects and Photoshop already talk the same language – the language of pixels – the dpi setting is irrelevant. Once your image is scanned, translating between pixels, inches, and dpi in the video workflow is not only unnecessary, it results in confusion.

This confusion is compounded by the mistaken belief that an image with a resolution of 300 dpi will look better than a 72 dpi image. In print, that may be the case. But with video, only the number of pixels in the width and height is important – there are no "inches" in video. Which will look better in your video animation, a 300×100 pixel image at 300 dpi, or 3000×1000 pixels at 72 dpi? The latter – because it has more pixels. The definition of "high resolution" in video is not lots of pixels per inch – it's lots of pixels. Period.

Another common misconception is that you should scan photos for video at 72 dpi. There is no perfect dpi setting, but use this rule of thumb: Capture enough pixels so that you can zoom into the image without ever setting the Scale parameter in After Effects past 100%.

Spend time exploring Photoshop's Image Size dialog, and make sure you understand how pixels, inches, and resolution balance against each other. Recent versions of Photoshop have a checkbox asking whether or not you want to resample the image. If unchecked, changing Resolution just changes the "inches" the image will take up, not the number of pixels in it. While After Effects assumes all images are 72 dpi, this is useful for programs that honor the ppi setting as it allows you to set the resolution without affecting the pixels themselves.

Full Frame: Crop 'n' Scale

If you want an image to just fill a video frame, with no zooming, scan the photo, then crop and scale the image to match your video output hardware.

- For 640×480 frames, Photoshop's Crop tool will do this in one step if you use the Fixed Target Size option set to 640×480.
- For D1 NTSC pixel aspect ratio, set the target to first crop to the square pixel size of 720×540; for DV NTSC crop to 720×534; for PAL crop to 768×576. If importing into an editing system, later scale in either Photoshop or After Effects to 720×486, 720×480, or 720×576 respectively. (More on pixel aspect ratios for NTSC and PAL in Chapters 39 & 40).

If you start with a low resolution file, the Fixed Target Size will scale up the image, blowing up pixels and softening the image. So make sure the resizing is reducing the file size. Save time in the future by recording Actions for these scaling steps.

For use in compositing apps like After Effects, we rarely crop scans in Photoshop to an exact frame size. If a full frame video image is needed, we create an oversized image of around 800×600 or higher. This applies to 3D renders as well. When you position and scale the image in a Composition, any pixels overlapping on the pasteboard are ignored (or cropped). For best results in After Effects, make the image size an even number of pixels wide and high.

Zooming: How Much Is Enough?

If you need to zoom into a detail of an image, you need enough pixels so that you don't exceed 100% scale in After Effects at the closest point. If a client requests that you "zoom in five times," this doesn't mean you scale to 500%. Plan on scanning a high resolution image and scaling from 20% to 100%.

Scanners tend to have their own preferred resolution, usually 300 or 600 dpi. We scan at either 300 or 600 dpi, depending on the size of the source, and avoid scanning at odd values like 137 dpi. If you let the scanner do its job, then resize in Photoshop, you'll get a better quality image. **The Direct Method:** Starting with an 8×10 inch photo, a 300 dpi scan creates 2400×3000 pixels.

Decide how tight you want to go in on an image (the white rectangle in this example), and make sure you scan with enough resolution so that you have enough pixels at this zoom amount to fill your comp without scaling past 100%. Image courtesy Paul Sherstobitoff.

If you're scanning a logo from, say, a business card, then 1 inch of source at 600 dpi will create 600 pixels. How many pixels is enough is determined by what you plan to do with the image.

Eyeball the scan to make sure that you have plenty of pixels to work with – this is easy to do by setting the Selection rectangle in Photoshop to a Fixed Size of, say, 640×480 and moving the selection marquee around the image. This indicates the maximum zoom level in After Effects before you'll start scaling up pixels. If you need to move in closer, rescan at a higher dpi or find a larger source to scan.

Thinking Ahead: Our preferred process is to first make a high-res scan, retouch dust and scratches, color correct, and create an alpha channel if necessary. It's not uncommon for this file to be in the 10 megabyte range. This may be overkill for video resolution, but it's insurance in case the design changes.

We save this high-res file, then save a smaller version for use in After Effects. The idea is that we have enough room to zoom in, but not excess pixels that will kill our rendering time. To test what this new size should be, we use the Photoshop Image Size dialog as a calculator:

Step 1:   Save the high-res file.

Step 2:   Select the area you expect will be the closest zoomed in view using the Constrained Aspect Ratio set to 4:3. Crop temporarily (Image>Crop).

Step 3:   Open the Image Size dialog (Image>Image Size) and set the Print Size popups to Percent.

Step 4:   Type in the desired Pixel Dimensions width and height (say, 640×480), and make a note of what percent that converts to. (If it's above 100%, you need a higher res scan.)

Step 5:   Hit Cancel, then Undo (to undo the Crop).

Use this percent value to resize the entire image, rounding up the value so you have some headroom. We save these smaller versions as "Image_50%" – the percentage is an indication that there is a high-res version available. If we later find that we still have excess resolution in After Effects (for example, scale keyframes only range from 0–50%), we may replace the image with an even smaller version of the high resolution scan to optimize rendering times.

7 Our Trusty Assistants

Tools to remove the tedium of tricky hand animation tasks.

A fter you've done a fair amount of animation, you quickly realize there are a few tasks that either you are performing over and over again, or that you find quite tedious to execute. Examples of these might be altering the velocity curves of a keyframe to get a smooth acceleration or deceleration, or giving an object a "nervous" jitter to its movement.

You might be tempted to program macros with a third-party utility program, or you might just wish that After Effects had a scripting language to allow you to execute such repetitive tasks with a keystroke or two. After Effects actually has something between the two: Keyframe Assistants. These are a number of routines, some of which come with the Standard version and more which come with the Production Bundle version of the program, that automatically create or alter keyframes and their values to execute a number of useful tasks. The assistants that help you animate layers are covered in this chapter.

Don't Lose Your Undos!

After you apply a keyframe assistant, avoid clicking around in the timeline – it will fill up the undo buffer with multiple "time changes." Instead, immediately launch a RAM preview. If you don't like the result, you can undo it more easily.

Example Project

Explore the 07-Example Project.aep file as you read this chapter; references to [Ex.##] refer to specific compositions within the project file.

Keyframe Assistants Roundup

After Effects ships with a variety of keyframe assistants. Assistants that include options have a floating palette interface (noted with an asterisk, below) and are available from Window>Plug-in Palettes. The other assistants execute when applied and are listed under the Layer>Keyframe Assistants menu. Those that relate to animating Transform properties are covered in this chapter, including:

Standard Version:

Easy Ease
*Motion Sketch**
*The Smoother**
Time-Reverse Keyframes

Production Bundle Only:

Exponential Scale
*The Wiggler**

The remaining assistants are covered in later chapters:

Standard Version:
Align & Distribute: Chapter 8*
Sequence Layers: Chapter 9

Production Bundle Only:
Motion Stabilizer: Chapter 33
Motion Tracker: Chapter 34
Motion Math: Chapter 35

Application for Employment

Assistants that you would normally apply once are found under the Layer>Keyframe Assistant menu, or by context-clicking on a keyframe. The others are found under Window>Plug-in Palettes – the reason is that these palettes remain open, so they are easy to apply multiple times.

A keyframe assistant is grayed out unless certain requirements are met. For instance, The Wiggler – which creates a number of randomized keyframes between previously set keyframes – is active only when two or more keyframes are selected. Exponential Scale, which creates a certain type of scaling curve, further requires that these keyframes be Scale keyframes.

Keyframe assistants differ from Effects in that once they are applied, they are no longer required by the project (you could apply an assistant that ships only with the Production Bundle, then open this project in the Standard version). If an assistant creates keyframes, these keyframes are not in any way "special" keyframes – you can manipulate or delete them just like regular keyframes after the assistant is done.

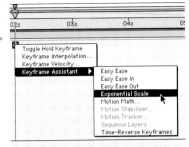

When keyframes are selected, context-clicking (Control+clicking on the Mac, right-click on Windows) on a keyframe will pop up a context-sensitive menu, where you can select most of the keyframe assistants. The others are found under Window>Plug-in Palettes.

Easy Ease

One of the most common telltale signs of inexperienced motion graphics artists is that their animations look too "linear." This criticism refers to motion where the velocity is constant – as in the ancient video game *Pong* – rather than motion with subtle velocity changes that add interest and sophistication.

The three Easy Ease assistants (Layer>Keyframe Assistants menu) tackle this problem by quickly setting the selected keyframes to have smooth beginnings or ends to their parameter changes. Easy Ease In changes the velocity curve "incoming" to a keyframe, Easy Ease Out affects "outgoing" from a keyframe. Easy Ease affects both in and out, and really should be called Easy Ease In & Out.

The Easy Ease assistants are handy but not magical – they don't do anything you couldn't do manually using the speed or velocity curves. For instance, applying Easy Ease In to a Position keyframe sets the incoming speed to 0 pixels a second, and the Influence handle to 33.33% – values you could simply enter in the Keyframe Velocity dialog by Option+ double-clicking on a keyframe.

On Edge

Of course, not all animations should be smooth. Unexpected, sudden changes in direction and velocity can impart an edgy or machine-like feel – the opposite of smooth and elegant.

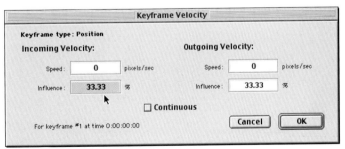

Now that you know what Easy Ease does, you can override the default settings by simply adjusting the curve or editing the values. You might not want a perfectly smooth stop every time, particularly if you're animating to music, and more rhythmic moves are needed. Smaller influence values make the action a little more hurried; larger values make it more languid around the keyframes.

Easy Ease sets the selected keyframe's parameter change velocity to zero, with an influence of 33.33%. Once applied, you can edit these values numerically, or change the velocity graph itself.

Coordinating Eases

You can apply the Ease assistants to virtually any keyframed parameter. Sometimes, it is desirable to apply the same ease (including influence amount) to more than one parameter, such as Position and Rotation. Comp **[Ex.03]** shows the benefits of this on a rolling tire.

Nervous Jitter

Motion Sketch is an alternative to creating nervous text using The Wiggler. The advantage of Motion Sketch is that you're in control – you can lightly shake a layer and then have it jump wildly in one direction. It also looks more organic. Try this with the layer in **[Ex.04c]**.

Composition [**Ex.01**] compares default linear moves (layer 1) to Easy Ease moves (layer 2), to slightly tweaked eases with more influence going out and less coming in (layer 3).

Before you get carried away with all this easy convenience, we don't recommend that you apply Easy Ease to multiple keyframes with the expectation that your animation will look better. If these keyframes were Position keyframes, for example, the layer would crawl to a stop at every keyframe. We tend to reserve eases for the first and last keyframes so that layers start and stop smoothly but continue their movement between keyframes. Preview each layer individually in composition [**Ex.02**]: Layer 1 shows ease on every keyframe while layer 2 shows ease just at the start and end, which is more natural. For the ultimate in smoothness, change the middle keyframes to Rove in Time (see Chapter 4); layer 3 shows the result.

Easy Eases are unquestionably the keyframe assistants we use most often. Fortunately, they also have handy keyboard shortcuts:

Easy Ease [In and Out]	F9
Easy Ease In	Option+F9
Easy Ease Out	Command+Option+F9

Motion Sketch

Although After Effects gives you a lot of control over creating and tweaking a motion path, it can still feel like painting with numbers rather than painting with your hand. The Motion Sketch keyframe assistant lets you trace out a motion path with your mouse (or pen, if you're using a digitizing tablet), allowing for more of a human touch. If the comp contains an audio layer, you'll hear the sound play as you sketch.

To use Motion Sketch, set up your work area in the Time Layout window to cover the period of time you will be animating over, select the layer you want to animate, then select Window>Plug-in Palettes>Motion Sketch assistant – or select its tab if you already have it open. It has a few parameters of interest: whether or not to draw a wireframe of your layer while you are dragging around, whether or not to make a snapshot of the background layers and keep that on-screen for reference, and speed. Since it can be hard to draw the exact motion we want at the speed we want it to play back at, you can slow down (or speed up) time – for example, a setting of 200% will give you eight seconds to sketch out a path that will actually take four seconds to play back.

Click Apply, and relax. When you're ready, position the cursor in the Comp window, press the mouse and drag it around the Comp window. The timeline progresses and automatically stops when the work area finishes. Mousing up also cancels the sketching, so if it keeps canceling prematurely you might be "tapping" the mouse instead of holding it down.

The Motion Sketch keyframe assistant: Your best friend in this window is the Speed control, which will allow you to sketch more slowly (or more quickly) than the path will be played back.

Once the sketch is complete, you'll notice Position keyframes created for every frame. Try this with comp [**Ex.04a**]. If you don't want to sketch to music, turn off the audio (layer 2) before you click Apply. When you're done sketching, hit the spacebar or 0 on the keypad to preview; if you don't like the results, try again. There's no need to undo first – since Motion Sketch creates a keyframe for every frame, it will replace all previous keyframes. Since it's practically impossible to edit the motion path created, check out The Smoother assistant if you need an editable path or want to remove some of the bumpiness in the motion.

Sketching to Capture Keyframe Values

It's common to create a small solid (Layer>New Solid, or Command+Y) and use it purely for capturing Position keyframes with Motion Sketch. You can then copy these keyframes and paste them into another compatible parameter, such as an effect point center, on another layer. In this way, you can mouse around to create the motion path, then apply these keyframe values to the action of, say, a Lens Flare effect. In comp [**Ex.04b-capture KFs*starter**], follow these steps:

Step 1: Apply Motion Sketch (as above) to the solid in layer 1, with the Keep Background option checked; move your mouse as you would like the lens flare to move.

Step 2: When you're done sketching, click on the word Position in the Time Layout window to select all the keyframes, and then Copy (Command+C).

Step 3: Turn off the solid layer, and move the time marker to the point where you want the action to start (00:00, say).

Step 4: In layer 2, click on the Flare Center parameter in the Time Layout window to activate its I-beam.

Step 5: Paste (Command+V) the Position keyframe values to the Flare Center track. This parameter also

Auto-Orient Sketch

To make an object like a buzzing insect really follow a sketched path, apply Auto-Orient Rotation (Transform>Auto-Orient Rotation, or Command+ Option+O). Add a rotational offset to the layer to initially align it to its path.

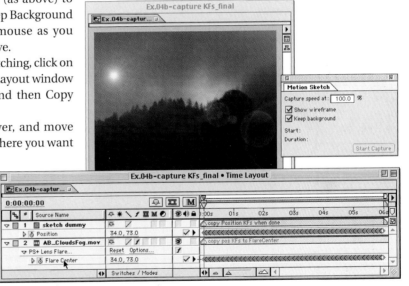

Use a simple solid layer to "capture" Position keyframes using Motion Sketch, then paste these values to the center-point of the PS+ Lens Flare effect. This technique works with any effects point parameter, so if you have a third-party effect that creates "pixie dust," say, you can create an organic motion path for the particles by simply moving your mouse or pen. Movie courtesy Artbeats/Clouds & Fog.

has values on the X and Y axes, albeit in layer space as opposed to comp space – but since in this case the comp and the movie layer are the same size, the copy/paste works as expected.

Preview to see the result. If you got lost, check out [**Ex.04b-capture KFs_final**]. We'll cover animating effects in more detail in Chapter 19, but in the meantime, bear in mind that this copy/paste trick works with any effect that has a parameter with an X and a Y axis (Bulge, Twirl, Write-on, Particle Playground, other third-party particle system effects, and so on). Remember to click on the name of the property you wish to paste into, otherwise the keyframes will likely paste to the Position track.

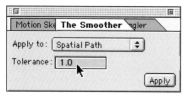

You will need to have at least three keyframes selected before you can use The Smoother.

The Smoother

The problem with the Motion Sketch keyframe assistant is that it creates a multitude of Position keyframes that are difficult, if not impossible, to edit as you would a regular motion path. And no matter how smooth we think we're drawing with the pen or the mouse, sketch paths rarely turn out as even as we would like. The Smoother keyframe assistant is designed to remove excessive keyframes, leaving behind an editable motion path. To use The Smoother, select the keyframes created with Motion Sketch (such as the ones you just created in [Ex.04] above). Then select Window>Plug-in Palettes>The Smoother, or click on its tab to bring it forward if you already have it open.

One of its parameters is a popup for Spatial or Temporal keyframes. Position keyframes in the Comp window are Spatial, because their values are on the X and Y axes. Properties that only change over time, such as fading Opacity up and down, are Temporal in nature. The Tolerance value changes depending on what type of keyframes you are editing – for example, when editing Spatial Position keyframes, it will define the number of pixels new Position keyframes are allowed to vary from the original path. Larger Tolerance values result in fewer keyframes and therefore generally smoother animation; make sure you don't overdo it.

Hit Apply and preview the results. If the animation requires further smoothing, it's a better idea to undo it and try again with different settings than to try successive applications of The Smoother. It may take a few tries to get it right, but it'll take far less time than trying to tweak dozens of keyframes by hand.

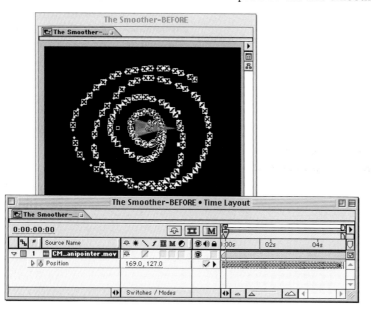

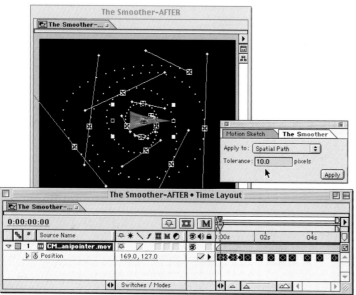

Motion Sketch creates one keyframe per frame (top). After applying The Smoother with a tolerance of 10 (bottom), the result is an editable path. Larger Tolerance values result in fewer keyframes.

Time-Reverse Keyframes

Ever built an animation, from the simplest right-to-left move to an involved dervish-like orchestration of position, scale, and rotation, only to decide it would probably work better going the other way? If you haven't, you will. And that's what this no-brainer keyframe assistant is for: flipping a selection of keyframes backward in time. No values are changed; just their location and order on the timeline. Note that this keyframe assistant works over multiple parameters and multiple layers.

Repeating an Animation in Reverse

The Time-Reverse Keyframes assistant is very straightforward, but we've set up an example for you to practice with anyway. This example also uses the technique of copying and pasting multiple keyframes.

Say you've created a nice animation of a layer scaling up while it also fades up. Now you want it to go away in the same fashion, just in reverse. In the accompanying project file, open [**Ex.05*starter**], which already has the initial fade-up move. Let's create the fade-out:

Step 1.   Select both the Scale and Opacity keyframes at the beginning of the layer (click Scale, then Shift+click Opacity), and Copy (Command+C).

Step 2.   Move the time marker to around time 02:00 and Paste (Command+V). Don't worry if the point in time you picked isn't exact, so long as it doesn't paste over any existing keyframes.

Step 3.   With these keyframes still selected, apply Layer>Keyframe Assistant>Time-Reverse Keyframes).

Step 4.   Move in time to the layer's out point (press O), or wherever you would like the layer to finish scaling down.

Step 5.   With the keyframes still selected, drag the last keyframe in the now-reversed sequence toward the time marker; add the Shift key to snap them to the time marker. The layer will now scale down and fade out over the same number of frames as the beginning, with the same velocity curves. The curves appear as mirrors of each other (see figure).

If any of this did not make sense, look at our version in comp [**Ex.05_final**] for comparison.

Reverse Keyframes, Not Frames

Time-Reverse Keyframes does not reverse the playback of frames in a movie. For that, you will need to employ Time Stretching (Chapter 10).

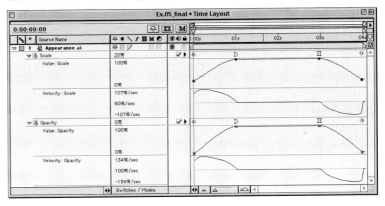

If we have an animation we like (above), we can mirror it by copying, pasting, and time-reversing the keyframes at another point in time. Note how the velocity curves are also mirrors of each other (below).

No Production Bundle?

If you don't have the Production Bundle, Exponential Scale comes with the *Adobe After Effects Classroom in a Book*. If you don't have that either, try to approximate the extreme velocity curve as closely as possible using the velocity handles in the Time Layout window.

Exponential Scale

By now, it's become obvious that a lot of After Effects is based on simple math. However, sometimes simple math lets you down. Take keyframing a simple scale, from 0% to 1000% over 10 seconds, as we've done in comp [**Ex.06*starter**] using an Illustrator layer that continuously rasterizes. With just two keyframes, After Effects neatly interpolates the scale 100% per second. But when you preview the animation, it doesn't look right at all – it starts way too fast, and ends way too slow. Why?

Our perception of scale is relative. Something scaled 200% looks twice as big as something scaled 100%. However, to look twice as big again, we need to increase the scale to 400%, not just another 100 to 300%. In [**Ex.06*starter**], twirl down Scale (S), and look at its value as you move the time marker around. From 01:00 to 02:00, it increases from 100% to 200%, but from 02:00 to 03:00, it increases only to 300%. The difference in the first second is relatively infinite – from 0% to 100% – but the difference in the last second is relatively small, from 900% to 1000%. All mathematically correct, but perceptually wrong.

The Exponential Scale keyframe assistant *(available only in the Production Bundle)* was created to cure this specific problem. When you select two Scale keyframes and apply it (Layer>Keyframe Assistant> Exponential Scale), it calculates what the scale should be at each frame to give a perceptually correct zoom. Try it with [**Ex.06*starter**]. To get a better idea of what is going on, twirl down the velocity graph for Scale and see how it looks before and after.

The only problem you might encounter with Exponential Scale is when you scale up from 0%, as the computer takes an inordinate amount of time to scale from 0% to 1%. After that it starts to pick up speed. If you're trying to get a layer to zoom toward you for a full 3 seconds in sync with a sound effect, the layer will be invisible for all intents and purposes while it scales from 0% to 1% or 2% – preview [**Ex.06*starter**] after applying Exponential Scale and see for yourself. To fix this delay, undo the keyframe assistant, and deselect (F2) both keyframes. Change the first keyframe from 0% to some small value like 2% or 3%; leave the second keyframe at 1000%. Select both keyframes again, and reapply Exponential Scale. Preview the animation, and the apparent dead time at the start of the zoom is removed. If you notice the image popping on at 2%, fade up the layer over a few frames. Our final compromise is shown in [**Ex.06_final**].

The problem with linear scaling occurs whether you are animating from 0% to 1000%, or 50% to 60% – it's just more obvious at the bigger leaps. You could apply it whenever you scale, if you wanted to be mathematically precise – and like scads of keyframes. We usually use it only in extreme zooms where we see a problem.

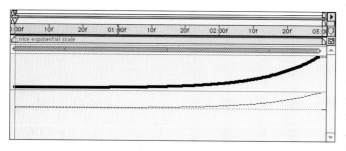

Note the velocity curve for an exponential scale – this gives a perceptually even zoom when you scale in large amounts.

The Wiggler

The Wiggler is a nifty keyframe assistant that can impart a nervous – or when used more subtly, a randomized and imperfect – quality to animations. It is most often used to automate the process of creating jumpy titles by randomizing their position values, but it's also invaluable for creating random values or deviations for any property or effect.

This assistant *(Production Bundle only)* creates new keyframes between the first and last selected keyframes, randomly offset in value from where a parameter would normally be at each keyframe's point in time. You could say it adds bumps in the road as a value interpolates from one location to the next.

To use The Wiggler, select at least two keyframes (they can even be the same value), and select Window> Plug-in Palettes>The Wiggler (or click on its tab if it is already open). The Wiggler is not affected by the work area. Options include:

Apply To: The choices are Spatial and Temporal. Spatial is available only for properties that have an X and a Y axis: Position, Anchor Point, and Effects Point. All other properties are Temporal – in other words, values that change over time.

Noise Type: Choices are Smooth or Jagged. In practice, there is little noticeable difference for many parameters. The biggest change occurs with Position keyframes, where Jagged has "broken" linear path handles in and out of the keyframes, compared with the more rounded motion of the tangential handles you get with Smooth.

Dimension: Some properties, such as Opacity, have only one parameter to change. If this is the case, the Dimension options are ignored. However, many properties – such as Position and Scale – have two dimensions (X and Y). You can choose if only one of them gets wiggled (and which one it is), if they both get wiggled The Same (same direction and same amount), or if they get wiggled Independently. All Dimensions Independently is a good default, but there may be occasions when limiting the randomness to either the X or Y axis, or moving on both the X and Y axes by the same amount, is useful.

Frequency: This is how often new keyframes are created, starting from the first selected keyframe. It can be thought of as the frame rate of the inserted keyframes. Note that if The Wiggler happens to run over a keyframe between the first and last ones you selected (because it happened to be exactly where a new one would be created by the Frequency's timing), it will overwrite that keyframe's value. Only the values of the first and last keyframe remain unchanged.

Magnitude: How much do you want a parameter randomized by? The amount of change will fall within the range set here, with larger values

The Wiggler has several options over how a keyframe's parameters are randomized.

Jagged Extreme

If the "jagged" Noise Type isn't jagged enough, select all the Wiggler created keyframes and change them to Hold keyframes (Layer>Toggle Hold Keyframes).

Simply Spatial

A common problem in getting The Wiggler to work is selecting keyframes that have values on the X/Y axes and wiggling with the Temporal option selected – try Spatial instead.

resulting in bigger changes. For instance, if the current value is 10, and the Magnitude is 8, then the keyframes created by The Wiggler will range between 2 and 18. If a property has natural limits (such as 0% and 100% for opacity), these limits will clip the amount of change. If a property (such as Scale and Rotation) can go negative, The Wiggler will swing between positive and negative, rather than getting clipped at zero.

After you have set your options, click Apply. If the Apply button is grayed out, make sure that you have at least two keyframes from the same property selected and that no other I-beams or keyframes from other properties are also part of the selection. After The Wiggler calculates the new keyframes, immediately render a wireframe or RAM preview. If you don't like the result, undo and try again. It often takes a few tries to get it right. Note that re-applying The Wiggler without undoing the first attempt will just further randomize the already-randomized keyframes you just created.

Nervous by Wiggling

Comp [**Ex.07a**] is another take on our "nervous" text we experimented with using Motion Sketch, above. Select the Position keyframes for the first layer, select The Wiggler, and try out different options. A high Frequency and low Magnitude (such as 15 and 4, respectively) are good starting points for a tight, buzzing nervousness. The other layers have some pre-wiggled keyframes for you to audition, but experimentation is the best path to understanding the effect.

If you're wiggling Position keyframes for a layer, you won't be able to easily reposition this layer in a comp unless you move all the Position keyframes by the same amount. It's a good idea to apply The Wiggler in a separate composition, then do your main positioning or motion path in a higher comp. This concept of "nesting" comps is covered in Chapter 16; in the meantime, check out comps [**Ex.08a**] and [**Ex.08b**].

Try, Try Again

The Wiggler creates a new set of random values every time you use it, even if the options are set the same. Undo and click on Apply again until you like the result.

You're not limited to the Smooth or Jagged options for The Wiggler. Once you've applied the keyframe assistant, select the resulting keyframes and change them in the Keyframe Interpolation dialog. For a really jagged animation, use Hold keyframes (shortcut: Command+Option+H on select keyframes).

Wiggly World

Remember that The Wiggler can be used to randomize values on any property or any parameter of any effect – don't limit yourself to just Position. For instance, to apply a luminance jitter for an "old movie" effect, you could animate Opacity. Open comp [**Ex.09*starter**], set two keyframes for Opacity, select them, apply The Wiggler, and preview the result.

If you find that many of the resulting keyframes have the same value and are not random enough, you may be seeding The Wiggler with the wrong starting values. For example, you'd like opacity to span a range from 50 to 100. You create two keyframes, both with the value 100%, and wiggle between them with a Magnitude of 50. However, this results in values that span plus

By wiggling Opacity values, you can introduce a luminance flicker to this old movie. The seed keyframe values of 95%, with a magnitude of 20%, result in many keyframes that are clipped to 100%. Retro Industry movie courtesy Artbeats.

and minus 50 from the starting value (100%). Since Opacity cannot support values above 100%, any would-be higher result will be assigned a value of 100. In a similar vein, if you apply The Wiggler to a parameter that cannot go below 0, any keyframes that result in a negative value will be clipped to 0.

The key to calculating the seed values and the appropriate Magnitude is to first decide on the range you'd like the keyframes to span. Use the center of this range for the value of the seed keyframes. For instance, to span a range from 50 to 100, the seed keyframes would have a value of 75. The Magnitude would be 25 (75 plus and minus 25 would span 50 to 100). Experiment to get a look you like. In [Ex.09], a seed value of 95% causes the opacity to occasionally "clip" at 100 – an effect that makes it appear the projector's light bulb is flickering.

A great way to further customize the feel that The Wiggler imparts to your animation is to change the keyframe interpolation type after it has created its new keyframes. For example, if you're applying The Wiggler to Position keyframes, both the Smooth and Jagged options create Bezier keyframes for Temporal, and Continuous Bezier keyframes for Spatial. Since both options smoothly interpolate between keyframes, if you really want a jagged animation, you'll need to change the interpolation type. Select all the keyframes, and change the Spatial or Temporal interpolation using the Keyframe Interpolation dialog from the Layer menu (or context-sensitive menu). For jagged animation, you might use Linear, or if you don't want any interpolation, then select Hold keyframes. (See Chapter 4 for a detailed description of each interpolation method.) Go ahead and try this on the wiggled text you created in [Ex.07a] above. To introduce further randomness to wiggled animation:

- Consider wiggling with fairly tight values, then manually editing a few keyframes here and there to more extreme values.
- Add additional keyframes between those created by The Wiggler.
- Move some keyframes in time to break up the frequency pattern.
- Fast animations look great with Motion Blur (see Chapter 11).

Connect

Auto-Orient Rotation was introduced in Chapter 5.

Motion Blur, which makes animation look more realistic, is discussed in Chapter 11.

Building chains of compositions through nesting and precomposing is covered in Chapters 16 and 17.

Animating effects, including editing their motion paths, is explained in Chapter 19.

Continuously Rasterizing Illustrator art is discussed in Chapter 28.

Motion Math, which can be useful for further copying and manipulating keyframes, is defanged in Chapter 35.

8 The Layer Essentials

Tips for managing multiple layers efficiently, hot keying to other programs and Layer Switches.

Scroll Layer to Top

When you twirl down a layer in the Time Layout window, the property or velocity graph you want to edit often ends up below the bottom of the window. Press X and the selected layer will scroll to the top of the TL window. (This does not re-order the layer in the stack, it merely auto-scrolls the window for you.)

Example Project

Explore the 08-Example Project.aep file as you read this chapter; references to [Ex.##] refer to specific compositions within the project file.

By now, you should know how to build a comp and how to animate layers, so let's step up to working with multiple layers efficiently. This chapter covers shortcuts and tips for managing and replacing layers, creating markers and snapshots, and editing images in their original application.

A large portion of using After Effects efficiently is to master some of the keyboard shortcuts. They may seem like brain twisters initially, but learning the most common shortcuts will mean you'll work faster – and go home earlier. After Effects usually presents more than one way to do any given task; as before, we'll concentrate on the shortcuts we use daily. Check out the Quick Reference Card, or select Keyboard Shortcuts from the Help menu, for other useful shortcuts. If you wish to practice manipulating layers, open [Ex.01] in the accompanying project file, or create your own layered composition.

Selecting Layers

Many editing techniques in After Effects affect all selected layers, so let's start with a roundup of the most useful selection shortcuts. If you use a third-party macro creation utility to create your own keyboard shortcuts, look for the selection techniques marked with an asterisk. You'll find these particularly useful as they don't rely on the screen coordinates of the Time Layout window when selecting layers:

Select a range of adjacent layers	Shift+select
Select discontiguous layers	Command+select
Select All*	Command+A
Deselect All*	Command+Shift+A (or F2)
Select layer above/below*	Command+up/down arrows
Select specific layer*	Type layer number on keypad (for Layer 10 and above, type fast!)
Invert Selection	Do from context-sensitive menu (context-click layer name or layer bar)

Moving Layers in Stack

How layers are stacked in the Time Layout window directly affects the front-to-back order of layers in the Comp window. When you add layers to a comp, these new layers are placed at the top of the stack, but you can easily move single or multiple layers up and down the stack by dragging them in the Time Layout window. Shortcuts that aid in reordering layers include:

Move layer to front	**Command Shift+] (right bracket)**
Send layer to back	**Command+Shift+[(left bracket)**
Bring layer forward one level	**Command+] (right bracket)**
Send layer back one level	**Command+[(left bracket)**

Moving Layers in Time

As you move a layer in time by sliding the layer bar along the timeline, the Info palette (Command+2) will display a realtime update as you drag. If you hold down the Shift key as you drag, the layer will snap to the time marker and other important events, such as the in and out points of other layers. This is a great boon in aligning animations. If you're moving multiple layers, only the layer you clicked on to drag the group will exhibit this snapping tendency – so choose the layer to drag wisely.

It is also possible to snap the beginning or end of layers to the current time, with simple keyboard shortcuts:

Move layer in point to current time	**[(left bracket)**
Move layer out point to current time	**] (right bracket)**

Duplicating Layers and Comps

If you want footage to appear in a composition more than once, you can drag the footage from the Project window to the composition a second time. However, if you've already animated a layer, you can duplicate selected layer(s) by selecting Duplicate (Command+D) from the Edit menu. This will duplicate all the attributes assigned to the layer, including keyframes, effects, and so on.

Another reason to duplicate a layer might be if you want to experiment with attributes, but don't want to ruin your original layer. After you duplicate the layer, turn off the visibility for one layer and experiment with the other. Delete the unwanted layer when you've determined whether the experiment worked or not.

You can also copy and paste layers, with all their keyframes intact, between comps. First, make sure that no keyframes are selected – you might even want to Deselect All (Command+Shift+A, or F2), then click on just the layer name(s) you want to copy. Then select Copy (Command+C), open or bring forward the comp you want to paste this layer into, and

You can also drag-select (or *marquee*) multiple layers in the Time Layout window, provided you're careful where you initially click. Start dragging the marquee from the # (layer number) column – you can finish dragging the marquee in the same or an adjacent column.

Trimming versus Dragging

Make sure you don't try to move a layer by dragging the triangles at the beginning or end of the layer bar – these "trim" a layer, rather than move it. We'll discuss trimming in more detail in the next chapter.

Layers, Go Home

To move selected layers so that they all start at 0:00:00:00, hit Home and then [(left square bracket). This is handy when you add new layers without first placing the time marker at the beginning of the comp.

Just the Keyframes, Ma'am

The über key (U) twirls down only the animated property tracks of selected layers in the Time Layout window, helping you focus on just the keyframes in a complex animation. A mondo shortcut! If you're opening a comp you're not familiar with, it's a good idea to select all (Command+A) and über them (U) to see what animation is taking place.

Returning to Source Name

If you've renamed a layer, and want to return it to the Source Name, hit Return, Delete (so the name is now blank), then Return a second time. This is handy if you use Replace Layer and the original Layer Name is no longer valid.

paste (Command+V). It will even remember its position in the timeline. If you had any keyframes selected (common mistake), then After Effects will copy only the keyframes, and you would either have pasted nothing into the new comp, or have pasted keyframe values into another layer (if you selected one by accident).

If you plan to experiment with multiple layers, you might want to duplicate the entire comp. To do this, select the comp from the Project window and Edit>Duplicate. The copy will be given the same name with an asterisk at the end to denote it's a copy – but you might want to rename one or both comps so you can keep track of which comp is which. (To rename a comp from the Project window, select it, hit return, type a new name, and hit return again.)

Renaming Layers

Every layer has a Source Name (the name of the source on disk and in the project window) and a Layer Name (the name of the source in a composition). Clicking on the Source Name panel header in the Time Layout window toggles between displaying Source and Layer names.

The Layer Name defaults to the source's name, but is easily changed: select the name, hit the Return key, type a new name, and hit Return a second time. Changing the name of one layer while in Source Name mode automatically toggles the panel to Layer Name view; layers that are not renamed will appear in brackets.

Renaming layers is particularly useful if you're using the same source multiple times. It also helps when the source material has an obscure name on disk, like FAB07FL.TIF, or is named by the timecode it was captured at on a certain reel (common with footage captured by nonlinear editors). You can't rename footage in the Project window, but you can add descriptive notes in the Comment field (see Chapter 2).

Replace Source

Here's one you won't want to forget. You spend time animating a layer, and are happy with the animation keyframes, effects, and other attributes you have set. But then you decide the source material needs to be changed (you want to swap out the source while keeping everything else). This is called *Replace Source*, and for some reason it's nowhere to be found on any menu. Practice the following steps to replace the source to a layer:

Step 1: Select the layer you want to replace in the Composition or Time Layout window.

Step 2: In the Project window, select the source you'd like to use instead.

Step 3: With the Option key held down, drag and drop the new source into the Comp or Time Layout window. All the attributes of the previous layer will be assigned to the new source. Instead of Option+dragging, you can also use the shortcut Command+Option+/.

You might run into a problem in which the new layer is added to the top of the stack instead of replacing the selected layer. This is caused by the program acknowledging that a layer has been added, but not recognizing that the Option key was held down. Try holding down the Option key a little longer (until the layer name updates or the frame re-renders); also, wait until any pending screen updates are finished rendering before replacing a layer to make sure the software is paying full attention.

Replace Footage

The above Replace Source feature works on a layer-by-layer basis. However, if you have a source in the Project window that's used multiple times in one comp, or even in multiple comps, you can replace the footage item in the Project window, which will update all instances in all comps. To Replace Footage, you must select the source in the Project window, and this window must be forward. From the File menu, select Replace Footage>File (Command+H).

If the new source has different attributes than the original footage, be sure to check the setting in the Interpret Footage dialog (Command+F) and make sure they are still appropriate for the new source. The biggest problem usually comes in replacing a footage item that did not have an alpha channel with one that has an alpha; you may need to re-interpret the footage if Alpha is set to Ignore.

Replacing Source or Footage does not change any new layer name you might have given a layer in a comp. After replacing, you might want to double-check the layer name to make sure it is still appropriate. If it's not, return it to the source's name: hit Return, Delete (so the name is now blank), then Return a second time.

Taking Snapshots

If you're familiar with taking Snapshots in Photoshop's History Palette, where you can revert back to a previous saved state at any time, we're sorry to say that you'll be disappointed with After Effects' interpretation of a *snapshot*. After Effects will save a snapshot as an image, but it cannot revert keyframes and other attributes back to the state associated with that snapshot. Having said that, we won't say no to any tool that helps when we're experimenting with a design. And if you keep track of what each snapshot represents, or if you can go back through the Undo buffer to revert to that state, snapshots are still quite useful.

The usual method for taking a snapshot is to click on the camera icon at the bottom of the Comp window (listen for the camera shutter sound effect). You then make a change to some attribute that updates the composition. Now click on the "man" icon to the right of the camera icon to display the contents of the snapshot, and quickly do a before-and-after comparison between the snapshot state and the current state. If you're experimenting with a color effect, for instance, and decide you like the old color better, use Undo until the old color is restored.

A snapshot taken in one window can be displayed in another window, so you can temporarily show a snapshot of the Comp window while in

Repeating an Animation

To create a second layer that has all the characteristics of an existing layer, duplicate the first layer, then replace the duplicate layer with a new source by selecting the duplicate layer, and Option+dragging a new footage item from the Project window into the Time Layout window. Both layers will animate in exactly the same manner. Now move the duplicated layer to the point in time and/or position in the Comp window that you need it to play at. This is a great trick for opening titles in particular, where all titles animate in a similar fashion, just offset in time from each other. Note that updating the first, original layer will not update any duplicates.

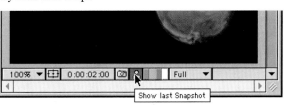

Two more odd icons explained: The camera icon allows you to take a snapshot of the current rendered state of a composition. After you make changes, you can compare the new current state to your saved snapshot by clicking and holding down the man icon (immediately to the right of the camera icon) to display the last snapshot.

Hot Keying to External Programs

You will find many occasions when you will be working with a piece of source material, have already partially animated it, then decide the source needs more work – for example, retouching a photo in Photoshop, or editing some Illustrator art. You could make the changes, then reload the footage. However, After Effects also lets you directly open the source in the program that created it and track changes when you're done – without having to find the file on your disk. This process goes by the names of Edit Original or *hot keying.* These are the steps:

Step 1: Select a source in any window, then Select Edit>Edit Original (shortcut: Command+E).

Step 2: After Effects will look at the file for a "creator" tag, then open the file in the program that created it (assuming you also have this program on your disk). You will need enough RAM to open both programs simultaneously.

Step 3: *Optional:* If you want to maintain a copy of this original file before you start editing, use the Save a Copy feature (not Save As) from the other application.

Step 4: Make your changes. When the changes are complete, save the file.

Step 5: Return to After Effects. As soon as After Effects is brought to the foreground, it will check to see if the file it's monitoring has been modified since you hot keyed, and if it has, it will automatically reload it.

If you're having problems making the hot key work, it's worth bearing in mind how After Effects is tracking the file. Let's say you select a Photoshop file and invoke Edit Original. After Effects sends the file to Photoshop and starts "watching" this file on disk. But it pays attention to only this particular file name, which is why protecting the original by doing a Save As with a new name in Photoshop (see Step 3) won't work – this renamed file is not the one being watched.

Also, the first time you return to After Effects after selecting Edit Original, it checks the source's "last modified date" on the hard drive – if it's been

If an original image had no alpha, and you add one when you hot key into Photoshop, when you return to After Effects the alpha channel will be ignored.

updated, the file is reloaded. Not only that, After Effects checks the status of this particular file only the *first* time you return: If you forgot to save and need to return to Photoshop, then you save the file and return to After Effects a *second* time, the file will not be reloaded. If that's the case, select the file in the Project window and manually invoke Reload Footage (Command+Option+L).

Another anomaly you will encounter is that if you add an alpha channel (in Photoshop, for example, by adding a New Channel) to what was originally an RGB-only file, After Effects will ignore the alpha channel when you return. Not only will it ignore it, but it will get into a weird state in which even Reload Footage or Replace Footage manually will also fail to update the source. The Interpret Footage dialog will even insist that the source has no alpha, period. The only way to update the source is to import the updated footage again and use the Replace Source feature to swap out the old source in the comp. Then delete the old source from the project list.

If you know you need to add an alpha channel, a better approach is to use Save As in Photoshop, give it a new name, then add the alpha channel. In After Effects, use Replace Footage to replace the old file with the new file. The Alpha will be set to Ignore in the Interpret Footage dialog, but at least you can override it and turn on the alpha. This method avoids the weird state noted above.

Hot keying is also useful for sources created in Adobe Illustrator, so you can quickly bounce back and forth adjusting titles and artwork. (Problems with alpha channels don't apply here.)

the Layer window or Footage window, and vice versa. This helps for comparing treated and untreated versions of layer, or for matching up different frames in time. You can also view just one channel from a snapshot: For example, click on the comp's alpha channel (the white button at the bottom of the Comp window) before displaying a snapshot to view the alpha channel only.

As of After Effects 4.1, there are four independent snapshots, which are found under the F5 through F8 keys (F5 being the original snapshot as described above). You need to use a shortcut to access these additional snapshots:

Take snapshot	Option+F5, F6, F7, F8
Display snapshot	F5, F6, F7, F8

Just remember that snapshots have no power to revert your comp to a previous state (instead, keep saving under new version numbers), and that they cannot be saved or rendered to disk. However, the four snapshots are retained in memory during a single After Effects session, even when different projects are opened. You can discard snapshots using Edit>Purge>Snapshots.

Align & Distribute Keyframe Assistant

When you're working with multiple layers, you'll find the Align & Distribute keyframe assistant handy for quickly and accurately tidying up the positions of layers in a composition. You access Align & Distribute from Window>Plug-in Palettes. To use this keyframe assistant, select more than one layer, and click on the icon for the option you want.

Align attempts to line up some feature of the selected layers (*whether they are visible or not* – be careful with your selections), such as their centers or an edge. Distribute spaces out these features equally, rather than forcing them to be the same. In some cases, the relative positions of the selected objects have a big effect on the result. Unlike what you might suspect, it does not look at a user-specified layer to be the reference or "anchor" for an alignment or distribution.

After Effects can "see" the edges of the full dimensions of a layer, or the edges of any masks you created for the layer inside After Effects. However, it cannot detect where the visible edges are for any alpha channel a layer might have (where's the "edge" of a glow or soft feather?). It also does not use the anchor point for any centering-based align or distribute. This reduces its usefulness for irregularly shaped or oddly framed sources.

If you decide to align the top, bottom, left, or right edges of a set of layers, After Effects will look for the top-most, bottom-most, left-most, or right-most edge of the selected layers and align all the selected layers to that point. For centering, it uses the average center point of all the selected layers.

After Effects Feng Shui

You can re-arrange and resize most of the information panels in the Time Layout window to create a layout more harmonious with your working practices. Context-click on the panel headers to hide and show panels.

What Does That Icon Do?

If you forget what some of the icons and switches in the various After Effects windows do, make sure Tool Tips are enabled (Preferences> General>Show Tool Tips), place your mouse cursor over them, and pause a few seconds without clicking. A short line of text explaining it will appear. If you're still stumped, remember the key words it displays, and use them to search the On-line Help.

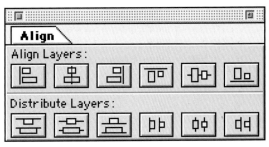

The Align & Distribute Plug-In Palette is handy for adjusting the positions of layers in a composition.

Mark That Spot!

One of the most valuable tools in After Effects are markers: tags you can add to a comp or layer in the Time Layout window. These help remind you where major (or even minor) events and other important points in time are. Once you've placed markers, you can use them to quickly navigate in time in a comp, as well as to Shift+drag layers and keyframes to more easily align events.

Comp Markers

There are a total of ten *comp markers* per comp, which can mark the major sections in the animation. Set a numbered comp marker by typing Shift+Number (0 through 9) from the keyboard (not the numeric keypad) – the numbered marker will appear in the timeline's ruler area. Once you've set some markers, jump to the marked times by typing just the number again (0 through 9). Delete comp markers by dragging them to the "marker well" on the right side of the timeline. You can also create comp markers by dragging them out of this well (the next unused number will be used). Add the Shift key while you're dragging to make them snap to other significant points in the Time Layout window.

Layer Markers

If you need to mark specific frames in a layer, use *layer markers* instead. Layer markers attach to the layer, so if you move the footage along the timeline, the markers move with it.

In addition to noting important events in the footage, they are particularly useful for marking audio events and beats (more on this in Chapter 30). You can create an unlimited number of layer markers per layer. Since they can contain comments as well, they are an excellent tool for annotating what is happening in the animation in a comp, either to remind yourself later, or before handing a project off to another animator. (Indeed, we've used this technique extensively in the example projects for this book.)

To create a layer marker, select a layer and position the time marker at the point in time where you'd like

Comp markers appear as numbers (0–9) along the timeline and mark points in time in the composition; layer markers are the triangular icons that are attached to layers; these can be named.

a marker to appear. Hit the asterisk key (* on the numeric keypad, not the keyboard), and a triangle-shaped marker will appear on the layer. You can double-click directly on the marker to name it, with a limit of 27 characters. If you know you want to name a marker before you create it, add the Option key (shortcut: Option+*) and name it as it is created. To delete layer markers, Command+click directly on the markers one at a time. Snap to layer markers by holding down the Shift key as you drag the time marker along the timeline.

When you nest one composition inside another, any comp markers in the first comp will appear as layer markers in the second comp, named with their respective numbers. However, layer markers created this way do not stay in sync if you later change the comp markers in the first comp.

Two Drag Markers Bugs

There are two odd little bugs associated with markers in After Effects:

• You cannot drag a comp marker all the way to the left in the Time Layout window; it stops one frame off. You can set a comp marker at that time, however; you just can't drag it there.

• When a comp is set to 29.97 fps, the Info palette displays the wrong time when dragging a layer marker; the time displayed is one frame earlier than the marker.

In the Distribute cases, After Effects has to do a little thinking. It looks at the relevant edges or centers of the selected layers, decides which two are at the furthest extremes in the dimension you have asked to distribute in, then sorts the remaining layers in order of their relevant positions. It will

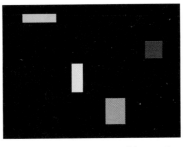

then reposition the layers between the two at the extremes, taking pains not to swap the relative positions of the middle layers.

Comp [**Ex.02**] is set up with a few different-shaped objects for you to experiment with. Just remember that you have to select at least two layers for Align and Distribute to do anything, and that you can always Undo (Command+Z). This keyframe assistant usually works as expected, but we've also seen some odd results that we can't explain...

Color-Coding

You might have noticed that different types of layer sources – such as movies, stills, audio, solids, and other compositions – tend to have different colored layer bars in the Time Layout window. There is rhyme and reason behind this: After Effects automatically assigns these different types of sources *Labels*. You can override

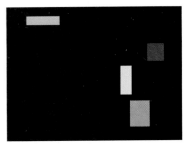

When distributing layers, After Effects looks at the relative arrangement of the selected layers in [**Ex.02**] to decide what to do. In this case (left), the two top-most objects are at the left and right extremes, while the lower objects are randomly placed between them. Distributing their centers horizontally (right) keeps the first two in their respective positions, since they are at the horizontal extremes, and averages out the horizontal spacings of the remaining layers without swapping their respective horizontal positions. Note that no vertical positions moved.

these label colors in three places throughout the program:
- In the Time Layout window. Context-click on the label for a layer, and select a new color. (If the Labels column is not visible, context-click in the Panels header, and enable Panels>Labels.)
- In the Project window. Make sure the Labels column is visible (same procedure as in the Time Layout window); you may need to open the Project window wide enough or resort the panels so that the Labels column is easily accessible. Context-click on the label for a source, and change its color. This new color will be used when you add the footage to a comp, but footage that has already been used in a comp will retain its original color.
- Change the default-assigned label color preferences (File>Preferences>Labels). This changes the color for any newly imported or newly created layer and their sources.

You can also select all similarly labeled items in the Project or Time Layout window through context-clicking on any color icon, which can be a handy shortcut for selecting a group of layers.

Connect

It's not possible to animate the layer order, but the Split Layer feature described in Chapter 9 provides a usable workaround.

Nesting compositions inside other comps is explained in Chapter 16; its relative Precomposing appears in Chapter 17.

Audio issues, including setting markers to beats in the music, are the subject of Chapter 30.

The Interpret Footage dialog is discussed in more detail in Chapter 36.

Other important chapter linkages are mentioned in the sidebar, *Beswitched*, on the next page.

Beswitched

The central hub of the Time Layout window are the switches that control everything from visibility to motion blur.

We've introduced a few of these switches here and in earlier chapters, and will explain more of the simpler switches below. Other switches are so involved that they benefit from a whole chapter to explain their inner workings and options, and these will indeed be covered in upcoming chapters, as noted below.

A/V Features Panel

This panel houses the switches for Visibility, Audio, and Lock, as well as the keyframe navigator arrows when a property is set to animate. The column defaults to the left side of the Time Layout window, but we personally prefer to move it to the right, adjacent to the timeline, where the keyframe navigator is more easily accessible.

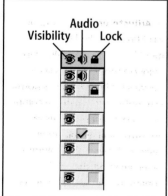

The visibility, audio, and lock/unlock switches are identified by eyeball, speaker, and padlock icons.

Toggle Switches Drag!

You can now drag your mouse up or down a range of layer switches to change the status of all the switches in one go. To change the status of a discontiguous group of layers, Command+click to select the layers and Option+click one layer to change all selected layers.

- **Visibility:** The eyeball turns on and off visibility for a layer. Layers that are turned off take no rendering time, unless they are used by another layer as a matte or an effect's map. Note that you can still set keyframes and other attributes for a layer that has its visibility turned off. You can "solo" a layer with the Hide Other Video shortcut (Command+Shift+V). However, Show All Video (Layer> Switches>Show All Video) does not revert – it turns on all layers regardless of their previous state.
- **Audio:** The audio switch turns on/off audio tracks, should the layer be audio-only or have an audio track attached.
- **Lock (Command+L):** When you lock a layer, you can no longer select it, delete it, move it, or edit any of its keyframes. This is typically used to prevent accidental changes. Layers that are locked will "flash" in the timeline if you

try to select them or move any of their keyframes. You can, however, change the status for many of the switches when a layer is locked, such as its visibility and quality. Command+Shift+L will Unlock All Layers (Layer>Switches menu) in a comp, whether the layers are selected or not.

Switches/Modes Panel

The Switches panel shares space with the Modes panel. Press F4 to toggle between them or click on the Switches/Modes button at the bottom of the Time Layout window. The Modes column is where you select Transfer Modes, Track Mattes, and Preserve Transparency (the T column) – these are all covered in later chapters (12, 14, and 15 respectively).

Back in the Switches column, if there is a gray box under a given column, this switch is available for a given layer. The Layer Switches consist of, from left to right:
- **Shy:** Layers that are set to be shy can be hidden from display in the Time Layout window, though they will still render and behave normally otherwise. To label a layer as being shy, click on the "Kilroy Was Here" icon and he'll go into hiding. Click the Shy switch again to Un-shy the Layer. To hide shy layers from displaying, click on the master Hide Shy Layers switch above the Panels.

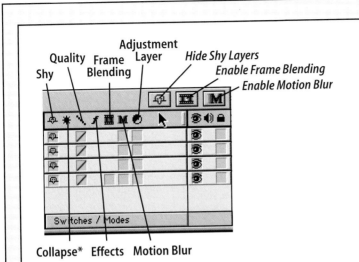

Quality **Adjustment**
Shy **Frame** **Layer** *Hide Shy Layers*
Blending *Enable Frame Blending*
Enable Motion Blur

Collapse* **Effects** **Motion Blur**

* Collapse Transformations or Continuously Rasterize

Switches define several important rendering and layer management properties, and the current values for any twirled-down properties are displayed in this area. Additionally, the three buttons along the top are comp-wide "master" switches for Shy, Frame Blending, and Motion Blur.

You might want to make layers shy to simplify the Time Layout window, or to hide layers that were failed experiments (in that case, be sure to turn the Visibility off as well). We also use the shy switch to indicate which layers are used as mattes or maps for other layers, and should render with their visibility off (we don't actually Hide Shy Layers, we just use the status of the shy switch as a guide); in a complex animation, it's easy to turn on a layer's visibility by mistake.

• **Collapse** (Chapters 18 and 28): This switch is available only when the layer is a nested composition (where it controls collapsing and consolidation of transformations), or an Illustrator layer (where it determines if the vector art will continuously rasterize or not).

• **Quality** (Chapter 4): This switch toggles between Draft and Best Quality. The default is Draft Quality. Click the dotted line to switch to Best Quality, which turns on anti-aliasing and subpixel positioning.

• **Effects** (Chapter 19): This switch is active only when effects are applied to a layer. You can turn on and off all the effects for a given layer with this one switch – a stylized "f" means effects are on; an empty gray box means they are off. Switches for individual effects appear in the A/V Panel when they are twirled down. Note that the effects switch can be overridden in Render Settings (Chapter 43).

• **Frame Blending** (Chapter 11): This feature will create new frames by blending together adjacent footage frames, if the footage has

been slowed down or otherwise has fewer frames per second than the composition. A check mark means it has been enabled; an empty gray box means it has not. The master Enable Frame Blending switch along the top determines whether enabled layers will display inside the Comp window with frame blending (which incurs an extra rendering hit); the comp's master switch can be overridden in Render Settings.

• **Motion Blur** (Chapter 11): Turning on this switch for layers animated by After Effects will render them with a natural, film-like motion blur. A check mark means it has been enabled; an empty gray box means it has not. The master Enable Motion Blur switch determines whether enabled layers will display in the Comp window with motion blur (which also incurs an extra rendering hit); as with frame blending, the comp's master display switch is overridden by the rendering controls.

• **Adjustment Layer** (Chapter 21): Effects applied to an adjustment layer will affect all layers below in the stack. This switch decides if a layer behaves normally (empty gray box in the column underneath) or becomes an adjustment layer (black/white circle is visible in this column). When enabled, the original content is ignored, and effects applied to the layer affect all layers below, using the adjustment layer's alpha channel and opacity setting.

9 Trimming the Fat

Learning how to edit layers through trimming, splitting, and sequencing.

After Effects is stronger vertically – stacking layers to create a single rich image – than horizontally – editing together various layers back to back in a linear fashion. However, there are several tools within the software to help in editing and sequencing layers. This chapter will cover trimming layers to remove unwanted frames, splitting layers in two so different pieces of time can be manipulated separately, and using Sequence Layers, a nifty keyframe assistant for automatically arranging multiple layers end to end, with optional overlaps.

In	Out	Duration	Stretch	:00s	01s	02s	03s
0:00:00;16	0:00:37;17	0:00:37:02	100.0%				
0:00:00;00	0:00:02;29	0:00:03:00	100.0%				
0:00:01;05	0:00:04;04	0:00:03:00	100.0%				
0:00:01;20	0:00:02;15	0:00:00:26	100.0%				
0:00:01;02	0:00:01;20	0:00:00:19	100.0%				

Expand or Collapse the In/Out/Delta/Stretch pane

Clicking on the "expansion arrow" (where the cursor is currently pointing, with Tool Tip open) reveals or hides the columns for in, out, duration, and speed of all the layers in a comp.

Example Project

Explore the 09-Example Project.aep file as you read this chapter; references to [Ex.##] refer to specific compositions within the project file.

The Ins and Outs of In and Out

Before we delve into trimming, let's sort out what we really mean by the terms *in point* and *out point*. They have different meanings, depending on whether you are talking about a layer or how a layer is being used in a composition.

As you've seen, when you add a movie to a composition, the position of the current time marker determines the initial in point of that layer in the comp. Depending on the duration of the layer, the out point will follow accordingly. You can move the layer to a different range of time inside the comp. You can also trim a layer's own in and out points to determine what portion of the layer is going to be used inside a comp.

If you want to numerically check where these end points (and a layer's duration) are in relation to this comp, click on the expansion arrow at the bottom of the Time Layout window. You will now get columns that list In point, Out point, Duration, and Time Stretch of each layer inside this comp. (We'll deal with Stretch – the speed – in the next chapter.)

Open the project for this chapter on the CD, and open comp [Ex.01]. Click on the center of the layer bar and slide the bar left and right to move it in time – notice how both the In and Out point values update, while Duration remains the same. Now double-click the layer to open the clip in its Layer window. The Layer window shows you the original, unedited source. Below the displayed frame is a timeline and another time marker. Notice that when you move the time marker in the Layer window, it also moves in the Time Layout window, and vice versa.

Below the Layer window's time-line is a trio of timecode numbers: these display the In point, Out point, and Duration of the layer, *regardless of where it is placed in the comp.* If the layer and comp both start at 00:00, the values in the Layer window and Time Layout window will appear identical. But don't let that lull you into thinking they must be the same thing. If any trimming or sliding takes place, then the time marker in the Layer window shows you where you are in time in the *layer*, relative to its current location in the comp.

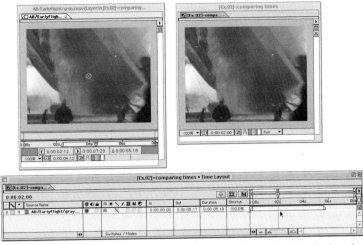

The Layer window (top left) displays the original source, before any attributes have been applied; it also shows any trimming you have done, regardless of where it is placed in a comp. If a layer does not line up with the beginning of a comp, note that their relative time markers – although synchronized – display different numbers, reflecting this offset. Hindenburg disaster footage courtesy Artbeats/Early Flight.

Trimming Layers

Trimming a layer instructs After Effects to "ignore" unwanted frames. These frames remain as part of the source and can be restored at any time. You can also trim audio tracks and still images, although since all frames are the same in a still, trimming merely changes the duration of the image in the animation.

There are two ways to trim a layer, and the results vary with the method. Depending on what you're trying to do, one method might be more convenient than the other:

Method A: Trimming in Time Layout Window

This is the more straightforward method. In [**Ex.02**], drag the triangles at the ends of each layer to trim out unwanted frames (watch the Info win-dow – Command+2 – for exact values). The layer bar becomes "empty" to denote the frames that have been trimmed. Add the Shift key as you drag to have the triangle snap to the current time marker. If you have the In/Out/Delta/Stretch panel open, note that the in and out points of the layer in relation to the comp change as you drag the triangles, and the duration will update accordingly.

Most importantly, the frames that you keep appear at the same rela-tive time in the comp's timeline as they did before – trimming in this manner does not slide the content of the layer relative to the comp. You can then drag the trimmed layer anywhere along the timeline, as needed.

The keyboard shortcuts for trimming with this method are so incred-ibly useful you'll rarely drag triangles – plus the shortcuts work across multiple layers. Select the layer(s), move the time marker to the correct frame, and type:

Trim IN point to current time	Option + [(left square bracket)
Trim OUT point to current time	Option +] (right square bracket)

Custom Panels

You can also context-click on the In/Out/Delta/Stretch panel to decide which individual parameters to hide or open.

Precision Trimming

Clicking on the In and Out point values in the expansion panel opens a dialog box; edit these values to move the clip in time. However, be warned that changing the value for Duration does not trim frames, it time-stretches the clip.

In the Layer window, clicking on the left curly bracket trims the layer's in point to equal the current time.

Out of Bounds

Frames that end up before time 00:00 or extend past the end of the composition are automatically ignored – there's no need to trim them.

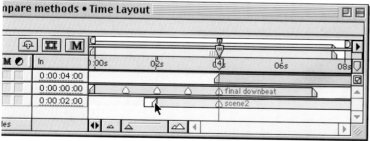

In comparing trimming methods in **[Ex.02b]**, you'll notice that trimming unwanted frames in the Time Layout window in Step 3 means that the cut point in the movie remained aligned with the downbeat at 04:00. This is not the case when trimming frames in the Layer window (Step 4).

Method B: Trimming in Layer Window

The second method for trimming requires that you double-click the movie to open it in the Layer window. Do this with the layer in [Ex.02a], find the frame you'd like as the new in point, and click the In button (the left curly bracket). Similarly, move to the frame you would like for your ending frame, and click the Out button (the right curly bracket). The Duration value for a layer changes as you trim. You can also drag the triangles to set the in and out points; the time code will display the new values in realtime as you drag.

So what's the difference between methods A and B? Make a note of the in point of the trimmed movie in the Time Layout window. Now change the in point again in the Layer window. No matter what frame you pick as your new beginning frame in the Layer window, the in point in the comp remains the same. In other words, *trimming the in point in the Layer window honors the in point set in the Time Layout window.* If you had determined that a movie needed to start at a specific frame in the entire animation, trimming with this method is the more direct route. However, the frames that you're keeping (and their associated keyframes) will move along the timeline when you edit the in point with this method, meaning the content of the layer will slide relative to the comp.

Comparing Methods

If the subtle differences between trimming methods are still unclear, compare both methods in the following scenario:

Step 1: Open [Ex.02b]. Frame 02:12 is where the second scene of the Hindenburg disaster starts (where it cuts to the close-up shot). A layer marker is placed on this frame. We've decided that this cut in the movie needs to sync to the final downbeat in the music at 04:00, which is where the title also pops on. We've set a comp marker there, so press 4 (on the keyboard) to jump to time 04:00.

Step 2: Drag the movie's layer bar so that the layer marker denoting frame 02:12 aligns with 04:00 in the timeline. The in point should now read 01:18 in the comp. Hit Page Up/Down to jog back and forth and check that the cut happens at 04:00 exactly.

Step 3: Method A: Now trim the movie layer's in point in the Time Layout window by dragging the triangle at the front of the layer. Drag the in point to 02:00, which aligns with another downbeat in the music. Note that the frame at 04:00 in the Comp window does not change, only the in point relative to the comp does. Double-click the movie to open the Layer window, and notice that the in point is at 00:12 in the movie.

Step 4: Method B: For comparison, undo (Command+Z), which will set the trim point back to 00:00 in the Layer window. Now trim the layer's in point directly in the Layer window to 00:12 – note that the layer marker (the cut in the movie) no longer synchs to 04:00 in the comp. By trimming in the Layer window, the in point in the comp remained static at 01:18, and the movie was forced to slide along the timeline.

Obviously, it's not difficult to slide the layer back so that the trimmed movie starts at 02:00. So, at the end of the day, there's not that much difference between both methods – except that one method will usually get you where you want to go more directly. So when you trim, try to determine whether keeping the in point in the timeline is important (trim in Layer window if so), or if it's more important to keep a specific frame in the movie aligned with a particular point in time (trim in Time Layout window if that's the case).

Don't Forget the Keyframes

No matter which trimming method you use, be aware that any keyframes applied to the layer are "attached" to specific frames of the layer, not the comp! The necessity of this should be obvious – if you drag the layer bar in time, the keyframes need to go along for the ride. The problem is that when you trim a layer,

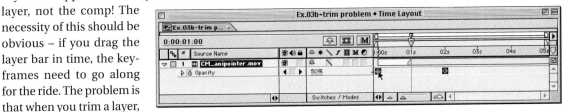

you will also trim out any keyframes attached to the unwanted frames. As a result, you may need to move the keyframes after trimming so that they begin at the new first frame. For example:

Step 1: Let's say you fade up a layer over two seconds, with Opacity keyframes from 00:00 to 02:00, as we have in comp [**Ex.03*starter**].
Step 2: Now trim out the first second of the movie by dragging the front triangle of the layer in the Time Layout window. At this point (1:00), the Opacity value is already at 50%, halfway through the fade-up, and the layer pops on rather than fading up from 0%. This is shown in [**Ex.03b**].
Step 3: To fix, select both Opacity keyframes, and move them so that the fade-up begins at 1:00. The final fix is in [**Ex.03c**].

Splitting Layers

You can split a layer at any point along the timeline, creating two separate layers from one. To see it in action, select a layer, move the time marker to where you'd like the in point of the second segment to begin, and invoke Split Layer (Edit>Split Layer, or Command+Shift+D). Open the In/Out/Delta/Stretch panel and make a note of how the layers align: The second layer begins one frame after the first layer ends. (In case you're wondering: Yes, splitting is the equivalent of duplicating a layer, and trimming the first layer's out point, and the second layer's in point. It's just more convenient.)

In Versus In

To hammer it home again: The in and out points in the Time Layout window represent the start and end points of the layer relative to the comp's duration, while the in and out points in the Layer window are relative to the original source movie. You could say that getting a handle on trimming depends on what your definition of the word *in* is…

Opacity keyframes at 0 and 2 seconds fade up a layer over two seconds. However, when the first second of the movie is trimmed, the keyframes will need to be moved also. This is a problem to watch for whenever you trim a layer, whichever trim method you use.

Careful with That Axe, Eugene

You can't "rejoin" two layers after you have split them (short of undoing); they are now two separate layers. However, since both retain a full set of their original keyframes, you can usually delete one and retrim the other to cover the original duration.

Sequence Layers

New in version 4.1 is a time-saving keyframe assistant, Sequence Layers. Layers can consist of movies or stills and be different sizes and durations. What Sequence Layers will do is organize the layers end to end, in the order in which you select them, beginning at the in point of the first layer selected. It can even add automatic crossfades.

To sequence layers, set up the layer stack in the order in which you'd like the layers to sequence, either from the top down or the bottom up (such as in **[Ex.06a]**). Select the layer that will be the first layer in the sequence, then Shift+click the last layer to select a range. Under the Layer>Keyframe Assistant menu, apply Sequence Layers. If you don't need any overlap, just hit OK, and the layers will be laid out sequentially along the time line.

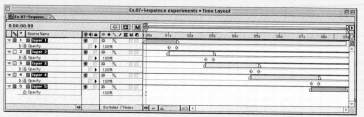

After you have selected a group of layers (left), Sequence Layers will arrange them in time, with defined overlaps and Opacity keyframes (below).

To apply an automatic crossfade, turn on Overlap Layers and set the overlap Duration. You then have the choice to crossfade the Front layer, or both the Front and Back layers. By *front* and *back*, After Effects is referring to the stacking order in the comp. In **[Ex.06]**, undo your previous Sequence action, and try out the various options, initially with a ten frame or so overlap. Twirl down the Opacity keyframes to see what is being done: the shortcut is to Select All (Command+A) and hit T. Preview the results to see how the crossfades look.

If you select to crossfade only the front layer, the layer on top in the Time Layout window will have Opacity keyframes applied to where it overlaps in time with a layer underneath, but the layer underneath will not get opacity keyframes over the same period of time. This is the preferred way to work if all the layers are full frame (or the same size and in the same position) – the one on top (in front) dissolves to reveal the one underneath, which is already at full opacity.

If you select the front and back option, the layer in front (on top) will be set to fade out while the layer in back (underneath) fades in over the same period of time where they overlap. This is preferred when the layers are different sizes, in different positions, if they have alpha channels (for example, text) or are otherwise irregularly shaped.

If you plan on using a transition effect, you can set the Crossfade type to Off and use Sequence Layers to just create the overlaps.

When sequencing a series of still images, you may wish for all layers to have the same duration. In this case, drag them to the comp as a group so they share the same in point. Then move in time to where the out point should be. With all layers selected, use the shortcut Option+] to trim all layers in one go. Now apply the Sequence Layers keyframe assistant to space them out.

Depending on the duration of each individual layer compared with the duration of the comp, some layers may extend beyond the end of the comp. If that's the case, undo, trim, or delete layers as necessary, and reapply Sequence Layers. Be careful that your transition duration is not as long as or longer than the layers; otherwise, Sequence Layers will not work.

There's nothing special about these two layers at this point – you could overlap the ends or crossfade one section into another if need be, or continue splitting one of the layers again.

Why and when would you split a layer? The most obvious reason is when you'd like a layer to change places in the stacking order in the middle of your animation, which allows for an object to appear to both go first behind an object and then in front of it. Comp [Ex.05*starter] shows an object animating behind a planet from left to right, then right to left. The idea is that the object should go in front of the planet for the right-to-left move:

Step 1: At time 01:00, the object (CM_anipointer.mov) is at its right-most extreme. Select it, and Edit>Split Layer. The layer will split into two sections.

Step 2: Move the second segment to the top of the stack in the Time Layout window. Preview, and now the object passes behind the planet, then in front.

Another important use is to avoid the rendering hit from an effect that's eating time, even though the parameters are set to have zero effect. If the effect doesn't start until the end of the layer, split the layer and apply the effect just to the second part. Most newer, well-written effects don't do this, but there are no doubt a few out there that still do. We also often split layers when frame blending and time remapping as blending incurs a render hit even when the speed is normal (100%).

One consequence of splitting a layer is that both resulting layers will contain all the keyframes applied to the original layer. However, since these layers after splitting are now completely independent from each other, their keyframes will not remain in sync with each other. If you make a change to one layer, you may have to copy and paste the keyframes to the other segment to avoid an animation glitch where the two segments join. If the changes are extensive, delete the other segment and repeat the split layer step. For this reason, it's best to avoid splitting a layer until the animation is locked down.

Advanced Technique: If the animation is constantly changing but you need to split the layer sooner rather than later, you might consider pre-composing the layer *before* you split it. Select the layer and Layer>Pre-compose; in the Pre-compose dialog, select Option #2 (Move All Attributes), and hit OK. Now all the animation keyframes will appear only in the precomp. Split the layer (now a nested comp) in the original comp as many times as you need. If you need to edit the animation, Option+double-click to open the precomp; any changes you make in the precomp will be updated automatically to all the split segments in the original comp.

Splitting a layer and re-ordering it so one segment is lower in the stack and the other is higher allows the same object to appear to first go behind the planet (top), then later go in front of it (above).

Connect

Time navigation shortcuts in the Time Layout window were discussed in Chapter 3.

Time-stretching is covered in Chapter 10.

Frame blending is explained in Chapter 11.

Precomposing is covered in more detail in Chapter 17.

Time remapping (time-stretching with curves) is unraveled in Chapter 31.

10 Stretch, Reverse, and Blend

Not a new aerobics exercise, but techniques to change the speed of movie clips and smooth out the results.

Reality is fine, but not always what you need. Sometimes, you need a captured movie to play back faster, more slowly, or even in reverse. In this chapter we'll discuss these techniques. Since keyframes usually get dragged along in the process, we'll also discuss how best to manage this. Finally, there is an option known as Frame Blending that can smooth over jerkiness in motion that can result from speed changes.

Time Stretch

The Time Stretch feature can be used to speed up or slow down video, audio, and nested comp layers. Time-stretching affects any animation already applied to masks, effects, and transformations, so speed changes also apply to keyframes. (If you need the speed change to vary over time and be keyframeable, you'll need the more advanced Time Remapping feature, covered in Chapter 31.)

When you speed up a movie (time-stretch value of less than 100%), frames in the movie will be skipped, as there will be fewer frames in the comp to accommodate all the source frames. Likewise, when you slow down a movie (a stretch value of more than 100%), source frames will be duplicated as necessary.

If you'd like to ensure that frames are duplicated in a consistent fashion, use a multiple of 100%. For example, a stretch value of 400% will play each frame four times. To blend the frames rather than simply duplicate them, turn on Frame Blending (see below).

If a movie layer contains audio, the audio will also be time-stretched and resampled. If you don't want to time-stretch the audio track, duplicate the layer and turn Audio off for the original and Visibility off for the duplicate. One layer can now play just video and be time-stretched, while the duplicate layer can be set to play the audio only, unstretched.

You can approach entering a time-stretch value from three angles:
• you have a stretch value that you'd like to use, or
• you know what duration the layer needs to be, or
• you know where you'd like the in or out point to extend to (but don't necessarily know what the duration should be).

You can experiment with these options with comp [**Ex.01**]. Expand the In/Out/Delta/Stretch column in the Time Layout window by click-

Stretching Stills

Don't stretch stills – particularly by large amounts. Keyframe precision will be compromised, and strange anomalies can occur. If you need to extend a still, drag the end triangle to extend its length. Then stretch selected keyframes by Option+ dragging the last keyframe.

Example Project

Explore the 10-Example Project.aep file as you read this chapter; references to [Ex.##] refer to specific compositions within the project file.

ing on the expansion arrow, and click on the value for Stretch. This opens the Time Stretch dialog (also available from Layer>Time Stretch).

You can enter a value for New Duration, or a value for Stretch Factor in % (higher being slower). Notice that when you change the Duration, the Stretch Factor updates accordingly, and vice versa. The Hold In Place option sets the origin point around which the stretching occurs (the layer's in point, current frame, or out point). Hold In Place defaults to Layer in-point, which is probably the most useful.

An easy way to time-stretch is to move the time marker to the point in time where you'd like the movie's out point to stretch to, and simply Command+click on the Out value in the panel. You'll usually end up with an odd value for the stretch amount, but it saves guessing values when you have a specific end time in mind.

• To stretch the in point of a layer to the current time, Command+click the value for In in the In panel, or use the shortcut:

Stretch in point to current time   **Command+Shift+, (comma)**

• To stretch the out point of the layer to the current time, Command+click the value for Out in the Out panel, or use the shortcut:

Stretch out point to current time   **Command+Option+, (comma)**

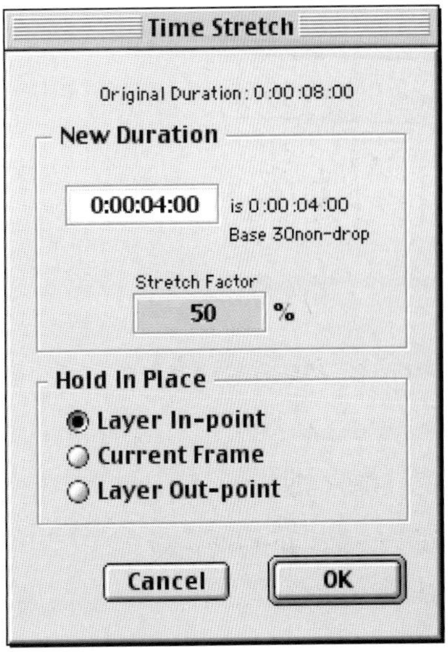

Stretching Animations

If the layer is a nested composition, time-stretching it will have the appearance of stretching all the layers in the nested comp. Any keyframes applied to layers inside the precomp will be adjusted accordingly, retiming the animation. This is a handy way to adjust the speed of an animation containing graphics and type animation, where the motion is later deemed to be too slow or too fast overall. If any of the layers in the nested comp are movies, though, you may want to avoid time-stretching them and stretch just their actual keyframes (see the related topics below), lest you also change their speed.

Going in Reverse

If you need a movie to play from back to front, you can easily reverse the playback direction using the following shortcut:

Reverse Layer   **Command+Option+R**

Practice using [**Ex.02**]. The layer bar will display with "barberpole" lines, and all keyframes applied to the layer will also be reversed. The shortcut will apply a time-stretch value of negative 100%, while also moving the in and out points so that the frames play in the same position of the timeline as before. (If you don't

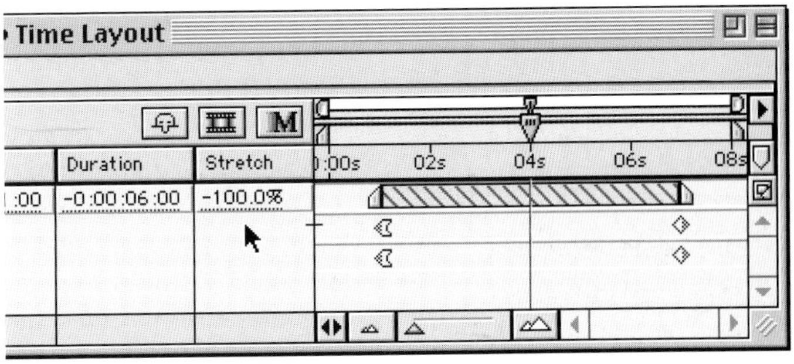

Target Frames

If you need a specific frame of a movie to appear at a certain time, without moving the in point, temporarily trim the out point of the layer to the target frame. Then move to the desired point in time, and Command+Option+, (comma) to align this temporary end. Then extend the out point back to its original point.

When a layer is reversed, the layer bar will exhibit "barberpole" lines; Time Stretch reads as negative 100, and the Duration is displayed as a negative value also.

Time Stretch

Original Duration : 0 :00 :08 :00

New Duration

0:00:04:00   is 0 :00 :04 :00

Base 30non-drop

Stretch Factor

50   %

Hold In Place

◉ **Layer In-point**
○ **Current Frame**
○ **Layer Out-point**

Cancel   OK

Time Layout

		Duration	Stretch	0 :00s	02s	04s	06s	08s
:00		-0 :00 :06 :00	-100.0%					

Stretching Effects

When creating a particle system effect, such as a tornado, the shape and velocity of the effect are usually co-dependent on each other. Create the shape of the tornado in Comp 1, nest this comp in a Comp 2, and time-stretch the nested comp to a desirable speed. The stretch factor should affect just the velocity while maintaining the original shape.

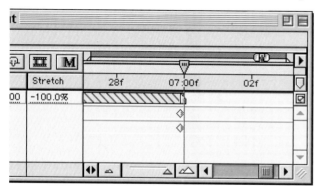

When you reverse a layer, the shortcuts for in and out point are reversed. Use the Go To In Point shortcut (I) to move the time marker to the out point. Zoom in on the out point, though, and you'll notice that the time marker has actually ended up one frame too far (it's a bug), so the frame appears blank. Also, keyframes are also reversed, but since they were attached to the beginning of a frame in time, they now align to the end of a frame so they appear a bit off. For these reasons, we recommend you reverse layers in a precomp.

use the shortcut and time-stretch by negative 100%, the layer will reverse itself around the in point, and you'll have to move the layer in time.) To return the layer to regular playback, reverse the layer a second time.

Backward Drawbacks

Once a layer is reversed, the shortcuts for in and out points are also reversed – confusing to say the least. You'll need to press I to jump to the effective out point, and O to jump to the in. Also, due to the manner in which After Effects calculates where a frame begins and ends, when you press I to jump to the last frame of a reversed movie, it will appear blank as you're actually one frame late. (Rather like moving to frame 10 in a ten-frame movie, where you have only frames 0 through 9.)

Navigating in time in the Layer window is also backward: Going forward in the original source now goes backward in the comp. More annoyingly, keyframes when reversed appear off by one frame in the timeline (since they are attached to the beginning of a frame in time, they attach to the end of a frame in time when reversed, which makes them appear to be one frame off).

Because of these drawbacks, we recommend you reverse the layer in a precomp. Not only will the layer shortcuts behave normally, but you can choose whether or not to reverse any keyframes:

Step 1: Open the [**Ex.03*starter**] comp. Select the AB_RetroHealthcare movie to be reversed, and select Pre-compose from the Layer menu.

Step 2: Give the precomp a useful name (such as Movie_reversed), and select option #1, Leave All Attributes. Click OK, and a new comp will be created that contains only the original source movie. Any keyframes will remain in the current comp, though you'll need to twirl down the layer again (or hit U to see animated properties).

Step 3: Option+double-click the precomp layer to open the precomp. Select the movie and reverse the layer (Command+Option+R).

Step 4: Return to the original comp. The layer will now play backward, but the keyframes will not be affected, and navigation shortcuts will work as expected. If you need to also reverse the keyframes, use the Time Reverse Keyframes keyframe assistant. If you get lost, check out the [**Ex.03_final comps**] folder.

The drawback to the "reverse in the precomp" technique is that you may lose your edits for the segment of the movie you wanted to see. If you have already trimmed the layer, open its Layer window, make a note of the in and out times, then precompose as above. Open the precomp and trim the movie to these same times in the Time Layout window; now reverse the layer. The same segment of the movie will be used in the original comp. Practice using [**Ex.04*starter**]; our results are in the [**Ex.04_final comps**] folder if you want to compare your version.

Frame Blending

Frame Blending is often used in conjunction with footage that has been time-stretched or time-remapped; otherwise, After Effects defaults to repeating or dropping frames for time-adjusted footage. Frame Blending interpolates between original frames and creates new blended frames, resulting in smoother slow or fast motion.

You don't have to time-stretch to use Frame Blending. You can frame blend any movie layer that does not have an original frame for every composition frame, so low frame rate movies (10 or 15 fps) can be blended in a 25 or 29.97 fps comp. Frame blending is desirable only when the source movie's frame rate is more or less than the comp's frame rate.

If you apply frame blending to a layer that has the same frame rate as the comp, it often won't appear to do much of anything, aside from slowing down your render (because it is still calculating, regardless). For this reason, don't use frame blending unless the effect is worth the rendering time and is actually needed.

Also, you may notice that footage fluctuates between blurred and sharp frames on some layers – trying an odd time-stretch value, instead of an even multiple of 100%, may help.

Frame-blended layers set to Draft Quality calculate blending using the two nearest frames. If the layer is set to Best Quality, After Effects will

Time Smear

Frame blending works for movies that have been sped up as well. If you render a high frame rate movie, use Frame Blend to get a "time smear" look.

Extreme Slo-Mo

Frame blending a movie that's been slowed down by a large percentage often staggers between blurred and sharp frames. We add the Wide Time plug-in from the Final Effects Complete package to blend the frames even more, then prerender this element.

Keyframe Behavior Tips

When you time-stretch or reverse a layer, any keyframes already created are also time-stretched. To avoid this happening, take your pick from the following workarounds:

- Before you time-stretch the layer, select any keyframes you do not want to have stretched. Cut these keyframes, then stretch the layer. Paste the keyframes back to the now-stretched layer – the pasted keyframes are unaffected by the stretch command.

- The built-in frame rate of the movie can be overridden in the Conform Frame Rate setting (select movie in Project window and File>Interpret Footage>Main). If you enter a lower or higher value, you'll slow down or speed up the movie before it even reaches the comp. For example, a 30 fps movie that has been conformed to 10 fps will play every frame three times, exactly what would happen if you had time-stretched by 300%. The advantage to

manipulating the frame rate by conforming is that you can change it as many times as you like, without ever having it affect keyframes. Since frame rate is calculated to 1/65536 fps, you can even conform to decimal values, such as 3.75 fps, and enter values as small as 0.01 fps. See also the sidebar *Slow Blended Grunge* later in this chapter.

- Apply the time-stretch in a precomp (see *Backward Drawbacks* for steps). This will time-stretch the movie before the keyframes, not after, and the keyframes will remain untouched in the original comp. If the movie is being slowed down, you'll also need to change the duration of the precomp, under Composition Settings, to match the new duration.

- Time Remapping (Chapter 31) is like time-stretching on steroids, plus it does its magic *before* masks, effects, and transform keyframes.

- If you forget to work around the problem, stretch selected keyframes back to their original position by Option+dragging the first or last keyframe.

In this sped-up explosion movie in **[Ex.05]**, compare no frame blending, blending in Draft Quality, and blending in Best Quality. Footage courtesy Artbeats/Reel Explosions 3.

use up to eleven frames: the current one (if the current time exactly lands on a frame of the source), plus five frames before and after – with a corresponding increase in render time. To see the differences in these looks, open comp [Ex.05] and solo the various layers.

Applying Frame Blending

To turn on frame blending for a layer, check the Frame Blending switch (the movie strip icon) in the Switches panel of the Time Layout window. The switch will be unavailable if the layer is a still image or nested composition; you can frame blend only a movie or sequence of stills.

Once frame blending has been checked on for a layer, you can choose whether to display the frame blending as you edit. The Enable Frame Blending checkbox determines whether the blending is calculated or not – it's common to check on frame blending for a layer, but leave the Enable

To enable frame blending per layer, set the checkbox under the movie icon for that layer. To see its results displayed in the comp, also turn on the Enable Frame Blending button (the larger film frame icon along the top of the window).

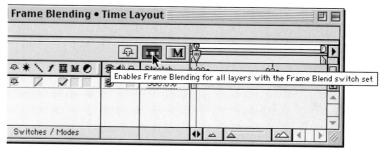

Frame Blending button off in the comp to avoid the rendering hit while you work. If you do turn on Enable Frame Blending and find the slow-down unacceptable, be sure to turn off the Enable button rather than uncheck the frame blend switch for the layer (unchecked layers will never render with frame blending on).

The Enable Frame Blending button can behave recursively: it also turns on the Enable switch in all nested compositions. Depending on how the Recursive Switches (File>Preferences>General) checkbox is set, press the Control key when you use Enable Frame Blending to use the opposite setting.

When you render your composition make sure that On for Checked Layers is set in Render Settings for the Frame Blending menu. This will ensure that all layers that have their frame blend switch checked on will render with frame blending, regardless of whether a comp's Enable button is on. It should be obvious that the frame blend switch is what's really important – the Enable button is for display only and can be over-ridden easily in Render Settings. The other options available when rendering are Current Settings, which indeed follows the status of the Enable switch, and Off for Checked Layers, which is useful for rough proofs as it will render all layers without frame blending.

Connect

The Time-Reverse Keyframes assistant was covered in Chapter 7.

Building hierarchies are the focus of Part 4, starting with Chapter 16. More details on Recursiveness in Chapter 18.

To time-stretch with velocity curves, see Time Remapping (Chapter 31).

The Posterize Time effect produces a "low frame rate movie" effect without slowing down the movie (Chapter 32).

More on Interpret Footage in Chapter 36.

When time-stretching movies that have had 3:2 removed, certain percentages produce more even results (Chapter 38).

Time-stretching audio is invaluable for keeping audio in sync if you've conformed the frame rate of a movie (Chapter 38).

More on Render Settings in Chapter 43.

Slow Blended Grunge

Working with grungy footage is a lot of fun, particularly if the client will let you go a little nuts. But if the job calls for something less than eyeball-popping, you can still use the grungy textures – just slow them way down and add frame blending.

This tutorial **[Ex.06*starter]** uses just seven frames from a film grunge movie from EyeWire's PaintFX CD. We're going to slow down the movie, frame blend it, and use it for a background:

Step 1: Select the movie EW_PaintFX.mov in the **[Ex.06*starter]** sub-folder in the project window, and note its duration – just seven frames long at 30 fps. Open the movie from the Project window and check it out; notice that each frame is quite different.

Step 2: Open the comp **[Ex.06*starter]** and add the movie to it. The movie will be very short compared with the comp's 10-second duration.

Step 3: With the Project window forward, select the movie and hit Command+F to open the Interpret Footage dialog (under File>Interpret Footage>Main). Under Frame Rate, type 3 for Conform Frame Rate; this will slow the movie down to 3 fps, or one frame every ten frames. Click OK. The movie will now have a duration of 02:10. Better, but not long enough for our 10-second comp.

Step 4: Reopen the Interpret Footage, and under Looping, set the movie to loop five (5) times. Click OK, and the move will be 11:20 in duration.

This edited movie from EyeWire's Paint FX CD has only seven unique frames, but slowing it down to 3 fps and looping it five times greatly increases its duration.

Step 5: In the composition, the layer bar will honor the original length of the layer, so drag the end triangle past the end of the comp's time line to extend it to a full 10 seconds.

Step 6: Preview or step through the comp, and notice that each frame of the source is duplicated ten times. Now turn on frame blending for the movie (check the movie icon checkbox), then check Enable Frame Blending along the top of the Time Layout window. Do a RAM preview.

Step 7: The frame rate is still fairly brisk, so try changing the frame rate back in its Interpret Footage dialog to a slower value of 1 fps. Remember that you need to select the movie in the Project window for Interpret Footage to be available. You can change the Conform Frame Rate setting at any time without affecting layer keyframes.

Once you've mastered this example, also see the *Blending Backgrounds* CD Tutorial, which takes this idea a step further: a sequence of frames are created from one high resolution image, the sequence is frame blended, and a loopable segment is created and prerendered. Creating a seamless movie avoids the rendering hit normally associated with frame blending a layer over a long period of time.

11 Motion Blur

Life's a blur – at least, to a camera it is.

Both lines of text are moving and rotating, but only the bottom one has Motion Blur enabled.

When images are captured on film or video, objects that are moving appear blurred, while static objects appear sharp. This is due to the fact that the camera is capturing samples of time, and the camera shutter is kept open for some or all of that time. The faster the object moves, the more distance it will cover while the shutter is open, and the less distinct the image. This motion blur makes for smoother motion and is a quality often lacking in computer-generated animation.

The computer samples the movement of an image at a certain frame rate, and when you view it frame by frame, all frames appear as sharp as nonmoving images. This introduces an unattractive "strobing" effect. And if you're trying to merge computer-generated objects into a live background, the composite will look less than convincing.

With After Effects, you can add *motion blur* to any layer. It will kick in only when a layer is animated using the Transform property keyframes, although some effects can also access the built-in motion blur. It is not capable of analyzing a movie or a still, or adding motion blur just to, say, a car driving past. However, if you pan this layer from left to right, you can add motion blur to the move itself.

Be aware that this Motion Blur feature is different from the Motion, Radial, Directional, or Vector blurs offered by some effects. These all apply the same amount of blur to any source, regardless of how it is animating. The built-in Motion Blur we're referring to in this chapter is a motion vector blur, and is based on the velocity and direction of each pixel in the layer. Compared with a directional blur add-on effect, this means it automatically tracks the position, scale, and rotation of an object from frame to frame, including changes in velocity.

Check the Motion Blur switch per layer you want blurred, then turn on the Motion Blur Enable button along the top of the Time Layout window to see it displayed in the comp.

Example Project

Explore the 11-Example Project.aep file as you read this chapter; references to [Ex.##] refer to specific compositions within the project file.

Applying Motion Blur

To turn on motion blur, check the Motion Blur switch (the M icon) in the Switches panel of the Time Layout window for the layer. Once motion blur has been checked for a layer, the Enable Motion Blur button determines whether the blur is calculated for previewing in the current comp. You may want to leave the Enable Motion Blur button off to avoid the rendering hit while you work, but leave the Motion Blur switch checked for the layer. In general, check motion blur on for fast-moving, small layers, not a slow-moving background layer where the rendering hit will be huge, with little benefit.

Preview the motion blur with Enable on, particularly where the motion stops and starts. If the animation stops suddenly, the effect is of a blurred image suddenly becoming sharp, often with an unattractive "pop." Add a little ease in and out of a sudden stop so that the motion blur has the time to ramp up or down. These are compared side by side in [**Ex.01**]; preview the comp to see the results. Also, layers rotated very quickly with motion blur enabled may appear to "grow" in size. This is demonstrated in [**Ex.02**].

If you're creating a hierarchy of nested comps, and the motion blur is not working for a layer, check that you turned on the Motion Blur switch in the comp that contains the animation keyframes. For instance, if you animate a group of individual layers in a precomp, each layer needs to be set to blur – you can't just check the Motion Blur switch for the nested comp layer in the second comp.

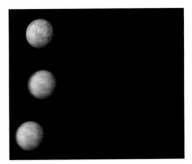

In [**Ex.01**], the top planet has no motion blur. The middle one has blur, and pops away from the side at full speed – that's why it has the most blur. The bottom planet is easing away from the side, with blur enabled; that's why it is lagging behind the others, and has less blur than the second one.

Render Settings

The Shutter Angle preference adjusts the intensity of the motion blur. It ranges from 1° to a maximum of 360°, simulating the exposure allowed by a rotating shutter in a camera. For example, in a 30 fps comp, each frame would play for 1/30th of a second, so 180° would amount to 1/60th

In Render Settings, you can override the default motion blur shuttle angle, and decide whether to follow or ignore the set motion blur switches.

of a second (50% of 1/30). Shutter Angle is set in File>Preferences>General Preferences, and defaults to 180°. The preference affects the amount of blur displayed in a comp, but it can be overridden in Render Settings.

The shutter angle value affects all layers rendered with motion blur. If you need a different shutter angle, or you want it to animate, animate the layer in question using the Transform effect (Effect>Perspective>Transform), where you can control motion blur with a keyframeable shutter angle.

When you render your composition, in Render Settings, make sure the On for Checked Layers popup is set for Motion Blur. This will ensure that all layers that have their Motion Blur switch checked on will render with motion blur, regardless of whether the Enable button is on. As you can see, the switch is what's important here – Enable Motion Blur is for display only and can be overridden in Render Settings. You can also override the Shutter Angle set in Preferences in the Render Settings, so each render queue item can have a different setting when you're batch rendering. Be aware that if you field render an animation, the motion blur intensity will appear to be half of that visible in the composition; since each field is half the duration of one frame, the blur takes place in less time.

Really Smart Blur

To add motion blur after the fact to moving objects in video footage, try the ReelSmart™ Motion Blur effect from RE:Vision Effects (www.revisionfx.com).

Connect

Building hierarchies are the focus of Part 4, starting with Chapter 16. Recursive switches are covered in Chapter 18.

Blur (and other) effects are discussed in Chapters 22 through 24.

For more extreme amounts of blur, you may need to add and manually animate the angle and length parameters of the Motion and Radial Blur effects (Chapter 23), or use third-party plug-ins.

Overriding the Motion Blur Shutter Angle and comp switch settings at render time is discussed in Chapter 43.

12 Transfer Modes

One of the most creative tools After Effects offers is blending images together using transfer modes.

Switch

To switch quickly between the Switches and Modes panels, use the F4 key.

More than One

Select multiple layers and hold down the Option key while choosing a mode to change all selected layers to this mode.

Example Project

Explore the 12-Example Project.aep file as you read this chapter; references to [Ex.##] refer to specific compositions within the project file.

We devoted the previous chapters to stacking multiple objects and moving them around in interesting ways. The next level of motion graphics mastery is combining multiple images together to create an utterly new image. And Transfer Modes are one of the strongest, most tasteful tools for doing so. In this chapter, we'll break down the method behind mode madness, and share a few of our favorite techniques for using them in real-world projects.

If you use Photoshop, you're probably already familiar with how modes work. However, most video editing systems don't currently offer modes, so if you're a video editor you're in for a treat. In the simplest terms, *Transfer Modes* are different methods for combining images together. They take some properties of one image and combine them with some properties of the underlying image, resulting in a new combination that is often far more intriguing than mere stacking. The results can vary from a relatively subtle enhancement of contrast or color saturation to total retinal burnout. If used with some semblance of taste and restraint, the result is often classy rather than gimmicky and cannot easily be identified as a specific effect. Transfer modes render fast, too.

Many artists use transfer modes through the "happy accident" method: They just try different modes until they find one they like. And that's a valid way to work, because it can be hard to predict exactly what the end result will be. But if you understand what's really going on, you'll find it easy to achieve a desired result more quickly – and even create or choose sources more intelligently, based on what you know about how they will blend together later.

Modus Operandi

To understand how transfer modes work, a quick refresher course on how After Effects calculates a final image in a composition is in order. After Effects starts with the bottommost layer in the Time Layout window, calculates the Masks, Effects, and Transformations applied to that layer, and saves this in a temporary buffer. It then looks at the next layer up, calculates its own Masks/Effects/Transformations, looks at that layer's alpha channel to see what parts of the layer underneath it should reveal and what parts to replace with the new layer, combines the two,

 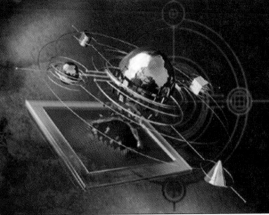

and temporarily saves off *that* composite. It then looks at the next layer up from the bottom and repeats the process a layer at a time until it reaches the top of the stack.

Important Concept No. 1: After Effects is usually thinking about only two layers at a time: the current layer, and the combination of everything underneath.

Transfer modes modify how this composite takes place. Normally, when the alpha channel of the layer on top is 100% opaque, After Effects replaces the corresponding pixels of the stack underneath with the pixels from the layer it is currently calculating. If the opacity is anything less than 100%, After Effects then mixes the pixels from the current layer and the underlying stack in a straightforward fashion – some of this, some of that. Transfer modes say: "Before we mix, let's look at some of the properties of these corresponding pixels (such as their brightness, hue, and so on), change the color values of the pixels of the current layer based on what we found underneath, *then* mix them together."

Important Concept No. 2: Transfer modes alter the pixel color values of the layer they are applied to. And these alterations are based on the image (stack of layers) underneath.

Each different transfer mode has a different set of rules (algorithms or math equations) on how it will alter the color value – the hue, saturation, and lightness – of the pixels in the layer it is working on. In many cases, a transfer mode is applied to just a grayscale layer, to enhance or reinterpret the layer underneath. However, when there is color involved (the red, green, and blue channels are different from each other), these colors further affect the outcome. This means you often see characteristics of the two layers coming through the final composite.

Important Concept No. 3: Differences in colors alter the final effect. Transfer modes do not replace or obliterate the normal masks, effects, and transformations calculated for a layer, and most important (except for modes discussed in a separate sidebar in this chapter), they do not change the transparency of a layer.

To demonstrate the effects different modes have, most of the examples in this chapter will use EyeWire's Reflections of Light movie (left) as the top layer, and a 3D illustration by Paul Sherstobitoff (right) as the underlying layer.

🔲	#	Source Name
▽ ☐	1	🎞 EW_Reflections.mov
	▷	Masks
	▷	Effects
	▷	Transform
▽ ☐	2	📄 PS_Mac3D.tif
	▷	Masks
	▷	Effects
	▷	Transform
		◀▶

If you need a reminder of the order of treatments After Effects calculates for a layer, twirl down its properties, and they will be listed in that order: Masks, followed by Effects, followed by Transformations.

Sample 1 • Time Layout

Sample 1

0:00:00:00

	#	Source Name	Mode	T	TrkMat	
▽ □	1	x3D_XrayTrumpet_loop....	Add ▼			◉
		Ŏ Opacity	75%			◉
▷ □	2	DV_AllThatJazz_singer....	Color Dodge ▼		None ▼	◉
▷ □	3	DV_AllThatJazz_trumpe...	Multiply ▼		None ▼	◉
▷ □	4	DV_NakedScared_gold.tif	Normal ▼		None ▼	◉

Switches / Modes

Click on the Switches/Modes button to toggle between Switches and Modes. The Transfer Modes are the left-most menu in the Modes panel.

After Effects offers an extensive list of transfer modes, most of which will be familiar to Photoshop users.

Normal
Dissolve
Dancing Dissolve

Add
Multiply
Screen
Overlay
Soft Light
Hard Light

Color Dodge
Color Burn

Darken
Lighten
Difference
Exclusion

Hue
Saturation
Color
✓ Luminosity

Stencil Alpha
Stencil Luma
Silhouette Alpha
Silhouette Luma

Alpha Add
Luminescent Premul

transfer modes

:00:03:10

	#	Source Name	
□	1	AB/SkyEffects..	
□	2	si Elliptic C	one
□	3	LR_0379.TIF	one

Film Glow

To add some of the magical puffiness and glow that film can impart to footage, duplicate the layer. For the top copy, apply a blur effect and select Screen mode; adjust opacity and blur amount to taste. This is demonstrated in [**Ex.08**].

Mode Swings

Every layer in a composition automatically has a transfer mode applied to it. The default mode is Normal, which means no changes in color value. Each layer can have only one mode, and you cannot animate mode changes on one layer (although we will often stack up multiple copies of the same layer, with different modes set to each, and blend them using opacity). The trick for many users comes in finding the mode switches, so you can indeed change them.

In the Time Layout window, under the Layer Switches panel, is a button labeled Switches/Modes. If it's not visible, context-click one of the visible panels and select the Switches/Modes option, or use the handy F4 shortcut to toggle back and forth. Click on it, and this panel will now change to display Modes (as in, Transfer Modes), T (Preserve Underlying Transparency, discussed in Chapter 15), and TrkMat (Track Mattes, discussed in Chapter 14).

Technically, transfer modes alter the color values of the layer they are applied to. You can alter the opacity of this layer and reveal more or less of the otherwise unaltered stack of layers underneath. Despite this, we find it easier to understand modes in terms of "what this layer does to the layers underneath." That's how we'll describe most of them, and you will come to see this as you work with the example projects and look at the illustrations throughout this chapter.

To simplify explanations, we will discuss stacking two layers, with the transfer mode always applied to the uppermost layer. If there are additional layers underneath, during rendering they will be composited into what becomes the "lower" layer, anyway. Some modes have the same effect regardless of the order of the layers – that is, of two layers, either one could be on top and have the mode applied to it; the final would be the same. Others look different, depending on which is being "moded" on top of the other.

Compositions [**Ex.01a**] and [**Ex.01b**] have been set up for you to experiment with different modes applied to the uppermost layer. [**Ex.01a**] uses a simple black-and-white radial gradient as the upper layer, which makes the lighting effects of different modes easier to see. [**Ex.01b**] uses two layers with colors. When you're done playing with [**Ex.01b**], set the layers back to Normal, reverse the order of the layers, then experiment with modes on the new uppermost layer to see the differences stacking order makes. The nonspecific examples shown in this chapter all come from [Ex.01b].

Lighting Effect Modes

These modes generally alter the brightness or darkness of the composited image. As a class, they are often used to make a section of the image brighter (sometimes to the point of blow-out) or darker (sometimes to the point of being completely "in shadow").

Add

Technically, the color values of the selected layer are added to the values of the layer underneath, resulting in a brightened image, clipping at full white. The order of the two layers does not matter. If one of the images is black, no change will take place; if one is white, the result is white.

Preview [**Ex.02a**] to see the effect of an all-white layer in Add mode being faded up over another image – the underlying images goes from looking normal, through an uneven blow-out (since brighter parts of the underlying image clip out at full white before the darker parts do), to all white. One of our favorite techniques is to composite a grainy film flash over a transition to hide a cut underneath such a blow-out, demonstrated in [**Ex.02b**]. The best flash layers go between all black and all white; you may need to increase the contrast of your "flash" layer with the Adjust>Levels effect (Chapter 24) to get the strongest effect.

Layers set to Add mode generally brighten the underlying image.

Transparency Modes

In general, transfer modes alter color values, not transparencies or alpha values. However, a few modes do indeed alter transparency. Some of these modes are covered in detail in upcoming chapters, and a brief summary of the others will be given here:

Dissolve

Dissolve creates a paint-spatter effect. It's based on a transition supported by many multimedia applications, since they often could not support partial transparency. A percentage of this layer's pixels are made transparent based on their opacity: lower opacity, more transparent pixels.

The result overrides normal opacity and alpha channel calculations, since there is no partial transparency with Dissolve. If the layer has no alpha channel or feathered masks and is set to 100% Opacity, this mode will appear to have no effect.

Dancing Dissolve

Like Dissolve, but self-animating. Which pixels are transparent changes every frame, even if their opacity is not changing.

Stencil/Silhouette Alpha/Luma

Transparency is cut out of all the layers underneath, based on either the alpha channel or the luminance values of the selected layer. See Chapter 15.

Alpha Add

Has essentially no effect unless the alpha channels of two layers share an edge or seam. In this case, Alpha Add will then help fill in that seam. See Chapter 15.

Luminescent Premultiply

Some sources with premultiplied alpha channels can have problems with their edges being overly bright – for example, some synthetic lighting effects (lens flares). Their color information is stronger than it should be for a true "premultiplied" image. If you are having edge problems with these images, Interpret Footage as Straight Alpha, and try using this mode to composite the layer in a comp. See TechTip 03 on the CD.

Multiply mode tends to darken images.

A black-and-white layer (left) applied in Multiply mode over another image (center) can appear to act as a matte (right), although transparency is not actually created. Footage courtesy EyeWire/TextFX and Senses.

Screen mode blends images as if projected on the same screen.

Multiply

Technically, the color values of the selected layer are scaled down by the color values of the layer underneath, resulting in a darkened image, clipping at full black. The order of the two layers does not matter. If one of the images is black, the result will be black (since you will be scaling the other layer with a color value of 0%); if one of the images is white, the result will be no change (since you will be scaling the other layer with a color value of 100%). Multiply has been likened to stacking two slides together and projecting the result.

Multiply is great for punching holes in or casting shadows over one layer based on the luminance of another layer. Comp [**Ex.03**] shows what

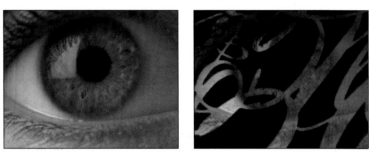

happens when a black-and-white text layer is Multiplied on top of an image; the black areas disappear, and the original image shows through the white areas – sort of like a matte. What makes Multiply different is that the alpha channel is not changed and the color – not just the luminance – of the multiplied layer influences the final outcome.

Multiply is particularly useful for compositing black-and-white images that were scanned and have no alpha channel – the fully white areas automatically drop out, saving the step of creating an alpha for them.

Screen

The opposite of Multiply: The color values of the selected layer are scaled above their original values based on the color values of the layer underneath, resulting in a brightened image, clipping at full white. (Technically, the inverse brightness values of one are multiplied by the inverse brightness values of the other, then the result is inverted. Got that?) The order of the two layers does not matter. If one of the images is black, no change takes place (the other layer is not scaled up to be any brighter); if one of the images is white, the result is white. Screen has been likened to the result of projecting two slides from different projectors onto the same "screen."

Screen can be thought of as a less intense version of Add, in that Screen does not clip as fast, and it does not approach full white as unevenly. The result can appear washed out, but if you reduce the opacity of the screened layer, it looks more like highlights, or adding light to a scene; depending on your sources, one may be preferable to the other. Go back to the comps in [**Ex.01**] and compare the Screen mode versus the previous Add mode.

Color Dodge

This transfer mode scales up the brightness of the underlying layer, based on the color values of the layer it is applied to. If the upper layer is black, the underlying layer will be passed through unaffected; if the upper layer is white, it will usually drive the result to white. The exception is if one or more of the R, G, or B channels of a pixel in the underlying layer has an original value of 0; in that case, just that channel will be left at 0 while the other channels max out, resulting in an otherwise fully bright and saturated color at that pixel. In general, it brightens the result. The order of the layers matters, with the underlying layer appearing to be more prominent in the result. If applied to the last visible layer of a stack, it will go black (since there is nothing underneath to brighten, and zero-value color channels stay at 0).

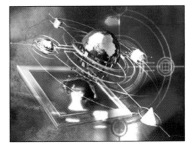

Color Dodge mode can brighten and intensify a layer.

Photoshop users will be familiar with this mode. It is often used to retouch areas of an image lighter than before, by applying a grayscale brush over the original. The fun in After Effects is that the color channels are factored in, resulting in some unusual color shifts the Color Dodged layer will impose upon the image underneath.

Color Burn

The opposite of Color Dodge: It scales down the brightness of the underlying layer, based on the color values of the layer it is applied to. In this case, a white layer will have no effect when it's color burned onto a layer underneath; a black layer will drive the image toward total black (although the alpha will still be intact); grays will evenly scale the brightness of the underlying image. In general, it darkens the result, and the order of the layers makes a difference: The underlying layer appears to be more prominent in the result. If applied to the last visible layer of a stack, it will go white.

Color Burn mode darkens and intensifies the image.

Shot on Black

Many pyrotechnic effects are shot against black, with no alpha channel. Likewise, some plug-ins create synthetic lighting effects against black. Apply the Add or Screen mode to them to drop out the black, and mix the nonblack parts of the image with opacity based on brightness. This is shown in **[Ex.02c]**. If the background is not pure black, bury its black level with the Adjust>Levels effect (Chapter 24).

An explosion shot on black (left) is composited over another image (center). The Add mode is applied to the explosion image to blend them (right). Explosion footage from Artbeats/Reel Explosions 3; background from EyeWire/FabricFX.

Altering Lighting

To add the impression of animated lighting to a scene, find a layer that has slowly changing white spots over black, experiment with Opacity, and composite with Overlay mode over your original scene. This effect is demonstrated in [**Ex.04**] and [**Ex.05**].

Overlay mode increases contrast, and as a result, apparent saturation.

The EW_Reflections layer we've been using in our examples (left) applied in Overlay mode over a movie with strong light and shadows (center) results in the light areas being affected, while the shadows stay dark (right). The Tint effect can also be applied to the lighting layer to convert it to black and white and remove the color cast. Bodybuilder courtesy EyeWire/Fitness.

Again, Photoshop users will be familiar with this mode. It is often used to retouch areas of an image darker than before. As with Color Dodge, the color channels are factored in, resulting in some color shifts as the mix grows darker and more saturated. The hardest part of Dodge and Burn is that their names may seem counterintuitive to video and film people, since "burn" usually implies an area of extreme brightness, rather than making something darker. If you find it confusing, think of these two modes as treating a negative.

Intensifying Modes

The following modes have the subjective result of intensifying the contrast and saturation in a scene. They are our favorites for creating a rich image that contains characteristics of both source layers.

Overlay

Technically, parts of the image darker than 50% luminance are *multiplied*, and the parts brighter than 50% are *screened*. In plain English, the lighter areas of the top layer will lighten the corresponding areas of the bottom layer, going to white; darker areas in the top layer will darken the corresponding areas in the bottom layer, going to black; areas that are 50% gray in the overlaid layer have no effect on the underlying layer. The result is increased contrast and particularly saturation, with the shadows and highlights still present, though altered. The stacking order makes a difference: The underlying layer appears to be more prominent in the result.

This mode is as close as they come to an "instant cool" effect, making something interesting out of almost any two layers. Once you get past the gee-whiz factor, start looking for layers that have good contrast between light colorful areas and shadows as being Overlay candidates; those dark areas will end up dark in the result, and the lighter areas will end up with an interesting color mix of both layers.

Comp [**Ex.05**] shows one typical application: The light playing across the bodybuilder's back is further infused with the color of the layer underneath, while the dark areas remain in the shadows. Given the increase in saturation Overlay usually brings, you might need to back off the opacity of the moded layer. But depending on your sources, you could also increase the intensity of the effect by duplicating the moded layer.

Soft Light

Areas lighter than 50% gray in the Soft Light layer appear to lighten the underlying image; areas darker than 50% gray appear to darken the layer underneath – although in neither case does black or white in the Soft Light layer force the final

mix to go completely black or white. Areas that are 50% gray in the upper layer have no effect on how the lower layer shows through. The stacking order makes a difference: The underlying layer appears to be more prominent in the result, but with a more even mix than some other modes. Soft Light often looks like a subdued version of Overlay, with less saturation shift.

The After Effects manual likens Soft Light to shining a diffuse spotlight on a layer. If you are going for a dramatic effect, you will probably be disappointed and feel it just looks washed out. However, if you are looking for a more subtle lighting effect without the strong contrast or tendency to go to black or white that several of the other transfer modes have, Soft Light, if you pardon the pun, shines.

Hard Light

Hard Light follows the same general math rules as Soft Light, but only much more so, with increased contrast and usually more saturation. Although an image can get both brighter and darker depending on the mix, in a similar fashion as Overlay, the result will be more

contrasty and saturated. The stacking order makes a difference, but in this case, the Hard Light layer tends to appear more prominent in the final mix than the layer underneath.

For example, if you use Overlay or Soft Light for a colorful layer on top of an all-white layer, the result will be all white; if you use Hard Light on this top layer instead, the result will be an overlit version of the Hard Light layer. If the bottom layer is black, Soft Light and Overlay give a black result; Hard Light just increases the shadows, contrast, and in particular, the saturation.

Hard Light is probably the most intense of what we call the *intensifier* modes. The After Effects manual (in case you haven't read it yet) likens it to shining a harsh spotlight on a layer. With high-contrast sources, it is more likely to be driven into saturation than clip the blacks or whites. Experiment with the various comps in the [**Ex.05**] folder on the CD, switching the mode on the uppermost layer between Overlay, Soft Light, and Hard Light.

Shot on White

An image or scene shot against a white seamless backdrop, with no alpha channel, can be hard to composite. Apply the Multiply mode to drop out the white background, and use the Levels effect to boost contrast if necessary.

Colorless

Some specific colors have no effect on the underlying image when they're used with specific transfer modes. This is not a problem; it's a feature: Select images that have these colors in the areas in the underlying image that you do not want affected, and apply the corresponding transfer modes. That way, only part of the layer on top will seem to affect those underneath.

black
> Add
> Screen
> Color Dodge
> Lighten
> Difference
> Exclusion

50% gray
> Overlay
> Soft Light
> Hard Light

white
> Multiply
> Color Burn
> Darken

Video Projection

Hard Light is perhaps the best mode to use when faking video being "projected" onto another surface. Receiving surfaces that average around 50% gray are the best; their shadows and highlights will affect the contrast of the projected layer without driving them completely to black or white in these areas.

A virtual video-cube wall was rendered in 3D, manipulating the lighting and surface color to average 50% gray (left). A video layer was then "hard lit" onto this surface (right), picking up the shadows in the creases as a result. Tai Chi movie courtesy Artbeats/Lifestyles Mixed Cuts.

Psychedelic Modes

These modes tend to create the strangest-looking (and – unless you're designing rave party or '60s acid-trip videos – arguably less useful) final composites. However, there is a hidden gem among them: Difference.

Darken

Darken mode does not just make a layer darker, but picks the darkest color from pixel to pixel.

Darken compares the color values of the two layers and uses the darker layer value. This tends to make the final result look darker. What makes this mode look so weird is that the relative brightness of each pixel is not compared; the value for each color channel – red, green, and blue – are compared individually, and the lower value for each channel is kept. If either one of the layers is not grayscale, color shifts will usually result. The stacking order does not matter, and both layers contribute somewhat equally to the final result. If one layer is white, the other layer shows through unchanged (since the other one is darker by default); if one layer is black, the result is black.

Lighten

Lighten mode is the opposite of darken – the brightest colors in each pixel are used.

Lighten is the opposite of Darken: The color values of the two layers are compared and the lighter layer's value is used. This tends to make the final result look lighter. What makes this mode look unusual is that the relative brightness of each pixel is not compared; the value for each color channel – red, green, and blue – are compared individually, and the higher value for each channel is kept. If either one of the layers is not grayscale, color shifts will usually result. The stacking order does not matter, and both layers contribute somewhat equally to the final result. If one layer is black, the other layer shows through unchanged (since it would be lighter by default); if one layer is white, the result is white.

Difference

Technically, the color values of one layer are subtracted from the color values of the other layer. You may think this would tend to make the result go toward black. The kink is, if the result is negative (a brighter color value is subtracted from a darker color value), rather than being clipped at black, the positive (or "absolute") value of the color is used instead. The result of this is that the stacking order of the layers does not matter, and both layers contribute to the result more or less equally. If one of the layers is black, the result is unchanged (since black has "zero" difference); if one of the layers is white, the result is an inversion of the other layer. As with Darken and Lighten, these calculations go on per color channel, resulting in often psychedelic color shifts.

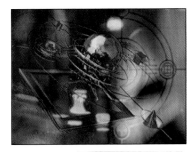

Difference mode tends to be the most psychedelic of the modes.

If both layers are very similar, however, the final image does indeed shift toward black. This opens the door to a very useful technique known as *difference matting* – when two layers are similar, only the differences between the two show through. An example would be shooting a scene with and without an actor. The result would be nearly black, except where the actor was present; here, the result would be the difference between the person and what was behind him or her. This can be used in conjunction with levels manipulation to pull a matte (see also Chapter 23). It's also handy for comparing two almost identical images to check for differences.

Exclusion

This mode is similar to Difference, except it tends to drive the final result toward gray, and the resulting color shifts are somewhat muted in intensity. The result of this is that the stacking order of the layers does not matter, and both layers contribute more or less equally to the result. If one of the layers is black, the result is still unchanged; if one of the layers is white, the result is still an inversion of the other layer. Its difference when compared with Difference is that when one of the layers is 50% gray, the result is 50% gray rather than wildly color-shifted.

Exclusion mode drives an image toward gray rather than psychedelia.

Quality Assurance

If we want to see if any artifacts or color shifts have been introduced into an image (such as by image compression), use Difference on the potentially changed version over the original, and look for any non-black pixels – these represent any changes in the image.

Alternatively, if you're having trouble lining up two copies of the same footage, use the Difference mode on the upper one and slide it in time and/or position relative to the other until the scene cancels out into black. These techniques are demonstrated in **[Ex.06]**. Actually, when a movie is offset in time and differenced, you get rather a neat effect!

Even Stranger Modes

If these transfer modes aren't psychedelic enough, apply Effect>Channel>Compound Arithmetic effect to a layer. It has even more math operations, and can apply the mode onto itself or other layers.

Hue mode combines the hue of the top layer (Reflections of Light) with the luminance and saturation of the layer below (the 3D image).

Saturation mode takes the saturation of the image on top and mixes it with the hue and luminance of the layer below.

Old to New

To suck the color out of a layer, apply a solid on top with any shade of gray, and apply either the Hue or Saturation mode to it. Since gray has no hue or saturation, it will remove any color from the underlying layer, with the result being a grayscale version of this layer. Varying the opacity of the gray layer on top will vary the amount of color removed. Animate for "black-and-white to color world" fades. This is demonstrated in [Ex.07a].

Conversely, if you want to add a color tint to a scene, try the Color mode: Add a solid on top with the color you want and set its transfer mode to Color. Opacity of this layer determines amount of tint. This is shown in [Ex.07b].

Property-Replacing Modes

The final set of modes we're going to look at takes one particular property of the uppermost layer and uses it in place of the same property for the layer(s) underneath. In this case, being able to think in HSL or HSB colorspace (rather than RGB) will be helpful in visualizing the results.

If you were to break down an image's color into three properties – Hue, Saturation, and Luminance – the following modes select which property to retain from the top layer and which properties to mix in from the layer(s) below.

Hue

Technically, the hue of the uppermost layer is combined with the luminance and saturation of the underlying layer. The final result gets the basic raw colors of the first layer, but with the brightness and intensity of the second layer. If the layer with Hue applied is a shade of gray (regardless of its brightness), the underlying layer will be shown reduced to grayscale, since the top layer has no hue. The stacking order matters, and the underlying layer will seem to contribute most strongly to the result.

Saturation

Technically, the saturation of the uppermost layer is combined with the hue and luminance of the underlying layer. The result gets the basic raw colors and brightness levels of the second layer, but with the saturation pattern of the first layer. If the layer with Saturation applied is a shade of gray (regardless of its brightness), the underlying layer will be shown reduced to grayscale, since the top layer has no saturation regardless of any colors underneath. The stacking order matters, and the underlying layer often seems to contribute most strongly to the final result. Compared with Hue, Saturation often results in less extreme color shifts, but it can occasionally result in a more posterized look.

Color

Technically, the color – the combination of the hue and saturation – of the uppermost layer is combined with just the luminance or brightness levels of the underlying layer. The result is the color wash of the top layer, but with the image details of the underlying layer. The stacking order matters; the underlying image is "repainted" with the colors of the top layer. You will probably find Color mode easier to control and predict than Hue or Saturation, since we often think of "color" as the result of these two properties rather than as individual parameters. Color mode is most useful for colorizing an underlying image. [Ex.07b*starter] has a movie layer that we want to tint. Create a solid (Command+Y), choose the color tint you want with the eyedropper or color picker, click on OK, and select the Color transfer mode for it. The underlying layer will now be tinted this color, with the highlights and shadows preserved. Vary the color tint layer's opacity, and you vary the amount of saturation in the solid's color. This works great for colorizing a stack of layers with a color wash – especially for tricks like adding an old-fashioned sepia tone to them.

Luminosity

Completing our roundup of these color property replacement modes, Luminosity impresses the color (hue plus saturation) of the underlying layer on the luminance or brightness values of the uppermost layer, which it is applied to. The stacking order matters, with the underlying layer stack "repainting" the layer on top that has Luminosity applied to it.

Luminosity is the exact opposite of the Color mode. If you were to swap the layers, and swap these modes, the results would be the same – swap the layers in [**Ex.07b**] if you don't believe us.

Luminosity mode is particularly useful for compositing an image with a strong contrast on top of a background, while maintaining the underlying color palette. [**Ex.09**] shows an example.

Summarizing H, S, L, and Color modes

To summarize the property-replacing modes, the name of the mode describes what is kept from the uppermost layer, which it is applied to. What is used from each layer can be described in this table:

top layer:	Hue	Sat	Color	Luminance
layers below:	Sat+Lum	Hue+Lum	Lum	Hue+Sat

Color (Hue plus Saturation) mode colorizes the underlying image, keeping the luminance of the layer below.

Luminosity inflicts the gray scale values of the layer on top onto the image underneath while retaining the color (Hue plus Saturation) of the underlying image.

Misc Samples

Transfer modes are one of the most effective and creative tools in After Effects. We've compiled various examples in the [**Ex.09-Misc Samples**] folder for you to explore and experiment with. You'll no doubt develop your favorites, and by understanding them better, you'll be able to pick an effective mode faster, and even design with specific modes in mind.

Images courtesy Digital Vision/All That Jazz and Naked & Scared. Trumpet 3D model treated with 3D Gear's EdgeFX.

Detective image © Corbis Images; microphone image courtesy Classic PIO/ Classic Microphones.

Connect

The Alpha Add transfer mode, which is useful in some specialized masking situations, is covered in Chapter 15.

The Compound Arithmetic effect allows many modes to be applied to any other layer, or onto the source layer without having to duplicate layers. How to use compound effects that can point to other layers is discussed in Chapter 22.

What is actually going on with Luminescent Premultiply is the subject of TechTip 03 on the CD.

13 All About Masking

*Masking tools create
transparency using
simple or Bezier shapes.*

Not all footage items look best full screen. And not all come with their own alpha channels to block out the parts you don't want to see. Therefore, we often use *masks* to "cut out" the alpha channels we need. Each new version of After Effects has improved the masking tools; version 4 introduced multiple masks and the Transform tool from other Adobe programs. Effects can use mask shapes and paths for creating animated strokes and text on a path. Masks can even be applied to simple, colored Solid layers for creating basic cel animation.

You can create masks in a variety of ways. You can draw a path using the mask tools in the toolbox, specify the dimensions numerically, or paste a path created in Illustrator or Photoshop. We'll start with drawing and editing simple rectangle and oval mask shapes, then move onto creating feathered edges. We'll continue with drawing Bezier masks, and build your expertise until you're comfortable editing multiple animated Bezier masks with Mask Modes.

Understand that as of version 4, masking got a lot more complex in After Effects; there also seems to be a lot of subtle inconsistencies that creep up when you're creating and editing mask shapes. Don't get bogged down in the details and minutiae – instead enjoy the power and flexibility they bring.

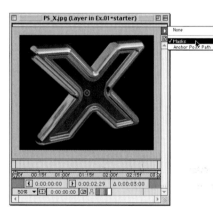

Double-click a layer to open the Layer window to draw a mask; make sure you have selected Mask mode with the Options menu in its upper right corner. X 3D render by Paul Sherstobitoff.

Example Project

Explore the 13-Example Project.aep file as you read this chapter; references to [Ex.##] refer to specific compositions within the project file.

Masking Basics

Masks are created in the Layer window, which you can open by double-clicking the layer. Do this with the "X" layer in [**Ex.01*starter**]. The first step is to make sure the Layer Window wing menu on the top right side is set to Masks, not Anchor Point Path. (Note that these two features are mutually exclusive – and it's easy to forget about this tiny menu that toggles between them, which can be frustrating when the masks you spent all day perfecting have disappeared…) If the layer window opened at 100% view, zoom down using the Command+ – (minus key on keyboard) shortcut. Arrange the Layer and Comp windows so you can see both of them clearly – although you draw the mask in the Layer window, the results are shown only in the Comp window.

Three tools in the Tools palette are used for masking: Rectangle, Oval, and Pen. You must have the Layer window forward for the rectangle and oval tools to be active.

To check out what sort of options masking offers, context-click (Control+click on the Mac, right-click on Windows) directly in the Layer window. These same options appear in the Layer>Mask menu; you can also call them up by context-clicking the Layer bar in the Time Layout window. But it's handy having the popup right in the window where you created the mask – plus the options relate only to masks.

Along with the regular selection tool, the toolbox has three other tools useful for masking: Rectangle, Oval, and Pen. Pen has uses beyond creating Bezier masks, so it is always available. The Rectangle and Oval tools are active only when the Layer window is forward as they are used strictly for masking. Let's do a quick tour through basic masking using the Rectangle and Oval tools:

Step 1: With the Layer window forward, select the Rectangle tool. Click on the movie in the Layer window and drag right and down to draw a mask. Note the result in the Comp window: The image area outside the mask is made transparent. (In other words, the layer's alpha channel is modified by the mask shape. The area outside the mask is filled with black, making the corresponding pixels in the RGB channels transparent in the Composition window.)

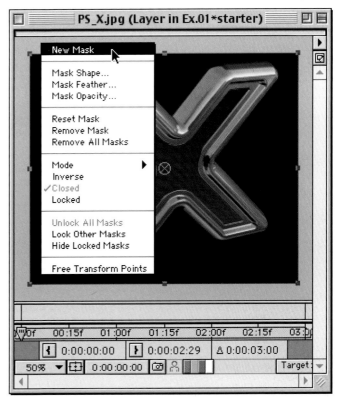

Context-click in the Layer window to bring up all the masking options. If you have not created a mask yet, only the first option – New Mask – will be active.

Simple Shape Shortcuts

The following shortcuts are handy when creating simple masks:
- Double-click the Rectangle tool, and a mask is created with the same dimensions as the layer. (You can also select New Mask from the Mask menu to create a new full-frame mask.) Warning: If a mask is selected when you double-click the rectangle tool, the existing mask will be replaced.
- Double-click the Oval tool to create an oval mask with the same dimensions as the layer. (Same warning as above.)
- Hold down the Shift key as you drag to constrain the Rectangle tool to a square, and the Oval tool to a circle.
- Press the Command key while dragging to draw a mask from the center out. Combine it with the Shift key to constrain the aspect.
- Reset Mask will convert any selected mask shape to a rectangle with the same dimensions as the layer, overriding the selected shape. Reset Mask can be found in the Mask menu.

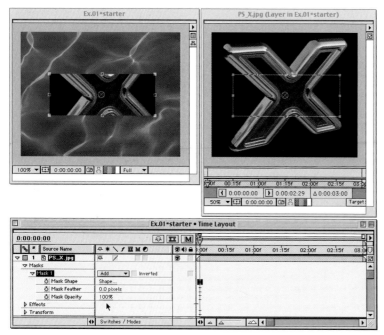

Step 2: When you create a mask, it gets added to the layer's properties in the Time Layout window. With it come several parameters, such as Shape, Feather, Mask Opacity. Background from Artbeats/ Water Textures.

Target Tip

If you're a masking novice and want to practice working with a single mask to keep things simple, create the first mask and change the Target from None to Mask 1. Each new mask you draw will replace the old mask.

If Mask Target (a popup in the lower right corner of the Layer window) is left at its default of None, every new mask you create is added to the layer's list. Select a layer as a target, and any new mask you draw or paste will replace it instead.

Step 2: In the Time Layout window, twirl down the master arrow for the PS_X layer, then twirl down the arrow for Mask. Notice that Mask 1 has three sub-categories: Mask Shape, Feather, and Opacity. The rectangle you've drawn is the Mask Shape component – we'll cover the others in due course.

Step 3: Every time you draw a mask, a new mask is created. We'll see later how to work with multiple masks, but at this stage, to avoid confusion, let's delete the first mask and reset to the starting position. The easiest way to do this is to context-click in the Layer window, which drops down the list of Mask options. Select either the Remove Mask or the Remove All Masks option.

Step 4: Select the Oval tool and draw a circular mask. Notice how the edges of the mask appear stair-stepped. This is an antialiasing issue (not a job for Feather!). Change the layer's quality from Draft to Best to antialias the edges. When checking the precision of a mask, it's worth taking the rendering hit of Best Quality to see smooth edges.

Target Practice

The unassuming Target menu at the bottom of the Layer window dictates how additional mask shapes are handled and may also affect how a mask is pasted. We'll cover targeting more in later examples, but even at this early stage it's worth introducing the concept. The default is Target:None, which means that any mask you draw is considered to be an additional, new mask. Likewise, if you paste a mask shape, it also creates an additional mask. When you have multiple masks, the Target menu will display them in the order in which they were created.

The reason to keep track of the Target is simple – it's all too easy to delete a mask shape accidentally. For instance, say you select Target: Mask 1 and paste a mask shape into this track. You then forget about the menu and draw what you think is a new Mask 2 – bingo, you've just replaced the original Mask 1.

There are few reasons to target a specific mask. You don't need to set the Target menu to simply edit a specific mask, and if you need to paste a shape, you can target a specific mask shape track by clicking on its name in the Time Layout window without setting the Target at all. However you work with it, just be aware of its current setting.

The Free Transform Tour

The Free Transform Points feature allows you to manipulate a bounding box to scale and rotate a mask shape. If you use Photoshop, you'll already be familiar with the Free Transform feature. However, After Effect's interpretation is more limited: It applies only to a mask shape in the Layer window (it cannot be used to distort the image in the Comp window), and the Skew, Distort, and Perspective options are not supported.

To access the Free Transform Points, double-click the mask shape in the Layer window. This will select all the points and load the bounding box. If you want to transform just part of the shape, select individual points and press Command+T to activate Free Transform. Once the Free Transform box is active, you have the following options:

• You can move the mask shape by dragging it anywhere inside the bounding box.
• If you want to resize the mask shape, the cursor changes to a Resize symbol (two arrows pointing in opposite directions) when over a corner or side handle. Drag a handle to resize; add the Shift key to maintain the aspect ratio.
• If you want to rotate the mask shape, the cursor changes to the Rotate symbol when it's just outside the bounding box. Drag to rotate; add Shift to rotate in 45° increments.
• Deselect Free Transform by either double-clicking on the pasteboard or hitting the Enter key. The mask shape will also be deselected.

The easiest way to activate the Free Transform bounding box is to double-click the mask shape in the Layer window. In this case, we have then placed our mouse cursor over one of the transform corners, activating the resize tool.

Nudging a Mask

With the Layer window forward, the arrow keys nudge the mask shape, or selected points, one screen pixel at a time.

Bounding Box Anchor Point

When a mask shape is rotated by using Free Transform, the transformation occurs around the anchor point for the bounding box. This is the tiny "registration" symbol that defaults to the center of the box. (Note that this is completely independent of the layer's anchor point, around which the layer scales and rotates; while the regular anchor point remains visible in the Layer window, it's not editable when you're masking.)

To change the anchor point for the bounding box, drag the symbol to a new position. Now when you rotate the mask, it will rotate around this new point. However, scaling the mask will behave as it did before – if you want to also scale around the anchor point, drag a handle with the Command key pressed.

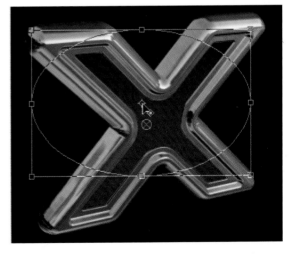

The registration mark symbol is the center, or anchor, around which free transforms take place. It can be repositioned. When the cursor changes (it has a second registration symbol at its tail), you can click and drag it to a new location.

No Free Transform Lunch

Although the Free Transform Points feature is extremely useful and usable, there are a few gotchas to watch out for:

• Free Transform works on selected points. If only some of the mask points are selected, the bounding box will scale or rotate these points

Simple Selection Moves

Sometimes just figuring out the simplest things can reduce your stress level…and so it is with selecting. As you've seen, masks are made up of a collection of points, and editing a mask requires you select a single point, multiple points, or the entire mask. Some rules of selection:

- When you first draw a mask, all points appear selected (they draw solid). If you carefully drag one point, you can move the entire shape. You might think that dragging a line segment will also move the mask, but it actually reshapes the segment.

- To select individual points, drag a marquee around all points you wish to select. All other points will appear as deselected.

- Shift+clicking a point will add and subtract points from a selection, as will Shift+marquee.

- If a mask is deselected (F2, or click on the pasteboard), no points will be visible. If you want to select a point that's not visible, drag a marquee around its general location. If you simply click where you believe the point should be, it's likely you'll select a line segment instead (which selects the two points on either end of the segment).

- To select all points on a mask, Option+click anywhere on the mask shape. Select All (Command+A) will also select a single mask (it actually selects all unlocked masks). And if the mask's name is visible in the Time Layout window, you can click on it, or on the words Mask Shape, to select the entire mask.

| When no mask points are selected in the Layer window, only the mask shape is visible. | When one point is selected, its vertex dot is drawn solid and bezier handles may appear; the other mask points are drawn hollow. | When all points are selected, they are all drawn solid, and the mask can be moved as a whole if you click and drag one of the points. | Clicking on and dragging a portion of the mask between mask vertex points reshapes that segment of the mask. |

Full Frame Masks

To create a rectangular mask the same size as the layer, double-click on the rectangle tool. To create an oval mask that reaches the edge of the layer, double-click on the Oval tool.

only. If you want to transform the entire mask, don't forget to double-click the mask shape to ensure that all points are active.

- Free Transform is an editing tool rather than a property, meaning that it works only for the current transformation. For instance, if you rotate a mask, then select Transform again some time later, the bounding box will not appear in a rotated position. (For comparison, when you're using the regular Rotation property, After Effects always keeps track of the rotation value relative to the starting value of 0°.)

- When a mask shape is animated over time and keyframes are created by using Free Transform Points to rotate the shape, check that the interpolation looks right between keyframes. While you might think the entire mask shape will simply "rotate" between keyframes, After Effects interpolates *each point on the mask independently to a new position.* This may result in the shape appearing to interpolate between keyframes in a strange way.

Masks of a Feather

We saw earlier how changing the layer quality from Draft to Best cleaned up the edges by antialiasing them. If you need more softness than this, or want to add a vignette effect, you'll need to add a Feather amount [**Ex.02.1**]. Each mask shape has independent Feather control, and it can be set numerically or with a slider:

• In the Time Layout window, twirl down the arrow for the mask you want to feather and click on its current value to open the Feather dialog. To access it from the Layer window, select the mask, context-click and select Mask Feather from the Mask menu. Command+ Shift+F also works. Set a value for Horizontal and Vertical feather and click OK.

• To set the feather amount with a slider, press Option as you click on the words "Mask Feather" in the Time Layout window. The "magic" slider will pop up; move the mouse on top of the slider to drag up and down. The Info palette (Command+2 to open) gives a realtime update of the value, while the Comp window will update as fast as it can.

The only gotcha to watch out for with feathering is that it occurs both inside and outside the mask's edge. If you apply a feather of 20 pixels, the feather attempts to draw roughly 10 pixels inside the edge and 10 pixels outside the edge. However, feathering cannot extend outside the dimensions of the layer, which can lead to feathered edges that don't ramp smoothly to full transparency and appear clipped.

Logic would dictate that if you apply any feather value, you should move the mask edge inside the layer boundary at least by half the amount. So for a feather amount of 20, move the mask inside all edges by 10 pixels. This may look okay in Draft Quality, but problems still appear in Best Quality, as can be seen in [**Ex.02.2**]. We've found that with the mask moved 10 pixels in from the layer boundary, you'll see a noticeable hard edge with even a 15-pixel feather, and a very hard edge with 20 pixels. (Pixels in the Feather dialog appear to be bigger than pixels in the image – go figure…) So check the edges with a critical eye with the layer set to Best Quality, not Draft. If you see a problem edge, adjust the feather amount accordingly, or inset the mask further.

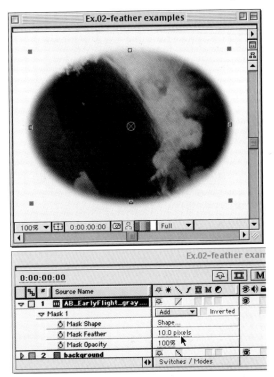

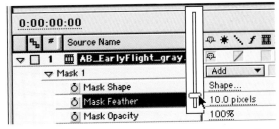

Increasing a mask's Feather parameter above its default of 0 results in a soft edge, centered around the mask's outline [**Ex.02**]. Click on its current value to open the Mask Feather dialog, you can set independent horizontal and vertical feather amounts, or keep them "locked" the same. Hindenburg footage from Artbeats/Early Flight.

Option+clicking on Mask Feather will open a popup slider for adjusting the value interactively.

The Mask Shape Dialog

If you need to create a mask shape with exact values, you can enter them in the Mask Shape dialog. Access this dialog by clicking on Shape in the Switches panel beside the mask you wish to edit. You can also select a mask and choose Mask Shape from the context menu in the Layer window. Or use the shortcut: Command+Shift+M.

Specify the size of the mask by entering values for the bounding box (Top, Left, Right, and Bottom) – Tab will move clockwise around the four entry boxes. The Unit's popup offers the option to enter values in Percentage of Source, handy if you want the same border on all four sides. Although you can select Rectangle or Oval from the radio buttons, don't be surprised when it reverts back to Bezier the next time you open the dialog (no, you're not going crazy).

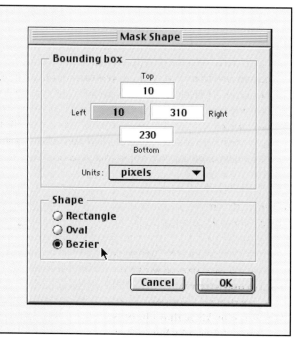

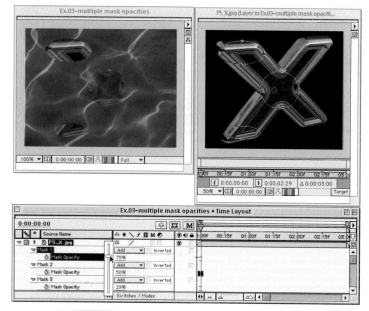

Each mask can have its own separate opacity, even if multiple masks are applied to the same layer [**Ex.03**]. The Option+click trick to bring up the interactive slider also works for Mask Opacity.

Mask Opacity

Next down from the Mask Feather property is Mask Opacity, and again, each Mask has a separate Opacity control [**Ex.03**]. As with Mask Feather, you can change the Mask Opacity value either numerically or with a slider:

• In the Time Layout window, click on the current value for Mask Opacity to open the numerical dialog. To access it from the Layer window, select the mask, context-click, and select Mask Opacity from the Mask menu.

• To set the Mask Opacity amount with a slider, press Option as you click on the words "Mask Opacity" in the Time Layout window. A slider will pop up – move the mouse on top of the slider to drag up and down, and watch the Info palette for a realtime update.

If you have only one mask shape, you should use the regular Opacity control to fade the layer up or down. But with multiple masks, having a separate and animatable fade up/down for each mask opens up lots of possibilities. We reckon this is one of those features you won't know you even need – until you really need it. For instance, you're rotoscoping a man with his arms by his sides, when halfway through the animation he moves his arm – creating a new shape between the arm and body. By animating Mask Opacity for this new shape (probably with hold keyframes), you can have a mask shape appear on the first frame it's needed.

Another use that comes to mind is fading up a list of headlines one line at a time. A mask is created for each line of text, and Mask Opacity is used to fade up each line, offset in time from each other. But since all the lines of type remain as one layer, you can then fade off the entire layer using the regular Opacity control. Also, any effect applied to the layer, such as a drop shadow, will apply to all the lines as a group.

Inverting a Mask

Normally the image inside a mask appears opaque, and portions outside of the mask are transparent. It is possible to inverse this behavior, however, so that the *inside* of the mask becomes transparent [**Ex.04**]. In the Switches panel opposite each mask is a checkbox that changes the mask to Inverted when selected. (No, you can't animate the Inverted option.) Meanwhile, the shortcut Command+Shift+I inverts a mask without having to hunt through the Time Layout window.

Inverting a mask is useful if you want to create a single hole in a layer. For instance, if you draw a mask around a window, you can invert it to see through the window to the layers behind. Note that when you're using multiple masks, After Effects uses Mask Modes (see below), rather than the Inverted option, to make one mask create a hole through another mask.

A circular mask is applied to a water texture movie, then Inverted – which opens a window, revealing the XraySkull layer behind. Water from Artbeats/ Water Effects 1.

Freeform Bezier Masking

Now that you've got the basics of how masking works, let's look at the most powerful mask drawing tool: the Pen. The most flexible way to create masks is to use the pen tool to create Bezier paths. Even when you think you've been creating oval and rectangular masks, you've actually been creating Bezier paths to make these masks. You can use these basic shapes as a starting point, or draw a Bezier path directly with the Pen tool.

The Pen can create a Bezier mask of any shape and include a combination of straight and curved segments.

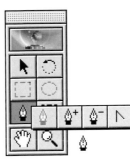

The Pen tool is used for drawing Bezier paths for masks. When you select it, the cursor changes to the pen. The keyboard shortcut is G; holding down the Command key also brings it up in the appropriate windows (or switches from the Pen to the Selection tool, if the Pen is already chosen). You can select variations on the Pen from the Tool palette, although there are keyboard shortcuts that are far handier.

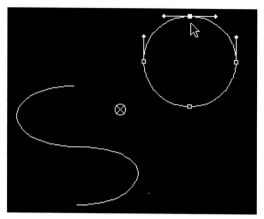

The masks can also be open or closed: A closed shape is required to create transparency, but even an open path can be of use to various effects (more on these later).

To draw a Bezier mask, select the Pen tool and draw your path directly in the Layer window. Practice this with the movie layer in [**Ex.05**]. After Effects' Pen tool works similarly to the Bezier drawing tool in other programs like Photoshop and Illustrator: A single click with the mouse creates a straight line segment, while a click+drag pulls out handles and creates smooth curves. To close the path, click back on the first point (or double-click the last point you draw). To create an open path mask, change back to the Selection tool when you've completed drawing.

Masks can be open or closed shapes. Even when you create a mask with the oval tool, if you click on one of its points, you will see the Bezier path editing handles.

Drawing with the Pen Tool

We promised in Chapter 4 that the techniques for creating a Position motion path and breaking and retracting direction handles would translate well to drawing with Bezier masks. And they do. If you'd like additional help learning the Bezier drawing tool, we recommend you check out After Effect's Online Help or the 4.1 user guide (pages 309 through 313) for step-by-step instructions for creating Bezier paths.

Under the main topic *Working with Masks and Transparency*, you'll find *Drawing a Bezier mask with the Pen tool*, with the subsections:

- Drawing Straight lines with the Pen tool;
- Drawing curves with the Pen tool;
- Tips for drawing curves.

If you're new to Bezier drawing, be aware that it takes a little practice. The key is to not draw curves by creating lots of straight lines (you know who you are…) and to create as few points as possible. Don't be worried if the mask shape isn't perfect as you're creating it. It's next to impossible to drag handles perfectly at every point and totally acceptable to just tweak it afterward. If you are already comfortable drawing with a Bezier tool in another program, and/or have completed Chapter 4, the following tips should be all you need to adapt your skills:

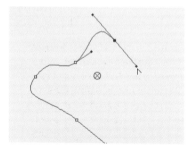

If you're drawing a mask shape with the Pen tool and you pass the cursor back over one of the handles before you've closed the shape, it will turn into an upside-down V: the "convert direction point" tool. Use this tool to drag the handle to break the continuous flow of the mask shape through this point, then continue with the rest of your drawing.

• When you're in the middle of drawing a mask with the Pen tool and you need to edit a point or handle you've already drawn, press the Command key to toggle temporarily to the Selection Arrow tool.

• While you're drawing a mask, if you need to break the continuous handles of a smooth point you've just created, move the cursor over the handle. The "convert direction point" cursor (the upside-down V) will appear. Drag the handle to break it, then continue drawing.

• If you accidentally deselect an active mask shape before you've finished drawing, you can continue where you left off. With the Pen tool active, Command+click on the end of the path – this will select the last point and make the mask active again. Just continue drawing and the new point will be added onto the end of the selected path.

Editing with the Selection Tool

Once the path is drawn, we switch from the Pen tool to the Selection (arrow) tool to edit it. The following info builds on the earlier tips for selecting points and entire shapes (see *Simple Selection Moves* above) and the earlier info on using free transform points:

• To break the handles of a smooth point with continuous handles, press the Command key and drag one handle. Repeat to snap them together again.

• Command+click on the point to convert it from "corner" to "smooth" (pop out handles if they are retracted), or from smooth to corner (retract handles).

• To adjust the shape of a line segment, drag the line. Be warned, though: Reshaping a line segment will force the handles on either side to be continuous. (We consider this a bug.)

• To add a point, press the Command key and place the cursor along the line segment between two points. The selection arrow will change to the Add Point icon. Click to add a new point, then drag it to a new position as required. *If the mask is animating over time, adding a point at one keyframe will add it to all points in time, but moving the new point will affect the current keyframe only.*

• To delete a point, click on it to select it and hit Delete. Note that all points will then be selected. *Be warned that if the mask is animating over time, this will delete the corresponding point and will reshape the mask at all keyframes* (see *Animating a Mask* below).

• To close an open path, select Closed from the context-menu (or Layer>Mask>Closed). A line will be added connecting the last point drawn to the first point.

• To open a path, select two points and select the Closed menu item (which will have a check mark by it) – it will now "unclose" the shape, removing the line segment between the two points you selected.

• To delete a mask, select it in the Time Layout window and hit Delete.

As you can see, you can edit a mask shape easily with just the Selection tool active. There's really no need to use the Pen tool except for drawing the initial mask. The problem with editing masks with the Pen tool is that it converts points from smooth to corner and vice versa when you click on them; it doesn't simply select the point. And if all points are selected when you click on one of them – whammo, you've just converted all your hard-drawn points to all corner points or all smooth points. Yes, you can undo, but this has to happen only a couple of times for you to realize that the Selection tool is safer. If you forget any of the shortcuts, you can use the Add Point, Delete Point, and Convert Point tools found by expanding the Pen tool in the toolbox.

Bezier Masking Practice

When you feel you're getting a handle on creating Bezier masks, practice cutting out the X in **[Ex.05.2]**. Try both its outline and the inner red X shape.

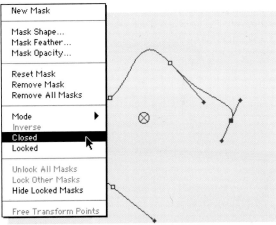

To close an open path, use the Layer menu or context-click in the Layer window and select Closed (above). The path will now be closed (below) and capable of creating transparency. To reverse the procedure and open a closed path, select two points and toggle the Closed option.

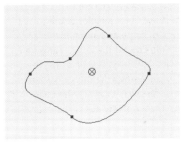

Animating a Mask

The most common method for animating a mask is to create the initial shape, make it the first keyframe, then change the shape of the mask by manipulating points. The mask shape will interpolate over time between keyframes just like any other property.

One of the most common uses for animated masks is to "wipe on" or reveal text. Open [Ex.06*starter] and try the following steps:

Step 1: Open the Layer window for the Revealing text. Use the Rectangle tool and draw a mask that comfortably encloses the entire word.

Step 2: In the Time Layout window, move the time marker to a point where you want the word to be entirely revealed. Select the layer, twirl down its Mask property (or hit M on the keyboard), and click on the stopwatch icon to the left of Mask Shape. This will set a keyframe for the word to be entirely revealed.

Step 3: Move the time marker back to 00:00. Look at the Layer window and note how the mask is drawn differently (larger spaced dotted line rather than a solid line). *The dotted line means the mask is set to animate, but the time marker is not currently parked on a keyframe.*

Step 4: Set the mask into free transform mode by double-clicking on it in the Layer window. Grab the right edge of the mask and slide it to the left until it is past the beginning of the first character. Note that a keyframe is automatically set for you in the Time Layout window.

Oops. What Happened?

After you finish drawing a mask, all points will be selected and the toolbox will revert to the Selection tool so you can edit it further. If you then reselect the Pen tool and click on one of the points, you'll convert every point on the mask to either all smooth points or all corner points. Use the Selection tool to tweak the mask.

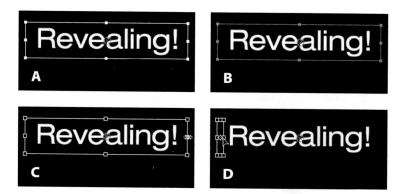

In the Layer Window in **[Ex.06*starter]**, draw a rectangular mask around the type (A). Go to the point in time where you want this end shape to land and turn on the stopwatch for this mask shape. Go to the start of the comp, and note how the mask is a dotted line (B) – this means it is animating, but you are not currently parked on a keyframe. Double-click the mask to enable Free Transform (C) and drag the right edge beyond the left of the text (D) – this is the first keyframe of your wipe animation. Preview the Comp window to see your type reveal animation.

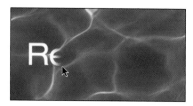

Adding some Mask Feather gives a soft edge to the wipe.

Step 5: Preview the Comp window and note the animation. To add some polish, select the layer, type Shift+F to reveal Mask Feather, and add some feather to the edge to get a soft wipe. Note that you need only feather it in the horizontal direction, since the edge of the mask doing the wipe is vertical. If you get lost, check out [Ex.06_final].

This "reveal" type of animation has a slightly different workflow in that we start where we want to end up. This makes drawing the initial mask shape easier. For more freeform animation, you can start at the start, of course. Practice this with [Ex.07*starter], using Bezier mask shapes, and setting more than two keyframes. Remember, you can use the same keyframe interpolation tricks you learned back in Chapter 4 as well.

Blind Speed

Once you've created an animated mask in [**Ex.07**], a twirly arrow will appear alongside Mask Shape in the Time Layout window. Twirl it down to reveal the Speed graph which controls how the mask interpolates. When there are linear keyframes, the velocity is always noted as "1.00 units per second" and the graph line appears totally flat, regard-

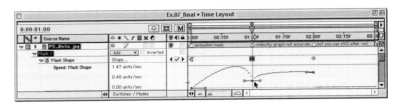

less of how much change in the animation is taking place. Since some points may be moving quickly while others remain stationary, this graph cannot be a clear indicator of the relative speed of the mask as it interpolates between different keyframes.

However, you can still use this graph to create ease ins and ease outs, using the same techniques you learned in Chapter 4, or apply the Easy Ease keyframe assistants (Chapter 7). Keyframes can also be changed to hold keyframes so that they pop into new positions rather than interpolate. And of course, anything you do with keyframes as far as copying, pasting, reversing, moving, deleting, and so on, are all fair game with mask keyframes. So treat the velocity graph as being a relative, rather than absolute, indicator of how fast the mask shape is changing.

Regardless of the details of the actual animation, mask velocity with linear keyframes always displays as "1.00 units/sec" in After Effects (top). However, you can still edit the velocity; this graph will now show relative changes in speed from keyframe to keyframe (above).

Wotating Wectangle

When a rectangle mask is rotated over time with Free Transform, interpolation occurs between *each point*, not the overall shape. This can yield some unexpected results – for example, the corners will head straight to their new positions rather than rotating in an arc to these positions. Preview this anomaly in [**Ex.09.1**].

If this is a problem, copy the mask shape and paste it to a same-size Solid layer. Then animate the solid using the regular Rotate property. Use the animated solid as an Alpha Track Matte (Chapter 14) for the original layer. This is demonstrated in [**Ex.09.2**].

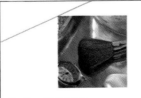

Starting mask shape

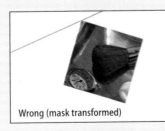

Wrong (mask transformed)

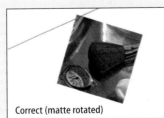

Correct (matte rotated)

When a rectangular mask shape (left) is rotated using the Free Transform tool, the corners follow a straight line to their new positions (center), making the mask appear to shrink while it's interpolating to its new position. To fix this, apply the mask shape to a solid, then rotate the solid and use it as an alpha matte (right). Movie courtesy EyeWire/Time Elements.

Using Interpolated Shapes

One of the hardest shapes to draw is an old rounded TV screen shape. Rather than draw it from scratch, in [Ex.08] we'll animate a mask from a rectangle to an oval, and find an interpolated shape in the middle that's close to what we need:

Step 1: At time 00:00, open the Layer window for the movie, and double-click the Rectangle tool (or select New Mask from the context-menu). A full-size rectangle mask will be created.

Step 2: Twirl down Mask 1 in the Time Layout window and turn on the stopwatch for Mask Shape to set the first keyframe.

Step 3: Move in time to 04:00. In the Layer window, set the Target popup to Target:Mask1. Double-click the Oval tool and the rectangle will be replaced by a full frame oval mask. (If you left it on Target:None, a new Mask 2 would have been created and the shapes would not interpolate.)

Step 4: In the Time Layout window, Option+drag the time marker between 00:00 and 04:00 and check the interpolated shapes. When you find a shape that's close to a rounded TV, turn off the Mask Shape

The final mask shape, with Levels, Tint, and Stroke effects added. Footage courtesy Artbeats/ Early Flight.

stopwatch in the Time Layout window. The shape you chose will now be used for the entire layer.

Step 5: Optional: Let's add a border to the edge of the mask. Select the layer and apply the Stroke effect (Effects>Render>Stroke). Set the Path popup to Mask 1 and the other settings to taste. The problem here is that because the mask points extend to the very edge of the layer, the stroke is being clipped. To fix this, in the layer window double-click the mask shape to load Free Transform Points. With the Command and Shift keys pressed, scale the mask slightly (the Command key forces scaling to happen around the bounding box's anchor point, while Shift maintains the aspect ratio). Tweak individual mask points to taste. See [Ex.08_final] for our result.

Living Large

You'll notice that many of the layers we're masking in the examples in this chapter are larger than the comp. It's easier to draw masks on larger images, since they have more detail in them. Mask first, resize later.

More Mask Animating Advice

When you're animating mask shapes, watch out for these gotchas:

• If the mask shape needs to be precise, draw and edit the shape with the layer set to Best Quality, the resolution set to Full, and the magnification set to 100%.

• When you're masking interlaced footage where the fields have been separated (Chapter 37), you will normally see only the first field of each frame in the composition. However, when you field render on output, both fields are used, and the mask will interpolate field by field. If the footage you're masking requires critical precision, you might want to check the mask on every field. To do this:

Change the comp's frame rate to double the existing frame rate (for NTSC 59.94 fps is double 29.97, while 50 is double PAL's 25 fps rate). Don't use 60 fps to double 29.97 fps, though – tiny increments in time are very important to keyframe placement. Youcould also change the Time-code Base (File>Preferences>Time) to 60 fps for NTSC and 50 for PAL.

Now when you navigate in time, you can check how the mask inter-polates for each field, even setting keyframes on the second field if you need to. When you're masking field by field, you might want to set up the footage being nested in its own precomp so you change just this comp's frame rate.

• When it comes time to render, bear in mind that animated mask shapes will interpolate at the frame rate set in the Render Settings, not the comp's frame rate. And if you field render, masks will interpolate at twice the frame rate. If you're masking field by field in an NTSC 59.94 fps comp, you don't need to return the frame rate to 29.97 fps before you render – just set it in Render Settings to 29.97 fps, with Field Rendering set to On.

• If a mask appears to be "slipping" in the rendered movie, even though it looks fine in the composition, there's another likely culprit – a mask is interpolating out of sync with the source frames. If your footage is not interlaced, you would mask this layer on whole frames in a regular 29.97 fps composition. But if you field render the entire animation, the mask will now interpolate at 59.94 fps and appear to be out of sync with the source.

Similarly, if you remove 3:2 pulldown from a clip (see Chapter 38) to return it to its original 24 fps film frames, then mask on whole frames at 24 fps, you'll have the same problem if you render at 29.97 fps, fields or no fields. The mask will interpolate at a rate that is not in sync with the source frames – even though it looks fine in the comp. If you need to field render the other layers, but not the layer being masked, prerender (Chapter 44) this one layer separately with an alpha channel so that the mask is locked down in position.

• We mentioned earlier that using the Free Transform Points feature to animate may create unexpected results. When you scale and rotate a mask to create a new mask shape keyframe, you might assume the shape would interpolate using this information, as in "Rotate mask shape 45° from time A to B." However, what happens is that each point on the mask individually interpolates to its new position. You may not even notice, but it's something to consider when animating masks.

Thinking Ahead

If you know you'll need to rotoscope (or even morph) footage ahead of time, try to shoot on 24 or 30 fps film or use a progressive scan camera. This will cut your workload in half compared to masking 60 fields a second…

Deleting Animated Mask Points

Whereas After Effects handles adding points to an animated mask gracefully, deleting a point from a mask is a different story. If you delete a point at one point in time, it will remove it for all keyframes throughout the animation. This will reshape the mask and you may lose valuable work. For this reason, the rule of thumb is to either start with the right number of points, or if the object you're masking changes shape, create the mask starting with the simplest shape. This way you'll be adding points as you create keyframes, not deleting them.

In After Effects 3.1, adding and deleting points related only to that particular keyframe and had no effect on other keyframes. The problem with this method, however, was that masks would often interpolate in unpredictable ways. For instance, you would start with twelve points, and at the second keyframe delete two points and add three new ones. At this point it was anyone's guess how points would interpolate between the two keyframes, and it was likely that every single frame (or field) would need a keyframe just to eliminate interpolation altogether. However, if you would like to use this older style of masking, turn off "Preserve Constant Vertex Count when Editing Masks" preference (File>Preferences>General).

Multiple Masks

So far we've explored simple and Bezier masks, along with animating a mask over time. The final piece of the masking puzzle is how best to work with multiple masks. You can have up to 127 masks per layer (don't worry, we won't go that crazy), and the Mask Modes control how masks interact with each other. Each mask has its own Mask Shape, Mask Feather, and Mask Opacity controls, and we refer to these three values as a "mask group." In the Time Layout window, each mask group has its own twirly arrow as a subset of the main Masks section.

Mask Modes

When you create multiple masks on a layer, the first mask creates transparency by modifying the layer's alpha channel. Any subsequent mask created on the same layer can add, subtract, intersect, or difference their transparency with the first mask, using the Modes popup associated with each mask group. You can also set a mask to None, which is very useful: You can draw mask shapes to be used later by effects without affecting the alpha channel of the image. Mask Modes can't animate over time, and open path masks don't have a Modes menu, as they cannot create transparency.

Modes can be a bit confusing at first, but try some examples and they should become clear. [**Ex.10*starter 1_eye**] has a layer already set up with different masks; experiment with different modes for the masks, then different transparency amounts. Create your own mask shapes if you like, or use your own source. Remember

The combination of multiple masks and mask modes allow for great flexibility. [**Ex.10*starter 1_eye**] uses four masks to isolate different areas (below). Try clicking on the comp's alpha channel view to see which areas are opaque and which are transparent. Eye image courtesy Digital Vision/The Body.

Renaming Masks

When you're working with multiple masks, give each one a unique name. To rename a mask, select the mask group name, such as Mask 1; in the Time Layout window, press Return, type a new name, and press Return again.

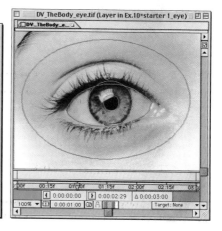

that masks are calculated from the top down as seen in the Time Layout window, so each mask operates based on the result of all the masks above it.

The Online Help also offers good examples of what each mask does. Search for Mask Modes (or see 4.1 User Guide, pages 334 through 335). In general:

• The top mask sets the underlying shape for the other masks to intersect with, and it is usually set to Add mode or Add Inverted. Try to avoid inverting the other masks, though – you should be able to create the required result with just the Add, Subtract, Intersect, or Difference modes; inverting masks makes the logic harder to follow. When Mask Opacity is set to less than 100%, the Lighten mode can be used instead of Add, and the Darken mode instead of Intersect.

• When masks intersect and create a new shape, whichever mask creates each side of the shape determines the amount of Mask Feather along that edge.

Practice also with [**Ex.10*starter 2_window**] where the private eye stands in front of a door. The idea is to cut out the white glass in the door so that it's a "window" to the sky background behind. We've cut out the top window shape, which uses an Inverted mask in Add mode; continue cutting out the window shapes, noticing how you need to mask just inside the edge to avoid a white fringe. Select the appropriate mask mode and turn on the background layer. Then study the other more complex examples in the [**Ex.10**] folder.

In [**Ex.10*starter 2_window**], practice Bezier masking by cutting out the rest of the white window shapes. Set the mask modes appropriately to reveal the sky movie behind. Private Eye image © Corbis Images; sky background in window from Artbeats/Sky Effects.

Problem-Solving Modes: Lighten and Darken

Mask Opacity refers to the opacity of the layer inside the mask shape. If you have multiple masks applied to a layer, each with a different Mask Opacity setting, the behavior of the alpha channel is such that the overlapping areas may appear more or less opaque. To solve this problem, there are two modes – Lighten and Darken – that are useful:

When multiple masks with different opacity settings overlay in Add mode, they will composite as if they were copies of the layer each with its own mask using regular Opacity settings. For instance, if two masks are both set to 50% Mask Opacity, both in Add mode, the opacity of the intersecting area will be 75%, appearing more opaque than either of the individual shapes. When more than two masks overlap, it gets even more complicated.

The Lighten mask mode is designed to counteract this problem in which semitransparent masks overlap and build up opacity. Its general rule is The More Opaque Mask Wins. For instance, in [**Ex.11.1**] where three masks of varying opacities overlap, the one with the higher Mask Opacity percentage controls the resulting opacity where they overlap. Intersecting areas will never be more opaque than the most opaque mask.

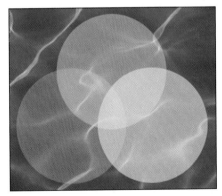

When overlapping masks have their own differing opacities, they behave as if they were separate partially transparent layers overlapping each other. This example is in comp [**Ex.11.0**].

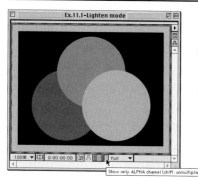

When three masks of varying opacities overlap each other and are set to Lighten mode (top left), the overlapping region is only as opaque as the least transparent mask (top right). This results in a more even overlapping. The "lighten" logic makes sense if you turn off the background layer and look at just the resulting alpha channel (bottom left): The "lighter" shapes in the alpha control the outcome.

Mask Opacity Feedback

To check the value of the layer's alpha channel when you're working with overlapping transparent masks, click on the Info palette to switch from 0–255 to Percentages. Now move your cursor over the mask shapes and read the value of Alpha % in the Info palette.

The opposite problem occurs when you set overlapping masks to Intersect: Their opacity values are scaled down instead of building up. For instance, if you set two masks to 50% Mask Opacity as in [Ex.11.2], with the second mask set to Intersect, the opacity of the intersecting area will be 25%, appearing more transparent than either of the individual shapes. The Darken mask mode is designed to counteract the reduction in opacity in Intersect mode. So for our two overlapping masks, change the second mask from Intersect to Darken, and the opacity of the intersecting area will remain at 50%. Where Mask Opacity values differ, the lower number will be used.

In practice, if you have soft feathered edges on masks and use the Lighten and Darken modes, the corners of the shapes can exhibit a strange "spikiness" that might be mathematically correct but isn't very attractive.

If all that talk of mask-opacity/alpha-channel/lighten-darken jargon has your head spinning, remember that if after creating multiple masks you only need a *single, consistent opacity value*, don't fool with the opacity of individual masks at all. Leave all the Mask Opacity settings at 100% and use the regular Transform>Opacity property as a master transparency control.

Managing Multiple Masks

Following are some tips for working with multiple masks:

• **Target menu:** We mentioned earlier the key role of the Target menu in the Layer window, which determines which mask track is used when creating a new mask shape. Targeting is essential when you're animating from one shape to another, as you can interpolate between only those masks that are on the same track. If the menu is set to Target:None, any mask shape you draw from scratch will create an additional mask. If you set the Target to a specific mask, any new mask you draw will replace the original mask on that track. Similarly, when you paste a mask, you can target the shape to paste to a specific mask track. If that particular mask is set to animate, a new keyframe will be created when you draw a new shape or paste a shape. Note that targeting affects only the Mask Shape property, not Mask Feather or Mask Opacity.

• **Turning Off a Mask:** If a closed mask is being used by an effect, but is not meant to create transparency, change the Mask Modes popup in the

Switches panel from Add to None. The mask shape will still appear in the Layer window for editing, but it will not create transparency. If you want to hide a mask in the Layer window that's set to None, you must first Lock it (see below), then Hide Locked Layers.

• **Copying Masks:** You can copy and paste mask shapes from layer to layer, or within a layer. If you copy a mask you've selected in the Layer window, you will copy only the Mask Shape property, not the Feather and Opacity values. Also, if you select the Mask group name from the Time Layout window and copy, only the Mask Shape data is copied (not very intuitive, we agree). To copy the three values as the group, marquee their I-beams in the Time Layout window and copy – you can also marquee keyframes if the mask is animating. To copy the Feather or Opacity values individually, click on the property name to select the value (and all keyframes on that track), and copy.

• **Pasting Masks:** When you paste a single Mask Shape property, the Target setting determines whether a new mask shape is created or an existing mask is replaced. However, you don't need to even open the Layer window to paste data. In the Time Layout window, select the Mask Shape track you want to replace (its I-beam will be highlighted), and paste. If the layer has no masks, a new mask is created. If you're pasting a mask group (Shape/Feather/Opacity values), click on the Mask group name or any of the individual properties and paste to replace all three values. (For some reason, you can't paste a group of values in the Layer window even with the Target popup set.) While you can copy multiple masks (or marquee multiple I-beams), you can paste multiple masks only as additional masks.

• **Reordering Masks:** When you have multiple masks on a layer, you can reorder them by dragging them up and down in the Time Layout window. This is useful when you use Mask Modes, as you may need to reorder the stack for masks to interact correctly.

• **Renaming a Mask Group:** You can rename a mask in the same way you can rename layers. Select the mask group name (Mask 1) in the Time Layout window, press Return, type in a new name, and press Return again. This comes in handy when masks relate to specific features, such as Left Eye, Right Eye, and so on. The new names appear in the Target menu also.

• **Selecting Multiple Masks:** We saw earlier how you could select all the points on a mask by Option+clicking the mask in the Layer window. You can also select the entire mask shape by clicking on the mask group name, or just the Mask Shape property, in the Time Layout window. This is a convenient way to select multiple mask shapes, as you can Shift+click to copy contiguous masks, or Command+click to select discontiguous masks. Remember that you're copying only the Mask Shape value when you select the Mask group name, not the Feather and Opacity values also.

Copy/Paste Mask Group

To copy Mask Shape, Feather, and Opacity as a group, select their I-beams in the Time Layout window. To paste as a new Mask group, select just the name of a layer and paste. To replace an existing mask group, select the Mask group name and paste.

Paste Replaces Mask

If a mask is selected in the Layer window when you paste a new shape, it will replace the existing mask, regardless of how the Target menu is set.

You can reorder masks in the Time Layout window by dragging them in the stack. A thick black line appears, showing you where in the stack you are dragging it to.

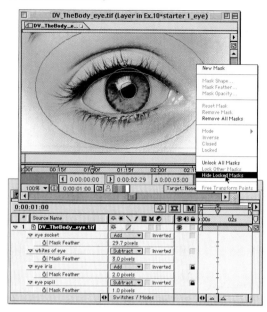

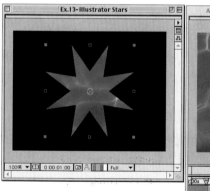

- **Deleting Mask Group:** Select a Mask group name, or Mask Shape, and press Delete to remove the mask group and all its keyframes. (Deleting a mask group in the Layer window works only if the entire mask is selected and the shape is not animating; otherwise it's more likely to delete the Mask Shape keyframe, or ignore you if there's no keyframe at that point in time.)
- **Locking and Hiding Masks:** When you're working with multiple masks, you can lock a mask to protect it from accidentally being edited. Just click the Lock box associated with each mask group in the A/V Features panel. Masks will still appear in the Layer window, but you won't be able to edit them or change any keyframes. To hide locked masks from displaying in the Layer window, context-click and select Hide Locked Masks from the Masks menu. To lock all selected masks, Option+click on the Lock switch for one of the selected masks. And remember, Unlock All Masks is just a context-click away.

Lock a mask to protect it from being edited accidentally. You can Hide Locked Masks to remove them from the Layer window, though they will still operate normally.

Using Masks from Illustrator and Photoshop

Although After Effects includes a number of mask modes for creating complex shapes, other programs may offer an even wider range of tools. For instance, Adobe Illustrator can create a new single shape from the interaction of multiple shapes with its Pathfinder options, can convert text to outlines, has automatic tools for creating spirals and stars, and offers effects for distorting paths. Shapes copied from Illustrator or Photoshop can be pasted directly to After Effects' Mask Shape property, then manipulated just like any other mask. Again, only closed paths can create transparency, but both closed and open paths can be used by an effect.

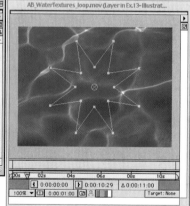

A star was created in Illustrator, copied, and pasted into an After Effects mask. The file IllustratorShapes.ai is included in the 13_Chapter Sources folder and contains several of the shapes used in **[Ex.13]**.

To use an Illustrator mask, simply create your shape in Illustrator and copy it. In After Effects, open the Layer window, set the Target popup to None, and paste to create a new mask. If you want to replace an existing mask shape, target that Mask Shape using the Target popup or click on its track in the Time Layout window to select it. You can also copy and paste multiple masks in one step.

Closed paths that are pasted from another program use the Difference Mask Mode as a default. This seems to work fine in most cases, but you're free to change the Mode if you need some other behavior.

If you want to animate from one Illustrator shape to another, you have to ensure that all the shapes are pasted to the same target Mask Shape track – otherwise, you'll end up with multiple masks that are independent of each other. Turn on the stopwatch for Mask Shape, and set the Target popup to target this Mask. Now, every time you paste another shape, you'll create a keyframe at that point in time.

In this way, you can easily animate between different "star" shapes, or even interpolate to a completely different shape, like a capital letter S – sometimes with odd results (preview the different layers in [Ex.13] to see some funky mask shape interpolation). The original Illustrator 8 file with these shapes are included on the CD in 13_Chapter Sources folder; better yet, practice by drawing your own shapes. Once you've created a keyframe for each shape, copy and paste these mask keyframes, rather than return to Illustrator each time you need to repeat a shape.

Type Outlines from Illustrator

If you create type characters in Illustrator, you must convert the font data to outlines using the Type>Create Outlines feature. Copy and paste the outlines only. Type with compound shapes, such as an O or a D, will paste as two masks, with the inside shape knocking a hole through the larger shape. As another example, using a word like *Swim* will paste a total of five masks – one for each character, plus the dot on the *i*. As a result, you may not want to use Illustrator type as masks on a regular basis.

In general, using an Illustrator file as an Alpha Matte (Chapter 14) is more convenient than creating an assortment of masks. However, it is the only way to get access to the *individual points* of an Illustrator layer, if you want to animate these points over time.

Masks for Effect

Effects that include a popup called Path are capable of using a mask shape to determine how a parameter behaves. An effect can access only masks created on the same layer, and they only see the Mask Shape – not the Feather or Opacity settings. To prevent the mask from creating transparency, set the Mode popup to None.

Some effects that use mask shapes are covered in the later effects chapters, including Audio Spectrum, Audio Waveform, Smear, Fill and Stroke (Chapter 23), Reshape (Chapter 24), and Path Text (Chapter 26).

Mask shapes don't always interpolate smoothly from one to another. This is because mask vertex points are just heading directly for their new position, not caring about what happens to the shape between them.

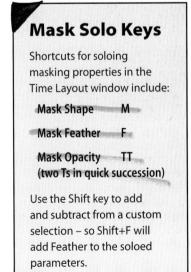

Masks to Motion

To copy a mask path to Position keyframes, copy the mask shape, click on Position in the Time Layout window, and paste. You can also paste to an Effects Point parameter, such as the center of a lens flare. (And yes, you can do all this vice versa.)

Mask Solo Keys

Shortcuts for soloing masking properties in the Time Layout window include:

Mask Shape   M

Mask Feather   F

Mask Opacity   TT
(two Ts in quick succession)

Use the Shift key to add and subtract from a custom selection – so Shift+F will add Feather to the soloed parameters.

Motion Paths Meet Masks

After Effects 4.1 allows for more choices in how you create paths. You can copy a mask shape to a motion path, and vice versa, and even copy and paste paths from Illustrator or Photoshop.

This chapter is focused on masking, but this new copy/paste feature applies also to Position (Chapter 4), anchor point paths (Chapter 6), and effects point animation (Chapter 19). Considering that many effects can access masks, but not motion paths, this flexibility opens up a whole host of new possibilities. For instance, a simple logo could be copied from Illustrator, pasted into Mask Shape, then moved into Position for use as a motion path. Or pasted to an effect point path, such as a particle system, so that fairy dust could animate over time around the edge of the logo.

To use an Illustrator path as a motion path in After Effects, select and copy the path, select the layer in After Effects, and paste. (If you run into an error dialog, make sure you twirl down and click on the word Position to make sure it's pasting to the right track.) The path will appear as spatial Position keyframes in the Comp window, and temporal

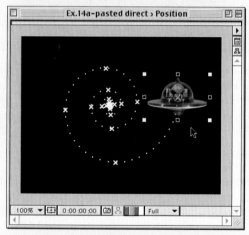

When you paste the Illustrator path directly to Position, the size of the path may be unsuitable. In this case, the spiral path is too small for our tastes – we want the spaceman to fly off screen at the end. Spaceman courtesy Classic PIO/Nostalgic Memorabilia.

Position keyframes in the Time Layout window. The timing of the animation defaults to 2 seconds, but since the middle keyframes convert as Roving keyframes, drag the first or last keyframe along the timeline to lengthen or shorten the animation. If the animation appears the opposite of what you expected, select all the keyframes and apply Time-Reverse Keyframes (Layer>Keyframe Assistant).

The only drawback we've found to this method is that After Effects assumes that the image being copied is at 72 dpi, so the size and position of the motion path when pasted directly to Position key-frames may not be suitable. It isn't easy to resize the motion path in the comp while maintaining its shape, because there is no Transform tool for a motion path (you can use a Motion Math script, but we won't scare you with that until later). If you find this a problem, try the following workaround, which uses a mask as an intermediary.

In this example, we used Illustrator's Spiral tool to create a motion path that would have been difficult to create from scratch in After Effects. Open the Illustrator 8 file IllustratorSpiral.ai from the 13_Chapter Sources folder that went along with this chapter's example project, or create your own path in Illustrator or Photoshop:

Step 1: Select the path in Illustrator and copy.

Step 2: In the After Effects comp **[Ex.14*starter]**, make a new solid (Layer>New Solid). Make sure you click the Comp Size button so that the solid is the same size as the comp. Turn off the visibility (eyeball) for the solid.

Step 3: Open the solid's Layer window (double-click layer) and paste – the Illustrator path will paste in as a mask. When it looks good, select it and copy the mask shape.

Step 4: Double-click the mask; this brings up the Transform tool. Resize and/or rotate the mask in rela-tion to the solid to simulate how you would like the motion path to appear in relation to the comp.

Step 5: In the Time Layout window, select the CP_Spaceman layer that will receive the new motion path, and twirl down Position. Click on the word

Rotoscoping Figures

While it is possible to create very complex shapes with the masking tools, bear in mind that rotoscoping moving figures out of a busy background is best done on a closed road by dedicated professionals: Be careful what you volunteer to do. If you need to composite a person into a scene, it's best to shoot the actor against a blue or green screen, and use the keying tools (Chapter 25) to drop out the background color. Despite the power of the Pen, it's simply not capable of creating soft transparency for swishing hair – plus it's extremely tedious work.

If you have a masochistic streak, you might not want to approach the project by creating a single mask for an entire human figure. Instead, break the figure down into separate shapes for the head, torso, upper arm, lower arm, and so on. It may seem like more work initially, but when the figure moves, you'll find it easier to keyframe the masks by concentrating on how each shape is changing. (It's sort of like learning to draw by visualizing a figure using simple shapes.) It may be possible to track some of the shapes, such as the torso, by simply moving or scaling its respective mask.

If the integrity of the shape is maintained, you can rely more on interpolated masks. After all, it's possible that the shape for the torso might need to be keyframed only every 10 frames, but the hand and fingers need

What's All the Commotion?

If you need to do rotoscoping on a regular basis, check out Puffin Design's Commotion (www.puffindesigns.com) – it's designed from the ground up for rotoscoping and includes additional tools, such as B-splines, that are tailor-made for the task at hand.

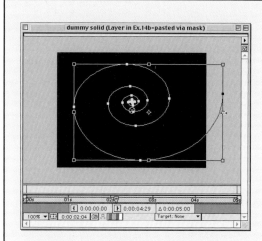

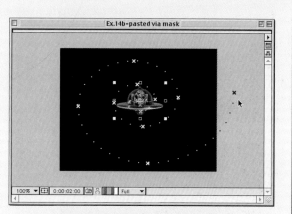

Position to activate that track (otherwise the default track will be Mask) and paste. The Mask shape will be pasted as a motion path, but the exact position of the keyframes in the Comp window will have been determined by the mask shape you created. Progress to this point is shown in **[Ex.14b]**.
Step 6: In our completed example **[Ex.14c]**, we used the Keyframe Assistant>Time-Reverse

By pasting the path to a mask first, you can use the Transform tool to resize the path to a suitable size (left). The mask shape is then copied and pasted to Position (right).

Keyframes so that the animation would start in the center and spiral outward. The final keyframe was edited so that the object moved completely off screen. The last keyframe was moved from the default 02:00 to 04:00, and Motion Blur was turned on (see Chapter 11).

AB_RetroHealthcare.mov (Layer in Ex.12*starter)

To tackle this rotoscoping job, we've divided it into the head, shoulders, and hand, worrying about precision in just the areas where they don't overlap. This is the first frame; practice doing the entire shot – then you'll understand why you should charge so much for rotoscoping frame by frame. Doctor footage from Artbeats/Retro Healthcare.

keyframes on every frame. If you were to cut out the figure using one single mask, you'd have a new keyframe on every single frame regardless.

Also, try to create the mask shapes just a little inside the shape being traced so that the mask creates a clean edge. You won't miss a pixel or two in most cases, and the mask will jitter less around the edges than if you try to follow every nuance on every frame.

If you want to get a taste for what hand-rotoscoping entails, open project [**Ex.12*starter**]. This is a relatively simple shot of a doctor staring at the camera, lowering his hand from his face. He is dressed in white, and it was shot against white, so there is no hope for color keying. (Note: The footage was originally shot on film and telecined to 29.97 fps video, adding fields. We've already removed the 3:2 pulldown and reverted the footage to 23.976 fps – this makes for less work than masking on each field at 59.94 fps. The comp is also set to 23.976 fps.)

We've created a set of starter masks: head, shoulders, and hand. They are set to Add mode, so they will add together to cut your final mask. Try animating the masks one at a time: First, do the head for the entire length of the clip; then the shoulders; then just where the hand and fingers appear outside the outlines of the head and shoulders – since they are all adding together, you don't need to be precise where they overlap. (With this example, you could also have created the first keyframe at the last frame, and worked backward.) If you think this is the long approach, delete all the masks and start from scratch with one mask. In the meantime, we'll get on with the rest of the book…

A Creative Alternative to Roto

You may come across a nightmare project where a figure needs to be cut out of a background, but the budget doesn't allow for time-consuming precise masking. Rather than cut out an object or character using a tight mask shape, create a funky mask outline loosely around the character. Animate the mask every few frames by moving the points. You might also try changing all the Mask Shape keyframes to Hold keyframes for a really jumpy look. Add the Stroke effect to outline the mask shape, or add a Glow or Drop Shadow. An example of this is [**Ex.12_cop-out final**].

Obviously, this doesn't suit every project – it works better when the subject matter is fun, or perhaps the audience is under the age of having taste. However, we once had a job that required minutes of footage to be cut out, and once the client agreed to go with this approach, it took us only days instead of weeks.

If it suits the job, consider wackier, creative solutions to otherwise tedious roto tasks. Background from Artbeats/Microbes.

Panning a Layer Inside a Mask

Normally when you move a mask in the Layer window, the "window" that reveals the image in the Comp window moves across the image. However, you may wish for this window to remain in a constant position in the comp, and to pan the image within this window. To do this, the program needs to adjust two values: the position of the Mask Shape (how the mask appears in relation to the layer in the Layer window), and the value of Position (which is the position of the layer in relation to the comp). To make these two changes in one move, After Effects created the Pan Behind tool. We'll explore how it works, ending with a tease for an alternate way of working...

The Pan Behind tool can be used to pan an image inside the mask directly in the Comp window. It changes the values for Mask, Shape, and Position in one step.

Open [**Ex.15*starter**] and open the Layer window for the movie layer. Notice the oval mask that's already created (hit M for mask if you don't see it). Then type Shift+P to also see the Position property in the Time Layout window.

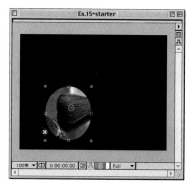

The easiest way to use the Pan Behind tool is to edit directly in the Comp window. Select the Pan Behind tool (Y is the keyboard shortcut), click inside the masked area in the Comp window, and drag the image to a new location. Notice that the mask is moving in relation to the image in the Layer window, and that the value of Position has changed.

The Pan Behind tool allows you to apparently animate a layer while keeping a mask stationary. You can see from the outline box that the layer is moving (left); release the mouse, and the layer has moved while the mask stays put (above).

The problem with the Pan Behind tool is that it changes the value of Position only *at the current frame.* This plays havoc with any motion path you might have already created, as it can't offset all the Position keyframes at once. If this is the case, you'll have to move the mask in the Layer window using the regular selection tool, then select all the Position keyframes and move the entire motion path so that the "window" moves back into position.

You can animate the Pan Behind effect, provided you turn on the stopwatch for both Mask Shape and Position. Practically speaking, the Pan Behind feature is useful only if you're animating how the mask moves across the image and you don't need to have a separate Position motion path. Personally, we find the Pan Behind feature too cumbersome to use and prefer to set up this kind of effect using two compositions. In this case, you would create the pan in the first comp, nest it in a second comp and apply the mask (more on this in *A Better "Pan Behind"* in Chapter 16).

Connect

How overlapping semitransparent layers interact are discussed in Chapter 5.

Track Mattes are discussed in Chapter 14.

Tips on how to combine masking with Motion Stabilization are discussed in Chapter 33.

You can save a lot of work masking film telecined to video if you remove the pulldown sequence first. This is covered in Chapter 38. Field issues are in Chapter 37.

14 All About Track Mattes

Mastering traveling mattes is a prerequisite for creating complex multilayered compositions.

Free Plug-ins

This chapter uses plug-ins that are included free on the book's CD, including Boris Tint-Tritone and Cult Effects' View Channel. Please make sure they're installed in your After Effects Plug-ins folder before opening the Examples Project file.

Example Project

Explore the 14-Example Project.aep file as you read this chapter; references to [Ex.##] refer to specific compositions within the project file.

We've been reinforcing the idea throughout this book that managing transparencies is the cornerstone of creating motion graphic composite images. But not all images come with their own transparencies – or ones we necessarily want to use. Therefore, we'll need to borrow another image to create those transparencies. This second image is called a *matte*.

A matte can be a grayscale still image, another movie, or an animated graphic such as text. At the end of the day, After Effects sees it as a 256-level grayscale image which it uses to define the transparency of another layer. Understanding matte logic and how to use mattes in a hierarchy of comps is one of the keys to creating complex animations.

What's in a Matte?

Creating an alpha channel in Photoshop is often the best option for simple still image composites. But what if you need to create an alpha channel for a QuickTime movie? For this effect, we use the After Effects' Track Matte feature. This feature has two options: Luma Matte or Alpha Matte. Whether you use the Luma or Alpha Matte setting is determined by *where* the grayscale information you want to use as a matte resides; there is otherwise no real difference between the two. If you create a grayscale image to use a matte, it's applied as a luma matte (see the sidebar *Under the Hood*). But if the grayscale information resides in another layer's alpha channel, it's an alpha matte. Either way, you're giving your movie a new grayscale image (or movie) to use as a transparency channel.

No matter which variation of Track Matte you use, there are three simple rules to follow to make it behave in After Effects:
• The Matte layer must be placed directly on top of the Movie layer.
• Set the Track Matte popup for the Movie layer, not the Matte layer.
• The Matte layer's visibility (the "eyeball") should remain off.

Creating a Luma Matte Effect

Let's jump in and set up a track matte. In this chapter's Example Project file, we've already imported a variety of sources and mattes for you to experiment with. We've also included a few final projects for you to see how things should have turned out. First, let's practice creating a track matte effect:

Step 1: Choose the movie you want to use from the Sources>Movies folder and drag it to the New Comp icon at the bottom of the Project window. This will create and open a new comp with the same size and duration as the movie.

Step 2: From the Sources>Mattes folder, drag in the xIL_GrungeSand to use as a matte. The matte should now be on top of the movie (if you drag sources to the comp in a different order, make sure the matte ends up on top).

Step 3: At the bottom of the Time Layout window, make sure the Switches/Modes button is set to Modes. The Track Matte is abbreviated to TrkMat, and is the rightmost popup. Select Luma Matte from the Track Matte popup for the Movie layer. Note that the name of the matte is included in the popup – this is a reminder that the Track Matte is using the layer *above* as a matte. (The matte layer has no popup available because there is no layer above *it* that could be used.)

As soon as you set the Track Matte popup, notice that the eyeball turns off for the matte layer, and a dotted line is added between the matte and the layer below. You will now see the movie you selected framed by the matte layer on top. If that's not the case, compare your results with ours in [Ex.01]. You may need to turn visibility back on for the matte when you're applying effects or animating it, but the eyeball should remain off when it's time to render. Also, if you move the movie up or down in the layer stack, make sure you also select the matte layer so they stay together as a group.

Just for fun, change the Track Matte popup to Alpha Matte. The matte appears not to work, but it does. Double-click the matte layer, and click on the white Alpha swatch at the bottom of the Layer window. Since this layer

A movie (left) is dragged into a comp first, followed by a grayscale matte image (center) on top. When the Luma Track Matte is applied, the result is the movie being "cut out" by the matte layer (right). Historical footage from Artbeats/NASA, The Early Years.

Black Eye

When you select a non-default Transfer Mode or Track Matte setting for a layer, its eyeball will fill with black. When you toggle back to the Switches column, the black eye will serve as a clue that a mode has been applied.

To tell the movie to use the layer above as a matte, the movie layer's Track Matte popup is set to Luma Matte, which then automatically turns off the visibility switch for the matte layer on top.

Head Scratching...

Matte not working? Make sure that the matte is on top of the movie and that the popup is set for the movie layer, not the matte.

Black Illustrator type against a black comp background can be hard to see, but if you look at just its alpha channel in either the Comp or Layer window, you'll see a matte in waiting.

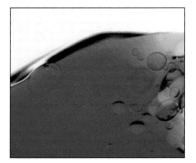

Our movie (left) is set to use the text layer above as an alpha matte. The movie now plays inside the type (right). Footage courtesy EyeWire/Liquid FX.

had no alpha channel, After Effects filled it with white. In fact, the movie's alpha channel is currently all white, for the same reason. So when you use the alpha as a matte, it displays the movie fully opaque just like it was before. Close the Layer window and revert back to Luma Matte.

The comp's background at this point might look like it's just black, but it actually represents transparency. Click on the comp's white Alpha swatch to display the layer's alpha – the luminance of the matte is now the comp's alpha channel. This transparency means you can either composite a background layer in the background, render this comp with an alpha channel, or nest it in a second comp so you can move both layers as a group (see *Building a Track Matte Hierarchy* later in this chapter).

Creating an Alpha Matte Effect

Creating a track matte using an alpha matte rather than a luma matte is very similar; the only real difference is the character of the source you're using for your matte. For example, Illustrator artwork usually works better as an alpha matte:

Step 1: Open comp [**Ex.02*starter**]. It may appear all black, even though there is a layer in it already. This is because the layer consists of black Illustrator text – not a very good luma matte, since it contains no luminance(!). To verify there is something there, either click on the Alpha swatch along the bottom of the Comp window, or change the comp's background color (Composition>Background Color) to something other than black.

Step 2: Drag a movie into the comp as well; we designed this example around EW_LiquidFX.mov, but feel free to try other sources, including your own.

Step 3: Now use what you've learned so far to apply the text as an alpha track matte for the movie layer.

(Having a problem? Remember to drag the movie layer below the matte and set the Track Matte popup for the movie layer, not the matte. This is the most common mistake – and some might say you learn best from your mistakes...)

You should now see the movie cut out by the Illustrator text map. In contrast, try the Luma Matte setting – the image disappears. This is because the matte layer is black in color, which means totally transparent to a luma matte. (For bonus points, select the type layer, hot key into Illustrator by hitting Command+E, change its color to white, save, and go back into After Effects. It will now work as either a luma or an alpha matte.) Again, changing the background color, or adding another layer at the bottom of the stack as a background, will illustrate these transparent areas more clearly.

Under the Hood

When deciphering how "Track Mattes" work inside After Effects, it may help to cover again how imported footage is treated. After Effects considers each footage item in a project as containing 32 bits of information: 24 bits of color information (Red, Green, Blue), and 8 bits of transparency information (Alpha). But that doesn't mean everything you import has to have four channels. If you import a regular QuickTime movie or any other 24-bit (RGB) source, the program will assign an alpha channel to it. Since it assumes you want the movie to be visible, this alpha channel will be completely white. Similarly, if you import a grayscale image, After Effects will place a copy of this image in each of the Red, Green and Blue channels, then add a fully white alpha channel.

So just because your grayscale matte may look like an alpha channel to you, this does not mean it will be transparent when it's added to a composition – these pixels reside in RGB colorspace. However, if you were to instruct After Effects to look at this layer's luminance, it would collapse the RGB image back to grayscale and use for a matte what in essence is your original grayscale image.

In short, when you're using a grayscale image as a matte, select the Luma Matte option. You'll use the Alpha Matte option when the matte image is defined

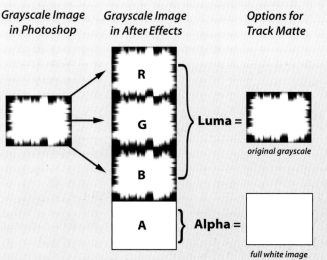

Grayscale Image in Photoshop   Grayscale Image in After Effects   Options for Track Matte

R
G
B } Luma =

original grayscale

A } Alpha =

full white image

Since After Effects always thinks internally in terms of R, G, and B color channels plus an alpha, even a grayscale image is divided into these channels (the same grayscale values are copied into each of the color channels), then its luminance is calculated.

by the alpha channel of the matte layer rather than by the luminance of its color channels, or when the matte is an Illustrator file.

Finally, a layer used as a matte or for an effect should have its visibility (the "eyeball") turned off. You don't want to see this layer; it's only in the comp to provide information to another layer. However, After Effects *does* see any masks, effects, or transformations you may have applied to this layer – it just uses them internally, rather than directly displaying them in the comp.

To Luma or To Alpha?

As you can see, alpha mattes behave just like luma mattes; they just look at different information in the source to create the matte. So how can you tell whether to use a luma or alpha matte? When you're starting out, you'll probably try one and if that doesn't work, you'll try the other. Most of the time, the right choice depends on whether the transparency information in the matte resides in the color or alpha channels. The rest of the time, it is a creative decision.

[**Ex.03**] contains our Kennedy movie that we used in earlier examples, a microphone for a matte, and a background layer. The microphone is from a still image "object" library, so it has an alpha channel cutting it

A   ALPHA

B   LUMA

C   ALPHA TRACK MATTE

D   LUMA TRACK MATTE

Some footage items work as either alpha or luma mattes. This microphone has both an alpha channel (A) and its own interesting luminance (B). It therefore can be used as an alpha matte (C) or a luma matte (D). Gray luminance values create partial transparency. Microphone courtesy Classic PIO/Microphones.

out from its background, but the image can also be looked upon as a luma map. Try both Track Matte options and compare the visual results.

Adding a Background

As we've started to show above, once you've created a Track Matte effect, the matte will create transparent areas. You can then add a background layer by simply adding a new layer to the comp and sending this layer to the back (Command+Shift+[is the shortcut). You don't need to also create an inverted matte for the background layer; the background will automatically fill the transparent holes.

A half black/half white luminance matte layer (left) is used to create a split-screen effect. When applied to the bodybuilder movie (below left), the black areas are transparent, allowing a second movie (below center) to show through in our final composite (below right). Footage courtesy EyeWire/Fitness and Backstage.

[Handwritten note: Matte -B/W (tif) / fitness - Luma / film - none]

An example of this is shown in [**Ex.04**]. Here, the matte is a "torn edge" split layer, with the luma matte applied to the Fitness movie. The movie of the film reels is added as a background, and it comes through on its own in the areas where the luma matte applied to the layer above it is transparent.

Soft Mattes

While it's common to use text or other well-defined shapes as mattes, you can also use blurry images and movies. This creates a softer falloff to the image being matted, leading to more interesting blends.

Soft-edged matte layers (left) can create very organic composites. Here, we've also tinted the Kennedy footage that gets the track matte (center) to use similar color tones as the film background (right).

In [**Ex.05**], we've prerendered a grayscale movie using the Cult Effects Noise Turbulent effect that we will use as a luma matte. Many effects can create great grayscale patterns, and some are even loopable so you can render just a few seconds and loop it in After Effects.

To finish the matte effect, we wanted the soft edges of the foreground movie (Kennedy) to blend well with the background movie (film reels). First we increased the contrast of the Kennedy movie, then we applied the Boris Tint-Tritone effect, using the Midpoint Color eyedropper to select a color from the golden background movie. Steps such as these add that extra bit of polish to composites and help make soft mattes in particular seem that much more natural and organic.

The final composite blends together into one unified color scheme.

Track Matte Inverted

So far, we've been applying mattes directly to movies to highlight a portion of them that we want to show through. However, it often makes sense to do the opposite: apply a matte inverted, so its white areas actually punch a hole through a layer, creating a picture frame effect. It now becomes easier to swap out movies behind this matted layer, without having to check or reset the Track Matte popup.

[**Ex.06**] is an example of this. The layer to be matted is footage of a flag waving. Double-click on the WiggleEdge map layer; note that its center is white with a black border. To punch a hole through the center of the flag with this matte, set the Track Matte popup to Luma Inverted. Now try adding other movies (such as the AB_NASAEarlyYears footage

Ex.06- Inverted Luma Matte • Time Layout

0:00:00:00

	#	Source Name	Track M
▷ ☐	1	⊞ xIC_WiggleEdge_loop.mov	Normal ▼
▷ ☐	2	⊞ EW_FabricFX.mov	Normal ▼
▷ ☐	3	⊞ AB_NASAEarlyYears.mov	Normal ▼	None ▼

No Track Matte

Alpha Matte "xIC_WiggleEdge_loop.mov "
Alpha Inverted Matte "xIC_WiggleEdge_loop.mov "
Luma Matte "xIC_WiggleEdge_loop.mov "
√ Luma Inverted Matte "xIC_WiggleEdge_loop.mov "

Switches / Modes

A typical matte has a white center and black border (left). If we want this to punch a hole through another layer and turn it into a "picture frame" where the white area is transparent, we need to set the Track Matte to Luma Inverted (above). Now we can place any source, or a montage of sources, behind this frame and it will show through the hole (right). Flag courtesy EyeWire/FabricFX.

with Kennedy) into this comp, dragging them below the flag layer – they'll show through this hole in the flag. Switch this popup between Luma and Luma Inverted if you're not clear on what it is doing.

The same "inverted matte" concept applies to alpha mattes as well. Go back to [**Ex.02-Alpha Matte_final**] and try switching it to Alpha Inverted; the water texture will now appear outside the type.

Using the Invert Effect

There are occasions when applying the Invert effect to a matte layer is *not* the same as using an inverted matte. This occurs when you are using a layer as a luma matte, and it also happens to have an alpha channel. When a layer is used as a luma matte, any alpha channel the matte layer has is also factored into the equation. This means that regardless of the luminance values of the image inside the alpha, any area outside the alpha (where the alpha is black) is considered to be luminance = black.

Yes, it sounds confusing, so let's run through an example. [**Ex.07a**] contains an alarm clock object; it so happens that this clock has a black face – which means when used as a luma matte, the face would be mostly transparent. If you wanted the layer being matted to show through this face, your first instinct might be to use an inverted luma matte. However, that "black" area outside the hole cut by the alpha channel becomes "white" when inverted – causing the matted layer to be shown through as well. Try it and see.

If you want to invert the effect of the luminance but still want the alpha channel of the layer being used as a matte to be obeyed, apply Effect>Channel>Invert to the matte layer; the default settings should work fine. This will invert the color channels of the matte (its luminance),

Open Effects Controls

If a layer has effects already applied, as in our final examples, select the layer and Layer> Open Effects Controls (or Command+ Shift+T) to view the effect settings.

CLOCK OBJECT

LUMA MATTE

LUMA INVERTED MATTE

CLOCK WITH INVERT EFFECT

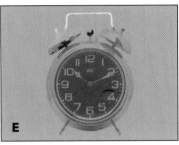

INVERT EFFECT + LUMA MATTE

When our alarm clock object (A) (shown against background color so you can see its alpha) is used as a luma matte (B), the liquid movie shows through the light silver case but is transparent where the face is black or the clock's alpha channel cuts it out. If you want the clock face to be opaque, an inverted luma matte will do that – but since it inverts the result of the track matte, the alpha is also inverted (C). However, if you apply Effect>Channel> Invert to the clock, this will invert its color channels (D). When used now as a regular Luma Matte (E), the result is that the clock's alpha is honored, and the face area is opaque as desired. Clock courtesy Classic PIO/Sampler.

but leave its alpha channel alone. This is shown in [**Ex.07b**]; select the matte layer and open Effects Control window (Command+Shift+T) to see the Invert effect settings. Note that Luma Matte is used, not Luma Inverted.

Increasing the Contrast of a Matte

When you're working with luma mattes, it is quite possible that the matte image you have does not contain quite the mixture of luminance values you want – for example, areas you want to be opaque may have some gray mixed in, resulting in partial transparency. Therefore, it is common to tweak the luminance values of a matte layer, using the Levels effect.

Open [**Ex.08*starter**] and study the layers – some footage of grungy black text on white is being used as a luma matte for a colorful image:

Step 1: Turn on the EW_TextFX layer; if you like this look, great. If you want the text to have more contrast, apply Effect>Adjust>Level to the text (matte) layer.

Step 2: When the Effects Control window opens, you'll see a histogram showing the range of luminance values that exist in the layer. Slide the black (leftmost) triangle underneath the histogram to the right to adjust the Input Black point – this pushes dark grays into full black.

Step 3: Slide the white (rightmost) triangle underneath the histogram to the left to adjust the Input White point – this pushes light grays into full white.

Step 4: When you're happy with the result, run the cursor over the Comp window and read the RGB values in the Info palette (Command+2). Black should read at 0 and white at 255. Don't forget to turn off the matte layer when you're done.

Luminance Adjustments

Layers used as luma mattes often benefit from some tweaking of their luminance values. Apply Effect>Adjust>Levels and adjust the image's Input Black and Input White points.

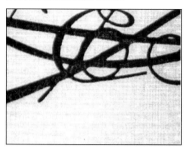

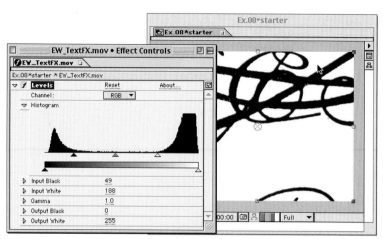

When a grungy black-and-white (and gray) text layer (above) is used as a luma matte, the light gray areas will not create full opacity. Increasing the contrast of the matte with Effect> Adjust>Levels (right) will convert more partial blacks to full black and partial whites to full white. Footage courtesy EyeWire/Text FX.

With the increase in the matte's contrast, note the difference it has in the final image: the text has much sharper outlines now, and more fully opaque areas. Check out [**Ex.08_final**] if you got lost.

If you need to increase the contrast of a matte's alpha channel, the Channels popup in the Levels effect can be set to modify the Alpha Channel only. There is also an Alpha Levels effect available from Effects>Channels that does the same thing, but without the histogram display.

Specifying One Channel as a Matte

Sometimes it's better to use just one channel of an RGB file as a matte, rather than a grayscale representation. In [**Ex.09*starter**], the blue-on-white EW_LiquidFX movie is used as a Luma Matte, but if you click on the comp's Alpha swatch you'll see that its luminance is rather flat.

Rather than applying a Levels plug-in to increase the contrast, turn on the eyeball for the matte layer, then select the Red, Green, and Blue swatches along the bottom of the Comp window in turn, looking for a color channel with more contrast. In this example, the Red channel is very close to a pure black-and-white image and would make a better matte than collapsing the RGB channels to grayscale.

Because the Luma Matte feature looks at the sum of the RGB channels, if you were to copy the Red channel into the Green and Blue channels,

Our liquid matte movie (left), while colorful, does not have enough contrast if viewed as a grayscale image (center), resulting in a washed-out composite when used by the eye movie as a luma matte (right). Footage courtesy EyeWire/Liquid FX and Senses.

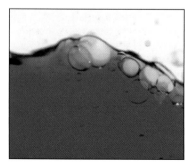

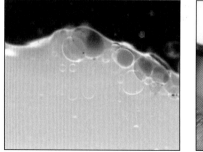

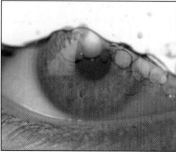

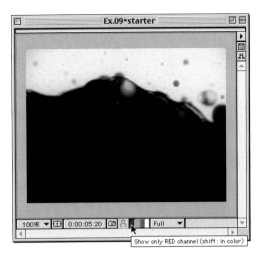

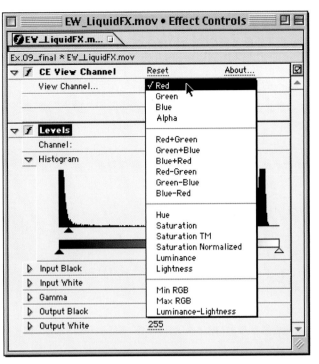

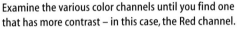

Examine the various color channels until you find one that has more contrast – in this case, the Red channel.

collapsing the RGB channels to grayscale will result in the same image as the Red channel alone (or expressed as a math equation…Red channel times 3, divided by 3, equals the Red channel). The following steps illustrate the process:

Step 1: Turn off any swatches, but leave the visibility on for the EW_LiquidFX matte layer. Select the layer and apply Effect>Cult Effects Xtras>CE View Channels.

Step 2: The default channel being viewed is Luminance. For this example, change the View Channel menu to Red.

Step 3: Turn off the eyeball for the matte. Click on the comp's Alpha swatch and note that the luminance of the matte is now represented solely by the original Red channel. To increase the contrast so that it's fully black and white, also apply the Effect>Adjust>Levels as in Example 08. See [**Ex.09_final**] for the final result; select the matte layer and open Effects Control window (Command+Shift+T) to see our effects settings.

An alternative to the CE View Channel effect provided by Cycore is the After Effects Shift Channels effects. It has fewer options, but you could either shift the Red channel into the Green and Blue channels for use as a Luma matte, or shift Red into Alpha for use as an Alpha matte.

Another alternative is to use the Set Matte effect applied to the movie layer (see sidebar on next page), set to point at the Red channel in the matte layer. There are disadvantages to using Set Matte though, as it is a compound effect (for more on compound effects, see Chapter 22).

To use just the Red channel as the luma matte, apply Effect>Cult Effects Xtras>CE View Channel. Set the View Channel popup to Red. You can boost the contrast further using the Adjust>Levels effect.

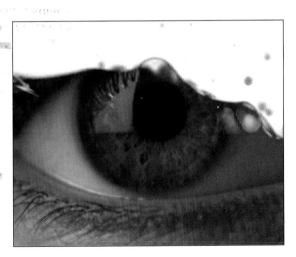

By using just the Red channel, and boosting its contrast, the result is a much stronger matte than could be achieved with a luma matte.

Using the Set Matte Effect

[Ex.10*starter] Before the Track Matte feature was added in After Effects v3.0, the usual way to apply mattes was to use the Set Matte effect. These days it's largely ignored and is included only so that legacy projects will be compatible. In fact, if you're still getting the hang of Track Matte, feel free to skip this section.

However, Set Matte has some advantages over Track Matte:

• Set Matte is applied to the movie layer, where it can select any channel from itself or another layer to use as a matte, regardless of their relative placement in the layer stack.

• Since the matte layer can reside anywhere in the layer stack, multiple layers can all point at a single matte layer. If you used Track Matte and need more than one layer to use the same matte, you would have to duplicate the matte layer for each movie as the matte must always be on top of the movie.

• The Set Matte effect determines the transparency of the movie, so if you follow Set Matte with Drop Shadow, the shadow effect will work as expected. (With Track Matte, you need to apply edge effects in a second comp.)

The biggest drawback is that Set Matte is a compound effect, so any effects or animation applied to the matte layer must take place in a precomp. The matte and movie layers should also be the same aspect ratio, so you may

need to prepare the matte by sizing it in a precomp.

To see how Set Matte works, follow along (or skip to Step 8):

Step 1: Open the comp **[Ex.10*Starter]**. The *matte* is the EW_LiquidFX layer, and the EW_Senses layer will be the *fill*.

Step 2: When using the Set Matte effect, the matte layer can be placed anywhere in the layer stack, but do turn off its eyeball.

Step 3: Select the EW_Senses layer, and apply Effect> Channel>Set Matte. The Effects control window will open. *Remember to apply the Set Matte effect to the movie layer, not the matte layer that's turned off!*

Step 4: In the Effects Control window, set the first popup Take Matte From to be the EW_LiquidFX movie. The effect will now look at the alpha channel for the matte layer – which happens to be a solid white rectangle, since it has no alpha.

Step 5: We determined in **[Ex.09]** that the red channel worked best as a matte, so set the Use For Matte popup to Red Channel. The movie will show up wherever the red channel is white.

Step 6: Turn on the Invert Matte checkbox so the opposite will be true.

Step 7: The other options in this plug-in are fine at their defaults. The Stretch Matte to Fit option determines what happens when the matte and the movie are

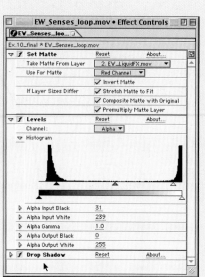

The Set Matte effect is a compound effect that uses either itself or another layer to determine the transparency of the layer it's applied to. In this example it's using the Red channel as a matte. The Levels effect then increases the contrast of this alpha channel. Since the transparency is created by the Set Matte effect, a Drop Shadow effect added later will work as expected.

different sizes (they aren't in this case). The Premultiply Matte Layer option is useful when the matte layer already has its own alpha channel; it factors it in.

Step 8: [Ex.10_final] is our version; select the EW_Senses layer and Layer>Open Effects Controls to see the effects applied. After the Set Matte effect, we added the Levels effect set to Alpha Channel to increase the contrast of the matte. We've also changed the background color to white and added the Effect> Perspective>Drop Shadow effect.

Fade the Movie or the Matte?

To fade in a movie with a track matte effect applied, you can fade up either the matte or the movie layer, as both will modify the transparency of the image. However, we suggest you apply Opacity keyframes to the *movie* layer. We demonstrate this in [**Ex.11**].

Why? For one, if you decide to remove the track matte, any opacity keyframes you applied to the matte layer will be removed too – meaning you lost your fade. If you create a track matte hierarchy (see below), we suggest you apply the Opacity keyframes in the second, higher-level composition – the idea being that you won't have to dig down into a pre-comp to edit the fade-up. And if you stay consistent, you'll always know where your fades are when you try to debug a project six months after you created it.

Slow Burn

To change the duration of "film burn" fades, change the Time Stretch value of the burn layer. Frame blending can smooth the result.

Head Burn Fadeout

Most of our examples for track mattes so far have been using still, or otherwise slightly animating, sources for our mattes. However, animated mattes that change their luminance over time can also be used. And since luminance affects transparency, these can be used for more complex fade-in and fade-out effects.

In this vein, one of our favorite sources for transitions are film head and tail "burns" that go from black (unexposed) to white (fully exposed) in interesting ways. [**Ex.12**] demonstrates this technique – it makes the footage fade in a flickering manner, characteristic of an old movie. This technique is also great for nervous text treatments.

To apply a matte transition such as this, you need to divide your movie into two segments, cutting it at the point where the transition is supposed to start or end. The tool Edit>Split Layer (Command+Shift+D) is handy for this. Leave the portion of the movie that is not supposed to have fades alone – i.e., no matte. For a fade-out, align your fade matte movie to the start of the second segment, placed above this segment in

Matte layers with luminance values that change over time can make for interesting fades in an underlying movie file. Film burn courtesy Artbeats/Film Clutter.

Ex.12-HeadBurn Fadeout • Time Layout

	#	Source Name	Mode	T	TrkMat		
▷	1	AB_FilmClutter_HeadBurn.mov	Normal ▼				head burn = matte
▷	2	AB_EarlyFlight_gray.mov	Normal ▼		Luma ▼		matte segment to fade
▷	3	AB_EarlyFlight_gray.mov	Normal ▼		None ▼		unfaded segment = no mattes

0:00:05:07

Switches / Modes

the Time Layout window. Set this second segment to Luma Matte. Your specific circumstances – whether your matte moves from light to dark or vice versa, and whether you're fading up or off – will determine whether you use Luma Matte or Luma Inverted to create the transparency.

To use track mattes for fades, divide the movie into two segments at the point where the fade starts or stops. Apply the track matte only to the segment to be faded.

The LiquidFX movie is matted by animating text and has its own luminance inverted. This is then transfer moded onto the original for effect.

Creating Animated Mattes

It's possible to have an animated matte simply by using a movie as the matte layer. But the matte layer can also be animated fully inside After Effects just like any regular layer, with all the keyframe and velocity controls you're already familiar with.

In [**Ex.14*starter**], Illustrator text is panned from right to left using two Position keyframes. This animated layer is then used as an alpha matte. Another way to look at this effect is as moving a "window" across the movie, rather than moving the movie itself. In [**Ex.14_final**] we turn on Motion Blur for the matte layer. To get more mileage out of the matte, we also added an Invert effect to the movie, which gets applied to a movie *before* its track matte is calculated. We then composited the track matte result over the original movie using the Hard Light transfer mode.

A larger layer is panned underneath its stationary matte, creating a moving texture through the title.

Animating the Fill

Conversely, you can keep the matte stationary and animate the fill. In [**Ex.15**], a metal-toned gradient was created in Photoshop using the KPT Gradient Designer filter, at a size that's wider than the matte. The texture is panned from right to left so that it moves inside the type created in Illustrator.

To animate the movie and matte together as a group, or to apply an edge effect (like a drop shadow), you'll need to build a hierarchy of comps…and that's what we're going to do next.

Building a Track Matte Hierarchy

One of the most powerful features of After Effects is its ability to create a hierarchy of nested compositions. Nesting is useful for project management and ease of editing, but it's also necessary to achieve specific effects. We'll cover the concepts of nesting and precomposing in detail in Chapters 16 and 17, but if you already know a little about nesting comps, you should be able to grasp the following specific information relating to track mattes. (If it proves too advanced, we suggest you complete Chapters 16 and 17, and return to this section later.)

In our first comp, we set up our basic track matte. The problem is, we can't animate the movie and matte as a group. Also, any edge effects need to be applied after the movie has been composited with the matte. Guitar footage courtesy of Desktop images.

Open [**Ex.16-Comp_1/matte**]. In this example, we've created a basic track matte effect. Note that in this composition, you can easily change the position of the matte independently of the movie (create a traveling matte), and move the movie layer independently of the matte (pan the movie behind the matte shape). You can animate each layer using keyframes just like you would animate any other layer, and apply an effect to one layer or the other.

However, you cannot easily move and scale both layers together without duplicating keyframes, which would spoil any independent motion paths the layers may have. You also cannot apply a drop shadow, glow, or similar filter to the edge of the movie *after* it has been composited with the matte. The reason is that according to After Effect's internal rendering order, effects such as Drop Shadow are added to the edge of the movie before the matte has been composited (when it's still a plain rectangular shape). For these reasons, it's best to use a separate comp to composite the movie with the matte. Once the track matte effect is complete, drag (or nest) this first comp into a second comp, where you can scale and position it as one layer, and apply a drop shadow to it.

[**Ex.16-Comp_1/matte**] is the first comp, where we apply the track matte. In this comp, we've scaled the matte to 90% and repositioned the movie inside the window. This first comp should ideally be the same duration as the movie layer; if the movie is shorter than the comp, any blank areas will show up as "empty calories" in the second comp. Neither do you want to trim any frames by making the comp too short: trim out excess frames in the second comp *after* you nest.

Synchronize Time

Force all comps in a chain to show the same frame by turning on "Synchronize Time of all related items" in File>Preferences>Display.

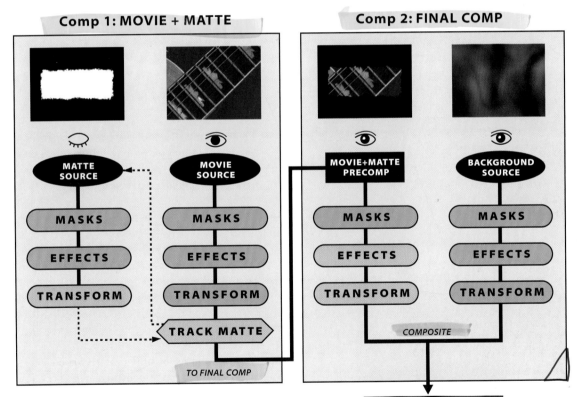

In Comp 1, the matte layer is turned off. When it's used by the second layer's track matte, the matte layer is triggered to run through its rendering order. Comp 1 is then nested in a second comp where the layer is positioned and scaled and a background added. The highlighted steps in the process are where editing has taken place: The matte animates in the precomp, and Track Matte is enabled for the movie layer. In Comp 2, the Comp 1 layer has been scaled and repositioned, and an effect (Drop Shadow) has been added.

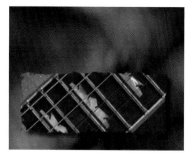

Once the first comp was complete, we created a second comp, [**Ex.16-Comp_2/fx**]. We then dragged in the first comp (nested it) and animated Scale and Position, which are applied to the movie and the matte as a group. We also applied Effect>Perspective>Drop Shadow and added a background layer. Edge-type effects (Drop Shadow, Glow, Bevel Alpha, and so on) applied in the second comp will work correctly, because the movie has already been composited with the matte in the first comp.

The hierarchy you've built is "live" until you actually render. The original movie and matte layers are still editable in the first comp. For more on nesting comps, check out Chapter 16.

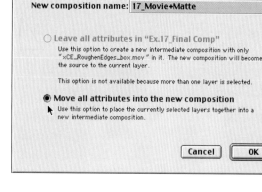

Comp 1/matte is nested in Comp 2/fx, where it is now one easy-to-manage layer. In this second comp, the matte composite is further animated, a drop shadow is applied, and a background layer is added. The result is a more complex yet manageable composite.

Precomposing after Track Matte

Nesting is by far the easiest way to set up a track matte hierarchy, but it does assume that you are planning ahead somewhat. What if you didn't plan ahead?

Let's say you built the track matte in one comp (let's call it Final Comp; it is [**Ex.17**] in this chapter's example projects), where you added a background and any number of other layers. Only afterward do you decide that you would like to move the movie and matte as one unit, and perhaps add a drop shadow. You can't nest this entire comp, as you would just be grouping *all* your layers – not just the two you need grouped. Don't panic: The Pre-compose feature lets you group the movie and matte layers together into their own comp (think of it as nesting backward). This new comp will then be rendered before your so-called Final Comp. Let's go through the actual steps involved:

Step 1: Open [**Ex.17-Final Comp**], where we've built a track matte effect and added a background. There could be many other layers as well. Now we decide that the movie and matte need to be panned from top to bottom as a group. Rather than apply the same Position keyframes to both layers, we'll group them using precompose, then move them as a group.

Select the two layers that make up your matte composite and Layer>Pre-compose (Command+Shift+C). Give this new comp you're creating a useful name, to make it easier to track later.

Step 2: To precompose, select both the matte (layer 1) and the movie (layer 2), and choose Layer> Pre-compose (Command+Shift+C).

Step 3: Give the new comp a useful name, such as **17_Movie+Matte**, and click OK. The two selected layers are replaced by one layer – the precomp – and this can be positioned and scaled as a group just as if you had nested it in the first place.

Step 4: Any keyframes or effects (attributes) that were applied to the precomposed layers have been moved to the precomp, where they are still live and editable. To open the precomp and add it as a tab, Option+double-click the new Movie+Matte layer. Now you can jump back and forth between the precomp and the original comp by clicking on the tabs. There's nothing special about this precomp; it's not much different from building the hierarchy by nesting.

The only drawback to precomposing the movie and the matte is that the new precomp will be the same size and duration

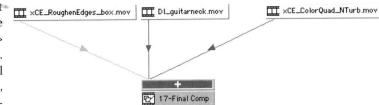

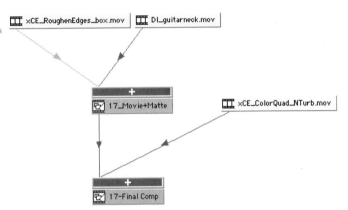

Before precomposing (above), all of our layers – matte, movie, and background – are in one composition. By selecting and precomposing the matte and movie layers, they are placed in their own comp, which then becomes a single layer in our original comp (below). (For this view, click on the Comp Flowchart Button, top right side of Comp window.)

as the Final Comp. This can be misleading if you have, say, a 30-second Final Comp, and you precompose two layers that are very short. The precomp will be 30 seconds in duration, and its layer bar in the Final Comp will indicate it's 30 seconds long – even though most of the precomp is empty. Chapter 17 covers precomposing in more detail and offers tips for addressing this problem. Below is another method of precomposing a track matte that avoids this problem altogether.

Precomposing before Track Matte

When you're building hierarchies of comps with track mattes, you can still think ahead even after you've already started. For example, [**Ex.18-Final Comp**] is a 30-second composition, with a background that spans the entire duration. The foreground movie is only 6 seconds long and has been scaled to 70%. We now decide that the foreground movie needs a more interesting torn edge effect, which we'll create by using a track matte. However, rather than adding the matte to this composition, scaling the matte to fit, then finding out that we have to precompose to create a group anyway, we'll precompose just the movie layer:

Step 1: Open [**Ex.18-Final Comp**]. Imagine you've just decided you need to create a track matte for layer 1, DI_guitarneck.mov. At this point, select the foreground movie layer and go Layer>Pre-compose.

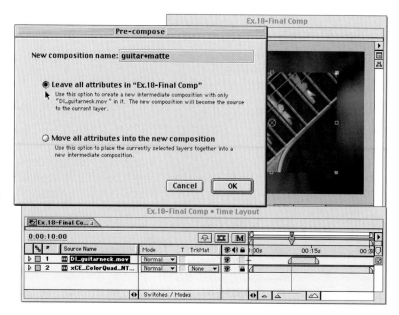

Step 2: In this case, we want to check the first Pre-compose option: Leave all attributes...This will make a new comp that is exactly the same size and duration as the movie we are precomposing, rather than one as long as the original comp (which was much longer than the movie we are moving).

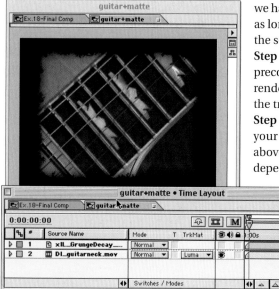

Step 4: In the precomp, we added the xIL_GrungeDecay layer as a luma matte for a torn edge effect.

Step 2: In the Pre-compose dialog, make sure you select the first option, Leave All Attributes. Don't forget to give the precomp a useful name, such as **guitar+matte** – we will be adding the matte in the next step. Click OK.

Step 3: The layer will be replaced by a precomp with the same size and duration as the movie. However, although the twirly is up, hit S and you'll see that the scale attribute remained in the current comp. (If we had checked the second option, this layer would now be as long as our comp, as opposed to our original movie, and the scale value would have moved down to the precomp.)

Step 4: Option+double-click to open the precomp. The precomp holds only the movie layer (at 100% scale) and is rendered before the Final Comp. Now is the time to create the track matte – *after* precomposing.

Step 5: From the Sources>Mattes folder, select a matte of your choice and drag it into the precomp. With the matte above the movie, apply either Luma or Alpha track matte depending on your matte. You can animate the movie and matte independently in the precomp.

Step 6: Return to [**Ex.18-Final Comp**], which shows the result of the track matte created in the precomp. You can now animate the movie and the matte as a group and apply Drop Shadow or other effects as you desire.

This is the same hierarchy you would have created had you planned ahead and created the track matte in one comp and then nested it. If you got lost along the way, check out our comps in [**Ex.18_result**].

Effects in a Track Matte Hierarchy

We will often further distress the outlines of mattes to make them more interesting. Effects that are capable of distorting pixels (blurs, scatter, wave warp, and so on) will give different results depending on what level of the hierarchy they are applied to, and whether they affect the movie, the matte, or both. You'll see that creating a track matte and using two compositions will give you the most flexibility in picking and choosing how effects are handled.

In the following series of examples [Ex.19-21], we've created a hierarchy you should be familiar with. The first comp in the chain (movie+matte) creates the track matte effect. This comp is nested in a second comp, Final Comp, where a background is added. We then experimented with three different variations that demonstrate the options available for adding a simple fast blur (Effects>Fast Blur). These options include blurring the movie and the matte, blurring just the movie, or blurring just the matte. You might want to close all open comps (Command+Option+W) before opening a new pair of example comps, just to keep things simple.

Adjustment Layers and Mattes

You can use an Adjustment Layer over track matte layers to add drop shadows and other edge effects to them – as long as there is no background behind them. Adjustment Layers affect all layers underneath. See Chapter 20 for more info.

The visual result of applying effects depends on where you apply them in the chain – for example, to a comp that contains both the movie and its matte (left), to just the inset movie but not its matte (center), or to just the matte shape (right). Footage courtesy Artbeats/Retro Healthcare.

▲ Effect Movie and Matte

Open the [Ex.19-Final Comp] and [Ex.19_movie+matte] comps. Notice the blur effect is applied to the nested comp layer in the second comp, after track matte is composited, and therefore blurs both the movie and the matte.

Close these comp windows with (Command+Option+W).

▲ Effect Movie Only

Open the [Ex.20-Final Comp] and [Ex.20_movie+matte] comps. Notice the blur effect is applied to the movie layer in the first comp. The blur is applied to the movie before the track matte is calculated, and therefore has no effect on the sharpness of the matte.

Again, close all comp windows.

▲ Effect Matte Only

Open the [Ex.21-Final Comp] and [Ex.21_movie+matte] comps. Notice the blur effect is applied to the matte layer in the first comp. The blur is applied to the matte before the track matte is calculated, and therefore has no effect on the sharpness of the movie.

Third-Party Edge Tools

If you have the Boris AE 3.0 package or higher, the Boris Alpha Process plug-in includes edge blurring for a softer edge that composites better. Alternatively, the Composite Wizard package from Puffin Designs has many useful edge tools, including Edge Blur, which you can apply after choking the matte.

Unmultiplying a Separate Matte

After Effects' Track Matte feature assumes straight-style alphas. The "fill" will appear larger than the grayscale matte, so when Luma Track Matte is applied, the edges will appear clean (the excess pixels will be outside the matte edge and therefore transparent). If you're outputting a separate fill and matte from another application, make sure you render with a Straight Alpha, not a Premultiplied Alpha (see TechTip 01 on the CD for more on Alpha Channels).

Many special effects stock footage CDs will supply separate mattes to use for their movies (they are separate files because the most common file format is JPEG, which doesn't support an alpha channel). However, these mattes are often derived from the original footage (such as an explosion), resulting in a premultiplied, rather than straight, alpha, because some of the background gets mixed in with the semitransparent parts of the image. An example of this is the Artbeats Cloud Chamber footage in [**Ex.22-Clouds-1/matte**].

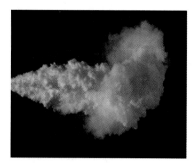
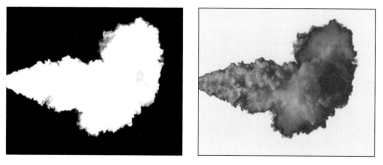

It is not uncommon for a special effects stock footage CD to supply both the image (left) and a separate matte created from the image (center). However, if you create a track matte using this matte pass, you may end up with fringing (right) – After Effects does not automatically know how to "unmultiply" the background out of the track matte. Footage courtesy Artbeats/Cloud Chamber.

This example uses a fairly common scenario in which the movie and the matte have been supplied as separate layers. You might also receive separate fill and matte from a 3D or editing program. In this case, the AB_CloudChamber movie was shot on film against a black background. No alpha channel in sight. By modifying the original movie, Artbeats managed to create an accompanying matte movie. The problem is that the fill and matte movies share the same edge. When a track matte is employed using this matte, the edges are premultiplied with black. This black fringe might be acceptable if you're compositing against a dark background (such as outer space), but not against a lighter background.

To remove the black fringe, or "unmultiply" it, you need to nest this comp into a second comp [**Ex.22-Clouds-2/remove fringe**]. In the second comp, the Effect>Channel>Remove Color Matting effect is applied, which helps to remove the black fringe. You cannot do this all in one comp, as the Remove Color Matting effect must occur after the track matte is already composited together because it's an edge effect (see *Building a Track Matte Hierarchy* above).

If the movie and matte were created precisely from a 3D program, it's likely that the edge would look fine at this point. But in this case, it helps

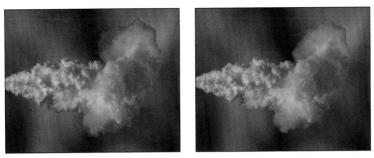

In a second comp, applying Effect>Channel>Remove Color Matting helps remove the fringe, although there still is some gray in the edges (left). Applying the Production Bundle's Effect>Matte Tools>Simple Choker with a value of +3 tightens up the matte the rest of the way (right).

to shrink the edge further. Therefore, if you have the Production Bundle, add the Effect>Matte Tools>Simple Choker with a value of positive 1 to 3 to "choke" the edge of the alpha channel. We use Simple Choker quite often to clean up these types of edges. You could also use the more advanced Matte Choker from the same submenu, if you find it works better for you.

Instead of creating a Track Matte effect, then trying to clean up the edge, we offer an alternative solution in [**Ex.22.1-Screen mode**]. Use the original "fill" movie and simply transfer mode it on top of your background using the Screen transfer mode. This will drop out the black background; although the result is quite different, it may be more pleasing depending on the images being used. Movies for fire, explosions, lightning, and so on often look better when you simply transfer mode them using Screen or Add mode. We discuss other alternatives to dropping out footage shot against black in Chapter 21.

When an image was shot against solid white or black, an alternative to creating a matte is to use transfer modes to blend an image into another layer.

Custom Transition Mattes

You can use any matte as a transition, provided that you animate the matte layer in such a way that at the beginning of the transition the frame is completely black, and at the end of the transition, the frame is completely white (or vice versa to wipe an image off instead of on).

You can use any shape, but those with a significant solid area in the center work best as a transition that zooms up and quickly fills the screen. Another option is to create an animation with white shapes that build on until the frame is filled with white. You could create this matte animation with an effect that spatters the frame with white particles, say, or use simple white solids in a precomp.

However you create the transition matte, we suggest that you apply the track matte only to the movie while it's transitioning. Once the transition is complete, Edit>Split Layer (Command+Shift+D) and turn off the track matte for the rest of the movie that plays normally (similar to the head burn fade-out in [**Ex.12**] above). This will save on rendering time; it also avoids having to extend a short matte.

Connect

Hot keying to external programs (such as Illustrator) is first described in Chapter 8.

Split Layer is covered in Chapter 9.

Nesting and precomposing compositions to build more complex hierarchies is detailed in Chapters 16 and 17.

Effects are covered in Part 5 (Chapters 19 through 25).

Choosing alpha channel type at render time is covered in Chapter 43.

Alpha channel types are explained in TechTip 01 on the CD.

Stencils and the "T"

Stencils are a great way to add transparency to multiple layers. And then there's that "T" switch…

The previous chapter was devoted to Track Mattes: having one layer create transparency for one other layer. Stencils, however, create transparency for *all* layers underneath. You can use a layer's luminance or alpha channel as a stencil, and invert it as well. This chapter also covers the Preserve Transparency switch and an obscure but useful layer mode called Alpha Add.

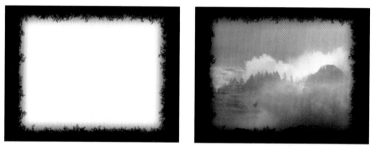

Three layers have been blended with transfer modes (left), meaning a simple single-layer track matte won't work in the same comp. We place our matte (center) on top; this will become the alpha channel for all underlying layers. If you set its mode to Stencil, it now cuts out all the layers underneath (right). Background montage images courtesy Artbeats.

Stencil Luma

In our first example [Ex.01*starter], we've composited three layers together using various transfer modes, and then added a matte layer on top which we'll use as a stencil. Turn on and off the top layer to view the layers below.

To access the options for stencils, make sure that the Switches/Modes button in the Time Layout window is toggled to Modes. The plan is to use the luminance of the grayscale image, xIL_GrungeDecay_matte, to set the transparency of all the layers below:

Step 1: Unlike with track mattes, make sure the eyeball is *on* for the top layer, and select Stencil Luma from the Modes popup. The grayscale image will disappear, and where the matte was white, the layers below are opaque.

Step 2: Click the comp's Alpha swatch on and off. The alpha channel is equivalent to the stencil's image. Areas that are black in the alpha channel denote transparency.

You can add additional layers *above* the stencil layer, and they will be unaffected by the stencil below. To temporarily disable the stencil, turn off the layer's visibility switch (the eyeball).

Example Project

Explore the 15-Example Project.aep file as you read this chapter; references to [Ex.##] refer to specific compositions within the project file.

		Ex.01_final • Time Layout				
	Ex.01_final					
0:00:00:00						:00s
	#	Source Name	Mode	T TrkMat		
▷ ☐	1	xlL_GrungeDecay_matte.tif	Stencil Luma ▼		👁	
▷ ☐	2	AB_ScenicWater.mov	Overlay ▼	None ▼	👁	
▷ ☐	3	AB_CloudsFog.mov	Screen ▼	None ▼	👁	
▷ ☐	4	AB_LiquidAmbience_loop....	Normal ▼	None ▼	👁	
			Switches / Modes			

The Stencil layer goes on top where it will cut out all the layers underneath. The differences with a track matte are that its Visibility switch must be on and that you select from the Mode menu instead of the TrkMat popup for this layer.

Stencil Alpha

No prizes for guessing that Stencil Alpha (demonstrated in [**Ex.02**]) is practically identical to Stencil Luma, except that the transparency is dictated by the stencil layer's alpha channel, not its luminance. In this example, the alpha channel of an Illustrator file is used for transparency. In addition, the stencil is animated using Position keyframes, which results in a moving window revealing the images below.

Just as with a track matte, you can apply effects directly to the stencil layer. For example, try adding an Effect>Stylize>Scatter and adjusting its scatter amount. Notice that when you apply Effects to the Stencil layer, they affect the edge of the stencil only, not the layers below. (To apply an effect to all layers below, you would use an Adjustment Layer, covered in Chapter 20.)

Layers with alpha channels – such as Illustrator artwork – can be used in Stencil Alpha mode. Note that you can also animate the stencil layers to make the mask move (this illustration shows the midpoint between two position keyframes we have set).

Effects applied to stencil layers affect the edges of the matte only, but not the layers underneath.

Stencils 101

After Effects' stencils are akin to the stencils you buy in art stores: masks with cutout centers where the characters or images are supposed to show through. The "transparent center" of a real-life stencil is the equivalent of an opaque area in After Effects, which is defined by the areas where the stencil layer's luminance or alpha channel are white. Black areas in the stencil layer mean block out or remove the image underneath; gray areas are partially transparent. Silhouettes are the opposite, and could be thought of as simply inverted stencils: They block out the areas where the luminance or alpha are white and allow the underlying layers to show through where the matte layer is black. They are the equivalent of the Luma Inverted or Alpha Inverted choices for track matte types.

STENCIL ALPHA

STENCIL LUMA

CLOCK OBJECT: Choice between
LUMA (left) or ALPHA (right)

SILHOUETTE ALPHA

SILHOUETTE LUMA

If a layer has both interesting luminance and alpha channel information, such as many object library images (above), they can be used as either alpha or luma stencils or silhouettes. Experiment with **[Ex.03]**, and compare the results of using this object as Stencil Alpha, Stencil Luma, Silhouette Alpha, and Silhouette Luma. Clock from Classic PIO/Sampler.

Silhouettes and Alpha versus Luma

A *silhouette* is nothing more than an inverted stencil (it sure would be easier to understand if that's what they were called). The options offered are for Silhouette Luma and Silhouette Alpha, based again on whether the luminance or alpha of the layer dictates the transparency.

Explore [**Ex.03**] on the CD. Just as with Track Matte, if the stencil layer has both an alpha channel and a non-solid-black image in its color channels, it may work well set to either Silhouette Luma or Silhouette Alpha. Using the CP_AlarmClock as your mask layer, compare the results of both stencil modes, and their inverted silhouette counterparts.

Adding a Background Layer

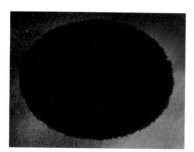

Arrange your stencil and the layers it is cutting out in their own composition (above), then nest and composite this comp over a background layer in a second composition. A bonus of this is the ability to add shadows and other effects to the stenciled result, shown here with the Glow effect applied (right). Mayhem, Liquid Ambience, and Retro Transportation footage courtesy Artbeats.

Because stencils, by definition, cut out all layers below, any background layer added to a comp will also be cut out by the stencil. To make them coexist, you will need to split them into two separate compositions. (We don't cover nesting compositions until the next chapter, but if you

already know a little about nesting, you should be able to follow this specific information relating to stencils. If it proves too advanced, we suggest you return to this section at a later date.)

First, create your stack of images to be stenciled in one comp, with your stencil layer on top. Then, create a second composition and nest the first comp into it. Now you can add a background layer to the second comp that will remain unaffected by the stencil, which is already composited in the first comp. An example of this chain is [**Ex.04-Comp-1/stencil**] and [**Ex.04-Comp-2/BG**].

As a bonus, you can now apply various edge treatments and effects to the stencil comp layer when it is nested in the second comp. For instance, we added Effect>Stylize>Glow in our second comp. Of course, you could apply Glow to an adjustment layer placed at the top of the stack in comp 1, but it's better applied in comp 2 where you can see how it relates to the background image. (Note: The Glow effect is a Production Bundle effect – but it's also free from Adobe on the accompanying CD.)

Preserve Transparency

When Preserve Transparency is turned on for a layer, the combined transparencies for all layers *underneath* affect the transparency of the layer you have turned it on for. This useful feature tends to get overlooked by many users. First, it shows up as a nondescript little T switch in the Modes panel. Second, if one of the layers in the comp underneath the one getting Preserve Transparency is full-frame, this switch will have no effect, since there would be no transparency to borrow. Hence, you

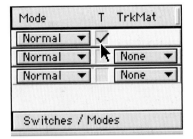

The nondescript Preserve Transparency switch is noted by a T when the Switches/Modes panel is showing Transfer Modes and Track Mattes.

might have relegated it to the "I wonder what that switch *does*" category… That's about to change:

Step 1: Open the [**Ex.05*starter**] comp , which consists of two objects each with their own alpha channels. Click on the comp's Alpha swatch, which displays the sum of both alphas. The white areas show where the objects are opaque, and

the black areas denote total transparency. Turn it off when you're done.

Step 2: Turn on the eyeball for the top layer, EW_Reflections, which obscures the layers below. Now turn on the T switch in the Modes panel. The top layer is displayed only where the underlying layers are opaque.

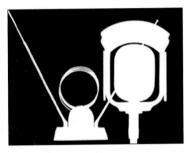

Step 1 starts with two images from the Classic PIO object libraries (left), each with their own alpha channels (right).

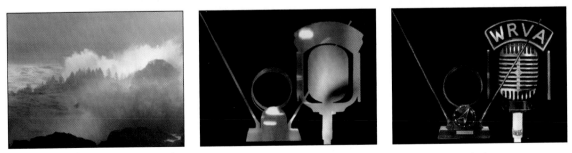

Adding a full-screen layer on top blots out those underneath (left). By switching on Preserve Transparency, the layer appears inside only the opaque areas of the alphas of the object layers below (center). Changing the top layer to Overlay Transfer mode uses just the highlights instead of the opaque image (right). Footage courtesy EyeWire/Reflections of Light.

Collapsing Stencils

Stencils and the Preserve Transparency option usually affect layers only in the comp they are in. However, if you nest the comp and set the Collapse Transformations switch (Chapter 18), their effect will carry into the second comp as well.

Spotlight - overlay - T
Tuattena 7 *w/ alphas*
microphone

A spotlight layer transfer-moded on top of underlying images shows both the spotlight and its effect on the layers underneath (at right). When Preserve Transparency is switched on for the spotlight layer, it's restricted to appearing only inside the alpha channels of the underlying layers (far right). The result is a subtle animated lighting effect.

Step 3: The top layer is otherwise just like any other layer. Change its transfer mode popup to Overlay so that the highlights in the movie are composited over the two objects, rather than obscuring them completely. This is shown in [**Ex.05_final**].

There's nothing you can do with Preserve Transparency that you couldn't do with a couple of comps and a track matte – it's just another tool to add to your growing arsenal of layering tricks, especially if you prefer to do as much as you can inside one composition instead of across several.

Glints and Highlights

Preserve Transparency is often used for adding glints and highlights to underlying layers. You can use Photoshop or After Effects to create soft-edged "glint" elements, then animate them across titles or objects to introduce subtle lighting effects. In [**Ex.06**] we moved a still image of a "spotlight" across the comp, and displayed it only inside the underlying layers. (The spotlight image was created using the Boris AE Spotlight effect, and saved as a still image with an alpha.)

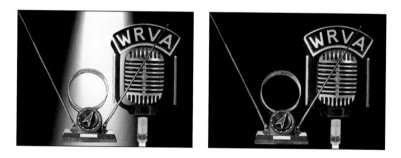

Stencil versus Track Matte

The Track Matte and Stencil features can both accomplish the same results, but they go about it in different ways:

• Stencils can affect multiple layers, but a track matte can be applied to only one layer using one matte. You'll need to group layers in a precomp if you need to apply a matte to multiple layers.

• You can have multiple stencils per comp, and you can create "doughnut" shapes or frames by combining stencils and silhouettes. Since After Effects renders from the bottom up, the lower stencil is calculated first, ending at the top stencil. You can't apply more than one track matte to a layer in one comp.

• Stencils affect all layers below them, so trying to add a background layer is futile – it will get cut out as well. You need to nest the stencil comp into a second comp and add the background there. You *can* add a background to a Track Matte comp, although you will have more flexibility if you also use a precomp (see Chapter 14).

• Track mattes and stencils can be mixed in the same comp so long as you keep track of their individual logic: A track matte takes its transparency data from the layer above, while stencils affect all layers below.

• Finally, with track mattes, the matte's visibility should be off, but with stencils and silhouettes, the eyeball needs to be on.

Preserving a Background

If you add a background layer to a comp where a layer has Preserve Transparency applied, the spotlight layer will become visible wherever the background is opaque. In this case, you'll need to composite the glint within certain layers only in the first comp, then add background layers in a second comp (just as we did when we combined stencils and backgrounds earlier in this chapter). This is shown in the chain [**Ex.07-Comp-1/spotlight**] and [**Ex.07-Comp-2/BG**].

Of course, compositing the spotlight over the full frame may look all right with some backgrounds – depending on the transfer mode used, it may look like a volumetric lighting effect. See [**Ex.07b-volumetric light**].

T Does Nothing

Remember that if the comp's alpha channel is fully white, Preserve Transparency will appear to do nothing.

Alpha Add with Stencils

Well, we promised you something obscure, and the Alpha Add mode is it. To keep track of what's going on, close all other comps (Command+Option+W), and open [**Ex.08*starter**]. Preview the animation and note how the two sides of a torn-edge matte meet at 02:00 – but not exactly seamlessly. What's wrong?

The left side is using stencil luma, and the right side is the same image using silhouette luma (exactly like the left side, but inverted). Where the alpha channels meet along the seam, both antialiased edges have identical transparency values. But instead of adding these values together, the transparency of both layer edges are honored and factored together (50% opaque + 50% opaque = 75% opaque, not 100%). Since this fails to result in a fully opaque pixel, you get an ugly seam.

When any mask or matte edge is combined with its inverted cousin, a seam will appear where their partial transparencies meet (above left). By selecting the Alpha Add mode for the one on top (see Time Layout window below), the complementary alpha values will be added together, and the seam will disappear (above right).

That can be fixed. Select the top layer, and from the Transfer Modes popup in the Modes panel, select the Alpha Add mode. The complementary alpha channels are added together, as opposed to compositing on top of each other, and the seam disappears.

If you're curious as to how this animation was created, check out the precomps for [**Ex.08**]. The first comp, [**Ex.08_layer group**], composites the layers that will be sliced in two. This is nested in both the [**Ex.08-Stencil_Left**] and [**Ex.08-Stencil_Right**] comps, where the stencils are applied. Any changes made to [**08_Layer_Group**] comp will reflect in both the left and right sides. The two sides are then nested in [**Ex.08-Alpha Add**] and animated so that they join to form a complete image.

Connect

How transparency values add is covered in the *Advanced Opacity* sidebar in Chapter 5.

Nesting is discussed in more detail in Chapter 16.

Adjustment Layers, which apply effects to all underlying layers, are discussed in Chapter 20.

16 Nesting Compositions

Creating complex motion graphics that are easy to edit requires building a hierarchy of compositions.

In this first of three chapters that show you how to build a hierarchy of comps, we emphasize creating complex animations that are easy to edit. We also delve further under the hood of After Effects' rendering order: Understanding how data travels through the hierarchy will help you troubleshoot complicated effects when the result is not exactly what you had planned…

If you've been following the book in a linear fashion, and don't feel quite ready to deal with this subject quite yet, feel free to jump ahead to the first chapter of Part 5, Chapter 19, *Applying Effects*. After you've had some fun in that part, come back here – especially if you want to more fully exploit the power of Compound Effects (the subject of Chapter 22).

Nesting 101

Graphics applications vary wildly, but advanced ones usually have one thing in common: a method of "grouping" items so you can transform multiple layers as easily as you can transform one layer. In After Effects, you edit layers as a group by giving them their own composition, and then by "nesting" this comp inside another. Nesting compositions also serve a second purpose: They allow you to build effect chains that need to go beyond the normal rendering calculation performed on a layer in a single comp.

Once you determine that more than one comp is necessary, the question becomes whether or not you were planning ahead. If you were, you'll find nesting comps to be quite straightforward and intuitive. However, if you discover a problem after the fact, you'll probably need to use the Precompose feature (which we cover in detail in the next chapter).

We have prepared many examples to show you how nesting works, and some of the tutorials projects on the CD that use hierarchies also show you how best to take advantage of (and troubleshoot with) the incredibly powerful nesting feature. But if this is your first time, let's run you through how to nest:

Step 1. Open this chapter's project [**16-Example Project.aep**] and make a new composition, 320×240, with a duration of 06:00. Name the comp Spheres-1.

Comp Won't Nest?

If a comp refuses to nest (it just bounces back to the project window), chances are you're accidentally attempting to set up an "infinite loop" of comps that would use each other.

Example Project

Explore the 16-Example Project.aep file as you read this chapter; references to [Ex.##] refer to specific compositions within the project file.

Step 2. Open the Sources folder, then the Objects sub-folder, and add three of the sphere images inside this folder at time 00:00 in your comp. Scale them all 50% and arrange them in a triangle around the center of the comp. You (or the client) now decide that what you really would like is to rotate and scale the trio of sphere images as a group. Have you just wasted your time? No!

Step 3. Rather than editing each layer's anchor point and applying rotation and scale keyframes to each layer individually, nest this first comp into a second comp. (Believe us, it's easier.) To do this, create another new composition, 320×240, with a duration of 06:00. Name this second comp Spheres-2. The number denotes it is the second comp in a chain called Spheres – naming conventions are very important when you're managing multiple comps.

Step 4. From the Project window list, locate the first comp, Spheres-1. Just as you would drag in any source to become a layer, drag the first comp into the second comp (Spheres-2). It will now appear as one layer, called Spheres-1. Move the layer around and notice how it moves as a group. Drag it back to the center of the comp.

Step 5. To add rotation to the group, make sure the Spheres-1 layer is selected in the Spheres-2 comp, type R, turn on the stopwatch for the Rotation parameter, and create two keyframes. We used 0° at the start of the layer and a value of 3 revolutions at the end. Preview the animation. The anchor point for the group defaults to the center of the nested comp layer so all three spheres will rotate around the same point.

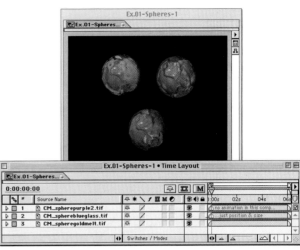

Step 2: Three spheres, scaled and positioned in a comp. But now we want to animate them as a group…

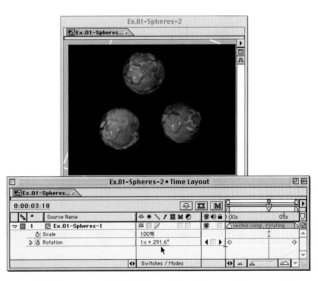

Step 5: The first comp with the three spheres is nested in a second comp and rotated as a group.

Keeping Comps in Sync

Before you get too far into nesting comps, you need to set one preference. Under File>Display Preferences, turn on "Synchronize time of all related items." This means that when you move in time in one comp, all comps in the same chain will synchro-nize and park their time markers on the same frame. This is particularly useful when your layers don't all begin at time 00:00, and it makes it relatively easy to synchronize keyframes across multiple comps in a chain. The program may feel more sluggish with this option on, particularly with an extremely complicated hierarchy, but the trade-off is usually worth it.

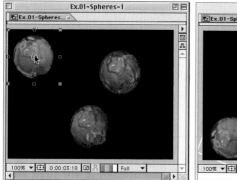

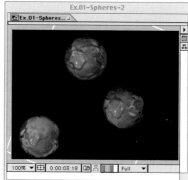

Step 8: Using nested comps means your source material is always "live" – for example, moving a sphere in the first comp (on the left) automatically updates the comp it is nested in (on the right).

Once you have animated a group of layers as a nested comp, you can add other elements such as a background in the second comp in the chain.

The Drop Shadow in the second comp applies to both the planet and title as a group, and renders with a consistent effect as they are both scaled 100% at this stage.

Step 6. Notice that you can reposition, scale, trim, and apply effects to the nested comp layer just as you would any single layer. In fact, the nested comp behaves just as if you had rendered the first comp and reimported it as a finished movie, with one very important difference: *The first comp is still "live."*

Step 7. At this point, the tabs for both comps should be visible along the top of the Comp window. Select the Spheres-1 tab and drag it out of its current window; this will create a second Comp window. Now you can see both comps side by side. The Time Layout window will reflect whichever Comp window is forward.

Step 8. In the first comp, move one of the spheres and notice how any change is automatically reflected in the second comp when you release the mouse. The first comp is rendered at the relevant time, and the resulting RGB+Alpha frame is sent to the second comp for further compositing.

Step 9. Note that the transparent areas of the first comp (where the background color is visible) are retained when the layer is nested. In the second comp, click on the Alpha swatch to confirm this for yourself.

Add any background layers to the Spheres-2 comp so they will be unaffected by the rotation keyframes; any images you add to Spheres-1 will be rotated along with the spheres. If you've gotten lost along the way, check out our versions: [**Ex.01-Spheres-1**] and [**Ex.01-Spheres-2**]. We used a background movie we created using Cult Effects as our background in the second comp.

Easy Editing for Effects

Nesting a comp not only allows for animating multiple layers as a group, it's also a convenient way to apply an effect to a group of layers at once. In [**Ex.02-Planet-1**] comp, the planet movie and the planet type animate independently of each other. In the second comp [**Ex.02-Planet-2**], the first comp is nested and a Drop Shadow effect is added.

Because the shadow applies to both the planet movie and the planet text as a group, it's easier to edit it than if you applied it to the layers individually in the first comp. Also, in the first comp, the planet movie is scaled 45%, while the type is at 100%. If you were to apply the drop shadow to each layer individually, the effect would be affected by the scale values since Scale happens after Effects (more on the rendering order later in this chapter). Scaling a layer with a drop shadow effect renders the shadow with less distance and softness, so the shadow on the planet movie would appear harder than the planet type, even with the same values for each parameter. This problem is not limited to Drop Shadow – many other effects, along with mask feather, are affected by scaling.

We've also used the second comp to fade out the nested comp as a group, which again is easier than duplicating Opacity keyframes for multiple layers. The more you start working with nested comps, the more opportunities you'll recognize for saving time and effort.

Example: Grouped Distortion

You'll apply an effect to a nested comp not only for expediency – it may be the easier (or the only) way to create a certain look. In [**Ex.03-Distort-1**], two animated skulls are positioned facing each other. This comp is then nested in [**Ex.03-Distort-2**] where a polar coordinates effect is added. Because the effect is being applied after the two skulls have already been composited into one layer, the distortion effect is capable of blending together pixels from both skulls.

This would be practically impossible to achieve in one comp. It would not look the same if you applied the effect to both layers individually. You can work around it with Adjustment Layers (discussed in Chapter 20), but then you couldn't place a background in this comp without distorting it as well.

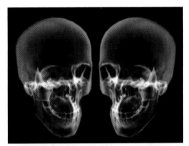

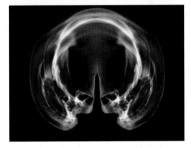

Two skulls are positioned side by side in one comp (top), then blended together using Effect>Distort>Polar Coordinates in a second comp (bottom).

Editing a Sequence of Video Clips

Although After Effects is not designed to be a video editing package, the concept of nesting comps can make managing edits much easier. An edit between several clips, or several different points in time in one clip, can be set up in one comp. Then this edited whole can be used as a "single" clip in another comp. This lets you re-edit or replace footage in the first comp without having undue pain and suffering inflicted upon the animation in the second.

For example, say you had a job of creating a regular 5-second segment for a news program. This week, the subject is the Hindenburg. You are provided with an 8-second historical clip (AB_EarlyFlight in the Movies subfolder of the Sources folder); you need to edit it down to 5 seconds.

| Ex.04-Editing-1 • Time Layout | | | | | | | | | |

Create a 320×240 comp 05:00 long and drag your footage into it. Preview the clip in its Layer window and place markers for any previously existing edits or other points that catch your eye. Chop it up (the Edit>Split Layer command is helpful), sequence it, crossfade it, and preview it until you are happy. An example of this is [**Ex.04-Editing-1**].

[**Ex.04-Editing-2**] contains the rest of the "look" for our show open: text, background, and animation accompany the video footage.

One use for nesting is to easily swap edited sequences of clips. The first step is to create our video edit in the first comp, [**Ex.04-Editing-1**].

[Screenshot of Ex.04-Editing-2 composition and Time Layout window]

We then swap our edited sequence in as a single layer in a composite, **[Ex.04-Editing-2]**, that's already built. Historical and background footage from ArtBeats/Early Flight and Liquid Ambience; aged film texture from IF Studios.

Theoretically, next week you could simply re-edit the footage in the first comp to update the animation automatically. Alternatively, you could build a new 5-second comp with a new video montage, then replace the current [**Ex.04-Editing-1**] layer in the second comp with your new edit (select the old layer, and Option+drag the new comp from the Project window into the Time Layout window). All existing attributes applied in the second comp will be retained when you replace the layer. As an exercise, build a new video edit for next week's show using the AB_RetroAmericana footage, and replace the layer in [**Ex.04-Editing-2**].

Size Doesn't Matter

You're already aware that layers can be larger, or a different aspect ratio, than your comp. This means you can pan around them or scroll them past your "virtual" camera to create interest.

The same, of course, can be done with compositions as layers. As of version 4.1, comps can be as large as 30,000×30,000 pixels (you'll need a lot of RAM, but hey). This gives you a lot of freedom to construct elaborate "stages" or "sets" in one comp, then nest this in a second comp that will act as an animatable camera through which you see the first comp. This approach to animation is another way in which After Effects differs significantly from traditional editing systems.

A simple example of this is [**Ex.05**]. In the first comp, we have built a vertical string of six 3D glass spheres in a comp that measures 200 pixels wide by 1200 pixels tall. This strip is then brought into a second comp, where it is scaled, positioned, and scrolled vertically, interacting with other layers behind it with the Hard Light transfer mode. A solid layer, with mask and feather top and bottom, serves as a track matte so that the top and bottom of the animated tall comp is matted out. This makes animation easier, because we had to keyframe the move of only one layer – the nested tall comp – rather than each sphere individually.

Nested Comps for Mattes

Sometimes, a piece of footage and its matte or key will be provided as separate layers. Marrying them together in one comp, and using that comp as a single layer elsewhere, makes handling them easier.

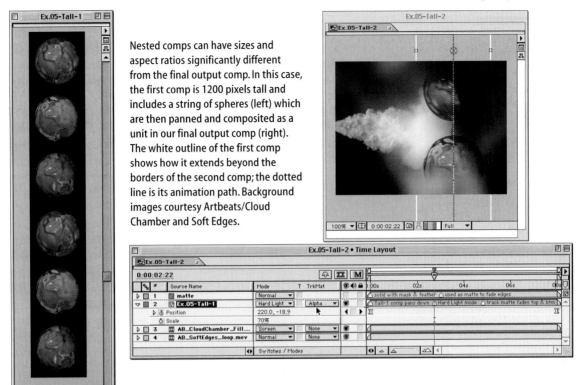

Nested comps can have sizes and aspect ratios significantly different from the final output comp. In this case, the first comp is 1200 pixels tall and includes a string of spheres (left) which are then panned and composited as a unit in our final output comp (right). The white outline of the first comp shows how it extends beyond the borders of the second comp; the dotted line is its animation path. Background images courtesy Artbeats/Cloud Chamber and Soft Edges.

The motion control technique for panning around photographs documentary-style, as covered in Chapter 6, should also be used when moving around a large composition. The general rule again is that if you're animating the Scale parameter to simulate a camera pushing in or pulling out, you should be animating the Anchor Point instead of Position, to ensure that all scaling occurs centered around the area of interest.

Greater than Two

Once you're familiar with nesting, you don't need to stop at just two. Building a complex animation may involve many nested comps. You should create as many levels in the hierarchy as necessary to make editing the animation easy and efficient. Managing an extra comp or two is usually easier than trying to keep layers in sync with each other. In the [Ex.06] series of comps, we use three comps to create our animation:

Wheel-1/rotates: A small comp (200×200) is used to animate the wheel and is only as big as the wheel image requires. This comp is longer in duration (12 seconds) than required.

Wheel-2/six up: The first comp is nested in a second, wide comp (1200×200, 8 seconds duration), where the rotating wheel is duplicated. Each layer is offset in time from the other to vary its appearance. Because the first comp was longer than this comp (12 seconds compared with 8), the offset layers don't come up short in time.

Opening a Nested Comp Layer

Option+double-click a nested comp layer to open the original comp rather than its Layer window. The nested comp will be added as a tab, allowing you to switch between comps easily.

Duplicates

When you're creating a series of similar comps, create one, duplicate it (Command+D in the Project window), and Replace Source (Option+drag) for just the item that differs from comp to comp.

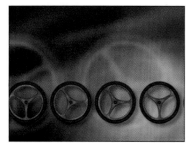

A chain of nested comps make complex animations easier to manage. A single wheel is rotated in the first comp; six of these are then arranged and offset in time in a wide second comp. This wide comp is used twice, at different scalings and animation speeds, in the final comp. Background courtesy Artbeats/Liquid Ambience.

Wheel-3/final: The second comp is then nested in a third comp where it is duplicated (Command+D). The foreground layer is scaled down, panned from right to left, and a drop shadow is added. The larger background layer – another copy of the second comp – also pans, but more slowly (24 pixels/sec, compared with 77 pixels/sec). A blur effect has also been added to help it recede into the background.

The beauty of this hierarchy is that the rotation speed of all twelve wheels is controlled by just two Rotation keyframes in the first comp. Change the second keyframe in this comp to another value, and see how the edit ripples through the chain. Go one better, and replace the original wheel source with one of the sphere images – now you have twelve spheres rotating. (Not that clients ever change their minds…)

Creating Master Colors and Logos

Nested comps do not need to be used in a strictly linear "this one goes into that" fashion. You could also create *master* comps for logos, colors, and so forth, so editing just the master updates every place that particular color or item is used.

Say you needed to create a number of credits for a show. The client hasn't decided on the color yet, but you need to get started anyway. First, create a Master Color comp that contains just a simple solid layer of the color you think is appropriate. In the first Credit comp you create, nest the Master Color comp, place it under the text layer, and its Track Matte popup to Alpha Matte – the master color will now show inside the outlines of the text layer above. Animate the credit as needed, and then duplicate this comp as many times as you have credits, customizing each credit as required.

Now, when the client picks the final color (for the umpteenth time, and at the very last minute), change just the color of the solid in the Master Color comp. The change will be reflected in all the Credit comps that use this master color. This chain is shown in [Ex.07]; open one of the credits, change the color in the master, and see how it ripples throughout all the credit comps.

The text layer merely acts as an alpha channel and is colorized by the master color comp. Changing the color there ripples through all the credit comps that use it.

General Nesting Tips

• The biggest and best tip we can offer is to *give comps useful names!* Otherwise, we guarantee that you'll waste valuable time poking around and wondering which comp does what.

• If you find yourself duplicating keyframes so that multiple layers are in sync, stop and ask whether you should be nesting comps instead, so you can manipulate multiple layers as a group.

• The general idea when building a hierarchy is that you don't scale down layers until the final comp. Once you scale layers, a smaller image is created and resolution is lost. (It's possible in some cases to recover resolution with Collapse Transformations – more on that in Chapter 18.)

Flowchart View

Version 4.1 includes a new feature that lets you see your chain of comps and layers within a comp in a diagrammatic "flowchart" view. This is helpful when you're trying to grasp a complex chain – particularly when someone else created a project that you now have to reverse engineer.

There are two Flowchart Views: one for the entire project file, and one for the current chain of comps. Project View tends to be a bit of mess, since it contains every comp chain in the project, but it can help you sort out which source comps and footage items are used where. Comp View shows the current comp and all its layers and nested comps, but not which comps use the current comp. The Flowchart View for the last comp in a chain (the one you will render) tends to be the most informative.

To access Flowchart View, click on the icon (it looks like a picnic table) in the upper right corner of the Comp window. This opens a resizable window, with comps and layers drawn as bars, connected by wires with arrows. You can drag items to new positions to make the flowchart more legible, but

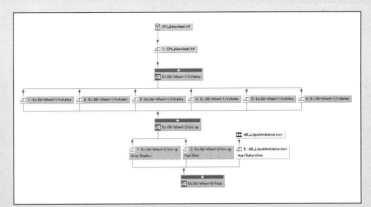

The full flowchart for Chapter 16's comp chain **[Ex.06]**, which shows a three-comp hierarchy. From top to bottom, the footage item CM_bikewheel is a layer in the comp **[Ex.06-Wheel-1]**. This comp is in turn used six times as layers in **[Ex.06-Wheel-2]**, which in turn is used twice as two separate layers – with different effects applied – in **[Ex.06-Wheel-3]**. This final comp also contains the footage item AB_LiquidAmbience as a layer, with its own effect applied.

you cannot change the "wiring" (or any other settings).

A light gray bar along the top of a comp with a black plus sign means the item is collapsed, hiding the hierarchy that made it; clicking on this bar inverts its color and exposes the hierarchy. The layer bars are numbered according to their order in the Time Layout window of the comp.

There are four option buttons in the lower left corner, indicated from left to right as:

Show Layers: Whether or not to expose the layers in a comp.

Show Effects: Whether or not to show any effects that might be applied to the layers (this automatically enables the "show layers" button). Option+click brings up a Justify slider for adjusting positions of bars.

Lines: Whether you prefer diagonal or right-angle lines to connect the items. Option+click to clean up lines.

Flow Direction: The default for flowchart direction is top to bottom, with the "last" comp at the bottom: that's what we used mostly for this book.

Double-clicking on an item in the flowchart opens it. If it is a footage item, it opens in its own footage window; layers in comps bring their comps forward, with that layer highlighted. Selecting a layer with an effect applied and hitting Command+Shift+T (F3) opens its Effects Controls window.

You access Flowchart View by clicking on the icon in the upper right corner of the Project window, and any Comp window.

Investigating the Chain

When you select a nested comp in the Project window, an info popup at the top of this window will report that it's "used X number of times." Click on the arrow to find out where it is nested; selecting one of the listed comps opens it.

• Make the nested comps big enough that you don't have to scale them past 100% in another comp; otherwise, they'll go soft.

• If possible, apply the Opacity keyframes in the final comp, so you don't have to hunt down keyframes in previous comps.

• When you're reorganizing a hierarchy, you can copy and paste keyframes between layers in different comps, as well as copy and paste layers themselves (we covered this in detail in Chapter 4).

• Creating a series of similar animations becomes less of a chore if you duplicate layers and comps and set up master colors and animations. However, you might need to create multiple animations that are related but otherwise unique. If possible, urge your client or boss to sign off on a sample animation before you duplicate and customize each instance.

• If you expect to make no further changes to a precomp, consider pre-rendering it and using it as a comp proxy (Chapter 44). This saves even more time if you're nesting the precomp more than once.

• When it's time to render, don't forget to render the final comp in the chain. It's all too easy to accidentally render an intermediate comp. You might use a symbol or other naming convention to guard against this (such as the ® symbol for "render me").

The Rendering Order

If you've ever been frustrated when you're trying to achieve a specific effect, it's probably because After Effects has a mind of its own when it comes time to render. The good news is that it's a very logical, predictable mind. The bad news is that its logic may not be exactly what you assumed. Unlike Photoshop, in which the user dictates the order that effects and transformations are applied, After Effects processes layers based on its own internal *rendering order*.

The first rule to understand is that the order with which you apply effects and transform objects is not necessarily the same order that's used when rendering. By understanding the default rendering order, and how to manipulate it – including by nesting compositions – you'll be equipped to troubleshoot many of your visual problems.

When you import footage into a project, the source's first port of call is the Interpret Footage dialog. In this dialog, the layer's alpha channel type, frame rate, field order, and pixel aspect ratio is set. If you don't change these settings, the footage uses the defaults assigned to it.

When you drag this footage into a comp, the layer is sent through different stages before the final image is rendered to the Comp window. Open [**Ex.08-Rendering Order 101**]. The default rendering order is listed in the Time Layout window:

Masks

Effects

Transform (Anchor Point, Position, Scale, Rotation, and Opacity).

After Effects' rendering order can be divined by just opening all the "twirlies" for each layer – the masks, effects, and transformations are calculated in the order they are drawn.

If there are no masks or effects applied, their twirlies will reveal no parameters when twirled down. If a layer's Opacity is at 0% or its visibility is off, the layer is not rendered. If there are multiple layers in the comp, they are processed from the back to the front. (A more detailed listing of the rendering order is included in TechTip 09 on the CD.)

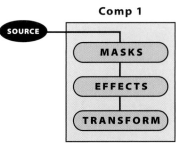

Existing render attributes

By trying to both mask and apply a Find Edges effect in one comp, we run into a problem – there's only one set of render order attributes. Since After Effects calculates Effects after Masks, the mask's "edge" is affected by Find Edges.

You can apply up to thirty-one effects per layer, which are processed from the top down. These are easily reordered in the Effect Controls window (not the Time Layout window, as the manual implies). However, *you cannot rearrange the main Masks>Effects>Transform order within a comp.* Most of the time, the default order is the preferred choice, but there are times when you need to be able to reorder these events.

Consider the problem displayed in the **[Ex.10-Mask+Effect]** comp. The planet image has a circular mask applied to drop out the background. The Find Edges effect is then added, but because the effect is finding the edge of the mask, an ugly dark line appears on the left side. (Don't worry; we'll show you how to fix that below.)

Two Comps Are Better than One

If you work with a single layer across two comps, the layer will have two rendering orders; all attributes applied in the first comp are calculated first, and the result is passed to the second comp where more attributes may be applied. This allows you to pick and choose which events happen in which order. Returning to the problem in **[Ex.10]**, the solution is to override the default rendering order (Masks>Effects) by creating the Find Edges effect in Comp 1, and the mask in Comp 2.

In the **[Ex.10-Fix-1/Effect]** comp, the planet movie would be the only layer, but the second comp, **[Ex.10-Fix-2/Mask]**, could be where you add other layers and build the final animation. The first comp needs to be only the same size as the planet movie, which conserves RAM. If the second comp will be the final comp, its size should be that required by your video hardware.

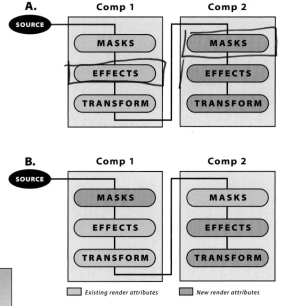

Existing render attributes   *New render attributes*

By nesting Comp 1 into Comp 2 (A), you'll have two render orders to work with. You can now move the mask attributes to the second comp (B), which reverses the default rendering order. The Find Edges Effect is applied in the first comp, which is calculated before the mask in the second comp, and the ugly edge is gone.

The Transform Effect

We stated earlier that you could not reorder the main Masks>Effects>Transform rendering order without using a second comp, and that is true. However, the Transform effect (Effect>Perspective submenu) is capable of doing all the same tricks, and more, as the regular Transform properties. And because it's an effect, you can force transformations to occur *before* your other effects, all in one comp.

To show you an example of why this is so useful, in [**Ex.11-Problem**] comp, we've set up a typical animation: a rotating wheel with a drop shadow effect applied. The presence of a directional shadow implies that a light source from the upper left is beaming down on our wheel, casting a shadow to the lower right. However, if you preview the animation, you'll see that the shadow is also rotating (the light source appears to revolve around the comp). This is because Rotation (a Transform property) is rendered *after* the drop shadow effect. We need the rotation to happen *before* the effect.

You don't need to re-create the animation across two comps when you notice this problem; just move the regular Transform keyframes to the Rotation property in the Transform effect. Try the following steps with the [**Ex.11-Problem**] comp:

In [**Ex.11-Problem**] comp, the default render order of Effects followed by Transform means that the Drop Shadow is affected by the Rotation property, so the light source appears to revolve around the object as the object rotates.

In Step 1, the Effect>Perspective>Transform effect is applied and dragged above Drop Shadow.

Step 1: Apply the Effects>Perspective>Transform effect. In the Effect Controls window, drag the Transform effect to the top; this will make it render before the Drop Shadow effect. Notice that Transform has a Rotation parameter.

Step 2: In the Time Layout window, move the time marker to the beginning of the comp (hit the Home key), click on the word Rotation to select all the existing regular Rotation keyframes, and cut them (Edit>Cut). Rotation should now read 0° with the stopwatch off; the object is static.

Step 3: Twirl down the Transform effect in the Time Layout window, and click on the Rotation property to highlight its I-beam. Paste (Edit>Paste) the Rotation keyframes. Preview the animation. The drop shadow should now remain at the lower right. (If not, compare your results with ours, [**Ex.11_Fix**] comp.)

Remember that Rotation occurs around the layer's anchor point. If you edited the Anchor Point, you should also cut/paste this value to the Anchor Point property in the Transform effect.

Step 3: Cut the regular rotation keyframes and paste them to the Transform effect that's calculated before the Drop Shadow effect, thus thwarting After Effects' normal rendering order, and fixing the rotating shadow problem.

Puzzle Solving

At this point, we hope you're feeling pretty confident that you can troubleshoot these sorts of visual problems, armed with the knowledge that:

• Visual problems are most often due to the rendering order of Masks>Effects>Transform, not user error.

• The answer to these problems is to use two comps. If the problem can be solved by swapping a transform property with an effect, use the Transform effect instead (see the sidebar, *The Transform Effect*).

We've shown you how to solve a few common problems, but there are many others that will crop up in a job when you least expect it. Instead of trying to show an example of every possible scenario we can think of, we'd rather arm you with the tools to troubleshoot *any* situation:

Step 1: Don't Panic.

Step 2: Get specific. Exactly which two properties are clashing? Until you narrow it down, you can't fix it. Consider [**Ex.11**] in The Transform Effect sidebar, for instance: The problem was not that "the shadow looks funny…" but specifically that "the shadow is being affected by rotation."

Step 3: Note what order these properties are in now; it might even help to jot it down on paper: *1=Drop Shadow, 2=Rotation*.

Step 4: Reverse this order: *1=Rotation, 2=Drop Shadow*. This is your blueprint for fixing the problem. If you can solve the problem with the Transform effect, go for it. Otherwise, use the blueprint as a guide for what event needs to occur in the first comp, and what attributes need to be applied in the second comp.

Remember that it's all too easy to identify the problem, create two comps, then re-create the problem. You need to reorder the two properties that don't work in the current rendering order to fix the problem.

The Best Laid Plans

In this chapter we've concentrated on building a chain of comps by nesting, which does entail some planning on your part. Of course, it's not always possible to preplan the perfect hierarchy, as the moment inspiration hits will dictate how comps are created and layers grouped.

When an additional comp needs to be added in the middle of the hierarchy, you can create a new comp and shuffle things around and relink the chain. But the Precompose feature covered in the next chapter is designed specifically for adding comps in the middle of a hierarchy. It is a bit less intuitive than nesting, though, so we suggest you get a firm grip on nesting before moving on.

Connect

All sorts of layer management tips, such as Replace Source, Markers, and Split Layer were covered in Chapter 8.

Building a hierarchy of comps also comes up when working with Track Mattes (Chapter 14), Stencils (Chapter 15), and Compound Effects (Chapter 22). This hierarchy is somewhat short-circuited by Collapse Transformations, the subject of Chapter 18.

The options in the Interpret Footage dialog are translated in Chapter 36.

Prerendering comps and creating Proxies is discussed in Chapter 44.

More detail than you ever wanted to know about the rendering order is revealed in TechTip 09 on the CD.

17 Precomposing

Continuing our tour of After Effects' rendering order, we prove that precomposing is easy once you know how...

Precompose Reality Check

Precomposing never solves a render order problem directly – it just gives you the opportunity to spread attributes over two comps so you can choose the order in which attributes are calculated.

In the last chapter, we used nesting to group layers and fix visual problems caused by the default render order. If you can plan ahead, you'll find nesting an intuitive way to create a chain of comps. However, predicting exactly how many comps will be needed to build a complex animation is difficult. If you need to insert a comp in the middle of an existing hierarchy, that's where precomposing comes in.

We recommend that you complete Chapter 16 on nesting before reading this chapter so you can compare how you might group layers and solve similar rendering order problems by precomposing instead. Many techniques can be learned by simply reading the copy and looking at figures; precompose isn't one of those. We suggest you either create some examples of your own or use the accompanying project file.

Precompose for Grouping

Precompose is used primarily for the same reasons you would use nesting – grouping layers and manipulating the rendering order. The difference is that nesting implies moving up the hierarchy; when you precompose, you're inserting an intermediate comp lower down in an existing hierarchy. You could think of it almost as nesting backward: The precomp created is always rendered first, before the current comp.

In the previous chapter, we used a nested comp to group three spheres so they could be rotated as one layer. In this chapter's example

Example Project

Explore the 17-Example Project.aep file as you read this chapter; references to [Ex.##] refer to specific compositions within the project file.

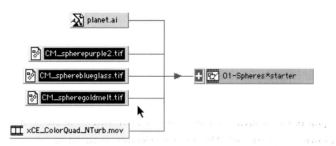

Before precomposing, the five layers are ungrouped in one comp. Click on the Comp Flowchart button (top right of Comp window) for the **[Ex.01-Spheres*starter]** comp to view this current hierarchy.

[**Ex.01-Spheres*starter**], we've created a similar design: three spheres, a background, and a title. Let's say it's not until this point that you decide the three spheres should rotate as a group. Stand by to precompose:

Step 1: Select the three sphere layers.

Step 2: Select Pre-compose from the bottom of the Layer menu.

Step 3: In the Pre-compose dialog, give the new composition a useful name, such as Spheres Trio. (Note that when multiple layers are selected, Move All Attributes is the only option available.) Click OK.

Step 4: The three spheres will be replaced with one layer, a nested comp called Spheres Trio. You can now add Rotation keyframes to the sphere group.

The new comp appears in the Project window just like any other comp, and as far as After Effects is concerned, the hierarchy is the same chain you would have created by nesting if you had planned ahead. The precomp is rendered first, so any changes you make in the precomp will ripple up to the original comp. Another way to look at it is that the original comp is now the second comp in the chain.

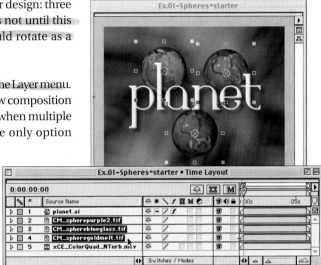

You need to rotate the spheres as a group. Select them, then select Layer> Pre-compose (Command+Shift+C).

To edit the three spheres separately in the precomp, Option+double-click the nested layer to open the precomp and add it to the list of tabs. Check our [**Ex.01_Result**] folder if you want to compare your result with ours. Also, click on the flowchart view again to see how the two comps are organized.

The three sphere layers were selected and precomposed using Move All Attributes; they now appear as one layer in the current comp. They can now be rotated as one.

Precompose Options

Precomposing a single layer is used to solve the same sorts of often-unforeseen rendering order problems we looked at in the previous chapter. The solution to problems with the default rendering order is to reverse the order of some events by spreading the layer across two comps, so you can pick and choose which step happens in which comp. If there's only one layer in the current comp, you have the choice to either nest the current comp in a second comp, or to precompose the layer. If there are other layers in the comp, precomposing is your best option to rearrange the hierarchy, as nesting would bring all other layers along for the ride.

The Pre-compose dialog offers two options: "Leave All Attributes in current comp," or "Move All Attributes to the new composition." Attributes refers to the values and keyframes for masks, effects, transformations, transfer modes, trimming, and so on. For a single layer, both options are available.

Current Comp

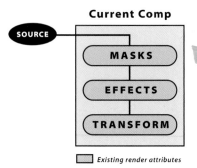

Existing render attributes

The basic render order – Masks, Effects, Transform – is also spelled out in the Time Layout window. The various attributes assigned to this layer will be calculated as Mask 1, followed by the Find Edges effect, followed by any transformations.

To compare the results of each option, we've set up two example comps for you to practice on:

Option #1: Leave All Attributes

From the Windows menu, select Close All. Open the [**Ex.02-Option #1*starter**] comp, and preview the layer. The CM_planet_loop.mov layer has attributes that include a mask, a Find Edges effect, and Position keyframes.

Step 1: Select the layer and precompose, making sure to chose the *first* option, "Leave All Attributes in current comp." Name the new comp "Precomp with #1." Click OK.

Step 2: The layer's master twirly in the Time Layout window will roll up, so twirl everything down again. Notice that the attributes remain in the current comp.

Step 3: Open the new precomp (Option+double-click precomp layer), and notice that the size of the comp matches the CM_planet source (200×200 pixels, same duration). If you get lost, check out our version in the [**Ex.02_Result**] folder.

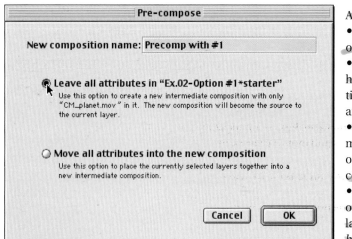

Selecting the first precompose option – Leave All Attributes – moves just the source of the layer into a comp of its own, leaving all masks, effects, and transformations in the original comp.

The result of precomposing is that you now have two full sets of attributes for the original source. If you used the "Leave All Attributes" option, the attributes you originally created stayed in the first comp.

To summarize Option #1, "Leave All Attributes":

• Option #1 is available for single layers only, including nested comps.

• After you precompose, the precomp will have one layer in it, and the size and duration of the precomp will be the same size and duration as *the original layer*.

• Any attributes (masks, effects, transformations, transfer modes, trimming, and so on) applied to the layer before you precompose will remain in the *current comp*.

• The precomp will have a fresh render order, and any attributes applied to the layer in the new precomp will render *before* the attributes in the original comp.

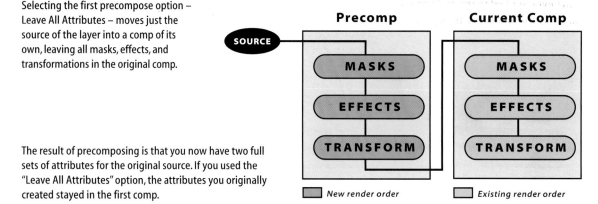

New render order   *Existing render order*

Option #2: Move All Attributes

From the Windows menu, select Close All. Open the next example, [**Ex.03-Option #2*starter**] comp, and preview. This is exactly the same animation as our [**Ex.02-Option #1*starter**]: The CM_planet movie has attributes that include a mask, a Find Edges effect, and Position keyframes.

Step 1: Select the planet layer and precompose, making sure to choose the *second* option, "Move All Attributes into the new composition." Name the new comp "Precomp with #2." Click OK.

Step 2: The layer's master twirly will roll up, so twirl everything down again. Notice that the previous attributes are gone. This is a fresh rendering order.

Step 3: Open the new precomp (Option+double-click precomp layer) and twirl down to reveal the Mask, Find Edges effect, and Position keyframes. Notice that the size of the comp matches the original comp (320×240), not the source. If you get lost along the way, check out our version in the [**Ex.03_Result**] folder.

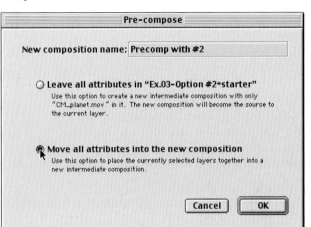

The second option in the Pre-compose dialog – Move All Attributes – creates a new comp the same size and duration as the current one, with the selected layer and all its attributes moved into the new comp.

When you precompose multiple layers, only the second option, "Move All Attributes," is available since the relationship between the layers can be maintained only if their attributes are kept intact. The layers that are precomposed will appear as one layer in the current comp so you can animate and effect them as a group, as in our spheres example above.

To summarize Option #2, "Move All Attributes into the new composition":
- Option #2 is available for both single layers and multiple layers, including nested comps.
- The precomp will be the same size and duration *as the current comp*.
- Any attributes (masks, effects, transformations, transfer modes, trimming, and so on) applied to the layer(s) before precomposing will be moved to the *precomp*.
- The layer in the *original* comp will have a fresh render order, and any attributes applied to this layer will render *after* the attributes in the precomp.

As before, the result of precomposing is that you now have two full sets of attributes for the original source. The main difference is that if you use the "Move All Attributes" option, the attributes you originally created have been copied into the new comp, and they reset in the original comp.

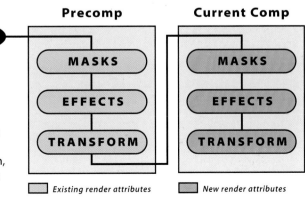

Fixing Render Order Problems

When you precompose a single layer, which option you choose depends on what the problem is and what solution you've devised to fix it. Let's run through one example.

From the Windows menu, select Close All – just to clean things up. Open example [**Ex.04-Planet+BG*starter**]. You'll recognize this as the same rendering order problem we saw in [**Ex.10**] in the previous chapter: The planet image has a circular mask applied, but the Find Edges effect is finding the edge of the mask, resulting in a dark line around the edge. This, of course, is due to the default render order (Masks>Effects>Transform) which dictates that masks are rendered first, followed by effects. We have also composited the planet movie using the Overlay transfer mode and animated it with Position keyframes.

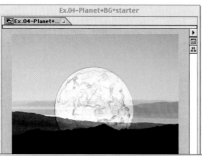

If we had foreseen this problem, we would have created a comp for the planet movie, with just Find Edges applied, nested it in a second comp, and added the mask there. Luckily, precompose allows us to fix this problem after the fact. As we saw above, precompose will spread a single layer over two comps, but it will maintain the existing render order intact – i.e., the mask will still render before any effects, it's just a matter of whether this all happens in the current comp or in the precomp. It's important to remember that neither precompose option will reverse the order of events and fix your problem *automatically*.

However, since both precompose options expand the layer across two comps, each with its own render order, you'll have the opportunity to copy and paste from one comp to the other. In this case, so long as you end up with the Find Edges effect rendering first in the precomp, and the mask rendering in the current (now second) comp, it might not matter how you get there. The question to ask before precomposing a single layer is: Is there any advantage to having the current render order happen first or second?

We've created an animation and composite, with one rendering order problem: The fact that masking occurs before effects means that the Find Edges effect is finding the edge of our mask, which is not what we wanted.

Adjusted Rendering Order

Adjustment Layers (Chapter 20) can also fix rendering order problems by applying their own effects after all other attributes are calculated for the layer(s) underneath. But this breaks down if you have a layer in the background that should remain uneffected.

Fixing the Edge

For fixing most render order problems with a single layer, we would usually pick the first option, "Leave All Attributes." Since a layer's attributes include transfer modes, which needs to interact with layers below, we don't want to bury modes in the precomp. It's also more convenient to keep as many of the keyframes as possible in the final comp so that keyframes can be easily synchronized. So let's fix the ugly edge problem using Option #1:

Step 1: In the [**Ex.04-Planet+BG*starter**] comp, select the CM_planet_loop.mov layer, and precompose using Option #1, Leave All Attributes. Name the comp "Planet_precomp" and click OK. The movie layer will be replaced with a nested composition layer. All the original attributes remain in the current comp.

Step 2: With the nested comp layer selected, choose Layer>Open Effects Controls (Command+Shift+T). Click on the name of the Find Edges effect (if not already highlighted) and copy (Command+C).

Step 3: Remove the effect from this layer by hitting the Delete key.

Step 4: Now let's paste the effect to the image in the precomp. Option+double-click the nested comp layer to bring it to the front. The precomp is a 200×200 comp, with just the CM_planet_loop.mov layer in it. Select the movie and paste (Edit>Paste) the Find Edges effect. Remember that this comp will render first, before the original comp.

Return to the 04-Planet+BG comp. The mask will now render after Find Edges and the ugly outline is gone. This comp has no knowledge of any effect that happened in a previous comp; it simply applies a circular mask to the composited RGB+Alpha image it receives from the precomp. The transfer modes and Position keyframes remain in the original comp and work as expected. Check our results [**Ex.04-Result**] folder if you got lost along the way.

And what of Option #2? (In case you're curious and want to try it out, we've repeated the starter comp in the [**Ex.04_why not try Option #2**] folder.) If you had instead used the "Move All Attributes" option when you precomposed, the existing render order would move down to the precomp. The first thing you would notice is that the Overlay transfer mode no longer works, as it's applied in the precomp where it has no effect (since there are no layers underneath). The original 200×200 planet layer would be replaced by a nested comp layer that's the same size as the current comp, 320×240. In order for the mask to render after the Find Edges effect, you would need to cut the Mask Shape from the precomp and paste it back to the layer in the original comp.

The problem with this method is that the mask was created to fit a 200×200 layer exactly, and if it's pasted to a 320×240 layer, it ends up off center. And the Position keyframes in the precomp are moving the image inside the mask. We think you'll agree that in this particular example, Option #1 is the better choice.

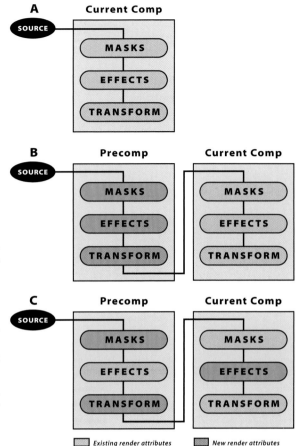

A single layer's render order highlighting the mask followed by a Find Edges effect which produces a dark edge (A). To fix the problem, the layer is selected and precomposed using option #1, Leave All Attributes in current comp (B). The Find Edges effect is then moved to the layer in the precomp (C).

By precomposing and performing the Find Edges in the first comp, we can mask the planet cleanly in the second comp.

Fixing a Clipped Layer

Some effects, particularly blurs and glows, can't draw outside the layer's original boundary, and instead are clipped at the layer's edge. (This was more of a problem with After Effects 3.1, but some third-party plug-ins still can't draw outside the layer's boundary.) For a quick fix:

Step 1. Precompose the layer using option #1.

Step 2. Open the precomp. Select Composition> Composition Settings (Command+K) and increase the comp's width and height (Composition Settings) by, say, 100 pixels all around. The layer will be centered in the enlarged comp because Anchor defaults to the center. Click OK.

Step 3: Return to the current comp and continue work. The size of the layer will now be dictated by the size of the precomp, and the effect will have space to draw into. (If the effect stills clips, repeat Step 2.)

This particular blur effect was not programmed to go beyond the layer's original boundary, causing clipping problems at high settings.

Trimming Out Empty Calories

One of the drawbacks to precomposing using Option #2, Move All Attributes, is that layers that are shorter than the current comp end up appearing longer when they're precomposed. To show you what we mean:

Step 1: Close all windows, and open the [**Ex.05-Short Layers*starter**] comp. This comp is 30 seconds long. The three sphere layers are shorter than the full duration.

Step 2: Scrub along the timeline (Option+drag the time marker) to get a sense of the animation. The first sphere fades up starting at 01:00, followed by the other two spheres staggered in time. The three layers are trimmed out at 25:00. The first and last 5 seconds of the comp have no spheres visible.

Step 3: Group these three spheres together by using precompose (let's say you want to, oh, rotate them as a group). Since you have selected more than one layer, your only choice will be Option #2 – Move All Attributes.

Numbering Precomps

Don't name a precomp with a higher number, as you might do when nesting. If the current comp is Comp 3, the precomp will be inserted between Comp 2 and 3 (so it's a 2.5, not a 4).

Before deciding we needed to precompose the sphere layers, we have animated them, slid them along the timeline, and trimmed their in and out points.

Step 4: After you precompose, the layer bar appears to extend for a full 30 seconds in duration. But scrub along the timeline again, and you'll see that the spheres are visible only between 05:00 and 25:00 seconds. The layer bar is misleading: The first and last 5 seconds are "empty calories." This is not a problem – unless you later assume that more frames are available to work with than really exist…

When you precompose with the second option (Move All Attributes), the resulting new layer seems to run the full length of the current composition, when in fact the layers in the precomp don't.

Removing Empty Calories by Trimming

An easy way around this misleading layer bar duration is to immediately trim the precomp's layer's in and out points after precomposing, to match

the first and last active frames in the precomp. When the empty calories are trimmed, the layer bar provides accurate feedback about which frames are "live." This solution is shown in the [**Ex.05-Result of Trimming**] folder.

You should probably trim the precomposed comp's layer bar to better represent its actual length.

Removing Empty Calories by Moving Layers

Another solution involves a few steps but provides an even cleaner result. Close All Windows and open the [**06-Short Layers*starter**] comp:

Step 1: Note where the first sphere layer starts in time (01:00, in this case) and where the last one ends (25:00). Precompose the three spheres again.

Step 2: After precomposing, open the precomp, select all the layers, and drag them back in time so that the first layer in time (layer #3) starts at 00:00. Extend all the layer bars to the full length of their new comp – you can trim excess frames in the original comp.

Step 3: Return to the original comp and move the in point for the nested layer to 01:00 (the original starting point) so that the first sphere starts fading up at 01:00. Trim the out point to 25:00.

The result is that any empty calories are removed from the head. You can also extend the nested comp layer at the tail knowing that the layer bar is not empty. Once the layers are moved, add rotation keyframes and fade the layers out as a group. Our results are in the [**Ex.05b-Result of Moving**] folder.

Connect

Masking is covered for the first time in Chapter 13.

The concept of building a hierarchy of comps via nesting is covered in detail in Chapter 16, as is Flowchart View.

Applying Effects is coming up in Chapter 19.

The Definitive Rendering Order is covered in TechTip 09 on the CD.

Collapsing Transformations

Our final leg of the Rendering Order tour pulls into the station...

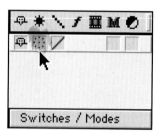

The Collapse Transformation switch in the default off position (above) is hollow; it fills in when it's on (below).

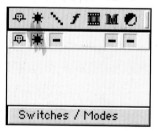

Example Project

Explore the 18-Example Project.aep file as you read this chapter; references to [Ex.##] refer to specific compositions within the project file.

Following the chapters on nesting and precomposing, we wrap up our focus on After Effects' rendering order by exploring the pros and cons of Collapse Transformations. This powerful feature allows for faster rendering and higher quality and is key to achieving infinite zoom animations. We consider this one of the more advanced concepts, so we recommend you use the example project to practice, rather than just read the copy. If you don't get it at first, don't panic. Skip ahead to some of the fun chapters on effects and type, and revisit Collapse Transformations when you feel more comfortable building hierarchies by nesting and precomposing.

Resolution Lost

If you've been with us for the previous two chapters, you know that After Effects renders in a series of discrete steps. The order of these steps is programmed, so the order in which *you* apply effects and transformations is largely irrelevant. You're probably also aware that when you set a layer to Best Quality, After Effects antialiases it whenever an effect is applied that distorts pixels as well as when the Transform properties (position, scale, rotation, anchor point, and motion blur) are calculated. Each time a layer is antialiased, pixels are altered and the image appears slightly softer. However, if you change your mind about how a layer is effected or transformed, at least these values are re-applied to the original source, so the image is not degraded with every edit.

The ability to re-edit a layer while maintaining its original resolution can be lost when you start building a hierarchy of comps. When Comp 1 is nested in Comp 2, the nested comp is "rendered": Effects and transformations are applied to each layer, which are antialiased if necessary, and all layers in Comp 1 are composited together. Comp 2 receives *only* the composited frame (a "flattened" image) and has no history of the layers in the first comp.

At least, that's how it works if you don't know about the Collapse Transformations switch. If you read the manual (yes, Jokes 'R' Us), Collapse Transformations is touted as a way to "speed up rendering and increase quality." But let's see just how free that lunch really is.

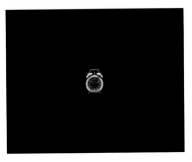

In Comp 1, the image is scaled down to 10% and reduced to just a few pixels.

Then it's nested in Comp 2 and scaled 1000% for a truly ugly result.

However, when the Collapse switch is turned on, the original resolution from Comp 1 is restored, as the two Scale values are calculated in one step (10% ×1000% = 100%). Alarm clock courtesy Classic PIO/Sampler.

Collapsing 101

You might already be familiar with the Collapse switch in the Time Layout window to Continuously Rasterize Illustrator files (more on that in Chapter 28). This same switch, when applied to a nested comp layer, becomes Collapse Transformations.

In the 18-Example Project file, open the [**Ex.01-Scaling-1**] comp. The CP_AlarmClock image is scaled down to 10%, where it's roughly 30 pixels wide. This comp is nested in [**Ex.01-Scaling-2**], where it's scaled back up 1000%. At this point, the small image is blown up ten times – and looks as ugly as you might expect. The Collapse Transformations switch for the layer in the Time Layout window is set to Off (it appears hollow), which is the default setting.

Time for some magic: Turn on the Collapse switch in Comp 2 for the nested Comp 1 layer. The lost resolution returns, as the Transform values applied in Comp 2 are combined with the values applied to each layer in Comp 1. A calculator will tell you that 10% times 1000% equals the original value of 100%. Of course, applying scaling values that result in a value larger than 100% would introduce degradation – you can't improve on the resolution of the original image. (That *would* be magic…)

The Good News…

Why exactly is Collapsing Transformations so useful? Let's consider another example, with multiple layers and motion paths:

Step 1: Open the [**Ex.02-Spheres*starter**] comp. Three spheres are scaled to 25% and animated using Position keyframes (which were created with the help of Motion Sketch, introduced in Chapter 7).

Step 2: Now you realize that the entire spheres animation needs to be larger to fill more of the frame. First, select the three spheres and use Layer>Pre-compose to group them together. Name the precomp "Spheres group" and click OK.

Step 3: Now scale this nested comp layer by 200%.

Step 4: Scaling past 100% would normally degrade the image, but turn on Collapse Transformations and the spheres will appear sharp again.

Step 1: After completing a complex, whizzy sphere animation, that nasty ol' client comes back again and says, "But can it take up more of the frame?"

Step 4: The solution is to precompose the animated spheres, scale this newly nested comp 200% (expanding the spheres and their motion path), then turn on Collapse Transformations to reclaim the lost resolution.

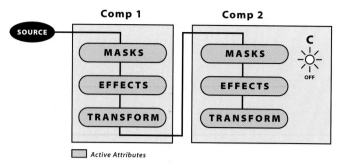

Active Attributes

With the Collapse switch off, layers in Comp 1 are composited together before flowing through Comp 2's rendering order of Masks/Effects/Transform.

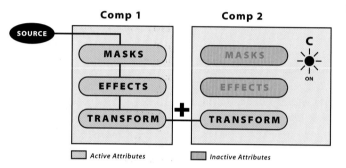

Active Attributes   Inactive Attributes

When you turn on the Collapse switch in Comp 2 for the nested Comp 1 layer, the Transformations applied in Comp 2 are combined with the values applied to each layer in Comp 1. Note that Mask and Effects are now not available in Comp 2.

In fact, you could scale up to 400% (100% ÷ 25% = 400%). Check out [**Ex.02_final**] if you get lost along the way.

Another way of looking at Collapse Transformations is that instead of rendering a final composited frame for the precomp, a "half-baked" comp is sent up to the current comp. Even better, the layers are antialiased only once for a faster render and higher image quality.

The Bad News...

When a nested comp is collapsed, the Mask and Effects for that layer are not available. This problem can be overcome by applying these attributes in the pre-comp, precomposing the collapsed comp and applying attributes in the current comp, or nesting the current comp into a new comp. Depending on your situation, you may also be able to use an adjustment layer (Chapter 20). Let's consider the pre-compose option:

Select Windows>Close All, and open the two comps in the [**Ex.02_Result**] folder. With the [**Ex.02-Spheres-final**] comp forward, try to apply an effect to the collapsed comp – a simple Adjust>Hue/Saturation effect will do. An error dialog will report "You can't do this because the layer is currently collapsed" and you'll be prompted to uncollapse the layer – of course, since you're scaling past 100%, click Cancel, as you don't want to turn off Collapse Transformations.

You'll also be informed that "you can still do this to any layer in the precomp." Since the precomp has three spheres, you could even apply the Hue/Saturation effect differently to each layer in the precomp. However, if you wanted to apply an effect that needed to be applied to the group of spheres after they've been composited together, the solution is to precompose a second time:

Step 1: Select the Ex.02_Spheres group layer and Pre-compose, using Option #2, "Move All Attributes." Name the precomp "Spheres scaled" and OK. This will move the Scale keyframes and the Collapse Transformations setting to the precomp.

Step 2: The current comp now has a fresh render order and is the third comp in the chain. You can apply any effect in this comp and it will apply to the spheres as a flattened image. We used Effect>Distort>Mirror, with Reflection Angle set to 90°.

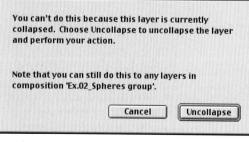

You can't do this because this layer is currently collapsed. Choose Uncollapse to uncollapse the layer and perform your action.

Note that you can still do this to any layers in composition 'Ex.02_Spheres group'.

Cancel   Uncollapse

You can't apply an effect to a layer that has already been collapsed.

If you get lost along the way, close all windows and check out our result. Open the three comps from the [**Ex.03-Plus Effects**] folder. To summarize, after precomposing the collapsed comp, the hierarchy became:

- In the first comp, [**Ex.03-Spheres-1/group**], the spheres are rotating as before, with the addition of a Hue/Saturation effect applied to the gold sphere only.
- In the second comp, [**Ex.03-Spheres-2/scaled up**], the first comp is scaled 200% and Collapse Transformations is turned on.
- In the third comp, [**Ex.03-Spheres-Final**], the Mirror effect is applied. With this comp forward, the Comp Flowchart button will display how the chain of comps come together.

Motion Blur and Other Switches

When Collapse Transformations is on, you lose not only the ability to apply masks and effects, but also transfer modes and track mattes. This is because collapsing in essence brings forward any modes, mattes or stencils from the collapsed layers into the current comp, and you can't apply these treatments twice to a layer. (More on the implications of this in a moment.)

The Quality and Motion Blur switches are also shown as unavailable, but you *can* set them for each layer in the previous comp:

Step 1: Bring the [**Ex.03-Spheres-2/scaled up**] comp forward. Notice that all the switches and modes are inactive. Clicking on the Motion Blur switch results in the now-expected error dialog, so cancel.

Step 2: Bring the first comp [**Ex.03-Spheres-1/group**] forward, turn on Motion Blur for all three sphere layers, and Enable Motion Blur. The motion blur is calculated once, based on the velocity of the combined transform values from this comp and the following comp, [**Ex.03-Spheres-2/scaled up**].

And the Unexpected...

When you apply Collapse Transformations, there are other issues in the rendering order that may be good news or bad news, depending on your situation. The Examples project encourages you to compare the results of turning on and off the Collapse switch for the following examples:

The Pasteboard

Once a layer's Mask, Effects, and Transform have been calculated, the rendering order includes a step we'll call "crop to current comp size," where any pixels that end up on the comp's pasteboard are trimmed. After this stage, the layer is composited with other layers using transfer modes, opacity, and track mattes.

[**Ex.04-Pasteboard-1**] has a large image panning across a 200×100 size comp. This is nested into [**Ex.04-Pasteboard-2**]. In this second comp, if you turn on Collapse Transformations, any pixels that spill onto the pasteboard in the first comp magically reappear, outside the layer's boundary handles.

Thinking Ahead

Collapse Transformations is a powerful feature that takes time to fully wrap your head around. The best advice we can give you is this:

- Turn on Collapse Transformations when scaling up a nested comp, but check carefully for any surprises.

- Don't turn on Collapse Transformations right before the final render because the manual said it would "speed up rendering and increase quality" (the manual just looks on the bright side).

- Don't scale layers down in the early comps, assuming that you can collapse the transformations later on. The resolution will be lost forever as soon as you apply a mask or effect in a later comp.

The image area outside the layer boundary handles was previously cropped by being on the pasteboard in the precomp, but collapsing the nested layer in this comp reveals this area.

Collapsing Recursively

In After Effects, some layer switches behave *recursively*, which means that changing their status in one comp changes the switch in the current comp and all nested comps. As of version 4.1, switches that behave this way include Resolution, Quality, Enable Motion Blur, Enable Frame Blending, and Collapse Transformations/Continuously Rasterize.

Whether or not switches are recursive depends on how the Recursive Switches preference is set (File> Preferences>General). The preference is enabled by default – if it's off right now, turn it on for the following example.

In most cases, recursiveness is a good thing. For instance, if you change the current comp's resolution from Full to Half to save render time, you would want all nested comps to also change to Half so they're not wasting time processing a high quality image.

Select the three example comps in **[Ex.09-Recursive Switches]** folder, double-click to open all three, and check them out. Bring the final comp, **[Ex.09-Recursive-3]**, forward.

• Change this comp's resolution from Full to Half (use the popup along the bottom of the Comp window) – all nested comps change to Half also. You can see this by clicking on the various tabs. (You could also drag out the tabs for each comp so that they each have their own windows, positioning them so you can see the Switches panel and Resolution setting simultaneously for all three comps.)

• Change the top layer from Draft to Best Quality – all nested comps change their layers to Best as well.

• If you're on a Mac, hold down the Control key when you change the Resolution back to Full and notice that only the top comp changes. The Control key temporarily toggles the preference, resulting in the opposite behavior. (Note: this keyboard modifier is broken in version 4.1 for the layer-specific switches Quality and Collapse Transformations. However, adding Control to the Quality shortcuts does work, as in Command+Control+U.)

• Now turn on the Collapse Transformations for the top layer. This also turns on Collapse Transformations in **[Ex.09-Recursive-2]** – which is not a good idea, as pixels from the pasteboard in **[Ex.09-Recursive-1]** have returned…

Summary: Collapsing transformations recursively is a really easy way to ruin your whole hierarchy. If the Collapse Transformation switch needs to be on in one comp but off in another, you'll have to carefully sift through the entire chain resetting switches. (In our opinion, collapsing comps is too dangerous a feature to have a mind of its own, and we hope to see it removed from the automatic recursive list soon.)

We suggest that if you never use Collapse Transformations, leave the Recursive Switches on for convenience. However, *if you intend to use Collapse Transformations, turn the preference to the Off setting*. If you're on the Mac, you can use the Control key to override the preference.

If you need to collapse this nested comp, and the excess imagery is a problem, there is a workaround. In the first comp, make a new solid (Command+Y), the same size as the comp. Use this solid as an alpha track matte for each layer that spills onto the pasteboard.

Trial Run

If your animation relies on being able to collapse transformations (for an infinite zoom effect, along the lines of the classic "powers of ten" animation), do a trial run with dummy sources to confirm that the hierarchy will work as planned.

Transfer Modes

When Collapse Transformations is enabled, transfer modes applied to layers in the nested comp will be passed through to the current comp. This is usually a good thing, as you can group layers in a precomp for animation purposes without losing the ability to have their individual transfer modes apply through to the background layer in the second comp.

As an example, in **[Ex.05-Modes-1]**, the foreground layer needs to be set to Screen mode in order to drop out its black background. The background

layer is also set to Screen, but it appears to have no effect as there are no layers below to interact with. However, in the second comp, [**Ex.05-Modes-2**], turn on Collapse Transformations, and the modes from the first comp will react with the background in the second comp.

Of course, you can always composite a nested comp using a transfer mode, but you would be limited to just one transfer mode for the entire group. Using Collapse Transformations, you could set each layer in the first comp to a different transfer mode, and still animate the group in the second comp where it's nested with Collapse turned on.

Adjustment Layers

Another surprise awaits when you collapse a nested comp when the first comp has an adjustment layer applied. In [**Ex.08-AdjustLayer-1**], our now infamous three spheres have an adjustment layer with the Bevel Alpha effect applied to it. The Bevel Alpha affects all layers below, after the spheres have been composited together. (This allows for the spheres to rotate individually, without the rotation keyframes affecting the direction of the Bevel's light source.)

If you beveled the spheres with an adjustment layer in a previous comp, just the spheres would get the bevel (top). However, if you now collapsed this layer, the underlying layers in the second comp get the effect of the Adjustment Layer – not quite what you intended (above).

When this comp is nested in [**Ex.08-AdjustLayer-2**], notice what happens when you use Collapse Transformations. Effects applied as adjustment layers in the first comp now affect all layers below in the second comp.

Opacity and Fade-Outs

When you fade down multiple layers individually from 100% opacity to 0%, you end up with a "staggered" fade-out. (See [**Ex.07-Fade Out Staggers**].) As the top layers fade out they become transparent, revealing the layers below. In our example, at time 04:00, the flag shows through the foreground layers. The solution is to apply the Opacity keyframes to the group of layers after they've been composited together.

So one solution is to not apply any fades in the first comp [**Ex.07a-Opacity-1**]. Nest this comp in a second comp [**Ex.07a-Opacity-2**] and apply Opacity keyframes to the nested comp as a group. However, if you now turn on Collapse Transformations for the nested comp layer, the Opacity keyframes are applied to the individual layers from the first comp, and the "staggered" fade returns.

Probably the easiest way to fade out a group of layers all in one comp [**Ex.07b-Fade Out Transform**] is to add an adjustment layer (Layer>New Adjustment Layer) and then apply Effect>Perspective>Transform to this layer. By setting keyframes for the Transform effect's Opacity parameter instead of the layer's regular Opacity keyframes, the animation affects all layers below after they've been composited as a group.

Stencils and Silhouettes

When you use a Stencil transfer mode, as in [**Ex.08-Stencil-1**], the stencil will "cut out" all the layers below. When you nest a stencil comp and turn on Collapse Transformations [**Ex.08-Stencil-2**], the stencil will cut out layers below in the second comp as well – not usually a useful result.

Connect

Motion Sketch, which is a fun tool for creating wild animation moves, was introduced in Chapter 7.

Chapters 16 and 17 cover the concepts of nesting and precomposing compositions; collapsing transformations applies only to these nested comps.

Applying and animating effects is coming up in the next chapter.

Effects and adjustment layers are covered in Chapter 20.

Precise details of what happens in what order during rendering is outlined in TechTip 09 on the CD.

Applying Effects 101

After animating layers comes treating their images with animated special effects.

One of the richest areas for exploration in After Effects is its "effects" side. The variety of effects supplied with After Effects ranges from the extremely utilitarian to the extremely wild, each with anywhere from one to one hundred twenty-seven parameters that you can adjust. Fortunately, virtually all effects share the same basic methods of adjusting and animating those parameters.

In this section of the book, we will start by giving an overview of how to apply and edit effects, then progress in the next few chapters to our favorite uses for many of these effects. If you're a beginner, feel free to dive into this introductory effects chapter once you're comfortable with basic animation techniques.

Each layer has a master effects on/off checkbox under the "f" column in the Time Layout window. Twirl the effects down for the layer (hit E on the keyboard), and each individual effect will be revealed, with its own on/off switch underneath the visibility (eyeball) icon.

Example Project

Explore the 19-Example Project.aep file as you read this chapter; references to [Ex.##] refer to specific compositions within the project file.

Applying an Effect 101

Applying effects is easy: Select the layer you wish to effect in either the Comp or Time Layout window, and click on the Effect menu. You will be presented with a list of classes of effects. Mouse down to the class you want, and a hierarchical menu will appear with all the effects in that class. Select the specific effect you want and release the mouse button – it is now applied to that layer.

After an effect has been applied, the layer will gain a new checkbox under the "f" column in the Time Layout window. The f switch is the "master effects" switch, and if an f appears in this box, all effects that are enabled will be processed. Click on the master f switch to turn off all effects. Hit E on the keyboard, and the names of all the effects applied to the layer will automatically twirl down. Each individual effect now has its own f box under the visibility column (the eyeball) in the Time Layout window; here, you can turn individual effects on and off.

[Ex.01] in the accompanying Examples project consists of a single layer (a painting by Los Angeles area artist Paul Sherstobitoff); select it, and add the Sharpen effect (Effect>Blur & Sharpen>Sharpen). In addition to the "f" column becoming active in the Time Layout window, a new Effect Controls window automatically opens. This window lists all the effects applied to a layer, as well as checkboxes to enable or disable each one individually, and you can twirl up or down each effect.

If you close the Effect Controls window and need to edit the effect further, select the layer, and then re-open this window with Layer>Open Effect Controls (Command+Shift+T). You can also double-click the name of the effect in the Time Layout window. Remember, if you want to re-edit an already applied effect, don't select it from the Effects menu or you'll just reapply it. This is how you end up with five Drop Shadow effects (you know who you are…).

To delete an effect, select it in the Effect Controls window and hit Delete. Cutting it (Command+X) will not remove it.

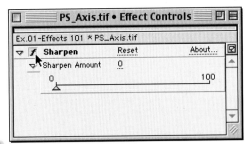

The Effect Controls window lists effects applied to a layer and is the best place to edit their parameters.

Parameters inside Your Control

There are two ways to edit the parameters of an effect. If you twirl down the arrow next to its name in the Time Layout window, the names of all its parameters will appear. Click on the number or description next to them, and a window where you can directly enter a new value will appear.

The more interactive way of editing is in the Effect Controls window. Most effects are edited using the same basic set of user interface elements. Each effect has an overall twirly to hide or reveal its parameters; each individual parameter also has its own twirly, if you want to conserve screen real estate by hiding its user interface element (its value usually stays exposed).

Beside the name of the effect are a Reset and an About button. Click Reset to revert the effect to the initial default parameters. Select About to see who created it – occasionally with a basic description.

Sliders

The most common effects parameter, the slider gives quick access to a range from a minimum to a maximum value, such as 0% to 100%. Dragging a slider changes its corresponding value; a big time-saving trick is that Option+dragging it updates the Comp window as you change its value – great for interactive adjustments. Try it with the Sharpen filter you applied to [Ex.01] above.

The numbers at the left and right ends of a slider are not necessarily the minimum and maximum values – they are just the end points of the effect creator's idea of what would be a useful range. Clicking on the underlined value above it opens a window where you can directly type in the number you want, and see what the absolute minimum and maximum ranges of the parameter are.

New in version 4.1, you can also customize most sliders to the range you deem useful. For example, set the Sharpness Slider's range from its default 0 to 100 so that the maximum slider value is 400. Play around with the slider to see how it behaves – it has a wider range, but less precise control, since the same length of slider is covering more discrete values. Try it again with a range of 0 to 50 for more precise control. Unfortunately, while After Effects remembers the value you chose, it does not remember the custom ranges when you close the project.

Delete versus Off

If you no longer want an effect, it's better to delete it than just turn it off, because Render Settings may override these switches and turn back on all the applied effects.

Stacking Effects

You can apply up to thirty-one effects to each layer in a comp. (If this is not enough, you can always precompose and apply thirty-one more…) The effects are processed in top-to-bottom order, as viewed in Effect Controls. To reorder them, drag them by their names up and down the list. Since some effects have long lists of parameters to drag past, you can always twirl up their parameters before dragging. Note that you can't reorder effects in the Time Layout window – despite what the manual says (oops).

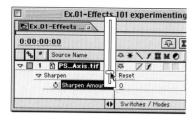

The magic slider introduced in previous chapters for transform properties also works for effects parameters with animatable ranges. Hold down Option and click on the name of the effect to get the slider; the Info palette shows the current value as you drag.

Parameters with sliders and dials also offer a handy popup slider in the Time Layout window: Option+click on the name of the parameter to see the slider, which maps to the parameter's default range.

In [**Ex.01**], select the PS_Axis layer, make sure its Effect Controls window is open (Command+Option+T), and if you applied it earlier, select and delete the Sharpen effect. Now apply Effect>Image Control>Color Balance (HLS). It has sliders for Lightness and Saturation. The Hue parameter has another type of user interface, which we call the rotary dial.

Rotary Dial

Most parameters that adjust an angle – such as rotation, drop shadow direction, or even color hue angle – use this circular controller. It has a line that points in the direction of the angle, with numeric confirmation above. To adjust it graphically, click anywhere inside or near the edge of the dial, and it will jump to this position; to further tweak it, hold the mouse down and drag it around the circle. As with any other parameter, it can be edited interactively by holding down the Option key as you drag.

There are two ways to enter a more precise value with the rotary dial. One is the fallback of clicking on the underlined value overhead and entering it numerically. If you prefer graphic editing, hold down the mouse, then move it further away from the dial's center – now as you rotate around the dial, you will have more control, since you are using a longer "lever" to tweak it with.

Rotary dials are used to adjust angle parameters. Click inside or around the edge of the dial and drag the cursor around the dial to reach your desired value.

Most effects with angle parameters allow you to enter multiple rotations. While the value 110° will look visually identical to two rotations plus 110°, it allows you to smoothly animate changes in value that "go through zero."

Color Swatches

There are many effects that allow you to colorize an element, and After Effects gives you two ways to set colors. Still in [**Ex.01**], delete any effects you have applied, then add Effect>Image Control>Tint. It has two colors to set: what to map the darker elements of an image to, and what to map the lighter elements to. These default to black and white; drag the Amount to Tint slider toward 100% and notice how the image now goes to grayscale.

Click on one of the small rectangles of color to open the "color picker" options of whatever operating system you are using. (We personally find the HLS or HSV pickers more intuitive to use than the RGB picker.) Select your color, click OK, and this new color will take effect. This is particularly handy if you need to match color values numerically.

Tint is an example of an effect that allows you to pick colors to use in a treatment. You can click on the swatches to edit the color, or use the eyedropper to pick a color from elsewhere on the screen.

The other method is to click on the eyedropper next to the swatch, then click on a color you want that is visible somewhere on the screen. If you have the Info palette open (Command+2), it will update the color values it "sees" – both numerically and with a temporary swatch of its own – as you move your cursor around. Note that it picks an average color of pixels around your cursor position.

We commonly pick colors in the images we are using as our starting points for tints and shadings. However, if you have already applied a filter such as Tint, it may not be able to see those original colors. You can temporarily turn off the effects, or open the Layer window, to see the original unprocessed image.

Popups

Some effect parameters have discrete choices rather than continuous numeric ranges. These are usually represented as popup menus. The most common menu choices are Horizontal and Vertical for blur directions and their ilk. To experience a moderately more complex set of popups, add Effect>Channel>Minimax to our test layer in [**Ex.01**], set a small value for the Radius slider, and try out the various menu options (we'll cover this plug-in more in Chapter 23).

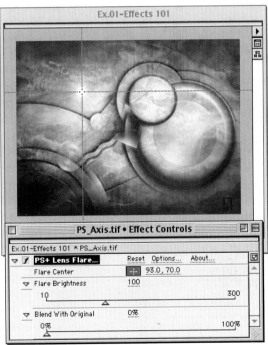

Popup parameter menus, shown here in Minimax, cannot interpolate between values, though they can be animated using Hold keyframes.

Effect Point

Several effects have specific points that they are centered around or that otherwise define the area the effect takes place over or between. Examples include the center of a lens flare or particle system effect, the center of a twirl, or the two points that define a lightning bolt. These are known as effect points and are represented by a crosshair icon in the Effect Controls window.

In our trusty comp [**Ex.01**], delete any other effects you currently have, and apply Effect>Render>PS+ Lens Flare. It will open a custom options dialog (more on those below); click on "35mm prime" and then OK. In the Effect Controls window, click on the crosshair icon next to Flare Center; your mouse cursor will change to a live set of crosshairs. Click on the point in the Comp window where you want the lens effect centered.

Effect points can be spotted and directly edited in the Comp window. They are identified as a small circle with a + symbol in it (contrasted with the anchor point, which has an X). To edit in the Comp window, make sure the effect is selected in the Effect Controls window and Effect Controls is enabled in the Comp window's own wing menu, then Option+drag the point for a real-time update.

The effect point's parameter has a value on the X and Y axes that is in relation to the layer, not the comp. You can animate the layer's position without messing up your effect points. However, this distinction makes it confusing to copy and paste values between effect point and position keyframes: Unless the layer and comp sizes are the same and the layer is centered in the comp, the same raw numbers will be describing different points in space.

Finally, the effect point can also be edited in the Layer window, which is useful if it is animated and you need to edit the motion path (see *Animating Effects*, later in this chapter).

Effect Points are identified by a crosshair icon in the Effect Controls window. They can be moved either by directly grabbing them in the Comp window or by clicking on this icon and then "placing" the crosshair center in the Comp window. Painting by Paul Sherstobitoff.

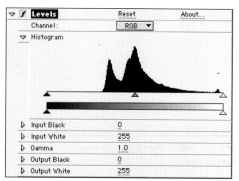

Effect>Adjust>Levels is an example of an effect with a custom interface; the "histogram" shows you the luminance distribution in the image.

Options

Some effects have special Options dialogs, such as the lens types in the PS+ Lens Flare effect we played with above. Another common Options dialog is entering font selections and text for the various Type plug-ins. Despite their varied uses, they have a few common rules:

- They usually appear when you first add the effect.
- You can edit them later by clicking on the word Options to the right of the effect's name in the Effect Controls dialog.
- You *cannot* undo them; you will need to manually change them back to their previous values.
- When you copy and paste, the values in the Options dialog are not included as part of the deal.

Custom Interface Items

Beyond the standard user interface items mentioned above, many effects – especially those from third parties – will have custom user interface elements. Some are intuitive; for those that are not, you can always consult the online help or the user's manual.

There is unfortunately a bug with custom interface elements that was introduced in version 4.0: If the custom interface draws a graphic based on the underlying image (such as the Histogram in Levels), and the underlying image changes from frame to frame (for example, a movie), it will not get redrawn if you go back to a frame that has already been stored in After Effects' image cache. To see this in action, open [**Ex.02**], select the one layer in it, and open its Effect Controls window. Note the shape of the Histogram display. Step forward a few frames; notice how it changes to show the luminance values of each new frame. Step back; notice it doesn't change back to its previous shape. Turning the effect on and off refreshes the cache and therefore the display for the entire layer. If you're setting values based on how these elements draw, toggle it on and off to be sure you're getting the right information.

Animating Effects

Animating effect parameters is very much like animating any other property of a layer – all the rules and tricks you've already learned (back in Chapter 4) about the stopwatch, keyframes, and velocity control apply. However, there are a few additional tricks for creating and navigating between keyframes from the Effect Controls window that are worth learning.

Tricks to Click

First, Option+clicking on the *name* of any effect parameter sets a keyframe for that effect. If that parameter has no keyframes yet, it turns the stopwatch on for that parameter and sets its first keyframe. This is very handy, because you don't have to twirl down a long list of effect parameters and scroll between them in the Time Layout window. Be aware, though,

Effects Quality

Many effects look drastically different in Best Quality mode than they do in Draft. Before settling on final parameter settings, set the layer to Best for a confidence check. Same goes for Comp Resolution – make sure you set the comp to Full before committing.

Some effects also have popups for antialiasing quality that further affect their render quality. These are usually indicated by Low and High (or additional) popup options. The Low setting they default to might be coarser than you like, but the effect will render faster compared with the higher settings. Fortunately, the High setting should kick in only when the layer is in Best Quality. This allows you to select High but continue to work quickly in Draft mode, where the effect defaults to the Low setting.

that if you're parked on an existing keyframe, Option+clicking will remove the keyframe.

Second, and new to 4.1, is context-clicking on a parameter's name (Control+click on the Mac, right-click under Windows). With most effects, this brings up a menu that allows you to set a keyframe (or remove it, if it has already been set), jump to the next or previous keyframe, or reset just this parameter to its initial value. If the parameter has already been enabled for keyframing, this last choice will set a keyframe at the current time with the reset value.

Of course, remember the trick of selecting a layer and hitting U to twirl down just the properties currently being animated; again, this is a real boon with effects that can have up to one hundred twenty-seven parameters.

Effect Point Animation

While you can edit an effect point in the Comp window and set keyframes, you can't see the motion path it creates. This has led many to believe you can have only linear movements with effect points. As it turns out, since the effect point has a value on the X and Y axes in relation to the layer (just like the Anchor Point), access to the motion path is in the Layer window.

To see this in action, in [**Ex.03**], we applied the Effect>Render>PS+ Lens Flare effect and animated the Flare Center parameter so that the lens flare moved around the frame. Double-click the layer to open the Layer window, and select the PS+ Lens Flare effect from the Layer Window Options menu

Favorite Memories

It can take a while to tweak an effect to the way you like it. Unfortunately, very few effects have the internal ability to load and save parameters. Which is why version 4.1 introduced a solution: *Favorites*.

After you have set an effect's parameters, select the effect in the Effect Controls window, then Effect>Save Favorite. A standard file dialog will appear, letting you save this effect and its settings anywhere on your disk. To recall it, select the layer you want it applied to and go to Effect>Apply Favorite. After Effects will also remember your most recent Favorites in the Effect>Recent Favorites menu.

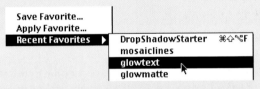

The accompanying CD-ROM includes many favorite effect settings used in this book, as you'll see in later chapters.

The additional power of Favorites comes in its ability to remember settings for multiple effects as well as any keyframes that have been set: just Shift+ or Command+click to select multiple effects applied to a layer, and all of them, including their order and keyframes, will be saved as one Favorite.

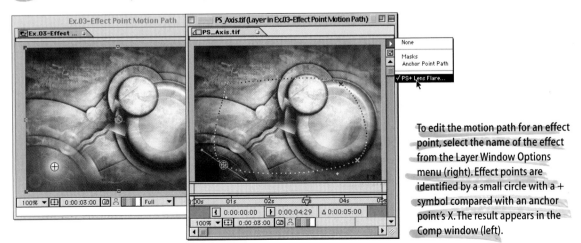

To edit the motion path for an effect point, select the name of the effect from the Layer Window Options menu (right). Effect points are identified by a small circle with a + symbol compared with an anchor point's X. The result appears in the Comp window (left).

Oops...

If you duplicate a layer (or an entire comp) and then open the Effect Controls window, all effects will be selected – including those scrolled off the bottom. Delete one effect, and they all disappear. To be safe, use Deselect All (F2) before selecting an effect to delete.

on the right side. The motion path will now be visible. The spatial keyframes default to Auto Bezier, but you can edit the handles just like the motion path for Position (as covered in Chapter 4). The Layer window shows only the motion path; the result appears only in the Comp window. Remember that the effect's name must be selected in the Effect Controls window to also see the effect point(s) in the Comp window.

Pasting Masks to Effect Point

Just as you can copy and paste mask shapes into position-related properties to create animations that follow their paths, you can also paste them into the effect point animation. This will come in handy if you've already traced an object or path in a layer and now want to animate an effect such as a Lens Flare or particle system to follow it:

Step 1: Select the mask shape in either the Layer or Time Layout window.

Step 2: Copy (Command+C).

Step 3: Select the effect point parameter name in the Time Layout window you want to paste into.

Step 4: Paste (Command+V).

Unfortunately, this will not work if the layer and comp sizes differ and if the layer is not centered in the comp. Effect points are defined by their position in the layer, not the comp (since the layer might also be moving in the comp). Those with a 3D background might know this problem as a

---

Copying and Pasting Effects

You can copy and paste effects between layers, but there are a few tips and gotchas you should be aware of:

• If you select the layer name in the Effect Controls window, copy it, and paste it to a layer that does not have this effect, the entire effect will be pasted. However, only keyframeable parameters will be pasted – parameters in any Options dialog (such as those for Basic Text) will not be pasted.

• Copying and pasting from the Effect Controls window copies a current "snapshot" of all its parameters at that point in time.

• If you paste an effect to a layer that already has the same effect applied, it just pastes its values, rather than the entire effect.

• You can duplicate a selected effect in the Effect Controls window using Edit>Duplicate (Command+D), which is handy for effects like Stroke, in which you might want to effect more than one mask shape (as in **[Ex.04_final]**).

• When you have the same effect applied multiple times, pasting values defaults to pasting to the topmost effect. To target another effect, move it temporarily to the top, paste it, then move it back down.

• You can select individual parameter values by clicking on the parameter name in the Time Layout window or by selecting its I-beam. If you copy these values and paste to another layer that already has the same effect applied, just the values for the selected parameter(s) will get copied across. If the effect is not already applied, the default values will be used for any parameters that are not part of the copy/paste process.

• If you select and copy effect keyframes in the Time Layout window, the keyframes as well as the effect will be pasted, with the first keyframe copied appearing at the current time when pasting.

• Command+click on the effect name in the Time Layout window to select all keyframes and values for an effect without having to even twirl down the parameter. Now you can copy and paste an animating effect in a jiffy.

Masks as Paths

Several effects let you create an effect that follows the outline of a mask. The parameter you need to set is called *Path* – this tells the effect which one mask shape to look at. In fact, some effects (such as Stroke) do nothing unless the Path popup points to a mask.

To practice, open comp **[Ex.04*starter]** and double-click on PS_Axis to open its Layer window. Note the three mask shapes that are already created. The masks are twirled down in the Time Layout window; note their names and the fact that they are set to None (off), since we don't want them to actually create transparency.

Now, apply Effect>Render>Stroke. Notice that its first effect parameter is a popup called Path. Click on it, and you get a list of available masks. Select each one in turn, and note that a different outline will now get the stroke. For additional fun, animate their Start and End points to draw these stroked paths. Our version is shown in **[Ex.04_complete]**.

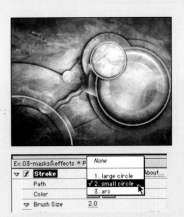

The Stroke effect can follow any mask shape currently applied to a layer, and even animated along the path.

difference between "local" and "global" coordinates. These two coordinate systems are the same only if the layer and comp are the same. However, there is a way to work around that if you have the Production Bundle – check out *To Effect Point* in Chapter 35.

Render Settings

Most effects take little to no rendering time when the effect has zero effect on the image. So when you animate a blur effect down to zero, the effect is essentially turned off from that point forward. If an effect is slowing down rendering even after the effect hits the last keyframe, split the layer (Edit>Split Layer) and delete the effect where it's not needed. Also, non-animating effects applied to still images should cache after the first frame rather than reapply on every frame in the comp. Exceptions include the Render>Ramp and Text>Path Text effects.

When it comes time to render your comp, the Render Settings includes a menu for Effects. The options are Current Settings, All On, and All Off. (More on Render Settings in Chapter 43.)

Generally, rendering with Current Settings is the safest option: any effects that are on will render, and those that are turned off won't be processed. However, if you've turned off an effect while you're editing because it's too slow, make sure you turn it on before you render.

The second option, Effects>All On, will turn on all effects, whether they're currently enabled or not. The danger here is that you will not only turn on that slowpoke effect you turned off temporarily, but other effects that you didn't want that you'd forgotten all about. In general, if an effect experiment failed, delete the effect rather than turn it off. That allows you the option to turn off slow effects temporarily and have Render Settings override current settings with the All On option.

Renaming Effects

You can rename any effect in the Effect Controls window by selecting it, hitting Return, typing in a new name (such as Blue/Orange Duotone), and hitting Return again. Note that these names are lost when you copy and paste effects.

Connect

Creating and editing masks were covered in depth in Chapter 13.

Precomposing was covered in Chapter 17.

Type effects are spelled out in Chapter 27.

Motion Fun, which among other tricks will let you copy a position path accurately into an effect point path even if the layer and comp are not the same size, is explored in Chapter 35.

Adjustment Layers

Ever wish you could apply the same effect to a stack of layers at once?

Adjustment Layers is a concept After Effects borrowed from Photoshop. Essentially, it's a dummy layer that you apply effects to. Everything under this layer gets treated by whatever effects have been applied to the adjustment layer. You can then manipulate the adjustment layer's opacity using masks and mattes in order to apply effects to selected areas, as well as add animation to the layer and the effects applied.

Adjustment Logic 101

An adjustment layer can be added anywhere in the layer stack, where it will affect just the layers underneath, while additional layers are untreated on top. It can also affect the entire frame or select just a region. Using an adjustment layer is often preferable to precomposing layers and applying the effects to the precomp. Internally, an adjustment layer in essence makes a copy of the underlying layer stack composite and applies the effect to the area where the adjustment layer is opaque.

Open comp [**Ex.01*starter**] – it contains a simple composite of several layers, scaled by different amounts. Say you wanted to give all the images except the large foreground sphere the same amount of blur. You could add a blur effect to each of the background layers individually, or you could precompose all the layers behind the forward sphere and apply the blur to that. Or, you could use an adjustment layer.

To try this, select Layer>New Adjustment Layer. A solid, the size of the comp, will be created with a default name, and with its "half moon" switch turned on in the Switches panel of the Time Layout window. This switch indicates that the image information in the layer should be ignored as it is going to be used only for adjustments.

Add Effect>Blur & Sharpen>Gaussian Blur and set the Blurriness slider to a value of 3 – all layers below are blurred. Now drag it down one layer in the Time Layout window so it is below the "gold melt" sphere. This sphere remains sharp because it is above the adjustment layer, while layers below are blurred. Experiment with reordering the layers to reinforce this idea.

The "half moon" icon in the Time Layout window is the switch that changes any ordinary layer into that superhero known as an Adjustment Layer. Here we've applied a Gaussian Blur effect to blur the composite of all layers below – the layer above is unaffected.

Example Project

Explore the 20-Example Project.aep file as you read this chapter; references to [Ex.##] refer to specific compositions within the project file.

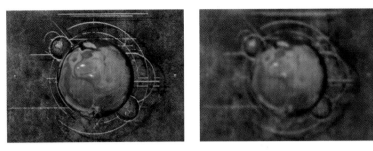

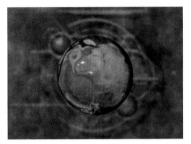

Remember that the content of the layer used as an adjustment layer does not matter; its image information is discarded and replaced with the image of the underlying layer stack. That's why After Effects uses a simple full-frame solid (Layer>New Solid) as a "seed" for an adjustment layer.

The "before" image of a stack of layers (left), all with equal sharpness. A new adjustment layer was created and the Gaussian Blur effect was applied which affects all layers (center). To keep the forward sphere "in focus," we moved it above the adjustment layer (right). Background image and underlying sphere textures courtesy Paul Sherstobitoff.

Edited Sequence

Adjustment layers are also useful for treating a sequence of edited layers, not just a stack of layers. In [Ex.02] we've given a sequence of movies a rich blue cast using the Boris Tint-Tritone effect (free on this book's CD). The effect is applied only in proportion to how opaque the adjustment layer is, so edit the adjustment layer's opacity value to mix back in the color from the original footage.

Additional Adjusting Tricks

Adjustment layers are easy – and fun – if you just keep their logic in mind: They are a region of a comp that you can apply effects to. This often saves having to precompose layers in order to affect them as a group. You can also apply multiple adjustment layers in a single comp, and these are processed from the bottom up (each adjustment layer sends its result to the adjustment layer above).

The sections of the adjustment layer that are opaque determine what portion of the underlying layer is affected. The layer's in and out times are also obeyed – no adjustments will take place before or after the layer is active in a comp. Apart from adjusting the Opacity value, there are other tricks for modifying the adjustment layer's opaque areas. The following examples include techniques covered in detail in previous chapters, as noted:

An adjustment layer can treat a sequence of edited layers with the same effect if it is applied on top of all of the clips. The footage in [Ex.02] is colorized with the Boris Tint-Tritone effect (free on the CD). Musician footage courtesy Herd of Mavericks.

Simple Selections

The simplest example of limiting the scope of the adjustment layer is to simply move it around the comp – the layers below are affected only directly under the adjustment layer, as shown in [Ex.03a]. Since this layer is simply a white solid that happens to have its "half moon" switch on, you can also open the Layer>Solid Settings dialog (Command+Shift+Y) and change the size of the solid.

Moving the adjustment layer down to the bottom of the frame limits the Channel>Invert effect to this area. Footage courtesy EyeWire/Cool Character and Water Elements.

Masking Shapes

For more interesting shapes, applying a mask (Chapter 13) to the adjustment layer will limit effects to the opaque area. In [Ex.03b], an oval mask was created, then inverted, so that effects would apply to outside the masked area (the adjustment layer is now opaque on the outside, and transparent on the inside). Gaussian Blur was applied to defocus the area on the left side destined for the titles. Don't forget to add a generous mask feather amount to blend the edges of the effected and original image. Additional mask examples for you to explore are included in the [Ex.03] folder, including a mask pasted from Illustrator.

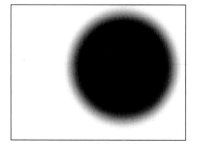

Applying an oval mask to an adjustment layer is a simple way to limit the effect to certain areas. In [Ex.03b] the mask is inverted (left) so the Gaussian Blur defocuses the opaque regions outside the mask (right). Stills © Corbis Images.

Any Alpha Will Do

Any layer can become an adjustment layer, though images with interesting alpha channel shapes work best. The image will disappear, but effects applied to it will modify all layers below based on its alpha channel. To practice this, open the comp [Ex.04*starter] where the top layer is a goldfish object. Turn on the half moon switch for the fish layer (the image will vanish – that's okay) and apply an effect to it. The effects will be applied to the water texture below based on the fish's alpha channel. We used Effect>Adjust>Hue/Saturation and Effect>Stylize>Scatter in our version [Ex.04_final].

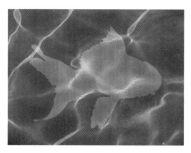

Any layer with an interesting alpha channel can be used as an adjustment layer. In this case, a fish image (left) is converted to an adjustment layer. Effects applied to it affect the water texture underneath based on the fish's alpha (right). Fish courtesy EyeWire/ Design Essentials; water footage courtesy Artbeats/Water Textures.

Animating Adjustments

No bonus prize for guessing that an adjustment layer can also be animated using the regular Transform properties (Position, Scale, Rotation, and so on) as covered back in Chapter 4 – this applies to both simple solids and layers with alpha. Try animating the position of the fish layer in [Ex.04] and see how the effects now move across the water texture. You can also animate parameters in the effects, as well as animate the mask shape when you're creating selections with masks. The [Ex.05] folder includes examples of adding animation to solids, alpha shapes, masks, and effects.

Transfer Modes

Effects applied to an adjustment layer can also be re-applied to the original image using a transfer mode (Chapter 12), using Opacity to further refine the mix. This is particularly useful for more subtle effects where mixing in the original image with just Opacity doesn't cut it. The [Ex.07] folder includes some examples, including applying the result of the Effect>Stylize>Find Edges effect back on the underlying image using the Screen transfer mode.

Luma Track Mattes

Any footage with an interesting alpha channel could make a good adjustment layer, but what if the footage is grayscale? In this case, create a new adjustment layer, then apply the footage as a luma track matte (Chapter 14). Remember to make sure the grayscale footage is on top of the adjustment layer, then set the adjustment layer to Luma Matte (or Inverted Luma Matte) in the Track Matte column. Effects will now apply to all layers below as dictated by the matte. Try this in [Ex.06*starter]; check out our version in [Ex.06-final].

Transforming Adjustments

The Transform effect (Effect>Perspective>Transform) may also be applied to an adjustment layer, allowing you to scale, rotate, reposition, skew, and fade the *contents* of the adjustment layer – i.e., the stack of all the layers underneath. This compares to the regular Transform properties, which change the region that will get adjusted. Experiment with comp [Ex.08], adjusting the scale, position, and rotation parameters of the Transform effect in the Effect Controls window (select the layer and hit Command+Shift+T). Chapter 16 covers using the Transform effect for fading a stack of layers to avoid opacity artifacts.

More Adjustments

To wrap up this chapter, we created three animations in the [Ex.09] folder for you to explore. These put to use the techniques discussed above.

In [Ex.06] a matte movie (above) is used as an inverted luma matte to modify a solid adjustment layer; the areas that are black in the matte are then blurred and washed out. Matte courtesy Artbeats/Cloud Chamber; footage for montage courtesy EyeWire/Cool Character and Water Elements.

[Ex.09a-Golf] uses a "torn edge" grayscale image as an animated luma track matte; effects Channel>Invert and Boris AE>Boris Tint-Tritone colorize the left side of the frame, inverting the moving text layer as well. The golf ball movie zooms up in Overlay mode. Golfer putting image © Corbis Images.

[Ex.09b-Recital] uses an animated Illustrator text layer (which includes an alpha channel) as an adjustment layer to invert the layers below. The Perspective> Transform effect then fades out all layers as a group. Piano player footage courtesy Herd of Mavericks; sheet music © Corbis Images.

[Ex.09c-Edgy Musicians] further refines the Find Edges effect with blurs and glows applied to the sequence of musician clips. This stack of effects is saved as a Favorite on the CD in the Goodies folder as **FindEdgesGlow_ch20.ffx**. Musicians footage courtesy Herd of Mavericks.

 That Ol' Black Solid

Many effects don't affect a layer – they outright replace it with their own imagery.

It's common to think of effects as filters that treat an image. Many of them indeed work that way. However, several very useful effects create their own images, such as stroked lines, text, and lens flares. Some replace the image they are applied to completely; some give you the option of having them draw on top of the image in the layer they are applied to. But even then, it is often more powerful to have them on their own separate layer, to be able to perform additional compositing tricks. Therefore, the most common layer to apply them to is a simple, often pure black, solid.

Divide and Conquer

Many of these effects will automatically turn off the underlying image and create their own alpha channel, ignoring any alpha or mask the original layer may have had. It is also not uncommon for them to present you with a number of compositing options, such as a Composite on Original checkbox (leave it unchecked to replace the source) or a Paint On menu (set it to Transparent to replace the source).

Even though these effects can composite directly on top of a host image, there are good reasons to want to separate them from an image we intend to keep. For example, if you create a text overlay with one of the effects such as Basic Text, you could apply it directly to the layer and check Composite on Original. Then, to give it a drop shadow, you might think you just apply Effect> Perspective>Drop Shadow as the second effect in line. However, this won't shadow the *text;* it will give a shadow to the *layer* the text is applied to. Check out the comp [**Ex.01a**] to see the results.

To fix this, we need instead to create a solid (Layer>New Solid, or Command+Y) to apply the text to and turn off Composite on Original so the text is the only image we see from this layer. Now our drop shadow will work [**Ex.01b**]. And now that we have it as its own layer, we can experiment with using Transfer Modes to make the composite more interesting – for example, [**Ex.01c**] uses Overlay mode so the text interacts more with the surface.

Effects that can optionally replace their source image often present this option as either a checkbox (Basic Text) or a menu (Stroke).

Example Project

Explore the 21-Example Project.aep file as you read this chapter; references to [Ex.##] refer to specific compositions within the project file.

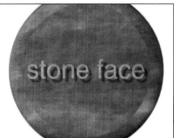

Dropping Out the Black

Some effects, such as lens flares, don't have an option to create their own alpha channels. However, the technique of applying them to their own solid is still valid.

Back in Chapter 19 when we showed how to apply effects, one of our examples was applying a lens flare to one of Paul Sherstobitoff's paintings. This is shown in [**Ex.02*starter**]. However, our control over the final look of this composite is greatly limited by the fact that the lens flare is applied directly to the image. Instead, try this:

Step 1: Select the layer PS_Axis, and delete its effect (Effect>Remove All).

Step 2: Select Layer>New Solid, name it Lens Flare, and click the Comp Size button. Make the color black, and click on OK to create the solid.

Step 3: With the black solid positioned above the image layer, apply Effect>Render>PS+ Lens Flare to this solid, accepting the default settings. The Effect Controls window will open, and you'll see the flare clearly on black.

Step 4: Change the Switches/Modes panel in the Time Layout window to show transfer modes, and experiment with different modes: Screen gives the most natural look; Add and Color Burn give more blown-out looks. You can also adjust the opacity of the lens flare layer to mix in the effect to taste.

Step 5: With the name of the effect selected in the Effect Controls window, Option+drag the lens flare center effect point around the Comp window to create different lens flare streaks from different areas. You can reposition the lens flare center and change the solid's rotation, scale, and position properties to better align the flare to how you want it to streak across the image. If your transformed flare starts to get cropped off,

When we apply text directly to a layer we want to see, adding Drop Shadow on top of it shadows the layer, not the text (left). If we give the text its own layer, it can now have its own shadow (center), plus we can use transfer modes for a more interesting composite (right).

Precomp to Group

A disadvantage of placing effects on their own layers is that animating them with their underlying layers as a group becomes trickier. Consider precomposing them together and animating the precomp instead.

A lens flare applied directly to an image (left) limits your compositing options. Instead, apply the effect to a black solid (center). Use the Add (or Screen) transfer mode to drop out the black background and change the flare color (right) or add other effects. Painting courtesy Paul Sherstobitoff.

Paint it Black

Remember, you can create a Solid layer with Command+Y (Command+Shift+Y edits it). The "comp size" button automatically makes it match the comp; this makes the effect point coordinates match the comp position.

Alpha Hunting

Some effects create an alpha, just not by default. DigiEffects Delirium's Fireworks (free on your CD) needs to be set to "Effect Only" to create an alpha if applied to a black solid.

Which Ones?

All of the effects in the Render and Text sub-menus are fair game to use with the techniques discussed in this chapter.

edit the solid's parameters (Command+Option+Y) to create a larger solid that can bleed off the edges of the comp. Since the lens flare exists separate from the underlying image, we can apply additional effects to just the flare. For example, Effect>Adjust>Hue/Saturation lets you change the color of the flare. We show the result of some of these adjustments in [Ex.02_complete].

Tracers

Although this chapter is about using black solids to create effects on separate layers for compositing, there's one exception to the black solid technique. When you're using an effect that "traces" the image below (as in using a mask to trace the route on a map), it's essential for the Layer window to show the mask shape against the original image and not a black solid. Tracing effects include Render>Stroke, which follows a mask shape, and Stylize>Write On, which draws along an effect point motion path (it is also edited in the Layer window, as we saw in Chapter 19).

If you need the effects on a separate layer, work on a copy of the image to draw your masks or paths. To do this, duplicate the layer (Command+D) and apply the effect to the duplicate (which should now be above the original in the Time Layout window stack). Create your paths or masks on this duplicate, Make sure you set your tracing effects to Paint On = Transparent so that they will create their own transparency. Now you can apply additional effects and use transfer modes to composite the effects on the original image.

If you're applying multiple copies of effects such as Stroke, you will need to set the first instance to Paint On = Transparent, and subsequent copies to Paint On = Original. This may sound odd, but with these settings the first Stroke effect will replace the underlying image, and will then in turn appear to be the original image to the second effect. Therefore, any further Stroke effects should also Paint On = Original, or the result of all previous effects.

If you need to trace a composite of multiple layers in the Layer window, nest or precompose the layers and apply the effect to the precomp.

Black Solid Calling Alpha, Over...

You may need to create an alpha channel from an effect applied to a black solid – it will give you a wider range of options in transfer modes, plus you can then apply additional effects that work on the alpha, such as Perspective>Drop Shadow or Bevel Alpha.

You can also render the effect with an alpha channel if you need to composite the effect over video footage in an editing system.

To create an alpha channel from an image set against black, download the Unmult effect created by special effects master John Knoll. It's available for free in exchange for registering on the Puffin Designs Web site (www.puffindesigns.com). Apply Unmult after, say, the Lens Flare effect, and Unmult will automatically extract black and create an alpha channel. It is especially useful with effects such as lens flares, but also for footage shot against black, such as most pyrotechnics stock footage.

A Solid Solution for Unsavory Alphas

Some third-party effects that create synthetic images do not create very clean alpha channels when they are composited. As an alternative (or last resort), alter the colors of the effect to have it create just white shapes over a black solid, with no attempt at alpha creation. Then use this as a luma track matte to reveal another solid color or image through the white shapes.

You can even try using this as a luma track matte for the original effect, which might give you a cleaner composite. Tweak the original to taste, turn off alpha creation if you have a choice, duplicate it, then set its colors to white (you may need to apply other Image Control effects as necessary to get a high-contrast matte). Use this as a luma matte for the original effect in a layer directly underneath. See Chapter 14 for more on creating track matte effects.

Of course, you don't need to apply these masks, paths, and effects to a duplicate of the original layer. If you created them on the original layer, you could copy and paste them to a black solid that is the same size as the original layer and still have access to transfer modes and additional tricks.

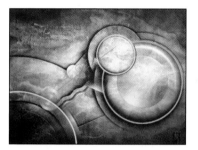 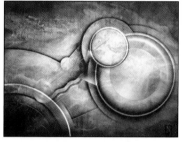

Applying the Render>Stroke effect directly to a layer yields only solid colors (left). Applying it to its own layer and using transfer modes gives more interaction (right).

Tracing Practice

Let's wrap up by putting a few of these concepts to work. In Chapter 19, we had an example project of animating strokes along mask paths over one of Paul Sherstobitoff's paintings. This is replicated in the project for this chapter as [**Ex.03*starter**]. The strokes animate over time; go to the end to see the final result.

The problem with this scenario is that you can't apply the strokes to the image using a transfer mode or apply any other effects, such as a drop shadow or glow. To fix this:

Step 1: Duplicate the layer (Command+D).

Step 2: Select the bottom layer and Effect>Remove All Effects – the effects are not needed on the background layer.

Step 3: Select the top layer and Layer>Open Effect Controls (Command+Shift+T). The three Stroke effects are all set to Paint On = Original, which is no longer appropriate. Edit the first Stroke effect so that its Paint On menu is set to Transparent – the first stroke will now become the original image to the next Stroke effect. All other Stroke effects should remain set to Paint On = Original.

Step 4: Experiment with various transfer modes to composite the strokes on top of the painting. Feel free to experiment with different stroke colors and use additional effects such as Drop Shadow and Bevel Alpha. Our version is in [**Ex.03_final**].

Connect

Transfer modes that work best on Black, White or Gray solids were listed in a sidebar in Chapter 12.

How to create and edit masks was taught in Chapter 13.

Nesting and precomposing comps were discussed in Chapters 16 and 17, respectively.

Effects Point and Lens Flare were covered more in Chapter 19.

Type effects are explored in greater depth in Chapter 27.

22 Compound Interest

Compound effects may seem nonintuitive at first, but they require learning only a few simple rules.

A *compound effect* is one that looks at a second layer to decide exactly how to treat the layer it is applied to. Examples of these vary from Compound Blur – which can selectively blur one layer based on the varying luminance values of another – to Texturize, which is great for creating those embossed station identity bugs most networks use these days, among other things. Note that you'll need the Production Bundle to follow the Displacement Map examples later in this chapter ([**Ex.03**] through [**Ex.06**]).

The "modifying" layer that a compound effect points to can range from a simple gradient to a second movie or composition. In most cases, the information being passed is an 8-bit (or 256 levels of gray) image, or the luminance values of a color image. These gray levels are then used by the effect to determine which pixels in the first layer are blurred, faded, displaced, and so on.

By pointing to a second layer, compound effects sidestep the normal rendering pipeline order of bottommost layer to topmost layer. As a result, mastering these effects requires a little forethought in preparing your sources, and quite often requires that you create the effect using more than one comp.

In this chapter we'll focus on three of these compound effects: Compound Blur, Texturize, and Displacement Map. These cover the gamut from fairly straightforward to fairly complex. Once you understand the logic behind compound effects, you should be able to adapt the techniques to any effect that uses a second, modifying layer.

The power of compound effects comes in selecting a second layer to affect the one the effect is applied to. If the default is None, no matter how many other parameters you change, the result will still be "no effect." So don't forget to select a modifying layer.

That Other Layer

Compound effects are easy to spot because they have a popup for you to select a second layer to work with. Most of these effects either default to None (which results in no effect, because no layer has been selected) or use themselves as the modifying layer. This popup automatically lists all layers in the current composition.

The modifier layer does *not* need to turned on in order to be used by a compound effect. In fact, if its image is not being used directly in the comp, it's best to turn it off to ensure it does not appear accidentally.

Example Project

Explore the 22-Example Project.aep file as you read this chapter; references to [Ex.##] refer to specific compositions within the project file.

Size Matters

As we mentioned above, the way compound effects work is to line up the modifying layer with the effected layer, pixel by pixel, and decide how to treat each pixel in the effected layer based on some property (usually luminance) of the modifier layer. If both layers are the same size, life is more straightforward. But what if the modifying layer is not the same size or aspect ratio as the layer the effect is applied to? For example, if you were to take a logo or bug that is, say, 300×300 pixels, and emboss it into a movie layer of 640×480, After Effects needs to know if it should:

• *Stretch to Fit,* which would stretch and distort the logo to 640×480 before applying it as a texture;

• *Center* the smaller logo in the 640×480 area; or

• *Tile* the logo, so that you see multiple logos, some of which may be incomplete if the two sizes do not match up exactly.

Short Circuit

While these options are often valid, they don't allow for the logo to be easily scaled and placed in the lower right corner of the screen à la a network ID bug.

The reason for this is the rendering order inside After Effects: When an effect is applied to the movie, and that effect is told to refer to a second layer for data, it's capable of seeing the modifying layer only at its "source" – *before* any masks, effects, or transformations have been applied to it. In other words, it uses the modifying layer as it would appear in its own Layer window – *not* in the Comp window. Hence, no scaling or positioning of the Logo layer is taken into account by the compound effect.

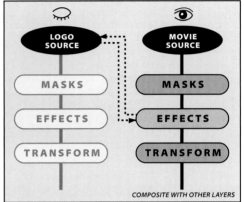

FINAL COMP

COMPOSITE WITH OTHER LAYERS

When a compound effect, such as Texturize, is applied to a layer, the effect looks at just the source of the modifying layer and ignores any masks, effects, or transformations that may be applied to the "map" layer.

Longer (and Better) Circuit

The trick, then, is to present the effect module with a modifying layer that's the same size as the layer being effected, and with the modifying layer already positioned and sized to line up with the layer we're treating. You do that by using a nested comp that is the same size as the layer being effected.

You can position, scale, and otherwise transform, as well as animate and effect, the modifying source in this nested comp, and the result will then be applied faithfully by the compound effect.

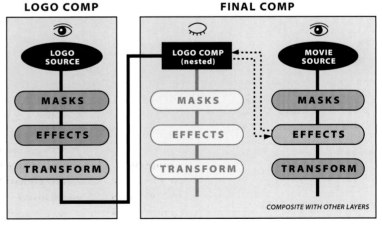

LOGO COMP   **FINAL COMP**

COMPOSITE WITH OTHER LAYERS

Apply any transformations (for example, scale and position the logo bug) to the modifying layer in its own precomp and nest it in the comp with the layer that gets the compound effect (Texturize). Now the effect will take the transformations applied to the bug into account when it processes.

Now that we have a general understanding of how compound effects work, let's look at them individually.

Compound Blur

This effect can be thought of as a variable blur, with the amount of blur controlled by the luminance of the modifying layer it points to. The amount of blur is calculated on a pixel-by-pixel basis: The brighter a pixel is in the modifying layer, the more blurred the corresponding pixel will be in the layer Compound Blur is applied to.

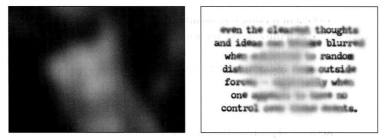

even the clearest thoughts and ideas can become blurred when subjected to random disturbances from outside forces – especially when one appears to have no control over these events.

Take a text layer (left), apply Compound Blur, and direct it to use a second layer with interesting luminance shapes (center) as a blur map. The result is selective blurring of our original image (right), based on the luminance values in the modifying layer. Soft Edges footage from Artbeats.

Composition [**Ex.01**] contains a text layer, a few animated texture movies for you to try out, and a white background solid layer.

Step 1:   Select the text layer and apply Effect>Blur & Sharpen>Compound Blur. The Effect Controls window will open.

Step 2:   The modifying layer is set to None – so no blur is taking place. Change the Blur Layer popup to the white background layer. The text will now go all blurry, since the modifying layer is solid white.

Step 3:   Change the Blur Layer to AB_SoftEdges movie, and now the blur varies across the text. Double-click the SoftEdges layer to open it in its own Layer window and compare how it looks with the blur pattern. Experiment with the other parameters in the Compound Blur effect, such as Invert Blur (means black areas in the modifying layer get maximum blur and white areas no blur), and the Maximum Blur amount. Try the other two blur map movies for comparison (the Cell Pattern movie looks better with a small blur amount) and try some grayscale images of your own.

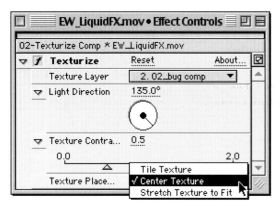

Remember that compound effects rely on the two layers being the same size in order to work. If they aren't, it needs to know how to interpret the modifier layer in order to force it to have the same number of pixels as the effected layer.

Texturize

Many will feel this effect should have been named Emboss, because that better describes the end result: It looks like an object has been embossed into the video screen of the layer it was applied to. We'll use the Effect>Stylize>Texturize effect to create a bug embossed in the corner of our footage.

As noted earlier in this chapter, Texturize is a prime example of a compound effect in which you may need to prepare the modifying layer in another composition so you can control the position and scale of the bug. You can take two different approaches to get there –

nesting or *precomposing* (covered in Chapters 16 and 17 respectively). The final solution is shown in [**Ex.02-Texturize Comp**] – open it now so that you know what the result should look like.

Texturizing by Nesting

If you're the type who likes to plan ahead, create a moving embossed effect by animating your bug in its own precomp, then nest this precomp with the movie in a second comp. Apply Texturize to the movie layer, using the bug precomp as the texture map layer. If you want to re-create our example, the steps are as follows:

Step 1: Make a new composition and name it Bug Comp. It should be the same size and duration as the movie you'll be effecting (320×240 if you're using our sources).

Step 2: Drag in the Sources>22_Chapter Sources>Aqua2000Bug.tif footage item. Our logo is a grayscale file with white text on black, which is ideal for the Texturize effect since it looks only at high contrast edges, not the alpha channel.

Step 3: Resize and position the bug in the bottom left hand corner and select Best Quality to antialias the layer.

Step 4: Make a second composition in which you'll create the actual effect. Do this by dragging the movie you want to effect to the New Comp button in the Project window. We used Sources>Movies>EW_LiquidFX.mov in our example. The new comp will open and contain the movie layer. Rename the comp (Composition>Composition Settings) Texturize1 Comp.

Step 5: Drag the Bug Comp from the Project window to this new comp.

Step 6: Turn off the Visibility switch (the eyeball) for Bug Comp, as it is not supposed to be visible. Move the Bug Comp layer to the back if you like.

Step 7: Make sure you apply the Stylize>Texturize effect to the *movie* layer (*not* the bug layer) and select Bug Comp in the Texture Layer popup. Since the movie and Bug Comp are the same width and height, the Texture Placement popup is now irrelevant. With all comps set to Full Resolution, edit the Contrast slider to taste. Sharp horizontal lines may flicker when they're field rendered, so we tend to use the 0.5–0.7 range for a softer effect. If you're having a problem, compare your version with the finished [**Ex.02-Texturize Comp**].

Step 8: *Optional:* Animate the bug layer in Bug Comp, and note how the Texturize effect now animates accordingly in the Texturize 1 Comp.

Safe Bugs

When you're creating logo bugs, watching the safe guides will help you keep them inside title safe. And remember to keep any "lower-third" graphics away from the bug zone…

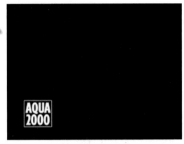

Steps 1–3: Our bug is prebuilt in one comp, where it is sized and positioned.

Steps 4–7: The logo bug is applied to our video layer in the second comp, resulting in an embossed effect. Background footage from EyeWire/Liquid FX.

Step 7: The Time Layout window of the second comp, where you can see how the effect has been set up.

Texturizer Tricks

The Texturize effect also has a set of criteria as to what constitutes a useful modifying layer. In our experience, high contrast images with sharp edges work best, so we usually use black text on a white background, or vice versa. You might think that the effect would consider the alpha channel of the logo layer, but that is not the case: It only sees the "luminance" of the RGB channels (the result of collapsing a color image to grayscale is the layer's luminance).

So if you need to use a layer's alpha, open the image in Photoshop, copy and paste the alpha channel to a new grayscale file, and use this as your source. Alternatively, and more useful if your map is a movie layer, you could use the Effect>Channels> Shift Channels in After Effects to take the Red, Green and Blue channels from the Alpha channel. The Effect>Render>Fill effect can also easily fill a layer's RGB channels with white.

Another potential troublespot appears when using Illustrator files. We normally create black text in Illustrator, and apply color later in After Effects. The problem is that black text on a comp's black background has no contrast, so the Texturize effect has nothing to work with. If you keep the text black and change the nested comp's background color to white, it still won't work; no matter what color you make the background, a nested comp's background is always "transparency," which is treated as black by an effect.

The workaround for black Illustrator files is to place the text over a white Solid in a precomp, since solids do exist in RGB space. Another alternative is to change the black text to white (using either the Image Control>Tint or Render>Fill effect), but this must be done in a precomp also in order for the tint effect to be seen by Texturize. All in all, it might be easiest to set Illustrator to Artwork mode, and create white text in Illustrator in the first place.

Filling with White

Make black Illustrator files white in a precomp to use them with Texturize. The Effect>Render>Fill effect will fill the RGB channel with a flat color; to use white, eyedropper the alpha swatch button in the Comp window.

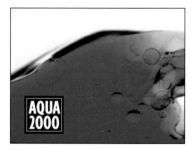

Step 2: the logo bug layer is scaled down and positioned in the left hand corner, in the correct placement to be an embossed bug.

Texturizing by Precomposing

If you forgot to plan ahead and already started to create the effect all in one comp, the following steps using precompose (Chapter 17) offer an alternate approach to building exactly the same Texturize effect. So let's start over again with a second scenario. By purposely making a couple of missteps, we'll also uncover a couple of gotchas common with precomposing:

Step 1: Select Window>Close All to start over. Make a new composition by dragging the movie you want to effect to the New Comp button in the Project window. Again, we used the Sources>Movies>EW_LiquidFX.mov in our example. The new comp will open and will contain the movie layer. Rename the comp (Composition>Composition Settings) Texturize2 Comp.

Step 2: Drag in the bug layer from Sources>22_Chapter Sources> Aqua2000Bug.tif. Resize and position the bug in the bottom left hand corner. Select Best Quality to antialias the layer.

Step 3: Turn off the Visibility switch (the eyeball) for the Bug layer, as it is not supposed to be visible.

Step 4: Select the movie layer (not the bug layer, remember) and apply the Stylize>Texturize effect. For the Texture Layer popup, select the bug layer as the texture. The result is that the frame is filled with large bugs, as the Texture Placement popup defaults to Tile Texture. But even setting this popup to Center Texture or Stretch Texture to fit will not show the bug positioned in the left hand corner.

Step 5: A bit of sleuthing is in order. Double-click the bug layer to open its Layer window, which displays the layer's source. The image in the Layer window tells you what's being fed to the Texturize effect applied to the movie layer. To have the Layer window display the bug positioned in the corner, we need to precompose the bug so the transform properties are calculated in a precomp.

Step 6: Close the bug's Layer window before you precompose. Select the Bug layer, and choose Pre-compose from the Layer menu. Name the new precomp Bug Precomp and be sure to select the *second* option, "Move all attributes into the new composition." It's essential that the transform keyframes are sent down to the precomp. Click OK, and a new comp is created that is the same size and duration as the current comp.

The new comp has one layer in it, the original Bug layer, and this precomp is nested in the Texturize2 Comp. So, the result is similar to nesting. (Of course, since the precomp defaults to being the same size as the main comp, it's important that the main comp is the same size as your movie or the Texturize effect may again have a placement problem.)

Step 7: After you've precomposed, you would expect everything to be hunky-dory. The Comp window's image is currently cached, and has not updated, so advance one frame to refresh the rendering. If you followed the above steps exactly, the logo bug will now disappear completely…

What's going on is that when you precomposed, After Effects turned on the visibility for the nested precomp layer. However, the eyeball for the bug layer you selected was in fact turned off, so it's still off in the precomp. This is a common user error. Option+double-click on the Bug Precomp layer to open the precomp and turn on the eyeball for the Bug layer. Return to the main Texturize2 comp and you'll see the Bug Precomp layer appear; now turn off the eyeball in this comp.

To summarize: The eyeball for the bug should be on in the precomp so that its data is sent to the main comp, but it should be off in the main comp as you don't want it to appear in the render.

Step 8: So we're now back in the main comp and…the Texturize effect is *still* not working. If you've been with us this far, this one is *not* your fault! When you precompose a layer that's used by a compound effect, the effect resets itself back to using None (or to using itself) as the modifying layer. Select the movie layer and open the Effects Control window (Command+Shift+T) if it's not already open. Re-select the Bug Precomp layer from the Texture Layer popup and…*success!* At this point, the result should be the same as both our [Ex.02-Texturize Comp] and the nesting method above.

Regardless of whether you ever use the Texturize effect, these two gotchas are worth remembering when you're precomposing with other compound effects. Once you understand the logic of how compound effects work, you can adapt these nesting or precomposing steps to almost any effect that uses a modifying layer.

At Step 4, the Texturize effect defaults to tiling the bug across the movie layer. Not exactly what we had in mind.

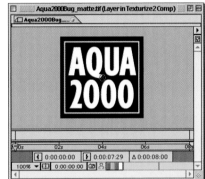

Step 5: The Layer window for the bug image shows the original source layer – before the position and scale properties have been taken into account. This is what the Texturize effect is receiving.

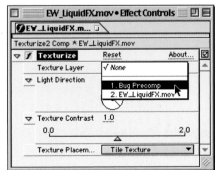

When you precompose a layer that's being used by a compound effect, the effect will reset itself back to using None as the modifying layer. In Step 7, re-select the Bug Precomp layer as your texture.

Displacement Map

A *displacement map* displaces pixels – in other words, moves them up or down and to the left or right – depending on the luminance values of the modifying layer. It's great for creating warped, liquidy effects, as well as making one layer appear as if it has been projected or painted onto an uneven surface. This effect is available only with the Production Bundle version of After Effects.

To see how this works, open [**Ex.03*starter**] comp. Layer 1 is a grayscale displacement map, and Layer 2 is the movie layer that will be displaced:

Step 1:   Turn off the visibility for the map in layer 1.

Step 2:   Select the movie in layer 2 and apply Effect> Distort>Displacement Map. Open the Effect Controls window so you can read the full parameter names. The Displacement Map Layer popup defaults to using itself as a map, so change this to point at Layer 1.

Step 3:   Choose what channel you want to use for Horizontal Displacement in the next popup; since the map is grayscale, you can use any of the Red, Green, Blue, or Luminance settings. Set the Maximum Displacement with the slider below. The next popup and slider control the Vertical Displacement in a similar way.

Step 4:   The Displacement Map Behavior parameter kicks in when the map is not the same size or aspect ratio as the movie it's displacing. Our map is 1440×480, and the movie is 320×240, so compare the Center Map and Stretch Map to Fit settings. The latter uses the entire map scaled to 320×240, so it has more extreme results.

Step 5:   The final trick to Displacement Map is the checkbox for Edge Behavior. If you displace pixels away from an outer edge of the layer, what fills in the space they left behind? Checking Wrap Pixels Around borrows part of the image from the opposite edge to fill in the gaps. If the layer has a fairly consistent color around its edges, this works particularly well, since the borrowed pixels will match. Preview the result.

To not displace an image, the modifying map needs to be 50% gray (RGB values 128/128/128), or its alpha channel must be transparent. Darker areas displace in "negative" directions (up and to the left) and lighter areas displace in positive directions (down and to the right), with the final amount controlled by sliders in the effect. You can select any number of characteristics of the modifying image to provide the map, such as the strength of a specific color. In contrast to Texturize, slightly blurred maps tend to work better than sharp ones; sharp contrasting edges result in disjointed displacements along those edges.

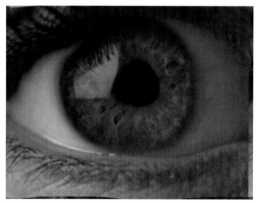

In [**Ex.03**], the displacement map (top) is 14440 wide by 480 high. When we applied it to the 320×240 movie, we used the Center Map setting (above).

The result: notice the edge artifacts even with Wrap Pixels Around turned on. Eye movie courtesy EyeWire/Senses.

Animating the Map

Displacement maps often look good when they're animating, and this is where the concept of animating the map in a precomp comes up yet again, just like with the Texturize effect above. For example, [Ex.04*starter] has our eye movie again, displaced by a wavy high-contrast map. That's nice, but the displacement isn't moving – even though the displacement map is panning from right to left. To have this animation affect the displaced layer, it needs to be placed in its own precomp. Follow the steps for precomposing in *Texturizing by Precomposing*, above, to move the animated map down to the precomp. If you get lost, compare your results with the [Ex.04_final comps] folder.

Different Sizes

We've seen how you need to animate a displacement map in a precomp. But what if the image or movie you're displacing is also animating? Or you have a stack of layers you want to displace?

In this case, you'll need to animate the movie or group the images together in a second precomp that's the same size as the map precomp. In the third and main comp, you nest both precomps, then create the displacement map effect.

You could think of these precomps as two sides of a "sandwich". When they come together in the main comp, the Displacement Map Behavior popup will be irrelevant because both precomps are the same size. This also gives you the opportunity to create the precomps a little larger than the main comp so that any edge artifacts are cropped off by the pasteboard in the main comp.

Larger than Life

To avoid edge artifacts when you're displacing images, create artwork and precomps that are larger than the comp size so that the artifacts will be cropped off by the comp's borders. [Ex.05] shows this in practice.

Alpha versus Luma

If the grayscale info you want exists in the map's alpha but the effect sees only the layer's luminance, the CE View Channels effect can move the map's alpha channel into each of the RGB channels.

[Ex.05] consists of a precomp (340×260) where the map pans right to left; a second precomp (also 340×260) where the hand image and text are animated and composited as a group; and a third, main comp (320×240), where the displacement map effect is created.

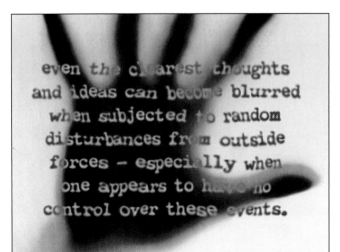

The main comp with the hand image and text displaced. The edge artifacts still exist, but since they're out on the pasteboard area they won't be visible in the final render. The text is composited using the Exclusion transfer mode (this is the first time we've ever gotten this mode to look good…). Hand from Digital Vision/The Body.

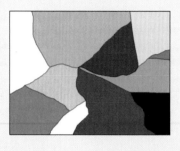
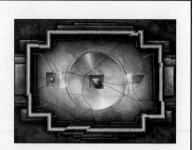

The Mirror Cracked

We usually suggest that displacement map sources do not have sharp transitions in luminance because these would cause sudden shifts in the positions of the displaced pixels. Of course, there are exceptions to every rule.

One useful exception is simulating a cracked reflective surface, such as a broken mirror. In [Ex.06], a painting by Paul Sherstobitoff (left) is displaced by a map where each faux mirror shard is given a different gray value (center), which results in a different amount of displacement per shard. We included black separation lines to help cover for the artifacts that result along sharp displacement edges – they serve as an alpha matte to make the pieces look like they are separated slightly (right).

Compound and Camera Blur

Compound Blur is a favorite effect for 3D artists attempting to fake depth-of-field effects, in which objects further away from the virtual camera get more blurred. Some 3D programs can automatically render a grayscale "depth map" image based on setting camera parameters for what distances are to be considered near and far; others fake it by making all their objects fully luminant white, then adding black "fog" to a scene to make objects that are further away darker.

Armed with this depth map, you'll find it is a relatively simple matter to apply Compound Blur to the main render, set the Blur Layer to this

Shy Maps

Layers that are used only by an effect should be turned off. If you make them Shy layers, then you can use Hide Shy Layers to hide them in the Time Layout window and reduce clutter.

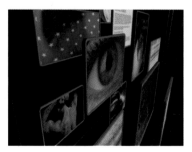
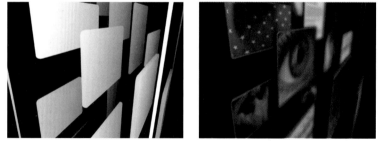

3D renders are typically crisp, regardless of how far away objects are from the camera (left). But if you can render or fake a depth map that indicates these distances (center), Compound Blur can keep near objects sharp and blur ones further away (right). Footage courtesy EyeWire.

depth map, and adjust the amount of blur to taste. Since many maps render white to be close and black to be far, you'll probably need to check the Invert Blur option. This has been set up in comp [Ex.07*starter].

Although interesting, this look does not accurately mimic the way a real camera works. An object or area is focused on to be sharp, and objects both nearer *and* farther away are progressively blurred, since

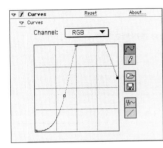

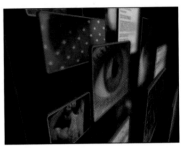

they will be out of the focus zone. There is a way to simulate this with conventional depth maps: by precomposing the map and applying Effect>Adjust>Curves to it. You can now sculpt a curve that converts the original whites and blacks in the depth map to black (out of focus), with a peak in the middle to select an area of intermediate grays that get shifted to white – in other words, in focus. Since some depth maps may have edge artifacts, a little Effect>Blur & Sharpen>Gaussian Blur after the Curves effect can smooth things out. This processing is in [**Ex.07a_curves_blur**].

There are a few shortcomings to this trick. One, having only 256 luminance levels is a bit coarse for really good depth maps, especially when they are re-curved. The result can be some banding in the image. Two, the Curves effects does not animate smoothly from one curve to another, making animated "rack focus" tricks close to impossible to pull off. A workaround is to use the Boris Tint-Tritone effect (included free on the enclosed CD); set the Black and White colors to black or a darker shade of gray, the midpoint to white, and animate the Midpoint parameter. This is demonstrated in [**Ex.07b_boris tritone**].

Fortunately, plug-in developers have started writing specialized rack focus effects; good ones exist in both the Composite Wizard and Image Lounge sets from Puffin Designs (www.puffindesigns.com). Also, if you have the Production Bundle, and use ElectricImage, Softimage, or another 3D application that can generate an RLA format file, you can take advantage of the 3D Channels effects – which include a depth of field effect. If you don't have one of the explicitly supported 3D packages, the *Z-Envy* CD Tutorial shows how to mimic many of these 3D Channel effects using regular depth maps.

By applying a Curve effect that is peaked somewhere in the middle and lowered on the ends (left), you can resculpt the depth map so that some middle distance ends up white – or sharp – and the other distances are progressively darker (center). The result is a more realistic depth of field effect (right).

Connect

Luma mattes and other track mattes were discussed in Chapter 14.

Nesting and precomposing compositions – nearly essential to getting the most out of compound effects – were covered in Chapters 16 and 17, respectively. The render order was also visited in Chapter 16.

3D Channel effects, which use additional "hidden" channels in a 3D render as opposed to a second layer, are discussed in Chapter 24.

23 Standard Effects Round-Up

Some of our favorite settings and applications for the Standard Bundle effects we use most often.

Try Before You Buy

Along with the free effects on the After Effects 4.1 CD and this book's CD, Toolfarm will also send you a free demo CD of virtually all the third party plug-ins. Check out their ad at the back of this book or log onto www.toolfarm.com.

Example Project

Explore the 23-Example Project.aep file as you read this chapter; references to [Ex.##] refer to specific compositions within the project file.

After Effects has long been blessed with the ability to add additional plug-in modules, especially for effects. While After Effects ships with a generous number of effects, a large number of third-party companies are also creating exceptionally useful plug-in packages of their own. However, this does not mean that just slapping on effects is the solution to every creative challenge – understanding what effects do and using them appropriately is the key.

How to best cover After Effects' effects is one of the subjects we've wrung our hands over the most. All of their parameters are already explained in the online Help (an underused resource). No recipe can solve every creative problem you may be presented with; there is no replacement for practice and familiarity. Some effects, frankly, are more obvious or less useful than others; neither would benefit from more words being written about them. And many of the best visual designs use surprisingly few effects, relying more on good taste, artful animation, and After Effects' built-in Transfer Modes.

That said, we *do* use effects every day. And despite all the documentation available, very few explain *how* you might want to use a particular effect, what the gotchas might be for some of their parameters, or whether a particular effect is even worth spending the time exploring.

Therefore, we've decided to share some of our personal favorite settings, tips, and advice on the effects we use most often. We're going to focus on the effects that come with the Standard program (the next chapter covers those that come with the Production Bundle). This doesn't mean that the others have no use; just that these are the ones that stand out for us or that benefit from some additional explanation. We will also suggest the occasional third-party package if it really stands out.

As we saw in Chapter 19, to apply an effect, select the layer, and then select the effect from the Effect menu. However, once you've applied the effect, you modify it in the Layer>Open Effects Controls palette (Command+Shift+T). Throughout the examples, turn the effects on and off to compare their results, and solo the different layers if there are more than one. If you find a setting you like, save it (Effect>Save Favorite); we have also saved a handful of our own Favorites that you can load (select layer, and Effect>Apply Favorite).

Adjust

Most of the color correction tools you would use reside inside this submenu. If you've been using After Effects for a long time, it's worth exploring some of the newer additions, such as Effect>Adjust>Hue/Sharpen over Effect>Image Control>Color Balance (HLS) and Effect>Adjust> Curves when Effect>Adjust>Levels can't quite reach the tweak you're after.

Curves

We normally use Hue/Saturation and Levels (see below) as our main color correctors in After Effects. However, Curves can allow more complex adjustments of the individual color channels: Rather than setting a simple hue shift or gamma correction, you can do tricks like decrease the blues in the shadows and increase them in the highlights. This is demonstrated in [**Ex.01**].

After Effects' Curves is related to the Photoshop Curves effect, with the difference that the After Effects version unfortunately gives you a lot less control and feedback when you're setting the control points. This is particularly important if you are trying to create a custom curve with mathematical precision. Fortunately, the settings files are interchangeable between the two: so in a pinch you could save a frame from After Effects (Command+Option+S), create a Curves setting you like in Photoshop, save your settings, and load it back into the Curves effect in After Effects by clicking on the folder icon in the Effect Controls window for Curves.

Hue/Saturation

Effect>Image Control>Color Balance (HLS) has more or less been replaced by Effect>Adjust>Hue/Saturation because it renders faster and provides far more control. Its default parameters work similar to Color Balance, but you can also select specific color ranges and alter just this range. Comparisons between these approaches are illustrated in [**Ex.02.1**]; solo the different layers to see the differences.

The secret is the Channel Control menu. Setting it to anything other than Master activates the Channel Range pointers underneath the top colored bar. The small vertical bars set the limited range of colors that will now be affected by the parameters underneath; the triangles set the "feather" region of colors over which it fades back to the original source. The new color mapping is reflected in the second bar below. The various popup choices merely default these pointers to default ranges; slide them around as needed. You can slide these bars past the left or right extremes; wrap them back on themselves and decrease the saturation, and you end up with a flexible "leave color" effect, as shown in [**Ex.02.2**].

There is a second whole effect hidden inside Hue/Saturation: Colorize. Click the checkbox by the same name, and the effect changes

Warped Curves

Effect>Adjust>Curves does not animate between two different settings gracefully; treat it as a static effect.

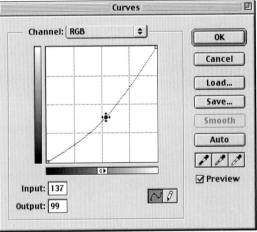

Photoshop's Curves allows more precise control, and its parameters can be saved and reloaded into After Effects.

Unwanted Posterize

Virtually any color correction aside from a simple Hue shift results in some posterization of the final image; be careful with extreme settings.

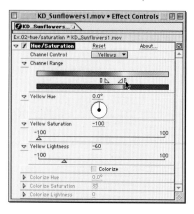

By wrapping the color range sliders back around on themselves and decreasing the saturation (left), Hue/Saturation becomes a flexible Leave Color effect (right). Footage courtesy of Kevin Dole.

identity, with a new set of parameters to tint a layer. Too bad it doesn't have a Blend With Original slider… For basic tinting, we use the Boris Tint-Tritone effect (free on your CD) as it has additional controls, not to mention that you can add a touch of a different tint to the whites.

To animate Hue/Saturation, you need to enable the stopwatch for Channel Range; to animate Levels, enable the stopwatch for Histogram. No, you can't animate each of the parameters directly.

Levels

We probably use this effect more than any other. Its main use is to increase the contrast of an image to make it look better. This feature is greatly enhanced by the visual Histogram that shows you what luminance ranges are present in the source.

To increase the contrast of an image, move the Input Black pointer up and Input White pointer down against the edges of the luminance range in the Histogram. An example is shown in [**Ex.03.1**] on some retro footage with its inevitably washed-out colors. More extreme uses include pulling a luminance matte out of footage shot against black or white.

You can further tweak the contrast within the midrange luminance values with the Gamma slider. [**Ex.03.2**] shows how you can lift more detail out of a dark image. You can do this for the overall image or individual colors. When individual color components need tweaking, though, we're more likely to go for another effect such as Hue/Saturation, Curves, Channel Mixer, or Color Balance, all found under the same Effect>Adjust submenu.

Histogram Caching

The Levels Histogram will not be automatically updated if you locate to a frame that has been cached in memory. Switch the effect off and on to refresh it.

Color Correction Favorite

Our most common color correction stack is Levels (to adjust contrast), followed by Hue/Saturation (to adjust color). This is saved on the CD as a favorite: **colorcorrect.ffx**.

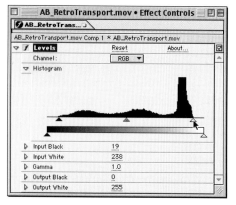

To maximize the contrast of an image, apply Effect> Adjust>Levels and drag the Input Black and Input White pointers to the active edges of the Histogram display.

Level's Gamma correction can lighten some of the detail from dark images, as seen in [**Ex.02**]. Footage courtesy EyeWire/Backstage.

Blur & Sharpen

Many of the effects in this submenu will no doubt be familiar to Photoshop users. Remember that After Effects has the ability to automatically add motion blur (automatic directional, zoom, and rotational blurs) to objects animated within the program, without requiring the application of a special effect (see Chapter 11 for more detail). However, you can still enhance this "built-in" motion blur with the Motion and Radial Blur effects or if the animation is being created with another effect that does not calculate its own motion blur.

Flicker and Blur

When you're using blurs to reduce video interlace flickering artifacts (see Chapter 37), remember you have to blur only in the vertical direction.

Channel Blur

The main use we have for Channel Blur is that it can blur the alpha channel independently of the image. This can help smooth rough or antialiased edges or just make images blend better into the backgrounds. We normally follow this with Effect>Matte Tools>Simple Choker to shrink the alpha back down to not include any background in the image (and have saved this as a Favorite: **edge blur/choke PB.ffx**), but doing so requires the Production Bundle. Another solution is follow it up with Effect>Adjust>Levels, set the Channel popup to Alpha, then set the alpha's Black In point to somewhere between 32 and 128. This is also saved as a favorite – **edgesmooth.ffx** – and demonstrated in [**Ex.04**].

If you find some of your elements to composite are too hard-edged (left), load the Favorite **edgesmooth.ffx** and tweak to taste (right).

Fast Blur

This effect was originally introduced when computers were much slower and Effect>Blur & Sharpen> Gaussian Blur took simply too long to calculate. In Best Quality, it looks remarkably close to Gaussian Blur, although there are subtle differences – Gaussian melts together bright areas slightly more quickly; Fast looks a little grainier at high settings. In Draft mode, Fast Blur also has an interesting "squinting" look to it. These are compared side by side in [**Ex.05**]. Remember that if you want to take advantage of how Fast Blur looks in Draft mode, your Render Settings need to be set to Current, not Best, quality.

Off to See the Wizard

If you do a lot of compositing of disparate elements, consider the Composite Wizard plug-in set (www.puffindesigns.com) – it contains a multitude of useful image blending effects, including some great Edge Blur and Feather effects.

Blur Shootout: from top to bottom, Fast Blur in Draft Quality, Fast Blur in Best Quality, and Gaussian Blur. Blur Amount = 18; an animation from 35 down to 1 is in [**Ex.05**].

Shrinking Edges

Both Fast and Gaussian Blur mix in black around the edges of a layer at higher blur values. Some third-party blurs, such as Boris AE Gaussian Blur and Image Lounge Super Blur (discussed in the sidebar below), don't.

Animated directional blur on type is seen everywhere these days. Water Effects 1 footage from Artbeats.

Gaussian Blur

Gaussian Blur still takes longer to render than Fast Blur, but faster computers have made it much less painful. Gaussian Blur looks the same in Draft or Best Quality and slightly smoother than Fast Blur (see [**Ex.05**]). If you find you need large amounts of Gaussian Blur on a regular basis and can't stand the rendering hit, know that this is one of the things that the ICE hardware accelerator card (www.iced.com) speeds up significantly.

Motion Blur

This effect should really be named Directional Blur. Whereas Fast and Gaussian Blurs allow you to set whether the blur direction should be just horizontal, just vertical, or both, Motion Blur lets you set any arbitrary angle. The Motion Blur algorithm also has a different "look" than the other After Effects blurs, resulting in dense areas streaking together more – this is illustrated in [**Ex.07.1**]. Animated directional blurs are also a popular type treatment these days; a simple example is [**Ex.07.2**].

Sharpen and Unsharp Mask

Those of you who come from a print background are probably used to using Photoshop's Unsharp Mask to enhance still images. Unfortunately, video and even film images have a higher noise content than many photos; as a result, sharpening often results in enhancing this noise as well (look at the gradients on the wall in [**Ex.08**]) – not to mention JPEG compression artifacts created by many video capture cards. Since this noise animates frame per frame, it is prone to "sizzling" when it's overly sharpened; therefore, use sharpening with caution. All that said, you can still use them to add punch to still images. Between the two choices, the one-slider effect Sharpen gets extreme more quickly than Unsharp Mask.

Special Blurs

Third-party blurs with different "looks" include Composite Wizard's Super Blur (faster than Fast Blur; slightly "boxier" look), Image Lounge's TrueCamera Blur (very realistic, but very slow), and Eye Candy's Squint (produces multiple images).

The first two are available from Puffin Designs; Eye Candy is from Alien Skin (www.alienskin.com). Also check out FE Vector Blur from ICE, which is included free on the CD with this book.

From top to bottom:
Composite Wizard Super Blur,
Image Lounge TrueCamera Blur, and
Eye Candy Squint.

Blur amount = 5; the last two dissolve very quickly at high blur settings.

Effects + Modes = Sex

One of our favorite techniques is to duplicate a layer, apply an effect to the one on top, and experiment with setting different transfer modes and varying the opacity of this top layer. You can often get some very interesting mixes that don't scream "I'm just a preset effect!"

For example, we have a trick we call Instant Sex: duplicate a layer, apply a generous amount of blur to the one on top, and mix it in with Screen or Add transfer mode. An example of this is in **[Ex.06]**. This puffs out the highlights in an image, reminiscent of blown-out film. Mix Opacity to taste; Add mode requires lower settings than Screen. We prefer to use the Boris AE Gaussian Blur (www.borisfx.com) for this effect, since it has transfer modes and matting built in. This is the blur effect we use most often as it's very flexible, uses one layer, and renders fast.

Instant Sex: Take an image that has highlights but is otherwise not exciting enough (left), and Add or Screen a blurred copy on top of itself (right). Retro Transportation footage from Artbeats.

Channel

This set of effects contains a potpourri of ways to exchange and otherwise mess around with the information in the color channels of a layer (or information that can be derived from the color channels, such as hue or saturation).

Blend

This is one of those secret gems that not all After Effects users are aware of. If you want to crossfade from one full-screen image to another, it's easy; just fade the one on top up or down. However, that does not work as well for less than full screen images or any that have transparency in their alpha channels – one image may not fully cover the other, so you

Channel Surfing

To re-arrange the color channels in an image, install CE Set Channel and CE View Channel from the CD – they are often easier to use than Effect>Channel>Set Channels and >Shift Channels.

When you're using Opacity keyframes to crossfade between two objects with alpha channels, they are both partially transparent, resulting in a luminance dip and the background showing through (left). By using the Blend effect instead, this transparency/opacity dip where they overlap is less objectionable (right). Objects from Classic PIO Radios and Telephones CDs.

The other Blend modes can help smooth crossfades even between full-frame layers (above). For example, using Lighten Only helps keep more clouds around during a sky crossfade (below). Puffy Clouds from Artbeats.

get "pops" at the transition point. Many try to work around this by fading one down and another up, but the result is often a dip in luminance as a result of mixed opacity during the fade.

Effect>Channel>Blend combines two layers in a way to avoid this luminance/opacity dip. It is a compound effect, meaning it is applied to one layer, and a second must be selected. Think of it as a "replace this image with another" effect with a parameter to blend between the original and this replacement, and it will make much more sense which layer you should apply it to and how you can fade it. Remember that compound effects look at other layers before masks, effects, and transformations have been calculated (Chapter 22); pre-process the second layer if needed in another comp. You will also need to trim or otherwise turn off the second layer right before the crossfade starts since you don't want two copies of it playing at the same time.

Examples of what can go wrong, and how Blend fixes it, are shown in [Ex.09] and [Ex.10]. It might be most illustrative to view the "bad" and "good" versions of these side by side, both aligned in time to marker #1, to see the differences. Also, turn off their backgrounds and run your cursor over them, paying attention to the Alpha channel strength in the Info floater. Where the objects overlap, the alpha value dips down to 192 (out of 255) for the Opacity crossfade; using Blend, it stays at full strength (255) where they overlap.

The other options for blending – such as Lighten and Darken Only – can also help smooth full-frame crossfades. Experiment with different modes on the second Puffy Clouds layer in [Ex.10.2].

Minimax

This tip comes from Kory Jones, one of the founders of Reality Check Studios (www. realityx.com). Kory likes to render his 3D animations in multiple passes, with different properties – such as just the specular highlights – in each render pass. In the case of specular highlights, he will then sometimes expand them with Effect>Channel>Minimax set to Maximum, blur the result, and use a transfer mode to apply this back to the basic underlying render. The result is "puffier" highlights, which some associate with more of a film look. Kory, we owe you a quarter. A starter Favorite is saved on the CD as **puffhilights.ffx**.

In addition to a highlight treatment, this effect can also create

Noise Killer

Video and film grain noise can unnecessarily "trigger" effects such as Minimax. Composite Wizard from Puffin Designs includes a great Denoiser filter to reduce video noise.

some nice "painterly" looks when they're applied to normal layers. Experiment with [Ex.11] to get a feel for the possibilities.

Minimax can be used to give a pointillist effect to normal footage. Footage courtesy Harry Marks, shot at the Wildlife Waystation (www.waystation.org)

Distort

If an effect bends, warps, or otherwise shifts around the pixels of an image, it is probably in the Distort submenu (the exception being effects that fake perspective – more on those later). If distortion effects are your bag, note that the Production Bundle includes many more.

Offset

This effect is an animatable version of its Photoshop equivalent: It can shift the image's position, and it wraps around pixels to fill in for those that would otherwise be shifted out of view. It is not a "tile" effect that makes a layer bigger than it was before, but if the layer already fills the comp, using Offset can make it seem to be infinite in size.

One useful application is with images that have already been made into seamless tiles, as is the case with most 3D texture libraries. You can keep "panning" along a surface without running out of image, as shown in [**Ex.12.1**]. Another use is endless scrolls, such as news tickers. Check out [**Ex.12.2.1**], where we created a "tickertape" precomp, which is then nested in a second comp [**Ex.12.2.2**]. In the second comp, we used Effect>Distort>Offset to continuously scroll the tickertape graphics.

The naming of Offset's parameter – Shift Center To – can be confusing. What this means is "move the center of the layer to this new location"; the effect will fill the rest with wrapped-around duplicates of the original.

Polar Coordinates

This filter that attempts to convert between two mapping systems has some creative uses. For example, when Type of Conversion is set to Polar to Rectangular, it attempts to take circular layers and stretch them into a series of vertical spikes. This results in some nice warps when the Interpolation is set to less than 25%, as shown in [**Ex.13.1**].

When Type of Conversion is set to Rectangular to Polar, this effect bends vertical linear lines into radial lines. This is handy for tricks such as mapping lines of text into circular, radial spokes of text (see [**Ex.13.2**]), bending straight brushed metal textures into spun textures, and so on. Square sources work best for this; otherwise, you might end up with a hole in the middle.

There are a few gotchas with Polar Coordinates. First, it is slow. Second, pixels will get stretched – consider applying it to a larger-than-needed source, then scaling the result down to cover some of the aliasing artifacts. With rectangular-to-polar conversion, hori-

Clone Theory

For traditional tiling, use Effect>Stylize>Motion Tile. If you need more control, check out FE RepeTile in the Final Effects Complete package from ICE (www.iced.com).

"Real" Spheres

Several third-party plug-in sets, such as Boris AE and Final Effects Complete, have effects that more realistically wrap layers around cylinders and spheres with much greater control.

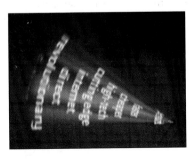

When Polar Coordinates is applied with rectangular-to-polar conversion, scrolling text in a straight line in one comp (right) results in it zooming radially from a center point (above).

Effect>Distort>Polar Coordinates was used to bend the words just under the grid in this 3D world into a pair of disks in this scene for client QAD Inc. (Buildings based on designs by Ridgley Curry of RCA.) Thanks to Dan Wilk of the After Effects team for figuring out the math to minimize distortion. This scene was also treated with the Instant Sex trick discussed in the sidebar *Effects + Modes = Sex.*

zontal lines get squished near the top and stretched near the bottom. (The Math: The width of the source gets spread across a number of pixels that is ~6.3 times the distance from the top.) You might want to consider prescaling your source material horizontally to compensate for this. An example of this prescaling is shown in [**Ex.13.3.1**]; note how it looks wider when used in [**Ex.13.3.2**] with Polar Coordinates applied.

PS+ Spherize

The PS+ designation means that an effect has been derived from a Photoshop filter of the same name. If After Effects also includes its own version of a filter, usually it is more powerful. For example, Spherize has a radius slider and keeps the distortion circular regardless of the layer's dimensions; PS+ Spherize assumes you want to do the entire image, even if it is not a perfect square (which would then result in an oblong "sphere").

However, one reason to use PS+ Spherize is that inside its Options dialog you can turn it into Cylinderize by distorting either just the horizontal or vertical dimensions. This is a useful additional distortion to have; check out [**Ex.14**] to see one application. Note that the distortion is a bit aliased at the edges of the layer; mask or scale to cover these.

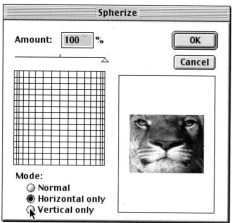

PS+ Spherize has the option to warp in just one dimension, turning it into a Cylinderize effect.

Smear

After Effects 4 added several distortion effects that are derived from morphing technology. Most ended up in the Production Bundle; Smear is available in all versions.

The online help does an excellent job explaining all the parameters of this effect, with a couple of small warnings: the labels for the Source mask and Mask Offset are reversed, and the shape of the offset indication is wrong – it should take on the shape of the source mask.

We have a few general tips to help you in your experimentation. First, don't think of it just as a smear but as a general purpose warping effect in which you move a masked region around a layer, forcing the rest of the layer to stretch to meet it. Second, the popup list of Elasticity settings are not different algorithms, as you might have assumed from their various fanciful names; they are just iterations of smoothness of calculation when a stretch takes place – with each step down the list improving quality, but also taking roughly twice as long as the prior one. And don't forget to crank up the Smear amount to see the effect – the default is 0%.

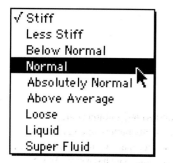

In Smear, each Elasticity setting takes twice as long as the last...

The Fabric of Space

The initial temptation with many of the Distort effects is to apply it to a layer, then animate how it warps the layer. However, another approach is to think of the various Distort effects as setting up "distortion fields" that objects are animated through.

One way to control this is to set up your animation moves in one composition. Then nest this comp in a second comp and apply the Distort effect of your choice to this nested comp. This gives you maximum flexibility since you can then further scale and position the distorted, nested comp in its new comp. An admittedly over-the-top example of this chain is demonstrated in **[Ex.15.1]**; a more practical use – to distress text – is shown in **[Ex.15.2]**.

You can also apply the distort effect using an adjustment layer in the first comp (Chapter 20) –

Text is panned in a precomp and distorted with Sphere in a second comp to make it appear to wrap around the globe image. Background textures from Artbeats/Liquid Ambience and Digital Vision/Naked & Scared.

which will affect all layers below. Nest this comp in a second comp where you can add any background layers that should not be distorted.

Image Control

The effects in this submenu are partners in crime with the Adjust group. Their primary purpose is altering the color of layers they are applied to. Some of them have been superceded by newer effects from Adobe and various third parties.

Color Balance (HLS)

This used to be one of most oft-used effects – it gave quick access to shifting the hue, increasing or decreasing the saturation, and tweaking the brightness of a layer. However, the newer Effect>Adjust>Hue/Saturation has replaced it, giving more control. Visually, Effect>Image Control>Color Balance (HLS) seems to add rather than scale saturation, resulting in more extremely colorized results at intermediate settings. This is demonstrated in [Ex.16]. On the other hand, Color Balance (HLS) is a little more direct to animate: You also have separate keyframing for its parameters instead of all being lumped into one as with Hue/Saturation.

Smear Campaign

For a more conventional smearing effect, check out FE Smear in ICE's Final Effects Complete. It is less flexible, but easier to use for simple applications.

Adjust>Hue/Saturation (left side) has a gentler effect when saturation is increased; Image Control>Color Balance (HLS) (right side) has a more extreme effect for the same intermediate values. Sunflowers courtesy Kevin Dole.

(Third-) Party Colors

If you prefer *not* to hand-roll your own color tables, third-party effects to check out include MultiTone Mix from Boris AE, and Evolution Colorama from Atomic Power (www.atomicpower.com).

PS Arbitrary Map

For those who have a little more time than money, this is a pretty neat tool for colorizing images. It requires that you create your color tables in Photoshop, then load them into After Effects.

The After Effects documentation suggests you use Curves to create these color mapping tables, but we prefer an approach that uses the Indexed Color tables in Photoshop. Open any still image in Photoshop or start one from scratch (we don't care about the image; we just need to edit a color table, and this is the only way to get to that dialog). Change its Image>Mode to Indexed Color, and set the Palette popup that will now appear to Custom. Select ranges of colors from the table by click-dragging across their tiles, and select the colors you want this range to fade between in the color picker dialogs that will now appear. Save your color table from this dialog, and cancel out of it. Image>Mode>Color Table gets you back to here if you want.

Return to After Effects, apply Effect>Image Control>PS Arbitrary Map to a layer. Click on the word Options along the top of its effect controls and select the color map you saved (to get back to this dialog, click on Options again). You can color cycle the table if you wish by animating the Phase control.

When you're using a table created through Indexed Colors, PS Arbitrary Map does not completely recolorize your layer at this point – it tints it. To completely replace the original image's colors with your map, apply Effect>Image Control>Tint *before* Image Control>PS Arbitrary Map (drag Tint above PS Arbitrary Map in the Effect Control window if you apply it later). Leave the Colors swatches at their default black and white and crank up the Amount to Tint parameter, which becomes a modified Blend With Original control. This converts the original to a grayscale image, and PS Arbitrary Map will then replace these grays with your new colors.

An effect Favorite with this stack is saved on the CD as **Arbitrary Colorize.ffx**; a black-to-blue-to-orange-to-white map is saved as **Blue2Gold.clt**. [Ex.17] uses these settings. To tint the result further, choose different colors for Tint or use in its place the Boris Tritone effect included on the CD.

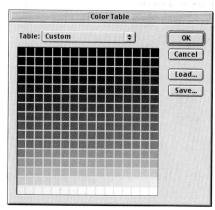

Create a Custom Indexed Color table in Photoshop (above) and save it. Take your image (A), apply PS Arbitrary Map, load the table you just saved, and it will tint the image (B). To use these new colors fully (C), apply Image Control>Tint before PS Arbitrary Map and increase its Amount to Tint.

Tint

This used to be one of our most frequently used effects. We create many graphic elements in Illustrator and bring them in either solid white or solid black. We would then always use Effect>Image Control>Tint to give them a color. However, we have started using Effect>Render>Fill for this purpose.

Tint is still one of the better ways to convert an image to grayscale: Use its default colors and set Amount to Tint to 100%. To our eyes, this looks better than decreasing a layer's saturation to 0%; check out [**Ex.18.1**] and see for yourself.

Ironically, Tint is not as useful when it comes to tinting colored layers. If you map Black to anything lighter than pure black, and White to anything darker than pure white, you'll lose contrast in your image, resulting in a washed-out look. Instead, try effects such as Boris AE Tint-Tritone (which Boris Effects graciously allowed us to give away free with this book) – it keeps the blacks and whites, tinting just the midtones.

Tint (on the right) often gives a more pleasing grayscale conversion than removing all the saturation (left).

Perspective

If there's an effect that helps give the impression that all your layers aren't strictly flat and stuck on top of each other, it's probably under this submenu. Oddly enough, so is the Transform effect (because it has a skew setting, in addition to duplicating the other normal transform properties); Transform is discussed in more detail in Chapter 16 and elsewhere.

Basic 3D

Basic 3D tilts layers as if they were slanted in 3D space. Perhaps the greatest cause of frustration when you're using this effect is that the swivel point is always in the center of the layer, regardless of where the layer's anchor point is currently set. To make a layer swivel around another point, first position it in a precomp, then apply Basic 3D to this nested comp. A second problem is that it does not automatically calculate motion blur. If these shortcomings bother you, consider using FE Advanced 3D from ICE's Final Effects Complete set.

Flat graphics with alpha channels can appear more dimensional with Basic 3D applied. This is demonstrated in [**Ex.19**]. Just know that this effect is slow to render; you might want to keep the layer in Draft Quality while working with it and force Best Quality in your render settings.

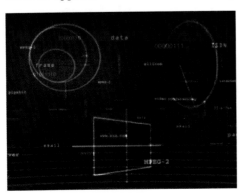

Basic 3D can tilt simple geometric objects in space, adding more interest to their shapes.

Shades of Gray

There are numerous recipes to derive grayscale images, such as applying Effect> Image Control>Tint with its default colors or desaturating an image with Effect>Adjust> Hue/Saturation. A great dedicated effect for this purpose is DE Grayscaler in the DigiEffects Delirium package (www.digieffects.com).

Another good approach is to preview its various color channels, pick the one you like, then apply Cult Effects Extras>CE View Channel (free on the CD) and pick the color channel you liked. This is demonstrated in [**Ex.18.2**]. We like View Channel because it also allows you to pick combinations of color channels along with other information, and is much faster than the old method of using Effect>Channel> Shift Channels and setting individual popups for each color channel.

Bevel Alpha's look can be extended in two ways: by picking a Light Color from the background, so the color of the layers interact, and by increasing Edge Thickness on characters of varying widths to get "lumps" in the text. Background image from Digital Vision/Naked & Scared.

The New Edge

If bevels are your thing, check out Carve from Alien Skin's Eye Candy – it has several different edge shapes. Also, Edge Lighting from Boris Effects offers more control over the bevel's highlight and shadow.

The Shadow Knows...

Two other great shadows are Real Shadows from Image Lounge (Puffin Designs) and Radial Shadow from Cycore's Cult Effects (free on the After Effects 4.1 CD). The former gives perspective fall-off on a floor; the latter simulates light on a distant wall.

Bevel Alpha *(use w/ tint)*

Another one of our favorite effects, Bevel Alpha looks great applied to text and Illustrator artwork to give it some dimension. The default settings use white for the Light Color, but consider picking a slightly different color. For example, apply Effect>Perspective>Bevel Alpha with the default white light, then eyedropper the resulting leading edge as the new Light Color – the result will be a little more natural. (For the 3D users out there, this is a concept similar to diffuse bias.) Another idea is to pick up a lighter color from the background so your beveled object will appear to be reflecting light from its environment.

When your object has greatly varying widths to its strokes and shapes, as is the case with many "grunge" fonts, try larger Edge Thickness amounts: This will give more apparent height variation and general lumpiness to the bevel, as they overlap each other. This and the background lighting concept are demonstrated in [Ex.20]; experiment with the Light Color and Edge Thickness parameters.

Bevel Edges

Bevel Edges affects the edges of the layer without regard for masks and alphas. It is an instant multimedia beveled button. The only use for it today is when you need a sharper edge than Bevel Alpha; this difference is demonstrated in [Ex.21].

Bevel Edges (left) has a much sharper shape than Bevel Alpha (right) and is useful only for simple rectangular shapes.

Drop Shadow

Also on the most-used-effects list. If we have one complaint, it is that the default is a hard shadow when you almost always want a soft shadow. An effect Favorite with better defaults is **DropShadowStarter.ffx**. Remember that the Scale property is calculated after effects like Drop Shadow; if you scale a layer down, you'll need to increase the Distance and Softness properties, or do your scaling with Effect>Perspective> Transform before you apply the shadow.

You can also get a nice halo/glow effect from Effect>Perspective>Drop Shadow if you set the Distance parameter to 0 and crank up the Softness parameter (~50 for 320×240 comps; ~100 for full video size). Unfortunately, the result is rather light even at 100% Shadow Opacity; you could simply duplicate the Drop Shadow effect but with 50% Shadow Opacity to beef it up. This is demonstrated in [Ex.22]. Some effect Favorites with this trick have been saved under the name **ShadowGlow*_*.ffx**; M means medium (320×240) and L means large (full video size). Of course, tweak to taste.

Don't forget that the Production Bundle includes a flexible Glow effect (which also appears free on this book's CD); we also like Alien Skin's Eye Candy Glow for simple applications.

Render

This group could also be called "how to create something from nothing" because all the effects involve After Effects creating – rendering – graphics without a need for image information in the underlying layer. Although you can apply them to an image, they are often better used in conjunction with simple solids; we explained this technique in detail in Chapter 19.

Most of the effects in the Effects>Render menu can also follow a path defined by a mask shape (see Masking, Chapter 13). Remember that mask shapes and paths do not need to be visible; you can create and animate them strictly for an effect to follow.

Audio Spectrum

The most common problem users have with this effect is that they assume they should apply it to an audio layer. Actually, it should be applied to an image (such as a solid); then a popup in its Effect Controls is set to point to which Audio Layer to use. An example of this basic setup is in [Ex.23*starter].

Effect>Render>Audio Spectrum works like one of those displays you see on some stereos, where different bars jump depending on the strength of the audio signal in different frequency ranges. You have a lot of control over exactly what is displayed and how; again, there is little substitute for reading the online Help and experimenting. But here are a few tips:

• The End Frequency parameter defaults to a number that is better optimized for voice. If your audio track will be full-range music, set it higher. You can Option+drag on this slider and watch for the point where no meaningful display is happening in the upper frequency bars, then back down from there.

• Audio Spectrum looks *radically* different at Best Quality than Draft Quality: Best can yield big glowing multicolor balls, while Draft just gives a bunch of mono-colored straight lines. Set the render quality for the layer *before* adjusting its parameters.

• Don't think of the Maximum Height parameter in terms of pixels; you'll need to set it much higher than you expect. Values in the thousands are common.

Audio Waveform

Waveform is similar to Spectrum except that the display is based on the actual vibrations of the sound wave, rather than the frequency components that make up the final sound. It would be more appropriate for an oscilloscope-style display.

Some of the advice given above for Spectrum applies here, such as how it looks much different in Best Quality than in Draft. The Maximum Height parameter seems to make more intuitive sense, however. Note

A pair of drop shadows with zero Distance and high Softness results in a nice diffuse glow effect. Background image from Digital Vision/Naked & Scared.

Instant Text Treatment

Text often gets Tinted (if it starts as black outlines from Illustrator), Beveled, and Shadowed. This effect Favorite is saved on the CD as **TextTreatStarter.ffx**. Tweak to taste.

O - PREVIEW

• - AUDIO PREVIEW

Audio Codec Issues

If you have problems with Audio Spectrum or Waveform not animating every frame or otherwise being unresponsive, it might be the audio codec. (We found problems with QDesign Music; try None or IMA instead.)

Audio Visual Aids

- A nature of sound is that lower frequencies tend to have a lot more energy or amplitude in them than higher frequencies. This makes the lower frequency bands almost always jump more strongly than the higher ones. Consider precomposing the audio track in question and applying one of the Effect>Audio filters or equalizers (discussed in Chapter 30) to pre-process the audio in a precomp and boost its highs. This is demonstrated in **[Ex.24]**.

- You can always turn off the audio layer that you are using to drive Audio Spectrum and Audio Waveform; that way, you can use a processed or dummy audio layer to drive the effect while you're listening to a different audio track for final output.

- With the above tip in mind, you can use some of the sound generating effects in the Production Bundle (also discussed in Chapter 30) to create raw tones to drive these effects. Pure, sustained tones often produce more predictable, usable results than complex sounds like music and speech.

- These audio render effects are also good at generating mattes. Rather than worrying about setting their color to something nice, set it to white and use the result as a luma matte for another layer. This is also shown in **[Ex.24]**.

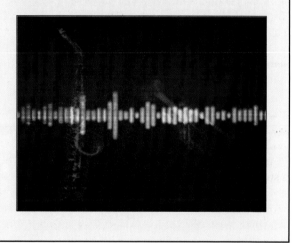

Effect>Render>Audio Spectrum (and Waveform) can be used to create mattes (above) to blend images together into a whole (below), as in **[Ex.24]**. Here, the matted image is from Digital Vision/Data:Funk.

Start ≠ End

Do not set Audio Waveform's Start Point and End Point to the same coordinates; After Effects might freeze.

that the amount of time displayed – the Audio Duration – can be set to longer than the frame of time being displayed; in this case, the waveform will seem to "travel" from the End Point to the Start Point coordinates. (The time duration of one frame is 1 ÷ [frame rate].) Otherwise, spend some time reading the Help file and experimenting – it is well worth the effort. A few ideas on how to use

Two different applications of Audio Waveform: dots emanating from the center of the circle at the left, and Lines outlining a pair of musical notes pasted from Illustrator into Mask Shapes in After Effects. No glow was added; the fringing came from balancing the Thickness and Softness parameters and using transfer modes. Background image from Digital Vision/Data:Funk.

Audio Waveform are contained in [**Ex.25**]. One of the applications just sends the wave out from an apparent point of origin in the background graphic by setting the End (not the Start) point there, and setting the Audio Duration time to a few times longer than a single frame. Maximum Height was set to match some framing horizontal lines in the background image.

A second idea involved creating some musical symbols using the Sonata font in Illustrator, pasting them into After Effects as mask shapes, and using Audio Waveform assigned to these masks to outline the notes, with a smaller Maximum Height parameter so they just get slightly perturbed by the sound bopping along.

Ellipse

Circles, lines, and "stuff" – that's what seems to make up a large amount of the cool graphics you see today. And After Effects includes an effect for creating circles: Effect>Render>Ellipse. It can be a little tricky getting a real smooth, broad, soft feather; try making the Inner and Outer Colors the same and using a high Softness value, or set Inner to white and Outer to black and use the result as a luma matte. You can always post-blur it, too.

A simpler effect is CE Circle from Cycore's Cult Effects, which is included free on the CD with this book. Since it does only circles, not ellipses, you can animate a circle with one slider, not two; it also has excellent feathering and antialiasing. A comparison between the two is included in [**Ex.26.1**] for you to experiment with.

An example of animating CE Circle to create a simple radio-wave look is shown in [**Ex.26.2**]; the parameters used are saved as **circlepulse.ffx**; adjust the end keyframe parameters as appropriate for your comp size. If you have the Production Bundle, there is also a Tutorial on the CD showing how to use this as the basis for a "ripple pulse wave" effect.

Fill

This effect fills the alpha channel of a layer with a solid color [**Ex.27**]. It took us a while to catch on to the idea that it can also be used to fill Illustrator text and logos with color, with fewer keystrokes than our old standby Effect>Image Control>Tint; we now regularly use Fill for this purpose.

If your source image's alpha fills the entire image, you can create an alpha by using masks – just don't forget to set the Fill Mask popup to the desired mask. Masks can also be set to None so they don't create transparency in the layer itself, in the event you want filled shapes. The Fill effect is useful if you want to have several animating shapes of different colors while you're using only one layer instead of multiple Solids; it is often used with the Stroke effect (see below).

Ramp

Please don't use this effect to create those simple two-color gradients we see all the time in corporate slide show presentations – that's all we ask.

Easy Waves

An excellent plug-in for creating animated radio-wave (and more) patterns is Radio Waves – part of the Evolution set of effects from Atomic Power.

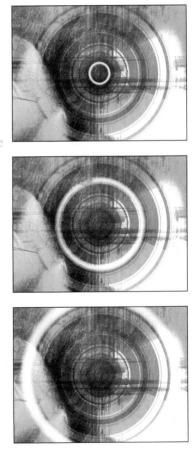

Ellipse and CE Circle both work well as luma mattes for other images to create softer, radio-wave looks.

Ramp Render Hit

Effect>Render>Ramp "renders" every frame, even if it is not animating – which can unnecessarily increase rendering times. Save it out as a still image, or create gradients in Photoshop.

This animated background in the Sources folder uses CE ColorsQuad plus CE Noise Turbulent from the Cult Effects package, both included free on the After Effects 4.1 CD courtesy of Cycore.

Where Ramp *is* useful is for creating luminance mattes and seeds for any compound effect or transition that uses luminance values to alter an image. Increase the Ramp Scatter parameter to break up any visible "banding" caused by not having enough luminance levels.

If you need more control – such as more individual colors, or more points that colors center around – there are third-party effects to check out. IL Alpha Ramp (free on your CD courtesy Puffin Designs) adds alpha channel fall-off along with simple gradient creation. DE MultiGradient from DigiEffects' Delirium package allows you to create a two-color gradient with an alpha value, to reveal an image underneath, or up to a 15-color gradient. Colorama from Atomic Power's Evolution package can colorize an image with a new palette and then cycle the palette; apply it after Ramp for a very powerful gradient and color cycling effect.

Taking a different approach, CE ColorsQuad (also free on the After Effects 4.1 CD, courtesy of Cycore) allows you to choose four colors and place their "centers" anywhere in the layer. We created the movie xCE_ColorQuad_Nturb in the Sources folder using this effect plus their Noise Turbulent (also on the 4.1 CD). Both effects are animatable.

Stroke

The Stroke effect is used several places throughout this book, including the subcomps back in [Ex.19]. The Stroke effect does nothing unless you select a mask shape for it to effect [Ex.27]. For creating graphical elements, create the mask shape on a simple Solid layer. When you apply the Stroke effect, don't forget to set the Path popup to look at the correct mask. To animate on the stroke over time, set keyframes for either the Start or End parameters.

Stroke can also create a dotted line – rather than just a solid stroke – if you set the Spacing parameter above 50% or so. This is where the Brush Size and Brush Hardness parameters really come into their own, controlling the size and fuzziness of the dots. Note that there is no guarantee that the dots will be perfectly spaced around a closed mask path at all settings; there may be a gap at the start point of the path. Balance the Spacing and Brush Size parameters to get an evenly spaced gap at this point.

Stylize

In contrast to Render effects, which create imagery from scratch, Stylize is a catch-all category for effects that alter the underlying image in creative ways:

Brush Strokes

The biggest strength – and problem – with this effect is that it randomizes on every frame rendered. This is okay for lower frame rates, but it often breaks into chaotic noise when you field-render video (which then randomizes at twice the speed of the frame rate). Apply Effect>Time> Posterize Time (explained in more detail in Chapter 32) to sample only every defined frame, or prerender the effect at a lower rate.

Different Strokes

If you like painterly effects, there are several other places to look besides Brush Strokes. Some still use Paint Alchemy from Xaos Tools (www.xaostools.com). Although primarily a Photoshop plug-in, it can be used inside After Effects and applied to layers. A stand-alone program that recently became an After Effects plug-in is Video Gogh from RE:Vision Effects (www.revisionfx.com). Two other dedicated After Effects plug-ins that create painterly effects are made by DigiEffects (www.digieffects.com):

a massive particle system/paint effect known as Cyclonist, plus DE Sketchist inside its Delirium set.

Although the focus of this chapter is on plug-ins that work inside After Effects, don't overlook the possibilities of processing footage in another application, then importing the result. The most recent darling of the painterly look crowd is the stand-alone program Studio Artist, from Synthetik Software (www.synthetik.com). And, of course, there is always the stand-alone natural media tool Painter, currently available from MetaCreations (www.metacreations.com).

Leave Color

This effect renders an image in grayscale except for those sections that match the chosen color. For many applications, you could use Effect>Adjust>Hue/Saturation (discussed earlier in this chapter) instead, and it's more controllable for what it does to the colors it removes. However, Effect>Stylize>Leave Color has the advantage of directly eyedroppering a color, and it also can have a lighter or "softer" look than Hue/Saturation. Compare the split screen in [**Ex.28**] and experiment for yourself. If you use Leave Color, try setting the Match Colors popup to Hue rather than RGB; it often makes it easier to select the desired color range.

Hue/Saturation (left side) can perform essentially the same function as Leave Color, although the latter can have a slightly lighter look (right side) – check out the leaves along the bottom for comparison.

Mosaic

This effect is normally used to simulate low-resolution computerish-style treatments. The parameters define how many slices you are breaking the original image into. To get an untreated image (for "fading" in and out of processing), they need to equal or exceed the number of pixels in the corresponding dimension of the original image. Note that an alternative Mosaic from Boris AE is also included free on the CD; you might find its parameters easier to animate, especially as it fades to 0. It also has a parameter that allows you to randomize still images, even if the block size stays the same – this is demonstrated in [**Ex.29.1**].

Of course, we encourage you to look for *abnormal* uses for effects – that's how to make your work look different from others. For example, if you set Boris Mosaic to display an otherwise unfractured image (Pixelate = 0), but animate the Scramble parameter we used above to randomize stills, you get an interesting "scatter" effect – this is shown in [**Ex.29.2**].

You can also get interesting looks out of either After Effects' or Boris's Mosaic if you set one dimension to show only one color, while the other is set high enough to draw fine lines. Apply to a colorful movie, and you get animated multicolored lines, which is a popular effect for background elements.

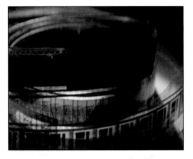

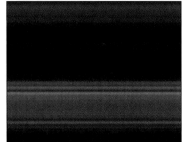

This technique is demonstrated in [**Ex.30**] and is saved as a Favorite: **mosaiclines.ffx**. Try setting the X dimension to a low value (between 2 and 6) and applying a strong horizontal blur for a different look; this Favorite is saved as **mosaicmelt.ffx** (decrease the blur amount for smaller-than-full screen images).

Since most Mosaic effects allow you to adjust the X and Y dimensions separately, with a little thought you can break an image (left) into single-pixel-high, full-width colored lines (right). Footage courtesy EyeWire/Backstage.

Motion Tile

As with most tile effects, Motion Tile can replicate a simple object to fill up a larger space. Note that the parameters Output Width and Height define the size of the additional tile created, not the final image – they are added onto the original image. More fun comes in animating parameters such as Tile Center or Phase – this allows you to move a whole flock of the original image.

A simple strip of four spheres (left) are tiled and animated, with Motion Blur, using Stylize>Motion Tile (above).

– mask out what you don't want.

What differentiates Effect>Stylize>Motion Tile from Effect>Distort>Offset is that multiple copies of the image can be made, filling more space than the original layer, and that automatic Motion Blur will be calculated for these moves when they are enabled for the layer.

Animating the Phase parameter is perhaps the easiest way to create animating tickertape effects, since one revolution (360°) is always one complete cycle of the source, with no need to measure pixels to calculate where the new center should be. Check out [**Ex.31**]: A string of our now-familiar spheres are set up in a small precomp, then tiled and animated in the second comp in the chain. The catch with Phase is that it will appear as if only every other tile gets animated, with the original center strip remaining stationary. Use a nested comp plus masking or a track matte to reveal just the strip you are interested in; this is also demonstrated in [**Ex.31**].

Size and Order

Beware of applying effects that change the apparent overall size of a layer before Motion Tile. For example, in [**Ex.31.2**] move Drop Shadow before Motion Tile for the second layer and see the result.

Noise

Of course, it is ironic that we spend money on the highest quality hardware we can get to reduce the amount of noise in our video captures and layoffs only to introduce it back into our designs. But sometimes adding a bit of noise roughens up an image appropriately or can hint at grainy film or surveillance video capture.

An interesting parameter to play with is Clipping. Checking it on gives a softer look that never completely obliterates the original image; unchecking it allows a complete noise-out and affects darker areas more than lighter ones. This is sometimes useful for science fiction "transporter" effects. These differences are demonstrated in [**Ex.32.1**].

We like using "real" noise whenever we can; it often has a less synthetic character. Some CD-ROMs such as VideoLoops from IF Studios and Film Clutter from ArtBeats have captures of actual film noise. We balance its gray levels with Effect>Adjust>Levels, then transfer mode it on top of the footage we want to grunge up. A comparison of synthetic versus real noise is shown in [**Ex.32.2**].

Strobe Light

Three quick tips: One, its time periods are calculated in seconds, not frames, so you'll have to do a little math: 1 frame (in seconds) = 1 ÷ frame rate. Two, it actually has a randomization parameter to create "nervous" style effects: 100% Random Strobe just inverts the effect with no randomization; 50% is maximum randomization. Three, it has built-in transfer modes but blends the chosen color with the original image. Since few transfer modes give something interesting with white, try changing the Color parameter to get stranger results, or use the Difference mode, which inverts the image [**Ex.33.1**]. In [**Ex.33.2**] we set the Strobe menu to Makes Layer Transparent instead of a flat Color to reveal the layers below – sort of like randomly set Opacity keyframes with Hold interpolation.

Write-on

Write-on is one of those effects that are initially frustrating: You apply it, and nothing happens. You figure out how to animate it, but it doesn't react the way you expect. For simpler jobs, you might consider using Render>Stroke and a mask path. However, Write-on offers a few more options that you might find useful.

For it to do anything, Brush Position must be animated. This effect then draws along the path defined by the animating Brush Position. You can hand-keyframe it (the path can be edited in the Layer window). If you change the middle keyframes to rove in time, you can have a complex path with smooth speed overall.

You can also copy a mask shape and paste it into Brush Position, though if the composition and the layer are different sizes, pasting directly from a mask into the Brush Position may result in position mismatches.

Another essential parameter to set is Brush Time Properties. For example, if you want the brush stroke width to be different sizes along the path, you need to set this popup to Size or Size & Hardness – otherwise, the width of the entire path will animate along with this parameter, including the parts already drawn. (If that's what you want, leave it at None.) These two results are compared side by side in [**Ex.34**].

Adding a blur after noise helps soften its effect. Here, CE Noise Alpha is used to punch holes in the text.

Noise Blast

Several third parties offer variations of noise. Included free on the CD is CE Noise Alpha, which features very controllable noise you can make crawl and loop – see [**Ex.32.3**].

Effect Point Tease

To edit the Effect Point for an effect in the Comp window, you must first select the name of the effect in the Effect Controls window. Option+drag it for a realtime update.

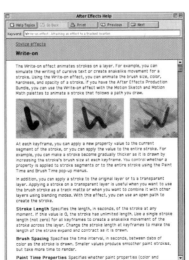

Write-on is an example of an effect with an extensive explanation in the online Help files. (This is a nice way of saying that we're not going to repeat all this info here…)

You can animate Write-on's Brush Size as well as Color (right side), but it will not remember it along the path if you do not set Time Properties properly (left side).

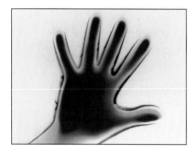

Combining techniques is where the real power emerges in effects. Here, Write-on is used as a matte for another layer and then beveled in a later comp. Hand image from Digital Vision/The Body.

Block Dissolve can be given many different looks, depending on how its parameters are set up. These simple black-and-white layers are then used as mattes or tinted and used directly as graphic elements. Below, left to right.

Effect>Stylize>Write-on does not draw a solid line – it draws a series of dots, spaced out in time according to the Brush Spacing parameter. It just so happens this defaults small enough to give the appearance of a solid line, because the dots overlap. But if your Brush Position path moves fast, you'll see your "line" start to break up. Reduce the Brush Spacing parameter to make it solid again. Also, if you need the line to be disjointed, use Hold keyframes for Brush Position so the line will jump to a new position – this is handy for dotting an "i" or stroking a "t".

Finally, this effect looks great combined with other effects (such as Effect>Perpsective>Bevel Alpha), or as a matte for another layer. Check out [Ex.35]: A mask shape was created, pasted in the Brush Position path, then Brush Size was animated to stroke selected portions of the path.

Transition

Several versions ago, After Effects added a set of transition effects to aid those who were attempting to do standard video edits in it as part of an overall project. True confession: At first, many of us groaned, but Transitions have certainly earned their keep over time. Most are obvious and therefore won't be covered here; the main tip is that they make portions of the layer they are applied to transparent, revealing whatever is underneath (as opposed to being a compound effect between two layers). However, one has emerged as our favorite building block for more interesting transitions, and another has even proven to be useful for creating design elements.

Block Dissolve

This transition is useful for either pixelated or soft, blobby wipe-offs of a layer (the Soft Edges checkbox yielding the latter effect). But more fun comes in distorting its settings to create interesting graphical elements, used both as mattes and as colored layers in their own right.

[Ex.36] contains a trio of different effects created using Effect>Transition> Block Dissolve. In most cases, they have been animated by using The Wiggler keyframe assistant on their Transition Completion parameter. Width and Height have been set to create the aspect ratio of the elements; this is further distressed in [Ex.36.3] by further scaling the layer (remember, Transformations happen after Effects are calculated). Applications for these elements are demonstrated for [Ex.36.2] and [Ex.36.3].

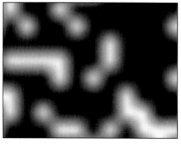
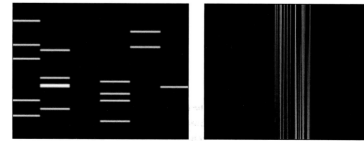

eye = on

eye = off

Wipe Out!

Requisite purchases for most After Effects users are Video SpiceRack Pro and OrganicFX from Pixélan Software (www.pixelan.com). Each offers hundreds of interesting gradient wipe seed images useful for transitions and distortions.

The luminance of a grayscale image is used by Gradient Wipe to transition between two clips. Gradient image from Pixélan's Video SpiceRack; Sunflowers courtesy Kevin Dole.

Gradient Wipe

Effect>Transition>Gradient Wipe is the ultimate in a customizable transition, as it looks at the luminance values of a second image as a "time map" of how to dissolve the image it is applied to: For example, the dark areas from the reference image dissolve first, followed by the intermediate grays, and finishing up with the whites.

The Gradient Wipe effect is easy to set up and manipulate. The challenge comes in finding interesting images to use as wipe maps. You can build your own maps, look at other interesting high-contrast images, or even point to the displayed image, so it directly affects the way it disappears. Experiment with [Ex.37], setting the Gradient Layer popup for KD_Sunflowers1 to the various layers in the comp. Most of these came from the Video SpiceRack collection (www.pixelan.com), a package of ready-made gradients that we highly recommend.

Any layer or movie could theoretically be used as the Gradient Layer, but those that include every gray level from 0 to 255 will create the smoothest transitions. You can also convert a layer to grayscale and use Effect>ImageControl> Equalize to help produce more consistent brightness levels across the image. Remember that Gradient Wipe is a compound effect (Chapter 22), so you'll need to pretreat the gradient layer with any color correction effects in a precomp.

The gradient layer can be selected from any layer in the comp, but specially prepared grayscale images tend to work best.

Connect

Roving Keyframes were included in Chapter 4.

Keyframe assistants, which help create and randomize keyframe values, were discussed in Chapter 7.

Motion Blur that is automatically calculated for moving layers was introduced in Chapter 11.

Many effects can trace the outlines of a mask. Creating masks was explained in Chapter 13.

Basics on applying and animating effects and saving Favorite settings are all covered in Chapter 19.

Vertical blurs are important tools for reducing interlace flicker in video. This technique is discussed further in Chapter 37.

Render Settings, where the current enable status of Effects as well as render quality can be overridden, are explained in detail in Chapter 43.

24 Production Bundle Effects Round-Up

New 3D Channel and warping-based Distort effects headline this chapter of Production Bundle tips and tricks.

Z Envy

If your application does not produce EIZ, ZPIC, or RLA files, but it does create grayscale Z-depth files, you can replicate most of the 3D Channel effects. Check out the *Z Envy* CD Tutorial.

Example Project

Explore the 24-Example Project.aep file as you read this chapter; references to [Ex.##] refer to specific compositions within the project file. *Don't forget to load the free plug-ins on the accompanying CD as well as from the After Effects 4.1 CD.*

One of the main reasons to purchase the Production Bundle version of After Effects is that it adds numerous powerful effects in several categories: 3D Channel, Audio, Distort, and Keying. Other effects included are a large particle simulation engine, Particle Playground, and other useful additions such as Glow (also provided free on our CD courtesy of Adobe Systems).

The Production Bundle has good explanations on effects in the printed Production Bundle Guide as well as in the online Help. Therefore, as with the Standard Bundle effects covered in the previous chapter, we'll restrict our comments to tips and tricks we personally find useful and some common gotchas. Note also that some of the following chapters will be devoted to certain classes of effects, such as Audio (Chapter 30) and Keying (Chapter 25), so we won't duplicate their descriptions here.

3D Channel

Some 3D applications let you save information beyond just color and alpha channel when they render. It is also not uncommon to be able to save *Z-depth* – the distance each pixel was from the virtual camera. You may save this as a separate file, or in the case of the RLA format, embed it in the file. Other programs can save additional channels of information, such as what object or texture material is visible per pixel in the frame. You may hear this extra information referred to as *auxiliary* or *G-buffer* information.

As of version 4.1, After Effects introduced this new class of 3D Channel effects that can access this additional information and allow additional processing such as selective proportional blur (for "depth of field" camera focusing simulations) or synthetic fog, or to create a variety of mattes that can then be used for other effects. Your 3D animation package will have more information on these file formats; we're going to give a couple of pointers on using them.

3D Channel effects work with only a few specific file formats. The most flexible one is the RLA format, which contains color, alpha, and a large number of additional channels of information in one file, which makes handling them easier. These files should be identified with the suffix *.rla*.

Softimage and ElectricImage users have access only to Z-depth information, which must be rendered into a separate file from the normal color plus alpha render pass. In both cases, the resulting files should have the same main name, with different suffixes. In the Softimage case, the normal file must be tagged *.pic* while the Z-depth render must be tagged *.zpic*; in the ElectricImage case, use the suffixes *.ei* and *.eiz*, respectively. When you import these files,

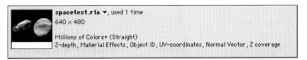

make sure both are in the same folder, and import only the normal 3D render – After Effects will then find the Z-depth file automatically.

When these files are imported and selected in the Project window, the additional channels they contain or reference will appear along the top of this window, just under the bit-depth information. They behave as normal color + alpha files until you apply one of the 3D Channel effects to them in a comp. At that point, selecting the effect in the Effect Controls window (Command+Shift+T to open) allows you to click on their image in the Comp window and have the additional channel information displayed in the Info floating window (Command+2). This information is very important: You will often have to set parameter ranges based on the information displayed here, since it will vary from render to render. Z-depth is the most critical in this regard; set the ranges incorrectly (or leave them at their defaults), and most of the 3D Channel effects won't work very well.

Set the layer to Best quality and view the Comp window at 100% to get the best idea of what's really going on; you'll need to be looking at edges of objects in particular for quality issues. The 3D Channel effect examples included in the 24-Example Project file are at 640×480 – you can zoom to 100% to see more detail.

When a file has 3D Channel information attached, selecting it in the Project window displays what additional channels are available underneath the Color information. This RLA file has numerous additional channels.

Apply Directly

3D Channel effects do not work when applied to precomps or to solids used as adjustment layers. Apply them directly to RLA, ZPIC, or EIZ format files.

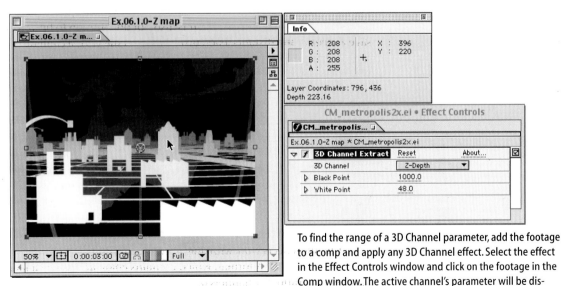

To find the range of a 3D Channel parameter, add the footage to a comp and apply any 3D Channel effect. Select the effect in the Effect Controls window and click on the footage in the Comp window. The active channel's parameter will be displayed for that pixel along the bottom of the Info window.

Oversampling

3D Channel information is often on/off per pixel, which results in an aliased edge to the matte that is produced. Rendering an image at least double size and scaling down in After Effects greatly improves this – at the cost of rendering time and disk space. A specific working practice for EI users is in TechTip 02 on the CD.

3D Channel Extract

This is the workhorse of this class of effects in that it creates a grayscale image based on information in the 3D channels. Indeed, you can use 3D Channel Extract and other processing and matting to re-create what most of the other 3D Channel effects do. At its simplest, you can use the result as a matte. You will also need to use this or the ID Matte effect (described later) if you want to do any processing with compound type effects, either from Adobe or third parties.

Practice using the [**Ex.01.1*starter**] comp. Select the image and apply Effects>3D Channel>3D Channel Extract. With the default Z-depth option selected in the 3D Channel popup, the White and Black Point parameters become active; these are very important. With 3D Channel Extract selected and the Channel option set to Z-Depth, click around the image in the Comp window and note the readings in the Info window for the nearest and farthest objects of interest. Enter these values as the White and Black Points, respectively. Traditionally, white is used for nearby objects. We typically set the Black Point a little bit "further back" than the last object so that this last object will be dark gray and stand out a bit from any holes in the background that might have distance of infinity (and therefore will be black); one result is in [**Ex.01.1_final**].

Unfortunately, you do not have Black and White Points with the other 3D Channel options, such as Object ID and Material ID. You will need to click around (or study the original 3D project) to find the range of objects that are in the scene. Apply Effect>Adjust>Levels and bring the Input White down until you have maximum contrast, as in [**Ex.01.2**]. If you need to isolate one Object ID, it is better to use Effect>3D Channels>ID Matte for this purpose and use the resulting alpha channel.

If you need to select a range of IDs, apply 3D Channel Extract and Levels as we did before, and follow with Effect>Adjust>Curves. Now "peak" the curve to make your selected objects white and the rest black. [**Ex.01.3**] is an example of creating a matte out of two sequential IDs; look at the Curves effect (select layer and hit Command+Shift+T) and turn it on and off to get an idea of what it is doing. If you need to select multiple discontinuous IDs, you will need either a trickier Curves setting or multiple copies of the layer with different settings, along with the Add transfer mode to blend them together to create your composite matte.

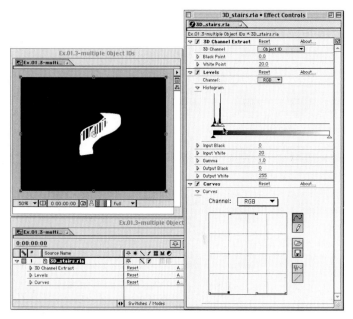

To create a high contrast matte from multiple contiguous Object IDs, spread out their gray levels with Levels, and "peak" them to white (and all others to black) using Curves.

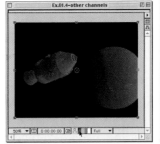

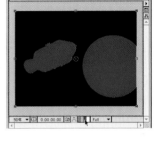

When 3D Channel Matte is used on RLA files and set to show Surface Normals (above left), each color channel shows an axis of which direction the surface of an object is pointing – red is the X axis, green is the Y axis, and blue is the Z axis. Image created by Frank DeLise.

Play around with the 3D Channel popup in [**Ex.01.4**] to get a feel for what the other channels available in an RLA file look like. Some of them, such as Texture UV and Surface Normals, result in multicolored files that may not make sense initially. But each color channel actually represents one of the dimensions of these channels.

For example, when you select Surface Normals – which indicates the angle the surface is "pointing" and therefore reflects light from – red indicates the X axis (black is negative X or to the left, white is positive X or to the right), green indicates the Y axis, and blue indicates the Z axis. You can temporarily view the individual color channels as grayscale values by clicking on the RGB swatches along the bottom of the Comp window; Shift+click on them to see the channel in color. You can isolate these color channels for further processing by following 3D Channel Matte with effects such as Channel>Shift Channels or Cult Effects Xtras>CE View Channel (included free on the CD).

Blending this raw information can help you set lighting to come from a particular angle and to fall "properly" on your rendered 3D object. For example, in [**Ex.01.5**], if you want to add lighting that appears to come from above (positive Y) a scene, set 3D Channel Matte to display Surface Normals, isolate the green (Y) channel, and use that matte for a solid that will act as your lighting. Applying Effect>Adjust>Levels and adjusting its Gamma parameter allows you to alter the fall-off of this lighting.

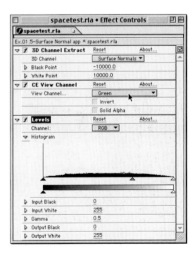

Here, we use 3D Channel Extract (above) to extract a matte based on how much the surface of an object is pointing up, or in the Y direction – carried by the green channel. This allows you to take an already-rendered 3D scene (far left) and apply directional lighting to it after the fact (left).

Tuning into RLA

To learn more about the 3D channels available in RLA files, download the RLA white paper from Discreet Logic: <www2.discreet.com/discreet/data/products/99-fset.html> These are also explained in the glossary of the 3D Studio MAX manual.

Depth Matte

Your first impulse might be to use this effect to "slice" a 3D render in half – all the information in front of a certain Z-depth in one layer, and all the information behind in another layer – and insert a new layer or image between the two. However, any problems you have with the Z-depth information not having enough resolution to create an antialiased matte will be amplified, because every object in the scene might be getting recut with this less-than-optimal matte. This is illustrated in [**Ex.02.1**].

A better approach is to think of it as a matte that can be used to cut out portions of the image you want to appear to be inserted in the middle of your 3D render. This requires only one application of the effect, resulting in faster render times and fewer parameters to adjust to animate the result. You'll also have less problems with matte edges.

To accomplish this, have an unaltered version of your 3D render as the back layer of a comp, then add the layer you want to insert in the "middle" of this render. Add a duplicate of your 3D render on top, and apply Effect>3D Channel>Depth Matte. This is illustrated in [**Ex.02.2**]. Set the Depth parameter to the distance you want your new layer to appear and turn on the Invert option at the bottom. Then set that new, middle layer to Alpha Inverted Matte mode – it will now have pieces matted out of it to make it fit into the layer underneath. While you're there, play around with the Depth parameter on the topmost layer to reposition the new, inserted layer.

Depth mattes are best applied as inverted alpha mattes for the layer you want to composite into your scene.

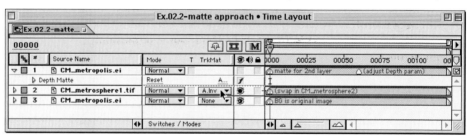

If you look closely at the result in [**Ex.02.2**], you may notice there are still some edge issues – especially between the top of the tall building on the right and the sphere we inserted in the middle. This can be improved by using a double-resolution Z-depth render; that result is in [**Ex.02.3**]. But there is still some white fringing between the buildings and sphere, and Depth Matte's Feather parameter does not seem to help this. This fringe can be cleaned up by applying Effect>Matte Tools>Simple Choker to the topmost layer (the one with Depth Matte applied), and setting Choke Matte to somewhere around 1.0; try it yourself with this comp.

Alternate Cameras

Good alternates to After Effects' Depth of Field effect are Composite Wizard's Super Rack Focus and Image Lounge's TrueCamera Rack Focus (both from Puffin Designs: www.puffindesigns.com). Use these with 3D Channel Extract set to Z-depth.

Depth of Field

This effect is helpful for creating selective "focus" effects based on the Z-depth information for a file. Animating the focus on even a rendered still is also a great way to add action to a scene. However, it seems to do nothing when you first apply it; you have to set the Maximum Radius (blur amount) parameter to some number above 0. Also set Focal Plane Thickness parameter to some number that seems to be a good slice of your total effective Z-depth range, or the effect will seem far too touchy to use, with only one value of Z-depth in sharp focus.

Since the effective Z-depth range will vary drastically from scene to scene, it is a good idea to apply this effect, and keeping your eye on the Info palette, click around the Comp window to get a feel for what your nearest and furthest objects are, and alter the Slider Range for the Focal Plane parameter to these limits. This slider will then be a lot more responsive.

This is also one of the effects that benefits greatly from rendering a higher-resolution Z-depth file – read TechTip 02 on the CD on Electric-Image issues, and compare the results in [**Ex.03.1**] (normal resolution Z buffer) and [**Ex.03.2**] (double resolution Z buffer). Note that the Maximum Radius parameter directly relates to how large the source file is; if you scaled it down to 50%, you would need twice as much blur for the same result.

Although a fun effect, the quality of this blur tends to "mush" images quickly. Use higher resolution source files, lower Maximum Radius values, or consider a third-party alternative.

Determine what is an effective Z-depth range for your scene, then enter these numbers in Focal Plane's Slider Range.

Fog 3D

Fog is very well explained in the online Help, so we have only a few tips here to share:

• The Fog Start and End parameters may be backward from your way of thinking: Just remember that Start is the least foggy point, or the point closest to you.

• Fog gets cut by the layer's alpha, which may give unexpected results – such as holes where there should be fog. There is a Foggy Back option, but it affects objects that are an "infinite" distance from the back – not objects that are cut out by the alpha. If you are using Fog 3D, you may need to make sure you render without an alpha channel, or at least plug up any "holes" in your model.

• Atmospheric effects tend to add a very pale sky color to objects, not pure white; consider choosing a Fog Color that is tinted slightly.

• Definitely exploit the power of choosing another layer to act as your fog. This layer can have a gradient applied, so the "ground" fog is denser than it is up in the sky. You can also animate it, either using stock footage of drifting fog or smoke from companies such as Artbeats. Or you can use various fractal noise effects such as the CE Noise Turbulent effect that comes free on the After Effects 4.1 CD-ROM. This is demonstrated in [**Ex.04**], which has a couple of tricks worth studying – such as "scaling" the fog layer to help make it appear to come forward in the room. Note that since the fog/smoke was created by an effect applied to an otherwise blank Solid layer, it needed to be precomposed, since compound effects (such as Fog 3D) do not see any effects applied to the layers they are pointed at. (Compound effects are covered in Chapter 22.)

If your 3D render has an alpha channel, this alpha will cut out the white fog – probably not the look you were expecting. (Hint: the areas between the continents should be fogged in as well.)

CE Noise Turbulent was used to create the smoke in a previous comp, which was then composited with Fog 3D. Room created by Shelley Green of 3D Gear.

Reflecting ID

When a material reflects other objects in a scene, some 3D software will assign the area of reflection to the ID of the reflected material – not the underlying material – regardless of who contributes more visually.

The original room is nice (above left), but the client decides they prefer rosier tones. To accomplish this, we isolate the floor and walls using ID Matte and colorize them using Hue/Saturation (above right) without having to rerender the image.

ID Matte

One of the real powers of the RLA format comes in tweaking colors of objects after the render. Imagine if a client, upon viewing your 72-hour render of a complex animation, told you, "It looks great, but could our logo be a little more blue?"

ID Matte allows you to isolate pixels in a render based on either their object or on material IDs. Rather than creating a matte, it creates a new alpha channel for the layer it is applied to, so you get the selected color pixels cut out of their frame. If you need just a matte, use this layer as an alpha track matte for a layer underneath.

Comp [Ex.05.1] contains the room used for the fog example above; it has a lot of material and object IDs for you to practice with isolating.

[Ex.05.2] shows one potential use of Material IDs, in this case isolating and tweaking the colors of the walls and floor by applying Effect> Adjust>Hue/Saturation after a material has been isolated. Don't forget that you will need a copy of the original image behind everything, to fill in the spaces that are not altered.

The Use Coverage checkbox often helps clean up color fringing of selected objects. Be careful, though; you may find some models actually introduce artifacts when this is turned on, as with the Apollo capsule in [Ex.05.3]. Change the comp's magnification to 100% to see this more clearly.

Also be aware that, unfortunately, the Feather parameter can often cause more problems than it solves because it spreads the alpha channel

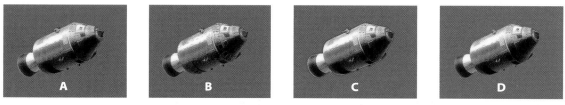

ID Matte can create alpha channels based on Object or Material IDs in RLA files, but with the occasional fringing (A). The Use Coverage option often improves this, but it can cause artifacts with some models (B). The Feather parameter spreads only the edge, worsening the problem (C). A better solution is to soften and choke the edge of the alpha, using tools such as Effect>Matte Tools> Simple Choker (D). Much easier than masking by hand…

beyond the object you are trying to isolate. Experiment with this parameter on the capsule in [Ex.05.3]. To bring in the edges of a selected object, try applying Effect>Matte Tools>Simple Choker (set around 1.00 for starters). Experiment with this in [Ex.05.4]: Simple Choker has already been applied; set the comp's magnification to 100% and turn Simple Choker on or off to see the result. (Note: there is a pair of effects Favorites on the CD – **edge blur_choke PB.ffx** and **edgesmooth.ffx** – that are designed for cleaning up edges.)

The gotcha in choking mattes is when two objects overlap, a gap may appear between them. This happens often when you're isolating a single object against a full frame background, where this is less likely to show up.

Channel

There is only one additional Channel effect included in the Production Bundle, and it is…

Alpha Levels

This is just like Effect>Adjust>Levels with the popup set to Alpha, but without all the other channels to distract you – and without the Histogram as a visual aid. Since the ordinary Levels effect is more flexible (and comes even with the Standard version), we tend to use it instead.

Distort

With version 4.0, After Effects added several effects that are based on morphing and warping technology. Most of these are included in the Production Bundle version of the program, and we'll touch on them here. We'll also cover gotchas on a few of the other more traditional distortion effects that come in this higher end bundle.

If you need to do an actual morph, consider a dedicated program, such as Avid's Elastic Reality (www.avid.com). If you do try to coax a morph out of one of the following effects, at the very least do the crossfade step in a precomp or use Effect>Channel>Blend. We use the new Distort effects to fix problems and add creative distortions to an image. As mentioned in Chapter 23, the Distort effects work particularly well as "distortion fields" applied to nested compositions, with the animation taking place in the precomp.

Remember that to edit the tangent handles for Bezier and Mesh Warp, you must select the name of the effect in the Effect Controls window. Option+drag tangents for a realtime update.

Bezier Warp

By pushing all the "tangent" handles proportionally away from or toward the center of a comp, you can introduce (or correct!) some forms of optical distortion. A very simple example of this is shown in [Ex.06]; turn the Effects switch on and off for the layer to see the difference. For simple distortions like this, you can leave the Elasticity popup at Stiff. If you select more accurate settings, you get a very small image quality gain, and a large render penalty.

More fun comes when you use Bezier Warp as a creative way to make static or flat objects such as text come alive, as shown in [Ex.07]. The text is cropped in a smaller precomp, to improve rendering times. All of these warps are slow, so perform them on as small an image as you can get away with. The vertices and tangents of the Bezier Warp effect are then animated to give a flowing motion to the text. Don't forget to turn the animation stopwatch on for all the parameters you wish to animate. If the warped object starts to display kinks, try one of the higher Elasticity settings (although the parameter consists of a series of names, there are not different algorithms; just smoother calculation accuracy).

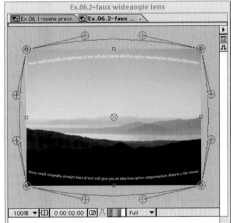

Bezier Warp can be used to take an image or a precomp (above) and introduce optical distortion (below). In this case, animate your action in a precomp and distort it in the second comp.

A creative use of Bezier Warp is to distort text in a flowing manner. Liquid FX footage from EyeWire.

Mesh Warp give you a series of crosshairs that you move around to distort the image. Image from Digital Vision/Naked & Scared.

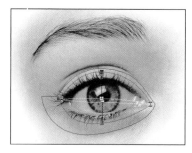

Setting up Reshape: The red mask shape captures the eyelashes and eye opening to fold down into the closed eye (the yellow shape). The blue mask shape outlines the portion of skin around the eye socket we don't want to stretch; the kink on the left side is to capture stray eyelashes. The inverted boxes are the Correspondence Points; they say "Move this portion of the image directly to this other point" (i.e., the corners of the eye). Image from Digital Vision/ The Body.

Different Elasticity settings obey the Boundary Mask with varying degrees of accuracy: Stiff (right) and Liquid (far right) are shown here.

Mesh Warp

Mesh Warp differs from Bezier Warp in that instead of warping just the corners and overall outlines of a layer, you get a series of crosshairs inside the layer to move and twist as well. Unfortunately, unlike some other implementations of this idea, you cannot create a custom mesh of control points *before* you start warping the image. There are three tricks to using this effect:

• The effect needs to be selected in the Effect Controls window (Command+Shift+T) to see the mesh.

• The crosshairs of the mesh don't become active until you click on them in the Comp window.

• To animate them, you have to enable the stopwatch for the single Grid Values parameter, which will store the position of all the crosshairs.

Since you have little control over where the grid lines fall beyond how many there are, you might consider positioning your source layer in a precomp and warping it in the next comp in the chain. This approach is demonstrated in [Ex.08].

Reshape

In our opinion, this is the most powerful and controllable of the new warping-oriented Distort effects. You set up two mask shapes: one around the region you want to move, and one representing where you want to move it to and what shape you want it to take on when it gets there. A third mask shape can serve as a protection boundary that says, "Nothing (much) beyond this region should move when the objects inside it are moving." You cannot cross this Boundary Mask, so make sure it encloses your other mask shapes.

How strongly the Boundary Mask is obeyed depends directly on the Elasticity settings – the higher the setting, the more strongly it is obeyed. The trade-off is increased rendering times. Be sure to give the Boundary Mask some extra room away from the features you don't want to move. In general, you should draw your masks so they enclose, not bisect or straddle, the feature or shape you are trying to move or protect.

An example of this issue is demonstrated in [Ex.09.1]. We have an image of an eye; we want to make it blink. The first thing we did is cut out an inverted mask shape for the eyeball to show through an undistorted copy of the eye layer behind – we don't want to distort the eyeball while

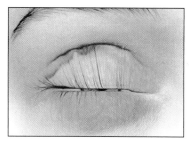

moving the eyelids. Next, we drew masks beyond the eyelid, trying to capture as much of the eyelash as practical, and inside the bone for the eye socket, since your bones don't slide down your face when you blink. However, the results are very sloppy with lower Elasticity settings – and the eyeliner painted

around the eye socket gets dragged in anyway. Try higher settings (and be patient while it renders) to see the difference in accuracy.

By the way, this example shows one of the most common problems with "realistic" warps: Parts of the image you want to move need to overlap parts you don't want to move. In this case, the eyelashes (which should move when we blink) overlap the eyeliner around the socket; this photo should be retouched to shorten the lashes before creating this effect.

Another good use for Reshape is to conform one shape to another. When the shape you want your selected layer to emulate exists on another layer (for example, stretching text to fit a shape on a background image), your life will be easier if you first make both layers the same size through prior trimming or precomposing. You can then draw the mask shape on the background layer and paste it into the layer to be reshaped. This arrangement is demonstrated in [Ex.10].

Through careful use of transfer modes, masks, Reshape, and its Correspondence Points (left), text can be wrapped onto the surface of another layer (right). 3D Glass by Paul Sherstobitoff.

SOuRCe Mask
Destination Mask
Boundary Mask

Distorting in 3D

Forge Freeform (www.forge.net) allows you to wrap and animate a layer in 3D space right inside After Effects.

Correspondence Course

One of the larger mysteries of Reshape are the Correspondence Points. This is a common feature of morphing programs, in which a point along the first shape will morph directly to a certain point along the second shape. If it's not set, you may find your warp drifting as parts head in directions you did not anticipate. On the opposite end of the spectrum, you can purposely move the Correspondence Points to rotated positions to cause a twisting animation as you warp.

Reshape defaults to one Correspondence Point. To set more, select Reshape in the Effect Controls window and Option+click on the Source or Destination Mask outline in the Comp window. When you position the cursor over one of these points, it will change to a four-way arrow. Drag the point to its new target destination. To delete an existing point, Option+click on it.

[Ex.09.2] has been set up for you to experiment with this. Here, the telephone dial is shrunk and spun as the Percent parameter animates. With the time marker at 00:00, select Reshape in the Effect Controls window (Command+Shift+T); study the Correspondence Points in the Comp window; and move, add, or delete them, observing the results.

Remember, too, that you can animate the Correspondence Points, either to follow the changing shape of an animated mask (which might be animating to follow a moving object in a movie) or to add further life to stills.

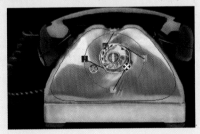

The dial on this phone is shrunken using Reshape, and twisted through manipulation of its Correspondence Points. Image from Classic PIO/Telephones.

Ripple

The first step after applying this effect is to set the Radius parameter to something larger than 0; otherwise, you won't see its effect. Beyond that, it is nice in that it self-animates, in a repeatable, loopable fashion – check out [Ex.11] for an example. To stop it, set its Speed parameter down to 0; you can then hand animate it using the Phase parameter.

The weakness of Ripple is that you can't create a single ripple to emanate from the center and die away. We've created a CD tutorial on how you can cook this up yourself using a displacement map, or you can use third-party plug-ins to achieve this (FE Ripple Pulse from ICE's Final Effects Complete, and Wave World from Atomic Power's Evolution).

Wave Warp

There are a couple of gotchas with Wave Warp. To start, it cannot warp a layer outside its original boundary. For example, you might think that to animate a thin line waving, you would create a thin Solid layer and apply Effect>Distort>Wave Warp. However, the waves would get clipped by the size of the solid. Therefore, you need to create a layer (be it a solid, Illustrator text, a nested comp, or something similar) large enough to accommodate the feature you want to see, plus the height of the wave, then mask it back down, if you wish, to the feature you want waved. This is demonstrated in [Ex.12.1] where a larger solid has been created, then masked down to the thin line we originally wanted.

Secondly, there is a slight glitch in the wave: When it crosses from "positive" to "negative" displacement, there is a small, discontinuous jump in the displacement, which is not always noticeable. The Boris Wave effect from Boris AE doesn't exhibit this problem.

As with Ripple, you can have the waves move automatically using the Speed parameter set to a constant value, or set the Speed down to 0 and animate the wave motion manually using the Phase parameter. The different Pinning options create a lot of different looks beyond the variety of the Waveshapes options already provided. Some simple line animations using different pinnings are put to work in [Ex.12.2].

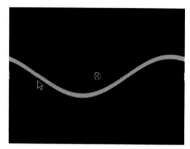

The cursor points to a slight glitch in Wave Warp's displacement.

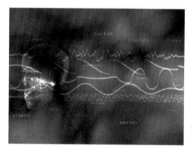

A variety of waveshapes and edge pinning applied to simple thin solids gives a variety of "electronic" lines.

Matte Tools

The two effects, Matte Choker and Simple Choker, in this submenu are most useful when color keying for cleaning up edges of alpha channels. (And so both of these are discussed as well in Chapter 25.) Matte Choker was designed to help clean up problematic color keys where there may be holes or tears in the edges. For tightening up less-tattered alpha channels, go with Simple Choker.

Beyond keying applications, the Matte Tools have some creative uses as well, such as blending a foreground object into a scene (demonstrated in [Ex.13]), cleaning up edges on objects with less than perfect alpha channels ([Ex.14.1]), and "eroding" the edges of text for a grungier feel – check out the example in [Ex.14.2].

1234567890

1234567890

The bottom is normal, boring Courier text; the top shows it eroded with Effect>Matte Tools>Simple Choker. Preview [Ex.14.2]; the Choke is animated to erode the text away to black.

Render

The Production Bundle adds one additional Render effect, and it is, shall we say, rather electrifying:

Lightning

This effect might be more appropriately named Electricity: It gives a constant electric arc bouncing between two points. At the risk of nagging you to eat your vegetables, the manual and online Help *do* have a lot of useful information on understanding this effect; it is certainly one that only gets more confusing if you just randomly poke at sliders. Note that Lightning's branches do not appear on the first frame (so don't set up the effect at time 00:00). We add a few additional tips:

• Lightning does not have a "replace" mode, making our "apply to a black solid" trick back in Chapter 21 a little harder to use. However, it does create its own alpha channel, which it adds to the alpha of the layer it is applied to. If you want to take advantage of After Effects' full complement of Transfer Modes with Lightning, create a solid, create a small mask in the Layer window, then drag the mask onto the pasteboard, in essence making the layer transparent. Apply Lightning to this now-blank solid. This approach is demonstrated in [Ex.15.1]. Experiment with the different modes in the Time Layout window.

• The default value for Width tends to be too large for realistic looks; try reducing it. The Core Width parameter also affects how "wide" the bolt will appear: smaller values make it more transparent and therefore apparently thinner; a Core Width of 0 snaps to looking blurry. (The Outside Color choice also has a great effect on apparent width; more on that below.) Smaller Branch Width settings (especially when you have a lot of branching and rebranching) will also get a more realistic, delicate look.

• The Inside and Outside Colors do not work the same as similar parameters in Effect>Render>Ellipse or other effects – they are actually glow colors rather than stroke and fill colors. As a result, you will rarely see exactly these colors; they *influence* the overall result instead. Brighter outside colors make the bolt appear much wider than you would expect since lighter colors glow more. High saturation values (90 to 100%) for the Outside Color swatch also make it swamp a white inside color.

• If you're going for lightning bolts rather than electricity, study real lightning – we've included a movie from Artbeats in [Ex.16], with markers at the major bolts. Note it is not on continuously; it flashes for a frame or two and then disappears for a while. Each episode of flashing also looks wildly different from the previous one. Therefore, get ready to do a lot of keyframing, of Opacity as well as the different bolt parameters.

To get more realistic bolts, experiment with thinner Width settings for the main bolt and the branches. To get a nice glow, reduce the Core setting and/or increase the Width Variation. This approach is demonstrated in [**Ex.15.2**]. Rabbit ears from Classic PIO/Television.

Swedish Storm Chasing

CE Lightning in Cycore's Cult Effects package (www.culteffects.com) includes the ability for bolts to trace around a layer's alpha – great for graphical treatments.

Real lightning flickers on and off and randomizes greatly. Even long continuous bolts vary considerably from frame to frame; here, you would need to animate Width and Branching parameters to re-create it. Footage from Artbeats/Storm Clouds.

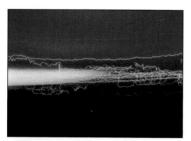

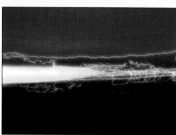

The default settings of Glow are good for taking an image with hot spots (top) and greatly intensifying them (above). Image from Digital Vision/Edge of Awareness.

Free Glow

If you don't have the Production Bundle yet, the Glow plug-in comes free on the enclosed CD, courtesy Adobe.

A less-than-obvious use for Glow is to have it turn highlights in an image (left) into a luma matte (right) for special treatments. This is saved as Favorite **glowmatte.ffx**.

Stylize

Of the two additional effects that appear in this submenu, one (Scatter) is self-obvious, and the other – Glow – is not. However, glow is a popular design element these days, so it is worth taking the time to master it.

Glow

What causes a lot of confusion with this effect is that there are two very different looks that are both referred to as "glow": one that adds hot spots of burned-in color to an image, and another that adds a halo around a layer's alpha. After Effects' Glow does them both, but with important differences in settings.

To get an idea of the first look, open [**Ex.17.1*starter**], select the one layer in that comp, and apply Effects>Stylize>Glow. Bang: You'll immediately get that "hot" glow look with the defaults. In this case, After Effects is looking for the bright spots of the image, puffing them out, and feeding them back onto the image. Decreasing the Threshold parameter increases the areas that are picked up and glowed. The Glow Operation popup is actually a full list of transfer modes that is used to composite the glow onto the image; experiment with different ones. This effect looks particularly nice on metal objects in a layer; try the same procedure with [**Ex.17.2*starter**].

If your image already has bright spots of suitably hot colors, like whites and yellows, you can leave the Glow Colors popup to Original Colors (those in the image) and ignore all of the other parameters below it. If you want to add a glow with a different color than is in the image to start with, select A & B Colors and choose them below (hint: black, the default for Color B, is pretty boring). Simple color cycles, such as setting Color Looping to Sawtooth and leaving Color Loops to 1.0, often work best; the A & B Midpoint parameter lets you balance off the two colors. This is shown in [**Ex.17.3**].

An unusual use for Glow is its ability to identify the brighter parts of an image to create a luminance matte. You can then use this matte for a

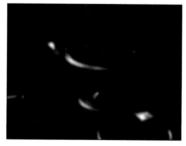

variety of purposes, from selective color correction to making sure new elements appear only in these "glowed" areas. This setting is saved as the effect Favorite **glowmatte.ffx**; a subtle use is demonstrated in [**Ex.17.4**]. Preview the comp to see it in action.

The other use for Glow is as a halo for objects with alpha channels, such as text. To see this in action, open [**Ex.18.1*starter**], select the text layer in it, and open the Effect Controls window (Command+Shift+T). These are the default settings that hint at this look, but a few tweaks are needed to go much further:

Particle Playground

The Production Bundle version of After Effects introduced a very powerful particle system called Particle Playground, where dots, text, and even other animated layers can be flung about the screen following a myriad of rules. Create a Solid (Command+Y), and apply Effects>Simulation>Particle Playground.

The possibilities are rather huge; the Production Bundle Guide dedicates 47 pages to very clear, detailed explanations of each of the parameters, and why and when you would use them. Rather than replicate that explanation here, Richard Lainhart of O-Town Media (www.otown.com) and JJ Gifford of Funny Garbage (www.funnygarbage.com) have contributed tips and tutorials for Particle Playground in the enclosed CD Tutorials folder – check them out.

In the meantime, be warned that the power of Particle Playground comes at a price: It can be rather slow, especially if particles are being emitted past the first frame. Several other plug-in manufacturers offer particle systems dedicated to a variety of tasks; they are also worth checking out if you need more specific looks. But if you want a lot of power to create completely different looks, expect to spend some serious play time.

Particle Playground particularly excels at tricks involving text, such as JJ Gifford's tips for blasting words to bits (left, Bonus Tutorial 19) and Richard Lainhart's tutorial for recreating the look of the opening titles for *The Matrix* (right, Bonus Tutorial 20).

Step 1: Change the Glow Colors popup to A & B Colors. If you like, go ahead and change the Color Looping and the colors to something more palatable; we prefer Sawtooth A>B for Looping.

Step 2: Change the Glow Based On popup to Alpha Channel. (If you do these two steps in the reverse order, you get an error message; ignore it.)

Step 3: To place the halo behind the object, change the Composite Original popup to On Top. Leaving this at the Behind setting gives a "hot" glow more akin to the default effect. A good starting point is saved on the CD as Effect Favorite **glowtext.ffx**.

Step 4: At this point, experiment with the Glow Threshold, Radius, and Intensity parameters. For a strong glow of a single color, make Color A and Color B the same – to wit, for an intense white glow, make both colors white.

To get even more intense looks, change Composite Original to Behind, and experiment with different Transfer Modes. Set the Glow Direction popup at the bottom to Vertical to get a trendy text treatment. Don't forget to save treatments you'd like to reuse (Effect>Save Favorite) so you can apply them easily in the future.

Using a vertical-only glow, with a large Glow Radius, yields stronger spikes than typical blurs – you can colorize it as well.

Connect

Many effects can trace the outlines of a mask. Creating masks was explained in Chapter 13.

Basics on applying and animating effects was the subject of Chapter 19. This includes saving and applying Favorite presets of effects.

The practice of applying certain effects to a black solid to take advantage of a layer's transfer modes was explained in Chapter 21.

Some tips on working with generic Z-depth files were discussed in Chapter 22.

Color keying – in particular, the Production Bundle's powerful Color Difference Keyer – is the subject of the next chapter (25).

The Render Settings determine whether Effects are rendered, and are explained in Chapter 43.

25 The Blue Riders

These two sample bluescreen shots are included in the Sources folder with this chapter's project on the CD for you to practice with: Alex (left) and Water (right). Special thanks to Photron, creators of the Primatte keyer, for permission to include these images.

Example Project

Explore the 25-Example Project.aep file as you read this chapter; references to [Ex.##] refer to specific compositions within the project file.

PB **C**ompositing images from one environment over a new background is one of the more common – and tricky – motion graphics tasks you will encounter. This technique often requires separating the foreground elements from the original background they were shot against. Even if the foreground comes with its own alpha channel (the result of a 3D render), getting it to blend nicely with its new background can still be a challenge.

Time for the bad news: Not all images can be cleanly separated from their background. Not all images can be seamlessly blended with their

new background. And the tools that come with the After Effects Standard Bundle are insufficient for either task under most conditions. But with proper forethought and preparation, plus the Keying Pack in After Effects' Production Bundle (or perhaps a select third-party effect, see later in this chapter), you should be able to produce professional results. This chapter will give you an overview of the issues, plus tips on using the tools at hand.

Keying 101

The process of *keying* footage means creating an alpha channel for it so that the objects or actions you want to keep are separated (or "pulled") from the background they were originally shot against. You can use a number of techniques to pull off this separation.

The most common technique is a variation on *color keying*. The actor or object is shot against a solid-color background. This color is hopefully one that does not appear in the object you want to keep – for example, blue when shooting people, because skin tones tend to be shadings on red. You then instruct your software or hardware to blot out this background color by making its alpha channel transparent in those areas, and to keep whatever is not the same as the background color by making its alpha channel opaque in these areas.

Key Personality Traits

There are a number of different keying techniques, as well as a number of keying plug-in effects. Not everyone uses the same names, even when they use the same techniques. Let's try to sort it out.

Binary or Simple Color Key: The most basic color keyer; comes free with the Standard version of After Effects (remember that you often get what you pay for). You select a color or range of colors to key (usually with a definable tolerance), it decides whether each pixel matches or not, and it makes it accordingly transparent or opaque – usually with feathering at the transitions. It can work on simple tasks, such as solid objects against solid backgrounds, but it cannot deal with semitransparent areas such as glass, smoke, and wispy hair.

Luminance Key: Uses the relative brightness of the image or one of its color channels, with some contrast adjustments, to determine final transparency. This type of key works okay if the object was shot against solid black or white. For a do-it-yourself luminance key, copy the clip, exaggerate and clip its contrast with Levels or Curves, and use as a luma track matte for the original layer. Add Effect>Channel>Remove Color Matting in a second comp to clean up the edges. We use the Knoll Unmult AE plug-in (available free at www.puffindesigns.com) to drop out black backgrounds from clips such as fire and explosions.

Linear Key: A refinement of Luminance keying, in which a pixel's transparency is based on its similarity to a chosen color. Preserves semitransparent areas and shadows, but does little to remove background color that is mixed into these areas. More sophisticated linear keys have additional contrast and smoothing parameters, and often the ability to "keep" a specified color (for fixing cases where holes develop).

Advanced Keys: More advanced color keying plug-ins have their own algorithms to determine the transparency of each pixel, plus additional color correction controls such as suppressing any "spill" of the background color onto the foreground object.

In addition to keying, other terms you may hear include *chroma keying* (chroma meaning color), *Ultimatte* (one of the oldest companies creating keying equipment), and *bluescreen* or *greenscreen* (describing the color of the background stage). A related technique is luminance keying, which creates an alpha channel based on the relative overall brightness of a scene rather than just its similarity to one color. This works well for white text on black title cards or for the occasional image shot against white seamless or a black set, but it does not work well for many other cases.

Although the basic concept may sound easy, things rarely work out so neatly in practice. Real images often contain a mixture of colors rather than pure ones. It is hard to paint and light a colored background perfectly evenly. Chances are strong that the light hitting this background is reflecting on the objects you want to keep, and as a result they'll take on some of this unwanted color. Then there's the issue of semitransparent parts of an image, such as wispy hair, shadows, and smoke. And that's just the obstacles in creating a key – now you have to convincingly blend the object into another world…

That's why any keying job should be treated in three phases: shooting, keying, and compositing. We'll cover them in order, while focusing on mastering After Effects' advanced Color Difference Keyer. Throughout this chapter, we'll often make the assumption that you are shooting against blue; the same ideas apply to green or other colors.

Through the Keyhole

The term *key* is short for *keyhole* – creating a keyhole in the alpha channel through which you see the object you want to keep.

Clean Pass

If the camera is locked down or under motion control, shoot a pass of the set without actors or objects. This will come in handy for difference mattes or Ultimatte's Screen Correction.

Realtime Key

Just because you can key footage in software does not necessarily mean you want to. Keying is one of the slower effects to render, so it can add significantly to your computing time. Transfers between tape and computer can also degrade the footage, making it harder to key.

That is why you should at least consider renting a hardware keyer, such as an Ultimatte system. If you have it on the set during the shoot, you can see right then and there if the key is going to work, for example, or if you need to adjust the lighting. You can also take your master tape and run a keying pass on it in a post-production house.

Either way, you will end up with two tapes: your original footage, and a keying pass that includes a high-contrast matte to use as a luma matte for your footage. Make sure they have been properly slated or time-coded, bring them both into After Effects, line them up in a comp with the matte layer on top, and set a track matte (Chapter 14) for the second fill layer. Conversely, create the animated backgrounds first, then composite the keyed footage over them in realtime at a post house. You can then use this already composited footage in After Effects, or directly in your nonlinear editor.

An Ounce of Prevention

Before you apply a single keying effect, 90% of the battle has already been fought. If the material has been lit, shot, and transferred correctly, your life will be much easier; if it hasn't been, you quite possibly will not be able to get an acceptable key.

It's preferable to attend the shoot, but for most of us in the trenches, that's not always an option. If the scenes have not been shot yet, encourage the producer to hire lighting and camera people with bluescreen experience. The lighting and shooting of the bluescreen stage is paramount: You want even lighting on the backdrop while still keeping realistic lighting (including lighting angles that match the new background you intend to use) on the foreground objects you wish to keep. You also want to minimize color spill from the background onto your foreground objects. Painting the backdrop with an actual bluescreen or greenscreen paint (such as Ultimatte Blue) isn't a bad idea, either.

If the camera is locked down or under motion control, have the lighting and camera people shoot a pass of just the blue set, especially if you're using the Ultimatte effect. This also comes in handy when you're trying to create a Difference Matte, where you key based on the similarities between two different images.

Shoot on the best format possible, even if the rest of the show is not being shot or posted in it. BetaSP should be considered the absolute minimum; DV's compression and reduced color space make it less desirable. DVC-Pro 50, Digital S, or Digital Beta are all much better. In the film world, the less grain, the better, making larger formats preferable (for example, 35mm over 16mm). Turn off any automatic edge enhancement at the camera (when shooting on video) or during the telecine transfer (if you originally shot on film); they can make edges harder to key.

When you transfer the footage into your computer, go for the absolute minimum compression – most recommend 3:1 or better. If the budget allows, get an uncompressed transfer. Use the best interconnects the deck has – analog component (YUV) at minimum; Serial Digital Interface (SDI) if you have it. Again, even if you're not doing the rest of the show this way, consider it for the bluescreen transfers. You can always recompress the footage for the nonlinear editing system that's being used after you have pulled the keys.

Figure out first which sections of which clips you will need in the final production. Setting up and performing a key are both enormously time consuming; you don't want to do this on footage you later won't be using.

Backgrounds for Bluescreen

If you find yourself creating images to act as backgrounds to keyed foreground subjects, and the key is less than satisfactory, you'll make your life a lot easier – and make the composite more believable – by designing the backgrounds using the same general color as the one you'll be keying.

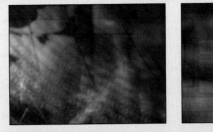
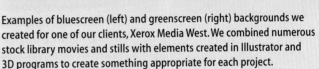

Examples of bluescreen (left) and greenscreen (right) backgrounds we created for one of our clients, Xerox Media West. We combined numerous stock library movies and stills with elements created in Illustrator and 3D programs to create something appropriate for each project.

Let's say you're keying a talking head shot again blue, and the subject is wearing glasses, has wispy hair, and lots of spill on the shoulders – *and* the key is less than perfect. Instead of choking the key to death, design an animated background with colors from that quarter of the color wheel. For bluescreen, you can use the range from purple to blue to blue-green. Greenscreen, unfortunately, forces you to design in the less desirable and more challenging yellow-green range.

When you add some fake lighting effects to the background, the mind is fooled into thinking that behind your subject is a live source that was casting bluish light onto the shoulders of the person being interviewed. Remember that unless the background looks like it emits some kind of light, the mind will find no explanation for blue spill.

Chapter 12 includes tips for using "lighting" movies, like those from EyeWire's Reflections of Light CD, composited on top of the other layers using the Overlay or Soft Light Transfer modes. If possible, create looping backgrounds and animations so you can repeat them for as long as needed to go behind any shot, no matter now long, either in After Effects or in your editing system.

After you get the footage captured, apply a "garbage mask" around the action you want to keep so you don't waste effort trying to get a good key on parts of the frame you don't care about. You might need to animate this mask to make sure it doesn't cut off any body parts or shadows as the action moves.

Now you're ready to start keying. As we mentioned earlier in this chapter, you'll really need the Production Bundle version of After Effects or a third-party keyer to get professional results. Unlike a typical reference manual, the Production Bundle's manual goes into excellent detail on using many of its additions, including its keying tools. The online help is also an excellent resource. Therefore, we're not going to repeat the manual here, especially for some of the easier-to-grasp tools such as the Extract Key (useful for pulling a key from white or black backgrounds, as well as extracting a range of gray levels); the Color Range Key; the Difference Matte (useful when you have a separate "clean plate" of the background without the foreground object present, in addition to the regular full shot); or the relatively easy to use Linear Color Key. Instead, we're going to focus on the powerful yet often intimidating Color Difference Key, or CDK.

Trial Run

Try to key samples of the footage before you sign on to do the whole job. Some footage simply cannot be keyed; a one-day bid for keying can easily turn into a week of rotoscoping hell…

The Color Difference Key's parameters: the default settings produces a low contrast matte, as viewed in the preview window on the right.

Our goal: create a better matte consisting of a solid black background (transparency), solid white foreground (full opacity), and soft gray edges (for semitransparent wispy hair).

The Color Difference Key (CDK)

When you first start using the CDK, the number of sliders and buttons can be quite overwhelming. But by going through the process of pulling a key, you'll see that most of the sliders and options are rarely, if ever, used. Once you start ignoring half of the sliders and focus on what's important, it won't look so daunting.

We'll first explain how to approach the CDK, then we'll work through an example of using it. The basic premise of the CDK is that there are three mattes. Let's say the keying color is blue:

• Partial A is the first matte, and it's based on the pixels in the image that are most *un*like the keying color (the foreground).

• Partial B is the second matte, based on the pixels that are most *like* the keying color (the blue background).

• By working on these two mattes, A and B, the result is that the third matte – the alpha matte – starts becoming higher in contrast. You can also work on the alpha matte directly, because at the end of the day, this matte is the one used for determining which pixels are actually made transparent by the keyer.

If you've owned After Effects for awhile, you might have noticed that the version 3.1 manual leads you down the path of working on the A and the B Partials separately, then finishing up by working on the final matte. By contrast, the 4.0 manual advises going straight to the Matte controls and using the Partials only if necessary. It's up to you how you prefer to work, but we find that working on the A and B partials separately is not difficult once you get the hang of it, and the results are usually superior.

The Goals

The goal is to create an alpha matte with solid black for the background (where there previously was blue) and solid white for the foreground (the subject you want to keep). The edges should have as broad a range of grays as possible from Black (0 RGB) to White (255 RGB).

Making a black-and-white matte is easy – just squeeze together the two Matte In sliders. What's difficult is keeping as wide a range as possible of gray values along the edge. The CDK pulls a matte based on the amount of blue in a pixel, so fluffy hair that's contaminated with blue will create semitransparent areas. If you end up with an alpha matte with mostly black-and-white edges and very little gray values, the composite will have pixels that are mostly on or off, resulting in an undesirable blocky edge.

It usually looks best to key all the really blue hair but keep some of the lightly contaminated pixels so you have a good "texture" for the hair edges. When you get to the final tweaking stage, these semitransparent edge pixels may be too blue for comfort. At this point, you have a choice to either darken the edge pixels in the matte (making the edge pixels more transparent) using Matte Gamma, choke the pixels (eliminating them altogether), or removing the blue color using Spill Suppressor (so you keep the nice texture, but remove the blue color). We'll look at all three options in detail later.

To Another Level

The next big picture to grasp is that the long list of sliders for Partials A, B, and Matte are basically three Levels filters. They contain three main sections:

- Input Black and Input White, which *increase* contrast;
- Output Black and Output White, which *decrease* contrast;
- Gamma, which changes the mid-point of the black-to-white range. This brightens or darkens the image without losing the black and white points already set.

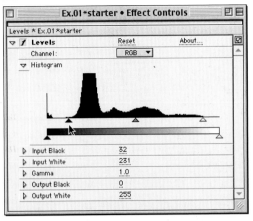

Our aim will be to increase the contrast in these Partials as well as the final alpha matte, so focus your attention on the In sliders. We have yet to come across a case in which it helped to decrease the contrast of the mattes, so you can usually ignore the four sliders with Out in their name.

If you've worked with the normal Effect>Adjust>Levels filter, you know it has a Histogram that shows the relative amounts of black, white, and grays in an image. If the Histogram does not reach the black-and-white extremes of its display, this is a sign that the footage does not have the maximum amount of contrast that it could. To alter that, you slide the Input Black slider up to the point where the blacks start in the Histogram and the Input White slider down to the point where the whites start. What Levels does then is stretch the luminance range so that the position of your Input Black slider will go out as value 0, and the position of your Input White slider will go out as value 255.

Unfortunately, the Color Difference Key does not have Histograms for adjusting Partial A, Partial B, and the Alpha. However, you can still see the results in the preview window in the upper right portion of the Effect Controls window, and even better feedback by setting the View popup to copy the partials out to the main Comp window.

To increase the contrast of an image, it is common to apply Effect>Adjust>Levels and to move the Input Black and White sliders up against the edges of the luminance range in the Histogram. This is basically what you want to do with the Partial A and B In sliders in the CDK – the shortcoming is that you are not able to see a Histogram directly.

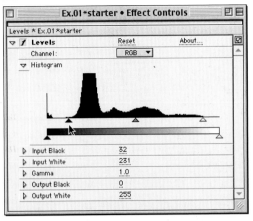

The default settings result in Matte Partials that are low in contrast (left). Therefore, we will be adjusting the In Black and White points for our mattes (middle) to increase this contrast (right).

Sectional Review

Now that we have an overall idea of what we want to do with the Color Difference Key, let's go over its specific parameter groups:

View: When you apply the CDK, the first thing to do is to set the View popup to Matte Corrected, which will show you the default key. As you build what looks like a good high-contrast matte, switch the View to Final Output to see how it composites against your background footage (or a dummy solid color, set to show up its shortcomings). You can also view all three mattes and the final in the comp, with the last option: [A,B,Matte] Corrected, Final. Make sure you leave it at Final Output when you're finished, or After Effects will render the black-and-white matte instead of the keyed image.

Key Color: If you're keying blue, the key color is not that important to AE. But go ahead and select the exact background (key) color as a feel-good exercise. If you're keying any other color, select the background color to key by using the Key Color eyedropper and either clicking in the source preview window or turning off the effect and selecting the color from the Comp window.

Color Matching Accuracy: Faster should work fine for bluescreen and greenscreen, but for any other color (such as orange), set this menu to More Accurate.

Eyedroppers: The top eyedropper between the Image and Matte thumbnails and the eyedropper for the Key Color swatch are essentially the same; they are for selecting the background (key) color. The Key Color eyedropper has the advantage that it can pick up colors from the Comp or Layer windows as well.

The next two eyedroppers set the In Black (center eyedropper) and In White (bottom eyedropper) for the matte currently selected by the buttons underneath the right-most thumbnail. Select an eyedropper and drag it around in either the left/original image, or the right/matte image. As you hold the mouse button down, the matte will update interactively; when you release the mouse, their respective parameters below will update.

Garbage Mask

Don't waste time trying to key areas in the corners that may be different than the color around your subject – create a mask (Chapter 13) to make these areas transparent.

A Second Opinion

There are several good Web sites, articles, and training tapes with additional information on bluescreen history, preparation, and execution. Our personal favorites:

**Alice in Bluescreen Land
(www.dv.com/magazine/1997/0697/bluescreen.pdf)**
An excellent article by Mark Christiansen that originally appeared in the June 1997 issue of *DV* magazine. It covers a project step by step from the shoot through the final composite and includes explanations for the decisions made along the way.

**Steve Bradford's Blue Screen / Chroma Key Page
(www.seanet.com/~bradford/bluscrn.html)**
This site contains a huge amount of relevant historical information on bluescreen and chromakey equipment and techniques. It will be of particular relevance to those making the jump from traditional video and film compositing equipment to the desktop.

The Ultimatte® Page (www.ultimatte.com)
Ultimatte is one of the pioneering companies of the bluescreen process. Its Web site contains many useful documents, including technical documents, test images, and an online version of its general manual which is essential for understanding Ultimatte's approach to the bluescreen removal process.

Masters of Visual FX (www.puffindesigns.com)
A valuable set of training tapes for all levels, created by working professionals and masters, that cover a variety of topics, including proper considerations for keying and compositing shots.

It's real easy to get carried away with these two "In" eye-droppers and create a matte with too high a contrast, resulting in the blocky edges we warned about. Use a light touch, especially when you're adjusting the Partial mattes – we use just the In Black eyedropper and adjust the In White points with the sliders.

Partials A, B, and Matte sliders: These are the Levels adjustments for the mattes we described above.

The Approach

Enough theory; let's get to work. Start with your own footage, or use the [**Ex.01*starter**] comp in this chapter's example project. You might also want to open the [**Ex.01_final**] comp and switch to it if you'd like to check the settings that worked for us. Here's the steps we typically go through when we're working with the CDK:

Step 1: Make sure the composition is at Full Resolution (Command+J) and set the layer to key to Best Quality (Command+U).

Step 2: Change the background color (Composition>Background Color) to the absolute opposite of the key color – for example, make the comp background orange or red if keying blue. By pulling a pretty decent key against the worse background color you could possibly imagine, it should look really good against a better matched background. This step is not required, but by setting up a challenge, you'll push yourself to try harder! Drag in the footage that you will be compositing your keyed footage over and turn it off for now; we'll check the key over this image after the key is pulled. We used AB_WhitePuffy.mov as our background.

Step 3: Double-click the layer to be keyed to open its Layer window and create a "garbage mask" (a rectangular or simple Bezier mask, see Chapter 13) around the image. Roughly cut out the action, and retain any shadows and hair. Animate the mask shape if the object moves a lot. This will save you from wasting time keying out the corners of the frame, where lighting tends to be uneven anyway. Close the Layer window when you're done.

Step 4: Apply Effect>Keying>Color Difference Key. Set up the effect in roughly the following order, but don't be afraid to adjust any slider at any time if you think it'll help the key. In general, our process is similar to that in the older version of the manual:

Step 5: Set the View to Matte Corrected.

Step 6: Pick the Key Color from the background, between your garbage mask and the subject you wish to keep, leaning closer toward the subject.

Step 7: Select the Partial A button under the right preview thumbnail, and using the Black Point eyedropper, set the Black In point to the lightest color in the background areas that really should be solid black. Remember to click in the Preview area for Partial A, not the Comp window. The Corrected Matte

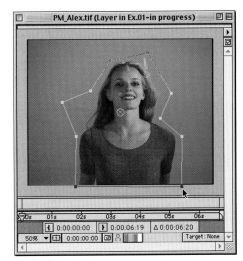

Step 3: Reduce your effort by creating a garbage mask that roughly encloses the foreground object.

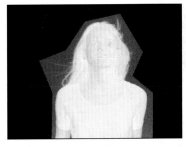

Step 4: The initial Matte (viewed in the Comp window by selecting Matte Corrected from the CDK's View popup) will probably start quite washed out.

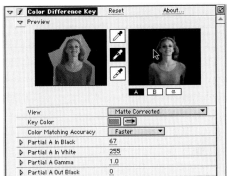

Step 7: Set the right thumbnail to show Partial A, select the Black eyedropper (the middle), and click on the lightest area of the background.

Step 8: After setting both Black points, the background in the Matte Corrected view should be pretty close to solid black.

should now have a darker background in the Comp window, and the Partial A In Black value will have changed.

Step 8: Select the Partial B button and similarly set the Black point also to the lightest color in the background that really should be solid black. The Matte being viewed in the Comp window should be pretty dark in the background area, and the Partial B In Black value will have changed.

Step 9: Next, instead of using the White Point eyedropper, set the White In point for both Partial A and Partial B (B might be more responsive), trying to turn the area you want to keep in the matte as close as you can to solid white. Keep the sliders in the high range; make sure increasing their values is actually helping. Don't overdue it, as overcranking the sliders can make the edges "spread" sometimes. If you can't get it solid white, don't panic; we have one more pair of sliders to set.

Step 10: To finish off, we need to make the alpha matte's background totally black and the foreground totally white. We do this by working directly on the alpha matte, using the Black In and White In controls.

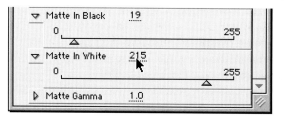

Step 9: Set both Partial's In White values using the sliders, not the eyedropper, for more exact control.

The important thing here is to increase the contrast by the *least* amount necessary: The more you crank the Black Point up and White Point down, the fewer gray levels you'll have in between. (This advice goes for the Partial A and B also, but it is more damaging with the matte values.) To see this, try moving the black-and-white slider so that they meet in the center at 128 each, and you'll get the point! Instead, start with the sliders at their initial positions, and let your cursor do the walking…

With the Info palette open (Command+2), run your mouse slowly around the background in the Comp window and read off the values of RGB. We need this value to be solid black, or 0, although you might initially find numbers in the double digits. Find the *highest* number that's not an aberration and make a note of it – say it is 20. Click on the value for Matte Black In from the Effects window, and type in this number. In this case, any pixels that fell in the range from 1 through 20 will now read 0 (remember how Levels works).

Step 10: After you determine what values the Matte In Black and In White should have, you can either drag the sliders or type in the values in their respective dialogs.

If you squeeze the Matte In settings too close together, you'll lose your grays (left), which will result in a harsh edge to the final key (right).

Similarly for the white foreground area, run your mouse over the foreground and make a note of what the *lowest* number is. Let's say you find values in the 230 range; type this number into the Matte In White value. Any transparent "holes" in the foreground area should now be solid white, or totally opaque.

If all is well, you should have a good texture in the edges of any fluffy hair, a solid black background, and solid white foreground.

Step 11: Switch the View to Final Output. Any blue spill areas will no doubt look pretty bad. Let's tackle those next.

Step 11: A good matte has solid black for the background, solid white for the body of the foreground object, and grays in the semitransparent areas and edges (left). Now you should have a pretty good key – but the fringes are blue (right). We'll use Spill Suppressor to tackle those next.

Step 12: To remove this blue fringing, use the Spill Suppressor effect – the default settings should work well.

Step 12: Apply Effect>Keying>Spill Suppressor, again from the Production Bundle. What this does is basically desaturate a chosen color (in our case, blue).

Make sure the cure isn't worse than the disease; you might want to skip ahead a step and turn on your background before going overboard reducing the spill, which might add a grayish tint to the edges. In fact, if the background already has a lot of blue in it (as ours does), then some blue spill might help "sell" the composite better.

Step 13: If you've used a challenging background color while pulling your key, the final image will probably look great against a better-matched background. There still is a slight halo, though; we'll need to tweak the matte just a little bit more in Step 14. Background courtesy Artbeats/White Puffy Clouds.

Step 13: Switch on the real background you're going to use for compositing with the keyed footage, and we bet your key appears a lot better than against red (particularly if the background has a lot of blue in it or is color corrected carefully to match the foreground).

Step 14: Finally, we decide whether the edges could be improved by choking. The first recourse is to select Matte Choker or Simple Choker from the Matte Tools submenu. These are great for real problem edges, but try this more subtle approach first: adjust the Gamma for the Alpha Matte in the CDK effect. By darkening the edges of the hair, you'll make those edge pixels more transparent, which is a mild choking effect itself. You might also adjust the Black In or White In points very slightly and see if you can't improve the key by tweaking some of the sliders you've already set. If you work a little harder you'll probably find that you don't need to apply a separate Matte Choker plug-in, saving render time later.

Fourteen steps hardly sounds easy. But if you've been poking around randomly in the Color Difference Key, now there'll be some method to the madness. Once you've got the hang of the CDK with [**Ex.01**], move onto [**EX.02*starter**] (the more challenging Water image). Our final versions of these two example comps include one possible solution – you'll find that with so many sliders, there can well be more than one solution.

Better Blending through Science

If you pulled a good key from some footage, you have reason to be happy. But it's no time to quit: That final bit of polish comes in matching your newly keyed foreground into its new background image.

A dead giveaway that a scene has been composited (aside from bad edges) is when the foreground and background images simply have different contrast and tonal ranges. You will see this sin left uncured even in feature films.

In [**Ex.03*starter**], the Water fountain footage is too green for the red sky (left) – an obvious giveaway. Color correct to taste to better match the red sky (right). Background courtesy Artbeats/Sky Effects.

Careful use of color correction can greatly aid in compositing disparate images, or further correcting a color cast in the foreground object caused by the lighting stage. For example, [**Ex.02_final**] has our water-drenched statue composited against a red sky. However, the statue, although very saturated, has a different tone than our sunset.

Open [**Ex.03*starter**] and experiment with different color correction effects to try to push the statue's color more toward its new background. Again, there is more than one right answer; we used the Effect>Channel> Channel Mixer to alter the red content of the image, then added a slight master hue shift with the Adjust>Hue/Saturation effect [**Ex.03_final**].

Other problems to watch out for are the black-and-white tones and the overall contrast. For example, in [**Ex.04*starter**] we took our statue and moved him out into the snow. He is way too dark for this scene, and needs lightening. A good place to start for these adjustments is Effect>Adjust>Levels. Gamma is usually the first parameter we grab – it leaves the black-and-white points intact and changes the gray levels between them. If the image needs more contrast, squeeze the Input Black and Input White sliders

closer together; if it needs less, squeeze the corresponding Output sliders.

With this vintage background shot, we also have a less saturated palette of colors to match. For an additional challenge, try blending the Water fountain with another backplate – the basic project is set up in [**Ex.05a**] with a variety of backgrounds to choose from.

We've also placed Alex against a new background in [**Ex.05b**], but be careful when color correcting not to change her skin tone to something too sickly!

The dark statue is out of place in this snow scene (left). Applying Effect> Adjust> Gamma and tweaking the gamma helps brighten it up, and Adjust>Hue/Saturation helps desaturate and shift its color to better match the scene (right). Background courtesy Artbeats/Retro Transportation.

Hire a Wizard

Throughout this book, we've made a point of sticking to solutions and techniques that use the After Effects Basic and Production versions of the program. However, there are some tasks that are simply made easier by other programs or third-party effects. One example of this is the Composite Wizard set of plug-ins from Puffin Designs (www.puffindesigns.com). If you are doing any amount of keying or other compositing work (such as blending 3D elements into scenes), this is a near-essential purchase.

The set includes a great selection of filters that feather, blur, and otherwise treat and improve the edges of layers being composited on top of other layers, as well as color correct them for a better match. One of the strongest effects of the set is Light Wrap, which takes the colors from a specified Background layer (or nested comp if you've more than one layer to wrap) and "contaminates" the edges of the keyed foreground image with the colors of the background. This helps fit the foreground keyed subject into the background by blending the edges better.

The difference between these two images is subtle but important. The first one (left) is an example of a regular keyed image; the second one (right) has Composite Wizard Light Wrap applied. Notice the highlights on the shoulders – this helps make the keyed footage look like it is interacting with the light in the scene, and melt into the background. Golf course background image © Corbis Images.

The Hue/Saturation effect can also be used to reduce the saturation of the key color (in this case blue).

Alternative Suppression

If you don't have the Spill Suppressor effect from the Production Bundle, you can also use Effect>Adjust>Hue/Saturation. This effect allows you to select a specific color range, then desaturate it. Selecting the color range from its Channel Control menu, tweak the range sliders underneath the first color bar to center around the color you're trying to remove and reduce the Master Saturation slider. See [**Ex.06**] for examples; it might help to turn off the key so you can see what effect the reduced saturation is having on the image.

Matte Tools

The Matte Choker effect was designed to help clean up problematic color keys where there may be holes or tears in the edges. The idea behind Matte Choker is to first spread the edges to fill in the holes, then choke them back in. Unfortunately, its default parameters are not ideal. For example, if you want to spread the matte first (which is what negative choke values do), the first Choke parameter should be negative, not positive.

Other Mousetraps

In addition to the keying effects available in the After Effects Basic and Production Bundles, numerous other companies have created their own keying filters for After Effects, either as stand-alone filters or as part of larger packages. Virtually all third-party effects developers have demo versions online for you to download and try for yourself. Here are our preferred alternatives to the After Effects keyers:

Primatte Keyer (www.puffindesigns.com)

Previously available as Photron Primatte for other high-end compositing systems, this After Effects newcomer yields excellent results – especially on hair and transparent edges. It's relatively intuitive and easy to use, focusing more on clicking on regions of the image than on manipulating sliders. Internally it works in three-dimensional RGB space, determining which parts of that space belong to the background, the foreground, or transitions between the two. You accomplish spill suppression and other correction by selecting specific colors and offsetting them from one of these regions into another. Primatte Keyer tracks the list of colors internally, and it uses its own Undo/Redo buffer. Our personal favorite.

Ultimatte (www.ultimatte.com)

The standard, available as hardware and as plug-ins for After Effects, Premiere, Media 100, Avid, and a number of other platforms. It works off a series of rules for color space manipulation, such as suppressing blue spill when blue exceeds green by more than green exceeds red. Unique to Ultimatte are filters that use a reference shot to remove background imperfections and an intelligent background grain/noise remover. It's complex – the parameters are not intuitive, and they balance off each other – but if you have some understanding of color space, and are willing to study the exceptionally detailed manual, you can get very good results.

Boris AE v3.0 (www.borisfx.com)

This pack of more than forty plug-ins includes several keyers, including variations on linear and luminance techniques, a stand-alone Matte Cleanup filter, plus its own advanced Chroma Key filter with spill suppression and a built-in garbage mask. It's easy to use and works surprisingly well on many (but not all) shots. If we had a complaint, it's a bit weak on spill suppression and hair, but it handled transparent water well.

Second, the higher the Gray Level Softness parameter, the less effect the Choke parameter has – and since the second Gray Level is set to 100%, you may think its Choke parameter is broken. Third, the Geometric Softness parameter is set a bit high for the first set of parameters (the spread pass) and low for the second set of parameters (the choke pass); try 2.0 as a starting value for both instead.

This effect can be used for softening edges, even if they are already clean. In this case, you can almost ignore the Choke parameters and treat Geometric Softness as an "amount of blur" parameter, with Gray Level Softness setting the blend. This application is demonstrated in [**Ex.07**].

For cleaning up less-tattered alpha channels, we use Simple Choker, particularly in cases where even correctly interpreting the alpha channel as Premultiplied still leaves a lingering black fringe or white halo around an object. This is a common problem with photos shot against a white background in

which the alpha isn't cut quite tight enough. A value of 1.0 or slightly under is usually a good starting point for Simple Choker.

This well-shot bluescreen footage was unfortunately mangled during the video transfer, resulting in rough edges (below left). To fix this, first blur the alpha, then choke it back in size (above). The result is a more acceptable edge (below right). Footage courtesy Artbeats.

Blur for Clarity

Another common trick for blending images into their backgrounds is to blur their edges so more of the background image will seem to leak around the foreground objects. This can also help repair bad edges of mattes that otherwise can't be pulled cleanly.

The best edge blurring tools are part of Puffin Designs Composite Wizard package. In a pinch, though,

you could use the built-in Effect>Blur & Sharpen>Channel Blur, which can blur each color channel, plus the alpha channel, individually. This means we can leave the color information sharp and smear just the matte. The downside of this is that the matte usually spreads out wider as a result of being blurred, revealing more of the background. You can rein the edge back in using Effect>Matte Tools>Simple Choker – positive values shrink the matte back down in size. Depending on your specific problem, you might have better results by reversing the order of the effects so you choke the edge first, then apply Channel Blur.

If there is a final piece of advice, it is not to beat yourself up looking for perfection. What looks unacceptable on a still image can be close to unnoticeable on moving video or film, when there is other action to watch as well as random interplays of noise, grain, and lights.

Connect

Using the Difference Transfer mode to find the differences between two layers was mentioned in Chapter 12.

Masking (including rotoscoping moving objects) was the subject of Chapter 13.

Track Matte techniques such as Luma Matting and the Remove Color Matting effect were explained in Chapter 14.

26 Plugging In Type

Managing effects that manage type.

O ne of the most important elements of motion graphics design is the effective use of type and numbers – for anything from clearly readable show titles to indecipherable background textures. Although we can't teach you design in one chapter, we can share with you some tricks for using After Effects' built-in text and number generators.

Solid layers default to Draft Quality, which looks pretty bad for text (top). Change the layer's Quality switch in the Time Layout window to Best to see the text properly antialiased (above) before tweaking any other parameters.

Basic Text

We rarely use Effect>Text>Basic Text for work that requires actual typography because it lacks flexibility in a couple of important areas. We use Effect>Text>Path Text (covered later in this chapter) for serious work, or we create the type in Adobe Illustrator. Having said that, Basic Text is great for simple titles and slates. It also has the advantage of allowing you to enter multiple lines of text with carriage returns inside one effect – unlike Path Text, which is limited to a single line.

Using Basic Text is easy. Just follow these simple steps (open comp [**Ex.01*starter**] if you want to practice while you read):

Step 1: Create a solid (Command+Y), the same size as the comp.

Step 2: Apply Effect>Text>Basic Text. The font dialog will open. This is where you specify which font you want to use and enter your text. Don't sweat these too much; you can change them later. Type in some words and click on OK.

Step 3: Your text will now appear in the Comp window, but it will look crunchy because it is not antialiased. Set the layer's Quality switch to

Example Project

Explore the 26-Example Project.aep file as you read this chapter; references to [Ex.##] refer to specific compositions within the project file. Most will use fonts we assume you already have, such as Helvetica, Arial, and Courier (the font used is mentioned in the Comments field in the Project window). Feel free to use whatever fonts you wish.

Font:	Style:
Courier	Regular

Direction:
- ● Horizontal
- ○ Vertical
- ☐ Rotate

Alignment:
- ○ Left
- ● Center
- ○ Right

Basic Text

☑ Show Font   [Cancel]   [OK]

When you add Effect>Text>Basic Text to a layer, you'll be asked to select a font and enter some text. Don't worry about getting it right; you can change the font and text later.

Best by clicking on it in the Time Layout window or by using the keyboard shortcut Command+U. You want to be in Best mode before tweaking any of the other settings.

Step 4: New to version 4.1 is the Display Options menu, where you can set the type to be drawn as Fill Only, Stroke Only, Fill Over Stroke, or Stroke Over Fill. The color swatches at the bottom control these colors. Note that the default bright red fill color is not broadcast-safe.

The other settings should be self-explanatory. If you need to change the font or text, click on the word Options near the top of Basic Text's parameter list in the Effect Controls window. While you can adjust the tracking (the overall letter spacing), there are no kerning controls to adjust space between individual characters. This is the main shortcoming of Basic Text for title design, unless you stick with monospaced fonts or fonts with good built-in kerning.

Basic Text can render significantly faster than Path Text. This is because once it is rendered for the first frame, the result is cached in memory and reused for subsequent frames. Hit the spacebar or play, or execute a RAM preview, and observe how quickly the comp renders to see this in action. Path Text has a number of parameters that can randomize from frame to frame; therefore it needs to be rerendered every single frame, slowing it down.

The Effect Controls window for Basic Text. If you want to change the font or text, click on the word Options along the top.

Isn't Kerning a Fruit Drink?

For those completely new to typography, it is important to know that most fonts do not look their best at their default settings – in other words, you can't just type in your text and leave it if you want to look professional. You'll need to learn about *tracking* (the average horizontal spacing between characters), *leading* (the vertical spacing between lines), and especially *kerning* (the space between individual pairs of letters). The first two are mainly aesthetic choices; the third is important to make sure your type doesn't look like it was created on a malfunctioning typewriter – you have to make sure characters aren't crowding each other or have so much white space between them that they look like breaks between words.

There are also other typesetting no-nos (such as using inch marks instead of real quotes) that you might like to brush up on, and there are a number of excellent basic typography texts available. Perhaps the best starting point is – depending on your operating system of choice – *The Mac Is Not a Typewriter* or *The PC Is Not a Typewriter* by Robin Williams, as well as her *Non-Designer's* series. She also has a book on font organization: *How to Boss Your Fonts Around.*

A Solid Tip

You can apply text effects directly to an image, though it's more common to apply them to a Solid layer on top of the target image. Then you can composite the type using a transfer mode and add effects such as drop shadows.

Effect Controls Panel

```
┌─────────────────────────────────────────────┐
│  ▤▤  Path Text 1 • Effect Controls  ▤▤ ▣ ▤  │
├─────────────────────────────────────────────┤
│ 🗲 Path Text 1      ▢◹                       │
├─────────────────────────────────────────────┤
│ Ex.02-Path Text 1 * Path Text 1             │
│ ▽ 🗲 Path Text    Reset  Options...  About...│▢│
│    Display Options      Fill Only      ▼     │▲│
│  ▽ Size                 36.0                 │▤│
│        0.0                          512.0    │ │
│             △                                │ │
│  ▷ Stroke Width         2.0                  │ │
│    Shape Type        ┌─────────────┐         │ │
│    Information       │ √ Bezier    │         │ │
│  ▽ Information       │   Circle    │         │ │
│        Font : Futura │   Loop      │         │ │
│        Text Length : 177.19  Line ▊│         │ │
│        Path Length : 198.99 └──────┘         │ │
│                             ▼                │ │
│  ▽ Path Control Points                       │ │
│        Tangent 1 /Circle Point  ⊹  80.0, 96.0│ │
│        Vertex 1/Circle Center   ⊹  64.0, 120.0│ │
│        Tangent 2                ⊹  240.0, 96.0│ │
│        Vertex 2                 ⊹  256.0, 120.0│ │
│    Path                  None ▼              │ │
│                       ▢ Reverse Path         │ │
│  ▽ Left Margin          0.00                 │ │
│     -2000.00                      2000.00    │ │
│             △                                │ │
│  ▷ Right Margin         0.00                 │ │
│    Alignment             Left    ▼           │ │
│  ▷ Tracking             0.00                 │ │
│  ▽ Kerning                                   │ │
│       ◀  │ Pa │  ▶                           │ │
│       ◀▶     0/1000 em  │Clear││Reset All│   │ │
│  ▷ Baseline Shift       0.00                 │ │
│  ▷ Character Rotation   0.0°                  │ │
│                       ✓ Perpendicular To Path│ │
│                         Vertical Writing     │ │
│                       √ Rotate Roman Characters│ │
│  ▷ Horizontal Shear     0.00                 │ │
│  ▷ Horizontal Scale     100.00               │ │
│  ▷ Vertical Scale       100.00               │ │
│  ▷ Visible Characters   1024.00              │ │
│  ▷ Fade Time            0.0%                  │ │
│    Mode                  Normal  ▼           │ │
│    Fill Color           ▢ │ ▭▶                │ │
│    Stroke Color         ▢ │ ▭▶                │ │
│                       ▢ Composite On Original│ │
│  ▽ Jitter Settings                           │▤│
│     ▷ Baseline Jitter Max    0.00            │▤│
│     ▷ Kerning Jitter Max     0.00            │▼│
│     ▷ Rotation Jitter Max    0.00            │▼│
│     ▷ Scale Jitter Max       0.00            │◹│
└─────────────────────────────────────────────┘
```

Path Text features a long list of parameters; many of the parameter subsets have been twirled open here for inspection. The first parameter you will need to learn is Shape Type; change it from the default of Bezier to Line to get normal, straight text.

Path Text

Users decried the basicness of Basic Text, demanding something more powerful. Ever accommodating, the After Effects programming team created Path Text, which floweth over with power. In addition to a variety of typographic controls such as kerning, Path Text allows text to follow a simple path or a mask shape. There are also numerous controls to randomize and animate the characters you enter. The biggest weakness is that you can enter only one line of text per application of the effect, with no carriage returns.

Applying Path Text is similar to applying Basic Text, and you can use it in place of Basic Text for most applications. However, it does feature a daunting number of parameters. The good news is that you can ignore most of them until the time comes when you decide you need a special look or feature. Open [**Ex.02*starter**], and follow these steps:

Step 1: Create a solid (Command+Y), the same size as the comp.

Step 2: Apply Effect>Text>Path Text. The font dialog will open. Here you specify which font you want to use and what text you want to appear. When you're finished, click on OK. Note that in Path Text, Return is the same as OK – it will not create a line break.

Step 3: Your text will now appear in the Comp window, but it will look crunchy because it is not anti-aliased. Set the Quality switch for the layer to Best by clicking on it in the Time Layout window or using the keyboard shortcut Command+U. You want to be in Best mode before tweaking any of the other settings.

Step 4: You will also note that your text is not in a straight line – it is in an arc, with a set of four path control points visible in the Comp window. These define a simple two-point Bezier path that the text will follow.

In the Effect Controls window, twirl down the Path Control Points to see the numeric coordinates for these points. Grab the control points in the Comp window and experiment with moving them around (if these points are not visible, make sure the name of the effect is highlighted in the Effect Controls window). The larger circles are the path end points; the smaller circles are the Bezier handles that bend the path. You'll notice the Path Control Points parameters update in the Effect Controls window as you drag. Hold down the Option key as you drag the handles for visual feedback as you edit.

Step 5: Select the Shape Type menu in the Effect Controls window. Change it to Circle or Loop. Notice that now the text is spread around a circle, with one control point defining the center and a second defining its radius. The two control points that are uncircled are unused now.

The difference between Circle and Loop is what happens if you have more text than will fit around the circle you've defined with the control points: Circle keeps spiraling on top of itself; Loop extends in a straight line off the end. If this is not obvious with your current text, click on the word Options along the top of the Effect Controls window, add more words, click on OK, then toggle between the Circle and Loop Shape Type settings.

To test how the text might animate around a circle or loop without setting keyframes, Option+drag the Left Margin slider. The radius control point (Tangent 1 in Pathspeak) decides where the circle begins and where the loop takes off if the text won't fit around the circle.

Step 6: Change the Shape Type popup to Line. The two Vertex control points now decide the end points of the line the text will sit along. If you have trouble dragging them to form a perfectly straight line, you can edit their coordinates numerically in the Effect Controls window – just click on the X/Y values to the right of Vertex 1 and Vertex 2. Note that you also can set these points by clicking on the crosshair

Path Text gives you up to four control points to manipulate the path your text will follow.

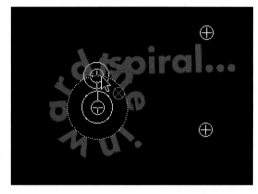

There are two options for circular text. Here, Shape Type is set to Loop, which means longer lines of text extend away from the circle in a straight line.

Kerning Tips

Path Text allows you to kern the spacings between characters – although the interface is a bit different than in other programs. Rather than being able to place a cursor between the letter pair you wish to kern, you need to open the Effect Controls window for the layer with Path Text applied and twirl down the arrow next to the word Kerning.

Select the letter pair to kern with the arrows to the left and right of the character display. The arrow pair below increases or decreases the kerning spacing in the minuscule increment of 1/1000th of an em space. (Compare that to Illustrator's default of 20/1000th of an em, which is on the large side.) Shift+ click on these arrows to kern in 10/1000 increments. Clicking and holding on these arrows also automatically increments and decrements the spacing.

Twirl down the arrow next to Kerning in Path Text's Effect Controls and click on the topmost pair of arrows to pick which letter pair you wish to kern.

Your new kerning will not be displayed in the Effect Controls window – watch the Comp window instead. Make sure the Path Text layer is in Best Quality, 100% magnification, and Full Resolution to accurately see your changes. **[Ex.03]** has been set up for you to experiment with.

Stopwatch Shortcuts

When an effect has lots of parameters (like Path Text), try this
trick: Option+click on the name
of a parameter in the Effect
Controls window to turn on the
stopwatch, then hit U to twirl
down animated parameters only
in the Time Layout window.

Hollow Words

Outline-only text is particularly
popular as a design element
these days. You can achieve this
look by setting Display Options
to Stroke Only.

icons in the Effect Controls window, then click where you want to place
them in the Comp window.

Step 7:   Experiment with the Left Margin slider in the Effect Controls
window; hold down the Option key as you drag the slider for instant
visual feedback. This parameter allows you to animate text along the
path you've defined. The Alignment menu further down this window
gives additional choices of how the text is spread out along your path.
Experiment with combinations of different Shape Type, Alignment, and
Margin settings.

Remember that you can animate these parameters – for example,
[**Ex.02_final**] demonstrates the combination of Loop and an animated
Left Margin. Animating the Left Margin is the preferred way to move text
around a circle or along a path, as opposed to animating the position of
the solid that Path Text is applied to, or its path control points.

Are we having fun yet? Good! You'll also notice that Path Text features
a host of typical typographic parameters, such as Display Options (the
Fill/Stroke and other options we discussed above for Basic Text), Size,
Stroke Width, Tracking, Kerning, Baseline Shift, Character Rotation,
Shear, Scale, and of course Fill and Stroke Colors. You can animate virtually all of them and can take advantage of the built-in Motion Blur (see
Chapter 11). Twirling down the arrow next to their names reveals a slider that can be Option+dragged for interactive adjustments. Experiment
with these and the rest of the parameters, referring to the online Help if
you're unfamiliar with any of their meanings. We'll also cover a few tricks
with Path Text that you may find useful.

Expansive Text

Here are a couple of tricks to add drama to words or phrases. The first is
very popular in commercials; the second is a less common trick that we
also like the look of.

The first technique animates the Tracking parameter. This expands
or contracts the spaces between characters and is demonstrated in
[**Ex.04a**]. Turn on motion blur if you expand or contract at a high speed
to avoid strobing.

Animated tracking yields the expanding
type look that is particularly popular in
commercials.

Note that if you have an odd number of characters and Alignment is
set to Center, the middle character will stay centered as the others
expand. You might want to add a space to the start or end to give an even
number of characters, and give this space a large negative Kerning value
so that its width doesn't offset your text too much.

The second technique animates the Horizontal Scale instead of
Tracking. The space between the centers of characters will not change;
however, the width of each character does. This results in each character emerging from a thin line – a peek-a-boo effect. It is demonstrated in

between the lines

between the lines

[**Ex.04b**]. The only weakness is that the characters scale from their left edges, not their centers, which can make letter spacing look a little funky during the animation.

The Typist

Previously, making text appear to type on required animating a mask with lots of hold keyframes. Now, it is just a matter of animating the Visible Character parameter in Path Text. A simple version of this technique is demonstrated in [**Ex.05a**]. If you don't like counting how many characters there are, Option+drag this parameter's slider in the Effect Controls window (or Option+drag next to this parameter's name in the Time Layout window to get the "magic slider") until the last character disappears and reappears to figure out the count.

To randomize the typing speed, you can use The Wiggler (Chapter 7). Select your Visible Character keyframes and apply Window>Plug-in Palettes>The Wiggler, set to be applied to the Temporal Graph, with low frequency and magnitude settings to prevent the typing from backing up. For starters, try 10 and 0.5, respectively.

Animated horizontal scale makes characters emerge from thin lines without expanding the overall width of the text.

Advanced Typist

If you like text typing effects, check out Text Typewriter in the Puffin Image Lounge set of effects (www.puffindesigns.com). It offers blinking cursors, raster scan lines, and grunge controls.

dissolve away · solve away

away

Also of use is the Fade Time parameter, which makes each character dissolve rather than pop on and off. Meanwhile, negative Visible Character numbers type backward (from right to left). These two techniques are demonstrated in [**Ex.05b**] and [**Ex.05c**].

Individual characters can also fade on and off as they type [**Ex.05c**].

$$pop\text{-}on = 0 \rightarrow 10$$
$$pop\text{-}off = (-10) \rightarrow 0$$

A Case of the Jitters

One of the most popular features in Path Text is its ability to randomize the movement of individual characters – great for nervous-style animations. This contrasts with using the keyframe assistants The Wiggler or Motion Sketch (discussed in Chapter 7), which are used to randomize the entire word.

To access these parameters, twirl down the arrow next to Jitter Settings at the bottom of the Effect Controls window. The baseline offset, kerning, size, and rotation of the characters can all be randomized. [**Ex.06**] demonstrates this randomized movement. Positive jitter values give smoother jumps; negative jitter values result in sudden jumps. In the case of negative values, these sudden jumps happen every frame; you might want to prerender an animation, re-import it, then slow it down to have the jumps occur at a slower pace. As with animated tracking, this movement honors the motion blur switch for the layer.

Path Text allows the size, scale, and position of characters to be randomized. The lower line also has motion blur enabled (Chapter 11).

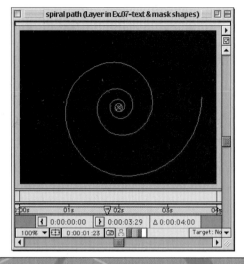

spiral path (Layer in Ex.07-text & mask shapes)

00s   01s   02s   03s   04s
0:00:00:00   0:00:03:29   Δ0:00:04:00
100%   0:00:01:23   Target: No

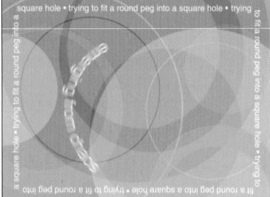

Text along a Shape

The fact that you can define a two-point path for your text to follow is nice, but nowhere near the end of the possibilities. As of version 4, you can use the Path popup to select any mask shape applied to this layer, allowing very complex paths. Also remember that you can copy and paste paths from Illustrator or Photoshop into After Effects (see Chapter 13 for details).

These techniques are demonstrated in [Ex.07]. One solid has a simple rectangular mask created inside After Effects. To orient the type in the direction we wanted, we needed to check the Reverse Path option; to keep the text confined to the closed path as it animated around it, the Shape Type must be set to Circle. A second solid has a path copied and pasted from the IllustratorSpiral.ai file (from the 26_Chapter Sources folder on the CD). We also animated the font's point size to emphasize the spiraling outward effect, and we enabled motion blur since it moves fast. In both cases, the Left Margin parameter was animated to move the text along these paths.

Path Text allows you to select a mask shape for its path. In [Ex.07], one of the paths (top left) was copied and pasted from Adobe Illustrator. The other was a simple rectangular mask. Background movie from the New Shoes/Cool Moves CD.

Credit Roll Issues

A common use of text is for credit rolls at the end of a program, where a long list of type scrolls up or down the screen. Although you can use Basic or Path Text to create this text, we prefer to typeset it in Illustrator and animate it as a single layer.

Due to the interlaced nature of NTSC and PAL video (explained in more detail in Chapter 37), there are some "magic" scroll speeds. Avoid any speed in pixels per second that is an odd multiple of the *field* rate of your video. For NTSC, this means 60, 180, 300, and 420 pixels per second; for PAL, the poison numbers are 50, 150, 250, 350, and 450 pixels per second. Using these numbers would cause details

of the text being displayed on only one of the two fields, resulting in a loss of half your resolution.

The best numbers are even multiples of the field rate: 120, 240, and 360 pixels per second for NTSC, and 100, 200, 300, and 400 pixels per second for PAL. Numbers between these might result in some strobing as the text moves an uneven number of lines per field; test-render and output to video to be safe. Softening the text with motion blur, shadows, and glows help smooth out artifacts.

For more hints, check out Adam Wilt's Web site www.adamwilt.com/Tidbits.html#CG – Adam spent nearly four years writing software for the Abekas A72 character generator, and he knows this subject well.

Playing the Numbers Game

Since the arrival of aliens and computers, animators have been asked to create graphical wallpaper with randomized numbers and symbols. The Numbers plug-in (don't worry – it's got nothing to do with math) was designed to help automate these tasks. Capable of creating random numbers and dates, the Numbers effect can also be keyframed to animate specific values and dates. The Numbers effect is fairly self-explanatory, and the After Effects online Help explains the individual parameters. We've included a few less obvious tips below:

• Numbers animate best when the font is monospaced, in which a 1 takes up the same space as an 8. To force a font to monospace, turn off the Proportional Spacing checkbox (new in 4.0).

• Numbers often generate unwanted characters, such as "0x" at the head of every Hex number, or the year when you need only the day and month. You might want to create your numbers in Comp 1 and mask out the unwanted areas in Comp 2. An alternate approach is to use a solid as a stencil alpha (see Chapter 15), which will exclude the unwanted data below. This is demonstrated in [**Ex.08**].

• The Value slider has a limit of 30,000. However, you have ten digits to the right of the decimal point, so if you animate between 0 and 1, you can count up to 9999999999 (although the precise step size might be a little uneven, due to internal rounding of numbers). Just mask out the unwanted leading number and decimal point. This is demonstrated in [**Ex.09**].

• Animated numbers usually look best changing at speeds less than 30 fps, so prerender at a slower frame rate and re-import, or render at 30 fps and conform the frame rate in the Interpret Footage dialog after you import it. This is simulated in [**Ex.10**] by slowing the comp's frame rate.

• Another trick shown in [**Ex.10**] is using the result as a matte, filled with another layer.

• The Random Values checkbox spits out random numbers. With the Value slider at its default of 0, values from –30,000 to +30,000 are generated. However, the numbers can be controlled: the Value amount sets the maximum value, positive or negative. For example, a Value of 99 generates numbers from 0 to 99 and avoids negative numbers. This is demonstrated in [**Ex.11**].

Numbers Wallpaper

Creating a "wallpaper" of random numbers often involves multiple uses of Effect>Text>Numbers. While this effect is pretty fast, we suggest you prerender a few seconds, loop, and reuse this movie at various speeds:

Step 1: Create a few seconds of randomized numbers in a small comp, at the largest size you'll need. An example of this is in the [**Ex.12**] folder as **Numbers_prerender**. Render at 30 fps uncompressed, with an alpha channel.

Randomized numbers look even more interesting when used as a matte for another image [**Ex.10**]. Texture from Digital Vision/Data:Funk.

must nest comp in order to see mask after effect.

The After Effects Numbers effect is used to create a movie of random numbers, which are then conformed to various frame rates and composited over an image using transfer modes. Background image from Digital Vision/Velocity.

Strange Math

Feed a strange font to the Numbers effect to simulate alien languages.

The Numbers effect can do more than just randomize numbers (1234567890) or Hex code (in which ABCDEF get thrown into the mix, with the sequence 0x always preceding it). Explore different fonts to create random masses of characters – particularly dingbats, which give a variety of symbols or hieroglyphics. Some fonts provide various engineering symbols (great for data readout simulations), while others hint at alien communications. The samples below show the ten numerals, and optionally 0xABCDEF, in the respective font.

On the **engineering** side, some favorites include:

• Adobe Universal Greek w/ Math Pi, which displays math symbols in place of numbers;

$$+ \quad - \quad \times \quad \div \quad = \quad \pm \quad \mp \quad {}^\circ \quad ' \quad ''$$

• Image Club Mini Pics Digidings, which includes various icons that suggest sound or light emanating, as well as a useful battery symbol for X in hexadecimal numbers;

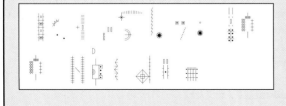

• Peter Grundy's DIY-Skeleton (published by FontShop as part of FUSE 15), which has glyphs that look vaguely like electronic schematic elements.

On the **alien communication** side, favorites include:

• Adobe Lucinda Math, which has a series of elegant minimalistic Greek-influenced symbols in its Extension weight;

• Fonthaus PF Household Items, which uses grids of dots in varying weights for numbers;

• A pair of circle-based iconic sets from FontShop's FUSE 10 collection: Atomic Circle and Robotnik-Uhura.

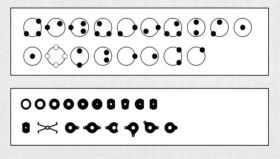

All of these would be great for random graphical elements or for purposefully indecipherable data displays. Of course, you can use them with the other text effects as well. If you can't find a font that has quite the symbols you want in the numbers positions, you can always hack your own using a font editing utility (such as Fontographer from Altsys) to copy and paste the desired symbols into the numbers' slots.

Step 2: Import the resulting movie. In the Interpret Footage dialog (Command+F), conform the Frame Rate to a lower rate, such as 15 fps. Loop as often as needed for the final animation length. The advantage of setting the speed by conforming rather than time-stretching is that you can change the frame rate without affecting any keyframes, and all duplicates will also be updated. However, time-stretching should work just as well if you're not applying keyframes.

Step 3: Import the movie a few more times, conforming each footage item to a different frame rate.

Step 4: Create a new "wallpaper" comp and drag in each of the number movies one by one, renaming each layer if you want to keep track of its frame rate. Then duplicate the layers as often as necessary, trimming layers so that they don't all start with the same first frame. Use the sources at different sizes, transparencies, transfer modes, and so on, for variety.

Inside the [**Ex.12**] folder is a sub-folder with our results. We took a slightly more complex path of arranging our numbers in a precomp, then using two copies of this in our final comp to create a fringing effect with blur.

Binary Numbers

One of the more time-consuming number tricks is creating a stream of seemingly random binary numbers, which vary only between 0 and 1. Unfortunately, the Numbers effect does not support this counting method. You could create a custom font in which you copy the 1 and 0 into the 2–9 slots, and use the Numbers plug-in, but here's a different approach, as demonstrated in folder [**Ex.13**]:

First we created several lines of random 1s and 0s in an Illustrator document (included on the CD in the Mattes_Maps_Spices folder), using the monospaced font Courier. The leading value was an easy-to-remember 50 points. A rectangle was created surrounding the numbers in a multiple of the leading value tall, in this case 600 points, and converted to Crop Marks.

When you import this 806×600 file into After Effects, create either a comp that's full size [**Ex.03a**] or one that crops off the numbers layer horizontally to the desired width, and a height that is some multiple of the leading value [**Ex.13b**]. A height equal to the leading (50) will display one line of numbers [**Ex.13c**].

Whichever size you create, you need to position the Illustrator binary numbers file so that it is nicely framed with no partially cropped digits. Apply the Channels>Offset effect – this tiles the source layer to an infinite size. Using Hold keyframes (Chapter 4), animate changes in the Y position value in the Offset effect that are again multiples of your leading. The binary numbers will seem to change randomly rather than just be moved to another position.

Copy and Paste Text

When you copy a text effect and paste, you paste only the settings, not the text and font. Duplicate the layer, or apply it as a favorite, to remember the text and font.

In a project for Xerox, we used random binary numbers animated in After Effects as a texture map (in Play's ElectricImage) to wrap around a model of a skull. To distress the perfectly clean Courier outlines, we applied the Production Bundle's Simple Choker to erode their edges.

Connect

Pasting paths from Illustrator to masks was covered in the *Motion Paths Meet Masks* sidebar in Chapter 13.

Chapter 19 contains explanations of the various effect parameter types.

27 Inside Illustrator

A few Illustrator survival skills for creating type and saving art to import into After Effects.

Adobe Illustrator is a vector-based drawing program that is often used to prepare type, logos, and other artwork. Because the art is vector-based, you can scale it to any resolution without losing quality. The following tips relate to preparing artwork for use in After Effects; these steps are compatible with Illustrator 8, which is recommended for use with After Effects 4.1. (The next chapter covers importing Illustrator files, and how best to rasterize the artwork inside After Effects.)

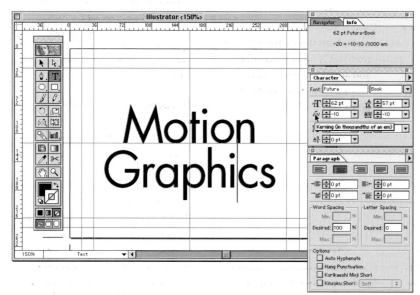

Illustrator 101

When you're preparing titles for video's 4:3 aspect ratio, the 8.5×11-inch page that Illustrator defaults to isn't all that helpful. Therefore, we've included ready-made templates on the accompanying CD with guides for action and title safe areas. There are four templates; these are based on the most common square-pixel video sizes (320×240 for tutorials, 640×480 for multimedia and older nonlinear editing systems, 720×540 for D1 NTSC square, and 768×576 for D1 PAL square).

Prior to After Effects 4.0, Illustrator type was rasterized (converted to pixels) in After Effects using Adobe Type Manager (ATM). Because ATM created problems for After Effects, such as strange kerning and out-of-memory errors, it was common to convert all type to *outlines* so that ATM would not be involved during the rendering process. More recent versions of After Effects use Adobe's CoolType technology to rasterize text, so saving as outlines is now optional.

Example Project

The 27-Examples folder includes examples of Illustrator 8 files with layers and outlines. The Goodies>Templates folder on the CD includes Illustrator templates for both video and film resolution.

You don't have to master Illustrator to set titles – all you need to master is the Type tool, plus the Character and Paragraph palettes.

Survival Guide

- **The bare essentials:** Using Illustrator, you can create multiple lines of type with different fonts and sizes for each line or character. But you don't have to be an Illustrator wizard to set good-looking type. If you're just getting started with Illustrator, avoid becoming overwhelmed by the feature list: Focus on the one chapter in the manual on creating type.

Most of what you'll use in Illustrator are in the Character and Paragraph palettes, available from the Type menu. Set the Fill color to Black and the Stroke to None (the / icon). Select the Type tool, click in the center of your frame, and type away. The type style may default to a tiny size and default font, so after you're done typing, select All (Command+A) to highlight the text and change the font size and leading.

- **Track and Kern:** If you don't want your title to look like it came off a cheapo character generator, spend some time tweaking the spacing between letters. It's guaranteed to pay off in a more professional-looking title.

Tracking adjusts the uniform spacing between more than two characters in highlighted type, while *Kerning* controls the spacing between two characters. So if the overall title is too loose or tight, start by adjusting the Tracking to a good "average" value. Since type for video tends to fatten up with antialiasing, don't tighten the letter spacing as much as you might for print output.

After you set tracking, kern character pairs that are too close together or too far apart. With the Type tool selected, place the cursor between two characters and close the space (Option+left arrow), or open the space (Option+right arrow). The value of each key click is set in the File>Preferences>Type & Auto Tracing, under Tracking, and is in 1/1000th of an em. We recommend a setting of 10 instead of the default 20.

- **Set Crop Marks:** Crop marks define the "layer size" (width and height) when your type is imported into After Effects. If no crop marks are set, the layer size defaults to strictly the size of the text. This is not a problem until you apply an effect that doesn't properly draw outside the layer boundary. If you use the supplied templates, the crop marks are already set to the full frame. Templates will import into After Effects with even increments in the width and height for maximum quality (see the *Resample* section in Chapter 4 if you've forgotten why this is important).

To define your own layer size with new Crop Marks, select the Rectangle tool and draw a rectangle around the art. Or click with the rectangle tool and define the exact size in a dialog. Either way, without deselecting the box you've drawn, select Objects>Cropmarks>Make. Voilà! The box is converted to crop marks.

- **Save as Illustrator:** Save the file as Illustrator 8 format. If necessary, convert type to outlines (select type with selection tool and then Type>Create Outlines). Save the outlines under a new name and import this file into After Effects.

Organize elements onto separate layers in Illustrator as you would like them to be grouped in After Effects. To move elements to a new layer, select them and drag the itsy-bitsy colored dot on the right side of the Layers palette to a new layer.

- **Layers:** To animate individual elements in your artwork, organize elements onto Layers in Illustrator – these will become separate layers in After Effects. Save normally. When you import into After Effects, use the File>Import>Illustrator as Comp option (more on this in the next chapter).
- **Sequences:** Crop Marks are critical when you're creating "cell animation" in Illustrator or making multiple files that need to be imported into After Effects in "register." Illustrator Sequences are handled like any other sequence format: Make a folder of same-size Illustrator files, numbered appropriately, import as a sequence and set the frame rate in the Interpret Footage dialog.

Working with Illustrator

Rasterizing Illustrator files in After Effects without annoying artifacts or error dialogs.

Verifying Versions

Occasionally, problems occur with certain combinations of After Effects and Illustrator. For example, After Effects version 3.1 and Illustrator version 7 had problems; After Effects 4.1 and Illustrator 8 work better together.

Example Project

Explore the 28-Example Project.aep file as you read this chapter; references to [Ex.##] refer to specific compositions within the project file.

Adobe Illustrator is a terrific complement to After Effects – its vector-based tools are powerful, and it creates complex typography quickly and easily. It also tends to be the program of choice for creating logos, so even if you don't use Illustrator yourself, you'll likely receive files in this format from clients and print designers. This chapter focuses on how best to use lllustrator art with After Effects and how to take advantage of the resolution independence of vector art.

Illustrator Art 101

After Effects can import Illustrator files from its regular File>Import> Footage Files menu option. You can use this to import a single layer Illustrator file, one layer out of a multilayer Illustrator file, or to treat all the layers in a multilayer file as a single layer (known as *merging*). You can also import a sequence of Illustrator files: save them with sequential numbers and import them as a sequence by enabling the "Generic EPS Sequence" checkbox in the Import dialog. Beyond these options, you can import a multilayer Illustrator file as an After Effects composition; we will discuss this in more detail later.

After Effects will automatically rasterize Illustrator vector-based files into bitmaps as needed, with very clean edges. The area considered the "paper" in Illustrator becomes transparent in After Effects, automatically creating an alpha channel upon import.

We tend not to color our shapes and text inside Illustrator; instead, we give them color with effects inside After Effects. Color isn't even necessary when Illustrator shapes are used as alpha track mattes. If you want to color your art in Illustrator, create colors using RGB colorspace – not CMYK – for best results. If you need white type in Illustrator, work in Artwork rather than Preview mode to be able to see it against Illustrator's standard white background.

It's a good idea to make your vector files large enough that you will not need to scale them over 100% in After Effects. If you do need to scale larger, you can turn on the Continuous Rasterization option in the Time Layout window, and they will cleanly scale to whatever size you need. However, you will incur a slight render time hit for this feature, and you won't be able to apply masks or effects to these layers (more later).

The Perfect Path

Any fonts used in Illustrator are converted to outlines when you import into After Effects – assuming you have the font installed and active on your system. If you move the project to another machine for rendering, or to set up a network render, you'll need to install and open the fonts on those machines as well.

If you'd rather have the flexibility to move the project without thinking to another machine to render, or share the project easily with others, create outlines from your text in Illustrator before importing into After Effects. To do this, save the original file with the font data in case you need to edit the type later. Then select the type with the selection tool

(not the Type tool) and go Type>Create Outlines. Save the file again and use this version in After Effects. *Note: All the Illustrator text elements in this book are saved as outlines so they will look exactly the same on your system.*

The disadvantage to outlines is that hot keying from After Effects to Illustrator (see Chapter 8) to edit a typo or make changes will open the outline file, not the original. You'll need to close the outline file, open the original, make your changes, and save. Then create outlines again and save over the first outlines file using the same name. When you return to After Effects, the outlines will be reloaded automatically since the file is seen as having been updated.

Illustrator as a Layer

Let's get some practice importing and setting up Illustrator files. Go to File>Import>Import Files (or Command+I), navigate to the book's CD, then to the Sources>Text subfolder. Select the file **nightlife_one layer.ai** and click on OK. Since this file contains only a single layer, it will be imported directly at this point. Open comp [**Ex.01*starter**] and drag this footage item from the Project window to the Time Layout window.

You'll notice three things at this point: the type is black (and therefore hard to read against the background image we already selected – even more so against the black default comp background color), not necessarily positioned where we want it, and very blocky or aliased in appearance. Let's tackle those problems, starting with the aliasing.

Click on the Quality switch for this layer in the Time Layout window and set it to Best (Command+U). The text will now look clean and antialiased. Move the layer into a nice position in the sky area above the city skyline.

Since the title is plain black Illustrator text, apply Effect>Render>Fill. This fills layers – including Illustrator artwork – with the color of your choice. Click the color swatch and pick any color; white is a good starting point. Compare your results with [**Ex.01_final A**].

All new layers in After Effects default to Draft Quality, which looks particularly bad for Illustrator files (left). The first thing we do after adding an Illustrator item to a comp is set its quality to Best, which results in very clean antialiasing (right).

Our Illustrator text antialiased, positioned, colored, and with a drop shadow in After Effects. Background courtesy Artbeats/Establishments Urban.

Crop Marks

If you do not place crop marks in your Illustrator file, After Effects will automatically crop the result upon importing to the edges of the outlines in the file. We prefer to set crop marks beyond these edges.

Hot Key into Illustrator

If you need to make changes to the Illustrator art from within After Effects, select the Illustrator layer and type Command+E. This will launch Illustrator. Make the necessary changes, save the file, and return to AE – the file is updated automatically. See the sidebar *Hot Keying* in Chapter 8.

If you'd like the color to animate, we suggest you *don't* animate the color in the Fill effect – color swatch parameters in general interpolate in a straight line across the color wheel, often going through unwanted saturation changes on the way. Instead, follow the Fill effect with the Adjust>Hue/Saturation effect and animate Hue instead (denoted as Channel Range in the Time Layout window).

Although After Effects is a flat, 2D program by nature, we like to give our layers a bit of depth. The most common treatment for Illustrator text and logos is to add Effect>Perspective>Drop Shadow to lift it off the background. We tend to increase the Softness and decrease the Distance parameters from their defaults. Drop shadows can shift the apparent position of a layer; you might want to nudge its position a little in the opposite direction from the shadow to rebalance the final image. The result of these treatments can be seen in [**Ex.01_final B**].

Other favorite treatments include Effect>Perspective>Bevel Alpha to give the text some dimension, Blur & Sharpen>Blur to make it recede, or Stylize>Glow (normally a Production Bundle effect, but included free from Adobe on your CD) when cool is called for. And since Illustrator files include an alpha channel, they can be used as an alpha matte by other layers (discussed in Chapter 14) for that classic video-inside-text effect, or just to fill it with an interesting texture.

Illustrator as Comp

As of version 4.1, you can now import Illustrator files as a composition, allowing you to animate separate objects inside After Effects more easily. In Illustrator, you would organize objects onto the same layer that should be grouped together for animation purposes, then place objects you wish to animate separately on their own layers.

Say you (or The Client) wanted the *Nightlife in the City* title from the first example above to be animated as two lines, one appearing later than the other. Rather than cut them apart from each other using masks, we saved a second version of the title from Illustrator with each line on its own layer. You could choose File>Import>Import Files twice, selecting the two separate layers each time. A quicker way of working would be to select the option File>Import>Illustrator As Comp. Navigate to the Text subfolder in the Sources folder that came on the enclosed CD and import **nightlife_two layers.ai**.

You should notice that two items have been added to your project: a folder and a composition, both with the name of the imported footage item. The folder contains a footage item for each layer in our Illustrator file. Each of them are 256×100 pixels, determined by the crop marks we placed when we created this file. There are several paths you can now take to get our background behind this type:

Approach 1: Assuming you have already started a composition with your background which you would now like to add your type to (such as [**Ex.02-Two Layers*starter**]), open the [**nightlife_two layers.ai**] comp that After Effects created when you imported this file, Edit>Select All (Command+A), then copy and paste these layers into your existing background comp.

Approach 2: Change the size of the [**nightlife_two layers.ai**] comp to 320×240 (the size of the background image we want to use), then add your background – such as the AB_EstabUrban.mov.

Approach 3: Use the comp After Effects created after importing as a precomp, and nest this precomp into a comp where you add or already have the background. For example, drag [**nightlife_two layers.ai**] into [**Ex.02-Two Layers*starter**].

Depending on your project, one of these routes will emerge as the obvious choice. Either way, the two lines of type are separate elements that you can animate as desired. [**Ex.02_final**] shows one approach, which uses Effect>ICE FEC>FE Vector Blur (free on your CD) applied to the title, and the subtitle animated with a mask – a technique explained in more detail in Chapter 13. Feel free to experiment with your own text treatments.

Whichever route you take, note that each layer is the same size as the original file. If you want to scale or rotate around the center of a line of type rather than the center of the layer (they often aren't the same), you'll need to move the anchor point to the center of the layer – see Chapter 6 if you forgot how.

Final Blur

[**Ex.02_final**] uses the intriguing FE Vector Blur effect from ICE's Final Effects package – it's free on the book's CD, courtesy ICE (www.iced.com).

Paths as Masks

Remember that you can copy a path in Illustrator and paste it into the Layer window as a mask. This gives you access to individual points to animate. See Chapter 13 for details.

Layer Size and Resampling

If you have not set crop marks in Illustrator, the source's size will be auto-cropped to just barely fit all the objects; if you have set crop marks, those will determine the size of the layer in After Effects. If you've been using workarounds like empty boxes or dots to force the layer size, check out the crop marks feature (covered in Chapter 27). Also, be sure to create crop marks when you're creating sequences so that every frame will appear to be the same size to After Effects.

Back in Chapter 4 we covered the problem of layers appearing softer because one or both of their dimensions consisted of an odd number. For instance, if the file was imported as 321 pixels wide, the layer would be resampled (antialiased) when it was placed in a comp that was 640 pixels wide, even at 100%. The same is true for the vertical dimension.

This is a problem for any file, but it's harder to control for Illustrator files than for Photoshop, which has a handy Canvas Size feature.

If you create your own crop marks in Illustrator, you might think that if you create a rectangle with no stroke and even dimensions and convert this box to crop marks, that will work. The irony is that creating an odd-sized rectangle for the crop marks has more chance of succeeding. Go figure.

To help you create Illustrator files with even dimensions, we've included ready-made templates in the Goodies folder on the accompanying CD. These templates have crop marks already set up to full frame size. There are four templates, based on the most common square-pixel video sizes (320×240 for tutorials, 640×480 multimedia, 720×540 D1 NTSC, and 768×576 D1 PAL), and they include guides for action and title safe areas.

Illustrator files are automatically rasterized at 100% scale (left). When scaled up to a larger value, such as 500%, they can look pretty ugly (center). Enabling Continuous Rasterization causes them to be rerasterized at their current scale value, resulting in crisp outlines at any size (right).

When applied to Illustrator layers, the Collapse switch in the Time Layout window (where the cursor is pointing) enables Continuous Rasterization.

Collapsing and Rasterizing

When an Illustrator file is imported into After Effects, you can think of it as being automatically rasterized into pixels at 100% of its original size. As long as you restrict this layer's Scale parameter to 100% or less, and its Quality switch is set to Best, it will be treated just like a pixel-based footage item and remain sharp and antialiased. However, if you scale it past 100%, things start to fall apart.

You can observe this in [**Ex.03*starter**]; make sure the comp is at Full resolution and 100% magnification. Notice how the text originally appears blocky and aliased. Set its quality to Best, and now it is antialiased. Adjust its scale to less than 100% (Option+drag to the right of the Scale parameter name in the Time Layout window to get the "magic" slider), and it continues to look sharp. Now click on Scale's numeric value, and enter a number larger than 100%, such as 500%: notice how ugly the edges appear. This is because After Effects is rasterizing the text at 100%, then scaling up these pixels five times.

Now for some real magic. In the Switches column of the Time Layout window, click once on the Collapse Transformations/Continuously Rasterize switch (the hollow circle below the "sunburst" icon) for our layer. Surprise! The edges are rendered sharp again. Better yet, no matter what size you scale the text, it remains crisp. This is because After Effects is applying the Scale value to the original Illustrator file, *then* converting the larger text to pixels. This process is known as *Continuous Rasterization*.

No Free Lunch

Since your problem is now solved, apply the Effect> Perspective>Drop Shadow to your 500% scaled, continuously rasterized text in [**Ex.03**], and knock off work early.

Not so fast, eh? After Effects flashed you with a dialog warning you that "You can't do this because this layer is currently collapsed." You'll get the same error message if you try to use the masking tools. If you uncollapse the layer to apply the effect, you're back to fuzzy text – with a fuzzy shadow thrown in (because transformations such as scale happen after effects). And if a mask or effect is already applied to an Illustrator layer, the Collapse switch is inactive.

> You can't do this because this layer is currently collapsed. Choose Uncollapse to uncollapse the layer and perform your action.
>
> [Cancel]   [Uncollapse]

The dreaded Uncollapse dialog – you can't directly apply masks or effects to a collapsed layer.

Rasterize 101

If you're a bit fuzzy on how the process of rasterization works inside After Effects, take a few minutes and run through this exercise in Photoshop – it should help you understand what's really going on.

Illustrator files are often referred to as having *resolution independence*. But to use them in video, they must be converted to pixels at some point. Once they're pixels, it's just as easy to make a mess blowing them up as it is with any other pixel-based image.

Both source files used below can be found in the CD>Example Projects>28-Example Project> Photoshop Test folder (or you can make a circle yourself in Illustrator and save it twice to disk).

Test #1: Open Photoshop, and then File>Open the Illustrator file **Rasterize_Scale source.ai**. The Rasterize EPS dialog will be presented. Select 100% for both width and height, 72 dpi resolution, and Grayscale mode. Check that Antialiasing is on, and click OK.

You'll see a small black circle on a checkerboard pattern. Flatten the image (Layers palette>Flatten Image); it should now appear against a white background.

Select Image>Image Size, set the Pixel Dimensions Width and Height popups to percent, and scale the image 1000% width and

In Test #1, the Illustrator circle has been rasterized first at 100%, then scaled to 1000% in Image Size. Notice the degradation around the edges. (This is the equivalent of scaling in After Effects with continuous rasterization off, where scaling happens after rasterizing.)

height. Click OK. The circle should look really fuzzy – this is because rasterization creates a small number of pixels which are then scaled up ten times.

Test #2: We saved the source Illustrator file twice, so File>Open the second file, **Scale_Rasterize source.ai**, but this time select 1000% for width and height in the Rasterization dialog. Click OK, and select Flatten Image again.

Notice that this circle has essentially the same number of pixels in width and height as the file in Test #1, but if you view both images at 1:1, the second file is noticeably sharper. The difference is the order in which the files were processed.

In the first example, the outlines are converted to pixels at 100%, giving you a 1-pixel-wide antialiased edge, then these pixels are scaled ten times. The result is that the image falls apart. In the second example, the scaling was done in the Rasterize EPS dialog so that the illustrator path was scaled *before* the path was converted to pixels, not unlike scaling the file in Illustrator itself.

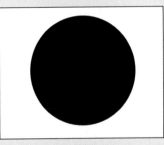

In Test #2, the same circle was processed in reverse – scaling was applied in the Rasterize EPS dialog, then the paths were rasterized. The result is a crisp, antialiased edge. (This is the equivalent of scaling in After Effects with continuous rasterization on, where scaling happens before rasterizing.)

What's this got to do with After Effects? Everything, as it happens, because After Effects uses the same code to rasterize Illustrator files. And just like in the above test, you can choose whether to rasterize before or after scale.

Now back to our scheduled programming…

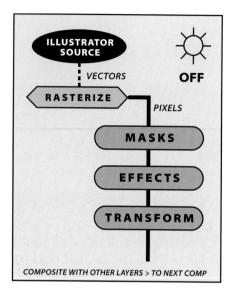

With Continuous Rasterization off (the default), the Illustrator file is converted to pixels at the source and is then treated like any other pixel-based image.

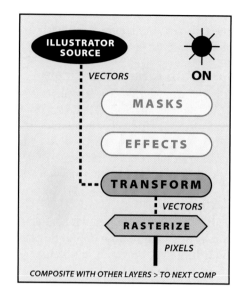

With Continuous Rasterization turned on, the Illustrator file bypasses Masks and Effects and is sent directly to Transformations for scaling. Mask and Effects can be applied in Comp 2.

Stating the Obvious

If you find yourself continuously rasterizing your Illustrator art, consider the obvious: you could always scale the text larger in Illustrator and use this larger text instead. Since there's now no need to scale the art in After Effects, you're free to apply masks and effects.

So a good rule of thumb is to avoid making small text in Illustrator that always requires scaling larger than 100% in After Effects. If you don't plan on the text being enormous, create it at the size you need, or a little larger to be on the safe size. Life will be simpler this way. Plus, when you scale between 0% and 100%, rendering will be fast and, at least to our eyes, it even looks a little sharper when it's scaled down. Reserve continuous rasterization for when large-scale values are called for and creating a huge Illustrator file is impractical.

Consider the rendering order for Illustrator files. There are two points at which a file can be rasterized, and the Collapse switch toggles between them. When the Collapse switch is off (hollow), the text is rasterized at 100%, then these pixels pass through the Masks, Effects, and Transform stages.

When the Collapse switch is turned on (filled in), the Illustrator outlines are passed directly to Transform, where Position, Scale, and Rotation are applied to the actual vectors. The newly sized outlines are then rasterized. The Masks and Effects stages are bypassed since they can't operate on paths, only pixels, and the pixels are not created until later in the rendering order.

So how do you apply a drop shadow to your text? Since the rendering order doesn't allow it in one comp, the solution is to do the effect over two comps. Zoom the text in Comp 1, nest Comp 1 into Comp 2, then apply any mask or effects in the second comp. This is shown in the [Ex.04] folder. If you turned on the Collapse switch in Comp 2, the Continuous Rasterization would be carried through from Comp 1 – you could scale it even further, but you would then have to apply masks and effects in Comp 3.

More Illustrator Tricks

Before we finish with Illustrator files, there are a few more tips and tricks we want to share with you.

Zooming with Exponential Scale

In Chapter 7 we discuss the Exponential Scale keyframe assistant (Production Bundle only), which makes zooming the scale of a layer look more realistic. This effect is particularly obvious for large changes in scale, such as from 0 to 1000%. Most footage items look bad at such extreme scalings, but continuously rasterized Illustrator files retain their sharpness, making them good partners for this keyframe assistant.

Dot Zoom

The *dot.com* bonus tutorial on the CD demonstrates using Exponential Zoom with Continuous Rasterization to zoom into a "dot"….

Gradient Shootout

If you create blends and gradients in Illustrator, you need to pay extra attention to how you handle these files. Oddly enough, Illustrator gradients look better when they are set to Draft Quality; set them to Best, and a series of odd lines appear in them, including artifacts in their alpha channels. Since we mentioned earlier that you should always set your Illustrator files to Best Quality, this is a bit of a conundrum.

The secret is to go into the Interpret Footage dialog for these items (Command+F from the Project window), click on Options, and set the Antialiasing popup to More Accurate. Gradients will now render smoothly at Best Quality as well. (The Interpret Footage dialog is discussed in more detail in Chapter 36.)

To see this in action, open [**Ex.05**]. You'll notice the middle example – the one in Best Quality – looks bad. Find the Gradient_illus8.ai file in the Sources>28_Chapter Sources subfolder in the Project window, and set its antialiasing option as above. For comparison, we've included a gradient created with After Effects' Render>Ramp effect; notice it renders smoothly as well.

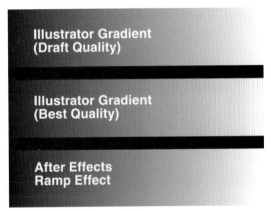

Some Illustrator blends and gradients do not rasterize cleanly at Best Quality (the middle example here). This can be fixed by setting their Interpret Footage antialiasing option to More Accurate.

Alpha Add with Illustrator Layers

If you use Illustrator, you might have used the Knife tool to cut up text and logos. (If not, take a break and try it out – it's kind of like being in a really cheap slasher movie, but no one gets hurt…) Shapes that have been "cut" with the knife always share the same edge, which is great when you need to line them up, but not so great when you find the edges are not seamless.

In [**Ex.06*starter**] you'll find two sides of a broken heart shape, slashed into two pieces using Illustrator's Knife tool. Each side of the heart is on a separate layer, as the file was imported using the Import Illustrator as Comp feature. Set the comp's zoom level to 400% so you can see the seam, and select the Alpha Add transfer mode (originally covered in Chapter 15) for the top layer. The seam will disappear.

Connect

The anchor point was the subject of Chapter 6.

The Exponential Scale keyframe assistant was animated in Chapter 7.

Masks were animated in Chapter 13.

Track mattes were revealed in Chapter 14.

Setting crops marks and creating layers in Illustrator was covered in Chapter 27.

Further mysteries of the Interpret Footage dialog will be uncovered in Chapter 36.

 Working with Photoshop

Turning Photoshop layers into After Effects layers.

Adobe Photoshop is the industry standard paint program many people use to create their pixel-based still image artwork. It is common to take Photoshop art into After Effects to animate or treat it further. We can't teach you how to use Photoshop in one chapter; fortunately, there are many excellent books and videos available to bolster your Photoshop skills. What we can (and will) show you are some tips and gotchas for managing Photoshop files inside After Effects.

Layered files need to be saved as Photoshop files to keep the layer elements separate. If only a Background layer is present in Photoshop's Layers window, then it is a single image file and can be saved to many different formats.

Photoshop Flavors

There are several ways to import Photoshop artwork into After Effects, and those options are affected by how you saved the file from Photoshop in the first place: as a single image or as a layered file.

A single image would consist of one *Background* layer (identified as such in Photoshop's Layers window), which you can save as almost any file format. If the Flatten Image command is grayed out in the Layer Options menu, then it already is a single Background image. Note that sometimes your Photoshop file will appear to have just a background layer, but it is in fact a layer with transparency. To export this image in a format nonlinear editing systems prefer, you will need to flatten it first, or use Save a Copy which will automatically flatten it during the save process.

When a file has layers, it must be saved as a Photoshop format file to retain those layers as individual elements. You can flatten the layers to merge them to a single background layer, which can again be saved in whatever format you wish, but the layers would then lose their individuality, making it near impossible to edit and animate them as separate elements later.

Fortunately, After Effects understands layered Photoshop files. If your goal is to eventually import the image into After Effects, there is no real reason to flatten in Photoshop, since After Effects can flatten (merge) layers upon importing or import the layers intact.

The type of file you save from Photoshop, and how you import it into After Effects, has an impact on what you get and how big the image is.

Example Project

Explore the 29-Example Project.aep file as you read this chapter; references to [Ex.##] refer to specific compositions within the project file.

Practice the last three options below with the TaiChiChuan.psd file in the Chapter Sources folder of this chapter's project. The available permutations are:

Import Single Image: Create or open a single image file in Photoshop (such as AB_LifestylesMixedCuts.tif in the Chapter Sources folder), or flatten layers for a multilayer file (such as TaiChiChuan.psd). Save to virtually any file format – PICT, TIFF, Targa, and JPEG are the most common. Import into After Effects using the normal File>Import>Import Footage Files command. The result is the same size as the original image; it may have just RGB color channels or RGB plus alpha. The alpha type will depend on how you created the file.

Import Merged Image: Create a layered image and save as a Photoshop format file. Import into After Effects using its normal File>Import> Import Footage File command. A second dialog box will appear, defaulting to the option Merged Layers. If this is what we want; click OK. This will create a single image in After Effects, the same size as the original canvas in Photoshop. All layers are merged, with any Layer Effects calculated, and their transparency summed to create an alpha channel premultiplied with white. Note only the merged option creates a premultiplied alpha; the other choices result in a straight alpha.

Import Single Layer: Create a layered image and save as a Photoshop format file. Import using the normal File>Import>Import Footage File command. A second dialog box will appear; select the name of the layer you wish to import and click on OK. This will create a single image in After Effects, *automatically cropped in size to the nontransparent borders of the image in that layer*, with a straight alpha channel. (Note that if you have only one layer, you might want to import as merged so the layer will be the same size as the original canvas in Photoshop.) This auto-cropping feature trips up many users who bring in layers one at a time, since they now have to manually realign the layers when they rebuild the original Photoshop image. Also, if the layer had any Photoshop Layer Effects applied, they are ignored.

Hot Keying

You can select a Photoshop file in After Effects and Edit>Edit Original (Command+E) to hot key to Photoshop. See Chapter 8 for more details.

Tai Chi Chu'an
raise hands play guitar grasp b
Background
Choose a layer: ✓ **Merged Layers**

[Cancel] [OK]

When importing a layered Photoshop file using the normal Import Footage command, you can select a specific layer in the file, or choose to merge (flatten) them together into one image.

Resampling

If a layer has an odd number of pixels defining one or both of its dimensions, it may not render as sharp inside After Effects in Best Quality as it appears in Photoshop. As we discussed in Chapter 4, an odd number of pixels causes the object to center on a half-pixel, causing After Effects to antialias it. To avoid this, use the Image>Canvas Size function in Photoshop to add a pixel in one or both dimensions as required so that they both end up with even numbers of pixels.

Another important tip is that you don't want to scale past 100% in After Effects – beyond this point, you're just blowing up pixels, which results in a fuzzier image. Make your image big enough in Photoshop to begin with. When we scan in images, we purposely scan them about twice the size we anticipate we need. If we need to do any masking, it's easier to cut precise masks with larger images. The downside is that the larger the image, the more RAM you'll need in After Effects, and the slower the image will be to manipulate. Therefore, we save the large version of the file for safety, then scale it down by half or so to create a thriftier version to import into After Effects. (More info in the *Dots, Pixels, and Inches* sidebar in Chapter 6.)

When you import a layered Photoshop file as a comp, it creates a folder with the individual layers and a comp where they are combined.

Import Layers as Comp: Create a layered image and save as a Photoshop format file. Import using the special File>Import>Import Photoshop as Comp command. After Effects will create a project folder that contains a footage item for each layer of the file, each with a straight alpha channel. Although the layer files are still auto-cropped, After Effects also automatically creates a composition the size of the original image, with all these layers already imported – and most important, properly aligned.

With the Import Photoshop as Comp function, Photoshop options used to blend layers – such as opacity, mattes, and transfer modes – will also be carried into After Effects. The real action occurs if you applied any of Photoshop's Layer Effects. After Effects will add a custom Photoshop effect to these layers, which can be edited and animated just like any other effect. The catch is that some of these Layer Effects require additional trickery such as their own transfer modes, preserve transparency switches, and even entire precomps to re-create, so the hierarchy can be initially confusing. At a minimum, you should rename the precomps (which After Effects gives the name *Layer Effects comp*) to help keep things straight. If you are intensely interested in further untangling the hidden secrets of Layer Effects, see TechTip 11 on the enclosed CD.

Nondestructive Editing

Import Photoshop as Comp is particularly useful for those who interface with a print-based art department that creates their artwork as Photoshop layers – you can import their files as compositions, with access to the individual layers, allowing you to animate their designs.

That said, we almost never work this way… If we know we're going to build a layered image, we'll do it directly in After Effects. Many of Photoshop's functions are destructive, in that pixels are changed and resampled far too easily. With After Effects, we can change our minds on issues such as scaling and effects as many times as we want, without losing resolution.

The exception to the above rule is when we need access to paint and cloning tools, which After Effects lacks. We perform jobs such as photo retouching in Photoshop, then import the file into After Effects for further manipulation. We'll also create some non-animating elements such as matte layers in Photoshop to save rendering time in After Effects.

On the flip side of the coin, print artists should seriously consider creating their images in After Effects – then they can enjoy the benefits of non-destructive editing and the ability to tweak their effects and transformations after they're applied. For example, the cover for this book was created completely in After Effects by co-author Trish Meyer.

After Effects version 4.1 increased the composition size limit to 30,000 pixels in each dimension, which allows it to tackle all but the largest print images (assuming you have enough RAM). When you're done, you can use Composition>Save Frame As to save as a still image, with or without alpha. If you need separate layers, use Composition> Save Frame As>Photoshop as Layers.

After building a rough composite in Photoshop, we imported the layered file as a composition, swapped out a movie for the background layer, and added some animation to the layers in **[Ex.02]**. Tai Chi footage from Artbeats/Lifestyles Mixed Cuts.

Sequence Cells

If you create cell-type animation, create each frame on a separate layer in Photoshop. Import Photoshop as Comp, select all layers, and use Layer>Keyframe Assistant>Sequence Layers (Chapter 9) to sequence them in the Time Layout window.

Photoshop Tai Chi

[**Ex.02**] contains an example of using a combination of Photoshop and After Effects to create a final animation. A single frame of the movie AB_LifestylesMixedCuts was exported from [**Ex.01**] as a still image (Composition>Save Frame As, or Command+Option+S) and opened in Photoshop to use as a reference background. Two text layers – one using a Drop Shadow Layer Effect and the other applied in Overlay mode – were added. The resulting composite was saved as the Photoshop layered file TaiChiChuan.psd and imported using the Photoshop as Comp option.

The composition After Effects built as a result of this command was renamed [**Ex.02**] and lengthened to 08:01 duration. We selected the background layer and Option+dragged our original AB_Lifestyles-MixedCuts movie from the Project window into this composition to replace it. We then precomposed the main title and its shadow layer together (Command+Shift+C) to make them easier to animate as a group. Of course, we could just as easily have deleted the shadow and applied After Effects' own Effect>Perspective>Drop Shadow directly to the title. [**Ex.02**] contains the beginning of an animation, fading up the main title and animating a mask to reveal the list of words down the side.

You Can't Go Back

There are a few gotchas when you use Import Photoshop as Comp. The biggest is that you lose some of the ability to edit the individual layers. After you've imported, if you select one layer and hot key into Photoshop to edit it – say, to change its position relative to the overall image – these changes do not ripple through to the comp After Effects created to reassemble all the component layers.

You also cannot add a layer to your Photoshop file and expect After Effects to automatically add it to the stack – you will need to import the new layers manually or re-import the entire Photoshop file and rebuild any changes as necessary. You may want to create your layered Photoshop file with a couple of extra layers you don't need so you have placeholders to go back and use later. (*Thanks to Kurt Murphy for that last tip.*)

Upgrade to 5.5

When importing layered Photoshop files created in version 5.0 into After Effects as a comp, a phantom Photoshop Solid Fill effect may be randomly detected, causing After Effects to create unnecessary precomps and to change the color of text… Either fix it manually in After Effects, or resave the files from Photoshop 5.5.

Connect

Importing Photoshop art was also covered in Chapter 2.

More details on using Photoshop paths as masks and position keyframes can be found in Chapter 13.

Tips on the correct image sizes for nonsquare pixel video work are included in Chapters 39 through 41.

Details on how After Effects re-creates Photoshop Layer Effects are revealed in TechTip 11 on the CD.

 Audio Basics and Effects

Learn how to "read" audio as clues for editing and animation, plus learn what the various audio effects do.

One of After Effects' traditional weaknesses has been handling audio. Audio has been supported since v1.0 in that you can import any QuickTime movie that has audio attached, or individual AIFF-format files. Once it's inside After Effects, you can set its level. However, earlier versions were less than optimal at controlling the levels of multiple audio files and mixing them together; they lacked refined tools, and distorted excessively if the total volume of the audio tracks in a comp was too high.

As a result, our personal workflow consists of creating and mixing our audio beforehand in other applications, then bringing the final mix into After Effects to spot for animation hit points. We can then render this already-finished audio track along with the rest of the project to create our final output.

This is still a good way to work. However, After Effects 4.0 greatly improved the way it handles audio – to the point where you can think about doing some of your audio mixing and sweetening inside After Effects. We're going to discuss spotting, mixing, and using effects inside this chapter. But first, we need to get a handle on how sound itself works – after that, everything else makes a lot more sense.

Note that some of the new audio effects discussed in this chapter are Production Bundle only (denoted by the PB icon). In the accompanying project file, you'll need these effects to use Examples 5, 6, 8, and 9.

The eyeball and speaker icons in the Time Layout window indicate whether a layer has image or audio data, or both. If you twirl down layer 3's parameters, you see Effects, Levels, and Waveform, which are covered in this chapter.

Example Project

Explore the 30-Example Project.aep file as you read this chapter; references to [Ex.##] refer to specific compositions within the project file.
Note that some examples use Production Bundle-only effects.

Seeing Sound

Import any source footage with sound into After Effects (such as the CM_Inglemuse.mov file on the accompanying CD) and drag it into a comp. All layers with audio, including any comps that have layers with audio, will have a little speaker icon in the Time Layout window's Audio/Video switches panel; clicking on this turns the audio on and off. Twirl down its audio parameters in the Time Layout window. If the clip contains both video and sound, you will see a new parameter added – Level – plus the word Waveform. If the clip was audio-only, all the normal masks and

transformations are missing, and nothing shows up in the Composition window, just in the Time Layout window.

Click on the twirly to the left of the word Waveform. See all those squiggles that appeared in the timeline? That's a visual representation of your sound. [**Ex.01**] contains the Ingelmuse music file for you to look at. Here's where those squiggles came from, and what they mean.

Those squiggles in the Time Layout window are the "waveform" of the audio, indicating how loud it is at each point in time.

Good Vibrations

For there to be a sound, something must vibrate. This vibration could be a guitar string swaying back and forth, a speaker cone pumping in and out, or pieces of glass shattering when a baseball flies through a window. These motions vibrate the air, pushing it toward you and pulling it back away from you. This in turn pushes your eardrum around, causing it to flex in sympathy. This stimulates nerves in your ears, which ultimately convince your brain that a sound has occurred.

The pattern and nature of these vibrations affect the character of the sound we perceive. The stronger the vibrations, the louder the sound. The faster the fundamental pattern of vibrations, the higher the apparent "pitch" of the sound. Humans can perceive vibrations from a speed of 20 back-and-forth cycles per second to as high as 20,000 cycles per second – a lot faster than the frame rate of video or film.

Sound is recorded by intercepting these vibrations in the air with a device akin to our eardrum – typically, a microphone – which converts them into electrical signals with a similar vibrational pattern. In a computer environment, these vibrations are frozen by *digitizing* or *sampling* that electrical signal. When sound is digitized, its instantaneous level (how much the air has been pushed toward or pulled away from the microphone) is measured (sampled) and converted into a number (digitized) to be stored in the computer's memory. A very short instant later, the signal is measured again to see how the air pressure changed since the last measured moment in time. This process is repeated very quickly over a period of time to build up a numeric picture of what the pattern of vibration was.

The speed at which it is performed is called the sample rate, and it is roughly equivalent to frame rate. The higher the sample rate, the more accurately high frequencies – which help make sounds intelligible – are captured. High end digital video cameras and digital tape recorders sam-

Instant Waveform

To directly access Levels and the waveform twirly, select the layer in the Time Layout window and hit L for Levels. To see the waveform, hit LL (two L's) quickly.

Tall Waves

To see more detail in the audio waveform, place your cursor over the thin embossed line just below it, and click and drag this line down. You can also zoom in the displayed range of the timeline to get more temporal resolution.

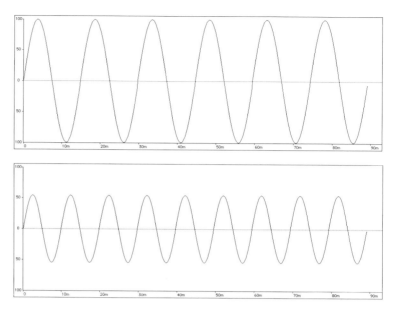

Here are a pair of simple waveforms displayed in an audio editing application, zoomed in the same amount. As the curve of the wave goes above the centerline, air is being pushed toward you; as it goes below, air is being pulled away. Time passes from left to right; the markings along the bottom are in 10-millisecond (hundredth of a second) increments – giving an idea of how fast sound vibrates. Since the up and down excursions for the second image are not as tall as for the first image, you know this sound is relatively quieter; since the up and down excursions are happening faster, you know it is higher in pitch.

Inaccurate Waveforms

Most programs do not display every sample of a waveform, so the same waveform looks different at different zoom levels. For critical edits, zoom in to single frame view (hit ; on the keyboard) for the highest display accuracy.

Audio in Precomps

Copy the audio layer with the layer markers to precomps to help you sync to audio events. Just remember that the audio feeds up to higher comps – turn off these audio switches in the main comp so only one version of the audio is rendered.

ple audio 48,000 times a second, usually expressed as 48 kHz (Hz = Hertz = cycles per second; kHz = thousands of cycles per second). Audio CDs use a sample rate of 44,100 (or 44.1 kHz); consumer DV uses a rate of 32 kHz; many multimedia applications such as CD-ROMs use a rate of 22.050 kHz.

The resolution at which these samples are digitized is defined as the number of bits per sample (akin to bit depth of a color image). Higher resolutions result in less *quantization distortion*, which is often heard as noise. Professional quality gear uses 16-bit resolution; 8-bit resolution sounds very noisy. The special 12-bit format used by some consumer DV cameras are just a bit short of the 16-bit format in quality.

This resulting *waveform* is typically displayed on a computer screen by drawing a point or line that represents the air pressure at one point in time, followed by additional points or lines that represent succeeding points in time. As a result, you can "read" a waveform from left to right to get an idea of the vibrational pattern. No one can look at the resulting squiggles and tell you what the sound was, but you can pick up some clues: louder points in time will be drawn taller than quieter points in time; cycles that take longer relatively to fluctuate up and down are lower in pitch than ones that fluctuate more quickly.

Spotting Audio

When we are animating or editing visuals to sound, the most interesting points in the audio tend to be the loudest ones: the moment a door slams, lightning cracks, a drum is hit, or a baby's crying reaches its crescendo. By looking for these *peaks* – taller points in the audio waveform – we have a tremendous head start in finding the more interesting audio events, which we can then use as a starting point for visual edits and effect keyframes. Strong drum beats produce these peaks, as do syllables

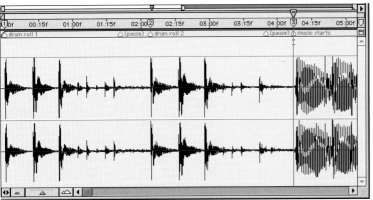

Starting the process of spotting important points in a piece of music. We've used both numbered Comp markers along the top, plus named Layer markers. Comp markers have the advantage of jumping directly to them using the numbers on the regular keyboard, but you get only ten per comp, so use them wisely. In contrast, you can have any number of Layer markers per layer, and you can type in your own notes.

in words. Areas with no peaks or other visible waveform indicate pauses between words and sentences.

Comp and Layer markers (see the sidebar *Mark That Spot* in Chapter 8) can be used to mark important beats in the music or words in the voiceover. We use the ten Comp markers to mark the major sections in the music or animation.

Since Comp markers are connected to the comp's timeline, if you move the audio track in time, the markers no longer line up. Layer markers, on the other hand, are attached to the layer. Use these to mark music beats and script highlights. If the audio layer fills up with markers, make a new solid (Command+Y) and call it "script notes." Turn off its visibility and add markers to this layer, leaving the audio track free for the music beats.

Our process is to view the waveform, locate these peaks both visually and by listening to the audio, and set Layer markers to remind us where they are. Then we twirl up the waveform display (since it has a relatively slow redraw), and animate based on the position of the markers.

For quickly adding Layer markers, use the "tap-along" method. Select the layer you want to place the markers on (the layer with audio, or a dummy solid layer as mentioned above), set the time marker to the start of the section you want to spot, preview the audio by pressing the period key on the keypad, and hit the keypad's asterisk key in time with the music. When the preview stops, Layer markers will appear. (You can adjust the length of the audio preview in File>Preferences>General.) If you're off tempo, slide the markers along the layer bar until they line up with the waveform peaks. Practice this with [**Ex.02*starter**].

Controlled Response

If you want effects that generate graphics from audio (see Chapter 24) to react only to certain portions of the audio spectrum, precompose the audio layer and apply audio effects in this precomp to focus in on the desired frequencies.

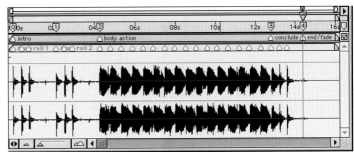

Finished spotting the musical beats, with script notes on a dummy layer above.

Once the music and script layers have markers, you can copy and paste these layers into precomps for easy animation decisions. Just make sure that at the top level, the audio switches are turned off for the nested precomps, or the audio will be doubled up.

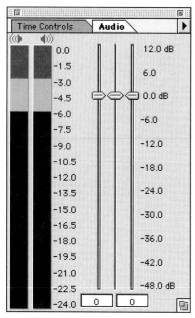

The Audio palette can be resized (bottom right) for more control. The meters on the left display the instantaneous level of audio being previewed; if the speaker icons at the top are red, you were clipping. They reset each time you play, or you can click on them to reset them. The sliders on the right are used for setting Levels parameters. Note that they always change values at the current location of the comp's time marker, even if you double-clicked on a keyframe at a different point in time.

The Audio Options window is opened from the Audio Palette wing menu; it affects how you enter and view Levels parameters using the palette's sliders. Since most Levels adjustments take place in a small range around 0 dB, you might consider setting the visible slider range down to something like –24 dB.

On the Level

In After Effects, you can change the relative volume levels of clips with audio and keyframe these changes if you wish. The way these parameter adjustments and keyframes work is a bit different from the way most other parameters inside After Effects work, however.

When you click on the Levels parameter for a clip with audio in the Time Layout window, instead of opening a dialog box, it brings forward the floating Audio palette. The Audio palette is usually tabbed together with the Time Controls palette; you can also open it via Window>Show Audio (Command+4). You can then either move the sliders, or directly enter values in the numeric boxes in this floater.

Note that if you double-click on a Levels keyframe, you might not be editing the values for that keyframe; the audio palette edits data only at the location of the time marker, regardless of which keyframe you selected. If keyframing is turned on for Levels, changing values in this palette will create a new keyframe at the location of the time marker or change the value of any Levels keyframe the time marker might be on.

There are two values, for the left and right channels of stereo audio clips. Dragging the handle between the two channel sliders moves them both at once. This slider reacts a bit differently from a normal linear parameter; most of the useful values for Level exist in a small area around the 0 mark. Unlike a parameter such as Scale or Opacity, 0 means no *change* rather than no effect.

You have two ways of viewing and entering Levels parameters: as a percentage of full scale volume, and in decibels (units of loudness). You can switch between these two methods by selecting the Options dialog for this palette (the wing menu arrow in the upper right corner). Unless you have an audio background, you will probably be most familiar (and comfortable) with the percentage scale; when we're reducing the volume of a music or sound effects track behind a narration track, we usually start at 50% volume and preview that to make sure the voice is intelligible.

Decibels is a *power* scale that more closely relates to the way we perceive loudness. When we're reducing the volume of music to help make any simultaneous narration clearer, we start at –6 dB from where the normal level was; it is not unusual to use values of –12 to –16 to really clear the way for more intelligible speech. To fully turn off the volume of

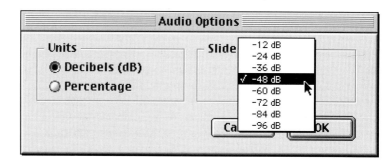

Previewing Audio

Audio cannot be previewed in all windows just by hitting the spacebar. In the Layer window, you have to Command+drag the time marker to "scrub" through it; in After Effects' Footage window, you have to either scrub it or do a RAM preview. If it was originally in QuickTime form, you can double-click it from the Project window and listen to it using the normal QuickTime player.

There are several ways to perform a RAM preview for audio inside a composition. The quality of the sound you will hear is controlled by the audio preferences, inside File>Preferences>General. The best choice is to use the same sample rate and bit depth as used in most of your source layers; it will take less calculation time and sound truer to your final result. We tend to use Duration settings of 10 seconds or longer since you can interrupt a preview playback at any time.

The easiest way to preview audio in a comp is to set the time marker to where you want to start, then hit the decimal point key (. on the numeric keypad of an extended keyboard). You can also use the menu item Composition>Preview>Audio (Here Forward). Hitting any key will stop playback. Note that hitting the spacebar to play the comp will *not* play the audio.

If you want to preview your images with audio playing, make sure the speaker icon is selected on the Time Controls palette, then click on either the

RAM Preview button or hit 0 on the numeric keypad. It will obey your work area and the Loop icon setting. Note that if your image is large or your video card is slow, the image may lag behind the audio; if so, the frame rate display in the Time Controls palette will turn red during playback.

Playing from RAM: 150 of 150
fps: 14.5/29.97 (NOT realtime)

To play back audio while previewing your visual animation, make sure the speaker icon is turned on in the Time Controls palette and click the RAM Preview button. If playback is not realtime, the frame rate display will turn red.

Finally, you can "scrub" audio by holding down the Command key (Control for Windows) while moving the time marker with your mouse. This will play a single frame of audio for each frame you move the time marker to. If you keep the Command key and mouse button held down after you have stopped moving, After Effects will then start playing a one-third second loop of the audio, starting at the current location of the time marker.

a clip with audio, you need to set its Level parameter to –96 dB for a 16-bit resolution clip. Since the sliders are so touchy, you might want to set the Slider Minimum to –12 or –24 dB in the Audio Options dialog, then manually type in –96 when you want to set a track to silence. When you're trying to even out the volume of a narrator that may be fluctuating from soft to loud on individual phrases, changes in the range of 0.5 to 1.5 dB are often sufficient.

You can increase the volume of clips by setting their level above 0. You may need to do this if the original audio was recorded too softly, but be careful; it is easy to scale the audio samples to the point where they *clip* and therefore distort. The same goes for mixing together several loud clips in a comp or project. If you preview audio for the comp and the volume meters in the Audio palette light up the top red indicator, you are clipping; reduce the volume of the audio track(s) slightly.

Enter, Then Preview

After typing in a Level value, hit Enter or Tab to accept the number before hitting . (period) to Preview the audio – otherwise, you'll type over your new Level setting.

Sample Rate Management

The final audio sample rate and resolution is determined by your Render Settings. You can combine files with multiple sample rates, and After Effects will perform the sample rate conversion automatically. Previous versions of After Effects did a fair job at this; version 4.x does a much better job. However, the best working practice is to either capture or pre-convert (in a stand-alone audio program) the audio sample rates of all your files to the target rate you intend to render at before bringing them into After Effects.

Dual Mono

Some systems, such as ProTools and the Media 100, represent stereo audio as two mono tracks. To use these properly in After Effects, you need to import both tracks, drag them into the same comp, apply Stereo Mixer to both, and turn the Right Level down to 0 for the first one and the Left Level down to 0 for the second. Now you can use Levels normally. This is shown in **[Ex.04]**.

After Effects interpolates between audio keyframes using the same unusual power-oriented scale as you see for the sliders. This results in fade-downs that can range from natural to slightly abrupt. Fade-ups, unfortunately, sound very unnatural, as they seem to linger at the lower volume, then suddenly rush up when they're close to the higher keyframe. You can smooth this out a bit by easing into and out of the higher volume keyframes for fade-ups and -downs.

Note that After Effects draws the audio waveform after it has been processed with the Levels parameters. This means you might want to spot your audio first, perhaps even with the level set artificially high (so you can see details in the waveform better), then do your Levels animation later.

Audio Processing Effects

The Standard version of After Effects comes with several audio processing effects; the Production Bundle adds more. They are all located in the menu item Effect>Audio. We'll go over some of the more interesting ones, including how they work and some suggested applications for their use. Of course, experimentation is the best way to master them.

An interesting side effect of some common audio effects is that they produce altered versions of the sound (such as echoes) that are supposed to exist after the original sound is finished. However, if you have trimmed an audio layer to end after the sound has stopped, the plug-in will stop there too: It cannot render audio that plays past the end of the trimmed layer. Therefore, when you're playing around with filters that create trailing versions of the processed sound, you might want to either trim them less tightly or precomp them – for example, a 1-second file in a 2-second comp – then apply the effect to this precomp to let it ring out. Another trick is to select the layer and apply Layer>Time Remapping (discussed in the next chapter); you can then easily extend the last "frame" of the audio layer as long as needed.

Note that some plug-ins create additional copies of or boost certain portions of the original sound, potentially increasing its overall volume. Make sure you preview your audio after adding Effects. In the worst case, you may now be clipping: This is indicated by the speaker icon at the top of the signal level meters in the Audio palette turning red. The result is distortion. Since Levels is calculated after any effects, you can't fix the clipping there. If an effect features Dry and Wet amounts (the level of the original and processed audio, respectively), you can reduce the level here; otherwise, place the Stereo Mixer effect first in the chain and reduce the volume there.

Our personal bias is more toward audio "sweetening" than special effects creation, and that will be our focus in the effects we discuss below. Almost any effect can be driven to extremes to create weird sounds. If this is really your goal, then you might want instead to consider a dedicated audio editing program, or Adobe's own Premiere application plus a pair of great special effects Premiere-compatible plug-ins: BIAS's SFX Machine and Arboretum System's Hyperprism.

Stereo Mixer

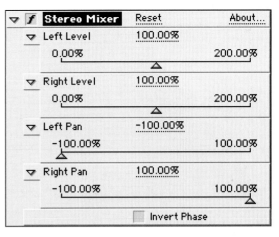

This workhorse effect has several uses. First is as an alternate Levels control, with parameter sliders that work on a scale easier for many to understand. Anything over 100% boosts the original volume of the layer; anything below cuts it. As always, watch that boosting doesn't cause clipping; preview after adjustments and watch for the red indicator at the top of the Audio palette.

The downside of using the Stereo Mixer for levels adjustments is that you have to adjust both the left and right channel parameters: There is no one slider to do both. The advantage is that more natural fades are easier to achieve. Compare the fade-up/down using the normal Levels in [**Ex.03a**], versus using the Stereo Mixer in [**Ex.03b**]. Default linear fades sound acceptable in most cases; for more natural fades, leave the first keyframe linear, then ease into the second keyframe of a volume change [**Ex.03c**]. A similar technique can be used at just the end of fade-ups using the normal Levels control [**Ex.03d**].

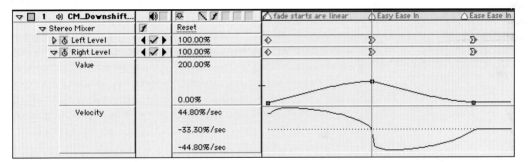

The Stereo Mixer effect is also a way to work around the rendering pipeline when it comes to audio. You can use it to pre-adjust the levels of different layers that might otherwise be too soft or loud compared with other clips, akin to using the normal visual Levels effect to tweak the gamma, black, and white points of source images. If another effect is causing the sound to be boosted into distortion, and you can't find a good balance of its parameters to tame it, reduce its volume beforehand with the Stereo Mixer. If you have already set up a series of Levels keyframes, and later find that adding audio effects has thrown your volume balance off, you can again use the Stereo Mixer to retweak the overall level of a layer without having to reanimate the Levels keyframes.

The Left and Right Pan parameters can be used to reposition a sound in the stereo field. If you need to swap the stereo spread of a sound (maybe you have a sound effect of a jet flying left to right, but your animation calls for it to go right to left), you can swap their default parameters to flip the stereo field. Many sound effects and most music

You might find it easier to control volume fades with the percentage-based Stereo Mixer effect than with decibel-based Levels keyframes. Easing into the keyframe at the end of a fade with a strong influence can often sound even more natural – see and hear this in [**Ex.03c**].

are recorded with a full left/right stereo spread, but you might want to narrow it down to make it seem like it is coming from a more definable location. For example, if you leave the Left control at –100 (full left) and set the Right to 0 (center), the result will be the sound still having a stereo spread, but being located a bit off to the left. As always, preview and watch for clipping; in this case, the Right audio channel is now getting added evenly into the left and right final channels in addition to the original Left channel going 100% into the left, potentially causing clipping in the resulting left channel. Reducing their respective level parameters inside the effect will bring it back in line.

▽ 𝑓 **Delay**	Reset	About...
▽ Delay Time (mi...	500.00	
0.00		2000.00
▽ Delay Amount	50.00%	
0.00%		200.00%
▽ Feedback	50.00%	
0.00%		200.00%
▽ Dry Out	75.00%	
0.00%		100.00%
▽ Wet Out	75.00%	
0.00%		100.00%

Delay

This plug-in is used to create echo effects. When it's rendering, it creates a copy of the original sound and plays it back delayed in time compared with the original. Delay Amount determines the relative volume of this echo. Feedback decides how much of this delayed sound to feed back through the chain, creating subsequent echoes. The higher the Feedback amount, the louder the echoes, and the longer it will take the final effect to die away. This is one of the reasons you might need to artificially lengthen sounds (as mentioned above), to prevent the echoes from getting cut off prematurely.

You can time the echoes produced by Delay to specific numbers of frames for rhythmic animation. All it takes is a little math (really):

[desired delay (in frames) ÷ frame rate] × 1000 = delay time parameter (msec)

The maximum delay time is 5 seconds (5000 milliseconds), which works out to just under 150 frames at 29.97 fps.

[Ex.05] demonstrates an echo trick using Delay. It also is an example of using Time Remapping (Chapter 31) to "freeze" the source audio at a specific point, but letting the layer continue in time so the echoes generated can continue past our freeze point.

Alternate Levels Control

If you find the parameter scaling in the Audio palette too touchy and unnatural to work with, instead apply the Stereo Mixer plug-in to your layer(s) with audio and adjust or keyframe your audio levels there.

Reverb

When we hear reverberation, we're actually hearing thousands of individual echoes smearing together. Instead of the archetypal echo case in which your voice bounces off against a canyon wall and bounces back to you, inside more normal rooms your voice (or any sound) is scattering out in all directions, bouncing off any surface it meets, and occasionally zooming past your ears on its various ways to other surfaces to bounce off. Get enough of these echoes and reflections together, and they start to blend into an overall ambiance rather than distinct sounds. Depending on how reflective the surfaces of the room are, the sound loses some energy with each bounce, eventually decaying away into silence.

Reverb is simulated in software by setting up a number of individual echoes of varying lengths, then feeding them back on themselves to get the additional reflections. After Effects' Reverb plug-in gives you direct access to these parameters: **Reverb Time** adjusts the spacing between the original reflections; longer times simulate larger rooms (where there are longer distances for the sound to travel between walls). **Diffusion** adjusts how random these individual reflections are: less diffuse means a more orderly room with patterns to the reflections; more diffuse means the reflections are more ragged in timing.

Decay is how strongly, and therefore often, the reflections bounce. Use smaller decay values to simulate carpeted and draped rooms where the reverb dies away quickly; larger decay values to simulate glass and stone where the reverb would linger much longer.

Brightness controls a very important (but often overlooked) parameter of reverb simulation: that imperfect real-world reflective surfaces tend to attenuate (reduce in level) higher frequencies more than lower frequencies. Crank this value up for more metallic sounds; keep it low for more realistic, organic sounds.

The default settings for Reverb are pretty good. It does not have quite the quality of a more expensive dedicated hardware or software reverb, but it can help add a sense of room (or distance) when it's used in small Wet amounts. Tweak the Reverb Time first to change the virtual room size, followed by the Decay to control how echoey it is. Varying Diffusion too much from its default quickly makes the simulation break down. Also, note that Reverb takes longer to render than most other audio effects do.

Sound Check

If you want to hear just what the reverb is doing, set the Dry Out to 0% and the Wet Out to around 30% to 70%, depending on how loud the original audio is. This is shown in [**Ex.06**].

Flange & Chorus

A funny thing happens when an audio file is delayed only a very short amount and mixed back in against itself. Rather than hearing two distinct sounds, they start to cancel or reinforce just certain frequency components of each other. This is what the Flange & Chorus effect produces.

When the Voice Separation Time is set to roughly 10 milliseconds or shorter, as in [**Ex.07a**], the phenomenon is known as *flanging* – so called because it was originally created by playing two identical audio tapes in synchronization, then dragging your hand on the tape reel flange of one of the copies, causing this slight delay. Some describe it as a "jet taking off" effect.

Voice Separation Time values of roughly 10 to 50 milliseconds, as in [**Ex.07b**], produce a phenomenon known as *chorusing* because it sounds like more than one singer or identical instruments trying to play exactly the same note slightly out of time with each other. The result is a more watery sound. Larger values get into very loose chorusing, to the point of being called a "slap back echo" – you can hear this in [**Ex.07c**] – because it sounds like an echo bouncing off a very near, hard object.

Typically, only one Voice would be used to create this effect, but this parameter can be increased to make it more deep and dramatic. Note that each voice is delayed by the Voice Separation Time; set both to their normal slider maximum values (100 msec × 10 voices), and you have a full second of machine-gun echoes for every audio event. (You can set these values even higher by clicking on the parameters and editing them numerically in the dialog box.) More Voices will also require you to reduce the Wet Out amount lest you start overloading. Enabling the Voice Phase Change parameters emphasizes some of the frequency-cancellation effects at lower Voice Separation Time settings.

The real secret to this class of effects is a touch of Modulation Depth and Rate. This causes the Voice Separation Time to wander (modulate), resulting in a slightly watery, unstable sound. Modulation Rate values of under 1.0 are most common; higher values produce more watery or even drunken effects. A touch of this effect will help add depth and "magic" to some sound effects such as cymbal crashes and jet engine takeoffs; musicians like to use it on vocals.

Intoxication Modulation

If you want to make your audio really sound drunken, try the Production Bundle's Modulator effect. This effect is aimed more at special effects creation than normal audio sweetening. Set its Amplitude Modulation to 0 and its Modulation Depth to higher values, such as 20% on up.

Bass and Treble

These are basic tone controls. They affect a broad range of frequencies: Bass affects those below 500 Hz; Treble affects those above 1000 Hz. When set to boost low (Bass) and high (Treble) frequencies, they have relatively subtle effects; they have a much more drastic effect when they are set to cut (negative values).

Boosting the highs can increase intelligibility but can also increase any hiss present; listen carefully. Decreasing highs can make sounds appear more distant, or less intelligible – which can be helpful if you have a music or sound effect track that is distracting too much from the voiceover.

Boosting Bass gives more low-end emphasis but can also quickly result in clipping distortion; preview and be ready to pre-lower the volume with the Stereo Mixer effect. These two effects are demonstrated in [**Ex.08a**] and [**Ex.08b**].

Preview the Bass and Treble parameters with the Effect switch in the Time Layout window toggled off and on to hear their effect.

If you have the Production Bundle, the High-Low Pass and Parametric EQ effects have more precision and more predictable results.

▽ *f* **Bass & Treble**	Reset		About...
▽ Bass	0.00		
−100.00			100.00
▽ Treble	0.00		
−100.00			100.00

Dry Out and Wet Out

Many of the audio plug-ins feature a pair of parameters called Dry Out and Wet Out. This is because many of the processings sound best if you mix together the unprocessed sound with the processed version. The Dry Out is the original version; the Wet is the processed one. Think of it as Blend With Original, but with more control.

A nice trick is to fade up the Wet Out from 0 to some nominal setting over time, causing the effect to fade in without reducing the volume of the original sound. Most of the plug-ins sound more realistic with relatively high Dry and low Wet amounts; some, like Flange/Chorus, work better set closer to a 50/50 mix.

High-Low Pass

The definition of a High Pass filter is one that passes frequencies higher than a set cutoff and tries to remove any frequencies present below that cutoff. A Low Pass filter, as you would expect, does the opposite – passes all frequencies below a set cutoff.

Why is this useful? From a purely corrective point of view, unwanted sounds often exist at the extremes of the audio spectrum. For example, traffic noise, wind across a microphone, and even some ventilation system noise often exists below 1–200 Hz in frequency; a High Pass filter with a Cutoff of 100 or so can help remove this while leaving most other sounds untouched. Likewise, hiss often exists at the highest end, above 10 kHz or so; a Low Pass filter with a Cutoff of 10,000 or higher can remove some of it with minimal damage on voice.

More creatively, reducing the portions of the audio spectrum we hear can be used to mimic lower fidelity devices, such as AM radios or the telephone. In these cases, you will probably need to apply this effect twice: one copy set to Low Pass, and one to High Pass. Setting the Cutoff of the High Pass to around 800 Hz and the Cutoff of the Low Pass to around 2000 is a good start at a cheap television or radio effect, as heard in [**Ex.09a**].

Most of the time, you will want to set the Wet Out to 100% and the Dry Out to 0% (not the 50/50 split that version 4.0 defaulted to; this was fixed in 4.1). If you are cutting out the frequencies you want, but otherwise find the effect too drastic, start adding in a little Dry Out until you get the mix you want.

This effect tends to reduce the volume of a sound; you may need to boost it back up again using Levels or the Stereo Mixer.

Parametric EQ

Parametric equalizers allow you to focus on specific bands of frequencies and either boost or remove them. This is the finest knife you have for altering the sound character of audio files. Examples of uses include making a voice more "present" by enhancing just parts of its range, reducing annoying harmonic peaks or *resonances* in a sound file, and cutting out specific narrow spectrum sounds such as fluorescent light buzz and ground circuit hum.

After Effects' Parametric EQ effect gives you three of these filters to work with; you can enable and disable each individually, and each is drawn on the frequency graph in its own color: red for 1, green for 2, and blue for 3. Inside the graph, pitch or frequency goes from low to high as you go from left to right; a curve that goes above the centerline is boosting a range of frequencies, while a curve that goes below that line is cutting them. Here are what the various parameters mean:

The **Frequency** parameter sets the center of the frequency spectrum range you are going to be targeting. Unfortunately, this slider (and the graph above it) visually has a linear range; our perception of pitch is

EQ Pointers

What frequencies should you use as starting points for equalization? Ground circuit hum in the United States starts at exactly 60 Hz, and in nasty cases, also appears at integer multiples of that frequency. In Europe, the magic number is 50 Hz. Since the narrowest Bandwidth setting – 0.1 – corresponds to roughly 200Hz, you'll have trouble making surgical adjustments down that low. Voice enhancement/adjustment usually takes place in the 100 Hz to 5 kHz range. Buzzes from bad dimmers and so on tend to happen around 8 kHz on up. You can also search and boost or reduce general musical instrument ranges using a similar technique.

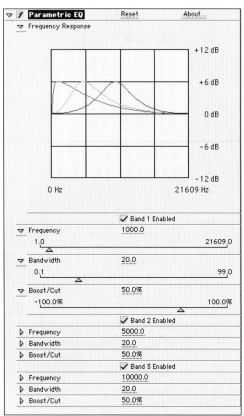

actually exponential. You'll find that the lower quarter of its range has the most audible effect, getting touchier as you get farther to the left.

Bandwidth sets how narrow or wide a range of frequencies you are going to be affecting. It is defined as a percentage of the total bandwidth of the original audio. Since professional audio sample rates (44.1 and 48 kHz) have a bandwidth of just over 20 kHz, this means that setting the bandwidth to 1% affects roughly a 200 Hz-wide swath of frequencies. (Note to those with an audio background: This is not the same as "Q" or width on typical audio equipment.)

The problem with this parameter is that the way we perceive pitch is not linear – a 200 Hz range is perceived to be a very wide range at lower frequencies and a very narrow range at higher frequencies. As you set the Frequency parameter higher, you may find you also need to set the Bandwidth parameter higher to get the same perceptual effect.

Boost/Cut sets how much you are increasing or decreasing the prominence of the selected frequency range.

A common working practice with parametric EQs is to set the Bandwidth fairly small (such as 2), the Boost/Cut to a moderate Boost (such as +6 or higher) and then go back and forth adjusting the Frequency and previewing the results until you have isolated the portion of the sound spectrum you want to work on. You can then adjust the Bandwidth to set how broad of an effect you want, and set Boost or Cut depending on whether you want to enhance it or remove it.

[**Ex.09b**] is another pass at our cheap speaker effect, this time using Parametric EQ to make it sound more akin to a telephone. (By the way, the audio for [**Ex.09**] comes from a short movie by Keith Snyder and Blake Arnold called *1 is for Gun*; that's Blake's voice and Keith's music.)

The Audio Rendering Pipeline

Elsewhere in this book, we've discussed the rendering pipeline and how important it is to wrap your head around it in order to understand how After Effects processes your images. Although it's not as critical, it is also useful to know the audio rendering pipeline. As with images, audio is processed in the order of its parameters when you twirl down an audio layer in the Time Layout window:

1st: *Time Remapping*
2nd: *Effects*
3rd: *Levels*
4th: *Stretch*

Unlike prior versions, After Effects 4.0 and later can varispeed the audio using the Time Remapping and normal layer Time Stretch parameters. This has made the Backwards effects essentially obsolete. Unfortunately, as of version 4.1, there still is no Conform Sample Rate in the Interpret Footage dialog.

Tone

Tone can be used to create sounds from scratch – the aural equivalent of a solid. It replaces any audio that came with the layer it was applied to, including any previous Tone effects – so you need separate layers if you want to mix multiple Tone effects together. If you add Tone to a layer that did not previously have audio (such as a solid), a speaker icon will appear for that layer and the Tone effect will work. However, due to a bug you will not initially get access to a visual waveform nor Levels keyframes for that layer – after applying the effect, close and re-open the Time Layout window to get at them.

Tone can create up to five pure pitched sounds with a single master volume for all five. The layer's Levels parameter can also adjust its volume. You can disable any of the five component sounds by tuning their Frequency parameters down to 0 Hz. You can also set only one Waveform, which is applied to all five component sounds. Their names describe the shape of their waves, and their general sound characters are as follows:

- **Sine** is the purest tone, containing no harmonics above the frequency it is set at.

- **Triangle** sounds just a touch brighter than a sine wave.

- **Saw** is short for Sawtooth and is the most raucous-sounding of the waveforms.

- **Square** is strong too, but has a more "hollow" sound than Saw.

Finally, you can set the fundamental frequency of each component sound. A human's typical hearing range is from 20 Hz to 20,000 Hz. The default slider range goes up only to 3000 Hz, which may seem a bit limiting (click on the parameter in the Effect Controls window to get access to higher values and to re-scale the slider range). However, waveforms other than Sine have additional higher-pitched components called *harmonics* that exist at integer multiples of the sound's fundamental frequency – 1×, 2×, 3×, 4×, 5×, and so forth.

At its simplest, you can use Tone to create the audio portion of the bars and tone reference signals that often get laid down at the head of videotapes. Apply Tone to a layer, leave the Waveform at Sine, set Frequency 1 to 1000 and all the other frequencies to 0, and Level to 100%. Now adjust the volume of your reference tone with the layer's Levels (–14 dB is a common reference that we use in-house). A basic test tone generator is set up in [**Ex.10**]; [**Ex.10_final-14dB**] is set up for a common –14 dB reference tone.

You can also create all sorts of sci-fi radio and electronic sounds by animating the Frequency of Tone.

▽ *f* **Tone**	Reset	About...
Waveform options	Sine ▼	
▽ Frequency 1	440.00	
0.00		3000.00
▽ Frequency 2	493.68	
0.00		3000.00
▽ Frequency 3	554.40	
0.00		3000.00
▽ Frequency 4	587.40	
0.00		3000.00
▽ Frequency 5	659.12	
0.00		3000.00
▽ Level	20.00%	
0.00%		100.00%

Connect

RAM Previewing was covered in Chapter 4.

Comp and Layer markers are in Chapter 8.

Nesting and precomposing were the subjects of Chapters 16 and 17.

Effects that generate graphics from audio were mentioned in Chapter 24.

Time Remapping, which can be used to pause a layer's source audio as an effect continues, is explained in Chapter 31.

The relative volume of the audio of a layer can also be used to control the parameters of a layer's effects or transformations. The Motion Math script to do this is discussed in Chapter 35.

31 Time Remapping

Ever wish you could make time stand still? Or just slow down at strategic points? The answer is Time Remapping.

Mixing Times

Do not combine Time Remapping and Time Stretching on the same clip – life will get too interesting…

Example Project

Explore the 31-Example Project.aep file as you read this chapter; references to [Ex.##] refer to specific compositions within the project file.

Time Remapping is another one of those concepts that seem a bit bizarre at first, but which are very useful and powerful when you get your head wrapped around them. It can be thought of as a form of "position" keyframes for time.

With Time Remapping, you can set which frame of your source will appear at what time in your composition. This remapping can be keyframed. If you have only one keyframe, this one frame of source is all that will be displayed – just as a solo position keyframe results in no movement. Indeed, freeze frames are one of the best uses of Time Remapping. When given two or more time remapping keyframes to work with, After Effects automatically interpolates between them, just as it would with any other property. Since the property being interpolated is *time*, the result is changes in the speed the clip is playing at.

You will not see Time Remapping listed as a default property of a layer when you play with the twirlies. It needs to be enabled by selecting the layer and invoking the menu item Layer>Enable Time Remapping (Command+Option+T). It will then be the first item in a layer's properties, because it happens before Masks, Effects, and Transform. You can then keyframe it just like any other property. Unlike Time Stretching (which Time Remapping is similar to), Time Remapping keyframes do *not* affect the timing of other keyframes already applied to a layer – it behaves as if you time-stretched the clip in a previous composition.

Getting Started (and Stopped)

More often than not, you'll use Time Remapping to make a clip longer than it originally was. Therefore, it's a good idea to start with a composition that's roughly twice as long as the clip you will be working with. Open the [**Ex.01*starter**] comp from this chapter's project, where you'll find a "Daring Men" movie clip of a car jumping over a house. The clip was originally shot on film at 24 fps, so we recommend you set your File> Preferences>Time>Timecode Base to 24 fps also when you're working with this footage. Double-click the clip to open its Layer window and play it until you're familiar with its action.

Close the Layer window, and with the clip selected, select Layer> Enable Time Remapping (Command+Option+T). Twirl down the property arrow to the left of its name in the Time Layout window and note that another layer property – Time Remap – will appear in the Time Layout

window above Masks, Effects, and Transform. The shortcut to twirl down just Time Remapping is RR (two R's in quick succession).

When you enable Time Remapping, two default keyframes are automatically created: one at the start of the clip, and another one frame after the clip's out point (see the sidebar *The Real Out Point*, later in this chapter). At any point, you can select Enable Time Remapping again to delete all keyframes. (Read: if you make a big mess as you learn how to time remap, toggle Enable Time Remapping off and on again to start over.)

Twirling down Time Remap's own arrow to see its value and velocity graphs will also be useful; it gives you a better idea of what is being done to the clip and what frame it is currently on.

Our sample movie for this chapter: an old car jumping a house (with predictable results). Footage courtesy Artbeats/Daring Men.

Freeze Frames

With Time Remapping enabled, the layer bar is now longer than the original movie's duration. Simply drag out the triangle at the end of the layer bar to extend the layer and freeze on the last frame. Option+drag the time marker around this end zone to confirm this.

To freeze on the first frame before the movie starts, click on the words Time Remap to select *both* default keyframes, then drag the first keyframe to its new time. The second keyframe will move by the same amount. For example, moving the first keyframe from 0:00 to 02:00 will produce a two-second freeze frame at the beginning of the clip. Note that you're moving its *time* keyframes, *not* the layer. To only create freeze frames, be certain to always move both keyframes together to keep their relationship the same as they slide along the timeline. Should they drift together or apart from each other, you will be introducing either a slow down or a speed up of the movie, not just a simple freeze frame.

When you enable Time Remapping for a clip, it gets two default keyframes, marking its normal start and end. The ghosted area to the right of the clip's original end shows you can now extend it, frozen on the last frame.

To start with a hold, then play at normal speed, make sure you drag *both* Time Remap (TR) keyframes – not just the first one.

Trimmed Time

If you have trimmed a movie, then enabled Time Remapping, immediately go to the new In point, click the TR keyframe checkbox, and do the same for the Out point. Now delete the two default keyframes. This will keep only the trimmed frames in play for freeze frames and editing.

Remapping Audio

Prior to version 4, After Effects could not Time Remap audio. Now that you can, it is a potential source of special effects and other weirdness, such as imitating DJ "scratching."

The Big Picture

Make sure you have twirled down the Time Remap arrow to reveal its graphs. All these numbers may be daunting at first, but most of them are largely irrelevant. The top (underlined) number is critical: This indicates which frame of the movie or comp is being viewed at the current time. The big picture first:

• A Time Remap (TR) keyframe denotes what "frame of the source" should play at a particular point in the timeline. Keyframes have interpolation types just like other temporal properties: Linear, Auto Bezier, Continuous Bezier, Bezier, and Hold (see Chapter 4 for more info). Remember that these are just regular keyframes underneath – but instead of having a value in *percent* (as in Scale) or *degree* (as in Rotation), their values are *frames in the source movie.*

• By setting multiple TR keyframes, After Effects will interpolate between these values, and the movie will play fast or slow depending on how many frames of the source movie are spread across a certain number of frames in the timeline.

• Should keyframes interpolate from a higher value to a lower value, the movie will play backward.

• Hold keyframes are used to freeze on a frame, and velocity curves add ease in and out control.

Doing Time

To add a TR keyframe, move somewhere to the middle of the clip, click on the underlined value, and enter a new frame number. After Effects will now play this frame of the movie at this point in the timeline and will interpolate between keyframe values, spreading the frames inbetween over time. You can also make a keyframe with the current value by clicking on the keyframe checkbox, and then Option+dragging the keyframe nubbin in the Value graph to edit the frame value.

[Ex.02] is an example of a comp that already has five of these keyframes placed, then moved in time. Preview the comp first to see how the action is time remapped. The Value and Velocity graphs can be read as follows:

Value:Time—The last frame of the movie (03:16 for the Daring Men movie in [Ex.01], assuming you remembered to set timebase to 24 fps in prefs) is at the top range of the cell, and the first frame (00:00) at the bottom. The Value line is a visual clue to which parts of the movie are used. When it ramps upward from left to right, the movie is being played forward (the frame number is increasing); when it ramps downward, the movie is playing backward (decreasing frame numbers). A flat line indicates it is holding on a particular frame.

Velocity:Time—The middle number is the important one, indicating whether the movie is playing slowly (less than 100%), normal speed (100%), faster (more than 100%), or backward (negative value). The top and bottom numbers indicate the "range" for the cell, which is the range from 0% to the fastest speed between the set keyframes. When this graph

Two Timelines

You can also create a... Layer window, whi... are easier to sel... The Layer win... when Tim... With F... to op... tim...

is flat, the clip is playing at a constant speed. If this flat line is... the scale, it is playing forward, at normal speed. If it is flat a... freeze frame. If it is below 0, the clip is playing backward.

Now, let's analyze the implications of our keyframes:

• In [**Ex.02**], place the time marker between KF #1–2: the movie plays at 50% speed (it plays 1 second of source material over 2 seconds, duplicating each frame to do so).

• Between KF #2–3, the movie plays at 100% normal speed (for every one frame of source, you have one frame in the timeline in which it plays). Note that the Value line has a steeper slope, and the Velocity line is higher – both indicators that the clip is playing faster than between the previous two keyframes.

• Between KF #3–4, the movie freezes for 1 second, on frame 03:00 into the clip (note we're at 04:00 in the comp's time, because we played the first portion of the movie at half speed). The Value line stays flat, and the Velocity line is at 0. Use Hold keyframes when you need the frame to really freeze, especially if you're also frame blending.

• Between KF #4–5, the movie plays backward at 200% (it plays 3 seconds of source over 1.5 seconds of time, but backward). The Value line has a strong downward slope, and the Velocity line is well below 0 – both indicators that the clip is playing backward.

Time remap keyframes can be dragged along the timeline as with any other property. Dragging keyframes with the Info palette open (Command+2) gives you feedback as to precisely which point in time you are dragging to. Start playing around with the keyframes yourself, sliding them to different points in the comp's timeline. Observe how the Value and Velocity graphs change, and Preview to reinforce what's going on.

When adjusting TR graphs, be careful that your velocity does not go negative, indicated by the gray line in the Velocity graph – this means your clip will back up. Unless this is the intended effect, hold the Shift key down to prevent the graph from crossing the line.

If you want to precisely align frames of the source with points in the timeline, double-click on a TR keyframe that has already been set. This lets you confirm the frame of the source movie being "pinned down" by this keyframe; change it to a new value if you wish.

Remapping a Comp

Time Remapping is great for applying a global velocity curve to a nested comp. This works best if the precomp consists of pure graphics – time-stretching movie layers can stagger playback.

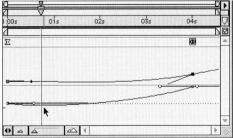

A gray line in the Velocity graph indicates your clip will back up – hold the Shift key down when you're editing handles to prevent the graph from crossing the line.

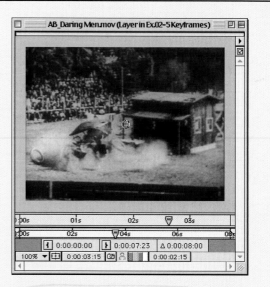

...nd edit TR keyframes in the
...ch is useful if the key "frames"
...ct visually than by timecode.
...dow has additional features
...Remapping is enabled:
...**[Ex.02]** still open, double-click the layer
...n the Layer window, and you'll notice two
...elines. The upper time ruler scrubs through the
...ovie frames and sets or edits a TR keyframe, while
the lower ruler corresponds to the layer bar in the
Time Layout window. Add the Option key to scrub
with realtime updates. Play the movie (hit spacebar)
from the Layer window and watch how the markers
scrub – kinda spooky!

To edit an existing TR keyframe, step to a
keyframe in the Time Layout window. Now, in
the Layer window, Option+drag the *upper* blue
time marker around to identify which frame of
the source you want on this keyframe. To create
a new keyframe, move the comp time marker
(the lower one in the Layer window) to the

desired point in time, then Option+drag the upper
time marker around.

When Time Remap is enabled, create masks in
a precomp or in a second comp. Otherwise, when
you set masks in the Layer window you'll inevitably
add or edit TR keyframes accidentally.

The Easy Life

Of course, you can alter the velocity of TR keyframes, just as you would
any other animated property. The Ease In and Ease Out Keyframe Assistants
(Chapter 7) are also useful for creating smooth acceleration and deceleration in a clip's speed. Our Daring Men footage starts with the car
already at full speed. Let's say you want to fake it starting from a stationary
position and gradually increase to full speed just as it reaches the ramp:

Step 1: Open **[Ex.03*starter]**, select the clip, enable
Time Remapping (Command+Option+T), and hit U
to see its keyframes. Step forward to about 00:22, the
frame where it has reached the ramp. Twirl down the
velocity graph.

Step 2: Click the keyframe checkbox to add a TR
keyframe at this frame of the movie. Decide how long
it should take to get up to speed. Select both the new
keyframe and the last one, and drag your new keyframe to the time
you've chosen. The last keyframe will move by the same amount.

Step 3: If you preview at this point, the motion is a little unrealistic.
To get a smoother start-up, select the first TR keyframe and use the
Layer>Keyframe Assistant>Easy Ease Out.

Step 4: Option+double-click the second
keyframe and ease into 100% speed by
entering a value of 1 second per second
in Keyframe Velocity. An Influence of
33% is a safe guess.

The Real Out Point

If you use the default time remap keyframes and apply velocity curves, you may not achieve a smooth entry into the last keyframe, particularly if you use a very long ease in. Since the second default keyframe is created one frame *after* the last real frame of the movie, the last real frame of the movie appears *before* the last keyframe and is then repeated if you freeze the end of the movie.

For example, in our Daring Men movie, which starts at 00:00, the last frame is 03:16 and it appears at 03:16 in the timeline (again, with the timebase set to 24 fps in prefs). But when you Enable Time Remapping, the second default keyframe is created at 03:17 – one frame later.

The reason is that After Effects assumes your source might be an interlaced movie, whereby you would be viewing only the first field of frame 03:16 at time 03:16. If the default Time Remap keyframe was created at 03:16 also, any freeze you create at the end of the movie would freeze on the first field of this frame. As a result, you would never see the second field.

This is nice, but the reality is that not all sources are interlaced – and now the actual image data from field 2 appears *before* the keyframe icon. This is a problem only if you have a slow ease into this keyframe. Let's say the image on the last frame is supposed to freeze at the big finale audio sound effect – the image from field 2 (or the last frame if the footage is not interlaced) will appear in the comp ahead of the audio. This is shown in **[Ex.04a]**. Our preference is to freeze on the first field of the last frame so that rounding errors like this don't occur **[Ex.04b]**.

We streamlined a workaround to fix this "feature." You can practice it in **[Ex.04c]**:

• *Before* you enable Time Remapping, select O to jump to the real out point (at 03:16), then Layer> Enable Time Remapping. Zoom In in time so you can see some detail.

• Check the keyframe box to create a new keyframe for the real last frame, at time 03:16. *Note: don't just drag the default keyframe back to 03:16.*

• Page down to advance one frame and uncheck the second default keyframe created at 03:17.

Step 4: To smooth the entrance to the second keyframe, don't use Easy Ease In; it would set the speed to 0 when we want to be up to full speed (100%, or 1 second of source per 1 second of timeline) at this point. Option+double-click on the second keyframe; this opens the Layer> Keyframe Velocity dialog. Set the Incoming speed to 1 and the Influence to taste (Easy Ease's default of 33% is a good starting point). Click OK. The graph should now ramp up to full speed.

Step 5: Preview again, and it should look much better; you might want to tweak the outgoing influence from the first keyframe to make it pick up speed faster.

Step 6: The last trick is enabling Frame Blending (Chapter 10) for the layer and the comp. Frame blending is an essential partner to "selling" time remapping, since it helps fake artificial frames between the original ones as you vary the speed. Preview your animation again, and check out [**Ex.03_complete**] if you got lost along the way.

Because Frame Blending incurs a big render hit, you might want to split your layer (Chapter 9) after remapping and turn off blending on the sections where it is playing at 100% speed [**Ex.03_split**].

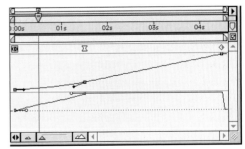

To make our already-moving car pick up speed from an artificial stop, we eased out of the first TR keyframe and ramped up to 100% by the second keyframe.

32 Time Games

A trio of effects for manipulating time: Posterize Time, Echo, and Time Displacement.

Adjusting Effects

You can apply any of these time effects to an adjustment layer (Chapter 20), which will affect all layers below. Depending on your hierarchy, you may then be able to create a difficult effect all in one comp.

Example Project

Explore the 32-Example Project.aep file as you read this chapter; references to [Ex.##] refer to specific compositions within the project file. *You will need the Production Bundle to use the Time Displacement examples.*

Earlier in the book, we covered the basics of manipulating time with frame blending, time stretching, and time remapping. After Effects also has a trio of effects – Posterize Time, Echo, and the Production Bundle's Time Displacement – that can further manipulate time. These particular effects often seem bizarre or of questionable use when you first apply them. However, Posterize Time is a solid problem-solver in addition to its uses for step-time effects; and Echo and Time Displacement are also very creative – once you get your head around how to use them.

Posterize Time

After Effects is surprisingly fluid in how it handles frame rates. The frame rate set in a composition controls only how you step through frames in that comp. The frame rate in the final Render Settings is what really controls how often comps, and all their sources, are "sampled" as the final frames are rendered.

This is often advantageous. However, it can work against you if you are purposely trying to fake a slower frame rate by setting a nested composition to a lower rate. For example, open [Ex.01.1] – this includes a Countdown movie that was rendered at 29.97 fps, but the comp is set to 6 fps. If you preview or step through the comp, you will see jumps in the motion compared with the original movie. This comp is nested in [Ex.01.2], which has a frame rate of 29.97 fps. Play this comp and you will see every frame from the source movie – the frame rate of the nested comp has been overridden!

The Posterize Time effect fixes this. It "wires in" a new frame rate for the source it is applied to. In [Ex.01.3], we applied Effect>Time>Posterize Time directly to the layer we wanted to stagger and set its Frame Rate parameter to 6. Even though the comp's frame rate is set to 29.97, this movie will still play only every fifth frame (29.97 ÷ 6, give or take some rounding error). Note that this changes the rate at which the source is sampled but does not affect any animation you applied to it, as transforms happen after effects. To posterize everything, set up the animation in a precomp and apply Posterize Time after you nest.

To posterize multiple layers in one comp, you could also apply the Posterize Time effect to an adjustment layer (Chapter 20) – the frame rate of all layers below will be affected. This is shown in [**Ex.01.4**].

Since Posterize Time rewires the rendering procedure somewhat, it has a few gotchas. For one, it ignores all effects that are applied before it – it must be first in line. It also ignores any mask applied to the layer (Masks render before Effects in the render order, and you can't mask a frame if its image hasn't been defined yet). Animating its frame rate is also dicey; that's why it allows only Hold keyframes to be used for this parameter.

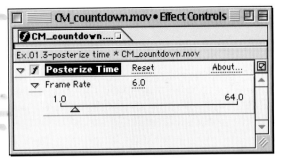

The Posterize Time effect can be used to force a layer to render at a slower frame rate than specified in Render Settings. It can be applied to both movie layers and nested comps.

If you want to mask a movie at a low frame rate and mix it with regular footage, you also have to consider that masks will be interpolated at the frame rate set in Render Settings, not the frame rate of the comp. Therefore, if you need to mask a movie you're also trying to step frame, do the masking in a composition set to that frame rate (say, 6 fps). Create a Layer>New Adjustment Layer, and apply the Posterize Time effect set to 6 fps. Now you can nest this comp in your regular 29.97 fps comp, and the masks should lock onto the correct frames when you render. Alternatively, you can prerender the mask comp at 6 fps and save rendering time later.

Let It Linger

In contrast to creating stutter, Posterize Time can also be used to "calm down" overly busy effects. Many effects that have a randomized action – such as Noise, Scatter, and Brush Strokes – randomize on every frame that is rendered, even when applied to a still. At higher frame rates (and especially while field rendering, which effectively doubles the frame rate), this randomization can turn into a buzzing distraction. Preview [**Ex.02.1**] to get an idea of this problem.

Add Posterize Time and set a lower frame rate, such as 10 fps, to reduce this nervousness and create a more elegant animation. Preview [**Ex.02.2**], which uses an adjustment layer with Posterize Time applied to slow down the buzzing of the Stylize>Brush Strokes effect all in one comp.

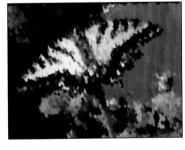

Applying Effect>Stylize>Brush Strokes to a still image results in it randomizing every frame – much too busy. Add an adjustment layer with Posterize Time applied and set to a lower frame rate.

The Frame Blend Smoothie

Frame Blending (Chapter 10) can smooth the look of most of the effects discussed in this chapter. Just be aware of the render hit involved when you enable it; you might want to set the layer to Draft instead of Best Quality to see if you can live with it. For example, these two settings look virtually identical when you're using Time Displacement, but the difference in render times is huge.

There are also numerous creative uses for frame blending, especially when they're combined with the "step time" concept discussed in the Posterize Time section. Check out the CD Tutorials that show creative uses for frame blending.

You'll have even more flexibility if you apply Posterize Time in a second comp. Here we've added a static edge effect with a luma matte and a background.

Another option using nested comps is shown in the [Ex.02.3] folder: the Strokes-1 comp creates the Brush Strokes, which is nested in the Strokes-2 comp and the Posterize Time applied. We can then also apply a luma track matte with a crinkly edge for a buzzing-image-inside-a-static-edge effect. You also have the flexibility if you spread your step frame effect across two comps to add a background movie in the second comp that will run at 29.97 fps.

A similar example of using two comps is the chain in [Ex.03]. A stylizing noise is created in the first comp; in the second comp, Posterize Time slows down the noise, and the result is transfer moded over a movie to add grain.

The classic need for Posterize Time is in conjunction with Effect> Text>Numbers. If you are randomizing or animating this effect, it will be changing every single frame – which again might be faster than you want. Preview and compare the results of [Ex.04.1] versus [Ex.04.2]: Having some numbers change at a slower rate reinforces that they may be tied to different parameters in the "display simulation" you might be creating.

If you're trying to create a data readout giving the illusion of many different parameters being active (above), it works better if the different layers update at varying rates. Posterize Time can vary those rates (right). Background image courtesy EyeWire/Information Technology.

Step Time

Now that we've suggested some good uses for Posterize Time, we're going to suggest that you use it infrequently. This is because of the significant render hit it entails, particularly when effects are in the chain: They are still getting calculated every frame, even if Posterize Time ends up throwing most of those frames away.

A more efficient strategy is to render out just the comp or layer that needs to get "posterized" after you've decided on an effect. Use a lower rendering frame rate rather than the Posterize Time effect. Re-import the result, then use this lower frame rate movie instead – it will save lots of rendering time later. You can also Enable Frame Blending at this point for a dreamier effect. For random elements such as the numbers in [**Ex.04**], you can even render one movie and use it several times, at different Time Stretch values, to get different "speeds."

It's ironic that now we've achieved full motion playback from the desktop, we're eager to drop frames for that neat jerky look – but it's a popular effect. The CD Tutorial, *Stepping Out*, includes tips on creating such effects in conjunction with Frame Blending.

An Original Echo

For many of us, the term "echo effect" conjures images of tacky, sparkling trails following flying logos in local car ads. Fortunately, After Effects is rarely tacky. Unfortunately, the Echo effect's defaults don't really show off the strength of this effect, and you'll often need to foil the default render order to get it to work at all.

Echo (Effect>Time>Echo) could be approached as a form of frame blending in which you have a fair amount of control over how many and how strongly the frames get blended. Frame Blending takes frames before and after the current frame, with very strong weighting toward the closest frame. By contrast, Echo grabs frames that are either in one direction or the other, depending on whether the Echo Time parameter is *negative* (frames from the past) or *positive* (frames from the future).

You can also use the Echo Time parameter to set how far apart the frames are that are used. This parameter is defined in seconds; if you want to calculate it in frames, you have to do a little math: The number of frames spacing, divided by the frame rate, equals the Echo Time in seconds. For a normal "use every frame" echo, it would be 1 ÷ frame rate (1 ÷ 29.97 = 0.03337 seconds; half that for interlaced material). Longer times start to give a sort of cloning effect; [**Ex.05**] gives an idea of what can be done by carefully setting Echo Time when you're using just three echoes.

The Number of Echoes parameter sets how many frames get used, and it can be varied up to a very large number (30,000 – although 10 or less is enough most of the time). Note that if you have a negative Echo Time (frames taken from earlier in time), and a large value for Number of Echoes, you'll need to move to a point in the timeline where the effect has built up some momentum.

Starting Intensity decides how strongly the "original" frame is in the final blend. The Decay parameter decides how much successively weaker the following echoes appear. Decay has a smaller useful range

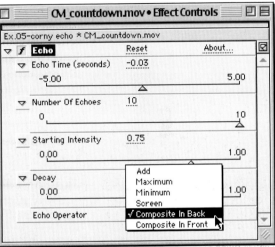

The Echo effect's parameters. It can be approached as a user-adjustable form of frame blending. Most unusual is the Echo Operator popup, which provides a few different forms of transfer modes to blend in the echoes.

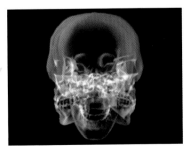

By setting the Echo Time to 2 seconds, and the Number of Echoes to 3, you can clone this movie of a rotating skull...

If your source material has an alpha channel that is changing over time, Composite in Back gives the most typical echo trail. Preview **[Ex.06]** and note how Echo affects the rotating dial and numbers.

than you might expect, since subsequent echoes get weakened by this amount – they go to being unnoticeable really quickly. The upper half of the range is best.

Note that the opacity of the original image, as opposed to the first echo, is affected by the Starting Intensity parameter. If you want your original image to be 100% strong and your echoes to start at a much reduced level, you will need to duplicate the original layer on top and play with the opacity of the echoes underneath. Such an echo trail effect is set up in [Ex.06].

The most intriguing parameter of the group is Echo Operator; this is similar to "Composite Original" in other effects but with the addition of transfer modes. Experiment with the following settings using [Ex.07], then swap in other sources to see how different movies react:

- The Add and Screen modes are akin to the transfer modes you should already be familiar with (Chapter 12) – they make the final image brighter. Add is the default Echo Operator setting.
- Maximum and Minimum produce more interesting blends, which contract or spread areas of contrast in the echoed image while often keeping the overall brightness somewhat similar.
- Composite in Front composites the original source on top of the echoes; it will have no visual effect if the Starting Intensity is at 1.0, unless the alpha channel of the source is moving (as in the Countdown movie in the previous example).
- Composite in Back is a straightforward opacity mix.

The power of Echo comes from its Echo Operator. These six variations show the result of different operators on the same image:
Top row: original image (left), the default Add mode (center), Maximum (right).
Bottom row: Minimum (left), Screen (center), and Composite in Back (right).
Note that Composite in Front looks like the original image as the source layer has no alpha channel. Footage courtesy Kevin Dole.

Echoed Animation

If you apply Echo to a layer that is getting its movement from animation keyframes, Echo may not seem to work initially. This is because effects are calculated before transformations, which yield most animation. In this case, you will need to animate the layer in Comp 1, nest this comp in Comp 2, then apply Echo. In the second comp, the animated layer looks like a "movie" with an animated alpha channel, so the effect works as planned.

A lot of fun can be had with extended Echo settings and fast, randomly moving objects. [**Ex.08.1-wiggler**] contains a simple object that was animated using the Wiggler keyframe assistant (you could also use Motion Sketch), with Motion Blur turned on. This comp is nested in a second comp – [**Ex.08.2-echo**] – with Echo applied. Be aware that render times can quickly stack up when a lot of motion blurred objects are being echoed (as is the case with this example). It also takes a while for the Echo effect to build up at the start, since the echoed frames are taken from earlier in time – and there is no time earlier than 0.

Note that because Echo reaches back to the source for data, animating an object using the Perspective>Transform effect, then applying Echo all on one layer doesn't create an echo trail. However, you could apply Echo to an adjustment layer above where it will then affect all layers below. An example of this is in [**Ex.08.3-adjustment layers**]: adjustment layer 1 with the Transform effect applied rotates the three spheres below, while adjustment layer 2 on top applies Echo to the result.

Echo following random animation can yield a complex swirl from a single still image. Internet @ symbol courtesy Digital Sorcery; 3D Spaceplane movie courtesy Lizard Lounge Graphics.

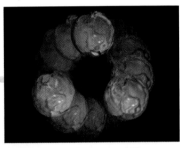

One adjustment layer rotates three spheres with the Transform effect, while a second adjustment layer on top applies Echo to the result.

Time Displacement

This Production Bundle effect is similar to its cousin, Displacement Map. It's also a compound effect (Chapter 22) that looks at the luminance values of a second layer to decide how to mess with the pixels of the layer it is applied to. But rather than displace the position of those pixels, Time Displacement grabs pixels from different points in time in the original source. The result is a strange time warpage of the layer that some might refer to as a *slitscan* effect.

There are a few rules to observe when you're using Time Displacement. Like any compound effect, it uses the source of the second "map" layer, ignoring any masks, effects, or transformations applied to the map in the current comp. If you need to edit or animate this map layer, you'll need to do it in a precomp. Time Displacement also ignores any masks created on the layer it is applied to; do any masking in a precomp also.

Darker pixels in the displacing layer reach back earlier in time to grab what pixels will be used in the effected layer; lighter pixels reach forward. Pixels that are 50% gray (RGB value 128) cause no displacement, so pixels from the current frame are used. The maximum amount of

The first step is to select the Time Displacement Layer that will do the displacing.

Fractured Alternate

If you like the "fractured mirror" example on the next page, but don't have the Production Bundle, you could get the same effect by duplicating your layer multiple times, masking each one to reveal a different section, and offsetting them in time.

reach is determined by the Max Displacement Time parameter. Since pixels earlier in time might be needed, this effect also takes a few frames to get up to speed (if that's a problem, trim the beginning of the layer). Time Resolution is most effectively set to the frame rate of the source being displaced; remember that interlaced sources have twice the effective frame rate.

This effect obviously needs things to change over time in the source to have any effect. If your motion is coming from effects and animations applied to an otherwise still object, do this animation in a precomp, then apply Time Displacement in the second comp.

Displaced Affections

Time displacement is one of those effects that often initially looks either ugly or unpredictable and is therefore quickly abandoned. However, there are many situations where it looks rather cool.

[**Ex.10**] on the CD has been set up as an experimentation comp for you to play with. The Time Displacement effect is already applied to the Countdown movie. With the time marker moved to the center of the timeline, open the Effect Controls window (Command+Shift+T) and set

---

Quality Issues

Using Time Displacement often results in aliased-looking images with rough edges. This is not the effect's fault; the problem is a lack of resolution in the material it is being fed to work on. This problem is demonstrated in [**Ex.09*starter**].

For example, there are only 256 luminance values available to calculate the displacement amount. This does not stretch seamlessly across video-sized frames which have 480 pixels or more in their shortest dimension, inevitably resulting in some aliasing or posterization. Even worse, source material frame rates are typically 30 frames per second or lower, not offering a lot of choices of where to grab new material from.

Time Displacement can result in aliased results (left), because there isn't enough image information to use. If the source has an alpha channel, applying some edge blurring will reduce some of the artifacts (right). Background: Artbeats/Soft Edges.

If you're shooting or rendering material specifically for a Time Displacement effect, consider using a higher frame rate (for example, shoot film at 48 or 60 fps, transfer to video frame per frame, and conform to the original frame rate in the Interpret Footage dialog). Material with less motion from frame to frame will also look smoother. If the source you are displacing has an alpha channel, you *can* clean up the aliasing a bit by blurring its edges. If you have the Production Bundle, you can check out our recipe in [**Ex.09_final**]. This is also saved as a favorite, **edge blur/choke PB.ffx**, in the Goodies>Effect Favorites folder on the CD. Better yet, if you have the Puffin Designs Composite Wizard plug-in set, use its Edge Blur effect.

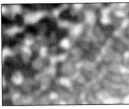

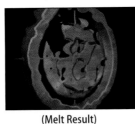

(Melt Map)   (Melt Result)   (Torn Map)   (Torn Result)

the Time Displacement Layer popup to the various Video SpiceRack maps. To try out other movie sources without reapplying the effect and starting over, select the Countdown layer, select another source in the Project window, and Option+drag the new source to the comp window (or use the Command+Option+/ shortcut). The sources EW_Senses and EW_Fitness both work well, or try your own sources.

    Here are some more examples using Time Displacement. Preview the comps to see how the displacement progresses:

Complex displacement maps result in melted and torn looks. Countdown courtesy CyberMotion; maps courtesy Pixélan's Video SpiceRack series.

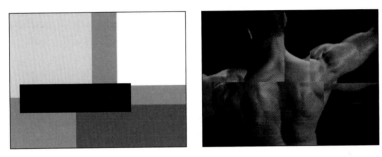

[Ex.14] A high-contrast displacement map with several levels of gray (left) results in a "fractured mirror" effect (right). Bodybuilder footage courtesy EyeWire/Fitness.

- The most typical Time Displacement effects are shown in the [**Ex.11**] folder. A gradient from top to bottom results in the wraparound effect demonstrated in the After Effects manual, and a radial gradient gives an emerging-from-the-center look.
- Complex displacement maps melt and rip apart images. The [**Ex.12**] folder contains examples of our Countdown movie being melted and torn by complex maps from the Video SpiceRack and OrganicFX series from Pixélan. Maps with smoother, more gradual gray transitions give more organic results; consider pre-blurring your map sources if your results are too torn.
- [**Ex.13**] uses the AB_SoftEdges animated grayscale movie as a map, which enhances the "I'm melting!" organic look. To tie in the displaced image more with what is displacing it, try blending it in with a variation of its displacement map. Remember: The map is taken before any masks, effects, or transformations are applied, so you can treat the same layer used for the displacement to make it look better, without affecting how it will displace the effected layer.
- Hard-edged displacement maps yield interesting "fractured time" visual effects [**Ex.14**]. The same thing could be accomplished by duplicating a layer, masking it, and giving it different offsets in time, but it is easier to experiment with just one layer and one displacement map.

Connect

Keyframe Assistants were covered in Chapter 7.

Time Stretching and Frame Blending were discussed in Chapter 10; Motion Blur in Chapter 11.

Nesting and Precomposing were the focus of Chapters 16 and 17.

The rendering order is discussed in several places, including Chapter 16 and TechTip 09.

Compound Effects were the subject of Chapter 22.

Time Remapping was in Chapter 31.

The Interpret Footage dialog, where you can conform frame rates, is discussed in detail in Chapter 36.

The Render Settings are covered in Chapter 43; prerendering and proxies will be elaborated upon in Chapter 44.

33 On Stable Ground

The Production Bundle includes the ability to stabilize wobbly footage. Learning it is the key to tracking objects, as well.

Motion Stabilization and Motion Tracking – the subjects of the next two chapters – often seem like magic…magic that you often can't quite get to work. Some of the problems come from improper preparation of footage (not all shots can be stabilized or tracked); some from less than ideal program defaults; some with choices the user makes. In this chapter, we'll learn the basics of good tracking and stabilization, plus navigating After Effects' user interface for these modules. In Chapter 34, we'll tackle applications for having one object track the movement of another.

Stabilizing 101

The point of Motion Stabilization is to remove drift, wander, or rotation in a footage item, making it appear rock solid. This drift might have come from a camera that was not perfectly steady or an object that was drifting off its mark.

To stabilize a footage item, it needs to have some high-contrast feature with an identifiable edge or shape that can be recognized and followed by the software. Dots are great; sharp corners also work well. Continuous lines or edges or otherwise indistinct features do not work.

You point After Effects at this identifiable feature, and After Effects will then track it as it moves around the footage item by looking for a nearby shape that matches the original. It will then create new Anchor Point keyframes to offset the apparent image center of the layer in a way that makes the overall image seem stable.

Setting Up

To stabilize a footage item, it needs to be a layer in a composition. Select it, then go to Layer>Keyframe Assistant>Motion Stabilizer. We'll be using [Ex.01*starter] on the CD for these examples.

The Tracking Region boxes are what you are most interested in. The inner box – the Feature Region – needs to be centered and resized around the feature you have decided will make a good target to lock onto. The outer box – the Search Region – is how large an area After Effects will search beyond the inner box to find a matching feature from frame to frame. To move both boxes together, grab them in the middle

Zooming In

Zooming in more than 100% will help you place Tracking Regions more accurately. The zoom indicator in the lower left corner is not a popup as it is in the Comp window; use the keyboard shortcuts Command and – (minus) or = (equals) to zoom out and in, respectively.

Example Project

Explore the 33-Example Project.aep file as you read this chapter; references to [Ex.##] refer to specific compositions within the project file.

of the inner box. To resize them, grab their handles on their respective sides or corners. Dragging the Feature Region too large "bumps" the Search Region larger. If you're having trouble editing the boxes, make sure the time marker in this window is set to the in point of the layer.

Minimizing the size of both these regions will speed up tracking, but going too small will make After Effects lose the track. Make the Feature Region large enough to just enclose the feature you are tracking, with at least a pixel of contrasting image inside the box. After Effects will reset the position of this region each frame as it finds the feature it is looking for. Make the Search Region just big enough to follow movement of the object being tracked from frame to frame – not how much it moves over the entire clip.

Remember that you can define the Tracking Regions only on the first frame to be tracked. If you are unable to get the handles to resize the regions, make sure the time marker equals the in time (or out time, if you are tracking in reverse – see below) for the track. Also note that the comp's work area does not apply to this window; however, a layer's in and out points will default to the tracker's in and out times. Check and possibly trim the in and out if you want to track less than the entire clip.

All that gray space beneath the in and out points are for giving numeric feedback before, during, and after the track. At this "before" stage, the first set of numbers are the four corners of the Feature Region; the second set of numbers

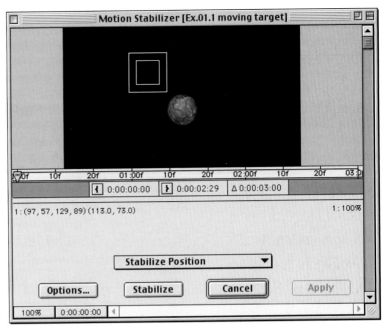

The Motion Stabilizer window. The top portion is a copy of the layer, with one or more Tracking Region boxes – the Feature Region (inside) and the Search Region (outside). In the middle is a timeline to define the region of time to track.

Below you choose what type of motion you want to stabilize: Position, Rotation, or both. Exceedingly important is the Options button in the lower left; you will want to change the defaults. Last are the buttons to go ahead and try to stabilize, apply the stabilization, or to cancel.

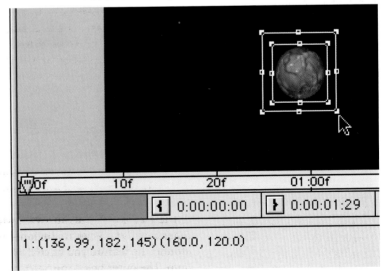

An example of making the Tracking Region boxes snugly fit our feature to track, with enough room to follow its movements from frame to frame.

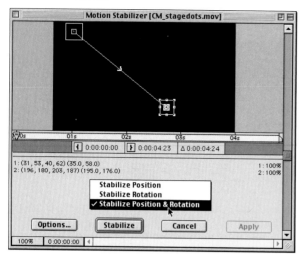

Set the popup at the bottom of the dialog if you want to track rotation instead of position. Rotation requires two Tracking Regions to calculate.

is where the initial anchor point will be set for the layer. The anchor point does *not* equal the middle of the Feature Region; it is controlled by where you dragged the regions to before you started adjusting their corners. If you want to set the initial anchor point to a specific value (such as the middle of the layer), you need to first drag the middle of the regions (the squares) to this point while watching these values. Then you need to set the regions without moving this anchor point, which can be accomplished by dragging just their corners and sides or by Option+dragging inside their boxes. If you drag normally, the Anchor Point will move as well.

You can stabilize just the position, just the rotation, or the position and rotation together of a layer. This is set with the popup at the bottom of the window. To stabilize the rotation, you need two points to track, and you will get two Tracking Regions connected by a line with arrows. The arrow travels from the pivot point to the second reference to decide how much the layer has rotated. The further apart these two regions are, the more accurately rotation will be stabilized.

Essential Options

There's at least one option you will need to change from its default to get a good track or stabilization, and it is worth knowing what the other options do in the event you have trouble. It is also possible to remember your settings, which makes experimentation much easier. Let's go over each of the options in order.

You can ignore the Apply Motion To options; they apply only to Tracking, which is covered in the next chapter. (All of the other options apply to both Tracking and Stabilization.)

The Time Options set how often the tracking data is calculated. For virtually every situation, you will want to track at the source's original frame rate lest you miss any details of the movement in the frames between tracking frames. If your source material has fields, you should

For best results, you need to tweak the Motion Tracker and Stabilizer Options, particularly the Subpixel Matching value (1/32 is a good setting to use).

strongly consider setting the Track Fields option as well. Lower frame rates result in looser tracks and stabilizations. Track In Reverse is usually not needed for stabilizing but comes in handy for tracking; we will cover it in the next chapter.

Stabilizing and Moving

Sometimes, you will want to stabilize just one dimension of movement – for example, if a camera panned left to right, you might want to keep the pan but stabilize any up-and-down bounce.

This is not a direct option in the Stabilizer, but you can do it indirectly with the following steps and a bit of Motion Fun:

Step 1: Duplicate the layer to be stabilized.

Step 2: Run the Motion Stabilizer on one of the copies of the layer (say, the original).

Step 3: Run Motion Math (also under Layer>Keyframe Assistant); the default script is Copy Values.

(If a different script was loaded during this session, Option+click on the Cancel button to reset.)

Step 4: Set Layer 2 to the layer you stabilized, and Layer 1 to the duplicate. Set the Property menu for both to Anchor Point.

Step 5: Change both Channel menus to the dimension you need stabilized – the Y axis in our example.

Step 6: Apply and turn off the layer you stabilized, leaving just the copy visible.

Note that you can also re-introduce camera moves like pans by stabilizing a layer, then animating its position along the path you want – even with smooth ease ins and outs, if you desire.

Track Options helps give After Effects a better scent to track. If the detail you are tracking has a strong change in brightness compared with its surroundings (such as a white table tennis ball on a dark object), use Luminance. When the difference is more in color than in brightness (a red dot on a green background), use RGB. All things being equal, Luminance calculates faster than RGB. Saturation is the option you will use the least; it comes in handy for rare cases, such as a bright red tracking point against a dull, rust-colored background.

Process Before Match helps with some problem footage. If the object being tracked is out of focus and therefore soft, but the footage is otherwise clean, check this box and use the Enhance option – it runs the equivalent of a "sharpen" filter on the layer just during the tracking stage. If the footage is noisy or grainy, instead use the Blur option lest a speck of dust or noise gets mistaken for a detail in the image to track.

Track Adaptiveness asks the question: "Is it more important to match what this thing looked like on the first frame of the track? Or from the most recent frame I just tracked?" If the former, type in a value closer to 0%; if the latter, type in a value closer to 100%. You would normally leave this at or near 0%. Setting it too close to 100% can result in a track "drifting" as it loses focus from frame to frame as to what feature it is supposed to be tracking. However, if there is a change in detail being tracked during the life of the track – such as a camera zoom (which results in a change in size in the object being tracked), or other lighting or focus changes – then try higher values for this number.

If the object you are tracking gets obscured by another object during the course of the track, or the track otherwise seems to randomly jump on a few frames, experiment with the Extrapolate Motion option. After Effects keeps a note of how accurately it feels it found the detail it was tracking in each frame; these numbers are remembered and can be viewed in the main tracker window after a track. If its guess falls below

Resetting Regions

Changing the "what to stabilize" menu resets your Tracking Regions; After Effects remembers it only if you go back to the same setting. To reduce frustration, set this menu, *then* set the regions.

Save and Load Remembers Regions

Save and Load remembers the position of your Tracking Regions as well as the settings in Options. Use Save before you track: this avoids having to reset the regions on subsequent attempts.

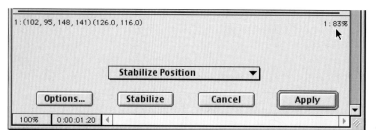

After a track, you can step through the timeline and see how accurately After Effects thinks it found the detail to be tracked in each frame. Above 80% is good.

No Undo in Tracker

Note that there is no Undo while in the Motion Tracker or Stabilizer dialogs. Use the Save feature before making drastic changes. If you need to, you can undo the keyframes after you apply the tracking data.

the threshold you set in this option, it will instead animate the anchor as if the object continued its current motion rather than use its poor match of the tracking detail for the new anchor keyframe.

The default for Subpixel Matching is one you really must change. A setting of 1/2 pixel will result in a jittery stabilization or track. The higher you go, the more accurate the track – and the longer it will take. To see for yourself, try tracking the object in **[Ex.01*starter]** with different Subpixel Matching settings, note the render times involved, and preview the results. Using today's hardware, we consider 1/32 to be a good trade-off between accuracy and speed.

You can Save and Load not just the Options, but also your Tracking Regions and previous tracking data (handy if you want to continue a track later). When you're experimenting with getting a good track – and it will often take more than one try – it helps to remember what settings you tried last time so you can see the effects of tweaking one parameter at a time. Get in the habit of using this feature; it will save a lot of time and fussing in a complex track. (Note that on the Mac, you can't load tracking data and immediately Apply because of a bug – you need to perform additional tracking for it to be enabled.)

Track and Apply

Once you have set your Tracking Regions, Options, and the in and out points of the segment of time you want to track, hit the Stabilize button and watch After Effects work. If you see the Tracking Regions wander off from the object you are tracking, stop and retweak your settings. **[Ex.01*starter]** is pretty easy to track; if you are having problems, load the settings **33_01.ms** from this chapter's project folder on the CD and try that. Note that tracking can be a slow process, especially if the frames of the movie are not already cached in RAM.

Once the tracking is finished and you are satisfied, hit Apply. Stabilize Position creates Anchor Point keyframes for every frame tracked; Rotation creates Rotation keyframes; Position & Rotation creates Anchor Point and Rotation keyframes – plus an extra Position keyframe just at the start of the track (which you're free to delete). Note that you can nudge Rotation keyframes further by selecting them all, parking the time marker on one of the keyframes, and using + and – on the keypad

During the tracking process, After Effects updates the Tracking Region to show if it still has a lock on the detail it is tracking.

Masking and Motion Stabilization

You will often want to mask or otherwise crop an image that has been stabilized. Consider, for instance, footage shot of a politician making a speech at a podium, such as in **[Ex.02]**. You use a basic rectangular mask (Chapter 13) so that only the head and shoulders of the person speaking are visible, and you use this as a picture-in-picture effect **[Ex.02 mask only]**.

However, the camera shake means that the figure is bouncing around inside the masked area. So you stabilize it. But since stabilizing animates the Anchor Point and transforms such as Anchor Point happen after masking, your mask will bounce along with the speaker, as demonstrated in **[Ex.02 wobble mask]**. It doesn't matter if you stabilize first or mask first – the render order will remain the same if you use only one comp.

To mask footage that is stabilized, you'll need to use two compositions so you can reverse the default render order. The idea is to stabilize the footage in the first comp and apply the mask in the second comp. If you want some practice:

Step 1: Open **[Ex.02*starter]**, which contains the footage to be stabilized. We used the gavel on the table as a tracking point. After you run Motion Stabilization, the Anchor Point will be animated.

Step 2: Create a new comp **[Ex.02-final]** and nest **[Ex.02*starter]** into it. Now apply a rectangular mask to the head and shoulders.

Step 3: *Optional:* You can also feather the edges or apply a bevel, drop shadow, or other edge effects to finish off the picture-in-picture effect.

The original source movie is stabilized in one comp, then masked in a second comp. Now the mask is unaffected by the Anchor Point keyframes. Edge effects have been added to the picture-in-picture layer, plus a background layer. Footage courtesy Artbeats/NASA, The Early Years.

Our comps appear in folder **[Ex.02_tracked "gavel"]**. The camera shake is removed – but unfortunately, our speaker leans to the right of the frame during his speech. In the "alternate" comp version, in the **[Ex.02_tracked "tie"]** folder, we stabilized the knot on his tie rather than the stage; preview both final comps and see which you like better. (The tracking setup data for these two versions is also saved on the CD in the 33-Example Project folder.) Know that stabilizing can be as much an aesthetic judgment call as a technical procedure.

to change rotation in one-degree increments. Or, use Effect>Distort> Transform to change the object's rotation (although this will resample the image a second time).

Preview the comp and note that the sphere stays pretty well centered instead of wandering around (which it does in its source comp **[Ex.01.1]**). However, it does not stay completely sharp or stable, which points up an important gotcha about stabilizing: the results are seldom perfect, so don't rely on it for absolute miracles. Also, if the object you're tracking had inherent motion blur, the object would appear to strangely blur in place when stabilized.

Tweaking Stabilized Position

Stabilize Position animates the Anchor Point, not the Position of a layer, so you can edit the Position value to recenter or further animate your tracked footage in a comp.

Broken Tracks

You do not have to track an entire clip with one Tracking Region definition. We once had to track a several-minute-long, continuous helicopter flight that went from the clouds into the front door of a building – needless to say, the best feature to track changed during the course of the shot. Just make sure you set your anchor point reference initially to where you need it to be. Track until After Effects starts to drift, back up the time marker to where the track was still good, reset the in point to this time, Option+drag the center (or drag just the handles) of the Tracking Region(s) to the new best object to track, and continue tracking.

Oops...

Sometimes, you might hit Apply before you intended to, or tracked too short of a work area, leaving yourself with a partial track. You do not have to restabilize the entire shot from scratch when this happens. Locate to the last Anchor Point keyframe that was created. Note the time and the Anchor Point value. Go back into Stabilizer and set the In time to the time of this last keyframe. Zoom in on the image, and drag the inside of the Tracking Region until the number in parentheses underneath equals that last Anchor Point value – this is where it will pick up from. Now drag the corners of the Tracking Region (but not the center!) around the feature you are tracking, and resume.

Full Resolution, Best Quality

Set your comp to Full resolution and layer to Best Quality before you track, especially if it is in a nested comp. Also, preview your stabilized layer in Best Quality, so it moves on subpixels.

Practice, Practice

Motion Tracking and Stabilization are something you get a feel for with experience. Below are a couple of real-world examples for you to practice on. Both were handheld shots taken by Harry Marks at the Wildlife Waystation, a refuge in Southern California for abandoned and injured animals (www.waystation.org).

Stabilize Position

Open comp [**Ex.03*starter**] and preview it. This close-up of a peacock was shot at a distance with a handheld camera at high zoom and there-

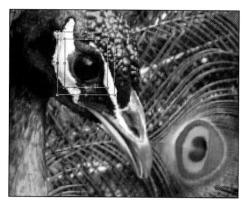

fore has some wobble in it. Your mission is to remove this wobble. Select the peacock layer, then select Layer>Keyframe Assistant>Motion Stabilizer.

The first decision is what to track. The big, round eyeball of the peacock is an obvious first choice; set up your Feature Region (the inner square) to surround it, making sure the Search Region (the outer square) is large enough to catch any movement from frame to frame. Go into the Options window, set the Subpixel Matching to 1/16 or 1/32, and decide if RGB color of your selected region is the best attribute to track, or if you should try Saturation or Luminance. Turning on Enhance might also accentuate the edge of the eye socket for tracking; try it if you have trouble getting a good track.

Setting up the Tracking Region around the eye of the peacock – include some of the color outside the eye to get better edges to track. Peacock footage courtesy Harry Marks.

Stabilize, Apply, then preview. Note that the head of the peacock now stays centered in the screen. With the background moving so much, you might experience the optical illusion that your tracked object is moving. Place your cursor over the eye, then preview again to check that the tracked area is indeed stable.

However, we have a problem insofar as the edge of the layer wanders in the comp, since the layer is being animated to keep the peacock centered. This "wanderlust" is a problem with most stabilized shots, unfortunately; take your pick from the following solutions:

- Scale the movie larger so that edges are not visible;
- Apply a mask in a second comp, to crop out the wandering edges; or
- Add a matte above the stabilized layer and use it as a luma or alpha track matte.

Go ahead and experiment with alternate Tracking Regions. For example, the spurs around the large white region behind the eye are good high-contrast regions. The leftmost one sets the pivot point (around which stabilization occurs) further back, which results in less neck movement but more beak movement after stabilization – perhaps a better trade-off. This is shown in [**Ex.03_final.alt**], where we also added

If an object is moving relative to its background and you stabilize the object, the background will usually move out of frame.

To avoid seeing wandering edges, we used a matte to mask the peacock down to a usable, stable region. (The matte is an animated loop created with the Wiggle Edges effect from ICE.)

Where to Start

A quirk in some footage is that the first frame may not be the best to start tracking on. If you can't get a good track, consider Tracking in Reverse, or retrimming the in time where you start your track.

a track matte to crop out the wandering edges. The end of the beak, on the other hand, would be a poor choice – you don't want the entire head and body pivoting around the end of its beak as it opens and closes!

Stabilize Position & Rotation

Comp [**Ex.04*starter**] shows a different perspective on our peacock. Preview it to again note the camera wobble; also note there is a slight rotation, as the right side seems to dip down slightly toward the end. This is a good example to try stabilizing both position and rotation. Lucky for you, a male peacock in display has built-in tracking dots: the "eyes" on its feathers.

Select the layer, open up the stabilizer, and change the popup to Stabilize Position & Rotation. Note that two Tracking Regions now appear. Select a pair of "eyes" on the feathers to track. Remember that the further

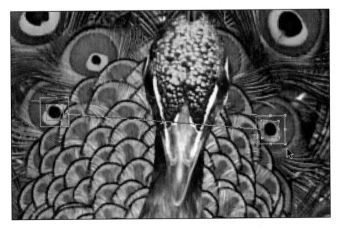

Peacocks, fortunately, have built-in tracking dots on their feathers.

Motion Myths and Madness

As great as being able to track and stabilize objects and footage is, there are a number of gotchas and trade-offs:

- Not all footage can be tracked or stabilized – sorry. And every shot is its own special case. Run tests before promising the client you can do it; have a Plan B ready in the event you can't.

- It is far, far better to plan ahead than to assume you can fix it later. If you know a shot is going to need to be tracked or stabilized, shoot it with tracking markers (such as table tennis balls or other high-contrast dots) placed on the tracking points. Make sure those points stay in camera during the shot. Shoot a backup plan in the event it doesn't work.

- When you stabilize an image, its useful image area will be reduced in size. This is because it is going to get cropped off at the edges as it wanders around. If the movement is too big to hide in the overscan safe areas, plan on cropping and framing the layer in some way in the final composition. You can also scale it up, but be aware that this will soften the image.

- When you stabilize, the image will inevitably get "softer." This is because you will be moving and rotating the image off its original, dead-on alignment, resulting in

pixels being resampled as they are moved about.

- Beware of sudden, quick camera moves, especially with long shutter times. Even if you can successfully stabilize these shots, the entire image will seem to have varying amounts of blur. This is from the natural camera blur caused by the camera's movement.

- Although the tracker and stabilizer in After Effects work quite well with proper preparation and understanding, in all honesty, there are better ones available. For tough jobs, consider using another application such as Puffin Designs' Commotion. You can even copy and paste tracking data from Commotion back into After Effects.

Connect

The Anchor Point was first discussed in Chapter 6.

Masking was covered in depth in Chapter 13, Track Mattes in Chapter 14.

Nesting and Precomposing were covered in Chapters 16 and 17, respectively.

Motion Math is covered in greater detail in Chapter 35.

Video overscan areas are discussed in TechTip 08.

apart they are, the more accurate the rotation will be; the smaller they are, the faster they will track. For our version, we locked onto the two small eyes to the left and right level with the top of the beak, but feel free to experiment.

Stabilize, Apply, and preview. Select the layer and hit U to note that both the Anchor Point and Rotation are being animated. As you step

Our peacock after stabilizing position and rotation. Note from the outlines of the original layer how it has been rotated to keep the bird stable.

through the composition, note that the rotation value is changing; you can also see this from the edges of the original layer as they creep into the comp. Again, you can mask this and recenter the layer's position in the comp; just note that After Effects adds a rogue Position keyframe at the start of the track – remove this so you can change the layer's position at any time in the composition without introducing unwanted animation.

34 Motion Tracking

In the last chapter, we covered the basics of using the Motion Tracking and Stabilization engine. In this chapter, we will cover the additional features required to make one object follow a feature in another layer, to make them appear they were originally shot together, or just to coordinate their actions. We have included several real-world examples for you to practice with.

Motion Tracking allows you to make it appear reality was different when you shot a scene.

Tracking 101

Everything you learned in the previous chapter relating to Motion Stabilization applies to Motion Tracking. The difference is that instead of creating Anchor Point keyframes for the original layer to make it appear stable, when the object is tracked, the tracking data is applied in the form of Position keyframes to a second layer. If the track is good, the second layer will follow a feature in the layer that was tracked and appear to be part of the scene.

To practice how this works, open the composition [**Ex.01*starter**]; it will look just like the first comp in the last chapter – except there is a new layer on top. Select the second layer (moving target), which is the one we want to track, and go to Layer>Keyframe Assistant. This time, a new option appears for you to select: Motion Tracker (note that this option is available only when there are two or more layers in a comp).

Track Point

The first thing you will notice is different is an additional + symbol. This is the spot that will be used to define the Position value of the second layer. If you're using a corner pin option, these are also used to define the corner positions for the pinned layer. Note that Track Points can be set to different places than the middle of the Tracking Region – you might need to pin the layer onto one feature, but another feature in the shot is better to track. For our purposes here, place it in the middle of the blue sphere. In any case, don't sweat its position for now – you can always nudge it later after you've applied the tracker.

Clicking and dragging somewhere inside the Feature Region (the inner square) but not on the Track Point itself moves both the Feature and Search regions as well as the Track Point as one unit. Option+dragging

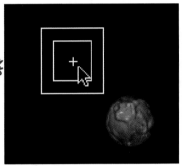

The + symbol that defaults to the middle of the Tracking Regions is the Tracking Point: where you want to pin the second layer relative to the feature you are tracking.

Example Project

Explore the 34-Example Project.aep file as you read this chapter; references to [Ex.##] refer to specific compositions within the project file.

Motion Tracker Options

Apply Motion To:
- ⦿ Layer: ✓ CM_spheregoldmelt.tif
  - Ex.01.1-moving target
- ○ Effect point control:

Time Options:
- 29.97 Frames per second
- ☐ Track Fields (doubles frame rate)
- ☐ Track In Reverse

Track Options:

Use:
- ○ RGB
- ⦿ Luminance
- ○ Saturation

☐ Process Before Match:
- ○ Blur 2 pixels
- ⦿ Enhance

Track Adaptiveness: 0 %

☐ Extrapolate motion if accuracy is below 80 %

☑ Subpixel Matching: 1/32 ▼ pixel

[Save...] [Load...]   [Cancel] [OK]

The two popups at the top become active for Motion Tracking – they decide what layer or effect point receives the tracking data from the current layer.

moves the regions while leaving the Track Point where you put it – this is very important when you're tweaking your regions. You might consider setting your Tracking Region(s) first, then locating your Track Point to avoid accidentally moving both of them together.

There are several different tracking types, which we'll cover after we get through the basics. The important thing to know about Track Position is that it creates Position keyframes for the second layer that follows this layer; it does not create Anchor Point keyframes as Stabilize Position does.

All of the Options are the same as for Motion Stabilization, except one set: the Apply Motion To menu. For simple tracking, select the layer that is supposed to follow the current one.

On the other hand, you might want to have the center of an effect – such as Bulge – follow a feature of the layer you are tracking. Apply the effect you want to the layer first, then use the Tracker. (When you've finished the basics in [Ex.01] check out [Ex.02] where this trick is applied to our hapless peacock from the previous chapter – begin with the *starter comp and see if you can figure out how to get to the _final comp.)

Motion Tracking can also apply to effect points, such as having the center of a Bulge track this peacock's eye. Experiment with this for yourself in **[Ex.02]**. Footage courtesy Harry Marks.

Once you have set up your Tracking Regions and Track Point and have set Apply Motion To as the gold melt sphere layer, click on Track, and if the track looked good, Apply. The gold sphere will now follow the blue one; if you set the Track Point to be the middle of the blue sphere, the gold sphere will now sit directly on top of it. Try tracking using a lower Subpixel Matching value, such as 1/2, and notice how the gold sphere now jitters about the center of the blue one – this is why it is important to use a higher value, even though it takes longer to track.

Experiment further with placing the Track Point in other positions, such as the upper edge of the blue sphere. To tweak the position after you've applied the tracker, select all the Position keyframes, park the time marker on one of them, and use the arrow keys to nudge the layer directly in the Comp window. You can also offset the Anchor Point of the gold sphere to change its relationship to the blue one as it follows it about.

Position and Rotation

There are several different flavors of trackings you can apply to another layer. The most basic, and the default, is Track Position. You can use Track Rotation, which will make one layer rotate the same way as the source – handy if you're trying to coordinate motion.

You can also use Track Position & Rotation; the manual gives a good example of placing a placard or other object in someone's hands that they wave about. By giving them a physical object to hold, their hands will be the same distance apart when you replace the placard later with a new object. (Note that the example in the manual cheated by having the

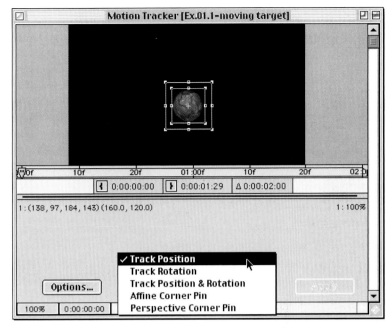

hands behind the placard – holding the edges would have entailed masking out the fingers that would appear in front of the sign...)

It is very important to set up the Track Points for Position & Rotation – otherwise, you will get position and rotation values that don't seem to make sense. Unfortunately (due to an anomaly), the Track Points are invisible in this option. Since you can't see the Track Points, before you open the tracker, you might want to move your cursor in the Comp window over the track point, and write down the values you see in the Info window. You can then set them by grabbing inside Feature Regions and

You can track combinations of position and rotation. There is also a pair of corner pin style trackings, which in essence mold one layer to fit inside the tracking points of another – great for replacing signs, license plates, and so on.

dragging, while watching the second set of position values for Track Regions in the numeric readout below (as described in the previous chapter). Then grab the handles on the regions to set the Track Regions.

To get an idea for what could go wrong, try the following exercise in futility with comp [**Ex.03*starter**]. Select the stage dots layer, apply Motion Tracker with the Track Position & Rotation option, and drag *just the corners* of the first (or leftmost) regions to center

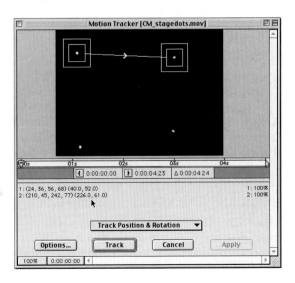

Track Position and Rotation uses two tracking regions: the arrow on the connecting line always points toward Rotation so you can tell which is which. The Position Track Point decides the position of the second layer. Unfortunately, the Track Points are not visible, so drag the center of the track regions and watch the second set of numbers underneath to verify their locations.

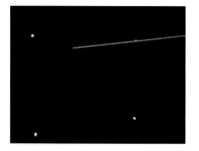

Even though our Track Regions were set to the upper two dots, the rod tracks the wrong dots, because we had "accidentally" set one of the invisible Track Points in the wrong place.

Adjust Separately

Option+dragging moves the Tracking Regions without moving the Track Point. Dragging the Track Point by itself does not move the Tracking Regions.

Cheat Sheet

If you are having trouble setting up the Motion Tracker, load our presaved options files that are in the same folder as this project on the CD. These files end in .mt.

around the upper left dot. Then drag the second (rightmost) Track Region from its center over the upper right dot. Apply this tracking data to the rod layer (set in the Options dialog) and notice how the left end is hanging out in space rather than sticking to the upper left dot that you positioned the first set of Track Regions around. Now do it right: Revert or undo and try again, paying attention this time to setting the invisible Track Points correctly (in other words, this time set the Track Points over the correct dots rather than drag the handles). Check our results in [Ex.03_final wrong] and [Ex.03_final right].

Corner Pinning Choices

The remaining two choices are variations on Corner Pinning. In both cases, they automatically apply the Perspective>Corner Pin effect to the second layer and create keyframes for the corners based on the Track Points plus Position keyframes for the rough center of what is being tracked.

Tracking with Corner Pinning is discussed in two of the examples below. For now, it is just important to know the difference between Affine and Perspective pinning. Normally, you will want to use Perspective pinning, which tracks all four corners and does whatever is necessary to fit your new layer over your tracked points. Affine keeps the opposing sides of the pinned layer parallel to each other, resizing and skewing the layer only if needed. To pull this off, only three of the four corners are tracked, since the fourth has to be calculated in a way to keep the sides parallel. Use this if the layer is not supposed to take on an angled, perspective look.

Real-World Examples

Every motion tracking case is different; that's why it is better to work through some actual examples. Here are three examples of projects you could expect to be asked to do.

Tracking across the Screen

The cameraperson has taken some nice continuous pans across a product, and the clients decide it would be cool to have their slogans track as if applied to the product. And they want them to start off-screen, track across on-screen, then continue off-screen in one smooth motion. Of course, there's no way to track a single point this far – you can't track something that's no longer in the camera's view. You need to track it in two parts, using one tracking region for half the move to pull the object on-screen, and another to push it off-screen.

Make sure Preferences>Time>Timecode Base is set to 30 fps, open [Ex.04*starter], and preview. This contains our footage of a continuous camera move along the neck of a guitar, and the slogan the client wants tracked. Shuttle around the first half of the shot (00:00 to 03:00) by Option+dragging the time marker, and look for good details of the guitar to track that stay in camera during this time – some of the fret ends and corners of the fretboard inlays are good candidates. Then shuttle around the second half of the comp (03:00 to 05:29), looking for a second point that stays in camera for this second half of the clip. Then position the time marker in the middle of the comp (03:00) and roughly position our slogan "Perfect Feel" in a place that looks good to you (we can tweak it later). Select the guitar layer and select Layer>Keyframe Assistant>Motion Tracker.

Let's do the first half first. Since we're going to start off-screen, this is a good candidate to track backward, starting where we want to end up. Set the time marker in the tracker window to 03:00, set the out time to equal this time (click on the right bracket icon under the timeline), go into the Options window, and enable Track in Reverse. While you're here, set a higher Subpixel value (such as 1/32), and consider if it would be better to track RGB or Luminance. Since we're tracking backward, 03:00 is the start of the track; therefore, this is the time to place your points. Place the Tracking Region around that first detail you wanted to track, then place the Track Point roughly where you want your tracked layer to be at this point in time (Figure A). Clicking on Track does the first half of the movie; you should see that the Track Point has been pushed off the top of the screen at time 00:00, meaning it will start off-screen (Figure B).

Now let's do the second half. Move the time marker to 05:29 and set the out point, go back to 03:00 and set the in point (click on the left bracket), turn off Track in Reverse, and select your second feature to track. *It is important that you Option+drag the Tracking Region to this new point* (Figure C) – otherwise, you will disturb the Track Point, which will throw off the continuous nature of the track we're trying to put together here. Go ahead and track again; note the Track Point is now pushed off the bottom of the screen by the end of the clip (Figure D). Click on Apply and preview the result. The text should move like it was stuck to the guitar. (If you're having trouble getting this to work, we've saved the tracking options we used; check out **34_04_pt1.mt** and **-pt2.mt** on the CD.)

The first Tracking Region (A) is set up at time 03:00 and will be tracked backward. After tracking (B), note that the Track Point (where the cursor is pointing) has been pushed off the top of the screen at time 00:00 – this means it will start off-screen. Go back to time 03:00, and set up a second Tracking Region (C) for the rest of the clip. After tracking (D), the Track Point (again, where the cursor is pointing) has been pushed off the bottom of the screen by the end. Footage courtesy Desktop Images.

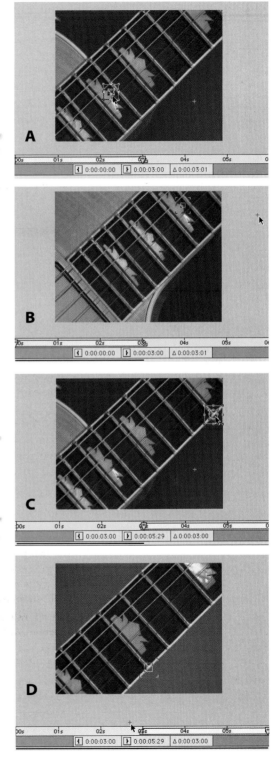

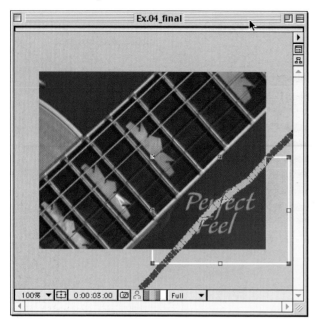

The text Perfect Feel now has Position keyframes that track the guitar neck, from start to finish, off-screen to on-screen to off again. The secret was tracking in two segments.

If you don't like the position of the text relative to the guitar, offset its Anchor Point to reposition it. Double-click on the text to open it in a Layer window, set the option menu in the upper right corner to Anchor Point, and Option+drag the anchor point in this window while looking at its new location in the Comp window.

Tracking with Dots

For motion tracking jobs, you really want to consider placing tracking dots on the object to be tracked – even if the object is a 3D render. In [**Ex.05*starter**], we rendered a videowall box on a virtual stage with a simple camera move around it. The face of the wall is left blank, so we can apply different movies later in After Effects (since 2D effects render much faster than 3D ones do). To make this easier, we rendered a second pass in 3D, with virtual table-tennis balls stuck on each corner of the face of the box. If you are doing a live shoot with a motion control camera that can automatically perform the exact same move over and over, you might consider shooting a separate take for just the tracking dots; this will come in handy as any other activity (such as an actress walking across a stage) might obscure the dots during the shot.

A virtual stage rendered in 3D (left), along with virtual tracking dots that were placed on the corners of the box and rendered as a second pass (right).

This technique gives us a far cleaner set of features to track than trying to follow the corners of a white box against a white backdrop. Select the stage dots layer, bring up the motion tracker, set the popup at the bottom to Corner Pin With Perspective, and place your tracking regions over the four dots. When done, locate your Track Points on the dots. Where you place these points is where the corners of your video will get pinned; in our case, the dots are centered on the corners of the box.

Better Blending

Some of the best tools to make objects blend into shots are the Composite Wizard plug-in set from Puffin Designs.

Set up the rest of your options to taste (the high contrast probably means you can use Luminance tracking; crank up the subpixel accuracy), make sure the video layer is chosen in the Apply To popup, then hit Track, and Apply. Preview, and the movie layer will now be pinned onto the videowall front.

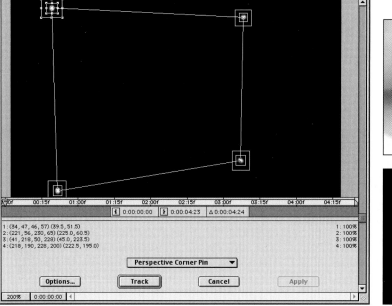

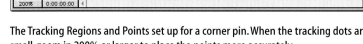

The Tracking Regions and Points set up for a corner pin. When the tracking dots are small, zoom in 200% or larger to place the points more accurately.

After tracking the dots, the video is perfectly pinned onto the front of our virtual videowall (top). To clean up the edges, we rendered a separate 3D pass of just the front face of the wall (above) and used that as a track matte. We also used a Hard Light transfer mode to allow the creases and shadows of the wall to show through the video. Musician footage courtesy Herd of Mavericks.

The final trick in a job like this is to clean up the edges. Most motion tracks still end up with some jitter, which gives the game away – particularly as the edges wander in relation to their frame. Consider creating a separate layer that is a matte for just where your tracked image is supposed to end up. In 3D, it's easy to render a separate high-contrast pass of just the face that is supposed to receive the tracked image; on a video shoot, perhaps paint this surface green or blue and key it later as your matte. In either case, set your Track Points slightly outside the area where the image will get matted to so you have some spill to crop off.

Motion Blur

One of the secrets to making motion tracked objects work in a scene – particularly when there is a lot of movement – is to use Motion Blur (Chapter 11). Enable it for the "applied to" layer, turn it on in the Comp, and preview to see if it helps. The Motion Blur Shutter Angle (File>Preferences>General) has a large effect on how well it works: too much angle, and the object will seem to overshoot its movements, even if the shot was tracked perfectly.

If you need this angle to be different for every other layer in the rest of your comps, consider using the Perspective>Transform Effect for your movement. It has its own shutter angle, which can override the program's default. Copy and paste your Anchor Point, Position, and/or Rotation keyframes from the normal layer properties into the Transform effect's properties. Of course, remember to go back and delete the original keyframes, or else you will get twice the motion.

Pinning with Wild Points

Say your clients have some footage of a series of buildings, and they want you to add a sign onto one of those walls. The camera is moving, so you will need to motion track it. However, there are no track points exactly where you're supposed to place the sign – just points like window sills and paint blotches roughly where the sign goes.

We call this "pinning with wild points." It is difficult, but it's possible with some planning:

Step 1: Create a comp with your layer to track (the footage of the wall, in our case) and the object to pin to this layer (our mythical sign). Apply Effect> Distort>Corner Pin to the sign. Drag its Corner Pin corners to their desired starting position you want in relation to the footage of the wall.

Step 2: Next comes faking After Effects into letting you set up Track Points for something you can't otherwise see. Create a second, temporary comp the same size as the original comp above. Nest your first comp into this temp comp – this allows you to see both the "tracked" and "applied to" layers (the wall and the sign) at the same time in the Motion Tracker's own window. Copy and paste the sign layer from the original comp into this temp comp as well; After Effects needs to see a second layer in the comp where the tracking takes place, or it won't let you select the tracker function.

Step 3: Select the layer with the nested original comp and select Motion Tracking. You should see both the wall and sign layers. Set up your Track Points to the corners of the sign's initial location (which you set with the Corner Pin effect in Step 1), and the Track Regions to whatever nearby features you can track on the wall layer. Go into Options and save this set of points; don't bother actually tracking just yet.

Step 4: Discard your temp comp. Go back to your original comp, delete the Corner Pin effect from the sign layer, and apply Motion Tracking to the wall footage, loading the points you just saved above from our fake comp. Don't move the Track Points – we have already set them in the temp comp to where you want your second layer to get pinned (Option+drag the Track Regions if you need to adjust them at this point). Make sure the layer to be pinned (the sign, in our mythical example) is selected in Apply To, hope the perspective difference between your track regions and points isn't too big, Track, and Apply.

(Although it is much better to simply tape track points onto the original object when you do the shoot in the first place…)

The shot of the sign changes from a close-up to a zoom-back, adding to our challenge. (The reason the sun and shadow patterns are so strange on the wall is that this was taken during a solar eclipse, turning the gaps between a tree's leaves into numerous pinhole cameras.) Footage courtesy Kevin Dole.

A Challenging Replacement

A common motion tracking task, from corny in-house videos to serious feature films, is to replace a sign or billboard in a shot with something more appropriate to the storyline. This usually requires Corner Pin with Perspective. In comp [**Ex.06*starter**], we have a rather challenging example for you to motion track of an interlaced DV NTSC shot of a street sign in France that we want to replace. Problem is, it's a handheld shot (lots of wobble), and the camera also zooms out – so the features we want to track change over the course of the shot.

Fortunately, the sign practically has tracking dots built in – the blue dots of paint in its corners. The sign corners are also fair game, though the sunlight patterns occasionally wash them out in contrast to the pale wall.

The biggest challenge is the camera pullback during the shot, because this means the size of the features we want to track are going to change. You can try tracking the shot in multiple segments (as with the guitar example earlier), or set the Track Adaptiveness parameter to a high value, such as 75% to 100%. As you remember from the last chapter, this option decides whether to try to match what was inside the Tracking Regions in the first frame, or the most recent frame of a track.

Ironically, this feature results in problems if you check the option to track on fields: Upper and lower fields interpolate into slightly different images from each other from field to field, which can confuse a highly adaptive track. Try it with and without the field option checked. You will have other decisions to make, such as whether to try the Enhance or Blur options, and whether to track RGB or Luminance. Expect to make several attempts. (If you get completely stumped, load the settings **34_06.mt**, then explore variations on its settings.)

After you have successfully tracked the old sign and corner-pinned on our new one (which says "Your Name Here" in French), you might notice it looks a bit flat and artificial. The unspoken second half of every motion tracking job is making the new object look like it actually belongs in the original scene.

For clues, look at the sign on the original video clip. Notice it has some thickness and a shadow where it does not mount perfectly flush against the wall. Perhaps it would be best to simulate these in the new sign. Try a couple of the Perspective effects, such as Bevel Alpha and Drop Shadow, to simulate this. Eyedropper colors from the original scene and adjust intensities to help improve the blend. A little blur might help as well, to simulate the camera focus. As you can see, there's no one answer to making a tracking shot "work." But start to view these tasks with an artist's eye, and it will be easier to solve their puzzles.

In addition to setting up the Tracking Regions, think about where to place the Track Points. The corners of the sign might not be a good idea, as the color of the sign bleeds into its surroundings (caused by the color undersampling inherent in the base DV format). Set the points out far enough that your new sign will cover this bleed.

Our final take on this shot includes Bevel Alpha and Drop Shadow to help make the new sign look more real. Place them before the Corner Pin effect so they get the same perspective distortion as the shot animates.

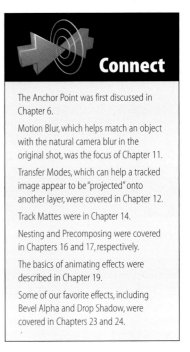

Connect

The Anchor Point was first discussed in Chapter 6.

Motion Blur, which helps match an object with the natural camera blur in the original shot, was the focus of Chapter 11.

Transfer Modes, which can help a tracked image appear to be "projected" onto another layer, were covered in Chapter 12.

Track Mattes were in Chapter 14.

Nesting and Precomposing were covered in Chapters 16 and 17, respectively.

The basics of animating effects were described in Chapter 19.

Some of our favorite effects, including Bevel Alpha and Drop Shadow, were covered in Chapters 23 and 24.

35 Motion Fun

Motion Math is the ultimate keyframe assistant. Unfortunately, its name and user interface scare off many users.

Scripting Fun

Enhanced scripts mentioned in this chapter are saved in the Goodies folder on the enclosed CD-ROM. To make scripts easier to find and load, mark them as a "remembered" folder such as with the Favorites popup in the MacOS Enhanced Open & Save dialogs (enabled in File> Preferences>Import). A networked studio might want to have a central script folder.

Example Project

Explore the 35-Example Project.aep file as you read this chapter; references to [Ex.##] refer to specific compositions within the project file.

Back in Chapter 7, we covered Keyframe Assistants: handy little functions you can run on your layers to either set or modify some of their keyframe values. Motion Math, available only with the Production Bundle, takes these further, allowing "scripts" to be written and modified so anyone can create his or her own assistants, which can affect the motion or almost any other parameter of a layer.

Adobe provides a number of these scripts, which can be run as is or tailored as needed. After Effects also provides a large tool set to create your own – which is either exciting or terrifying, depending on your mind-set. To help alleviate the fear some experience in trying to use this assistant, we will refer to it throughout this chapter as *Motion Fun*…

Before we begin, locate the Motion Math Scripts folder – the default location for the scripts from Adobe is the same folder as the program (although scripts can be located anywhere on your drive). We've also included several of our own enhanced scripts in the Goodies folder on the enclosed CD-ROM. *To make it easy to navigate between the different scripts used in this chapter's examples, drag the Motion Fun Scripts folder to your After Effects folder, or even merge them with your existing scripts in one folder.*

Relatively few users are of the programming persuasion; they prefer to use tools rather than create them. For those who *are* so inclined, the After Effects Production Bundle Guide has a very detailed section on programming Motion Math; teaching programming here would take another entire book. Therefore, we're going to focus on how to use the scripts Adobe provides – with enough about the scripts that you can tweak them as needed to get the results you want.

Basic Fun

As with most assistants, the goal of a Motion Fun script is to help animate something that would otherwise be tedious to do by hand, with a precision that would otherwise take a calculator and a lot of number writing.

Basically, Motion Fun creates keyframe values. It usually does this for only one layer at a time, over the period of time defined by the work area, and only one parameter of that layer, such as position or rotation. Like most other keyframe assistants, it can affect nearly any parameter of a layer, although there are some parameters that don't make sense for particular scripts. You can choose how many keyframes a second a script creates, and you can always undo the result if you're not satisfied, or just delete the keyframes that are created.

The most common use of Motion Fun is to have the behavior of one layer affected by the animation of another – for example, for the position of one to affect the rotation of another, or to have a second object appear to be dragged behind the first as if attached by a spring. There are some other handy utilities, such as a great bouncing ball simulation, and more targeted tricks, such as an automated way to make the opacity of a layer (such as an LED display) blink continuously over time.

A Fun Dialog

To apply Motion Fun, select any layer or group of layers in a composition, then select Layer>Keyframe Assistant>Motion Math. If you selected only one layer, it will default to the layer that will get the new keyframes. But don't sweat it too much; you can select any layer in a comp once you're inside this dialog.

In order to run, Motion Fun needs a script. It automatically loads the CopyValues script, which does what it says: copies one set of values from one layer to another, including some additional scaling along the way, such as 100 pixels = 360° of rotation. You can load another script, either a default script or one supplied with this book, as we'll see later.

We know some users who immediately hit Cancel once they see the Program Text window. However, you can ignore most of the contents of this window. Just start by reading the lines at the top that begin with the double slashes (//) – they describe what the script does and what the main popups below do. For some scripts, you might need to look at one or two more lines of the script itself; we'll cover those later.

Skip the next row of popups (Functions and its friends – they're for programming), and go to the Layer/Property/Channel popups. The first one is the *to* layer: which layer, and which parameter of that layer, is going to get the new keyframes. The Layer popup is a list of all layers in the current comp; the second is a list of all properties available to be manipulated for the layer – including all transformations and nearly all

The Motion Math dialog is initially gray and daunting (above). Focus just on the main parameters for executing scripts, namely the Layer/Property/Channel popups, the "Sample at" rate, and the Load, Save, and Apply buttons. With a little imagination, you could visualize a kinder, gentler, and more colorful Motion Fun dialog (below)…

Jerky Movement

If you want jerky, nervous keyframes rather than smooth ones, enter a lower frame rate in the Motion Fun dialog, run the script, select the keyframes that were created, and change them to Hold keyframes (Layer> Toggle Hold Keyframe or Command+Option+H).

effects properties. The Channel popup is only for when a property has more than one dimension, such as X and Y for position and scale. It will let you choose if one or all of the dimensions are affected.

Some scripts can look at one layer to affect another. The second set of popups is usually the "looked at" or *from* layer. This is one of the confusing parts of Motion Fun: The selected layers tend to go in the order *Paste To* and *Copy From*, not Copy From and Paste To as you might expect.

Skip the Errors box (it is usually empty); at the bottom is where you set how often keyframes are generated. Motion Fun creates only linear keyframes: If you are tracking a layer that has all sorts of eases and other acceleration changes, you will probably want to sample at the frame rate you intend to render at, to make sure you don't miss anything. This does generate a lot of keyframes; you can always run The Smoother keyframe assistant (Chapter 7) on it later. If the result is still an overly busy animation, you can try lower frame rates, then change their keyframe interpolation to something like Auto Bezier.

Fun and Games

Let's practice running a script. Open comp [**Ex.01*starter**] and hit 0 on the keypad to preview it: it's an animation of one wheel turning, with the other (currently) stationary. We've turned Motion Blur on, to reduce the strobing of the wheel as it rotates fast; if your previews are taking too long, click off the Enable Motion Blur switch in the Time Layout window. If the Rotation parameter is not visible, select the layer and hit R; note that it has several keyframes.

What if we want to rotate Wheel 2 based on the rotation of Wheel 1? Select the second wheel layer and then select Layer>Keyframe Assistant>Motion Fun. The default script is Copy Values, which is exactly what we want. Make sure Layer 1 is Wheel 2 (our To layer) and that its Property is Rotation; Layer 2 should be Wheel 1 (our From layer) and its Property should also be Rotation. The Sample At parameter should default to the comp's rate (29.97); leave it. Click on Apply and hit 0 to preview. They both rotate the same now.

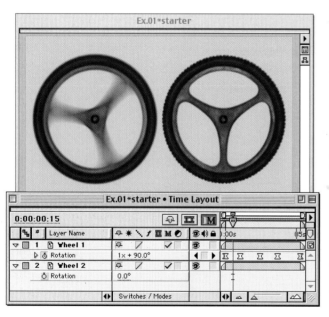

Two wheels, but only Layer 1 is rotating, as you can see from the keyframes and motion blur.

Select the Wheel 2 layer and reveal its Rotation property if it is not showing already. Note that it has a keyframe every single frame – this may seem excessive, but at least the rotations track exactly. This is shown in [**Ex.01_final**]; turn off the Motion Blur switch along the top of the Time Layout window if it takes too long to preview.

Undo until these keyframes disappear and bring up Motion Fun again, setting the Sample At rate to 3; apply; and preview. Notice that Wheel 2 does not track the changes in rotation for Wheel 1 as closely.

Notice also that the speed tends to bounce awkwardly; this is a side effect of linear keyframes. Select Wheel 2's rotation keyframes and change their type to Auto Bezier (Command+ click on one of them). Preview again; the speed changes in the rotation of Wheel 2 are at least smoother now – as if it's playing catch-up to Wheel 1. This result is in [**Ex.01_final_alt**].

The Power of Fun

The exercise above is a lot of work when all you needed to do was copy and paste keyframes from Wheel 1 to Wheel 2. But what if you wanted Wheel 2 to rotate in the opposite direction of Wheel 1, and at twice the speed, as in our [**Ex.02_final**] example? That's where the fun comes in. Try it for yourself with the comp [**Ex.02*starter**]: select the Wheel 2 layer and run Motion Fun again, setting up its layers and parameters just as you did above for [**Ex.01**] – but don't click on Apply yet.

Notice that the description of the Copy Values script in the Program Text says it sets the value of the popup, "multiplied by a scale factor." Look down a little further to the first line of text without a // in front of it, and you'll see the statement **scale_factor = 1.0**. This is the multiplier it was talking about. We'll refer to numbers you can enter and modify as *variables*. When Motion Fun scripts have variables you can enter to alter the behavior of the script, they're usually near the top of the code portion of the script, to make them easy to find.

Change the 1.0 to –2.0, being careful not to delete the semicolon at the end of the line. Set the Sample At rate to 29.97 if it isn't set already, and apply. Now when you preview, Wheel 2 rotates in sync with Wheel 1, just backward and twice as fast – which otherwise would have taken a bit of hand-keyframing and a calculator to figure out.

Scale down Wheel 2 to half of its original size, and place it so its rim just touches the rim of Wheel 1. When wheels or gears touch, their relative speed is related to their relative size – so a half-sized wheel would be driven twice as fast. Preview, and now you see how Motion Fun can be useful. This script is saved in our Motion Fun folder as **doublereverse.mm**.

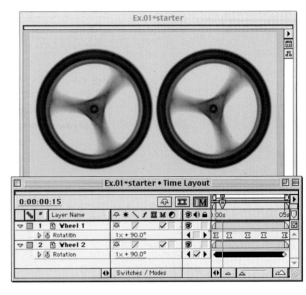

[**Ex.01**] After running Copy Values, the rotations are now the same – although admittedly, it took a lot of keyframes to do it.

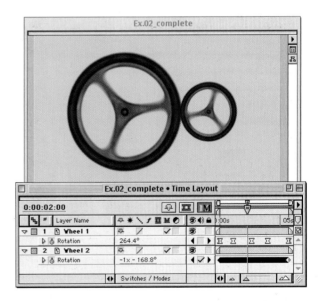

[**Ex.02**] Motion Fun can scale transformations, such as making sure the half-size wheel on the right rotates twice as fast as the larger wheel it is touching.

The Rules of Fun

The rest of this chapter is dedicated to using the Motion Fun scripts that come with the Production Bundle, including applying them in real-world applications. Getting the most out of the scripts will usually require tweaking one or two numbers, as in the **[Ex.02]** example. Therefore, let's go over some of the basic rules of editing scripts. (If you feel like graduating to actual programming, the Production Bundle Guide will take you from here.)

• Lines that start with **//** are comments, not actual code. If you want to add your own comments to a script, or temporarily disable a line (such as a variable you might have set), start the line with **//**.

(Don't type in a novel – although a script can theoretically hold more, the Motion Fun window tops out at about 4000 characters. If you can't type in any more or the computer freezes after running a script, your script may be too big.)

• If there is a value you can or should enter to modify the behavior of a script, Adobe will identify it with a name, followed by an equal sign and a default value. For example, at the start of the Copy Values script is the line **scale_factor = 1.0**. We call these variables; they are usually the only detail of a script you need to read, other than the comments at the head.

• Each line of code must end with a semicolon (;). You might think it was a carriage return instead, but that's not the case; you add those just to better format the text. Don't delete those semicolons; add one at the end of any line of code you might write. An exception is any line that ends with a { or a } – these are program loop points that should be left alone. Comments also don't need semicolons at their end.

• When you're changing variables or otherwise adding numbers and you enter a number that is less than 1, there must be a 0 in front of the decimal point or you'll get an error.

• Speaking of errors, if you accidentally messed up a script or entered an illegal statement, After Effects will let you know in the Errors section at the bottom of the dialog before it creates keyframes. Don't worry about crashing or getting illegal keyframe values.

• You can use normal math statements if you want to further alter values. For example, in the Copy Values script, if you wanted it to add 10 to the value of every keyframe rather than just scale it, change the end of the last line from **scale_factor;** to **scale_factor + 10;**. Use the asterisk (*) and slash (/) for multiply and divide (which is how they appear on many numeric keypads).

• You don't need to leave a space between math functions and numbers, but it's good practice to do so. If you want to enter a negative number, don't place a space between the minus symbol and the number or variable.

• If you modify a script, try using variables to make things clear later. Here is an example of a modified Copy Values script (in our Motion Fun folder on the CD as **copyscaleoffset.mm**) that allows you to both scale and offset, using variables at the start of the script:

```
scale_factor = 1.0;

offset_value = 0;

value(pop_layer(1), pop_property(1))
[pop_channel(1)] =

 value(pop_layer(2), pop_property(2))
[pop_channel(2)]

    * scale_factor + offset_value;
```

• When a script has a **minimum** and **maximum** value, it does not center its results around the middle between the two – it starts at the minimum, then adds to that. You may need to fudge these numbers to get the results to center on a desired value.

• Scripts do not need to end with the letters **.mm** – it just makes the scripts easier to spot or search for. Just make sure you save them in plain text format, should you decide to edit them in a word processor rather than After Effects.

Applied Fun

Let's go through what the scripts supplied by Adobe do. Don't be discouraged if you can't figure out how to make one script do exactly what you need – it simply might not directly change the parameter you want. It is therefore common practice to set up one or two dummy solids, run a script on those, then copy the results from them to the parameters you want. Therefore, we'll cover the various copying scripts first, then move on to the more creative ones. (The actual name of the scripts is in parentheses, followed by the names of any enhanced scripts we've included on the enclosed CD-ROM.)

Copy Values (copyvalu.mm, copyscaleoffset.mm)

This script has been covered earlier in this chapter in detail. It copies one set of values, such as position, into the keyframes of another layer, and lets you scale the result. It will probably be the script you will use most often, copying and scaling keyframe values created by the other scripts below. Use the **copyscaleoffset.mm** script included on the enclosed CD to both scale and offset values without having to hack the script yourself.

Copy Relative Values (parallax.mm, parallax2.mm)

Can you say "instant multiplaning"? That is one of the primary uses of this script, although it is also a good alternative to the normal Copy Values script when you need to remember the original position or other transformations.

The main difference is that Copy Relative Values remembers the initial value of the property you are affecting, then creates new keyframes relative to this initial position, rather than just copying them across, as in [**Ex.03_final**]. To understand this difference, open comp [**Ex.03*starter**], select the B layer, and run the default Copy Values script, setting the pop-ups to copy Position from layer A (the second set of popups) to B (the first set of popups). Preview, and note how B sits on top of A as it moves. Undo until the keyframes are removed, make sure the B layer is still selected, run Motion Fun, and load Copy Relative Values (**parallax.mm**). Again, set the popups to copy the Position parameter from layer A to layer B. Apply, and preview the result. Notice that B now moves in the same way as A, but stays the same distance away during the move as when they started.

Copy Relative Values also has a **scale_factor** value you can set, but it takes on new meaning thanks to the "relative" nature of this script. If you set it to less than 1.0, the layer getting the new keyframes will still get the same motion (or other value changes) from the second layer, only less so. This is shown in [**Ex.04_final2**]. If you set it higher than 1.0, the affected layer will get the second layer's motion (or whatever you assign), but exaggerated.

This is exactly what you need when you're trying to fake multiplaning, in which objects further away appear to move more slowly than objects

Come Back...

If you ever want to revert to the default Copy Values script, Option+click on the Cancel button. (It should say Reset…)

Atomic Multiplane

One of the free plug-ins on the CD is a four-layer version of the powerful Multiplane effect from Atomic Power. See it in action in Bonus Tutorial 21 on the CD.

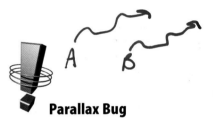

Parallax Bug

There is a minor bug in the Copy Relative Values script where the initial parameters of layer 1 are not remembered. Either manually set a keyframe before running the script or use **parallax2.mm** on the CD-ROM.

Blur and Distance

Adding progressively more blur to "further away" layers helps sell multiplaning illusions.

Copy Relative Values makes it easier to make a "distant" layer move proportionally less than a "near" layer, creating a multiplaning effect.

Synchronicity

To make different layers of a composition seem like they're all being influenced by each other, try scripts such as Copy Relative Values between different parameters – like the position of one layer influencing the rotation of another.

that are near, even if they are moving at supposedly the same speed in the real world. To try this out, open comp [Ex.04*starter] and notice how the larger text layer moves across the frame. Select the smaller text layer, open Motion Fun, load Copy Relative Values (parallax.mm), change the scale_factor to equal 0.6, set the layer popups to copy the position of the "near" layer to the "far" layer, and Apply.

Now when you preview, the smaller layer moves the same as the bigger layer, only more slowly, faking a multiplane move. Compare your result with [Ex.04_final1] to make sure you selected the right parameters. If the layer we were applying keyframes to was supposed to be closer rather than farther away, we would have chosen a value larger than 1.0. It takes a bit of trial and error with scale_factor and the initial settings of the slaved layer to get the most realistic effect, but in the end it can save time over hand-keyframing.

Copy Relative Values is also useful when you want one layer to appear to be just influenced, rather than fully controlled, by another layer. For example, run this script on the "far" layer again in [Ex.04_final1], but this time choose the Rotation values from the popups, with scale_factor set to 0.7. The smaller layer will now rotate as the larger layer does, only less so. This result is shown in [Ex.04_final2].

Apply from Effect Point (frmeffect.mm)

Several effects have their own internal position coordinates. These can be used to center a bulge, align a piece of text, define the corners of a corner pin, and so on. What makes them trickier to deal with is that this position is relative to the layer, regardless of where the layer is positioned in a comp. Because of this, if you want to copy an Effect Point position to the actual position of another layer, you can't use Copy Values (unless the layer happens to be the exact same size as, and centered in, the comp).

Apply from Effect Point does the necessary translation of coordinates for you. It will even track any Position animation in the layer with the Effect and take both into account when it's tracking another layer to it. If you want a relative influence rather than an exact tracking, set the scale_factor variable in the script to something other than 1.0.

The After Effects Production Bundle Guide has a good example of having already animated a Bulge effect traveling around an image, then using Apple from Effect Point to have a magnifying glass track the bulge. If you try this trick, remember to set the anchor point of the layer that is doing the following to where you want the layer centered relative to the Effect Point.

Another example is [Ex.05*starter]. We've used Corner Pin to make a text layer warp and twist in space. Now our client comes back and says, "Very nice, but could we have something tracking the corners of this text layer so its outline is better defined?" We need to make sure the Visibility switch (the eyeball icon in the Time Layout window) is on for the four spheres also in the comp, select one, run Motion Fun, and load the Apply from Effect Point (frmeffect.mm) script. We also need to make sure Layer

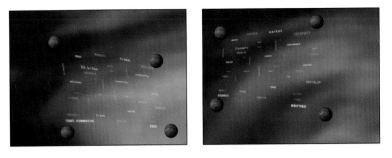

Four spheres set to track the corners of our corner-pinned text, using the Apply from Effect Point script. Background from Artbeats Liquid Ambience.

1 is the sphere, with its Position property selected; Layer 2 should be the text, with one of the corners of the Corner Pin selected – say, upper left. We then Apply and repeat for the other three spheres, assigning each one to a different Corner Pin corner. The result is shown in [**Ex.05_final**].

Apply to Effect Point
(toeffect.mm, toeffectplusoffset.mm)

The opposite of Apply from Effect Point: You have a normal layer position value that you want an Effect Point to track, but you aren't ready to break out the calculator and try to translate between the two different coordinate systems (absolute comp position versus relative layer position) by hand.

In comp [**Ex.06*starter**], we have two spheres flying around in space. Our client now decides it would be cool if a line of text ran between them, as if centered on an imaginary string connecting the two spheres together. You can do this easily with a combination of Motion Fun and Path Text. Select the Text layer, then run Motion Fun. Next, load the Apply to Effect Point script (**toeffect.mm**). Make sure Layer 1 is the Text layer and set its Property popup to Path Text/Vertex 1/Circle Center – this is the left reference point for our text. Set Layer 2 to Sphere 1, and select its Position property. You can then Apply, and do the same thing again, this time setting the destination as the text's Path Text/Vertex 2, and the source as Sphere 2's Position. The result is shown in [**Ex.06_final**].

Apply to Effect Point has a **scale_factor** as well, if you want an "influenced" move rather than an absolute position. If you need an off-

By applying the position of our two spheres to the end points of our Path Text, our text acts as if strung on an invisible rod that intersects the two.

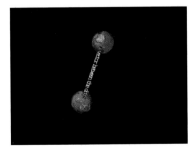

set to the position, you can add (or subtract) it on the last script line after **scale_factor**; a modified script with this offset as a variable is saved on the CD as **toeffectplusoffset.mm**. If you need to offset X and Y separately, run the script twice, selecting the axis you want in the Channels popup.

Scale All Layers (scaleall.mm, scalefromcenter.mm)
Scale Layers by Comp Size (scaleby.mm)

These two scripts were made somewhat obsolete by After Effects version 4.0. But don't skip ahead just yet; we've modified them to have more uses.

The problem with changing the composition's size during the middle of a project was that the Scale parameter of all the layers did not get updated to match this new size. So, if you were animating in a 320×240 comp, then changed its size to 640×480, all of your layers kept their original scale, with all their motion now happening in the upper left corner of the comp. These scripts resized the scale of the layers, and repositioned them to help match the new comp size.

As of version 4.0, After Effects added a new Anchor parameter to the Composition Settings (Command+K) that allowed you to resize a comp from its center, rather than the upper left corner. This kept your layers centered in the resized comp, but did nothing to rescale the layers or expand their movement proportionally to cover the comp's new area.

Unfortunately, these scripts still assume the resizing happened from the upper left corner, throwing your position keyframes out of whack. Therefore, we've created a modified script – **scalefromcenter.mm** – that allows you to resize the scale and the position animation of your layers around any "center" point you enter. It can also be found on the enclosed CD-ROM.

In addition to fixing changes in the comp's size, this script will be handy if you have already animated a group of layers. But now the client asks you to "make them bigger" or "make them smaller" – motion paths and scale included.

This script has four parameters for you to set, some of which take a little preplanning. The first is our ubiquitous **scale_factor** – how much do you want to expand or contract the layers? If you resized your comp, enter how much you scaled the comp by – for example, 2.0 for scaling up from 320×240 to 640×480. Second is **scale_center**. If you are resizing the animation of a group of layers, before you run Motion Fun, make sure the Info window is open (Command+2), move the mouse to the perceptual center of the group that you want to scale around, and enter that number, separated by a comma – such as **160,120**. Again, in the comp case, enter the center of your new comp size (half of its overall dimensions).

The Layer popups themselves mean nothing in this script; Scale and Position are always the properties that are modified. The layers to be affected are defined by **start_layer** and **end_layer**. Observe the layer number(s) in the Time Layout window and enter them by these constants. The default for **end_layer** is **num_layers**, which is After Effects' internal way of saying "the last layer there is."

Lightning Strike

To make an electrical shock seem to flow from one object to another, regardless of their animation paths, copy their positions to the start and end points of Effect>Render> Lightning (Production Bundle effect).

Scaling Past 100%

Remember that scaling past 100% softens a layer. If it's an Illustrator file, or another comp, try turning on the C switch (Continuous Rasterization or Collapse Transformations, respectively) to maintain maximum resolution.

Comp [**Ex.07*starter**] has a cluster of buzzwords animating from a central point. After designing them to look good in the half-resolution comp you were viewing, you realize they're too big when viewed at full size (Command+= to zoom the comp out to 100%), and they overwhelm the background image. Set the time marker to 00:00, move the cursor to the apparent center of their animation, and note this value in the Info palette (Command+2); also note which layers are the text. Run Motion Fun, and load **scalefromcenter.mm**. Enter the position you just noted for **scale_center**, leave **start_layer** at 1, and enter the number of the last layer for **end_layer**. Decide how much you want to scale them down by – say, 75% – and enter this number (0.75) for **scale_factor**. Apply, and preview.

For a different effect, select a smaller range of layers to scale – now you will have a mixture of original and more compact moves. [**Ex.07_final**] shows what we came up with. This technique can also be used to achieve a type of multiplaning effect.

Gravity (gravity.mm, gravitywithborders.mm, gravity_splat.mm)

One of the most popular Motion Fun scripts is Gravity, because it helps create a bouncing-ball effect. It affects the position of one layer, bouncing it off the edges of a comp. Although the Position keyframes are replaced, the positional velocity of the layer at the start of the work area (which is where all Motion Fun scripts start their work) will be the initial speed and direction of the layer that gets bounced – so you can simulate tossing a ball in the air and letting it fall, for example.

The parameters for this script are buried; read down a little in the Program Text to find them. **damping** is the air resistance the object encounters as it flies and bounces around. This is a very touchy parameter; play around with very small changes between 0.90 and 1.0 to go between mud and the center of a golf ball. **grav** is how strong the gravitational pull is; lower values will give a dreamy moon bounce effect.

grav_dir is the direction gravity is pulling. It is a little strange to edit. The first number is pulling in the positive X direction (left to right); the second number is pulling in the positive Y direction (up to down). Ignore the third number and leave it at 0. The range you should play with for X and Y is –1 to 1, with negative values meaning that gravity is pulling in the opposite direction. Having a non-zero number for both X and Y means gravity is pulling at an angle – for example, {**1,1,0**} means it is pulling toward the lower right corner.

Comp [**Ex.08.1**] has our rotating planet from earlier examples. Select it, run Motion Fun, load the Gravity script (**gravity.mm**), and click on Apply. Our planet will bounce off the bottom of the comp; if it is not already visible, twirl down the Position property, then twirl down its velocity to get a feel for what is going on. Undo to remove the keyframes, and apply again, playing with different values for **damping**, **grav**, and **grav_dir**.

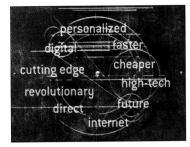

Several layers have been animated and scaled (above), but we're displeased with the final result. By running **scalefromcenter.mm** on different ranges of them with different scale values, we get a more varied, multiplaning effect (below). Background image by Paul Sherstobitoff.

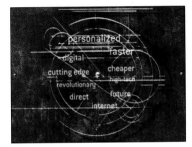

```
if (time() == start_time) {
    vel = tmap (time() + step_time, value(pop_layer(1), position)) –
        value(pop_layer(1), position);
    damping = 0.95;        // Damping force (0 = infinite friction, 1 = none)
    grav = 0.9;            // magnitude of gravity force
    grav_dir = {0,1,0};    // direction of gravity
    accel = grav * grav_dir;  // gravity vector
```

The parameters to edit for **gravity.mm** – highlighted here – are buried a bit down in the script.

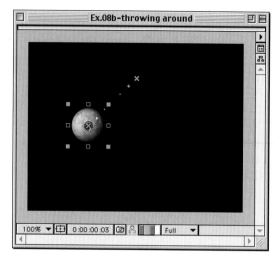

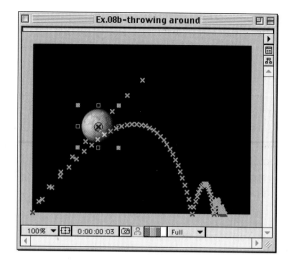

[Ex.08.2] The initial direction and velocity of an object's Position (left) affect how it gets bounced around a comp (right).

You'll note that the center of our planet, not the bottom of the planet, is bouncing off the comp bottom. What is really "bouncing" is the anchor point. Try moving the anchor point to the bottom of the planet or selecting all the keyframes and nudging them up after applying the script. The result is shown in [**Ex.08.1_final**].

Now let's experiment with throwing our planet around. [**Ex.08.2**] contains a pair of position keyframes, with the planet being aimed at the lower left corner. Run the Gravity script on it, and watch it bounce around the comp. The result is shown in [**Ex.08.2_final**], if you want to verify what you're doing. Undo, and try altering the planet's second Position keyframe to see the results of throwing it in different directions.

Enhanced Gravity

Two weaknesses of the Gravity script are that it doesn't take the size of the bouncing object into account – its anchor point bounces instead – and the bounce walls are limited to the comp's sides. On the CD is a bonus script called **gravitywithborders.mm** that fixes these two shortcomings. It is full of comments to help you understand how to use the new parameters. Try running it as is on **[Ex.08]** and notice how the planet stays "inside" the comp now. Edit the **xxxx_edge** parameters to make the object bounce inside a virtual box (which can be larger or smaller than the comp).

An additional not-so-obvious weakness of the original Gravity script is that it takes air resistance

into account, but not how "bouncy" the object or the walls are. To make an object bounce less, you have to increase the **damping** parameter, which also slows down how it travels through "air."

Therefore, also on the CD are a pair of scripts with the name **gravity_splat.mm**, which add a **splat** parameter to control bounciness in the **gravitywithborders.mm** script, as well as a **skid** parameter that adds rolling resistance when the object hits a side or rolls along the bottom. This may yield results closer to what you were expecting. The **_a** version of this script also more accurately calculates how an object would bounce away from a wall, at the price of occasionally looking a little odd with motion blur turned on; the **_b** version seems to "hit" the walls better, at the price of slightly less accurate bounces.

This is another example in which combining scripts comes in handy. What if you want a wheel or gear to act like it has been wound up, is let go, and slaps against an end stop, as in [**Ex.09_final**]? In this case, decide how far wound up (in degrees) you want the spring to be initially, create a dummy layer with a solid, and position its height this many pixels above the bottom of the comp. Try this out in comp [**Ex.09*starter**]: Let's say you want the wheel to spin 360°. Since your comp is 240 units tall, make the initial Y position 240 – 360 = –120 pixels; for 180° of rotation, start it at 240 – 180 = 60 pixels for Y. Place your solid here and run the Gravity script on it – it should fall from this height and bounce off the bottom. Now, run the Copy Values script, copying the Y position of your dummy solid to the Rotation of your wheel. You can turn off the dummy solid when it's no longer needed.

Our wheel is wound up and comes to rest against an end stop, bouncing (using the gravity script copied to rotation) until the wheel gradually comes to rest.

Spring (spring.mm)

You could think of this as the "puppy dog" script, since its job is to make a second layer chase another around, flying past, rebounding, and bouncing into position as if attached by a spring to the first layer.

There are two parameters in this script to play with. The first, **rest_length**, acts like the length of the spring. When everything comes to rest, this is as far away as the second layer's center will end up from the first layer's center. However, the results of a length longer than 0 can be a bit unpredictable, since you have no control over what direction the spring "hangs" in when it is done. This can have the advantage of making your animations less predictable; otherwise, start with it equal to 0 – you can always offset the position later using our **copyscaleoffset.mm** script or by selecting and nudging all the position keyframes.

The second parameter, **damp**, is how springy the spring is. As with gravity, it is very sensitive; try small changes in value between 0.9 and 1.

To get a feeling for Spring, open [**Ex.10.1**]. Select the second layer, called Leader, and run Motion Fun. Load the Spring (**spring.mm**) script, and set the **rest_length** parameter to 0. Make sure Layer 1 is Leader and Layer 2 is Follower, Apply, and preview; compare your results with [**Ex.10.1_final**]. You'll see the second layer spring past the first, bouncing back and forth until it comes to rest directly on top of it. Undo or delete Follower's position keyframes, and run Spring again, experimenting with different initial positions for Follower, as well as different values for **damp** and **rest_length**. Note that if Follower starts out exactly the **rest_length** away from Leader, there is no spring action, since they already are the rest length apart from each other.

Things get more interesting when the leader layer is moving as the follower layer tries to snap to its position. Open [**Ex.10.2**]; here the Leader layer has a simple motion path. Select this layer, run Motion Fun, load the Spring script, set **rest_length** to 0, make sure Layer 1 is Leader and Layer 2 is Follower, Apply, and then Preview. This result is shown in [**Ex.10.2_final**]. Again, experiment with different initial positions for the Follower layer and try tweaking Spring's parameters.

 **Drunken Motion**

If a layer is already moving, it can be "springed" to itself. The result is a jittery, wobbly motion path.

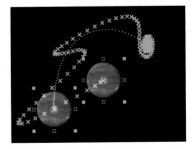

The Leader layer (disc on lower left) has a simple lower left to upper right motion path; after Spring is applied, the Follower layer's path goes through all sorts of gyrations to keep up.

Spring can have similar uses as Gravity, but without the hard bounce. [**Ex.11_final**] has our wheel and dummy solid again, but this time there is a second solid for our dummy solid to bounce around. Re-create this example using [**Ex.11*starter**]; run Spring on Leader, as you did above, making Follower (Layer 2 in the script) bounce around it. This time use Copy Values to transfer Follower's X position to the rotation of the wheel.

Double Spring (dbspring.mm)

This script varies from Spring in that rather than one object following another, here both objects are "let loose" when the work area starts, and they spring toward each other, separated by the **rest_length** parameter. This is shown in [**Ex.12_final**]. The position animation of both is overwritten, but their direction and velocity at the start of the work area is taken into account, akin to Gravity where we were playing with throwing objects against the wall. As with Spring, the script parameter **damp** affects how springy the spring is.

Sprung Parameters

It is easier to use Gravity, Spring, and Double Spring to generate position keyframes to be copied to other properties if you restrict the movement to just the X or Y axes. Do this by aligning the objects before running Motion Fun.

The trick to having this initial velocity truly affect the result is to have the work area start somewhere between two keyframes. If the work area starts at the same time as a position keyframe, the two layers will just spring towards each other, ignoring their "initial" movement. Try this with [**Ex.12*starter**]: Make sure the work area starts at time zero, select one of the layers, run Motion Fun, load Double Spring (**dbspring.mm**), make sure the two layers appear in the two popups, Apply, and preview. Not very exciting – because they didn't have any motion yet to cause them to bounce around. Undo back to where you started, set the work area to start at time 00:02 (a point in time where the objects are already moving toward each other), and run the script again. The result is far more interesting, with the two objects swinging around each other. Play around with different keyframe positions (these will result in different initial velocities), and observe the results.

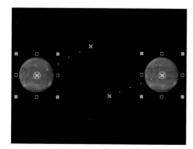
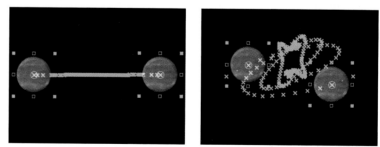

The initial motion path of the objects (left) has no effect on Double Spring if the work area starts at a keyframe (center), but has a great effect if the work area starts *between* position keyframes (right).

Double Spring is another example of a good keyframe generator for other effects, as you can see in [**Ex.13_final**]. Try this example in comp [**Ex.13*starter**] with the two spheres we played with earlier. It also includes a line of text done with Path Text; observe how far apart Vertex 1 and Vertex 2 are in the Path Control Points (or measure using the rulers – Command+R), about 200 pixels. Run Double Spring on the spheres, as above, to make them spring back and forth in relation to each other, but in this case, set **rest_length** to the desired text width – in this case, 200. Run Apply to Effect Point (**toeffect.mm**) on the text layer twice, first mapping Sphere 1's position to the text's Vertex 1, then Sphere 2's position to Vertex 2. The text will now stretch and contract as the springs do. If you don't like the text overlapping the spheres, click on Path Text's Options and pad it with a couple of spaces before and after.

Span (span.mm, span2.mm, span2squash.mm)

This Motion Fun script is handy to run in conjunction with many other scripts, such as Gravity and Spring. It takes a third layer and stretches it from top to bottom to "span" the distance between the anchor points of two other layers, including rotating and scaling its length as necessary, as shown in [**Ex.14_final**]. As fate would have it, there are a couple of bugs in the script Adobe supplies: The layers are backward, and if their Y positions are the same, the layer flips 90°. Instead, run the script **span2.mm** supplied on the enclosed CD-ROM.

Most Motion Fun scripts use one or two layers; this one uses a third – which means it has an unusual parameter in **span_layer**. Here, you enter the name for the layer you want to bridge the other two. If you gave it a new name in the current comp, use that name instead. You can also just enter the layer's number, which is easier (less chance of typos). If you use the name, surround it with quotes; a layer number does not get the quotes.

A Spanner in the Works

There are a pair of bugs in the **span.mm** script. Use the script **span2.mm** on the enclosed CD-ROM.

Precomp a Span

If the layer you are using to span between two others is not oriented, sized, or offset from its sides the way you want, do this in a precomp, and Span this comp. An example of this is [**Ex.14.1**].

Span is a handy script in that it stretches, positions, and even rotates a third layer between the anchor points of two other layers.

[**Ex.14*starter**] is similar to [**Ex.13**] in that we have our two globes springing toward each other (we already ran the Double Spring script on them). However, the text has been replaced with a comp that has an animation of a metal spiral. Note its layer number, select any layer, run Motion Fun, and load Span (**span2.mm**). Select Sphere 1 and Sphere 2 for Layers 1 and 2 respectively (the spanning from and to layers), and enter the spiral's layer number in place of **"your name here"** (delete the quotes as well, since we are using the layer number rather than its name). Apply and preview; note how the metal spiral stretches and compresses between them now.

Blink (blink.mm, blinkany.mm)

This simple script was designed to blink the opacity of a layer on and off, following a gentle sine wave pattern, as in [**Ex.15_final**]. The parameters are easy to manage: **blink_speed** is how fast it blinks, in on/off cycles per second; **low_opacity** and **high_opacity** set how transparent and opaque the layer will get at its extremes. It works automatically on the layer you selected when you ran Motion Fun; the blinking will start at the **high_opacity** value at the start of the work area.

Span and Squash

The script on the CD called **span2squash.mm** has the additional feature of scaling both dimensions of the spanning layer to give a character animation "stretch and squash" effect. Preview [**Ex.14_squash**] to see the results.

Not All Effects

For some reason, not all parameters of all effects will appear in Motion Fun's popup list. The oft-used Levels is unfortunately one of these effects, since it bundles multiple parameters into a single Histogram keyframe.

By now in this chapter, you should be thinking, "What other parameter could I apply this Motion Fun trick to?" The answer is any, including various effects parameters, as well as rotation and scale. That's why we included our modified **blinkany.mm** script on the enclosed CD – it has been altered to allow you to select any parameter in Layer 1's second popup. The parameters are similar, except that _speed has been changed to _value.

For example, a more realistic light blinking might be achieved not by varying a layer's opacity, but its brightness. [**Ex.15*starter**] has a layer with the effect Brightness & Contrast applied. Experiment with the Brightness slider in its Effect Window (Command+Shift+T) to see what range from darkest to lightest you like. Select it, run Motion Fun, load **blinkany.mm**, and set the second popup to Brightness & Contrast/Brightness. Set **low_value** to the dark value you liked and **high_value** to

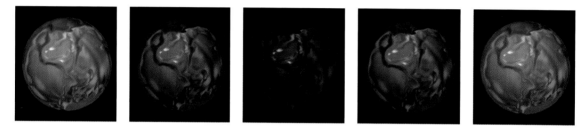

Our **blinkany.mm** script can be applied to almost any parameter, such as Brightness (to get a more realistic light blinking effect).

the value you liked for its brightest. Apply and preview – the result is shown in [**Ex.15_finalalt**]. Feel free to try this with other effects, such as Hue & Saturation or Tint.

Point At (pointat.mm, pointxat2.mm, pointyat2.mm)

This simple script allows one layer to automatically point at another that is traveling around the composition, as in [**Ex.16_final**]. This also comes in useful for simulating instrument display overlays. Unfortunately, Point At also has a bug in it where the pointing layer will jump to an incorrect angle at certain positions. Run our two fixed scripts instead – **pointyat2.mm** assumes your pointing layer is originally aimed straight up; **pointxat2.mm** assumes your pointing layer is aimed left to right when at rest.

Point Where?

If the layer being tracked happens to be right on top of the pointing layer, it will assume it is to its left.

These scripts are easy to run. Select the layer that is your pointer, run Motion Fun, load the Point At script that best describes how your pointing layer is oriented (if you need to re-orient it, do it in a precomp), and select the layer to track in the Layer 2 popup. Apply, and you're done. Remember that the anchor point of the second layer is what will be pointed at. The anchor point of the pointing layers is also what its rotation will be centered around.

Tracking Video

Point At is another good script to combine with Motion Tracking: Track an object on a background shot, then run this script to have an indicator point at it as it travels around the screen.

[**Ex.16*starter**] has been set up for you to experiment with. Select the anipointer layer in this comp as Layer 1 in the Motion Fun dialog. Which script will work best – **pointxat2.mm** or **pointyat2.mm** – is left as an exercise, to make sure you're clear on the difference.

Layer Audio (layeraud.mm)
Comp Audio (compaud.mm)

These two scripts vie with Gravity for the most often used Motion Fun tricks. Their goal is to take the loudness of the audio in either one layer (Layer Audio script) or all layers (Comp Audio script) in a composition, and map this to any parameter for a layer you can select inside the Motion Fun dialog. Scale is used most often, but you can use any transformation and most effects properties as the destination. See our results in [Ex.17_final].

These scripts work by looking at the average audio loudness within each frame of time, then using the result to create a parameter that varies from the **min** to the **max** you set inside the script. The trick is that this script indeed looks at the *average* – not the absolute loudest point inside that frame of time. This average is usually around 70% for material that is "full" loudness; this has an effect on the **min** and **max** ranges you want to set.

For example, if you want to vary the opacity of a layer based on loudness, you would set the **min** parameter to 0 but you might consider setting the **max** parameter to around 143, instead of 100 (100 ÷ 0.70 ≈ 143). Otherwise, the effect might end up lower on average than you expect. It *is* possible for some audio to average higher than 70%; it is also likely for it to average lower. You might need to run the script a couple of times and tweak these parameters to get the best result, but a good starting rule of thumb is to divide the highest parameter value you want by 0.7.

The results of this script are often very jittery, both because it normally creates a keyframe every frame (unless you enter a lower Sample At number in the Motion Fun dialog), and because this "average" value can vary from frame to frame, even for apparently constant-loudness sounds – especially if they are low in frequency. This is the script for which you will most likely want to run The Smoother keyframe assistant (Window>Plug-in Palettes>The Smoother) afterward.

Remember that you can run this script on dummy audio tracks to get certain results. For example, comp [Ex.17*starter] has three copies of our soundtrack. Two of them have had the Low/High Pass Filter audio effect added, one set to Low Pass (so it has only lower frequencies passing through), and one set to High Pass (to get the higher frequencies). Since these filters can weaken the loudness of an audio track, and since this script is based on loudness, we increased the Level of each layer so that their audio meters touch maximum as they play. You can solo and preview these (period on the numeric keypad) if you like. Then play with the scale of the spheres in this comp to get a feel for what you would like their minimum and maximum sizes to be.

Select the blue sphere layer, run Motion Fun, and load Layer Audio (**layeraud.mm**). Make sure the blue sphere is selected for Layer 1 and set its property to Scale. Select the low pass version of our audio track in Layer 2. Enter the scale sizes you decided upon for **min** and **max** in the script,

No Audio?

A layer must have audio and its audio switch turned on to be processed by these Audio scripts. Remember to turn dummy audio layers off after running the script.

Stereo Scaling

When a parameter has two channels, such as position or scale (X and Y), the left and right channels of the audio are used individually for these two channels. If the parameter has one channel (such as Rotation), only the left audio channel is used, regardless of which you pick in the audio layer's Channel popup.

remembering to divide by 0.70 (or even less) when calculating the **max**. Apply, and now do the same for the other sphere: select the gold sphere for Layer 1 and the high pass version for Layer 2. Apply, and turn off the audio for the low and high pass audio tracks, since we don't want them in the final mix.

When you preview, you should notice that the blue sphere jumps with the bass, and the gold sphere jumps with the higher pitched sounds, such as the snare hits. If the results are too nervous and jumpy for your tastes, try a lower Sample At frame rate, or apply Window>Plug-in Palettes>The Smoother; for the latter, values between 1 and 3 seem to work well in this case.

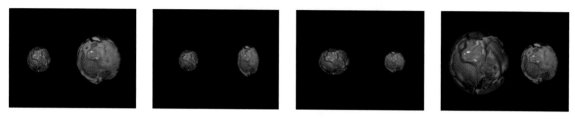

You can process the same audio track differently to get different results out of the Audio scripts, as was done for the left and right spheres here.

Stopping Scripts

If you want to stop a script before it has finished Applying, hit Command+. (period).

Stereo Positioning (stereops.mm)

A new Adobe script that is not in the manual, Stereo Positioning can help make a sound appear to follow a layer around the Comp window by altering its left and right Level parameters to match the X position of a layer. Select the audio layer you want to manipulate, run Motion Fun, and load **stereops.mm**.

This script will automatically calculate the relative position of the object selected by the Layer 2 popup relative to the comp's boundaries, clipping it if it goes beyond the edges of the comp (so you don't have to worry about runaway volumes). There are two parameters to adjust: **min_DB** and **max_DB**, which you set to the minimum and maximum volumes you want the audio to have as the tracked layer moves around. The defaults are a touch extreme; you might want to try −12 and 0 respectively to start.

Layer Audio to Time Remap (layer audio remap.mm)

This deceptively named script (also a new addition that is not in the version 4.0 manual) has a subtle but interesting effect on any assignable parameter of a layer, including its Time Remapping velocity. If the audio of a selected layer is getting quieter on average, it will reduce the value of the selected property in the layer to affect. If its loudness is getting higher on average, it will increase the value of the selected property. Rather than completely replacing keyframes, the parameter values before the script is run are taken into account and modified by the result of looking at the trends in audio volume.

If you want this script to affect Time Remapping, you first have to enable it (Command+Option+T) for the layer you want to remap. Select this layer, run Motion Fun, and load **layer audio remap.mm**. There are two parameters inside the script you can alter – **max** and **min**. They are set to pretty small initial values (0.02 and −0.02); these work well for subtle

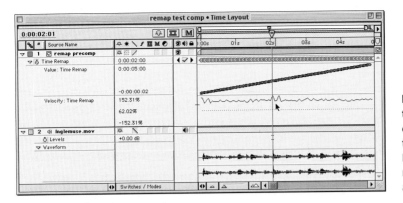

Layer Audio to Time Remap alters the velocity of a parameter's normal changes based on changes in an audio track's loudness. Normally, the Time Remap Velocity line would be a straight ramp; see how it jitters in relation to the audio waveform below.

Time Remapping, but you might want to increase them for a larger effect. If you want to adjust another parameter, you will need to increase these; somewhere between ±1 to ±10 is a good start for properties such as Scale. Select your audio source in Layer 2 and Apply. The result is the animated layer slowing down and speeding up its progress in relation to the music.

This is undoubtedly the most obscure of the Motion Fun scripts. However, if you want something like a simple motion path to slightly deviate, jump, and jive in response to a music track, it can "randomize" keyframes in a manner that makes sense. This script is another good candidate to sample at a lower rate or to run The Smoother on afterward.

Relative Corner to Absolute Corner (cornpin.mm)

Our final Motion Fun script for this chapter is just a utility that can make some work easier after you've applied the Motion Tracker using its Perspective Corner Pin option. The result of the motion tracking operation is that both corner pin values and the layer's position value will all be animated. If you then run Relative Corner to Absolute Corner on this layer, the Position value will now be frozen in place, with the corner pin values offset to compensate. Compare the result in [Ex.18_final], and note that layer 1's Position is static – you might find this result easier to work with than the original layer 2.

To see this in practice, open [Ex.18*starter]. It contains two identical layers, both the result of a Perspective Corner Pin tracking operation as above. Their keyframe parameters should be twirled down in the Time Layout window; if they aren't, select the layers and type U. Now, select the top layer, run Motion Fun, load Relative Corner to Absolute Corner (**cornpin.mm**), and Apply. This script will now pick a new Position for the layer that does not move and alter the corner pin keyframes to give the same visual result as before. Step through the comp and notice the differences in keyframe values between the top and bottom layers. Since position is no longer animating, you can turn off its stopwatch for this layer (since Motion Fun will still place a keyframe every frame, even though the Position parameter is no longer changing). You can then reanimate the position, if you like.

Connect

Managing the work area was introduced in Chapter 2.

Keyframe interpolation types, such as Hold and Auto Bezier, were discussed in Chapter 4.

The Smoother and other keyframe assistants were covered in Chapter 7.

Align Objects appeared in Chapter 8.

Turning on Motion Blur, which helps sell many animation tricks, was discussed in Chapter 11.

Nesting and Precomposing comps were the subjects of Chapters 16 and 17.

Collapse Transformations was explained in Chapter 18; Continuous Rasterization in Chapter 28.

The uses of audio, including the audio filters, was covered in Chapter 20.

The use of Path Text was discussed in Chapter 26.

Time Remapping was sorted out in Chapter 31.

Using the Motion Tracker, which is good to combine with some of these scripts, was taught in Chapter 34.

36 Interpret Footage

This dialog box decides how comps will read your sources.

The Interpret Footage dialog is where you can indicate how After Effects interprets and handles your source files as it hands the images off to your comps. We call it "the money box" because most mysterious problems in final rendered output can be traced back to incorrect settings in this dialog. In this chapter, we will discuss the Interpret Footage dialog's various settings and their general implications. In the next few chapters we will show how these parameters are used in specific situations.

Interpret Footage

Interpretation for "02.3 Z rays dbl/FX.an5"

Alpha
- [Guess]
- ○ Ignore   □ Inverted
- ● Treat As Straight (Unmatted)
- ○ Treat As Premultiplied (Matted with color)

Frame Rate
- ● Use frame rate from file: (24.00 fps)
- ○ Conform to frame rate: 24 Frames per second

Fields and Pulldown
- Separate Fields: Off   □ Motion Detect (Best quality only)
- Remove Pulldown: Off
- [Guess 3:2 Pulldown]

Pixel Aspect Ratio   **Looping**   **Options**
- Square Pixels   Loop 1 times   [Options...]

[Cancel] [OK]

The settings in the File>Interpret Footage>Main dialog sit between your source and every comp you may use it in. You can set alpha interpretation, frame rate, and how interlaced video frames get pulled apart to form their original source images.

Example Project

Explore the 36-Example Project.aep file as you read this chapter; references to [Ex.##] refer to specific compositions within the project file.

Alpha

The top portion of the box is a repeat of the alpha channel dialog that usually pops up while it's importing files that have alphas. If you feel you might have made a mistake with your initial alpha interpretation, you can go back and change it any time here. If you are having problems with colored fringes on objects with alphas, there's a good chance that changing alpha type from straight to premultiplied with black or white will clean it up.

[Ex.01] contains a still image that has this problem. When you open it, notice the slight white fringing around the horn and base of the megaphone. This is the result of After Effects' incorrectly guessing "straight" for its alpha type. In the Project window, locate the file footage item CP_Entertainment.tif inside the Sources>Objects folder. Select it and go to File>Interpret Footage>Main (Command+F). If you change its alpha type to Ignore and click OK, you will notice that it was shot on a white background – a clue as to what may be bleeding into the edges. Change the Alpha type to Treat as Premultiplied (Matted with color), change the color swatch to white, and click on OK. The white halo will disappear.

The premultiplied color always defaults to black, but some source material is originally shot on white – such as still image object libraries. If their masks were cut right on the edges of the objects, chances are some of the white background got mixed in; selecting Treat as Premultiplied and changing the swatch to white will usually improve them. If a different background color was used, you can eyedropper its background to see if that improves the edges. (To see the background clearly, set the Alpha type to Ignore; now you can eyedropper the color directly.)

Frame Rate

The next pane is dedicated to frame rate and applies only to movies or sequences of stills. Movies come in with a rate already embedded in them; sequences have their default rate set via the File>Preferences> Import dialog. However, you can change or *conform* that rate to a new one inside After Effects for either practical or creative reasons.

For example, the VideoLoops sequence, VL_FilmCrud, in the Sources> Sequences folder was imported at its film rate of 24 fps. As you step through the movie in comp **[Ex.02]**, which was created at the NTSC video rate of 29.97 fps, you will note that some frames are repeated because the frames rates do not match. Since this sequence is just film crud and noise, its speed is not critical; open its Interpret Footage dialog and set its Frame Rate to 29.97.

You also may need to change the frame rate because it was mislabeled. For example, NTSC video runs at 29.97 fps, but many people render 3D animations and label stock footage at 30 fps. Leaving these sources at 30 while you build your comps and render at 29.97 fps will result in skipped frames, because your source will be feeding frames at a faster rate (30.00 fps) than they are being requested (29.97 fps) by the comp or rendering engine. These frame jumps will occur roughly every 33.33 seconds, usually starting with the first frame. If you are separating fields (discussed below and in Chapter 37), the frame rate effectively doubles, and a field (a half-frame) will slip roughly every 16.67 seconds.

Object libraries with alpha channels that are shot against white are usually incorrectly guessed as having a straight alpha, as in **[Ex.01]** – this results in white fringing around the object (left). Set the alpha type to premultiplied with white to remove the fringe (right). Image courtesy Classic PIO/Entertainment.

Grayed Out?

The Interpret Footage menu item will be grayed out unless you select the footage in the Project window. Then you can use the shortcut Command+F.

Inverted Alphas

Some files have inverted alpha channels: black represents visible or opaque areas; white represents transparent areas. Examples of this include mattes created by some hardware keyers and film systems.

Copy and Paste Interpretation

If you have a number of footage items that all need to have their Interpret Footage parameters set the same – such as Straight Alpha, 29.97 fps, Lower Field First – you can copy and paste from one item to many. Set up one the way you want, select File>Interpret Footage> Remember Interpretation (Command+Option+C), select the other items to get these parameters, then select File>Interpret Footage> Apply Interpretation (Command+Option+V). This can save you countless keystrokes early in a project. The only parameter this does not work for, as of version 4.1, is the EPS antialiasing option.

The Real 29.97

We strongly suggest that if you are working in NTSC video, you set all of your compositions to 29.97 fps and conform all of your video-rate footage to 29.97 as well. Using 30 instead will inevitably result in trouble. As it turns out, even some footage labeled as 29.97 fps can have trouble because of a mislabeled frame or subtly different definitions of what is the correct rate.

The frame rate of NTSC video is not 29.97 fps, but technically 30000 ÷ 1001 frames per second. The difference will rarely come up, but the makers of QuickTime are moving to standardize this exact ratio (not the 2997/100 ratio used by many other programs, such as After Effects through at least version 4.1).

If you are having strange problems with NTSC footage, such as the very first frame repeating in a composition, reconform its frame rate to 29.97 exactly. You can also create an Interpretation Rule (see the sidebar at the end of this chapter, as well TechTip 10 on the CD) that will do this automatically for you:

conform any movie close to "29.97" fps to AE's "29.97":

*, *, 29.97, *, * = *, *, 29.97, *

Other corrected frame rates that are of importance are conforming 60 fps to 59.94 fps (NTSC's field rate), 24 fps to 23.976 fps (the real speed telecined film is run at), or 24 fps up to 25 fps, since many films are simply sped up for playback on PAL video. In the case of our VideoLoops film grunge sequence, you could conform it to 23.976 fps for "true" playback at NTSC rate, or 25 fps for PAL work.

There are also creative uses of frame rate manipulation, such as faking staggered and other similar looks. One of our favorite tricks is to bring in a sequence of stills, set a low frame rate such as 1 fps (you can go as low as 0.01), then frame blend between them to create a dreamy background. Higher frame rates can be used for nervous grunge sequences and treatments. (See the sidebar, *Slow Blended Grunge*, in Chapter 10).

The EW_TextFX movie consists of rapidly changing random frames (left and center) of text. Slow down the frame rate and it becomes less nervous; turn on Frame Blending, and the frames between become more dreamy (right).

In [Ex.03*starter] is a movie of rapidly changing random text. If you preview it, you will see it is quite nervous and fast. Experiment with changing the frame rate of its footage source (EW_TextFX.mov); slower rates make it less nervous. Reduce the rate to around 2 fps and turn on Frame Blending: it is more dreamy than grungy. With the frame rate reduced, check out [Ex.03_final] to get some ideas on how you can use these movies with mattes to create abstract backgrounds.

Fields and Pulldown

Behind door number three are different ways to pull apart the separate fields that often make up a video image. Most single frames of video consist of two "fields" or are partial images taken at different points in time. They are woven into one frame through a process known as interlacing. You usually want to unweave them into the separate images that they came from, for maximum processing flexibility and quality. This popup is where you help After Effects know how to unweave or separate them. *More detail on this, including how to test your own video card to learn its field order, is discussed in Chapter 37.*

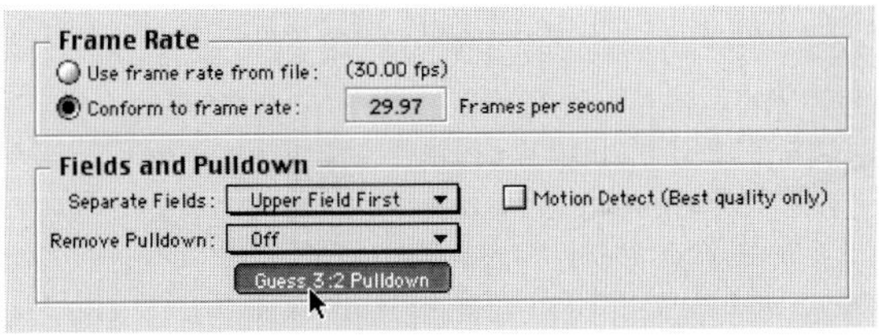

[handwritten note: □ - Square - Computer; ▱ - non square - Avid]

[screenshot of Frame Rate and Fields and Pulldown settings panel showing: Frame Rate — Use frame rate from file: (30.00 fps), Conform to frame rate: 29.97 Frames per second; Fields and Pulldown — Separate Fields: Upper Field First, Remove Pulldown: Off, Motion Detect (Best quality only), Guess 3:2 Pulldown]

If you have selected one of the popup options for separating fields, an additional popup underneath – Remove Pulldown – activates. When 24 fps film is transferred to nominally 30 fps video, a special process called *pulldown* is used to spread four film frames across five video frames. Sometimes it is desirable to remove this pulldown and get back to the original film frames. Clicking on the Guess button underneath sends After Effects off to try to detect if pulldown was used in the movie under inspection and to set the field order and pulldown sequence accordingly; if not, no settings are changed. *Remove Pulldown is discussed in more detail in Chapter 38.*

If you have NTSC video footage that originated on film, After Effects can remove the pulldown sequence that was added to it when 24 fps film was telecined to "30" (29.97) video.

Pixel Aspect Ratio

Fourth on the hit parade is Pixel Aspect Ratio. Although most computer displays tend to be based around square pixels (they are as wide as they are tall), many video and film formats project pixels differently, resulting in what initially appears to be stretched or squashed images when they are viewed on a computer. For example, "anamorphic" film images are only half as wide on the film than they ultimately appear on the screen; in this case, a special lens is used to stretch the image back out upon projection. In video, the issue becomes how many pixels are spread across one horizontal scan line of a video monitor.

Things can get really confusing when you try to combine images with different pixel aspect ratios, or try to do something as simple as draw a "perfect" circle with squashed pixels. By telling After Effects how the image was originally captured or created (with normal square pixels, or with a particular nonsquare pixel aspect ratio), it will handle these differences internally and protect you from a lot of potential confusion. You can even mix and match sources with different individual pixel aspect ratios.

Most artwork you scan in or create on your computer uses square pixels, so this setting is left at its default. However, After Effects keys off of certain "magic numbers" (such as 720×486) for image size when sources are imported, and it will automatically set the pixel aspect ratio if the image matches one of these magic numbers. Some image sizes can have more than one valid pixel aspect ratio (normal TV versus widescreen); the software assumes the non-widescreen case – but you can always set

Motion Detect

What's the deal with the Motion Detect checkbox? The process of separating fields requires interpolating image data to fill in missing lines as a single frame is pulled apart into two fields. When Motion Detect is on and little or no change is detected in a portion of the image from frame to frame, After Effects will just copy the original pixels rather than interpolate new ones. However, given the realities of video noise and film grain, it is very rare that this ever occurs; it requires extra processing time to calculate regardless. The consensus is to just leave it off.

Pixel Aspect Ratios

Following are the common image sizes that typically have nonsquare pixels. After Effects autodetects most of these and automatically sets the pixel aspect ratio popup accordingly; you can always set it to something else yourself (maybe the image was really widescreen, instead of normal). The horizontal scaling used on projection is in the rightmost column.

These are the numbers that are hard-wired inside After Effects. Some of them are open to debate (as detailed in TechTip 05 on the CD).

After Effects through version 4.1 does not have explicit popups for most of the Advanced Television Standards Committee's Standard Definition TV specification (ATSC SDTV for short). They come in three sizes: 640×480 square pixels, 704×480 nonsquare, and 704×480 widescreen nonsquare. The good news is you can leave the first case alone (since it is square), and use the D1/DV NTSC equivalents for the 704x480 cases. The default Interpretation Rules that come with 4.1 set this automatically.

image size	format	image aspect	pixel aspect
720×480	DV NTSC	4:3	0.9
720×480	DV NTSC widescreen	16:9	1.2
720×486	D1 (ITU-R 601) NTSC	4:3	0.9
720×486	D1 NTSC widescreen	16:9	1.2
720×576	D1/DV PAL	4:3	1.0666
720×576	D1/DV PAL widescreen	16:9	1.4222
1440×1024	D4	4:3	0.9481481
1440×1024	D4 anamorphic	8:3	1.8
2880×2048	D16	4:3	0.9481481
2880×2048	D16 anamorphic	8:3	1.8
varies	anamorphic film	2:1	2.0

(handwritten margin note: non square)

the popup to the widescreen case. The accompanying *Pixel Aspect Ratio* table details the numbers that are recognized automatically.

It is a good idea not to create square pixel images at these magic sizes in programs like Photoshop because After Effects will assume that it must treat them as nonsquare, causing image distortions. (You can always set them back to square in their Interpret Footage dialog.) In general, if you don't lie or attempt to fool After Effects about aspect ratios, everything will be fine. *Chapters 39 through 41 focus on working with video formats that have nonsquare pixels,* including some tutorials that mix square pixel images with them to see how everything lines up. Note that you can set up additional Interpretation Rules (see later in this chapter) to accommodate more ratios, or to override After Effects' guesses.

Looping

You may loop any movie or sequences to repeat more than once – in fact, up to 9999 times (compared with the limit of ninety-nine loops in version 3.1). This is great for extending the running time of stock movies and other animations that have been built to loop seamlessly. For example, our

VideoLoops grunge sequence is very short – just over a second. The comp we played with it in, [**Ex.02**], is 6 seconds long. To make the footage longer, go back to its Interpret Footage dialog, increase the number of loops, and extend its layer bar in the timeline.

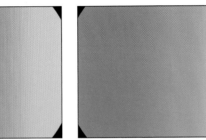

Our grunge sequence movie is originally not long enough to fill the timeline. If we increase the number of times it loops, it now has a ghosted bar showing its potential to fill the comp's time (as shown here); all we need to do now is drag out its out point to the end of the comp.

Options

What, there's more? Not usually. The After Effects programming team members left themselves a handy trap door to add more features with this Options button. Currently, the source types that take advantage of it are EPS and Illustrator files. In this case, the Options button allows you to render Postscript color blends more smoothly by changing the Faster option to More Accurate.

After Effects defaults to rasterizing EPS blends Faster (left) which may show artifacts. To fix this problem, open the source's Interpret Footage dialog, click on the Option dialog, and select More Accurate (right).

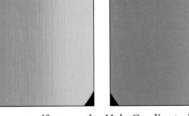

To see this for yourself, open the Ugly Gradient.ai in the 36_Chapter Sources subfolder in this project and change its Interpret Footage option. This item is also in comp [**Ex.04**]; note the quirk that it actually looks better in Draft Quality than in Best with the option left at Faster.

Interpretation Rules

When you import footage items into a project, After Effects makes several guesses on how to set the Interpret Footage parameters for an item. Some guesses are based on tags embedded in certain files; you are also given the opportunity to set or have After Effects guess the alpha channel type. These concepts are covered in Chapter 2.

As of version 4.1, After Effects added a feature called Interpretation Rules. This is a form of scripting, in which the program looks at certain parameters of a file, compares it with a set of rules in the file *interpretation rules.txt* that resides in the same folder as the program, and automatically sets many of the Interpret Footage parameters based on these rules if it finds a match. Of course, you can always override these automatic settings later in the Interpret Footage dialog.

The default rules After Effects ships with include some helpers for a few common file types. If you want to learn how to modify and write your own rules to help filter specific file types and image sizes, see TechTip 10 on the CD for an explanation of the scripting language. This TechTip also includes some of our own personal rules.

Connect

Importing Footage was originally discussed in Chapter 2.

Frame Blending was in Chapter 10. Using the Time Stretch parameter discussed in that chapter is also an alternative to reconforming the frame rate of a movie.

Track mattes were explored in Chapter 14.

Fields and their separation are covered in detail in Chapter 37.

Pulldown is demystified in Chapter 38; additional film issues are covered in Chapter 42.

More NTSC issues are discussed in Chapter 39; PAL in 40. Chapters 39 through 41 also deal with pixel aspect ratio issues in depth.

Alpha Channels are explained in more detail in Tech Tip 01 on the CD; Interpretation Rules are covered in TechTip 10.

37 Playing the Field

A video frame is more than it seems to be: One frame can represent two different points in time, known as fields.

Video is full of seemingly arcane rules and exceptions that we have to take into account when we're creating motion graphics. One of the most arcane (and important) has to do with fields – the half-frames that make up an interlaced image. Understanding them results in improved smoothness of motion. Getting them wrong results in all sorts of visual side effects. Even on their own, fields can introduce flicker artifacts that require careful blurring to hide. We'll cover the theory, input, output, and flicker aspects of fields in this chapter.

Two Faces

When you shoot footage with a video camera, it usually does not record whole video frames at a time. Instead, it captures half the lines of an image (and these lines alternate – lines 1, 3, 5, and so forth). It then goes back and captures the remaining lines (lines 2, 4, 6, and so on) to fill in the blanks. These sets of lines are called *fields*.

Fields are placed one after the other on videotape. When this tape is played back to a video monitor, it draws one set of lines – again, skipping every other line – then it uses the next field to draw in the remaining lines. Most important, these fields come from (and are played back at) different points in time, at a speed twice the frame rate. In other

Individual fields – half frames – of an image are captured and placed one after the other on videotape.

Example Project

Explore the 37-Example Project.aep file as you read this chapter; references to [Ex.##] refer to specific compositions within the project file.

Pairs of fields are interwoven, or *interlaced*, when they are captured as a frame inside the computer.

A video frame with fields (left) often exhibits a comb-like effect around moving objects. This is merely showing the difference in motion between the two different points of time. When we de-interlace them into their original fields, two distinct images appear (center) and (right). But which came first in time?

words, the field rate of NTSC video is 59.94 fields per second (29.97 × 2); it is 50 fields per second for PAL (25 × 2). Although each field has only half the resolution (number of lines) of a whole frame, this doubled rate makes motion appear much smoother.

For better or worse, most computer software and file formats do not think in terms of individual fields, but in terms of whole frames. When video is captured into a computer, two fields are woven or *interlaced* into a whole frame. This may initially seem easier to handle, but since alternate lines are from different points in time, it is dangerous to treat an interlaced frame as a whole frame.

Therefore, we must separate the frames on input back into their individual fields to best handle them. We then render a field at a time, and re-interlace them back into frames to save into files. After Effects is capable of doing both. The tricky part of both procedures is knowing which field in a frame comes first in time.

After Effects names the field order of frames according to which comes earlier in time – the first or *upper* line, or the second or *lower* line. If the first line came first, the frame is considered to be upper field first. Most 720×486 and both NTSC and PAL DV 720×480 pixel systems are lower field first; all 640×480 pixel NTSC systems, non-DV PAL formats, and all US ATSC video formats that have interlaced frames are upper field first.

Degrees of Separation

When After Effects imports an interlaced movie, it looks to see if there is a resource saved with it that already indicates the correct field order (After Effects often adds this resource to movies it renders, and some NLEs such as the Media 100 insert it as well), or if it has an Interpretation Rule script (discussed in the last chapter and in TechTip 10) that tells it how to separate the fields for this kind of file. If it finds neither, it then treats the video as if it were non-interlaced (or as if the entire frame belongs to the same point in time).

Field Order ≠ Field Dominance

Many systems use the terms *field dominance* and *field order* interchangeably. Unfortunately, this is not accurate – one refers to edit points; the other refers to how fields are packed in a frame. These concepts are explained in more detail in TechTip 08 on the CD.

If you don't separate fields on video, and then scale (left), rotate (right), or perform virtually any other processing on the footage, different fields will get scrambled together in undesirable ways – notice the moiré patterns in the basketball. This is what we call *field mush*.

If you then use this source in a composition and scale or rotate the layer, you'll most likely mix information from the two different fields – and therefore two different points in time – onto the same new line. Even if you field-render on output, a mixture of these different fields would end up on each field in the output movie. The result is a shuddering mess, often referred to by a highly technical term we coined: *field mush*.

To avoid field mush, every time you import an interlaced movie, select the footage in the Project list, go to File>Interpret Footage>Main, and choose either Upper or Lower Field First for the Separate Fields popup. This tells After Effects to separate each frame into two separate fields and space them 1/59.94th of a second apart (1/50th of a second for PAL). Then it constructs a full frame out of each field (using field interpolation at Best Quality, or field doubling at Draft Quality), which is then displayed in the Comp window.

Now when you Field Render your animation, interlaced source footage will be processed correctly (information from the first temporal field of the source will end up on the first field of the output movie, and pixels from the second field of the source will be routed to the second field on output).

Progressive Scan

A feature gaining popularity in many cameras is a progressive scan mode, in which the entire frame is captured at one point in time rather than split over two fields. It is felt that this approach better simulates the look of film, which does not have fields and which also typically has a lower frame rate than video.

If the camera's shutter is kept open for the same percentage of time per frame, and the frames are on screen longer (either because of a lower frame rate or because only whole frames – not two fields per frame – are being shot), then it follows that more action is being captured per frame, resulting in an increase in natural motion blur.

Progressive scan playback is also an option in all of the Advanced Television Standards Committee (ATSC) digital video formats. If you work entirely in progressive scan, you can blissfully ignore this chapter. We should all be so lucky.

If you don't separate fields correctly (above), motion will seem to stagger back and forth – for example, look at the position of the basketball. Separate correctly (below), and motion will progress as expected.

Before you can Separate Fields, of course, you'll need to know whether the source is Upper Field First or Lower Field First. If you're not sure of the field order, guess Upper Field First, then open the movie into After Effects' player by Option+double-clicking it from the Project window. After Effects' player will display each field, interpolated to a full frame. (If you merely double-clicked on it, you would open the standard QuickTime player, which does not show individual fields.) If your guess was correct, a moving object would make steady progress as you step through or play the movie; if you guessed wrong, the object will appear to stagger back and forth as the fields play out of order.

To try this out, open the 37-Example Project. Inside folder [**Ex.01**], you will find a file called CM_interlaced.mov. Option+double-click on it, and you will notice it looks slightly messy – the rightmost digit seems like a mixture of a 1 and a 2; the bar at the bottom is divided into thin lines. These are normal artifacts of viewing interlaced footage (if there are no scan line artifacts, and the fields have not been separated yet, then perhaps your movie was shot or rendered in progressive scan mode). Step through it using the page up/down keys, and you will notice these artifacts persist.

Select the movie in the Project window, and open the Interpret Footage (Command+F) dialog, and set the Separate Fields menu to Lower Field First. You will notice the text looks a bit crunchy; this is a natural side effect of

What's My Line?

Some systems use the terms *even* and *odd* instead of *upper* and *lower* to define field order. Unfortunately, this is ambiguous, since some systems consider the first line to be number 0 (an even number) and some consider it to be 1 (an odd number). In Adobe Photoshop, Apple Final Cut Pro, and products from Radius/Digital Origin, even is the lower field. In Play's ElectricImage, Apple's JPEG-A and JPEG-B codecs, and some Discreet Logic products, even is the upper field. If you are not sure, run tests back and forth to your hardware before committing to a long render. See also the After Effects User Guide, Chapter 11, *Testing the Field Rendering Order*.

frame 10/field 2

frame 10/field 1

When you initially open the field-rendered movie in the **[Ex.01]** folder (left), the interlaced fields are obvious in the mixed 1/2 and the red bar underneath. When you separate its fields (right), it looks crunchier because you are seeing only one field, but notice that we also see only one field number, and the red bar is whole now.

seeing only one field, with every other line being interpolated. Step through the movie frame by frame (shortcut: Page Up/Down); you will notice the bar along the bottom moves in a jerky fashion, and the numbers don't count in the right order. Change the Separate Fields option to Upper Field First, and now all the elements will progress as you would expect as you step through it. This is how you know you separated fields correctly.

Composition Frame Rate

Remember that a composition's frame rate does not affect the source material's frame rate. If you separate fields, resulting in a field rate of 59.94 per second, there is no need to increase a comp's frame rate to 59.94 – you can continue working at 29.97 fps. Just remember that as you step through a comp, you will now be seeing only the first field of each frame (which has a lower resolution, because every other line is interpolated). Likewise, you will still be placing keyframes at the start of every frame; there will just be two fields inside each of those frames. Open [Ex.02] and step through the timeline. You will see only Field 1 of our interlaced movie we played with above. The second field isn't missing; you're just stepping through time a frame at a time, temporarily leaping over every other field. Compare the difference between Draft and Best Quality – the field is doubled in Draft, and interpolated in Best.

The Between Value

If you want a parameter, such as Position, to jump cleanly from one frame to the next, don't place normal linear keyframes one frame apart. When you field render, there is an extra field in time that gets rendered between these two keyframes, exposing the move. Use Hold keyframes (Chapter 4) instead.

If you want to see every field, you can double your comp's frame rate to 59.94 (50 for PAL) frames per second. In [Ex.02], open Composition Settings (Command+K) and type in 59.94 for the rate. Now as you step through the comp, you will see both Field 1 and Field 2 of our movie. Although this is not essential, this can be a good confidence check that nothing is slipping by you as you step through a comp, and it is useful when you're editing mask keyframes for accurate rotoscoping (Chapter 13).

Note that the act of doubling a comp's frame rate does not increase the temporal resolution of your source material: If its rate was 29.97 and you did not separate fields (or there were no fields to separate), you will not magically get a new image every 1/59.94th of a second – you will see each frame duplicated only as you step through the comp at this finer increment of time.

Rendering with Fields

How can you take advantage of the extra temporal resolution of fields when you render? By *field rendering* your output. This makes After Effects double the rate at which it renders a composition. It will render an image at the beginning of a frame, then temporarily store this image. It will then forward its internal clock one-half of the frame rate asked for when rendering – 1/59.94 of a second when working in NTSC – and render another image using information at this point in time. If you have any footage at this frame rate with separated fields, one field will get used in rendering the first image, and the other field will get used when rendering the second image. These two rendered images are the two fields of the newly rendered frame.

After Effects will then combine these two images into a final frame, using the interlacing method described earlier in this chapter: Every other line is kept from one image, with the remainder thrown away; these lines are replaced with the corresponding lines from the second rendered field and the interlaced frame is saved to disk. Which field starts on the top-most line is set by the Field Order menu in the Render Settings dialog (discussed in more detail in Chapter 43).

Gone for Good

The term *de-interlace* is more often used when a field is removed and thrown away – as you might need to do if you're using interlaced footage for multimedia applications.

Field Mismatches

If your source footage has the same field order as your final render, and you remembered to separate fields, everything works fine. If your sources are the same size as your final render, and are always used centered and full-screen, the lines that got separated into individual fields will be the exact same lines kept during field rendering and re-interlacing on output. If any scaling, rotation, effects, or other treatments were performed on the footage, you are still okay, as long as you told After Effects to separate the fields into two new "frames" to process individually.

A subtle gotcha creeps up when you're working with full-frame material and the field order of your source material is different from your render, or if the frame sizes or positions don't line up. The basic rule of thumb to remember is this: *Moving an unscaled image up or down an even number of lines keeps its field order; moving it an odd number of lines reverses its field order.* And if you render the "wrong" fields, the resulting image will be softer.

In this chapter's project, open [**Ex.03-field render test**] which consists of our interlaced movie already separated as Upper Field First. Now open the Render Queue window (Command+Option+0). You will notice that this composition has already been placed in the

Fields and Multimedia

Remember that video often has fields, but computers do not. When creating content for multimedia and the Web, separate the fields in footage on input, and don't introduce them on output when rendering. This will take only the first field from each frame of the source movie and interpolate the single field out to a full frame. This is the same effect you would get with Photoshop's De-Interlace filter on a single frame. (Draft Quality in After Effects equals Photoshop's Create New Fields by Duplicatation option, while Best Quality is akin to the Interpolation setting.)

When you're converting a 640×480 interlaced movie to 320×240 non-interlaced, don't just render a 640×480 comp at Half Resolution. For the highest quality, after Separating the Fields, scale the movie to fit a 320×240 comp, and render that. Alternatively, render at 640×480 and scale down in the Output Module. Either way, remember to set the Render Settings to Best Quality for interpolated fields.

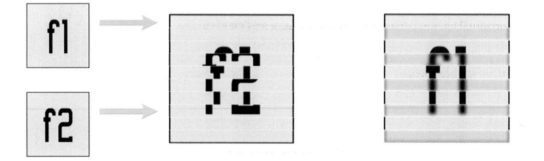

As shown earlier, a video frame often consists of two interlaced fields, as with alternating the yellow and blue lines above (left). When they are separated into two individual frames, the lines that belong to another field are re-created by interpolating between the lines that are kept. These interpolated lines are shown as gray (right) and are softer in focus than the original lines because they are interpolated. If you field render, but use a different field order on output, *only the interpolated lines are kept during the interlacing process,* resulting in a softer final image overall.

Best Fields

To get better field interpolation, set the Quality switch for interlaced layers to Best. In Draft mode, separated fields are merely duplicated.

render queue twice, with names already specified as "test upper" and "test lower" – they have been set to render this comp to two different field orders in Render Settings. Click on the first file name, select where you want to save the movie to, and click on Render. (If you opened the project directly on the CD and try to render both movies at the same time, you'll get an error because After Effects won't be able to write its log file back to the CD; either move the project to your hard drive or simply render one movie at a time.) When the first movie is done, repeat for the second render queue item.

When finished, both movies will have automatically re-imported themselves into your project. Double-click (not Option+double-click) to open them and step through them – you will notice the "test lower" movie is fuzzier than the "test upper" movie. This is the result of misaligned fields from input to output. Compare the results also when you separate the Right movie as Upper Field First and the Wrong movie to Lower Field First, and step through them field by field (Option+double-click).

The most common occurrence of this is mixing D1 and DV footage. Most NTSC D1-size footage is 486 lines tall, lower field first. All NTSC DV footage is 480 lines tall, lower field first. If you set up a 486-line tall comp that intended to render lower field first, then center a piece of DV footage in this comp, there will be three blank lines at the top and bottom, meaning it got shifted down three lines – an odd number. The lower field of the DV footage now lines up with the upper field of your intended final render, resulting in your using only the softer, interpolated fields. Move it up a line, and the fields line up again.

The same applies to PAL footage – DV and D1 sources have the same number of lines, but opposite field orders. You will also encounter this when you're centering a 640×480 upper field first footage item in a 720×480 lower field first DV comp: the fields misalign. Lower the 640×480 source a line, and everyone is happy again.

Again, this is not an issue if you are scaling and otherwise altering the source footage, since there is no longer a clean one-to-one correspondence between fields in and fields out.

Managing Interlace Flicker

One side effect of the interlaced, field-based nature of video is that adjacent horizontal lines are drawn on a monitor at different points in time. Coupled with the tendency of the illuminated picture phosphors on a screen to decay (go dim), high-contrast horizontal lines or detail in an image tend to *flicker* (or vibrate) on video screens, even if no movement is happening. Similar objects that are moving horizontally slowly over time might also exhibit an odd *crawling* effect, seeming to get shorter and taller as they move – particularly annoying for credit scrolls. This is a different issue from field mush described earlier and is a problem inherent in video. To fix it, you will need to intelligently blur parts of your image.

First, let's look at the problem. These examples will be more evident if you have a video card in your computer that can drive a video monitor directly. Open composition [**Ex.04**], and if you have such a video card, drag it and center it (Command+Shift+\) on that monitor. Layer 4 (grid) should be the only one on right now. Look closely: notice how the vertical lines of the grid don't vibrate, but the horizontal ones do. Interlace flicker affects only horizontal lines. Turn off Layer 4 and turn on Layer 3 (text). Again, vertical lines and rounded areas do not flicker, but horizontal lines – such as the bars on the F and the radio's grill – do. Turn off Layer 3 and turn on Layer 5 (the radio). Again, note that the round portions of the dial and speaker opening don't vibrate, but you may notice that the horizontal lines of the speaker grill and dial detail do. If you were to open any of these sources on your computer monitor (double-click to open their Layer windows), they would look fine.

Which Blur?

To reduce interlace flicker, many use Gaussian Blur. However, at its default settings it blurs in all directions instead of just the vertical direction you need, resulting in softer images. Either set the Blur Dimensions to Vertical, or instead use the Motion Blur effect with Direction set to 0°.

High-contrast horizontal lines – such as the horizontal bars in the F and L, as well as the speaker grill on the radio – are prone to flickering when they are displayed on interlaced video monitors. Image courtesy Classic PIO/Classic Radios.

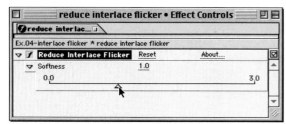

Reduce Interlace Flicker blurs images in just the vertical direction (above), or you could just as easily use the Motion Blur effect (below) set to 0° direction.

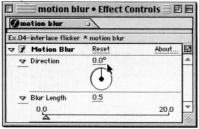

Crawling Titles

When scrolling credits and titles, avoid any speed in pixels per second that is an odd multiple of the field rate of your video. Using these numbers causes details of the text being displayed on only one of the two fields, resulting in a loss of half your resolution. See Chapter 26.

There are several ways to solve this. After Effects has a Reduce Interlace Flicker effect (Effect>Video> Reduce Interlace Flicker) designed to blur images in just the vertical direction, resulting in less contrast between horizontal lines (since pixels are now being blurred between them). Turn on Layer 1, which is an adjustment layer with this effect. Notice how the vibrating suddenly stops. Go ahead and enable the various image layers (3 through 5) to see the effect this filter has on them. Select Layer>Open Effect Controls window and set this filter to taste, balancing blur against flicker; as little as 0.5 can kill most problems.

However, we've noticed in some circumstances the Reduce Interlace Flicker effect introduces some visible artifacts of its own. Therefore, we prefer using the Motion Blur effect (Effect>Blur & Sharpen>Motion Blur, not to be confused with the layer's Motion Blur switch) set to a Direction angle of 0° (to keep the blur vertical). To see the Motion Blur effect, turn off Layer 1 and turn on Layer 2 (an adjustment layer with Motion Blur effect applied), and again play around with different values. A blur length of 0.5 roughly corresponds to 1 in the Reduce Interlace Flicker effect.

For comparison, turn on layers 3 through 5 and create a snapshot (Option+F5). Turn off Layer 2, and turn back on Layer 1 (the Reduce Interlace Flicker effect). Now load the snapshot (F5) and compare both results, particularly the edges of the radio.

Scaling and Blurs

You can apply either one of these effects directly to the offending images, rather than an adjustment layer that affects all layers underneath. However, keep in mind that scale and rotation take place after an effect is applied. If you scale an image down, you are also scaling down the amount of blur – and therefore might need to increase it to compensate.

Turn off all layers in [Ex.04] except Layer 5 (the radio). Apply the Motion Blur effect to it, and set the Blur Length to 1 in the Effect Controls window. If you've been viewing in on a video monitor, the flickering should stop. Now, scale down the radio to 25% of its original size – notice that the flickering returns! You need to increase the blur length accordingly: 1 (blur length) ÷ 0.25 (scale) = 4 (new blur length to try). Enter 4 as the length, and the flicker will improve considerably – although it may not be perfect. You might need to increase the value to 6 or more to kill all the flicker – which now results in a rather blurry image.

De-interlace versus Separate Fields

There is an important difference between the Photoshop filter Video>De-Interlace and After Effects' separation of fields. The Photoshop filter throws away one field entirely and interpolates new lines from the field it kept to make one new image. After Effects creates two images – one from each field. Use the Photoshop filter only if you need to clean up a still captured from video. Remember that still images – photos, scans, and so on – don't have fields, so they don't need de-interlacing or separation.

Selective Blurring

When only part of the image is causing a flicker problem, you might want to consider selectively blurring just that part of the image. Open comp [Ex.05]; only Layer 2 should be turned on. Center it on your video monitor and observe the flicker. Now, turn on Layer 1. This is a copy of the radio, masked down to just the most offensive areas of flicker – the speaker grill and dial detail. You can temporarily solo Layer 1 if you wanted to see what areas have been masked. Motion Blur has been applied to just this layer. The result is blurring just the worst areas of flicker, while keeping the rest of the image sharp.

    You could now animate this comp as you would the original radio. If you don't like handling two layers in place of one, you could also perform this selective masking and blurring in Photoshop, making sure to save the original unblurred version in case you need to revert later.

If blurring an entire object to reduce interlace flicker is overkill, mask out the portions that have been causing flicker and blur just these areas.

Covering the Edges

Quite often, problems with interlace flickering do not occur within an image but around the outside edges of the image, as with the text example, above, or when you're shrinking an image down for a picture-in-picture effect. Sometimes, this flicker can be fixed by adding a glow or shadow around the object, softening the contrast between horizontal lines. If this works, you can reduce or eliminate the amount of blur you might otherwise need to apply to an object.

    If the object is moving vertically – for example, a typical credit scroll – you might also see if normal motion blur, rather than the applied effect, blurs the edges enough to reduce flickering. With the animation keyframes already set, enable motion blur for the layer and in the composition. Remember you can alter the shutter angle amount of motion blur in a preference (File>Preferences>General) and change it later when you render if you wish – the maximum shutter angle is 360 degrees.

    In comp [Ex.06], turn motion blur (the checkbox under the M icon in the Time Layout window) on and off to see this potential effect. (For more clues on credit scroll speed issues, see the sidebar *Credit Roll Issues* in Chapter 26.)

    A fact of life: standard definition video does not have enough resolution to hide all the artifacts of a pixel-based medium. You may have to compromise to work around these shortcomings. Some images will simply give you trouble. For instance, computer screen dumps come to mind, as interface designers tend to use thin lines on a contrasting background. If the intention is that the viewer be able to read the information being displayed, this is a case where a multimedia-based presentation may give better results, at the expense of gee-whiz effects.

Connect

Motion Blur was covered in Chapter 11.

Masking was the subject of Chapter 13.

Credit Roll Issues was a sidebar back in Chapter 26.

Setting up renders, including how to alter rendered frames as they are saved, and creating render templates, are covered in Chapter 43.

If you want to permanently reorder the fields in a footage file, you can render it back out again with the fields shifted. This is covered in Chapter 44.

Interpretation Rules were covered in Chapter 36, and in TechTip 10 on the CD.

More information on video issues, including Field Order versus Field Dominance, may be found in TechTip 08 on the CD.

38 3:2 Pulldown

Film and NTSC video run at different rates. To transfer film to video, some trickery is required.

Footage originally shot on film and transferred to video using the telecine process can be used just like regular video. However, there are situations – such as frame-by-frame masking and rotoscoping – in which reverting back to the original film frames can be a big time saver. It will also improve the smoothness of speed changes and frame blending. In this chapter we'll discuss what this *pulldown* process is and how to remove it.

Film to Video

Film is most commonly shot at 24 frames per second. NTSC video runs at 29.97 frames per second, and PAL runs at 25 frames per second. How are these differences in frame rates resolved?

In countries that use PAL, the footage is often just sped up from 24 to 25 fps, with the audio either sped up or time-stretched to match. However, the difference between 24 and 29.97 is too large to simply varispeed between them. Instead, the film frames are parceled out among video fields to make their average effective frame rates match.

First, film is slowed down 0.1% to 23.976 fps – the same difference as between 30 and 29.97 – to keep the math simple. The rates of 24 and 30 (or 23.976 and 29.97) have a fairly simple math relationship between them: 4 to 5. The simplest pulldown method, *repeated fourth frame*, does exactly that – it transfers the first four frames of film to four frames of video, repeats the fourth film frame for the fifth frame of video, then repeats this overall sequence. You rarely see this method employed, except with government and military video. Although it's simple, the motion is not exceptionally smooth.

Five video frames can be thought of as ten fields of video. The *3:2 pulldown* method takes the first film frame and spreads it over two video fields. The next film frame is spread over three video fields. Likewise, the third is spread over two fields, and the fourth over three fields, yielding four film frames to ten video fields – or five video frames. This sequence is then repeated as long as necessary.

film frames

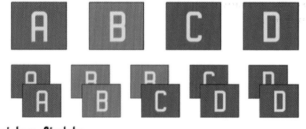

video fields

3:2 pulldown is the process of spreading every four film frames across a sequence of ten video fields.

Example Project

Explore the 38-Example Project.aep file as you read this chapter; references to [Ex.##] refer to specific compositions within the project file.

Just a Phase

Open composition [**Ex.01**] and step through it in the timeline. This is an example of a film movie originally created at 24 fps, slowed down to 23.976 fps, with 3:2 pull-down added to bring it up to 29.97 fps, placed in a normal video-rate comp, with field separation left off for now. Each individual film frame is represented by a sequential number. Step through the movie and notice how some frames are interlaced *(split)* and some frames look complete *(whole)*. Depending on where the trim in point was made in the preliminary editing process, the clip could have one of five possible *phases* of Whole (W) and Split (S) frames. (After Effects refers to these phases as WSSWW, SSWWW, and so on in the Interpret Footage dialog.)

A large amount of television we all watch originated as film and was transferred to video through this process – so obviously, it works well enough. However, there are some gotchas for those of us in the production stages. A film editor working in video has to consider many issues to later conform the edit decisions back to the actual film. Our points of concern are simpler: Video fields are being redundantly padded out (we'll call them *bonus fields* for short), and the footage has an irregular motion stagger that shows up when it's time-stretching.

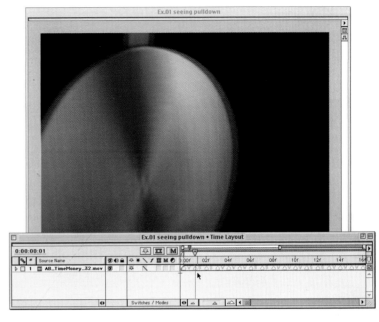

In [**Ex.01**] is a movie with 3:2 pulldown. We've marked which frames are whole (W) and which are split (S). This frame is split; you can see the interlaced lines in the image. Original footage courtesy Artbeats/Time & Money; we specially modified it to simulate a source exhibiting 3:2 pulldown behavior.

Varispeed and Audio

There may be times you want to revert back to the absolute original film rate of 24 fps. You would do this by conforming your 29.97 fps footage to 30 fps, then removing pulldown. However, if the file also had audio attached, After Effects will give you a warning that "audio may not synchronize." As of version 4.1, After Effects still won't conform audio.

You have a few options to keep the two in sync. One is to not conform the file in the Interpret Footage dialog and instead time-stretch the layer in a comp by 99.9%, undoing the 0.1% telecine slowdown. Another is to conform the footage and time-stretch just the audio as its own layer – but make sure you keep the original in points lined up, or you could drift out of sync.

PAL Pulldown

When the speed-up from 24 to 25 is not tolerable, there is a system in which the 12th and 24th film frames get spread across three video fields each instead of two, making 24 equal 25. This yields a huge number of potential phases, plus half the video frames will appear split in a program like After Effects.

Under Fields and Pulldown in the Interpret Footage dialog, click on the Guess 3:2 Pulldown button, and After Effects will attempt to discern the field order and pulldown phase of your file. If it succeeds, the corresponding popups will be set, and the effective frame rate will be slowed down by a 4/5 ratio. If After Effects cannot figure it out, you can manually set the field order and phase.

No Pulldown Please

To save time, money, and disk space, have the telecine film-to-video transfer done at 30 fps (one film frame to one video frame). The footage will play fast from the video tape or digital disk recorder, but you can easily Conform the footage to 23.976 fps in After Effects' Interpret Footage dialog. You'll save 20% if you're paying a per frame charge for the DDR transfer, need 20% less disk space for sources, and enjoy faster rendering (thanks to fewer frames to retrieve from disk). Plus you avoid the hassle of removing pulldown.

Removing Pulldown

When a video clip requires rotoscoping, it's common to expand the roughly sixty video fields that occur during a second to sixty interpolated frames for editing. In this case, you would separate the fields of a 29.97 fps clip and add it to a 59.94 fps comp, where you could now step through and edit the clip field by field.

But if the footage originated on film and has had pulldown added, only twenty-four of these sixty frames are "real," and reverting back to the film frames can save hours of tedious editing. To remove the pulldown, select the clip AB_TimeMoney_32 in the [**Ex.01**] folder of the Project window and choose File>Interpret Footage>Main (or Command+F). In the Fields and Pulldown section, click on Guess 3:2 Pulldown. The program scans the first ten fields of the clip, figures out the field order and the phase, and reverts the footage to its original 23.976 whole frames per second. Step through either the clip or its associated comp, and you will see only whole frames now.

You will notice that a message indicates that the 29.97 fps video clip now has an "Effective frame rate of 23.976 fps" rather than 24, which accounts for the slowdown that occurs during the telecine process. (Just to confuse you a little more, AE often displays the 23.976 rate rounded up to 23.98 fps – rest assured that the internal frame rate is accurate enough that no rounding of frames is taking place.) If you're working on a non-video project, you might want to Conform Footage to 30 fps – removing the pulldown will now produce an effective frame rate of an even 24 fps (which divides in half to a Web-friendly 12 fps).

Pulldown Miscues

After Effects will beep if it's unsuccessful in guessing the pulldown phase. When you're capturing footage, you may want to trim out fades so that the first ten fields of the clip are clean and have some obvious motion.

To check that the footage has reverted correctly to the original film frames, Option+double-click the clip from the project window for After Effects' player (which takes the Interpret Footage settings into account). Play or scroll through the entire clip – *there should be no visible interlaced frames*. If interlacing is visible, manually select the different phases until you arrive at the correct one. Occasionally we've encountered a single clip with a mixture of phases, and can only assume that it was time-stretched during editing (read: you're hosed). Also, when a comp is at Half Resolution, don't panic if you see interlacing – it will disappear at Full Resolution. (If it bothers you, you can prerender the source at 23.976 fps and permanently remove the pulldown.)

If footage consists of multiple edits, the 3:2 phase may be changing throughout. If so, edit the video capture so that each scene is a separate footage item to After Effects, and apply Remove Pulldown to each clip separately. If that is not an option, import the unedited source clip multiple times and manually set the phase for each segment you plan to use.

Advantages of Removing Pulldown

There are two areas where removing pulldown from telecined footage will make your life much easier: masking and time-stretching.

Problem Unmasked

When you're masking a moving object in interlaced video footage, you often need to set your comp rate to 59.94 fps, and either mask on every field, or at least check every field to make sure the mask isn't wandering as it interpolates between keyframes. If the footage was originally shot on film and has pulldown added, the 3:2 pattern will add an irregular temporal stagger which makes smooth mask shape interpolation even more difficult. However, if you can remove this pulldown, you'll have only 23.976 frames per second to mask, and each frame will progress in even increments.

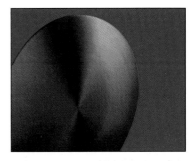

Life is good – until you go to render. If you don't take precautions to lock the mask down, it can still slip if you render at the 29.97 fps video rate, especially when fields are introduced. This is because After Effects looks at the comp rate only for display and setting keyframes; when it renders, it uses the final render rate to sample the sources.

If the mask is not locked down with Hold keyframes or the Posterize Time effect, it will look correct when the frames align (above), but will slip (below) when you field-render the footage that you originally removed pulldown from.

Comp [Ex.02.1] contains a swinging pendulum, from footage with pulldown removed, masked at 23.976 fps. If you step through it, you will see that the mask follows the motion correctly. This masking comp is nested into comp [Ex.02.2], which is running at video field rate (59.94 fps); we will use this comp to simulate our field rendering process. As you step through this simulation comp, the mask now slips in relation to the pendulum, because the mask shape is interpolating between fields.

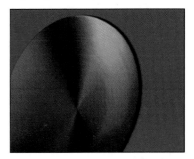

The obvious fix is to prerender the masked layer at 23.976 fps with an alpha channel and to re-import – this locks down the mask to each frame permanently. There are two other ways to fix this that don't require more disk space. The first is shown in [Ex.02.3], where all the mask key-

frames have been changed to Hold keyframes (Command+Option+click on keyframes, or Layer>Toggle Hold Keyframe). Now no matter what frame rate you render at, each Hold keyframe is locked to each frame of the source. This method will work, however, only if you have a mask keyframe on every frame; otherwise, you will lose some mask shape interpolation you may have been relying on between keyframes.

Changing the mask keyframes to Hold is one way to fix the slippage, as shown in [Ex.02.3].

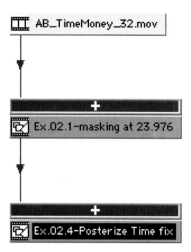

Another solution is to mask our movie AB_TimeMoney in one comp at 23.976 fps ([**Ex.02.1**]), nest it in a second comp ([**Ex.02.4**]), and apply Posterize Time to the nested comp layer using the frame rate of our source (23.976).

The other approach is to use the Posterize Time effect (covered in Chapter 32). Open [**Ex.02.2**], where the original [**Ex.02.1**] masking comp is nested, and apply Effect>Time>Posterize Time to the nested comp layer. Set the frame rate to 23.976 to match the first comp (after you OK, this is displayed annoyingly as 24 fps in the Time Layout window). Now, as you step through the frames, the mask should not slip. This is also shown in [**Ex.02.4**] if you got lost. Note that Posterize Time must be applied in a second comp so it occurs after the mask has already been keyframed; it will not work if you apply it directly to the footage you were masking in the first comp (more on Posterize Time in Chapter 32).

Stretching by Numbers

When telecined footage is time-stretched, the "three fields, two fields" staggered pattern is slowed to the point where it can become distracting. Comp [**Ex.03**] again has our pendulum, with pulldown removed. Make sure only the first layer is turned on; this features the pendulum time-stretched 300%. Invoke RAM preview (Composition>Preview>RAM Preview, or hit 0 on the keypad). Notice the stagger, even with Frame Blending turned on.

You can smooth the motion with a little math (we know; we keep saying that – but a *little* math isn't bad). You want to use a time-stretch value that will evenly place one film frame every certain whole number of video frames. For instance, if you time-stretch a 1-second clip (twenty-four film frames) to 80%, the new duration of 00:24 will place one film frame per one video frame. A value of 160% will place one film frame per two video frames. An easy calculation method is to multiply the percentage by 80% to account for the difference between 30 and 24: for example, to stretch eight times = $8 \times 80\% = 640\%$. Using similar logic, there are two fields per video frame, so you can stretch by 40% increments and have a film frame every whole number of video fields.

The other layers in [**Ex.03**] feature these different stretch amounts. Solo and preview a few; note that their pattern in a little smoother.

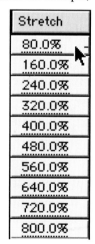

Time-stretching by multiples of 80% on footage that has had 3:2 pulldown removed will result in smoother motion.

Removing Repeated 4th Frame

After Effects does not remove Repeated 4th Frame pulldown automatically. We've personally used several different techniques to do this, including hand-removing the repeated frames from a movie or still sequence.

Our current favorite 5:4 removal recipe is to carefully line up a 29.97 fps movie in a 23.976 fps comp, until you find an arrangement where it naturally skips the redundant fifth frame. The steps:

Step 1: Import the movie, making sure field separation is turned off and the frame rate is conformed to 29.97.

Step 2: Drag it into a new comp with a frame rate of 23.976.

Step 3: Step through each frame of the movie, looking for repeated frames. If you find one, slide the movie one frame later (or earlier, if you can afford to lose some its head) in the timeline, and repeat.

Step 4: Once you find the offset that results in no repeated frames, render back out at 23.976 fps, without fields. You now have a clean film-rate movie to work with.

Rendering with 3:2 Pulldown

Now that you've been working happily at film rate on whole frames, how do you get back to video? Very simple: After Effects can add pulldown during rendering on the way to creating a video rate movie.

The easiest procedure is to just render at 29.97 fps, with fields, and After Effects will naturally introduce pulldown as it samples 23.976 fps source material during the rendering process. You can set the final comp to 29.97, drag your film rate Comp into a comp set to 29.97, and render that, or you can alter the render rate in the Render Settings dialog. If you have been mixing video and film sources, or want additional sources to render with smoother motion, this is the way to go.

However, it is often stylistically a better match if all the sources are rendered with the same motion. To do this, set up your compositions at 23.976 fps and use this rate to add and keyframe your additional elements such as titles and other graphics. Add the final comp to the Render Queue. You can then add 3:2 with the Pulldown feature during rendering. In the Render Settings, set the Field Render popup to Upper or Lower as your hardware requires and (unless you are specifically matching back to edits in film, where you might need to match a specific phase) select any phase from the 3:2 Pulldown menu. The comp will be sampled at 23.976, but a 29.97 fps movie with an overall 3:2 pattern will be interlaced and saved to disk, using the same process as a telecine.

The advantages are faster rendering (since you are sampling the comp at 23.976 fps, not 59.94 for normal field-rendered video), and the look of all your motion will match. The disadvantage is that the lower frame rate of 23.976 fps can cause visible strobing with faster movements. If this is a problem, you might try cranking up the Motion Blur Shutter Angle in the Render Settings dialog to 360°.

A Grand Compromise

There is a middle ground between the smooth motion (and long render times) of interlaced video, and the fussiness of working with 24 fps film with pulldown added: work at 30 (or 29.97) fps, with no fields. For instance, film can be shot at 30, not 24, and transferred to video a frame to a frame. Also, many video cameras have progressive scan 29.97 fps no-field modes as well. Create 3D animations at 30 fps, and conform to 29.97 upon importation. Either way, you work at 29.97, and render without fields. Rendering goes faster, and motion will be more film-like without quite the tendency to strobe as 24 fps film.

Film-like 3D Motion

A popular trick among 3D animators is to render at 24 fps to better simulate the motion characteristics of film. Import these renders into After Effects, and render with pulldown added at 29.97 fps. Turn on motion blur in your 3D app, or try ReelSmart Motion Blur from RE:Vision Effects in After Effects.

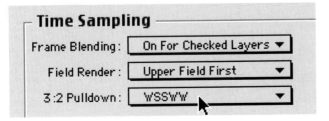

To add pulldown to a 23.976 fps comp, and raise it to 29.97 fps interlaced at the same time, queue it up to render, set its Render Settings to set the field order you want, then select a phase in the 3:2 Pulldown popup. The frame rate will automatically change to sampling the comp at 23.98 (23.976) and rendering a movie to disk at 29.97.

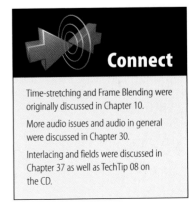

Connect

Time-stretching and Frame Blending were originally discussed in Chapter 10.

More audio issues and audio in general were discussed in Chapter 30.

Interlacing and fields were discussed in Chapter 37 as well as TechTip 08 on the CD.

39 Working with D1/DV NTSC

The world may be round, but not all pixels are square.

D1 and 601

The spec that defines most digital video is ITU-R BTU.601-4. The first digital tape format to use this spec was D1. As a result, many use the terms *D1* and *601* interchangeably, even if your footage never touches a D1 deck.

Example Project

Explore the 39-Example Project.aep file as you read this chapter; references to [Ex.##] refer to specific compositions within the project file.

Computers break images down to a series of tiny picture elements called *pixels*. On computer screens, pixels are square: they are as wide as they are tall. In most high-end video formats, however, pixels are not square; they project on a video monitor differently from the way we see them on our computer screens. We often have to mix the two worlds. Here's how to keep them straight. (We'll also discuss simpler issues such as common NTSC field orders and frame rate.)

Square and Nonsquare

The most common proportions, or image aspect ratio, for a television image is four units wide to three units high – a 4:3 aspect ratio. Most computer monitors also follow this image aspect. The most common computer resolution for years was 640 pixels across by 480 pixels wide, which also works out to a 4:3 ratio. As a result, many early computer video systems were based around a 640×480 size, and virtually all computer software products assume pixels are square when they create and edit content.

The most common digital video specification – ITU-R BTU.601-4 (sometimes known a CCIR-601, or just 601) – has a different idea about the size of an image. The aspect ratio of the viewed screen is still 4:3. However, this standard defines 486 scan lines for NTSC video (the standard for North America), not 480. It also defines 720 pixels across, not 640. Of course, 720:486 ≠ 4:3; what's going on?

In ITU-R 601, the pixels that make up an image are not square. When they are seen on a video monitor, they are drawn taller than they are wide. They are captured this way, and displayed this way, so everything works out. However, our computer monitors – and most of our computer software – can only conceive of pixels being square, and as a result, display and think of these 601 images as being wider overall than we would expect. Not only is this visually confusing, it creates real problems when we try to combine the two worlds – such as when we try to add square-pixel text on top of a nonsquare image.

For those few who actually like math, you can derive the pixel aspect ratio for 601 NTSC video: 486 lines × 4 ÷ 3 = 648 for a square-pixel image; 648 ÷ 720 = 0.9 for the pixel aspect ratio After Effects uses. (Not all agree with that precise number; see TechTip 05 on the CD for the details.)

On the left is how the wheel appears in its native environment, a perfect circle with either square pixels on a computer monitor or rectangular pixels on a D1 NTSC monitor.

The center image shows the compression that occurs when a square-pixel image, wrongly tagged as NTSC D1, is displayed on a rectangular-pixel monitor.

On the right are NTSC rectangular pixels widened as expected when viewed on a square-pixel monitor.

Pixel Aspect Ratio 101

To mix square and nonsquare pixel sources, you need to determine what is the "native" pixel aspect ratio of each source and make sure this is set correctly in the Interpret Footage dialog. Luckily for us, so long as we tag each source correctly as square or non-square and create our comp with the correct pixel aspect ratio, After Effects does all the math to blend these two worlds.

Let's consider artwork generated on the computer in the square pixel world. When you scan a photo of a wheel on a desktop scanner, the photo is being sampled at a resolution of a certain number of pixels per inch, and the result is an image of a round wheel. What you really have are many individual square pixels, each with a value of Red, Green, and Blue, that form a recognizable image when arranged in a specific pattern. The wheel will have the same circular proportions provided it's viewed on a square-pixel monitor.

But let's say you have an NTSC video card out-putting 720×486 rectangular pixels. If you were to drag the wheel image from the RGB computer monitor to the D1 NTSC monitor, the image would appear compressed horizontally; if you had a PAL video card outputting at 720×576, the image would appear stretched horizontally. Each individual square pixel is now displayed as a rectangle, and the result is that the entire image appears squashed – your wheel has become egg-shaped. Drag the image back to the computer monitor and it looks correct again. In practice, scans and art created in Photoshop, Illustrator, and most other graphics programs are square-pixel natives, and look correct only when viewed in a square-pixel world.

Now let's say you capture video of a wheel with your DV camera and transfer the clip to your computer. When you view the wheel on the NTSC monitor it looks perfectly round, but on the computer monitor the wheel looks fat (if you captured in PAL, it would instead look skinny, because PAL's pixels are rectangular in a different dimension than NTSC's pixels). Since the digital camera sampled the scene and created rectangular pixels, the video needs to be displayed on a rectangular-pixel monitor to look correct.

After Effects doesn't recognize an image as being a circle or an egg – to After Effects it's just a bunch of pixels. But unless you display each pixel in its native environment, the entire image will appear distorted.

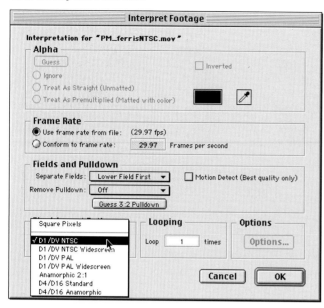

Each footage item has its pixel aspect ratio defined in the Interpret Footage dialog; many preset sizes trigger the popup to be set automatically, otherwise the default is square pixels. After Effects uses the source's pixel aspect ratio to determine how the footage should look when added to a composition, which itself can be defined as square or nonsquare pixels.

The world has been further complicated by the introduction of the DV (Digital Video) standard. Its NTSC size is 720×480 pixels. Fortunately, it can be treated like a 601-size image, just with six lines missing (two from the top and four from the bottom). Its pixel aspect ratio is the same as for 601. Likewise, one of the specifications for standard definition ATSC television is 704×480 pixels; it too uses the same pixel aspect ratio as D1 and DV.

Tracking Aspects

Fortunately, After Effects can compensate for different pixel aspect ratios. Whenever a footage item is set to have a D1/DV NTSC pixel aspect ratio in its Interpret Footage dialog (Command+F), After Effects knows those pixels were originally 0.9 as wide as they were tall when the footage was captured or created. If you use this footage in a composition that has been set to Square pixels, After Effects will automatically scale the width by 0.9, in essence converting the footage item to square pixels. (You can see this in action by opening the Scale parameter dialog box for a layer with this aspect ratio and watching the values as you toggle the Include Pixel Aspect Ratio switch on and off.) This way it will mix naturally with square-pixel footage, and all effects will be calculated correctly.

The Composition Settings dialog (Composition>Composition Settings, or Command+K) has the same pixel aspect ratio menu as you see in the Interpret Footage dialog. This tells After Effects how to preprocess the footage items inside it. Since it is easy to forget to set this menu, get in the habit of selecting a composition preset (the rightmost popup) when appropriate; presets automatically set the pixel aspect ratio for you.

If you drag the same piece of tagged D1/DV NTSC pixel aspect footage into a comp that has been set to also have D1/DV NTSC aspect pixels, no scaling will take place. After Effects will automatically take its nonsquareness into account when it's processing effects, so everything will keep the right proportions when it's rendered and played back to a video monitor.

However, if you drag a footage item tagged as having square pixels into this same nonsquare comp, the square pixels will get stretched to match the aspect ratio of the composition (and the D1/DV NTSC footage also in the comp). When played back on an appropriate monitor, the pixels will get resquished and appear at their original proportions.

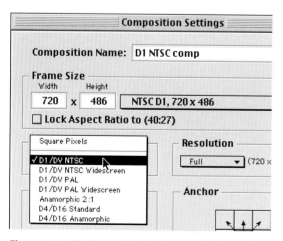

The presets in the Composition Settings set the size and pixel aspect ratio automatically. Using the presets avoids mistakes (such as creating a 720×486 square-pixel comp).

The great thing is that After Effects will do all of this automatically – as long as you have your footage, and your comps, tagged correctly and you didn't incorrectly prepare any footage items before you brought them into the program. Make sure that you never mislead the program about what the aspect ratio of the pixels really are! And to do that, you need to keep track of where images came from, and where they are going.

Comps and Footage

In the example project that goes with this chapter, we've started three comps for you to experiment with – [**Ex.01-D1**], [**Ex.01-DV**], and [**Ex.01-Square**]. Select them individually and type Command+K to see what their settings are:

- The DV comp has been set up for 720×480 and for nonsquare D1/DV pixel aspect ratio.
- The D1 comp is 720×486 in size, and is also nonsquare D1/DV pixel aspect ratio.
- The Square comp has been set up for 640×480 square pixels, which is a common size for older and lower-end video cards and editing systems, and is another one of the standard definition sizes defined by the ATSC for digital television.

Another common square-pixel size to work at is 648×486, following the math outlined earlier. This is actually a good compromise size for NTSC work: you lose a little horizontal resolution, but you keep your comps square and with the correct number of lines, which makes designs easier to visualize on a computer display. You can change [**Ex.01-Square**] to this size if you like.

Option+double-click the footage item HD_golfball.jpg in the project's 39_Chapter Sources subfolder. This is a frame exported from a D1 720×486 movie. Notice how it looks stretched horizontally compared with what you might expect; this is because it was captured with nonsquare pixels. Now open either the [**Ex.01-D1**] or [**Ex.01-DV**] comps, and drag this footage item into them. Notice it looks the same – this is because the footage item and the comps both have been set up to the same nonsquare pixel aspect ratio, so After Effects does not perform any adjustments.

This NTSC DV capture looks right through the viewfinder or when it's played back on an NTSC monitor (left), but it appears stretched horizontally on your computer monitor (right). This is because DV and D1 pixels are not square, while your computer's pixels are, causing it to be displayed this way. Footage courtesy Herd of Mavericks.

NTSC and 525 Lines

We're using the term *NTSC* for video that will eventually be broadcast in this format. Some would have us refer to it during production as *525-line* standard video.

Best Stretch

When you're mixing square and nonsquare footage items and compositions, make sure to render in Best Quality, even if you don't scale them – After Effects itself is scaling them to make up the difference in pixel aspect ratios.

Now open the [**Ex.01-square**] comp and drag the golf ball image into it – notice how it squishes horizontally and the ball looks more round. This is because After Effects is correcting the pixel aspect ratio of the image to match the comp, which is square. If you have both it and one of the nonsquare comps open at the same time, click back and forth between the two tabs and note the difference.

A special note about DV footage: Since it has lines missing compared with D1-sized images and has a different field order than 640×480 captures, in most cases it needs to be moved up one pixel so that its Y Position = 242 in a 486-line comp (rather than its center 243). Similarly, you would place a D1 source at Y Position 241 in a DV comp, rather than its center (240). This aligns its field order so it will render more sharply. More on this later in this chapter.

The sphere and golf ball on the right are actually round; they are just displayed on our square-pixel computer screen as being wider because the pixels in this nonsquare comp are skinnier than the computer displays them.

Square Sources

Now, let's play around with how our square-pixel computer-generated images interact with our nonsquare footage and comps. In the Objects sub-folder of the Sources folder, you will find one of the spheres that we have used throughout this book; in the Movies folder is a 3D animation of a golf ball rotation. Both are square-pixel sources. Drag either one into the [**Ex.01-square**] comp – they keep their normal round shape, as you would expect. Now drag them into one of the nonsquare comps, and notice that they stretch horizontally. Rotate them, and they stay stretched horizontally. It is important to understand that the object *itself* has not changed; just the way it is being *displayed* has changed.

This may initially look wrong, but it is actually right – these square-pixel footage items are getting pulled into the same "world" that our nonsquare footage exists in. When they are played back later, they will get squished back again automatically and appear round on a TV monitor.

Stills, Scans, and Vector Art

Virtually every source file other than video that you will be using will be created with a square-pixel aspect ratio. This includes scans, still image stock footage libraries, Photoshop files and other paint programs, and Illustrator artwork including text and logos. So the next question becomes: What size should you be creating new images at?

The size you should *not* be creating still artwork at is 720×486 or 720×480 pixels. Even though these match D1 and DV image sizes for NTSC, remember that these sizes imply nonsquare pixels, while your artwork uses square pixels. Import these images into After Effects, and it will assume they have been pre-stretched horizontally by the 9:10 ratio discussed above – and therefore tag them to be treated this way. The fact that they appear round in a nonsquare-pixel comp (such as [**Ex.02.1**])

leads you to believe that you must have done something right. Don't be fooled. When they are displayed later on a video monitor, they will then get squished and look out-of-round (this is simulated in [**Ex.02.2**]). The difference is noticeable – especially to clients who happen to like nice, round circles, rather than squished egg shapes, in their logos. The rule is that when you add square-pixel artwork to a D1 comp, the images *should* look wider than normal.

A common size to create still artwork for D1 NTSC is 720×540 pixels (720×534 for DV, since it has six lines missing). After Effects will treat this as a square-pixel size and rescale the image horizontally as necessary to mix with nonsquare footage. You then scale these images to 486 pixels tall in your D1 compositions (480 for DV), either manually, or by using the handy fit-to-comp shortcut (Command+Option+F).

Try this yourself by opening [**Ex.03.1**] and dragging the image rightsize.jpg from the 39-Chapter Sources subfolder into it. It will stretch wider, and you will notice from the white lines in the pasteboard region

Intuition may tell you to create your artwork at a D1 or DV size such as 720×486 or 720×480 (left). However, when they are displayed later on a video monitor, they will be squished horizontally (right), because the pixels were assumed by After Effects not to be square in the first place. Background image from Digital Vision/Naked & Scared.

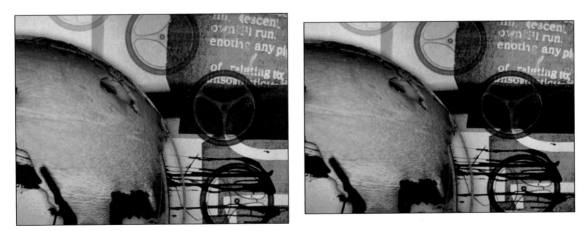

Create your artwork at a square-pixel size that matches the overall aspect ratio of your final image, such as 720×540 (left). Then scale it to fit inside your final comp – 720×486 for D1 size. It will look stretched on a computer monitor (right) but will look correct when mixed with captured footage and displayed on a video monitor later. Background image from Digital Vision/Naked & Scared.

Fit to Comp Size

The Command+Option+F shortcut will stretch any layer to exactly fit the size of a comp. While this may distort the aspect ratio of the image, it's handy for automatically stretching 720×540 comps to 720×486.

540 Fields – NOT!

If you create 720×540 D1 square comps, remember never to field-render these comps directly, which creates 540 fields. Always nest them in a final 720×486 comp and scale to fit. (And don't scale in the Output Module – this scales after the fields have been created.)

of the Comp window that it is bigger than the comp. Scale it to fit the comp (Command+Option+F), and it will look stretched (the globe will look flattened) – but that's okay, as this is a nonsquare comp. Now open [**Ex.03.2**], which is a 648×486 square-pixel comp, with [**Ex.03.1**] nested inside. This display-only comp simulates how it will look on playback, and you can see that the circles are round once more.

There is no rule that says your nonvideo sources have to be the exact same width as your composition; just that you remember they have square pixels, and that you don't use one of the sizes After Effects automatically assumes to be nonsquare, such as 704×480, 720×480, or 720×486 (or for that matter, any of those listed in the Pixel Aspect Ratio table back in Chapter 36). Quite often, we create images, crop pictures, and render animations at 800×600 or even 1024×768 pixels, which still have an image aspect ratio of 4:3, but also have extra resolution to allow us to scale or nudge their position slightly in the composition.

The 720×540 Route

When they're working on a design that *does not* incorporate full-screen video, some artists like to set up their compositions at 720×540 pixels (534 for DV final output) so they can see everything "normally" on their computer monitors and keep maximum resolution.

However, you should never field-render this 720×540 comp – or you'll create 540 lines, not 486 as required. When it's time to render, create a 720×486 D1/NTSC comp, and nest the 720×540 comp into it. Scale the layer to fit (Command+Option+F), and turn on Collapse Transformations for maximum quality (see Chapter 19 for more on collapsing). This chain of comps is shown in [**Ex.04**].

It is important that you do the scaling in a final comp rather than the Output Module! Otherwise, the Render Settings will create an interlaced frame that is 540 lines tall, and the Output Module will then squish those 540 lines down to 486, resulting in field mush.

29.97 fps, Usually Lower

We'll end this chapter by recapping a few general issues surrounding NTSC video. For example, as you know by now, NTSC video runs at 29.97 fps, not 30. Unless you are specifically playing with alternate rates, it is a good idea to make sure all of your footage is conformed to 29.97 and to set up your comps at 29.97 – this will greatly reduce potential problems later when you're playing your final renders through a video card or importing into an NLE.

Both DV and D1 NTSC footage tends to be lower field first. However, DV has 480 lines, compared with 486 for D1. If you center full-size DV footage in a D1-sized composition, the result will be three blank lines top and bottom. However, offsetting an image an odd number of lines vertically aligns it with the wrong field. If you were to render this comp out lower field first, it would become visually softer, because you would be using only the interpolated pixels.

To keep maximum sharpness, you will want to shift these footage items up one line (position value 360, 242) in a D1 NTSC composition. Conversely, if you are using full-size lower-field D1 footage in a DV comp, shift these footage items down one line from center (position 360, 241) for maximum sharpness.

The 704×480 standard definition size for ATSC (Advanced Television Standards Committee) digital video is actually upper field first, not lower. This means that when you're working with full-frame footage, you can center it in a D1 comp and vice versa. However, again: DV footage will need to be shifted up one line in a 704×480 comp, and 704×480 footage will need to be shifted down a pixel in a DV comp.

All of these little shifts are of no relevance if the footage is being moved or scaled vertically, is rotated, or is otherwise mangled by effects, since pixels are getting moved around between fields anyway. You can also ignore these one-pixel shifts if your footage is noninterlaced (30 fps film or DV shot progressive scan, for instance), since there are no fields to separate and interpolate.

Drop Frame and Non-Drop Timecode

When you're working at NTSC rates, you want to set your Timecode Base (File>Preferences>Time) to 30 fps. You will then be presented with an additional menu called NTSC with a choice of either *Non-Drop Frame* or *Drop Frame*. This affects how the numbers in the Time Layout window are counted in this timebase. It also is the source of almost as much confusion as the rate 29.97 fps.

There is no such thing as a 29.97 fps counting timebase, because there is no good way to count with fractional frame numbers (1/29.97, 2/29.97, and so on) – that's why we use 30. However, 29.97 is slightly slower than 30. If we count at 30 and run at 29.97, when running in realtime, eventually the frame numbers in a long composition will drift behind the "clock on the wall."

That's why SMPTE created an alternate counting method known as Drop Frame. Contrary to the belief of many, this does not mean any frames are actually "dropped" – just that certain frame *numbers* are skipped so that for longer projects, the frame count and realtime (i.e., the clock on the wall) match more closely.

To pull this off, the first two frame numbers of each minute – for example, 0:01:00:00 and 0:01:00:01 – are skipped, meaning in this case the counter in the Comp and Time Layout windows would jump straight from 0:00:59:29 to 0:00:01:02. The exception is every whole tens of minutes (00, 10, 20, and so on), where we would count normally.

Confusing? You bet. That's why most people use the Non-Drop counting method, unless the duration of the program is getting over a half hour or so, and they need to carefully track running time for commercial breaks, and so forth. Unfortunately, After Effects defaults to Drop Frame; set it to Non-Drop as soon as you get a chance.

Wrong Rate Timecode

Effect>Video>Timecode has a major flaw: you cannot set it to 29.97 fps, the speed of NTSC video – so it will drift. If you need to add visible timecode, prerender the effect at 30 fps, import, and conform the timecode movie to 29.97 fps.

The Time Preferences allows you to count in Drop Frame or Non-Drop Frame timecode. This is applicable only when your comp is set to 29.97 fps.

Connect

The Interpret Footage dialog and Interpretation Rules were in Chapter 36.

Fields and interlacing were first discussed in Chapter 37; additional issues with video are discussed in Tech Tip 08 on the CD. Also, TechTips 04 and 05 on the CD contain additional information about luminance ranges and pixel aspect ratios.

The Render Queue – including the Output Module – is studied in Chapter 43.

 Working with D1/DV PAL

*Like NTSC, PAL has
nonsquare pixels – but
in a different direction.*

P AL – the most common video format outside of North America – has several advantages over NTSC. Its frame rate, 25 fps, is much cleaner mathematically and close enough to film that pulldown is often not used. The three most common PAL digital formats – square pixel, D1, and DV – also have the same number of scan lines. However, the D1 and DV variants still use nonsquare pixels, which are ultimately displayed on a video monitor wider than they do on most computer monitors. Therefore, it requires a little thought and planning to mix nonvideo elements with this.

A Different Size; A Different Squish

The most common proportions, or image aspect ratio, for a television image is four units wide to three units high – a 4:3 aspect ratio. Most computer monitors also follow this image aspect.

PAL video (often referred to as 625-line video) has 576 lines of image area that we're interested in. Therefore, early PAL digital video systems took $576 \times 4 \div 3 = 768$ pixels across as a good size to work at.

The most common digital video standard – ITU-R BTU.601-4 (also known a CCIR-601, or just 601) – has a different idea about the size of an image. The overall aspect ratio is still 4:3. However, it decrees there should be 720 pixels across, not 768. Of course, $720{:}576 \neq 4{:}3$; what's going on?

In ITU-R 601, the pixels that make up a PAL image are not square. When they appear on a video monitor, they are drawn wider than they are tall (compare that with D1 NTSC, where pixels are drawn taller than they are wide). Since they are both captured and displayed this way, everything works out.

However, our computer monitors – and most of our computer software – can only conceive of pixels being square, and as a result, display and think of these 601 images as being skinnier overall than we would expect. Not only is this visually confusing, it creates real problems when we try to combine the two worlds – such as when we try to add square-pixel text on top of a nonsquare image.

For those few who actually like math, you can derive the pixel aspect ratio for 601 NTSC: $756 \div 720 \approx 1.0667$ for the pixel aspect ratio, which is what After Effects uses. Since video standards are often expressed as

Déjà Vu
You may notice this chapter is largely similar to the previous one on NTSC; the difference is that PAL stretches pixels in a different direction, and by a different amount. Read the chapter that pertains to your country.

Example Project
Explore the 40-Example Project.aep file as you read this chapter; references to [Ex.##] refer to specific compositions within the project file.

ratios of whole numbers (such as 4:3 rather than 1.333:1), you might also see this ratio described as 16:15. (This precise ratio is the subject of some debate; see TechTip 05 on the CD for more details.)

Tracking Aspects

Fortunately, After Effects can compensate for different pixel aspect ratios. Whenever a footage item is set to have a D1/DV PAL pixel aspect ratio in its Interpret Footage dialog (Command+F), After Effects knows those pixels were originally 1.067 as wide as they were tall when the footage was captured or created. If you use this footage in a composition that has been set to Square pixels, After Effects will automatically scale the width by 1.067, in essence converting the footage item to square pixels. This way it will mix naturally with square-pixel footage, and all effects will be calculated correctly.

The Composition Settings dialog (Command+K) has the same pixel aspect ratio menu as you see in the Interpret Footage dialog. This tells After Effects how to preprocess the footage items inside it. Since it is easy to forget to set this menu, get into the habit of selecting from one of the composition presets to the right of Frame Size when appropriate; they will automatically set the pixel aspect ratio for you. However, these presets don't set the frame rate automatically; enter 25 for PAL.

If you drag the same piece of tagged D1/DV PAL pixel aspect footage into a comp that has been set to also have D1/DV PAL aspect pixels, no scaling will take place. After Effects will automatically take its nonsquareness into account when it's processing effects, so everything will keep the right proportions when they're rendered and played back to a video monitor. If you drag a footage item tagged as having square pixels into this same nonsquare comp, the square pixels will get squished horizontally to match the aspect ratio of the composition (and the D1/DV PAL footage also in the comp). When they are played back on an appropriate monitor, the pixels will get restretched and appear at their original proportions.

The Composition Settings dialog (Composition>Composition Settings…, or Command+K) has the same pixel aspect ratio menu as you see in the Interpret Footage dialog.

On the left is how the wheel appears in its native environment, a perfect circle with either square pixels on a computer monitor or rectangular pixels on a D1 PAL monitor.

The center image shows the stretching that occurs when a square-pixel image, wrongly tagged as PAL D1, is displayed on a rectangular-pixel monitor.

On the right are PAL rectangular pixels compressed as expected when viewed on a square-pixel monitor. See the *Pixel Aspect Ratio 101* sidebar in Chapter 39 for why this occurs.

Disorderly Conduct

D1 and square-pixel PAL video are both upper field first, and fortunately have the same number of lines, which greatly simplifies mixing together footage from different sources. However, there is one kink in the system: PAL DV has the same number of lines, but a different field order. Mix D1 and DV full-frame footage together, both centered in a composition, and one of them will go soft due to field interpolation (explained in greater detail in TechTip 08).

The great thing is, After Effects will do all of this automatically – as long as you have your footage – and your comps – tagged correctly and you didn't incorrectly prepare any footage items before you brought them into the program. Make sure that you never mislead the program about what the aspect ratio of the pixels really are! To do that, you need to keep track of where images came from, and where they are going.

Comps and Footage

In the example project that goes with this chapter, we've started a pair of comps for you to experiment with – [**Ex.01-D1/DV**] and [**Ex.01-Square**]. Select them individually and type Command+K to see what their settings are. The D1/DV comp has been set up for 720×576 and for nonsquare D1/DV pixel aspect ratio. The square comp has been set up for 768×576 square pixels, which is a common size for older video cards and editing systems.

Option+double-click the footage item PM_ferris.mov in the Sources> 40_Chapter Sources folder. Notice how it looks squished narrower horizontally than you might expect; this is because it was captured with nonsquare pixels. Now open the [**Ex.01-D1/DV**] comp and drag this footage item into it. Notice how it looks the same. This is because the footage item and the comp have both been set up to the same nonsquare-pixel aspect ratio, so After Effects does not need to perform any further adjustments.

Now open the [**Ex.01-square**] comp and drag the Ferris wheel movie into it – notice it stretches horizontally and the wheel looks more round now. This is because After Effects is correcting the pixel aspect ratio of the movie to match the comp, which is square. If you have both it and the nonsquare comp open at the same time, click back and forth between the two tabs and note the difference.

Square Sources

Now, let's play around with how our square-pixel computer-generated images interact with our nonsquare footage and comps. In the Objects subfolder of the Sources folder, you will find one of the spheres that we have used throughout this book; in the Movies folder is a 3D animation of a golf ball rotation. Drag either footage item into the [**Ex.01-square**] comp – they keep their normal round shape, as you would expect. Now drag them into the nonsquare comp and notice that they squish horizontally. Rotate them, and they stay squished horizontally. It is important to understand that the object has not changed; just the way it is being *displayed* has changed.

This may initially look wrong, but it is actually right – these objects are getting pulled into the same "world" as our nonsquare footage. When they are played back later, they will get stretched back again automatically and appear round on a TV set.

The sphere and golf ball on the right are actually round; they are just displayed on our square-pixel computer screen as being skinnier, because the pixels in this nonsquare comp are actually wider than the computer displays them. Ferris Wheel footage shot by JD Wilcox of ProMax Technology.

Stills, Scans, and Vector Art

Virtually every source file other than video that you will be using will be created with a square-pixel aspect ratio. This includes scans, still image stock footage libraries, Photoshop files and other paint programs, and Illustrator artwork including text and logos. So the next question becomes: What size image should you be creating new images at?

The size you should *not* be creating still artwork at is 720×576 pixels. Even though these match the D1/DV image size for PAL, remember that these sizes imply nonsquare pixels, while your artwork uses square pixels. Import these images into After Effects, and it will assume they have been presquished horizontally by the 16:15 ratio discussed above – and therefore tag them to be treated this way. They will continue to look round in a nonsquare-pixel comp (such as [Ex.02.1]), but when they are displayed later on a video monitor, they will then get squished and look out-of-round (this is simulated in [Ex.02.2]). The difference is noticeable – especially to clients who happen to have nice, round circular shapes, rather than eggs, in their logos.

Instead, consider working at 768×576 pixels. After Effects will treat this as a square-pixel size and automatically rescale the image horizontally as necessary to mix with nonsquare footage. Square-pixel PAL video captured on older systems will also be this size. These images will look skinny on your computer screen while working in a 720-wide comp (assuming you remembered to set the comp's pixel aspect ratio menu correctly, or let the PAL preset frame size menu do it for you), but will be restretched when they are later displayed on video.

There is no rule that says your nonvideo sources have to be the exact same size as your composition – just that you remember they have square pixels and don't use one of the sizes After Effects automatically assumes to be nonsquare, such as 720×576. Quite often, we create images, crop pictures, and render animations at 800×600 or even 1024×768 pixels, which still have an image aspect ratio of 4:3, but also have extra resolution to allow us to scale or nudge their position slightly in the composition.

Create your PAL full-screen artwork at 768×576 pixels (left). After Effects will automatically scale it horizontally to fit in your PAL D1/DV compositions. Circles will look squished on a computer monitor in these comps (right), but will look correct when displayed on a video monitor later. Image from Digital Vision/Data:Funk.

Connect

The Interpret Footage dialog was discussed in Chapter 36. Interpretation Rules were also discussed there, as well as TechTip 10 on the CD.

Fields and interlacing were first discussed in Chapter 37; additional issues with video are discussed in TechTip 08 on the CD. TechTips 04 and 05 contain additional information about luminance ranges and pixel aspect ratios.

The Render Queue – including the Output Module – is studied in Chapter 43.

Working with Widescreen

As television production moves to a wider aspect ratio, pixel aspects and working practices change as well.

Film started out having a 4:3 image aspect ratio. When television – a perceived threat to film – appeared with the same aspect ratio, film differentiated itself by adopting a wider aspect. Today, television is chasing film by moving to widescreen aspect ratios – typically, 16:9. There are several different approaches that achieve this; we'll discuss some of the most common ones, starting with so-called "standard definition" video solutions.

Widescreen Approach 1: Faux Letterbox

When film production switched to a widescreen approach, in which the image is anywhere from 1.85 to 2.35 as wide as it is tall, the film often did not get wider; the projection cropped off the top and bottom of the 4:3 (1.33) image to make it appear wider.

Some fake widescreen in video by using the same approach: The top and bottom of a normal 4:3 image are masked off. This is sometimes referred to as *letterboxing* an image. A few cameras also reportedly do this in what they call (somewhat misleadingly) *widescreen mode*. The result is less resolution – fewer active pixels are being used to convey an image – but it gives the look some people prefer.

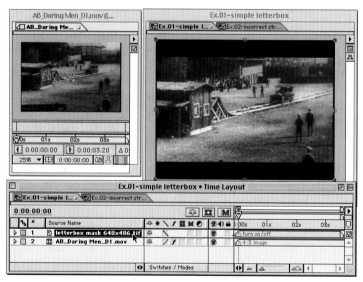

A quick and dirty approach to widescreen is to merely mask off the top and bottom of an image with black solids. On the left is the original in the Layer window; the right shows the result. Footage courtesy Artbeats/Daring Men.

Letterboxing is easy to achieve in After Effects by simply creating black solids to obscure the top and bottom. We've included several prerendered letterboxing masks for common frame sizes in the CD>Goodies> Templates folder – just add the appropriate image to the top of your layer stack. An example is shown in comp [**Ex.01**].

What size should this letterbox hole be? One method of calculation would be taking the square-pixel dimension of a full video frame, such as 648×486, multiplying its width by 9/16, and using the result for your

Example Project

Explore the 41-Example Project.aep file as you read this chapter; references to [Ex.##] refer to specific compositions within the project file.

height. In this case, it yields 364.5 pixels. It is best to round it to the nearest even number – 364 – to have the same, whole number of masked pixels (in this case, 52) above and below the mask in a comp. Make your mask the entire width of the comp, regardless of the pixel aspect ratio in use.

A common cheat many people use to fake a filmic letterboxed look is to take 4:3 aspect footage and scale it down vertically (rather than crop it) to simulate a widescreen aspect ratio. The result is an image that looks stretched horizontally; see [**Ex.02**]. It's not accurate, but you may like it as a stylized look. Just be cautious when you're doing any vertical scaling to interlaced material; even separated fields may not scale gracefully.

Widescreen Approach 2: Anamorphic

The most common standard definition video approach is to squeeze the captured image horizontally into the pixels used for a normal 4:3 aspect video image. Upon playback they are stretched back out to their original width. During production on a square-pixel computer screen, the images look skinnier than they are. This allows normal video equipment to be used to capture, store, and play back these images; you just need to know how to handle this squeeze during production.

Square Pixels

D1 /DV NTSC
√ D1 /DV NTSC Widescreen
D1 /DV PAL
D1 /DV PAL Widescreen
Anamorphic 2:1
D4/D16 Standard
D4/D16 Anamorphic

After Effects cannot tell the difference between 4:3 and anamorphic 16:9 footage because the frame sizes are the same; you'll need to set the Pixel Aspect Ratio yourself for widescreen footage in the Interpret Footage dialog.

This "anamorphic" approach is really just a variation of the nonsquare pixel examples of the previous two chapters. For D1, DV, and ATSC NTSC, the pixel aspect ratio used by After Effects is 6:5 (1.2); for D1 and DV PAL, the aspect ratio is 64:45 (~1.4222). (These precise numbers are the subject of debate; see TechTip 05 on the CD.) However, since the image sizes as defined in pixels for this anamorphic footage are the same as for the normal 4:3 image aspect ratio cases, After Effects assumes this footage is 4:3; you will need to set the Pixel Aspect Ratio menu in the Interpret Footage dialog (Command+F) for these footage items to be treated as widescreen.

Whenever a footage item is set to have this widescreen pixel aspect ratio, After Effects knows those pixels were originally much wider than they are on the computer's screen. If a comp has also been set up to use a matching widescreen pixel aspect ratio, no scaling will take place. However, After Effects will automatically take the nonsquareness into account when it's processing effects applied to these layers, so everything will keep the right proportions when it's rendered and played back to a widescreen video monitor.

The most common approach to widescreen video production today is to take a 16:9 image (left) and squeeze it horizontally to fit a 4:3 video frame (right). Background image from Digital Vision Naked & Scared; foreground 3D scene by CyberMotion based on icons designed by Ridgley Curry for QAD Inc.

Viewing Anamorphic Comps

The unusual pixel aspect ratio of anamorphic compositions can give you pause when you're making artistic decisions. There are a couple of ways to display them with their correct aspect ratio.

One is to have a video card in your computer, driving an NTSC or PAL monitor that has a 16:9 switch on it, as most newer monitors do. Another is to set up a comp in square-pixel dimensions (864 pixels wide for NTSC, 854 for ATSC SDTV, 1024 for PAL) with square aspect pixels for viewing purposes only, and drag your working comp into this viewing comp. If you've tagged your comps correctly as having widescreen or square pixels, your working comp should automatically stretch to fit the viewing comp. Keep this open somewhere on a square-pixel computer monitor (perhaps in half size and resolution to reduce rendering time and screen real estate) to glance at for a confidence check. If the slight pixelation from the wide/square stretch bothers you, set the working comp layer to Best Quality in your viewing comp. An example of this is **[Ex.03.1]**.

If you drag a footage item tagged as having square pixels (such as scans, stock photos, vector art, and so forth) into this same nonsquare widescreen comp, the square pixels will get squished to match the aspect ratio of the composition (and the widescreen footage in the comp). Try this with [**Ex.03**]: Drag other D1 or square-pixel footage items in the Sources folder into this comp and notice how they become squished horizontally. After Effects will even track the pixel aspect ratio of Solid layers and effects (such as text) applied to them, squishing them down inside an anamorphic comp. (Solids automatically take on the pixel aspect ratio of the comp they are in.)

Widescreen comps and footage will look skinny on your computer monitor, but when they are played back on an appropriate monitor, the pixels will get restretched and appear at their original proportions. Working in this artificially skinny world can become confusing, especially when you're adding nonvideo elements such as text and photos. Therefore, you might want to adopt a hybrid approach in which you work on some elements in a square-pixel widescreen comp, then combine them later with video elements in an anamorphic comp. Working in square pixels for widescreen is what we're going to discuss next.

Widescreen Comps

After Effects does not have comp presets for widescreen images, so you will have to remember to set the Pixel Aspect Ratio popup to Widescreen yourself.

Widescreen Approach 3: Square Pixel

Another popular way of working in widescreen is to create your comps at the widescreen 16:9 ratio using square pixels. Depending on what format you will ultimately render to, it's easy to calculate what comp size you should use. For example, in NTSC specs with 486 lines, $486 \times 16 \div 9 = 864$ pixels wide. Make sure to set the comp's pixel aspect ratio to square, not one of the widescreen choices (which are anamorphic, or nonsquare).

You can now create (and view) your nonvideo artwork normally. When you drag a properly tagged anamorphic footage item into this comp (such as the case with the CM_metrowide layer in comp [**Ex.04**]), After Effects will automatically stretch it to its correct aspect. Drag in any other square-pixel footage items, and they will keep their normal aspect.

Unfortunately, in North America there are no square-pixel video standards until you get into high definition TV – all "standard definition" widescreen video is anamorphic. Therefore, unless you are working in hi-def, you will need to squeeze your work into one of these formats for final rendering. This can be done two ways:

Method #1: Create a for-rendering composition that matches your target video format (such as D1), set its pixel aspect ratio to a matching widescreen choice (such as D1/DV NTSC Widescreen), and drag your final design composition into this rendering composition. After Effects will automatically squish it down to fit. Turn on the Collapse Transformations switch to maintain maximum quality through this chain. Render this composition normally. We have set up **[Ex.04.1]** in this way, and added it to the Render Queue (Command+Option+0) for you to check. As you drag footage items into **[Ex.04]** to experiment, periodically glance at **[Ex.04.1]** just so you are clear about what is going to happen to your image when you go to render.

Method #2: Queue up your square-pixel widescreen composition for rendering, then squeeze it down using the Stretch section in the Output Module of the Render Queue to match your target format. The **[Ex.04]** comp has already been added to the Render Queue and squeezed in this way. Remember, never scale interlaced footage vertically; it will mess up your fields. Therefore, it is important that you set up your comps with the number of lines in your desired render target format. If necessary, you can crop off lines top and bottom from D1 NTSC to fit it into DV's 480 lines.

Future Proofing

If you are creating standard definition compositions today that might be redesigned at hi-def in the future, try to use vector art whenever possible so you can continuously rasterize it to keep resolution at larger sizes.

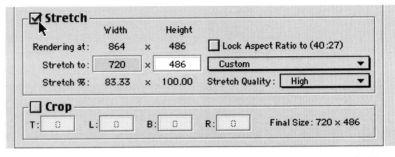

A square-pixel widescreen composition can be squeezed into an anamorphic frame at the rendering stage in the Output Module dialog.

Widescreen Approach 4: High Definition

In the United States, the Advanced Television Standards Committee (ATSC) has designated a number of image sizes that can be used in digital television. In addition to the Standard Definition Television (SDTV) sizes that have been discussed in the past few chapters, there are two sizes for High Definition (hi-def):

720 line: 1280 W × 720 H

1080 line: 1920 W × 1080 H

Fortunately, both of these specifications are 16:9 and use square pixels. This means that no special pixel aspect ratios must be set for their footage or compositions, and that they will display with the same aspect ratio on a computer screen as they will ultimately be viewed on a high-def video monitor. So, there are no special tricks to worry about.

The distressing part of the equation comes in the interlacing and frame rate choices. According to the ATSC's documents, the 720-line format is

Framing for Two

How you shoot the source material depends on what you feel your most common distribution format will be. For example, films are typically framed for their widescreen theater presentation, with an effort to make the set clean above and below the action so the full frame can be used later for 4:3 television. On the other hand, since television is still predominantly 4:3, much of the prime-time television being shot for both widescreen hi-def and ordinary 4:3 television is framed for a 4:3 image, with the set dressed to make sure the areas to the left and right of the action are clean for widescreen formats.

Editing also enters into the equation. For example, if an actor enters the scene from offstage, the point at which he or she becomes visible changes depending on whether, and how much, you are cropping off the sides. Editing two versions of the program is ideal; compromises are often necessary.

When all else fails, remember to satisfy your primary audience and protect for your secondary audience.

progressive (referred to as *720p*), but the 1080 line format can be progressive (*1080p*) or interlaced (*1080i*, which is upper field first). The 720-line format can run at 23.976, 24, 29.97, 30, 59.94, or 60 frames per second; 1080p can run at 23.976, 24, 29.97, or 30, and 1080i can run at 29.97 or 30. Production standards for the most popular rates, and how to transcode between them, will fall out over time. In these early days (early 2000), the standard NTSC and film rates are initially proving the most common.

Designing for 16:9 and 4:3

During the next several years, as we transition to various advanced and digital television standards, the chances are strong that clients will ask for you to deliver both 16:9 widescreen and 4:3 normal versions of a project. The two formats have quite different aesthetics. There will be many occasions when artistically it will just be better to design and deliver two different versions. However, if you want to minimize the amount of work, there are a few different approaches for going from one to the other.

The early consensus seems to be that whatever path you choose, design for widescreen initially, then consider how to convert it to an acceptable presentation in the 4:3 format. All of the following paths are based on this assumption, with the exception of the BBC approach, which uses a compromise size as the initial design goal.

Pan and Scan

One potential conversion technique is to keep the full height of the image, chopping off part of the sides to make it fit. Depending how the action is framed, it might be best to cut more off of one side than the other, or to vary which portions get chopped during a scene. This is the *pan and scan* technique often referred to when transferring motion pictures to a 4:3 video format. This is demonstrated in [**Ex.05**], where we're trying

 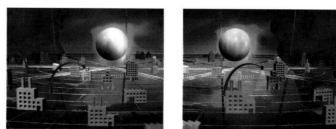

Panning and scanning means taking a widescreen image (left), deciding which area to use or "scan" (center), and perhaps panning it (right) to follow the action in a shot.

to keep the focus on the light pole and the building in front of it. To understand how the original image is being panned, look for the white outline of the layer on the pasteboard in the Comp window, and note how its location changes over time. In some extreme pan and scan cases, the image might even get scaled horizontally.

The one area where pan and scan probably works least well is titles. A title that is a comfortable width in widescreen suddenly becomes large – possibly even encroaching on safe areas – when it's cropped down to 4:3. For example, work with the 4:3 comp [**Ex.06**] and see if you can find a balanced position for this widescreen title, keeping safe areas in mind (hit the apostrophe key to overlay them on the Comp window if they are not already visible).

A title that was designed to balance a widescreen frame (left) may be hard to center without crowding when cropped down to 4:3 (right). Images courtesy Digital Vision/The Body and Naked & Scared.

On the other hand, if you design with safe areas of 4:3 in mind, you'll have large unused areas to the left and right in widescreen. Even if you choose the pan and scan approach, you might consider re-doing the titles and other text-based scenes specially for 4:3.

To minimize the gyrations that need to be performed at the pan and scan stage, some people will shoot widescreen but keep the action centered inside a 4:3 image inset in the middle of the 16:9 stage. Keep the sides of your sets dressed to minimize unwanted garbage at the left and right extremes for when it is broadcast widescreen.

Protected for Full Aperture

As mentioned earlier, most film has a raw aspect ratio of 4:3. Many are careful when shooting film to frame the action vertically in the center for widescreen, but also to keep the top and bottom of the frame clear of props, microphones, lights, and so forth (a practice sometimes referred to as *protected*) so they can use the full aperture of the film later for 4:3 without any panning and scanning. This is a good technique to keep in mind if your footage is originating on film. It is less practical for standard definition video, since it would mean shooting at 4:3 and using fewer lines (and therefore, less resolution) to blow out to fill a 16:9 screen.

It is common practice to frame shots based on widescreen presentation but to protect the areas above and below (tinted white in this photo) for clean 4:3 playback as well.

Whether shooting on video or film, this technique is also worthwhile to consider if you decide to design for 4:3 first, then convert for widescreen later: shoot full frame, but frame your shots so the action happens inside the smaller vertical 16:9 area. Part of the top and bottom will be cropped in the 4:3 version by the safe areas, anyway. It will then be a relatively simple matter to throw a letterbox mask on it later (the first widescreen technique discussed in this chapter) for quickie widescreen.

Hard Masks

When you're scaling your master comp in a second comp to hit various presentation aspect ratios, turn on the Collapse Transformations layer switch to maintain maximum quality (see Chapter 18). You'll need to watch out for areas on the pasteboard in your master comp becoming visible in the output comp. To guard against this, create black solids in the output comp to mask or hide unwanted pixels.

For example, in **[Ex.08.2]** turning on Collapse Transformations displays an unwanted portion of the image that was previously cropped by the comp's size in **[Ex.08.1]**. Turn off the black solids in **[Ex.08.2]** and turn on/off the Collapse switch if this concept isn't clear.

If you use a particular output size often, prerender the black solids as a still image with alpha so you can simply add the image as a top layer in the future. We've already created letterbox masks for the most popular sizes (Goodies>Templates folder). Now that you know how easy a "hard" mask is to make, you can create new masks as needed.

Letterbox Presentation

Another approach is to shoot for 16:9 and present the 4:3 version letterboxed. This uses the full visible width of the screen while using less of the height and filling it in with black.

Within the letterbox presentation approach, there are several schools of thought. The most straightforward approach scales the 16:9 image evenly so that its width just fits into 100% of the width of the 4:3 image; 75% all around is typical. This is demonstrated in **[Ex.07.1]**. The 4:3 version does not contain any more or any less image than the widescreen version.

For some people this leaves too much black area above and below. Therefore, they will not scale the 16:9 image down quite as much, resulting in some of the original 16:9 image getting cropped off the left and right

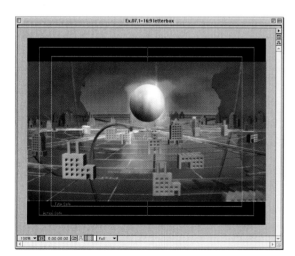

The most aesthetically pure approach is to take a widescreen image and rescale it to fit inside a 4:3 frame, with black bars above/below. The side effect is that the image looks "smaller" on a 4:3 screen. Note the safe areas; they crop just the sides.

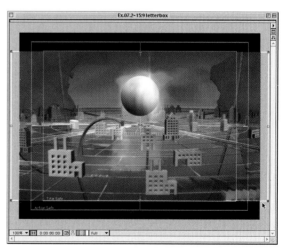

Another common approach is to scale the original 16:9 image so that only a 15:9 aspect of it fits inside the 4:3 comp. Notice the white lines on the pasteboard to the left and right; this means some of the original image is getting cropped off.

side, but with smaller black bars above and below. The most common approach is to aim for a 15:9 or a 14:9 final aspect ratio of the image to be fitted inside the 4:3 final, working out to an overall scaling of 80% and 85.7%, respectively. These are demonstrated in [**Ex.07.2**] and [**Ex.07.3**]. Double-click the layer to see it uncropped and to get a better idea of how much you are losing.

Frank Capria, who works on shows such as *The American Experience* for Boston PBS station WGBH and was one of the first to tackle high-def production for the station, says that how the footage was originally shot often "determines the letterbox format more than how much black we are willing to tolerate on screen. If the material was shot in 16:9 protecting for 4:3 (meaning the action was centered in the 4:3 area), then we are more likely to settle on 14:9 or 15:9. If the material was shot using the full 16:9 canvas, then we are most likely to use 16:9 letterbox."

Whether you choose to present a 16:9, 15:9, or 14:9 aspect of your original image inside a 4:3 image will be determined by how much of visual interest appears at the left and right edges. Meanwhile, the top and bottom will be fully visible – overscan and all. It is also best to choose an aspect as early as possible so materials can be shot and created with these croppings in mind.

14:9 Compromise

Several people have attempted to strike a balance between 16:9 and 4:3 by picking a ratio between the two and presenting both with black bars filling in the unused portions of the respective formats. For example, the BBC has been promoting 14:9 as a compromise. When it's projected in 16:9, the full height is used, with some black on the left and right; when it's projected in 4:3 (which equals 12:9), the full width is used, with some black – less than with a normal 16:9 letterbox – at the top and bottom. The feeling is that with safe areas cropping out part of these bars anyway, the results would be least noticeable to either viewer. However, as with most compromises, few are satisfied; 14:9 has yet to catch on in a big way in the United States.

A design framed for a 14:9 aspect ratio (top) has black bars on the sides in 16:9 (middle) and along the top and bottom in 4:3 (above). Images from Digital Vision Velocity and The Body CDs.

There are several approaches to this production inside After Effects. For standard definition NTSC, one would be to set up your design compositions to be 756×486 with square pixels, which is a 14:9 aspect ratio. When you need to do a 16:9 output, center this inside a 864×486 square-pixel comp and do the anamorphic squeeze when you render. For the 4:3 version, place the 14:9 square-pixel version inside a 4:3 comp (640×480 square or D1 as needed), and scale it to fit the width of the comp. This hierarchy is shown in the [**Ex.08**] folder, where [**Ex.08.1**] is the 14:9 master, and the other comps are set up for various output sizes. Note that black solids are used as masks (see the *Hard Masks* sidebar).

Special thanks to Frank Capria of Kingpin Productions (www.dtvpix.com) for sharing his invaluable experience in producing widescreen programming for PBS station WGBH, which influenced much of the content of this chapter.

Connect

All the issues surrounding Collapse Transformations were discussed in Chapter 18.

The Render Queue, Render Settings, and Output modules are explained in more detail in Chapter 43.

TechTip 05 on the CD-ROM goes into meticulous detail about pixel aspect ratios for various formats.

 Working at Film Resolution

The Big Screen requires big hard drives – and lots of planning.

Once you've mastered working with video in After Effects, it's not much of a leap to working at film resolution. There are obvious differences, but the biggest obstacle is usually disk space. To cover working with film resolution would take a book in itself, so we will concentrate on working with the most popular "2K" film resolution – 35mm Academy Aperture – including the popular Cineon file format with its log-based color space.

An Academy Aperture film frame as it might appear on a contact print for projection. (The optical audio track is added for clarification only.) The grayed-out area at the top and bottom, though captured on film and rendered, will not be seen in the theater (resulting in a projected aspect ratio of 1.85:1), but will be used when the film is later transferred for TV and video (1.33:1). Image courtesy Cinesite Los Angeles (www.cinesite.com).

Film Flavors

It's easy to be overwhelmed by the number of aspect ratios, formats, and film systems that are available. What makes it even more confusing is that quite often the entire film frame is exposed, but only a portion of it is projected, with bits on the top and bottom masked upon projection. We're interested in the aspect ratio of this projected area, although quite often the rest of the frame – a 4:3 aspect ratio – will be used later for video.

Just to add another layer of confusion, part of the film frame is usually also reserved for an optical soundtrack. The bible on film systems, the *American Cinematographer Manual*, differentiates between the full frame and the area minus soundtrack as follows:

- *Full Aperture* (also known as *camera aperture* or *silent aperture*) refers to the total area between the 35mm perforations, including the area normally reserved for the soundtrack.
- *Academy Aperture* refers to that area of the negative excluding the soundtrack area.

Example Project

Explore the 42-Example Project.aep file as you read this chapter; references to [Ex.##] refer to specific folders and compositions within the project file. *You will need to increase the RAM allocation above the default – 64 megabytes at a minimum.*

Which Road to Travel

Different types of jobs, such as film titles or live action visual effects, can all be done on the desktop, but they require different approaches to achieve the best results with the minimum amount of pain. The pivotal decision is whether it is best to work in your computer's normal linear color space, to get comfortable with the Cineon format's log color space, or to do the composite outside the computer.

Option 1: Pure Graphics

If you are creating graphics from scratch – such as a 3D render – that are not composited over any previously shot film, the simplest approach is to work in normal linear color space. Then, the file format you will typically output is a series of stills saved in SGI-RGB format. This format has an RLE (run length encoding) option, which means it can use a lossless compression scheme that is essentially the same as PICT files.

Note that there is a small advantage in saving your graphics out to the Cineon log color space and file format instead (discussed later), because it will give the operator who's doing your final output to film some additional flexibility in exposure control.

Option 2: Composited Images

If you are treating previously shot footage or adding graphics on top of footage, you will want to do everything possible to retain the original color range and detail that was in the original film. Therefore, you should consider working in a log color space, based on the Cineon file format developed by Kodak.

In this workflow, you keep the source footage in log space throughout and convert any computer-generated graphics from their native linear space to log to composite with this footage. You can temporarily convert the final image to the linear space for checking your work or making video proofs, but you will ultimately render to the Cineon log format. Fortunately, After Effects has built-in support for this

format, and we'll discuss how to manage this process in this chapter as well as a case study in the Bonus Tutorials on the CD; TechTip 06 also contains a pair of technical articles that will be of interest.

It is not required that you perform these jobs in log color space; for example, we composited titles over the opening footage of the movie *Now and Then* in linear color. However, this puts a lot more pressure on the film scanning operator to aesthetically fit the extended dynamic range of film into the reduced linear range most computers use (occasionally requiring rescanning).

Option 3: Optical Composite

If your contribution consists of relatively simple solid-colored titles to be overlaid on a film scene, it might work out faster and cheaper to build the graphics just as white on black and save them to the SGI-RGB format (as with Option 1). These images would then be composited over the film using an optical printer; you can even color your titles at this stage and add fades. We won't be covering this method here, as it's more often used for stills as opposed to animation, but keep it in mind as an option.

Option 4: Resizing Video

With the advent of relatively inexpensive, high-quality digital video cameras, an increasing number of people are shooting on video and having a service bureau scale it up to film. For best results, this requires you to collaborate closely with the service bureau you will be using.

Again, the focus of this chapter is working on actual film frames inside After Effects, but a couple of video-to-film tips would include using progressive scan (interlacing and film do not get along), checking out the dropping price of high-definition video cameras, and considering working in PAL, since its frame rate is much closer to that of film (25 versus 24 fps).

The most common aspect ratio in the United States is 1.85 or Academy Aperture, while in Europe, 1.66 is more popular. This ratio is determined by dividing the width of the image by its *projected* height. (In reality, an Academy Aperture image as shot has a 1.37:1 aspect ratio, but the top and bottom is cropped upon projection.) You'll often see these ratios written in formats like 1.85:1, but it's referred to as "one-eight-five." Before you start work, confirm the aspect ratio with the client.

Pixel Dust

Film is usually scanned to fit the final output: If you plan to output Academy Aperture, then have the film house scan only the Academy area. Most of the time, you won't need the additional image that appears in the Full Aperture area, and your scans will be properly centered without worrying about where the optical soundtrack is. (Of course, there are exceptions to every rule; occasionally you will need some extra image to play with to reframe shots or perform other adjustments. In these cases, assuming the shot was not cropped with a hard matte as it was filmed, you may need to request a "Full Ap" scan and reframe yourself for Academy.)

If you're outputting computer-generated animation to Academy Aperture, it's a waste of render time and disk space to create files at Full Aperture size – no one will see that extra image in the soundtrack area.

While recommended pixel sizes can vary slightly between different post houses, the standard Cineon sizes are below:

Academy Aperture: **1828 W × 1332 H**

Full Aperture: **2048 W × 1536 H**

(Some scanners/recorders use 2048 × 1556; ask to be sure.)

Note again that the usable area of the film is close to a 4:3 aspect ratio, not the 1.85 (or 1.66) you thought you were getting. The reason to render the extra pixels is so that the movie won't be letterboxed when it's eventually transferred to video or shown on TV. Make sure that any important action happens in the vertical center and that titles are safe for the 1.85 aspect ratio (not just the TV title safe area). Examples of both Full Aperture and Academy Aperture, with templates overlaid to show title safe areas, are demonstrated in this chapter's **[Ex.01]** folder.

With that advice given, be aware that occasionally you will be asked to design only inside the widescreen film window. It is very important then to establish if the 4:3 video version will be presented letterboxed (so you'll see the entire widescreen area, minus a small amount off the sides for video safe areas), or if it will be "panned and scanned," which means substantial portions of the sides will get chopped off. This latter approach has substantial implications on how you design your titles or images – you can't spread your elements out too wide without causing major grief downstream. Ask early, ask often, and get it in writing.

If you do design your animation at Full Aperture size (2048×1536) when you really need Academy output, make sure that your service

Thumbs Down

When you're working with film res sources and comps, the Project window will bog down drawing thumbnails. Speed up redraw by checking the Disable Thumbnails in the Project Window preference (File>Preferences>Display).

The Real Center

When designing for one-eight-five (Academy), titles should be centered across 1828 pixels wide, not 2048. If you center for 2048, they will be offset to the left when they are projected.

provider can scale your animation to fit the Academy image area, and that you tell the service provider to do so – otherwise, your animations will appear off center, since the Academy "window" is offset to the right to make room for the optical soundtrack.

Occasionally a post house will ask you to render a Full Aperture frame, with your Academy Aperture animation positioned inside it. You can do this by nesting your 1828×1332 animation into a second comp created at 2048×1536 for output, as demonstrated in [**Ex.02**].

Academy Aperture size overlaid with 1.85 and TV safe zones.

Timeless Templates

Film frame sizes are often referenced in inches, in relationship to the film – for example, Academy Aperture is typically 0.864×0.630 inches. Obviously, that's not very helpful in the digital world. Over the years, various service providers have obliged us with their definition of how inches relate to pixels. After collecting quite a few templates, we built our own versions in Illustrator.

Check out the Goodies>Templates folder on the accompanying CD for these Film Templates. The Academy Aperture templates at 1828×1332 fit the common Cineon size, and there are also templates that place this frame inside Full Aperture (2048×1536). They are supplied as white TIFFs with alpha channels – drag them on top of your design and turn them on temporarily when you're sizing and placing graphics. This is demonstrated in the comps in [**Ex.01**].

If you need to design your film titles in Illustrator, we've included an 1828×1332 Illustrator template, with not only guides but also a 12-field chart, which divides the frame into twelve even increments in all directions from the center. When the editor makes a request for you to "move the title up one field," he or

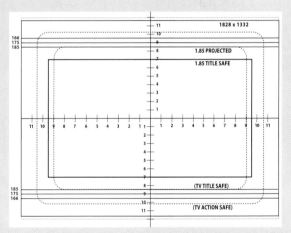

Templates in the Goodies folder of the CD will help you visualize the safe areas for a number of common film formats.

she is referring to a "field" (grid line) in the 12-field chart – not a video field. We've also included a separate 12-field chart template, which you can overlay in a comp as a handy guide when you're repositioning or measuring titles.

Note: *As far as we know, these templates are as accurate as anything currently out there, but we make no guarantees as to whether they are scientifically correct to the exact pixel.*

Film Preferences

There are a number of Preferences in After Effects that are made for working with film:

- Since you'll be creating Comps at 24 fps, set the Display Style to 24 fps also (File>Preferences>Time). You can also set the Display Style to Feet+Frames, or Frames.

- Change the default frame rate for newly imported sequences to 24 fps (File>Preferences>Import>Sequence Footage).

- Be aware that the "start numbering frames at" dialog controls both Feet+Frames and Frames. Film scans usually come in frames starting from 1, while a film editor using an Avid Film Composer counts in feet+frames starting from 0. However, since the preference sets the starting number for both Frames and Feet+Frames, you'll need to be on the ball when you're cross-referencing numbers and switching back and forth.

- Despite the large sizes, you can work efficiently with film res comps set to quarter resolution and 25% zoom, which is slightly smaller than full-frame video.

- You might also want to "Disable thumbnails in project window" to speed up the Project window's reaction times (File>Preferences>Display).

Warning: *Preferences are saved on an application basis, not per project, so don't forget to reset these preferences if you switch back to working at video res.*

Sizing Up the Job

A 2K Academy SGI-RGB frame of 1828×1332 pixels requires about 7 megabytes of RAM when it's opened. Because of the noise inherent in film grain, it is usually not much less when it's saved on disk. Since film runs at 24 frames per second, one second of film takes up nearly 170 megabytes of disk space. One minute of film – 1440 frames – takes up about 10 gigabytes. If your design calls for working with the 10-bit Cineon file format, which requires a 32-bit file per frame (two bits are unused), a 1828×1332 frame will consume 9.3 megabytes each.

Working at film resolution usually leads to a shopping spree for cheap, fast, and large hard drives, which fortunately continue to fall in price. You could also resave source footage with a slight amount of JPEG compression to save space, but thanks to those falling prices, this is not as necessary as it once was.

Bear in mind that you don't need to have the entire job on line at once. Fortunately, pixels are more stable than film; they don't expose differently depending on the room temperature and day of the week they're processed. For very large projects, load in part of the job (up to a good break point), render, back up, off-load, and then continue with the next section. The complete job can be output to film either continuously or in sections.

To process film resolution frames, you'll also need a sizable amount of RAM. The amount will depend on the number of layers you're rendering and the effects being used. An individual film frame requires seven to nine times as much RAM as a video frame, but you're usually using fewer layers and applying fewer effects, so the RAM requirements don't scale up proportionally. As a general guide, dissolving between two frames while overlaying a title is no more taxing than a complex video project, but 256 megabytes or more is recommended for special effects with nested compositions. Make sure to test that you can render your design at Full Resolution and Best Quality well before the deadline, which should also give you a good estimate of how long rendering might take.

For title sequences, plan on also creating at least one *textless* version, which is used for international distributors. Try to plan how this can be achieved without rerendering the entire sequence – for example, rendering "patches" just for the frames or scenes where the titles came up in the *texted* version. You might want to coordinate the output of the textless version to coincide with the texted version so that the project is still online at the film house.

Scanning the Horizon

In order to have film scanned, or your animation output to film, you'll need some heavy-duty equipment – your slide scanner won't cut it. This means working with a post house with a film scanner and a film recorder. (Make sure you're sitting down when you get the estimate...)

Film is typically scanned and recorded by a device connected to an SGI (Silicon Graphics) computer. While most post houses have integrated desktop computers into their production environment at some level, be prepared to spend a little time working out the optimum method for transferring files to and from your desktop. Your service bureau will prefer file formats that the SGI reads quickly, such as SGI-RGB (8-bit linear) or Cineon (10-bit log). Targa or TIFF (both 8-bit linear) are other options, although they are accepted less. Fortunately, After Effects can read and write all of these formats. If you insist on a file format not on their preferred list, expect a delay and a possible extra charge for format conversion.

The preferred media will be up for discussion as well, with DLT or Exabyte computer tapes being the usual common denominators cross-platform. SGIs read and write to tape using the Unix TAR (Tape ARchive) format. If you're on Mac or PC, you'll need a utility that can read or write TAR and has drivers for your tape drive. Don't forget to factor in the cost of the media – DLT tapes in particular can add up fast.

Time Prefs Recall

If you bounce between video and film projects on the same computer, be warned that Preferences are not saved on a per-project basis. When you re-open a project, check that time is being displayed in the format and frame rate you expect.

TAR and Feathered

An increasing number of film houses are able to handle Mac or PC formatted media. However, you should assume that they'll prefer a tape format such as Exabyte or DLT, written as a Unix Tape ARchive (TAR).

On the Mac platform, the preferred TAR application for Exabyte tapes is Missing Link (from Puffin Designs – www.puffindesigns.com), because it is user friendly and handles Abekas DDR tapes as well. For other formats such as DLT and AIT in addition to Exabyte, the choice is Backup, which is part of the QuTape set (available from CyberComp – email cybercomp@earthlink.net). On the PC side, we've heard WinTAR-SCSI from SpiralCom Communications (www.spiralcomm.com) is a cost-effective choice.

TAR has a set of options concerning how large the data chunks written to tape are: block size and number of files per archive. Check with the film house you are working with to get its preferred block size; 16 sectors (8192 bytes) is common. If no one can give you this information, ask for a sample tape. Many TAR programs have an auto-detect option while reading; write back the tapes using the same setting as detected while reading.

TAR's one-file-per-archive option is convenient, because each frame will become its own archive, making locating individual frames easier. That said, your film house may prefer that you save all the files in one archive, because they read and write much faster than the one-file-per-archive option.

Speaking of which, don't forget to leave lots of time not just for rendering, but also for transferring to tape. In fact, the faster computers get, the more the tape transfer becomes the bottleneck. For long projects, we set up a production pipeline where frames are rendered to a removable hard drive. This drive is then moved to a second machine that transfers them to tape, while the first machine continues rendering the next section.

Macintosh users have a couple of additional issues to be aware of:

• On the reading side, Mac files require a file type and creator to be set when using CyberComp's Backup utility; in the Preferences, *before you read the tape*, enter SDPX for the Type and AVIM for the Creator.

• On the writing side, After Effects tags each frame with a preview icon for viewing in the Finder. This additional icon can show up as a separate file when it's saved to TAR, which can be confusing to the service bureau. If you have this problem, look inside the Goodies folder on the CD; Adobe has provided a plug-in to work around this issue.

Bits and Pieces

If you deliver your animation on multiple tapes or cartridges, but need continuous output, be sure to specify this – otherwise it may be output in pieces.
If you built in break points, note these as well in case there's a problem while recording out.

Film on a Video Budget

If you can't afford to shoot on film, check out the Cinelook and Cinemotion plug-ins from DigiEffects (www.digieffects.com). The Cinelook manual is on the CD (Free Plug-ins>DigiEffects) if you'd like to know more.

When you decide on a service provider, test the entire production path at the beginning of the job – make sure you can read their files; make sure they can read yours – and work closely with them during the project. Once you have the general file path sorted out, you'll need to settle on what size the film frames are to be scanned and output at. As noted earlier, there are a lot of choices, and film scanning and output are both very expensive to re-do, so make sure everyone involved agrees on formats in advance.

Getting What You Want

When you're completing an order form for scanning or recording, you'll need to know the frame size (Full Aperture, Academy Aperture, and so on), color depth (10-bit log or 8-bit linear), file format, and tape format. If there's a checkbox for Resolution, Full Resolution refers to 4K frames; Half Resolution to 2K (which means either 2048 or 1832 pixels across, depending if the scan is Full or Academy), and Quarter Resolution would be 1K. You also specify what film stock to print to and the number of prints required, both of which will normally be dictated by the film's editor or production office. Obtain an order form in advance of output so you can check that you have an answer for every checkbox.

If you provide a long sequence over multiple tapes, make sure that the frame numbers are sequential and that you specify Continuous Output. Otherwise, you may find each tape will be output and processed separately, rather than as one piece of film.

Scanning In

The biggest issue on the scanning side, after general issues of frame size, file format, and precisely which frames you want (see the sidebar *Telling Time*), is color correction. Film is a lot more subjective than video, with each film stock looking different, and a wide range of adjustments available on both input and output.

Most desktop computer monitors do not look like projected film – the gamma does not match and they are typically set to a much higher color temperature than film (9000K versus 5400K). And, chances are, the person who shot or edited the footage is already in love with the way it looks on the prints he or she has already seen. Therefore, we take the approach of making the absolute minimum amount of color correction to the original footage in our computers, pushing the task of making it "look right" up to the scanning stage. We then match our graphics to look good when they're composited with the footage we received.

To achieve this end, we ask the film's production department to supply the scanning room with a sample, either in the form of a *match clip* or a *guide clip*. A match clip is a handful of the exact frames being scanned in, with a color gamut the Powers That Be are already happy with. A guide clip contains frames that aren't from the exact scene being scanned, but that can serve as an overall color guide. We then ask the scanning operator to match these colors.

If the scan at the default settings doesn't match, the operators can either re-adjust their scanners, or if they're using the Cineon format, color correct the frame digitally in 10-bit log color space on monitors that are expertly calibrated, then supply color-corrected Cineon frames to us for compositing. If the frames were scanned into the linear format, chances are good that the film will have to be rescanned, since this format does not contain any real latitude for post-correction.

If you get saddled with color correcting a scene or two anyway, try to isolate a clip you know the client is happy with, and match the tonal balance of the clip you are correcting to this reference. Another approach is to get a match or guide clip yourself, tape it over a white area on your monitor, and compare it with a linearized image in After Effects – either to calibrate your monitor or to create an adjustment layer that will bring your footage around to match. If you do any correcting, test-outputting a *wedge* (discussed below) becomes even more important.

A Switch in Time
Command+click on the frame number display in After Effects to toggle it between the three different counting methods: SMPTE, Frames, and Feet+Frames.

Telling Time

In addition to the differences in frame rates, film does not count time using SMPTE; instead it counts the physical measurement of feet+frames. With 35mm film (the most common format), there are 16 frames to a foot and typically 24 frames to a second. Similar to SMPTE, the frames are counted 0 to 15, not 1 to 16.

There are occasions when you may deal strictly in the number of frames since the start. For example, when your film is scanned, each frame will have a unique number – not a feet+frame indicator – that usually counts from the beginning of the clip. In this case, be aware that most film scanning facilities count the first frame as 1, while many computer people count the first frame as 0.

In any case, you can set the counting method in After Effects in the File>Preferences>Time dialog. Calculators are available that convert between the two; you can also Command+click on the frame number display in After Effects to toggle it between these different counting methods.

Each individual reel of film stock is identified by a unique keycode (or Keykode™) number. This is printed along the edge of the film stock in a format readable by both humans and machines. Video dubs of film should have these numbers "burned in" along with the feet and frames timing; they may also have the video SMPTE timecode burned in.

When you receive a video dub of the footage to make your selects, it will have a variety of numbers burned in over the image. In this case, the numbers along the bottom from left to right indicate the video dub's timecode, the keycode numbers (two letters followed by six numbers), and the feet+frame measurement from the start of the reel.

When you're ordering a segment of film to be scanned, you will need to provide both the keycode number and the feet+frames readings for the in and out points. Also add a few frames of handle on to the front and back for safety, and clarify whether the in and out points requested include or exclude the handle. You cannot go back and ask for just a few more frames later on; you will inevitably experience slight shifts in color and position from scan to scan.

Four Lumps, or Five?

After Effects defaults to five digits for the frame number. However, many film houses prefer four. Delete one of the # symbols in the default filename to save with four digits.

Icon Begone

When the Mac version of After Effects saves a sequence of stills, it normally writes a preview icon for each file. Some film systems don't like this. Adobe has provided a plug-in in the CD>Goodies folder that disables this feature.

Saving Templates

To save the Output Modules in our example project for use in your own projects, select Make Template from the bottom of the Output Modules menu. This will add them to your Prefs file.

Finally, don't assume just because the scanning equipment costs more than your house, that any problem with the supplied scans is your fault. If the color looks odd, question it before you composite the titles and record it back to film. Many film projects we've worked on have had to be rescanned – we even received a shot where the film was loaded into the scanner backward…

Recording Out

In After Effects, render to a sequence, at 24 fps, with field rendering off. In the Render Settings, enter a Custom Work Area to render only enough frames to fit whatever tape format you're using (1000 Cineon frames will fit on a 10-gigabyte DLT, for example). By setting a Custom Work Area, you can easily rerender the section by simply Duplicating the render queue item. In the Output Module, make sure you set Starting# to match the frames being rendered for each render item.

The common file path for film TAR files is a folder with the movie's name, which then holds a folder with the frame size as its name (1828×1332). Place the frames inside that folder. End the frame's name with an underscore, the frame number, a period, then the file type code (cin for Cineon, rgb for SGI-RGB). An example as it appears in the Render Queue would be **titleseq_[####].cin** – note that the number of pound symbols denote how many digits the frame number will have. Examples of this naming convention are also already loaded into the Render Queue (Command+Option+0) in the example project.

You can create a video proof at the same time by selecting the item in the Render Queue and choosing Composition>Add Output Module. Edit the output module to "Stretch" (actually, squeeze) this movie to 640×480 or 720×486 (or whatever your video card supports). Select your hardware's codec, or render to a QuickTime JPEG movie. Then render both the film and QT versions simultaneously. You'll now be able to quickly step through the QuickTime movie to check for any problems.

The example project's Render Queue has various comps set up to render, which you can explore. Specifics on the Cineon file format are discussed below.

Before you output a large sequence of frames, it is best to order a trial output of a few frames or seconds at different exposures. This is commonly called a *wedge*. Call the clients in to view it projected at the film house. Have the clients pick which exposure they like best, or go back and tweak your graphics based on their feedback.

If you have a long sequence to record, ask if the film house can output the entire job continuously, and note this on your order form. Remember that you can't "insert edit" on film: If there's a mistake, you have to output a section again between two hard cuts. If it's a long title sequence, design the animation with *break points* (hard cuts at major scene changes). If there's an output problem, or a credit needs changing later, these break points give you and the film house the option of re-outputting between two break points rather than starting over from the very beginning.

The Cineon File Format

Throughout this chapter, we've been referring to Cineon files and log color space. Kodak designed this format to better mimic the characteristics of film so that film could be copied digitally without losing any of its detail. This format is probably new to users with a video or multimedia background, and its logarithmic response is not native to the way most computer software displays color. However, After Effects has a set of tools to allow you to work in this truer-to-film space.

The Cineon file format can represent each color channel as a 10-bit range, with 1024 possible values. When neutral test cards are shot on film and scanned into this format, 2% reflection (black) is set at a Cineon value of 180, 18% reflection (neutral gray) at 470, and 90% reflection (stark white) at 685. Since the entire range of values of 0 to 1023 are not used for nominal black to white, there is extra room left to capture (and recover) darker or brighter than normal portions of a scene. In the case of film that was purposely overexposed to trade off reduced highlights for less noise in the shadows, increasing the exposure on the film one "stop" raises all these values by 90.

Film is typically exposed just above the "toe" where the darker luminance values round off, allowing lots of headroom for specular highlights. This nominal luminance range is usually mapped to values 180 to 685 inside Cineon's 1024 potential values per color channel.

Cineon in After Effects

When you initially open a Cineon format file in After Effects, it will look like noise. This is because the 30 bits of a Cineon file's RGB color information are being spread across the 32 bits of a typical RGB+alpha file, scrambling the expected data somewhat. Applying Effect>Cineon Tools> Cineon Converter tells After Effects to re-interpret the information and to present it as its normal 8 bits per color channel, with no alpha.

In addition to decoding the bit packing of a Cineon file, the Cineon Converter can then remap the data between log and linear color spaces. At this point, it works like a special version of the Levels effect, with the ability to set the Black and White Points, Gamma, and an additional Highlight Rolloff parameter to tweak the brightest areas. The 10-bit values are the input, the 8-bit values are the output for Black and White Points.

The Conversion Type popup defaults to Auto Log to Linear, which guesses whether it is applied to an 8- or 10-bit file, and converts it to the linear color space using com-

More Converter

TechTip 06 includes a feature from *DV* magazine, written by Johnathan Banta, on how best to use the Cineon Converter – with additional tips and insights.

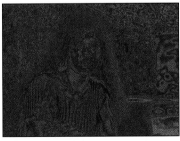

An uninterpreted 10-bit Cineon file can look like a noisy mess (left). Apply Effect>Cineon Tools>Cineon Converter to convert it to 8 bits. The default settings assume you need 8 bits linear. When it's changed to the more useful 8-bit log, the image looks washed out (right); this is due to its gamma and the location of the Black and White points. Rest assured that it will look fine when it's recorded back to film.

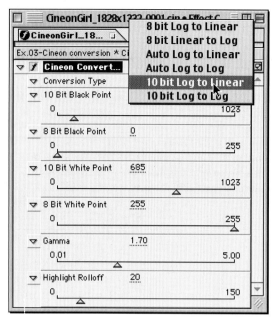

The Cineon Converter dialog looks like an enhanced Levels effect. Selecting various options in the Conversion Type popup will change the other parameters automatically.

mon defaults – just what you need to see a Cineon file "normally" in your computer. (Note the 10-bit Black Point is set to 95, which is Cineon Black.)

[Ex.03] has a raw Cineon file in a comp; practice applying Effect>Cineon Tools>Cineon Converter to see what it does. Since we know this is a 10-bit log file, it is safer to change the Conversion Type popup to 10-bit Log to Linear; the "auto" function can get tripped up occasionally during fades. You can play around with the sliders to get a feel for what effect they have on the conversion, but note that most of the time you will be leaving them at their defaults, unless you have a shot that needs correction because it was overexposed or has problems in the highlight areas.

Reverse Logic

Now that we've shown you how to convert a Cineon log file to linear color space, we're going to tell you not to do it: you'd be throwing away a lot of image information. The preferred path is to keep all log scans in the log format and to convert your computer-created images, which are linear, into log space. To work this way, you need to organize your layers as follows:

• The background Cineon file is the bottom layer, with the Cineon Converter applied. The Conversion Type menu set to Auto Log to Log will work most of the time; set it explicitly to the bit depth of log file you have, if you know it. This unscrambles the Cineon file into something After Effects can read. If you've already converted the 10-bit original

To keep scanned film in its Cineon color space, you need to convert your added graphics into log space. The Adjustment Layer converts everything underneath back to linear space for proofing on your computer monitor or to video.

frames to 8-bit log, you won't need to also apply the Cineon Converter at this point (see the sidebar *Saving Space and Proxies*).

• Non-Cineon graphics layers, such as titles, are layered on top of this. Apply the Cineon Converter after any other effects applied to these layers (such as Tint and Drop Shadow for text), with Conversion Type set to 8-bit Linear to Log. Your graphics will now be in the same log color space

Render	⊞	#	Comp Name	Status	Started	Render Time
▽	☐	■ 1	Ex.04-Convert Clip w/proxy	Unqueued	–	–

▷ **Render Settings :** ▼ Best Settings/nofields/ALL	**Log :** Errors Only ▼
▷ **Output Module :** ▼ TIF seq 24bit RGB only	**Output To :** Film01_8LOG_[####].tif
▷ **Output Module :** ▼ JPEG MOV_med_%640×480	**Output To :** Film01_proxy.mov

Saving Space and Proxies

After Effects is still only an 8-bit per channel program, even though it can read 10-bit Cineon files. It is throwing away two bits of information per channel, but this is not as great a loss as you might expect so long as you convert to 8-bit log, not 8-bit linear.

The Cineon Converter can handle both 10-bit and 8-bit log files, and in fact it is common practice to resave the source 10-bit Cineon log files back out as 8-bit log files to save disk space and speed up working. You can also save a proxy file at the same time. To do this:

Step 1: Read in the 10-bit Cineon frames from tape.

Step 2: Open After Effects and File>Import the original 10-bit log frames, making sure to check the Cineon Sequence checkbox in the Import dialog. They should read in at 24 fps if the File>Prefs> Import>Sequence Footage was set to 24 fps. If not, Conform the sequence to 24 fps in the File>Interpret Footage>Main dialog.

Step 3: Drag the footage to the New Comp icon at the bottom of the Project window, which will add the footage to a new composition with the same specifications. Apply the Cineon Converter and set the Conversion Type popup to **10-bit Log to Log**. This will convert it to 8-bit log.

Step 4: Render to virtually any RGB file format, though we suggest you save the 8-bit log version to another sequence format, rather than a movie, so you can touch up individual frames in Photoshop if necessary. In the Output Module, set the Starting Number to have the same starting frame number as used by the service bureau – this will make it easier to replace a bad frame if you need to reread a frame from tape.

Step 5: You can also save a video-size proxy at the same time you render your 8-bit log file by adding a

The Render Queue shows the first output module will resave the original Cineon source as a 24-bit TIF sequence, while a second output module creates a proxy version as a QuickTime Photo-JPEG movie, scaled to 640×480.

second Output Module and scaling the frames to 640×480 using the Stretch area in the Output Module dialog. We usually render proxies using the Photo-JPEG codec. Save these proxies to a separate folder – you can trash them at the end of the project.

This process has been set up inside the comp **[Ex.04-Convert Clip w/proxy]** and is the first item set up in the Render Queue. Examine the two output modules and select Make Template from the Output Module popup to add them to your own prefs.

After you convert the frames to 8-bit log, you can discard the 10-bit log frames (but keep the source tapes, just in case) and enjoy the disk space savings. Import the 8-bit log files and begin the design process; rendering will also be faster as there's less data to retrieve from disk. You will still need to apply the Cineon Converter as an adjustment layer to convert log to linear and check your work.

After you import the 8-bit log sequences, link them to their respective proxy file: select each footage item in the Project window, and select File>Set Proxy>File. After the proxies are applied, you can work much faster inside After Effects since the frames being retrieved from disk are smaller and there are fewer pixels to process. To seamlessly switch between displaying the high-res film version and the low-res proxy version, click on the icon to the left of the footage item in the Project window. The Proxy Use popup in the Render Settings dialog includes options for rendering with either version. Be sure to set it to Use No Proxies for the final render. See Chapter 44, *Prerendering and Proxies*, for more information on working with proxies.

Cineon for Techies

TechTip 06 on the CD includes white papers on the Cineon file format, courtesy Cinesite Los Angeles (www.cinesite.com).

Cineon Alpha Warning

Cineon file format packs the color data into all four channels, and the Output Module must be set to RGB+Straight Alpha. If you're creating masks or tracks mattes, make sure the comp does not have an alpha channel: fill the background with a full-frame black solid.

Case Study: Film Title Sequence

The film work flow can be initially confusing – even more so if audio is involved. Therefore, the final tutorial on the CD consists of a case study that walks through a project from start to finish, based on titles we've animated for movies like *The Talented Mr. Ripley* in which both scanned footage and synchronized audio were involved. Lock in these concepts the rest of the way by examining the process in context.

as the film layer underneath, complete with altered black-and-white points and gamma curve.

• On top of this goes an adjustment layer (Layer>Adjustment Layer), also with the Cineon Converter applied, this time set to 8-bit Log to Linear. Turn this layer on only when you want to see your comp in linear color space – while you're working at your computer, or when rendering a video proof. *Do not render your film output with this layer on!*

• An option is to apply any overlay grids on top of this, again remembering to turn this layer off when you render.

Examples of this working method are included in [**Ex.05**]. Try turning the layers on and off; note in particular how the colors change when the adjustment layer is turned on and off. Try changing the color of the type (set by the Tint effect on layer 3) with the Cineon Adjustment Layer turned on, and you will see the "mind warp" part of working in log color space: You cannot directly pick colors, because they will be changed by

In [**Ex.05**], the comp is set up to output as log (left). When the adjustment layer is temporarily turned on (right), the image is converted to linear, offering a preview of how it might appear on film.

the color space conversion. You'll have to get used to nudging colors created in After Effects in the direction you need to make the linearized display look right.

One exception to this working practice is if you plan to create only pure white text. In this case, you can create or tint the text with the color Cineon white (67% white, or 171/171/171 in 8-bit linear color space), with no need to apply the Cineon Converter to this layer. This is demonstrated in [**Ex.06**].

Rendering to Cineon

To render out to the Cineon format, in the Output Module dialog you must select the format Cineon AE Sequence and make sure the Channels menu is set to save RGB+Alpha. This repacks the data into a 10-bit-per-channel Cineon file.

Major warning time: As your animation will end up packed into all four channels using a straight alpha channel, your comp's alpha channel must not contain any interesting alpha information, just solid white. This means that if you're masking or creating mattes, or just have titles over a black background color, you *must* put a full-frame black solid in the background. This solid will force the layers to composite (or multiply) against black before being packed into the 32 bits of the Cineon format. If your comp is 8-bit linear, then a pure black solid is fine. If the comp is created as 8-bit log space, apply the Cineon Converter to this black solid and set it to 8-bit Linear to Log, to shift it into log space with the correct black value. Of course, the solid doesn't have to be black – to create titles against another color, create a colored solid instead.

In the Output Module, click on the Format Options button to view the Cineon Conversion Parameters – which are a bit confusing. It is not asking, "What format is this comp I am rendering?" but instead, "What do you want me to do with this comp?" For example, if your comp is already in log color space and you are rendering to Cineon, you do *not* want to do any conversion – therefore, you will select Linear as your File Type and click on Full Range for your Values. This is the case with [**Ex.05**]; check the Output Module options for the second item in the Render Queue.

If, on the other hand, you have a comp that is in the linear color space, you need to convert it to log at this output stage. Therefore, you need to set File Type to Logarithmic and click on Standard in Predefined Conversions (unless you want to purposely set different Black and White Points – for example, to print an overexposed or "heavy" negative). This is the case with [**Ex.07**]; check the Output Module options for the second item in the Render Queue.

Of course, if you're going out linear, you don't have to save to the Cineon format. Make sure your comp is in normal linear space (as in [**Ex.08**]) and save to the SGI-RGB format (the last item in the Render Queue). Particularly if you're only saving titles against a black background or rendering animated mattes – the SGI-RGB format includes an RLE option, which losslessly compresses frames to as little as 300 kilobytes, instead of more than 9 megabytes!

To save any of these templates for use in your own projects, select Make Template from the bottom of the Output Modules menu in the Render Queue. This will add them to your Adobe After Effects Prefs file.

Thanks to Tim Sassoon of Sassoon Film Design and Richard Patterson of Royal Garden Post for their help in compiling the information in this chapter.

Cineon Conversion Parameters

Conversion Parameters
Black-Point (10 bit): 0
Black-Point (8 bit): 0
White-Point (10 bit): 1023
White-Point (8 bit): 255
Current Gamma: 1.0
Highlight Expansion: 0

File Type
○ Logarithmic ● Linear

Predefined conversions
[Standard] [Video] [Full Range]

File Format
● FIDO/Cineon 4.5 ○ DPX

Presets
[Load...] [Save...]

[OK]

The Format Options for Cineon can be confusing; what they are really asking is, "How do you want me to change this file before I save it?" The settings here are suitable for saving a comp that is already in log space.

Connect

TechTip 06 on the CD has additional information for working with Cineon file format, including a feature written by Johnathan Banta for *DV* magazine, and a white paper from Cinesite Los Angeles.

For more information on working with video and film, also check out:

American Cinematographer Manual: Seventh Edition, by the American Society of Cinematographers (published by The ASC Press).

Non-Linear: A Guide to Electronic Film and Video Editing by Michael Rubin (Triad Publishing Company).

43 Join the Queue

The Render Queue is where you set up and manage the creation of your final work.

To create a movie or still image from your animations and arrangements, you have to render a file. After Effects is very flexible in allowing you to set up and override certain parameters when you render, as well as to create multiple files with different aspect ratios and file formats from the same render pass. You can also create and save templates of these render and output settings.

Internally, After Effects treats rendering a movie as a two-step process: Calculate an image, then decide how to save it to disk. These two steps are presented to the user as two different sets of options for each comp

Saving Time

A discussion of what kills rendering times, what buys it back, and general things to watch out for is in the Online Help under Topic: Managing Projects Effectively>Techniques for Working Efficiently.

A comp in the render queue, with the Render Settings and Output Module details twirled down for inspection (they default to twirled up). After clicking the Render button to start the render, twirl down the Current Render Details twirly to see how long each stage is taking (great for spotting a slow effect) and how large the final movie will be.

43-Example Project.aep • Render Queue

All Renders
Message: Rendering 1 of 1
RAM: 167M free of 195M
Renders Started: Sat, Feb 12, 6:03 PM
Total Time Elapsed: 24 Seconds

Pause   Stop

Log File: None

Current Render
Rendering "Final Comp" Elapsed: 24 Seconds Est. Remain: 32 Minutes

0:00:00:00 (1) 0:00:00:03 (4L) 0:00:07:29 (240)

Current Render Details
Rendering
Composition: Final Comp
Layer: 2
Stage: Gaussian Blur

Frame Times
Last: 7 Seconds
Difference: -1 Seconds
Average: 8 Seconds

Output Modules

File Name	File Size	Est. Final File Size	Free Disk Space	Over- flows	Current Disk
Final Comp-D1/29L/an	2.0M	157M	2448M	0	CMG CD

Render	⊞	#	Comp Name		Status	Started	Render Time
▽	☐	1	Final Comp		Rendering	Sat, Feb 12, 6:03 PM	-

▽ Render Settings: ▾ Best Settings/LowerFF/ALL   Log: Errors Only ▾
None

Quality: Best	Frame Blending: On For Checked Layers	Time Span: Comp Length	
Resolution: Full	Field Render: Lower Field First	Start: 0:00:00:00	
Size: 720 × 486	Pulldown: Off	End: 0:00:07:29	
Proxy Use: Use No Proxies	Motion Blur: On For Checked Layers	Duration: 0:00:08:00	
Effects: Current Settings	Shutter Angle: 180.00	Frame Rate: 29.97 (comp)	
Storage Overflow: On	Skip Existing Files: Off		

▽ Output Module: ▾ QT Anim RGB only (no alpha)   Output To: Final Comp-D1/29L/an
CMG CD:CreatingMG CD:Chapter Example Projects:43-Example Project:Final Comp-D1/29L/an

Format: QuickTime Movie	Channels: RGB
Output Info: Animation Compressor	Depth: Millions of Colors
Spatial Quality = Most (100)	Color: Premultiplied
	Stretch: -
	Crop: -
Output Audio: Off	Final Size: 720 × 486

Rendering 101

When you render in After Effects, at a minimum you select a composition, add it to the Render Queue (viewed by going Window>Render Queue, or Command+Option+0), give it a file name to use when it is saved to disk, then tell After Effects to start rendering. The settings used will be the default templates (see *Creating and Editing Templates* later in this chapter), though you can choose a new template or modify the current one.

Multiple comps can be dragged to the Render Queue, which After Effects will then render one after another as a batch. The batch in the Render Queue is saved with the Project; you can quit and render later. While you can't render multiple projects at once, you can create a new project and then use File>Import>Project to merge multiple projects and their render queues.

Renders can be paused or stopped. You cannot change the contents of the project or a comp while you are rendering. If the comp being rendered is currently open or under a tab, it will bring that window forward and update it as it renders.

The basic size of the frame that will be rendered is set by the comp's size, so try to build it at the correct size to begin with. If that's not possible, you can alter it in another comp and render this new composition instead, or scale plus crop it in the Output Module.

Conversely, the frame rate of a comp can be overridden during rendering. Render Settings defaults to the same rate, but you are free to change it. Changing the render frame rate does not speed up or slow down the speed of the *motion* in the comp or any of the source material used in it; it merely changes the *intervals of time* at which the rendering engine steps through the comp to decide what to render next. You will find many advantages to this scheme, such as the ability to field-render without having to work at the field rate, or to work at film rate in a comp, and then introduce 3:2 pulldown later when you render.

A number of composition switches – such as whether or not effects, proxies, frame blending, and motion blur are rendered – can be set or overridden at the render stage. It can often be useful to work with processor-

intensive enhancements such as frame blending turned off as you build a composition, then turn it on at the rendering stage. You still need to preset the layers in your compositions with your intentions; the render modules can do only large scale overrides such as *ignore all effects, set all layers to best quality*, and *turn on frame blending for all checked layers*.

Note that the Collapse switch must be set manually per layer – there is no Render Settings override to continuously rasterize all Illustrator files, for instance.

How you queue up a composition to render depends on what it is you want rendered: a movie, a still, or your most recent RAM preview. In all cases, you must enter a name for the file; the name of the comp will be automatically entered as a default basis for the name – but you can change it if you like. You must then click on the Start button in the Render Queue (or hit Return or Enter) to start rendering. As noted above, you can tweak the render settings and output module before you hit Start, with the exception of Save RAM Preview, which launches the render as soon as you've named the movie.

in the Render Queue: *Render Settings* and *Output Modules.* You can twirl down the arrows to the left of these tags to see the parameters that have been set, or click on the name to the right to open a dialog to change these settings.

In this chapter, we will first discuss the general difference between rendering (and saving) a still image, a movie, and a RAM preview. Then we'll go over the two parts involved in rendering a movie: the Render Settings and the Output Module. Finally, we will cover making templates

No Fields in RAM

RAM Previews are not field rendered. Saving a RAM Preview will not allow you to interlace a movie or add pulldown. Any alpha channels are premultiplied with the comp's background color, not the standard black.

Queueing Up

After Effects renders the queued compositions in their current state when you hit the Render button – not the state they were in when you added them to the Render Queue. If you queue up a comp, After Effects does not memorize the state of the comp when you queued it – so be careful of any additional changes you make between queuing and rendering. A common mistake is to queue a comp, turn on a layer, queue it again, turn on another layer, queue it again, and *then* render, thinking you're rendering three variations of the same comp (you know who you are). In fact, you are rendering only the comp in its most recent state, three times. Either render one version at a time, or duplicate the comp to create variations.

so you don't have to keep typing in all the numbers and setting all the switches that exist in the Render and Output sections.

After Effects has long supported a simple form of distributed rendering. It requires having duplicate projects, files, and copies of After Effects on each of the rendering machines and having them all render into the same shared folder. As of version 4.1, distributed rendering became considerably more advanced. After Effects Production Bundle now comes with a "render engine" version that can be installed on as many computers as you like with just a single license. There is also a new feature – Collect Files – that makes it easier to gather just what is needed to render a composition, which is also a great aid in backing up or handing off a project to someone else. *Both distributed rendering and Collect Files are covered in TechTip 07 on the CD.*

Movies

The most common item you will want to render is a movie of your composition. To do this, you need to add it to the Render Queue. You can do this several ways; the most common is to either select or bring forward the comp you want, and hit Command+M (Composition>Make Movie). You will be presented with a dialog to name the file and select a destination; do so, and click on OK. The Render Queue will then come forward; you can then change the render and output parameters, queue up other comps, or go back to work – just don't forget to eventually click Render in the Render Queue.

If the Render Queue window is open and visible, you can also drag compositions directly from the Project window in the Render Queue window – this is a good way to queue up a group of compositions quickly. They will be unnamed at this point; you need to give them a name and destination (click on the words *Not yet specified* in their respective Output Modules) to do so. In either case, you can define in the Render Settings the time segment you want rendered: the entire comp, the already-set work area, or a custom-entered region of time.

Stills

To render a still of a frame in a composition, locate to the desired time in the comp with the time marker and hit Command+Option+S (Composition>Save Frame As>File). Give it a file name when prompted, then click on the Render button in the Render Queue to render it.

You can change the time the still will be taken from after queuing, but it is good to get in the practice of locating to the correct time as a confidence check before you queue it. Again, you can batch up multiple stills before rendering; just be careful not to accidentally change a comp you haven't rendered yet. In the Mac version of the program, you can also save the current frame in After Effects' Footage window directly to a PICT file (no Render Queue involved) by pressing Command+Option+Control+S. Another option, which will be of interest to Photoshop users, is saving a still in the form of a layered Photoshop file: Composition>Save Frame

As>Photoshop Layers. Effects, masks, and most transformations will be pre-computed; transfer modes and opacity settings will be carried through to the new layered file. Track mattes will not be computed, but the track matte layer will appear in this file, turned off, for further use as a selection in Photoshop if needed.

RAM Preview

New in version 4.1 of After Effects, you can queue up your most recent RAM Preview and easily save it to disk as a movie. What After Effects does is simply take the work area of your current comp, give you an opportunity to name it, add it to the Render Queue with the Render Settings set to "Current Settings," and automatically starts rendering it – an "auto" version of the normal render movie procedure.

To save a RAM preview to disk, select Composition>Save RAM Preview. If the preview has not been cached to RAM, After Effects will cache it, as if you invoked a RAM preview first. At this point, you can pause or stop it. If you already RAM previewed the current work area (0 on the keypad), the rendered frames will already be cached in RAM, and the Render Queue will come forward immediately. In this case, the "rendering time" is reduced to just the time it takes to save it to disk. The Output Module used will default to the template set for RAM Preview (setting templates is discussed later in this chapter).

Render Settings

These parameters decide how the composition is processed when After Effects renders – basically, you enter all the information After Effects needs to create an uncompressed frame (RGB and Alpha channels). Some may appear to just be duplicates of other switches available in the program, but in fact the ability to reset them during rendering can greatly enhance your workflow. To access the Render Settings, click on the underlined text to the right of the words Render Settings. The settings default to those of the current template as selected from the menu (click on the arrow to see all available templates). Let's go over each one of the parameters and their settings, including tips on when to use which option, and the gotchas associated with some of them.

Files Missing

When you initiate a render, After Effects will warn you if any files used by the selected comp are missing. However, it does not tell you the names of the missing items; you will need to search through the Project list looking for *names in italics,* which indicate the footage cannot be found. (Missing items also appear as color bars in a comp.) After Effects does not look at the section of time you are rendering – the files could be used before or after the segment you are interested in.

The Composition Settings interprets or overrides various comp and project switches; the Time Sampling section determines which points in time to render. The result is an RGB+Alpha uncompressed frame which is then sent to the Output Module for saving.

Quality

Affects how each layer is calculated. Usually, this popup is set to Best, which means every layer is forced into Best Quality during rendering, which is usually what you want. Otherwise, if you accidentally left a layer in Draft (either for speed while working, or because you forgot to change it from its default), you might miss out on antialiasing and sub-pixel positioning during the render. If it's set to Current Settings, it obeys the current Quality switch for each layer, be it Best, Draft, or Wireframe. This is useful on those occasions where you purposely left some layers in Draft mode, to exploit artifacts and the lack of antialiasing. Draft and Wireframe forces all layer to these quality settings, which are useful only if you need to crank out a fast draft.

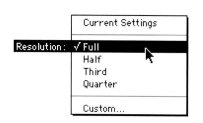

Resolution

This is identical to the Resolution settings for comps. For the final render, you will want Full, since it will force every comp in the chain to full resolution. Choosing a lower resolution renders less than every pixel and produces a smaller sized movie – for example, 720×486 set to Half would render a 360×243 image. The size of the image that will be rendered is displayed under this menu as a quick confidence check. It is quite common to set various nested comps to different resolutions while working; if you use Current Settings, those settings would *not* be overridden, and each comp would render using the resolution you'd set for it manually.

    If you are rendering a lower-resolution proof (Half for video, Quarter for film), these menus will override the current settings in the comp chain and drastically reduce rendering time, since a quarter or an eighth of the actual pixels would be computed. However, changing Resolution does not yield the highest quality if all you're trying to do is create a smaller version of your animation – do that by rendering at Full Resolution and then scaling in the Output Module, or by scaling in another comp in the chain.

Half Res or Scale?

Rendering a 640×480 comp at Half Resolution will render every second pixel and output a 320×240 movie. For a higher quality 320×240 version, render at Full Resolution, no fields, and scale it in the Output module to 320×240.

Proxy Use

Proxies will be explained in more detail in Chapter 44, but in short, they are prerendered stand-ins for footage files or entire compositions. They are usually created either to save time (by prerendering an otherwise time-consuming comp that will need to be rendered time and time again), or as lower-resolution or even still image placeholders to make the program more responsive while you're animating. Typically, if you used proxies just as placeholders, you'll choose Use No Proxies; if you're using them as prerenders, you'll probably want Current Settings. Comp Proxies Only will render proxies applied to comps but not to footage.

Effects

When this options is set to Current Settings, What You See Is What You Get: an effect has to be enabled for a layer to be rendered. If you are the type to stack up three or four different effects on a layer to quickly compare their results and then forget to delete the unused ones before rendering,

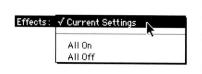

selecting All On will turn on all effects in the final render. Naturally, this leads to much confusion and wasted rendering time. However, some effects are so processor intensive that they drastically slow down navigating around a comp, so you might turn these off when you're working. Select the All On setting, and they will be used for the final render. All Off is used only to blast out a quick proof and is less useful.

The best advice we can give you is to decide how you like to work with effects, and try to remain consistent. Do you prefer to not delete unused ones (which means Current Settings would work better), or do you tend to temporarily turn off slow ones (which means All On would be best)?

Frame Blending

Frame Blending certainly falls into that category of a great-looking effect when you want it, but too slow to leave on while you're working. We usually turn it on for the layers we want blended, turn it off at the comp level for speed, then set this render parameter to On For Checked Layers to be included in the final render. Again, if you're just blasting out a quick proof, use Off For All Layers. Current Settings will render according to which comps have Enabled Frame Blending turned on.

Field Render

When it's turned on, Field Render effectively renders at twice the rate set in the Frame Rate parameter below. One entire frame is rendered at the start of the frame; After Effects then moves forward a half-frame in time and renders another complete frame. These two frames are then interlaced into a single frame, taking alternating lines from each. The order of the lines taken is determined by the Upper and Lower Field First choices. Set this menu to match the hardware you will be playing back through. (The field rendering process is covered in detail in Chapter 37.)

Note that selecting field rendering does not create new source material if it did not previously exist – for example, if you had rendered a 3D animation at 29.97 fps, selecting field rendering here will not magically give it fields – the rendered frames will look the same as they did before. Field rendering works when the source material was interlaced, with its fields separated, or if you want your animation moves created inside After Effects to look smoother on video playback.

3:2 Pulldown

Pulldown is a special technique of interlacing frames that is relevant only when your source material originates on 24 fps film (or you are trying to simulate the "motion" of 24 fps film), but you need to render a file for NTSC video playback. If you're not doing this, leave it off. Otherwise, work at 24 or 23.976 fps in your comps (we suggest conforming to and working at 23.976), set the field rendering order your hardware needs, then pick one of the five pulldown phases from the popup. (All phases render essentially the same; the only time you need to pick a specific one is if you are trying to exactly match the pulldown phase of a scene

Caps Lock

Engaging Caps Lock stops After Effects from updating the Comp window, which can save time during rendering.

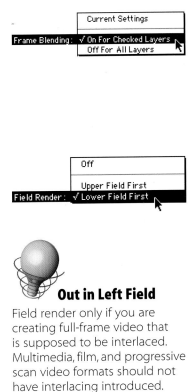

Out in Left Field

Field render only if you are creating full-frame video that is supposed to be interlaced. Multimedia, film, and progressive scan video formats should not have interlacing introduced.

Hot Ice

The combination of Integrated Computing Engines' BlueICE accelerator card and their special "iced" version of After Effects essentially eliminates the render hit that comes with using Motion Blur.

Locked Work

If you want to "freeze" the work area for a newly queued item, set Time Span to Work Area Only, then click on the Set button, and click OK. This changes the popup to Custom, and altering the work area will no longer change the time span.

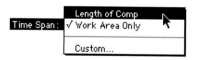

You can set a custom time span to render sections of a comp independently of the work area, or to "lock in" the work area. Be warned though that this span may "stick" even if you later pick another template entirely.

you will be splicing this render back into.) Then, make sure you enter 29.97 fps in the Frame Rate parameter below.

If Pulldown is enabled, After Effects will then render the comp at 23.976 frames per second, saving a considerable amount of rendering time, and updating keyframes animations only at the film rate. These rendered frames will then be split across video frames and fields as they are saved to disk, following the sequence described in Chapter 38. Note that if you field-rendered the same comp at 29.97 fps, the same result will occur for 23.976 fps source material; however, all of your animation moves will be sampled at 59.94 fps (the field rate) instead, and rendering overall will take longer because more points in time are being calculated.

Motion Blur

This switch works similarly to the Frame Blending setting, above: Since Motion Blur takes so long to calculate, it is usually checked for individual layers but left off at the composition level so you can work faster. When it comes time to render, you can override the comp switches and render with it on (without having to go manually set the switches in all precomps) by setting this menu to On For Checked layers. Legal values are 0° to 360°. Current Settings will render each comp according to whether Enable Motion Blur is on or off.

Below this popup is a setting for Shutter Angle. Normally, the shutter angle set in the preferences (File>Preferences>General) is used; you can override it at render time if you decide to use more or less blur. When rendering low frame rate versions (such as for Web examples), remember that the virtual shutter is now "open" for a longer period of time, resulting in longer blur streaks; if we lower the frame rate, we lower the shutter angle proportionally if we want to keep the same "look." Larger shutter angles also take longer to render.

Time Span

As we mentioned earlier in this chapter, you can direct After Effects to render the entire queued comp, the work area set in that comp, or another section of your choosing. The first two choices are obvious from the menu; the third choice can be invoked either by selecting Custom or by clicking on the Set button.

This will open a new dialog where you can enter the time range desired. The timebase selected in File>Preferences> Time is used; entering a number in any one field automatically updates the other two. A duration of one frame in essence means render a still, at the Start time specified.

Note that if you select Work Area from the popup, After Effects will look at the work area as defined at the time you click on the Render button, not as set when you queued up the comp to render. This is pretty slick if you know what it is doing, and another big gotcha if you don't – because you might end up rendering a different time stretch than you intended.

Frame Rate

One of the most important concepts about rendering in After Effects is that the comp's frame rate at render time is overridden by the value chosen here in Render Settings. This does not change the *speed* of anything; just the increments of time at which new frames are calculated.

The comp's frame rate is indeed chosen as the default, but you can type in a new number here. If you need a quick proof of a 29.97 fps comp, set the frame rate to 15 fps – don't change the comp's frame rate as keyframes will shift slightly. Also, if you've set up a comp at 59.94 fps (50 fps for PAL) to edit a mask on fields, you can render normal frames on output by setting the frame rate (29.97 or 25, for NTSC or PAL) here, and setting the Field Render option as appropriate for your hardware.

Use Storage Overflow

If you run out of disk space during rendering, you can tell the program to automatically overflow the excess to other drives you designate in Drive Contingencies under File>Preferences>Output. Set the amount of space to leave before overflowing in this preference as well. If this limit is hit during rendering, After Effects will automatically start a second file on the first overflow partition you have specified. However, if you use removable drives (as we often do) then After Effects will complain when they are dismounted. Instead, we tend to simply check the Render Details after a render is launched to make sure there's adequate space.

Skip Existing Files

Prior to version 4.1, it has been tricky to have multiple computers render out segments of the same movie. One way is to copy the entire project and its media to a second computer, set up both machines to render a different Custom segment of time (that will later splice end to end), and hope you balanced the load fairly between them. Another way is to copy your projects and media to more than one machine, but network them and point them at the same folder on one of the machines to render to. Render as a sequence of stills rather than as a movie (discussed below under *Output Module Settings*) with Skip Existing turned on. Each machine will now look at this one folder, see what is the next frame number that does not already exist, create a placeholder for that next frame, and start rendering it. The end result is a nicely load-balanced network render, since each machine can proceed at its own pace and the final render will be built sequentially in one folder without having to marry segments together later. Note that Skip Existing is available only when you render a sequence of stills – it does not work for movies.

This feature is also a good trick to fall back on if your render crashed and you don't want to calculate what time to enter to restart it, or if you (accidentally or intentionally) trashed some already-rendered frames. It just requires that you render a sequence of images, rather than one already-appended movie.

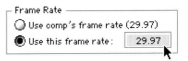

Filename and Path

Twirl down the Output Module to see the file directory path, even after rendering.

Storage Overflow and Skip Existing cannot co-exist, since the latter depends on the rendered files being in one specific folder. Checking one will gray the other out.

The Output Preferences. Here, you can tell After Effects to start a second file or folder for your render if it's about to run out of disk space, or make too large a file to fit on a certain piece of removable media (such as a Jaz cartridge). Limiting the number of stills it will put in one folder can also speed up render times – we set this number quite low and merge the folders later.

Output Module Settings

Composition "Final Comp"

Format: QuickTime Movie ▼   ☐ Import into project when done

☑ Video Output

[Format Options...]

Animation Compressor
Spatial Quality = Most (100)

Channels: RGB + Alpha ▼
Depth: Millions of Colors+ ▼
Color: Straight (Unmatted) ▼

☐ Stretch

	Width	Height
Rendering at:	720	× 486

☑ Lock Aspect Ratio to (40:27)

Stretch to: 720 × 486   Custom ▼
Stretch %: ×   Stretch Quality: High ▼

☐ Crop

T: 0   L: 0   B: 0   R: 0   Final Size: 720 × 486

☑ Audio Output

[Format Options...]

44.100 KHz ▼   16 Bit ▼   Stereo ▼

[Cancel]   [OK]

The Output Module Settings dialog is where you decide what to do with your rendered frame: what format to save it in, what to do with the color and alpha channels, whether or not you want audio, and if you need to do any scaling and cropping to the image as it is saved.

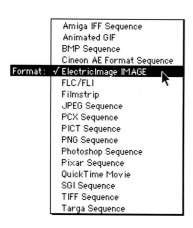

Format: ✓ ElectricImage IMAGE
- Amiga IFF Sequence
- Animated GIF
- BMP Sequence
- Cineon AE Format Sequence
- ✓ ElectricImage IMAGE
- FLC/FLI
- Filmstrip
- JPEG Sequence
- PCX Sequence
- PICT Sequence
- PNG Sequence
- Photoshop Sequence
- Pixar Sequence
- QuickTime Movie
- SGI Sequence
- TIFF Sequence
- Targa Sequence

Output Module Settings

Now that After Effects has rendered a frame, it has to do something with it – namely, save it. Sounds simple, but there are some decisions that have to be made before that happens, such as file format, color depth, whether you want audio and/or video, and if you need to do any scaling or cropping to the image. These parameters are set up in the Output Module.

One of the best features in After Effects is that *a single render can have multiple Output Modules.* Every render must have at least one, and it gets one as a default when queued; to add more, select the comp in the Render Queue, then select Composition>Add Output Module. For example, some editing systems require that audio and video be separate; you can render video with one module and audio with the other. Perhaps you need to render a 720×486 uncompressed movie for online work, but also want to render a 640×480 compressed version for a confidence check to play on an inexpensive board in your own computer – again, just set up two modules. During film renders, you can save the high-res film frames to one folder and also scale them down to create a proof movie at video resolution.

In these cases, you have to render (which is your big time killer) only once, and can set up multiple output modules to take your render and save them in as many formats as you need. However, since the frame rate and field rendering decisions have already been made in Render Settings, in some cases you may need to render two different versions – for instance, a 640×480 interlaced movie at 29.97 fps would have to be rerendered if you also needed a 320×240 15 fps version without fields.

To change the settings of any of the modules, click on the underlined text to the right of the phrase Output Module.

Format

After Effects can render to any of a number of formats, which can be self-contained movies (QuickTime for most nonlinear editing systems) or a sequence of still images, one for each frame (SGI RGB or Cineon files for film). You select the basic format here and set its parameters in the Video Format Options below. The best format depends completely on your particular application – but we most often use QuickTime, SGI, Cineon, and PICT sequences and ElectricImage IMAGE (which favors its own file format).

Import into Project When Done

This option is very straightforward: When the render is finished, do you want After Effects to automatically import it? It's handy for checking your renders without leaving the program, but make sure you remove files from the project before archiving if you've trashed them – they'll just create confusion later on.

Video Output

Do you want the video portion of the render saved with this Output Module? If yes, check this; if you are rendering just the audio portion of a comp, uncheck this. Don't worry about wasting rendering time; After Effects is smart enough to look first if any of the Output Modules have Video Output checked before bothering to render any images.

Format Options

Depending on what format you chose above, any options it may have can be accessed under this button. If you selected QuickTime movie, the standard QuickTime codec dialog will be opened. Other typical options include bit depth, whether or not to RLE or LZW encode the file to save disk space (check with the people receiving the file to make sure they can read these encodings – for example, some software companies won't pay the LZW licensing fee and therefore can't read LZW-encoded files), and other operating system-specific features (such as PC versus Mac byte order, or OS/2 versus Windows BMP formats). Not all formats have Format Options; if they don't, this button will usually be grayed out. Using the QuickTime format gives you the bonus of having its settings displayed underneath this button.

Starting

This parameter appears only if you have selected a format that is a sequence of still images, such as a PICT sequence. The successive rendered frames will get auto-incremented numbers, starting at the number you enter here.

When you select a format of sequential frames, After Effects will automatically add _[#####] to the name of the file entered. You must have this somewhere in the name in order for frames to be numbered predictably. The pound symbols (#) indicate how many digits you want in the number; the program will automatically pad with leading zeroes. You can remove or add pound symbols if you want. Because After Effects thinks only file extensions should start with a period (.), it uses an underscore (_) to separate the number from the rest of the name. Position the number somewhere in the name before the file extension, if you are using one.

QuickTime Dialog

The standard QuickTime codec dialog has a few twists that relate to After Effects:

- Setting the Color popup will also automatically set the Channels and Depth options in the Output Module dialog.

- Quality is the normal codec slider; some codecs disable it. It tends to be "sticky" and jumps over some values; hold down the Shift key while you're dragging it to get finer control.

- Frame Rate will be ignored – it is taken from the Render Settings module.

- Key Frame affects how data is saved in the movie – it creates reference frames at the rate specified in the parameter box to its right and remembers just the differences in frames inbetween. This saves disk space, but some programs – After Effects included – often have difficulty navigating these movies. Leave it off unless you absolutely need it.

- The Limit Data Rate parameter is used by some video cards to set target data rates to maintain a certain quality or smooth playback. The gotcha is that QuickTime defines the rate in kilobytes per second, while some systems define it as kilobytes per frame. To translate, multiply the frame size by the frame rate: For example, 150 kilobytes/frame $\times$ 29.97 frames/second $\approx$ 4495 kilobytes/second.

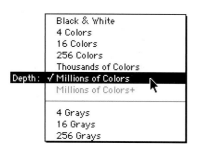

Alpha Output

Remember – you must choose a codec or file format that supports 32 bits (Millions of Colors+) in order to select Channels>RGB+Alpha.

Channels

The Channels, Depth, and Color menus are all somewhat interrelated; together they control which channels (RGB, Alpha, or both) are saved and whether the alpha is straight or premultiplied. If you need to save an alpha channel, select RGB + Alpha, but make sure to select a 32-bit file format in Format Options (QuickTime Animation at Millions of Colors+, for instance). If your nonlinear editing system doesn't support embedded alphas, you will need to use two output modules: one module renders Channel>RGB only with Color set to Straight, and the other renders Channels>Alpha only.

Depth

What bit depth of color do you want the file saved at? Different file formats will give you different choices, and setting the Channels will often limit the Depth choices. Usually, you will want Millions (24-bit color), although you could also specify 256 Grays if you are just creating a matte. If you are also saving an alpha channel, your only choice will be Millions of Colors+ (24-bit color plus an 8-bit alpha).

Color

This deceptively named popup does not have color choices. Instead, it determines how the RGB channels should be rendered if there are also transparent areas in the alpha channel. The alpha type choices are Straight (in which the color information extends, full strength, past the edges of the alpha) or Premultiplied with Black (in which the color information extends only as far as the alpha). *Alpha channel types are explained in detail in TechTips 01 and 03 on the CD.*

If you select Channel>RGB+Alpha, you will normally want the Color menu set to Straight (unmatted) so that the background color is not premultiplied. If you are rendering Channels>RGB only, be sure to set the Color menu to Premultiplied to composite the color channels over black.

The Channels/Depth/Color menus control which channels are saved and whether the alpha is matted or unmatted. We applied a white glow to this TV object and rendered using the following variations: RGB with alpha premultiplied (left), RGB with straight alpha (center), and alpha channel (right). TV © Corbis Images.

If you select both Channels>RGB and Color>Straight, After Effects will display a warning message: "you should also output an alpha channel to use straight color." Heed this warning – otherwise, your color channels will have an image area extending beyond the alpha area, but you will have no alpha channel to cut it out. The only time you should ignore the warning is if you are outputting the RBG and Alpha channels separately, using two output modules. In this case, the alpha channel *is* being output, just as a separate movie.

Stretch

We're going to treat all the parameters in this section of the Output Module as a whole, since they interact so strongly. Here, you can resize your rendered composition before you save it to disk.

The *Rendering at* line shows the original size of the comp you rendered, factoring in any Resolution reductions you may have selected in the Render Settings. In the *Stretch to* section, you can type in the new size you want, larger or smaller than the original. To facilitate typing in numbers, you can check the *Lock Aspect Ratio* box to make sure you don't distort your image, or select a preset size from the popup to the right of these boxes – it contains the same list of sizes as in the Composition Settings dialog. The *Stretch %* line underneath shows you how much you stretched by; the *Stretch Quality* popup determines how smooth the scaling is (leave this at High for best results, obviously).

Note that changing the size here does not change the size your original comp will be rendered at – by the time the image gets to this setting, it has already been rendered; we're just resizing it here.

Common uses for Stretch are to go between video sizes with minor variations (squash a 768×576 square-pixel PAL comp down to its 720×576 D1 PAL size) or to create a scaled-down proof of a noninterlaced film-size render in a second module.

Crop

In addition to, or as an alternative to, stretching an image is just chopping parts of it off. This is done by the Crop parameters. You can set the number of pixels that get chopped off the top (T), left (L), bottom (B), and right (R) of the already-rendered image before it is saved to disk. Your final size is updated automatically to the right, as a confidence check that you've entered the right parameters. These are often used in conjunction with Stretch to resize between video standards – for example, cropping a 648×486 comp to fit into a 640×480 codec.

A not-so-obvious trick is that you can use negative numbers to pad extra pixels around the image. The added pixels will be black in both the

☑ **Stretch**			
	Width	Height	
Rendering at:	720 ×	486	☑ Lock Aspect Ratio to (4:3)
Stretch to:	648 ×	486	NTSC, 648 × 486 ▼
Stretch %:	90.00 ×	100.00	Stretch Quality: High ▼

☑ **Crop**							
T: 3	L: 4	B: 3	R: 4		Final Size: 640 × 480

Stretched Fields

If you selected Field Rendering in the Render Settings, do not ever, ever, *ever* set the Stretch Height to anything other than 100%. Doing so would cause the already-interlaced fields to get scrambled between lines, resulting in field mush.

Duplicating Queued Items

In the event you need to rerender a comp but otherwise want to keep the exact same render and output settings, you can duplicate an already-queued item. Selecting it and hitting Command+D duplicates it but leaves its name unentered; Command+Shift+D duplicates the original name as well.

alpha and color channels. This is commonly used for resizing video. For example, you can pad the 480-line NTSC DV format up to 486-line NTSC D1 format by adding two lines above and four lines below; you would do this by cropping Top –2 and Bottom –4.

Audio Output

This section will also be discussed as a group. If you want audio saved with the file, check this option. Note that some video editing systems

(such as Scitex/Accom Sphere and Media 100) need the audio in a separate file from the video; otherwise, they need to go through a lengthy Import procedure. In this case, add a second "Audio Only" output module.

There is a Format Options box, but as version 4.1, it is always grayed out. If you want to compress your audio using a special codec, you will have to do it in another program, such as the pro version of the QuickTime Player.

After Effects provides a long list of common (and some not-so-common, such as the 47.952 kHz rate used by the Scitex Sphere) sample rates; choose the one that matches your desired target system – typically 44.100 or 48.000 kHz for higher-end video, 32.000 for consumer DV, 22.050 for low-end multimedia.

Available bit depths are 16- and 8-bit; almost no one uses 8-bit anymore because of its high levels of quantization distortion. Finally, you can select Stereo or Mono. All of the audio tracks inside After Effects are inherently stereo; mono sources are automatically converted to stereo, centered in their pan position. If combined to mono, the levels of the left and right channel are scaled by 50% before mixing down to one, to end up with an average volume without risk of clipping. This may result in a slight perceived loss of volume in a few cases.

Unfortunately, After Effects cannot currently load or save stereo audio in the "dual mono" format used by some systems, such as ProTools and the Media 100. Render audio separately, and let your editor separate the channels on import.

The Render Queue Window

Now that we've covered what goes on when After Effects renders, and the parameters you can set to customize the rendering process, let's talk about managing renders in the Render Queue window.

You can queue up as many compositions as you want to render. They will be rendered in top-to-bottom order in the queue. To re-order items in the queue, grab them by their comp names and drag them up and down the list, but you must do this before you start rendering the first item. You can twirl down the Render Settings and Output Module displays to check their settings before you render.

There is a bar of panels between the render details portion of the window above and the queued renders below. Most of the fields can be re-ordered

Audio Tips

QuickTime interleaves audio and video into the same stream. How often a chunk of audio is stored is set by the Audio Block Duration parameter inside File>Preferences> Output. The default of one second works well. If the block size is longer than the movie, all the audio will be stored first in the file – good for some multimedia applications.

For the absolute highest audio quality, you should pre-convert all of your sources to the audio sample rate you intend to render at, preferably in a program dedicated to processing audio – not video. Fortunately, the quality of After Effects' own sample rate conversion improved considerably as of version 4.0.

by dragging, as well as re-sized, just as panels in the Project and Time Layout windows can. Context-clicking on these panels allows you to hide some or reveal an additional Comments panel (useful for handing a project over to someone else to render).

After Effects will render only the comps that have a check in the box in the Render column and a legal name (if the name is in italics, click on it and enter a name and destination). Only items that are "Queued" in the Status column will be rendered when you click the Render button. After a render finishes, the Status will change to either Done, Stopped by User (if you clicked on Stop before it was finished), or Failed (if a problem arose during rendering). The render item remains in the queue until you select and delete it; in this state, you can still twirl down the settings windows, although you can no longer edit them.

If a render did not finish successfully, an unqueued copy of it will be made and appended to the end of the render queue. If it was stopped by you, its Time Span (in Render Settings) will be automatically updated to cover the unrendered portion. If the render failed, you can't count on the Time Span being correct; check it before proceeding.

Render Progress

While After Effects is rendering a composition, it keeps you well informed about its progress. Twirl down the Current Render Details section of the window to see which step of which layer of which comp After Effects is currently on, plus how long each frame took. This is a good way to see if a particular layer or effect is bogging things down. Be warned, though, that the *Estimated Time Remaining* is a best guess and is based only on the average time each previous frame took to render multiplied by how many frames remain to be processed. If the layers and effects are fairly balanced from start to finish in your animation, this estimate is pretty accurate.

Along the top of the Render Queue window, in addition to some book-keeping, you can track how much RAM is being used to render. After Effects tries to keep as many sources and partially rendered images in RAM as it can, to save time refetching them from disk or recalculating them. If After Effects does not have enough breathing room, it will either slow down or in severe cases give you the dreaded "out of memory" error. Having said that, throwing more RAM at the program may actually slow it down, seeing as it has to do more RAM management.

The Current Render bar shows you how far along the current render you are. When it's done (or if it the current render fails), After Effects will automatically start the next render in the queue. When all queued renders are finished, you will hear a sound we call the "happy happy joy joy" sound. Note that the same sound is played even if some renders in a batch failed; check the individual comps' Status and the Message bar along the top.

The Current Render Details also tracks file sizes and free disk space, so you can tell ahead of time if you're going to run out of room. This window does take time to update during a render, slowing things down a bit; untwirl it when you are done watching the paint dry.

The Render Log

√ Errors Only
Plus Settings
Plus Per Frame Info

After Effects can create a text log file of how your rendering progressed. The normal setting is Errors Only, which means create the document only when something went wrong. If you render more than one item in a queue, it will also create a log file explaining when each started and ended, and where it was written to. These logs are inside a folder the program will create in the same folder as the project.

If you select Plus Settings, this log file will contain all of the parameters in the Render Settings and the Output module(s).

The Plus Per Frame Info selection saves the rendering settings, as well as how long each single frame took to render. This allows you to go back later and see if there was a particular stretch of frames that was killing your overall render time, but this information is overkill for most cases.

RAM and Rendering

In general, more RAM is good, because After Effects can then cache more images and partial internal renders. In the MacOS version, the percentage of RAM it sets aside for caching is set under File> Preferences>Cache. (This replaces the RAM cache patch for version 4.0 of the program.) During rendering as well as normal operation, After Effects will period-ically pause to clean up and re-arrange its caches; more RAM means longer pauses as it cleans up more space. Selecting Favor Speed in this preference reduces the number of times After Effects does this cleanup. It can reduce the number of frames you can cache under RAM preview, but it also supposedly improves the per-formance of some third-party effects.

Stuck in Time

Be warned that if you set a Custom Time Span for a render queue item, this custom time will "stick." So even if you select another template, and that template is set to render the whole comp or just the work area, you'll get the custom time span anyway.

Creating and Editing Templates

Render Settings and Output Modules contain a large number of para-meters to set every time you render. Fortunately, you can create as many preset templates as you like for both and assign them to any item in the Render Queue. Both are accessed under the menu item File>Templates. If you disagree with the templates, go ahead and edit them. For example, we always change the *Lossless* Output Module template to RGB+Alpha (Straight). Creating a useful set of templates is another way to streamline your After Effects work flow.

The Render and Output templates behave pretty much the same. They are both just copies of the parameters you would normally set in their respective dialogs. The Output Module templates even remember the Format Options settings, including file encoding for stills and codecs, quality settings, and codec data rates for QuickTime movies. The differences are that you can create and edit them without having a com-position in the render queue. You can then give them names, and save them for later application. To change their settings, open them from the Edit menu and click on New or Edit; you will get the same editing dialog as if you had a comp in the Render Queue. The current templates are selected by a menu in their respective dialogs; select one to see its settings, duplicate or edit it.

Very handy is the ability to set the *tem-plate defaults:* the template that will be used whenever you queue a new still or movie to be rendered. Changing the default does not change the settings for any currently queued items. The Output Module Templates also have a default for RAM Preview – define the RAM Preview template before you select Composition>Save RAM Preview.

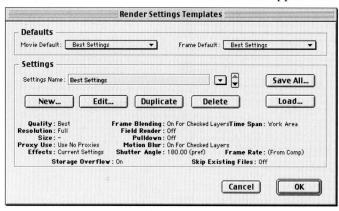

The File>Templates>Render Settings Template dialog. You can create tem-plates and choose which ones are used as defaults. There are separate defaults for saving a movie versus saving a frame.

After templates are created, they are selected in the Render Queue by the menus that appear directly to the right of the Render Settings and Output Module titles for a queued item. As of version 4.1, templates are automatically sorted by name in alphabetical order. To group similar templates together, give them the same first few characters in their names.

Once in the Render Queue, you can still pick another template from the menu (the current Default is at the top of the list), edit the current template for this one instance (by clicking on the template name), or save current settings you may have just created as a new template. Also, holding down Command while selecting a new Render Settings or Output Module template will automatically change the default to the selected template, which saves a trip to the Preferences.

You can also change multiple comps in the render queue to the same Render Settings at the same time. Shift+click (or Command+click) on their names to select them, and pick a new template – all selected comps not already rendered will now use this template. To change multiple items to have the same Output Module template, select them by clicking on the name of the current Output Module, not the item names themselves.

Template sets can be saved to disk or loaded from previously saved files. Note that Load is actually a merge; all of your current templates plus the templates you loaded will appear in the list. If there are identical templates, After Effects will not delete the duplicates; it will just add a number onto the end of them. This may require some sorting and deleting on your part after a Load.

We use templates a lot – the Output template changes almost every job, depending on what our target is; the Render Settings template changes depending on whether we are rendering proofs or final renders. Our templates take into account many different hardware devices and video formats we might output to and need to convert between.

Odd Lines Flip Fields

If you are adding lines to the top or bottom of an already-interlaced render, be careful: even numbers of lines keep the same field order, where odd numbers of lines reverse the field order. For example, if you rendered a 720×486 composition lower field first and are saving the file to the DV 720×480 lower field first standard, don't crop three lines off the top and bottom – crop two off the top and four off the bottom.

Memory Loss

Templates are stored in the Preferences file on your drive; deleting or swapping the prefs file will wipe out your templates.

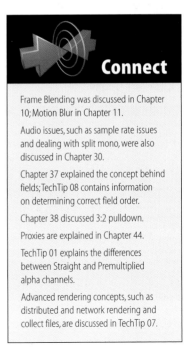

Connect

Frame Blending was discussed in Chapter 10; Motion Blur in Chapter 11.

Audio issues, such as sample rate issues and dealing with split mono, were also discussed in Chapter 30.

Chapter 37 explained the concept behind fields; TechTip 08 contains information on determining correct field order.

Chapter 38 discussed 3:2 pulldown.

Proxies are explained in Chapter 44.

TechTip 01 explains the differences between Straight and Premultiplied alpha channels.

Advanced rendering concepts, such as distributed and network rendering and collect files, are discussed in TechTip 07.

Output Module Templates

Defaults

Movie Default: Lossless   Frame Default: PICT seq RGB

RAM Preview: RAM Preview

Settings

Settings Name: Lossless

[New...] [Edit...] [Duplicate] [Delete]   [Save All...] [Load...]

Format: QuickTime Movie   Channels: RGB + Alpha
Output Info: Animation Compressor   Depth: Millions of Colors+
Spatial Quality = Most (100)   Color: Straight
Stretch: –
Crop: –
Output Audio: Off   Final Size: –

[Cancel] [OK]

File>Templates>Output Module Templates also has separate defaults for saving a movie versus saving a frame, along with the additional Default for RAM Preview.

44 Prerendering and Proxies

Planning (and rendering) ahead can save time later.

Ⓞne of After Effects' strengths is that you don't have to prerender anything – all of your sources, layers, and manipulations are "live" all the time, allowing you to make unlimited changes. However, calculating everything all the time can slow down both your work and your final render. Prerendering complex comps can speed up your workflow, and using proxies for footage and comps can streamline that process further.

Prerendering

Prerendering is the practice of creating a movie or still of an intermediate composition, or one that you intend to reuse as an element, and then swapping this rendered movie into a project in place of the comp that created it. The reason is to save processing time while you're working, as well as rendering time later on. You can create prerenders for various reasons and purposes, but you should be clear on whether the prerendered element is temporary, or whether it could be used to speed up the final render:

• When you're satisfied that a precomp is final, you could render it at this point to save processing time later. This really adds up if it is nested multiple times by other comps, or if you expect to be rendering a lot of proofs. This precomp might contain, say, a stack of background movie layers with transfer modes, masks, and blurs; when it's nested it might be colorized or manipulated further, but the basic precomp design is locked down. Once you've prerendered this comp, only one movie needs to be retrieved and no further processing is needed, rather than retrieving frames from disk for four movies and processing them. If you're prerendering a logo or element that will be manipulated further in other comps (which we sometimes called *sprites*), make sure to save the prerender with an alpha channel.

• You might have one layer that has a very slow effect applied (such as a particle system). Prerender this one layer, with an alpha channel if needed, and re-import the movie. Turn off the original layer (don't delete it in case you need to make changes), and use the prerendered layer instead.

• You could also create a still to stand in for an animated composition. For instance, say you created animated wallpaper or other background elements that change from frame to frame, but it is not important to see

Freezing Temporarily

If you don't have time to prerender a slow precomp that's not changing much, apply Time Remapping and create a temporary freeze frame. Find a representative frame and create a time remap keyframe here, then delete all other time remap keyframes. A single image will be rendered and cached as you work along the timeline. Just don't forget to turn off Time Remapping before you render!

these changes while you're working on the foreground elements. This is particularly useful if you don't have time to prerender the comp, but you need to work a bit faster.

• Likewise, you could export one frame from a source movie and use that in place of the original footage while you're designing the rest of the project. Since this still image will be cached in RAM, no slowdown will occur retrieving frames from disk as you move about the timeline.

In all cases, you can import the prerendered element normally and use the prerender in place of the original. To swap the prerender where the original comp was nested, use the Replace Layer (Option+drag) technique covered in Chapter 8. However, there is a slicker way to manage these stand-ins: Proxies.

Proxies

A *proxy* is a file that is designed to stand in for another file or an entire composition. It can be used temporarily, to speed up editing, or the proxies could be used in the final render. What makes proxies handy in After Effects is that it is easy to turn them on or off on an individual basis, or on a project-wide basis when you're rendering. After Effects will also automatically scale a lower resolution proxy to match the size of the footage or comp it is standing in for. And when it comes time to archive the project, you can trash the proxies without ruining your hierarchy – just remove the proxies to return the project to its original structure.

There are various situations when we use proxies, some of which are the same as the reasons we create prerenders:

• To prerender a composition, to save time during both working and rendering. This prerender is created at the full size of the composition, interlaced if necessary, and is referred to as a *Comp Proxy*.

• To prerender a still of a composition, to save time while working. This is also considered a Comp Proxy, though you would not use it during final rendering.

• To create a reduced resolution version of movies to save time when working; you would need to prerender this proxy in After Effects or another program, taking care that it is the same length as the original movie. The original footage would be used during final rendering. Creating smaller-sized versions of movies is recommended only when the original footage is at film resolution (see Chapter 42 for more on working with film). Otherwise, the comp's Resolution setting is designed to drop all footage to Half or Quarter resolution on the fly.

• If you have an extremely large background still image that's slowing you down, create a low-res proxy for just the background layer (open the hi-res image in Photoshop, scale to 25%, and save under a new name). Now you can work at Full Resolution to design the foreground layers, while the background layer alone is at "quarter resolution."

• Exporting just one frame from a "talking head" movie and using it temporarily as a Footage proxy. Now, instead of retrieving frames as you move about the timeline, this single frame is used and cached instead.

Don't Lose It

You do not want to lose any image quality if you prerender elements that will be used in the final render. A good choice is a QuickTime movie, using the Animation codec set to Best (Quality = 100) with the keyframing option turned off – it saves in the same color space as After Effects (RGB) and is lossless.

Note that most "uncompressed" video cards use the YUV color space, and the inevitable translation between RGB and YUV can potentially result in a slight loss in quality, especially if the codec does not support 10-bit YUV. Some companies, such as Digital Voodoo, have put an extra effort into making this translation perceptually lossless.

For the highest quality, especially for sprites that will be transformed further, render without fields, at double the frame rate (59.94 fps for NTSC)– you'll have the extra visual information you need when you transform later.

Otherwise, if you are pre-rendering a full-frame layer that will not be scaled or animated further and your output will be field-rendered, go ahead and field-render the prerender – there is no point in rendering and saving more data than you need. Whether you render uncom-pressed is up to you.

```
┌─────────────────── AE4.1 refblend 3 ──────────────────┐
│ □                                                  ⊞ ☰ │
│ ┌────┐  counter v22 D1/30 Comp 1   counter v22 601/D1/29/an5 │
│ │    │  720 × 486, D1/DV NTSC      720 × 486, D1/DV NTSC     │
│ │    │  Δ 0:00:06:01, 29.97 fps    Δ 0:00:06:01, 29.97 fps   │
│ └────┘                             Millions of Colors        │
│ ┌────┐                             Animation Compressor       │
│ └────┘                                                         │
├──────────────┬───────────┬───────────┬──────────┤
│ Name         │ Comment   │ Duration  │ Type     │
├──────────────┴───────────┴───────────┴──────────┤
│ ▷ 🗀 footage                              Folde  │
│   🗐 counter M main           Δ 0:00:06:01  Comp │
│   🗐 counter M ref            Δ 0:00:06:01  Comp │
│ ▣ 🗐 counter v22 D1/30 Comp 1  Δ 0:00:06:01  Comp │
│   🗐 reflection edit          Δ 0:00:06:01  Comp │
└──────────────────────────────────────────────────┘
```

After you have assigned a proxy, a black box (the proxy on/off switch) appears to its left, and two item information thumbnails appear overhead – the right one is for the proxy. The item whose name is in bold is the one that's currently active.

Mixing Resolutions

When you're working with film or high-definition video, use low-res proxies for background footage. Now you can set the comp to Full or Half resolution when you're designing titles while the backgrounds retrieve quickly from disk.

Applying Proxies

After you have prerendered your proxy, select the footage item or composition it is supposed to stand in for in the Project window, then select File>Set Proxy>File (Command+Option+P), and select your proxy file from disk. Two things will change in the Project window: a black box will appear next to the comp or footage in the list, and when you select it, two information thumbnails will appear along the top of the window. The left one is for the original file/composition; the second one is for your proxy. You may need to widen or scroll the Project window to see both.

In this case, since we rendered the selected comp to create its proxy, the size and duration match. If the proxy's size was smaller, After Effects would automatically scale it up so it appears to be the same size as the original. If you need to change any of the Interpret Footage settings for the proxy (for example, to separate its fields or set it to loop), select File>Interpret Footage>Proxy.

The black box next to the item is the Proxy Switch. Click on it to toggle it off and on. The current status is echoed in the top of the Project window: the source being used, proxy or original file/comp, will have its name in bold. Proxies can be globally ignored or used at render time in the Render Settings. To change the proxy file, use Set Proxy again; don't Replace Footage. To remove a proxy, use File>Set Proxy>None.

Proxy Behavior

When a proxy is assigned to a file, it is as if you replaced the file, with the exception that low-res proxies will be scaled to the original dimensions of the file it is standing in for. These proxies may look a little pixelated,

---

Placeholders

If you know a footage item is coming, but it hasn't been provided yet, After Effects allows you to create a simple Placeholder object: File>Import>Placeholder. You can set its dimensions and duration; it will default to the frame rate set in File>Preferences>Import under Sequence Footage. After Effects will create a fake movie of color bars, which you can now animate, mask, and add effects to as desired. When the footage arrives, you can use File>Replace

Footage, and this new file will be swapped in for the temporary color bars.

Having said that, you're free to use any dummy image or title, or even a simple solid (Layer>New Solid), as a placeholder. You might like to create or choose images that are visually more representative of the footage you expect to get than just a set of bars. However, Placeholders have the advantage of having "fixed" durations, which make them more like movies to handle and edit once in a comp.

but the auto-scale feature has the great advantage in that all your transformations and effects settings will work the same for the proxy as for the original file. If you had simply replaced the file with a smaller version, this would not be the case as you would have had to scale up the proxy (perhaps in a precomp) to match the original's size.

When a proxy is used for a composition instead of source footage, stepping through time in the comp actually steps through time in the prerendered proxy – but there is no indication of that in the comp window. Editing layers in the comp the proxy is applied to will *not* change what you see in the Comp window, which can be disconcerting. Of course, further comps that use this comp won't care if the layer they are accessing is a comp or a prerendered image or movie, and navigating higher up the chain will be much faster when the proxies are enabled.

You can, of course, turn off the proxy in the Project window, which will now make the comp "live" again. Make your changes, and observe the effects downstream in the comps that use this comp. If you end up liking your new variation, render a new proxy and swap it in, or simply remove the proxy and render normally.

Collapsing and Proxies

The one instance where behavior of a comp and a comp proxy differ is if you switched on Collapse Transformations (Chapter 19) for this comp layer in another comp. Collapse looks beyond the frame size of a nested comp and can access images on the pasteboard; a comp proxy does not have this information anymore. If you're depending on using collapse transformations, see if you can prerender from higher up the chain.

Rendering with Proxies

When it comes time to render, you can use or ignore your proxies, and this is set in Render Settings under the Proxy Use menu. You

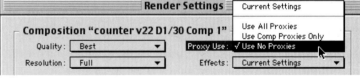

typically want to ignore proxies if they were low-resolution versions of your footage; you typically want to render the proxies that are prerenders that stand in for computationally intensive compositions.

The normal choice is Current Settings, which means obey the current status of the proxy switches in the Project window. This means the final comp will render exactly as you are viewing it. The other choices override the Project window settings.

If you were using low-resolution footage proxies, but the prerendered comps were final versions, choose Use Comp Proxies Only for your final render. This will use the original footage, but still use any composition proxies you may have prerendered to save time. This is our usual default.

If you used stills to stand in for comps, remove these proxies in the Project window before the final render, or select Use No Proxies. Of course, if you've already prerendered horribly slow comps, Use No Proxies will start rendering everything again from scratch (been there, done that…).

Looping Comps

To loop a comp, prerender it, re-import, and set the prerendered movie to loop in File>Interpret Footage>Main. If you apply it as a proxy, select Interpret Footage>Proxy and loop the proxy; then extend the original comp's duration to see the proxy repeating.

Archiving Proxies

Since they are just stand-ins, you could archive your project without saving the proxies. However, if they took a long time to create, it may be worth the time to archive them as well.

You can override your proxy switches in the Render Settings dialog.

Connect

Importing Footage was originally covered back in Chapter 2.

Collapsing Transformations was the subject of Chapter 18.

Field rendering was covered in Chapter 37.

Rendering in general was in Chapter 43.

CoSA Lives

The story of the company behind After Effects.

Many assume that companies make software. Not true: a handful of real, live, breathing, unique people do. We've had the pleasure of knowing a very special group of people – those who brought After Effects into this world – from the first day the tiny Company of Science and Art showed a promising animated graphics program named "Egg" to the public. This program has changed our lives, and those who created it have become our friends. Therefore, we asked one of the original creators of After Effects – David Simons – to recount what it was like in those early years, and what in the world they were thinking when they started down this path.

Afterword by David Simons

After Effects was originally created at a small start-up company in Providence, Rhode Island. We ended up with a focused application, but the path we took was far from planned.

It all started officially in June of 1990, when Greg Deocampo, David "DaveF" Foster, David "DaveH" Herbstman, and I ("DaveS") sat down with our new lawyers to incorporate The Company of Science & Art. We had high hopes. We knew the odds were against us, but the idealism of four recent college graduates trumped the 90% failure rate we were warned about. Providence's Brown University was our common connection. Greg had graduated in 1988, and we three Daves had just graduated that spring.

Greg had a plan, and we all wanted to help make it reality. The Company of Science & Art – "CoSA" for short – would become a world-class content provider for the new electronic age. Greg predicted a time when all computers would be connected and electronic information publishing would become much more important than paper-based methods. He also saw CD-ROM, a

new technology at the time, as the first enabling medium for mass distribution of cross-linked multimedia information: *hypermedia*. According to the business plan, CoSA would become an electronic publishing conglomerate in five years.

But first we needed an office, because all the preliminary meetings so far had been held in my apartment, which I shared at the time with my girlfriend and two housemates. It was nice to wake up to Greg bringing over doughnuts every morning, but my girlfriend made it clear that CoSA needed its own office.

After searching all around Providence, DaveF found a great space near downtown in the recently refurbished Imperial Knife Building. A great open space with huge factory windows and sandblasted brick and wooden support beams, it seemed perfect. DaveH negotiated the rent down to $1,000 a month, and we were in business. With the help of some friends, we postered the Brown campus looking for furniture. It was a buyer's market, since most of the graduating seniors had little need for their desks ($15), chairs ($10), and bookcases ($5) anymore. Greg's couches from home rounded out the comfortable décor.

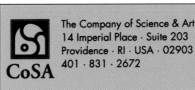

The Company of Science & Art
14 Imperial Place · Suite 203
Providence · RI · USA · 02903
401 · 831 · 2672

CoSA

The four CoSA founders clearly needed help to carry out the master plan, so we immediately started hiring others. The only capital we had was Greg's $30,000 investment, so the main thing we were offering was the fun of working at a start-up where the next big thing would be born. This was a hard sell, but Greg is a very convincing person.

Greg had saved a lot of time by picking a name for the company before anyone joined. However, CoSA didn't yet have a logo. The majority of our first few weeks (months?) were occupied with making pencil sketches and holding meetings, trying to decide on a logo. In case it's not obvious, the CoSA logo we picked is composed of a stylized C, o, S, and A. The response from most people is "Oh – I thought it was a parrot's head."

The basic premise of CoSA's business plan was to have artists and programmers working side by side to produce multimedia content. CD-ROM production was our first task. Macintosh computers were the most advanced multimedia platform at the time, so we planned out a system for authoring electronic magazines using HyperCard and custom plug-ins. Microsoft Word RTF documents with hyper-link information were "flowed" into a multipage multicolumn layout, with space for in-line advertisements.

MacWorld Expo Boston was coming in August, and it was a big marketing opportunity. We decided that we needed to prime the pump by giving away a free, compelling CD-ROM to show off what we could do. This was before America Online™ diluted the value of CD-ROMs by flooding the country with junk mail CDs.

Our first hypermedia publication was called *Connections: The CoSA Journal*. Designed to show off the new medium, it was a varied collection including an art gallery, virtual steel drum, and articles on the history of music and Canyon de Chelly. We tried selling advertising pages on the CD-ROM, but we couldn't find anyone willing to pay. We dropped the price to $0 and still had very little interest.

When we got the CDs back from the mastering plant, we were crushed to find out that our images and animations were *painfully* slow when they played back from the CD. Back then, the one thing we couldn't really test before mastering was the performance of the CD-ROM itself, and none of our testing had prepared us for the end result.

We had already rented out part of a MacWorld booth from a chip merchant, and couldn't let the opportunity slip by. But *Connections* was not going to impress anyone. So instead of giving out a free CD, we gave the *promise* of a free CD. In our tiny booth, we put a big "FREE CD-ROM" sign over our heads and collected the names of a lot of interested people. The hundreds of fruitless *Connections* discs were later used around the office for art projects, as Frisbees, and as microwave-oven fodder.

We later discovered that *Connections'* abysmal performance was mainly caused by a certain extremely slow brand of CD-ROM drive we happened to own. But it turned out to be a blessing in disguise, as the slowness of the animations was the impetus for us to write

Promises, promises – but every electronic publishing conglomerate has to start somewhere…

PACo, the PICS Animation Compiler. PACo allowed platform-independent, low-bandwidth streaming animation playback with synched sound.

Work on PACo continued through the fall of 1990, and we even were able to generate some income by building custom animation-playback HyperCard plug-ins for trade show displays and museum kiosks.

It became increasingly clear that PACo was more likely to produce real income than hypermedia publishing. We simplified our custom animation tools into a coherent product, and in May 1991 PACo 1.0 shipped. Bill O'Farrell, who had been hired on as president earlier in the year, worked a deal with Paracomp to sell PACo, under the name QuickPICS, that was bundled with Paracomp's 3D program ModelShop. PACo and QuickPICS sales provided enough income to allow CoSA to limp along, paying very low wages to the non-founders (typically $1,000 a month). Founders didn't get any salary. We each had our ways of surviving – mine was the generosity of my parents.

> **Excerpt from the CoSA business plan, circa early 1991:**
>
> The potential of hypermedia is only now becoming clear…. In the long run hypermedia may be as significant an invention as the television. It will allow the computer to act as the television, telephone, newspaper, shopping mall and library, all in one. Users will be able to tune into television programs, make phone calls, select articles from magazines, buy clothing, research a topic of interest and much more.

The office rent was usually paid on time, but the heating bill that winter was getting out of hand. Suite 203 in the Imperial Knife building was a cavernous space, and to get the lower 6 feet warmed up we had to heat the 15 feet above as well. To save money, we kept the heat way down. It was a surreal sight to walk into the CoSA office and find half a dozen jacketed people, each in front of a glowing Macintosh screen, with a task-lamp positioned – not to light their work – but rather a few inches over their hands to keep them warm. I also liked to use cutoff-finger gloves for added comfort while programming.

When we started work on PACo, we didn't know that Apple Computer was secretly working on a new technology called QuickTime. We had a hint that something was up when we had an opportunity to demo PACo to Apple CEO John Sculley during his visit to Brown University's computer science department. He was *very* interested when we showed him a single digital video file that was playing back with synched sound on a Mac, PC, and Sun Sparcstation.

CoSA circa 1991. *Left to right:* David "DaveH" Herbstman, David "DaveS" Simons, David "DaveF" Foster, Greg Deocampo, Ben The Dog, Sarah Lindsley, and Josh Hendrix.

When Apple announced QuickTime in June 1991, we decided it was time to change our plan. CoSA was in no position to compete with Apple, and we didn't want to be, as DaveH is fond of saying, an "ant running in front of the steamroller."

PACo Producer 2.0 would eventually ship on February 29, 1992. But in the fall of 1991, we had already started planning for the "next big thing." We gathered everyone in the company together to discuss future products. No idea was turned down for discussion. We even considered turning the "meal plan" in our shared house (where by then DaveH, David "DaveT" Tecson, Greg, and I all lived) into a commercial endeavor. The front-running ideas were a full-media-indexer – like full-text indexing and retrieval but extended for images, sounds, and movies – and some type of animated effects program.

In the end, the animated effects idea looked like it had the most promise, and seemed like the most fun. Greg had used Photoshop to repeatedly apply filters like Twirl, saving out each frame individually and running the frames through PACo to produce distortion animations. Josh Hendrix, our friendly blond-ponytailed tech supporter had been known to stay up late at night repeatedly applying random permutations of Photoshop filters just for the reward of the resulting eye candy. And those of us with cable television had watched countless hours of MTV to inspire our effects imagination.

Since we knew nothing about the effects market, we had to find some experts for advice. *MacWeek* happened to run a special article on people using Macs for digital video work. DaveH threw some darts and picked a few people to call. Lucky for us, Harry Marks was one of the names. Without knowing anything about us, Harry offered to meet in his Hollywood office to discuss our plans for a new digital video product. It wasn't until months later that we found out about Harry's legendary status in the motion graphics field. We scraped together a few other industry connections, then DaveH and I took off for a week of research in San Francisco and Los Angeles. The information we gathered from Harry and others was used to plan our new product, code-named *Lort* after a favorite entrée at Apsara, a nearby Cambodian-Vietnamese

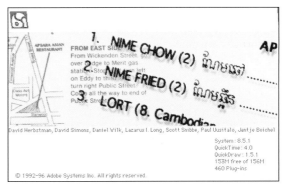

restaurant. Subsequent code names were also pulled from the same menu (see the secret "About" dialog in After Effects 3.1).

We gathered lots of ideas from our trip. After PACo shipped in February, fellow engineer Sarah Lindsley (now Sarah Allen) and I started planning Lort's architecture. After weeks of design work, we had created a monster architecture. Lort would be able to process any type of media in any way. Anything from MIDI musical data to a word processing document, all of it time-based. The only problem was, CoSA would surely go out of business before we were half finished.

I slapped together a very simple mock-up of the user interface to show to potential investors. Bill pitched our idea to various companies, including Aldus Corporation and Adobe Systems, but no one was interested in paying us to develop such a beast.

PACo was selling well enough to support us for a while, but we really needed to ship something new in six months or it would all be over. We gutted the Lort plan, leaving only the most crucial elements. The next item on Apsara's menu was Egg Roll, so we called our new project *Egg*.

We started coding for Egg in earnest during the spring of 1992. CoSA had turned into a software company instead of a media company. By this time DaveF had moved onto other pursuits, and Greg had stepped back from day-to-day operations to be more of a hands-off CEO. We never did give away a free CD as promised – software development became our focus.

We hired two engineers as summer interns to help out: David "DaveC" Cotter for user interface work and Dan "Filter-Boy" Wilk to write effect plug-ins.

There's a 50% chance my name is Dave.

DaveC (now known as Lazarus Long) also helped bring our Dave count back up. Both ended up joining us full time and are still on the team today.

At a point when half of CoSA's employees were named Dave, DaveT produced a T-shirt with the CoSA logo on the front and "There's a 50% chance my name is Dave" across the back. That T-shirt is often remembered as our most successful product. Besides the T-shirt, DaveT was also responsible for the After Effects packaging and documentation.

Our first press demos were held in a private suite at MacWorld Boston in August. We had varied responses – most reviewers were impressed or at least interested, some were confused and a bit hostile. We were excited and proud to see a headline in *MacWeek* soon after (naturally with a pun about hatching an egg).

Egg was demonstrated to the public for the first time at a multimedia show in Santa Clara, California, in September. Bill and DaveH were on hand to give a demo to Chris and Trish Meyer,

who asked to be beta testers on the spot. Needless to say, taking them on worked out well!

Our schedule started to slip, but by cutting some features it looked like we could finish in time for MacWorld San Francisco in January 1993. As popular as the name Egg had become, we needed a real name. Every meal and social gathering was spent suggesting and ruling out possible names. My favorites were Video Banana and MovieTwist, but the top vote-getter was Effecstacy.

Most of us were about 24 at the time, and fairly liberal-minded. At 30 years, our president Bill was the old-timer of the group, and therefore the voice of reason. Bill wouldn't stand for the drug-related implication of the name Effecstacy. His veto was honored, and after further debate we all agreed on After Effects. In memory of the naming crisis, After Effects' four-character operating system identifier is still FXTC.

As evidenced by our naming choices, we saw Egg as an *effects* program. In hindsight, it is now obvious that Egg was a compositing application with effects as just one of its tools. At the time, we didn't know that compositing in and of itself was an avenue we could explore. We were lucky that the layering architecture we started with was a great base upon which to build a compositing application.

With the name chosen, we still had many features to finish and bugs to fix. We had a small group of dedicated beta testers to help us find bugs, since our QA department was only one person. As MacWorld approached, it became clear that a few of our beta testers were really hardcore. Chris and Trish Meyer were particularly productive. Late one night I was talking to Trish on the phone about a bug, and we

The CoSA Timeline	
June 1990	CoSA incorporates
September 1990	PACo starts
May 1991	PACo 1.0 & QuickPICS 1.0 ship
February 1992	PACo Producer 2.0 ships
April 1992	*Lort* starts
June 1992	*Egg* starts
January 1993	After Effects 1.0 ships
May 1993	After Effects 1.1 ships
July 1993	Aldus buys CoSA (fifteen employees)
January 1994	After Effects 2.0 (*Teriyaki*) ships
April-June 1994	Ten CoSA employees move to Seattle
October 1995	After Effects 3.0 (*Nimchow*) ships
April 1996	After Effects 3.1 ships
May 1997	After Effects 3.1 Windows (*Dancing Monkey*) ships
January 1999	After Effects 4.0 (*ebeer*) ships
September 1999	After Effects 4.1 (*Batnip*) ships

CoSA as of August 1993.
Left to right:

David Herbstman,
David Tecson,
David Cotter
(now Lazarus Long),
Karen Schoenfein,
Charlie Donaldson,
Ben Dubrovsky,
Sari Rosen,
Dan Wilk,
Russell Belfer,
Erin Hurley,
Sari Gilman,
and Sara Daley.

realized that DaveH was talking to Chris on another line, while Trish faxed in a bug report at the same time on a third line!

The 1.0 release of After Effects was declared ready for shipping just a day before we had to leave for MacWorld SF. A few plug-ins weren't quite ready yet – Basic Text in particular was being worked on right up until the flight out. We had a little party in the foyer of the office, and hand-built the first few dozen boxes for sale on the show floor.

Showing After Effects 1.0 to the public for the first time was an exhilarating experience. We had a tiny booth, and people were packed ten-deep at times trying to get a glimpse of DaveH's exuberant demo. Looking back on it now, version 1.0 seems incredibly simple: no Time Layout window, one effect per layer, no transfer modes, no motion blur, one mask per layer (no Beziers). But sales were good, people were starting to pay attention, and we were motivated to add more features.

Potential customers weren't the only ones paying attention. Now that we had a shipping application and companies like Apple promoting the digital video field, larger software companies were interested in CoSA. Six months after MacWorld, we agreed to be acquired by Aldus Corporation. It was both scary and relieving – scary to give up control, relieving to have a steady paycheck.

A year after the acquisition we moved to Seattle just as Aldus merged into Adobe Systems. Through all the corporate changes, the After Effects team stayed together, and even today many of the same people are working on the product. I'm still managing the After Effects engineers with Dan Wilk, but some of the other founders have moved on. Greg is Chief Technology Officer at IFILM, a Web forum for filmed entertainment. DaveF founded Photerra, makers of fotoZap.com. DaveH, after working on After Effects up to version 4.1, is now studying pottery techniques in Japan. Unfortunately, I don't have the space here to mention all of the other teammates over the years who have been vital to our success.

We currently have about twenty dedicated employees working on After Effects in Adobe's Seattle office. It's a fun program to work on and a great team of people. After Effects' success has been a pleasant surprise for all of us who have worked on it. The ultimate reward is seeing the amazing things our users produce – you continue to challenge and inspire us.

I'm not allowed to discuss unannounced versions, so I can't say much about our future plans. One thing that I can say is that we decide what to do based on your feedback. Email with suggestions for new features can be sent to **aftereffects@adobe.com** – please help us design the next version!

David P. Simons
Seattle, December 1999

Bonus Tutorials

How the tutorials are organized and other useful information...

The CD-ROM that accompanies this book contains 22 Bonus Tutorials for you to explore. They range from simple techniques to full graphic designs to a case study on how to tackle a film opening title sequence. Overall, we have tried to focus on teaching skills you will find useful in actual work. Several are written by guest artists, including a pair designed to teach Particle Playground – an important addition to the After Effects version 4 Production Bundle.

The unifying theme behind these tutorials is that they bring together multiple skills learned throughout this book. A list of those skills, plus the chapter they are introduced, is included in each tutorial's description. In general, the earlier tutorials are aimed at beginning level users; the later tutorials assume more experience. Each tutorial is graded for **Style** and include:

- *Step-by-Step* – shows you how to build the project from scratch.
- *Guided Tour* – dissects an already-made project layer by layer.
- *Poke Around* – a more informal tour of a project.
- *Case Study* – indepth project analysis.

The **Difficulty Level** is also noted and is based on a hiking guide theme of Easy through Strenuous. The exact levels are *Easy, Easy–Moderate, Moderate, Challenging,* and *Strenuous*.

 This icon is used if the tutorial requires the Production Bundle version of After Effects.

The **Trail Head** description inside each tutorial will give you an outline of what will be covered, and any special actions you must take such as installing the free plug-ins included on the CD.

We hope you enjoy these bonus tutorials.

The following folders on the CD are used by the Tutorials:

▶ CD Tutorial Projects

Each tutorial folder contains a PDF file of the tutorial itself (.pdf suffix), an After Effects project file (.aep suffix), additional source material (if required), and a QuickTime movie of the final result (.mov suffix) where applicable. Note that you will need Adobe Acrobat Reader to open the PDF file; the Reader is included in the book's CD>_Installer folder if you don't already have it.

The final movies can be played from any QuickTime player utility, from within Acrobat Reader, or from the Catalog of Tutorial Movies – an Extensis Portfolio catalog which serves as a visual reference to the final movies. This catalog is included in the main CD Tutorial Projects folder; if you do not already have Portfolio, run Portfolio Browser (PortBrws.exe for Windows users) in the Installers folder.

Opening Projects: The tutorials can be run directly from the CD by opening the After Effects project file. If you copy the Tutorial folder to your hard drive, you may need to relink the source material to the master Sources folder on the CD, or a copy of it on your drive. If files are "unlinked", they will appear in *italics* in the Project window. Simply *double-click the first missing item*, which opens the Open dialog, and navigate to it on the CD or your drive. Select this item and After Effects should relink to all other missing items.

▶ Free Plug-ins

Many of the tutorials make use of the free plug-ins included on the CD from Adobe, Atomic Power, Boris FX, Cycore, DigiEffects, ICE, and Puffin Designs. If you haven't already installed them, now is the time!

▶ Sources

The Bonus Tutorials use the movies, music, mattes, objects, stills, sequences, and text elements from this folder. Each footage item has a two-letter prefix that identifies its creator; a key to the companies, artists and musicians who provided the footage and audio sources is on page 466.

TUTORIAL 01

Getting Animated

If you're relatively new to using After Effects, this tutorial will be a good workout for you to practice some layer editing and keyframing skills. We're going to build a mock environmental public service announcement combining movies, still images, and text, synchronized to a pre-marked soundtrack. You'll also learn to import footage items, including other projects and layered Illustrator files, and keep your Project window organized.

Before tackling this tutorial, we suggest you at least read the first five to ten chapters, or have worked through other tutorials such as in Adobe's Classroom in a Book. We'll carefully step through each part of the process. For those with a bit more experience, at the end we'll suggest several enhancements you can try on your own to improve the final composition.

Footage credits
Artbeats/Establishments Mixed Cuts
Digital Vision/The Body
Corbis Images

Music by
Chris Meyer

EASY

STEP-BY-STEP

Chapters & Skills

▶ 2 – importing footage & projects ▶ 4 – animating position ▶ 5 – scale and opacity
▶ 8 – managing layers ▶ 9 – trimming layers ▶ 10 – time stretching
▶ 19 – applying effects ▶ 28 – Illustrator artwork ▶ 30 – spotting audio (optional)

TUTORIAL 02

All That Jazz

A popular documentary practice is to perform "motion control" camera moves over historical photos of a subject. This technique can be replicated with finer control inside After Effects by animating a layer's Anchor Point, which in essence aims your virtual camera. Since scale changes are also centered around the Anchor Point, camera zooms will work better as well.

In this tutorial, we will use this technique to animate stills so that they will blend better with other already-moving footage. Both zoom and camera pan styles moves will be demonstrated, including motion paths and velocity curves. Then we'll break down an already-finished project using these concepts.

Footage credits
Digital Vision/All That Jazz
Herd of Mavericks/musician footage

Music by
Sonic Desktop Smartsounds™

EASY-MODERATE

STEP-BY-STEP +
GUIDED TOUR

Chapters & Skills

▶ 4 – keyframe animation ▶ 5 – scale and opacity ▶ 6 – anchor point animation
▶ 9 – trimming layers ▶ 19 – applying effects (optional) ▶ 28 – Illustrator artwork
(optional) ▶ 30 – spotting audio (optional)

TUTORIAL 03

Slip Sliding Away

Sliding a layer in time in a composition also moves any animation keyframes applied along with it. This can be a problem if you already had fade and other effects carefully timed against other layers, and merely wanted to play back a different section of the footage you're editing.

    The solution to this problem is to precompose the footage itself into its own composition, and to edit it in time there. Your animation keyframes are then applied to the precomp layer in the main composition, allowing much greater freedom. We'll step you through this procedure with the realistic example of editing a video insert that resides inside another composite.

Footage credit
Artbeats/Early Flight

EASY

STEP-BY-STEP

Chapters & Skills

▶ 4 – keyframe animation ▶ 8 – managing layers ▶ 9 – trimming layers
▶ 16 – nesting compositions ▶ 17 – precomposing

TUTORIAL 04

Blending Backgrounds

Abstract looping background textures can be used as a background in a composite, or as a subtle lighting effect when applied to other layers using transfer modes. After all, this is *motion* graphics; there is no need to be resign yourself to still image backgrounds – and having loopable footage means it can be extended to play as long as you need.

    There are several good CD stock footage libraries of backgrounds available, but sometimes you need something custom. We'll show you how to roll your own loopable backgrounds using a sequence of still images plus frame blending. You can select or create your own stills, or use sections of a single high-resolution image – another technique we'll demonstrate here.

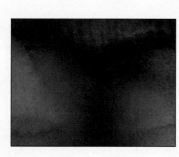

Footage credit
Paul Sherstobitoff/painted wash

EASY

STEP-BY-STEP

Chapters & Skills

▶ 2 – importing sequences, frame rates, looping ▶ 3 – creating compositions
▶ 4 – animating position, hold keyframes ▶ 5 – animating rotation
▶ 10 – frame blending ▶ 19 – applying and animating effects (optional)

TUTORIAL 05

Enhancing 3D

3D animation programs allow you to create your own virtual worlds, right down to the surface textures and lighting. However, we tend to be so busy creating our models, keyframing realistic animation moves, and worrying about rendering times that we rarely have the chance to get those lights and colors exactly the way we like.

The secret to great-looking 3D is to post-process it in a program like After Effects. A combination of layered, multipass renders, color correction, blurs, and transfer modes allow you to perk up – or grunge down – any 3D render. In this project, we'll walk you through our standard procedure to add sex appeal to our renders. *(Special thanks to Kory Jones of Reality Check, who originally showed us many of these techniques.)*

Footage credit
CyberMotion/Countdown animation

Chapters & Skills

► 3 – creating compositions ► 5 – altering opacity ► 12 – transfer modes
► 19 – applying effects ► 20 – adjustment layers (optional)

EASY-MODERATE

STEP-BY-STEP

TUTORIAL 06

Ramp It Up

One of the cornerstones of creating successful composites is managing transparency. For example, you might need to fade away a portion of a layer to reveal something more interesting behind it. In the first part of this tutorial, we will explore different techniques for creating "vignettes" (controllable regions of transparency), comparing their rendering times, ease of use, and most importantly – their look.

We will then move on to a step-by-step of how to apply these techniques to merge together different layers, using Puffin Designs Alpha Ramp effect to create a vignette. Final polishing-off techniques – including color correction, transfer modes, blurring adjustment layers – will also be demonstrated, along with using mask opacity to animate on the title.

Footage credits
Herd of Mavericks/drumming
New Shoes Design/Cool Moves

Music by
Keith Snyder

EASY-MODERATE

GUIDED TOUR +
STEP-BY-STEP

Chapters & Skills

► 12 – transfer modes ► 13 – masking, including feathering and animating opacity
► 14 – track mattes ► 19 – applying effects ► 20 – adjustment layers
► 28 – Illustrator artwork

TUTORIAL 07

Revealing Type

One of the most challenging (and potentially tedious) tasks is simulating a word being handwritten onto the screen. In After Effects, we use the Write-On effect to accomplish this – but not to actually write on the text; we use it to *reveal* lines and strokes of text that have been specially prepared in Photoshop.

This multipart tutorial will lead you by the hand (so to speak) on how to prepare your text, and then reveal it in a fluid motion to simulate handwriting. This technique will then be used in the context of creating an opening title for a documentary about the Irish famine, set to the music of Troy Donockley. The guided tour will also cover animating text precisely, and using masks to reveal lines of text quickly and easily.

Footage credits
Corbis Images/Irish still images
EyeWire/World Flags

Music by
Troy Donockley

CHALLENGING

STEP-BY-STEP +
GUIDED TOUR

Chapters & Skills

▶ 4 – animating position ▶ 5 – animating opacity ▶ 6 – animating the anchor point
▶ 12 – transfer modes ▶ 13 – animating masks ▶ 16 – nesting compositions
▶ 23 – Write-On and Stroke effects ▶ 28 – import Illustrator as comp

TUTORIAL 08

Ripple Pulse

This is one of those tricks that started as a puzzle, which became a challenge, and has ended up as a tour into some of the tweakier ways to manipulate the Production Bundle's versatile Displacement Map effect. You'll notice that several of these Bonus Tutorials are based around displacement mapping techniques; it is an effect worth understanding and mastering.

In this tutorial, the goal is to create a singular pond wave or ripple pulse. After Effects' own Ripple effect generates waves continuously, which makes it hard to simulate individual water drops. After you've brushed up on how displacement mapping works in Chapter 22, try your hand at building a nice-looking, liquidy ripple that you can reuse in your own projects.

Footage credit
Digital Vision/The Body

CHALLENGING

GUIDED TOUR

Chapters & Skills

▶ 15 – preserve transparency switch ▶ 16 – nesting compositions
▶ 22 – compound effects

TUTORIAL 09

Projected Text

We're very fond of the interplay of light on moving objects, such as projecting an image or text onto blowing cloth or flowing water. To create this digitally, you might think you need a 3D program to model these dimensional objects. However, it is possible to fake these "projected" effects in a 2D program like After Effects through use of its Displacement Map effect.

This tutorial contains two examples. The first consists of projecting text onto the rippling muscles of a body builder. In addition to using displacement mapping, we will also use transfer modes to alter the coloration as well as the shapes of the characters; a lesson on animating type using Path Text will also be included. Our second example will use these techniques to project text onto flowing water.

Footage credit
EyeWire/Fitness

Music by
Flow of Soul

Chapters & Skills

▶ 4 – animating position, motion paths ▶ 12 – transfer modes
▶ 16 – nesting compositions ▶ 19 – applying and animating effects
▶ 22 – compound effects ▶ 26 – Path Text effect

MODERATE

GUIDED TOUR

TUTORIAL 10

Texture Mapping

A popular 3D texture mapping technique consists of applying an image onto a surface, and then giving the surface a bump map so it has more apparent texture and depth. Additional maps can optionally be used to weather the appearance of the originally mapped image. This look can be simulated in After Effects with a combination of displacement mapping, transfer modes, and track mattes.

Here, we take on the challenge of painting a warning sign onto a sidewalk. We'll show how to blend the paint onto the concrete, make it run into the pockmarks and cracks, and then wear it away to give the impression of years of weathering and foot traffic. *(Special thanks to Alex Lindsay, formerly of ILM and now founder and CEO of dvGarage, who showed us the weathering trick.)*

Footage credit
Artbeats/City Surfaces

Chapters & Skills

▶ 12 – transfer modes ▶ 16 – nesting compositions ▶ 19 – applying effects
▶ 22 – compound effects ▶ 24 – track mattes

EASY-MODERATE

STEP-BY-STEP

TUTORIAL 11

Z Envy

Footage credit
CyberMotion/3D render

CHALLENGING

POKE AROUND

The Production Bundle version of After Effects 4.1 introduced the new 3D Channel class of effects. These can look at additional information rendered by 3D programs such as ElectricImage, Softimage, or 3D Studio MAX, and create masks based on distance from the camera, add fog to a scene that gets thicker the further away you are, plus other tricks. These are discussed in Chapter 24.

But what if you don't own the Production Bundle? Or one of the 3D programs named above? We'll show you how to recreate most of the 3D Channel effects using mainly Standard version effects (Depth of Field requires the Production Bundle or a third party effect) plus more common Z-depth renders – and even show you how to fake those. Tricks for cleaning up mattes and edges, plus creating entirely new looks, will also be discussed.

Chapters & Skills

▶ 4 – scale and opacity   ▶ 12 – transfer modes (optional)   ▶ 15 – stencils (optional)
▶ 16 – nesting comps   ▶ 17 – precomposing   ▶ 18 – collapse transformations
▶ 19 – applying effects   ▶ 22 – compound effects   ▶ 24 – 3D Channel effects

TUTORIAL 12

Digital Gogh

Footage credits
Kevin Dole/sunflowers movie
Artbeats/Cloud Chamber & Soft Edges

Music by
Giovanna Imbesi

MODERATE

GUIDED TOUR +
STEP-BY-STEP

It's not always obvious how you might apply effects to regions of a movie, as opposed to the entire frame. One method is to use track mattes – layers that allow you to set transparencies for the layers immediately below them. By duplicating a layer, treating it with effects, and then masking off parts of it with a track matte, you can achieve a variety of interesting framing effects.

In this tutorial, we will be using mattes in a variety of ways, including colorizing selected portions of a layer, and creating two copies of text with different scalings moving across the frame at the same time, fragmented by a matte. Boris Mosaic is used to good effect, and we dive into the PixelChooser section of the Boris AE plug-ins, which gives their effects built-in mattes and transfer modes to exploit.

Chapters & Skills

▶ 4 – animating position   ▶ 5 – rotation   ▶ 11 – motion blur   ▶ 12 – transfer modes
▶ 14 – track mattes   ▶ 16 – nesting compositions   ▶ 19 – applying effects
▶ 36 – looping a movie

TUTORIAL 13

PB ## Dotcom Zoom

Continuous rasterization of vector-based art from
Adobe Illustrator opens up a few neat tricks, such as being able
to "zoom" through sections of text or a logo while keeping your
shapes completely sharp.

This tutorial comes in two parts. First, we step you through how
to set up Illustrator text for continuous rasterization, using the
Production Bundle's Exponential Scale keyframe assistant to keep
a consistent speed through the zoom. We also show you how to
animate the anchor point to zoom through the center of the "dot"
in dotcom. Then, we guide you through a tour of how we applied
the result as a track matte to create an interesting animation
where the inside and outside of the text are related but different.

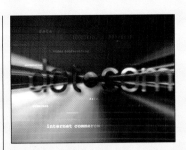

Footage credits
Lizard Lounge/slitscan render
CyberMotion/additional elements

Music by
Chris Meyer

EASY-MODERATE

**STEP-BY-STEP +
GUIDED TOUR**

Chapters & Skills
- ▶ 4 – keyframe animation ▶ 5 – animating scale
- ▶ 6 – animating the anchor point ▶ 7 – exponential zoom
- ▶ 11 – motion blur (optional) ▶ 28 – continuous rasterization

TUTORIAL 14

Cool Moves

The client wants a cool, animating background. But of course,
they have no source material. Sound familiar? Take heart: A lot
can be done by animating simple shapes created in Illustrator,
and combining them using a variety of scales, opacities, and
transfer modes.

Guest artist **Brenda Sexton** of New Shoes Design, creator of the
Cool Moves CD of creative stock footage backgrounds, shared with
us the project and source material used to create one of her Cool
Moves animations. As we walk through it, you'll pick up useful
tips on making animations loop seamlessly, rasterizing Illustrator
artwork, offsetting anchor points to make layers wobble as they
rotate, and working at NTSC D1 size and pixel aspect ratio.

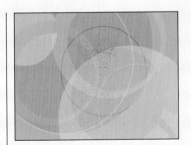

Footage credit
New Shoes Design/Cool Moves

Music by
Giovanna Imbesi

MODERATE

POKE AROUND

Chapters & Skills
- ▶ 5 – animating rotation ▶ 6 – moving the anchor point ▶ 12 – transfer modes
- ▶ 16 – nested compositions ▶ 18 – collapse transformations
- ▶ 20 – adjustment layers ▶ 28 – Illustrator art ▶ 39 – D1 NTSC

Circles, Lines, and Stuff

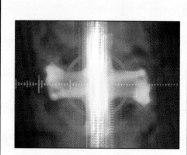

Footage credit
Digital Vision/Data:Funk

Music by
Chris Meyer

MODERATE

POKE AROUND

Current popular motion graphics design work has several recurring themes, including the use of simple geometric shapes such as squares, circles, and lines, and other engineering-related shapes such as audio waveforms. There is also a heavy emphasis on other abstract background elements (which we call "stuff"), as well as hot, glowing looks.

Continuing our theme of creating cool-looking work with virtually no resources, we'll take a pair of interesting still images and add a bunch of "stuff" to them using Illustrator artwork, and effects such as Block Dissolve, Audio Waveform and Spectrum, CE Circle, Ellipse, and Stroke. Cycore's CE Noise Turbulent is used to create an organic lighting effect as well as mattes. An audio soundtrack will be used to drive some of these effects.

Chapters & Skills

▶ 4 – keyframe animation ▶ 7 – the wiggler ▶ 12 – transfer modes
▶ 13 – mask shapes ▶ 14 – track mattes ▶ 16 – nesting compositions
▶ 19 – applying and animating effects ▶ 21 – black solids ▶ 23 – numerous effects

Time Warp

Footage credits
Paul Sherstobitoff/TV,
Artbeats/NASA, The Early Years and
Liquid Ambience, EyeWire/Backstage,

Music by Jeff Rona

CHALLENGING

STEP-BY-STEP +
GUIDED TOUR

In today's soundbite culture, it is common to be asked to edit an interview or speech down to a single phrase. However, the speaker is often talking before and after this soundbite, resulting in either unprofessional freeze frames or embarrassing lip flapping while the audio is off.

In the first part of this tutorial, we show how to use a combination of time remapping, frame blending, and audio levels animation to create clean handles on edited footage where there were none before. We'll then walk through an example of a news factoid spot where you might need these sound bites, showing a number of tricks involving track mattes, transfer modes, color correction, blurring, and a special application of Boris Mosaic (free on your CD) to create the currently trendy "stretchy lines" look.

Chapters & Skills

▶ 9 – trimming layers ▶ 10 – frame blending ▶ 12 – transfer modes ▶ 14 – track mattes ▶ 16 – nesting compositions ▶ 19 – applying effects ▶ 23 – gradient wipe and block dissolve ▶ 30 spotting audio and animating levels ▶ 31 – time remapping

TUTORIAL 17

Better Than Average

Smearing time is often used to enhance the natural motion blur of an object, imply speed, or create surreal or dreamlike effects. There are a number of effects available to create variations on this look, such as After Effects' Echo and built in frame blending, Final Effects Complete's Wide Time from ICE, and ReelSmart™ Motion Blur from RE:Vision Effects. But it's also possible to create your own.

We'll show you how to build a composition that recreates a version of the "averaging" effect. This comp can then be used as a template to preprocess your own footage items, with as many frames of blending as you desire, plus the ability to add your own surrealistic twists such as effects and transfer modes. While doing so, you'll also gain a much deeper understanding of how opacity is calculated inside After Effects.

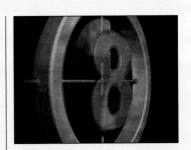

Footage credit
CyberMotion/Countdown animation

EASY

STEP-BY-STEP

Chapters & Skills

▶ 3 – creating a composition ▶ 5 – setting opacity ▶ 10 – time stretching (optional)
▶ 12 – transfer modes (optional) ▶ 16 – nesting compositions

TUTORIAL 18

Stepping Out

A technique commonly used by the "grunge" or "nervous" movement of graphic design is to shoot footage at a low frame rate. This results in jerky movements that resemble a series of rapid stills, plus generous amounts of natural motion blur. But how can you create that look if all the footage has already been shot normally?

In this tutorial, we will walk through two different approaches that use a combination of frame blending and frame rate manipulation to create a "step time" look from previously smooth footage. We will then extend this technique by compositing film dirt and grain on top of our footage, using Levels and transfer modes to simulate a blown-out overexposed film look.

Footage credits
Herd of Mavericks/piano
IF Studios/VideoLoops

EASY

STEP-BY-STEP

Chapters & Skills

▶ 3 – changing composition settings ▶ 10 – frame blending
▶ 12 – transfer modes ▶ 36 – setting frame rates in interpret footage
▶ 43 – render settings ▶ 44 – prerendering

Text Bounce

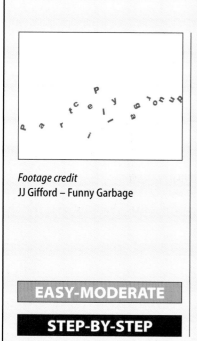

Footage credit
JJ Gifford – Funny Garbage

After Effects version 4 introduced Particle Playground: a complex particle physics simulation effect, that can toss text, dots of color, and even other layers around a frame based on a set of rules you can control. This major addition has proven to be as daunting to many users as it is powerful. Therefore, we've asked a pair of artists who have already conquered Playground to share their tips, in addition to example projects.

In the first tutorial, **JJ Gifford** of Funny Garbage helps demystify Playground, and shares numerous tips to better control it as well as reduce rendering times. He follows this up with a simple Playground project (a contradiction in terms?) to make the individual characters of a word fall away and bounce around the screen. This is an excellent first project for anyone new to Playground.

EASY-MODERATE

STEP-BY-STEP

Chapters & Skills

▶ 3 – creating a composition   ▶ 13 – creating a rectangular mask
▶ 17 – precomposing   ▶ 19 – applying and animating effects
▶ 22 – compound effects

Matrix Playground

Footage credit
Richard Lainhart/O-Town Media

If you're ready to seriously tackle Particle Playground, check out this tutorial by **Richard Lainhart** of O-Town Media. In it, Richard recreates the look of the opening title of the recent smash movie *The Matrix*. Originally created by Animal Logic, the title consists of characters of randomizing text falling down the screen like raindrops running down a window pane. As part of accomplishing this feat, you will learn advanced concepts of how to create Property Maps that control both the randomization and opacity of the "particles" you are animating – the text itself.

Be sure to read the second document in this tutorial's folder, where Richard helps put Particle Playground in the context of both physics simulation systems, as well as the "tweening" practiced by animators as they fill in the motion between key frames of action.

STRENUOUS

STEP-BY-STEP

Chapters & Skills

▶ 4 – animating position   ▶ 5 – scale   ▶ 16 – composition hierarchies
▶ 19 – applying and animating effects   ▶ 22 – compound effects
▶ 43 – rendering stills   ▶ 44 – composition proxies (optional)

TUTORIAL 21

Multiplane

After Effects is what's known as a 2D program: you can move objects left/right and up/down, but there is no inherent sense of near/far. There are numerous ways to fake depth, such as scale, blurring, drop shadows, and other perspective effects, but from an animation point of view, you still aren't explicitly moving objects closer to you or further away.

Fortunately, several third-party effects have been released recently that allow you to explicitly move layers in that third dimension. The most versatile such effect is Multiplane, from Atomic Power's Evolution set, and a four-layer version of this effect is included free on your CD. In this tutorial, guest artist **Trevor Gilchrist** of Five Short Stories gets you thinking in three dimensions as you make two objects orbit around a third.

Footage credits
Trevor Gilchrist/3D objects
Artbeats/Liquid Ambience

Music by
Jeff Rona

Chapters & Skills

▶ 4 – basics of animation ▶ 7 – easy ease keyframe assistant (optional)
▶ 19 – applying and animating effects ▶ 22 – compound effects
▶ Atomic Multiplane PDF manual (on CD-ROM)

CHALLENGING

STEP-BY-STEP

TUTORIAL 22

Film Title Case Study

We've had the opportunity to composite and animate several film title sequences in After Effects over the years. Although every project brings a unique set of challenges, there are several recurring themes and concerns: what film format will you be working in, how much disk space will you need, file and tape formats for interchange with your service bureau, maintaining audio sync, and making sure the final output to film is as envisioned.

In this case study, we will discuss these overall issues, and then walk through *The Talented Mr. Ripley*, a film title we animated in conjunction with Deborah Ross Film Design. Issues that arose during this project include working in the Cineon color space, managing the tremendous amount of disk space required, and conforming the scanned film frames according to the assembly list and offline video created by the film's editor.

© EyeWire/Backstage

Chapters & Skills

▶ 38 – 3:2 pulldown ▶ 42 – working at film resolution
▶ 43 – render settings and output modules ▶ 44 – prerendering and proxies

CHALLENGING

CASE STUDY

ARTIST CREDITS

We would like to acknowledge and thank the numerous companies, studios, and artists who contributed the visual and musical content that illustrate this book and are used in the Chapter Example and Bonus Tutorial projects. To find out more about these companies and artists, check out the Credits and Info folder on the CD-ROM. Additional contact information is also included in the Portfolio Catalog of Sources.

Stock Footage Suppliers

AB	**Artbeats**	www.artbeats.com
CI	**Corbis Images**	www.corbisimages.com
CP	**Classic PIO Partners**	www.classicpartners.com
DV	**Digital Vision**	www.digitalvisiononline.com
EW	**EyeWire**	www.eyewire.com
VS	**Pixélan Software**	www.pixelan.com

> Please read and understand the End User License Agreements (EULAs) included on the CD; you are agreeing to abide by these whenever you use the content on the CD.

Studios & Artists

3D	**Shelley Green**	3D Gear	www.3dgear.net
CM	**Trish & Chris Meyer**	CyberMotion	www.cybmotion.com
FD	**Frank DeLise**		www.frankdelise.com
DI	**Rex Olson**	Desktop Images	www.desktopimages.com
DS	**Anthony Pittari**	Digital Sorcery	tand@rcn.com
FG	**JJ Gifford**	Funny Garbage	www.funnygarbage.com
H5	**Alex Bigott**	H5B5 Media AG	www.h5b5.com
HD	**Lee Stranahan**	Herd of Mavericks	lstranahan@earthlink.net
HM	**Harry Marks**		www.apple.com/applemasters/hmarks
JR	**Jeff Rona**	Silkscreen Music	www.jeffrona.com
KD	**Kevin Dole**	SunSpots	www.kevindole.com
KS	**Keith Snyder**	Woolly Mammoth	www.woollymammoth.com/keith
LL	**Christopher Mills**	Lizard Lounge Graphics	www.lizardlounge.com
NS	**Brenda Sexton**	New Shoes Design	www.newshoesdesign.com
OT	**Richard Lainhart**	O-Town Media	www.otownmedia.com
PM	**Scott Gross**	Photron USA	www.photron.com
PS	**Paul Sherstobitoff**		home.earthlink.net/~sherstobitof
PT	**JD Wilcox**	ProMax Technology	www.promax.com
TD	**Troy Donockley**	*(courtesy Alliance Music/SGO)*	www.troydonockley.co.uk
TG	**Trevor Gilchrist**	Five Short Stories	www.fiveshortstories.com
TT	**Giovanna Imbesi**	TuttoMedia	www.tuttomedia.com
VL	**Tony McShear**	IF Studios	www.ifstudios.com

Note: *All images appearing throughout the book not explicitly credited were created by CyberMotion.*

INDEX

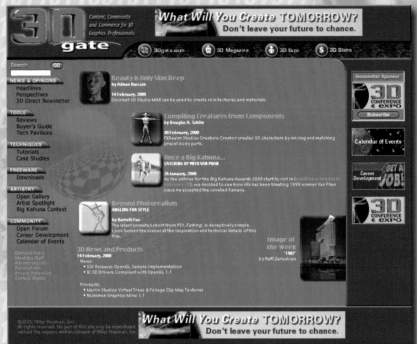

Digital Video

DV.com

delivers

CHOICES Search the only comprehensive, **online buyer's guide** with descriptions of more than 1000 digital media tools.

CREDIBILITY Before you buy, check out the most extensive collection of **independent product reviews** written by industry authorities.

COMPETENCE Develop your expertise with the largest selection of **practical, relevant tutorials** by digital video specialists.

CONNECTIONS Boost your career with these **valuable resources:** DV magazine, DV Web Video *magazine*, DV Expo, Web Video Expo, and the DV Store.

COMMUNITY Share digital video problems and solutions with your peers on **message boards** hosted by industry experts.

Strengthen your position in the digital video industry.
Visit **www.dv.com** today! Priority Code: OOCMGAE
